BLACKWELL ANTHOLOGIES

# Native American Women's Writing, c.1800–1924

## An Anthology

*Edited by Karen L. Kilcup*

# BLACKWELL ANTHOLOGIES



Blackwell Anthologies are a series of extensive and comprehensive volumes designed to address the numerous issues raised by recent debates regarding the literary canon, value, text, context, gender, genre and period. While providing the reader with key canonical writings in their entirety, the series is also ambitious in its coverage of hitherto marginalized texts, and flexible in the overall variety of its approaches to periods and movements. Each volume has been thoroughly researched to meet the current needs of teachers and students.

BRITISH LITERATURE

*Published titles*

Victorian Women Poets: An Anthology
*edited by Angela Leighton and Margaret Reynolds*

Romanticism: An Anthology. Second Edition
*edited by Duncan Wu*

Romantic Women Poets: An Anthology
*edited by Duncan Wu*

British Literature 1640–1789: An Anthology
*edited by Robert DeMaria, Jr*

Chaucer to Spenser: An Anthology of Writings in English 1375–1575
*edited by Derek Pearsall*

Renaissance Drama: An Anthology of Plays and Entertainments
*edited by Arthur F. Kinney*

Old and Middle English: An Anthology
*edited by Elaine Treharne*

Restoration Drama: An Anthology
*edited by David Womersley*

The Victorians: An Anthology of Poetry and Poetics
*edited by Valentine Cunningham*

Renaissance Literature: An Anthology
*edited by Michael Payne and John Hunter*

Gothic Novels: An Anthology
*edited by Nicola Trott*

Modernism: An Anthology
*edited by Lawrence Rainey*

*Forthcoming*

Medieval Drama: An Anthology
*edited by Greg Walker*

AMERICAN LITERATURE

*Published titles*

Nineteenth-Century American Women Writers: An Anthology
*edited by Karen L. Kilcup*

Nineteenth-Century American Women Poets: An Anthology
*edited by Paula Bernat Bennett*

American Gothic: An Anthology 1787–1916
*edited by Charles L. Crow*

Native American Women's Writing, c.1800–1924: An Anthology
*edited by Karen L. Kilcup*

*Forthcoming*

Early African-American Literature: An Anthology
*edited by Phillip M. Richards*

# NATIVE AMERICAN WOMEN'S WRITING c.1800–1924

## AN ANTHOLOGY

EDITED BY **KAREN L. KILCUP**

First published 2000

2 4 6 8 10 9 7 5 3 1

Blackwell Publishers Ltd
108 Cowley Road
Oxford OX4 1JF
UK

Blackwell Publishers Inc.
350 Main Street
Malden, Massachusetts 02148
USA



*British Library Cataloguing in Publication Data*

A CIP catalogue record for this book is available from the British Library.

*Library of Congress Cataloging-in-Publication Data*

Native American women's writing : an anthology, c. 1800–1924 / edited by Karen Kilcup.
p. cm. — (Blackwell anthologies)
Includes bibliographical references and index.
ISBN 0-631-20517-9 (alk. paper) — ISBN 0-631-20518-7 (alk. paper)
1. American literature—Indian authors. 2. American literature—Women authors.
3. Indian women—Literary collections. I. Kilcup, Karen L. II. Series.

PS508.I5 N374 2000
810.8′09287′08997—dc21

99-086315

Typeset in 9½ on 11 pt Garamond 3
by Ace Filmsetting Ltd, Frome, Somerset
Printed in Great Britain by T.J. International, Padstow, Cornwall

This book is printed on acid-free paper.

*This volume is dedicated to anthropologist Phyllis Rogers (Cherokee), whose work has inspired me and whose friendship sustained me through difficult times*

# Contents

# Preface

Completing this anthology has helped transform my view of nineteenth-century American literature as a whole – its shape, its voices, its ambitions, and its aesthetics. I hope that it will have a similar effect on readers. Although the volume is envisioned in part as a text for courses on Native American women's writing, Native American literatures, nineteenth-century American literature, Women's Studies, and American Studies, I also seek to provide scholars with the resources for further conversation in the field and to engage general readers. The basic principles of selection for this collection are analogous to those for my earlier collection, *Nineteenth-Century American Women Writers: An Anthology*: to include as diverse a group of writing and genres as possible, and to offer complete texts, or, where selections are included, internally coherent and independent pieces. Because of the Cherokees' early education in English, writers from this group occupy an especially prominent space. Some writers, like Pauline Johnson, Sarah Winnemucca, Ora Eddleman Reed, and Zitkala-Ša, were particularly prolific; hence, they represent a significantly larger portion of the collection than those like Jane Johnston Schoolcraft and Annette Leevier.

Because of space limitations and because many of the writers included here retell versions of traditional oral narratives, I have opted to deemphasize those collected by white ethnographers, offering only a small selection from the most strongly represented tribes in the anthology in the hopes that these examples will provide a framework for understanding the individuals' work and inspire readers to seek additional sources. I have also deemphasized songs for these reasons, as well as because their performative contexts are erased by placing them in print. In including oral and as-told-to work, I am obviously construing the terms "writer" and "writing" broadly.

The choices of selections were often dependent on context and the interrelationships between writers. For Mary Jemison, I have included those selections that have been identified as principally her own. For Narcissa Owen and Buffalo Bird Woman, I have chosen chapters that I thought would be most accessible to contemporary readers and that also provide interesting and productive connections with other writers in the collection (all the selections, in fact, have been chosen with an eye toward such connections). Buffalo Bird Woman's autobiography is taken not from Gilbert Wilson's published text, *Waheenee*, but from his field notes, which represent her voice in a much less mediated form. For writers whose work is extensive, such as Johnson, I have attempted to indicate their diversity and range. Seeking to aid readers in approaching the materials, I have divided the well-represented writers' work into the very broad generic categories of poetry, fiction, and nonfiction prose. Although genre is itself a Western concept, it can provide a useful conceptual tool for understanding the literatures, revealing, for example, that these writers' works are impressively diverse, including short fiction, novel, poetry, political writing, autobiography, humor, oratory, children's writing, and many others.

Because of their strong publishing history, Zitkala-Ša and Pauline Johnson presented the question of which text to select among multiple versions. I have chosen to work from their collections, and readers unfamiliar with these materials should be aware that many of the pieces were published earlier – sometimes, as in the case of the former's "Impressions of an Indian Childhood," originally published in the prestigious *Atlantic Monthly* in 1900, much earlier than the collection in which it ultimately appeared. This choice means that writers are represented in some cases by revised work; while often both interesting and informative, these revisions cannot be traced here.

In addition to providing brief headnotes that attempt to outline the writers' lives and to offer some connections between and among the writers, I have supplied brief bibliographies of primary and secondary materials for each writer; these are intended to be indicative rather than complete. Although I have attempted to be as accurate as possible with biographical details, for some writers such details have been difficult to confirm; for others, the existing biographies are contradictory. In the latter cases, I have relied on what I believe to be the most reliable sources. Footnotes, as in all anthologies in the Blackwell series, are offered only where necessary to explain terms or references not readily available. In some instances I have been unable to locate references after considerable investigation and have simply omitted them. Because of space considerations, and because this volume is conceived principally as a literary text rather than a collection of historical documents, I have not attempted in every case to confirm the accuracy of individual facts in writers' accounts of tribal history, choosing instead only to remark briefly, where appropriate, on their apparent reliability. For the purposes of literary study, it is more appropriate to ask why a writer has altered her "facts" and to consider what those alterations may reveal about her perspective than it is to catalog them.

In terms of the texts themselves, I have retained the original spelling and punctuation except in those cases where errors clearly represented mistakes in proofreading or typesetting. The exceptions to this rule are the early Cherokee women's texts, where I have made some slight alterations for readability. As with all Blackwell anthologies, the emphasis here is on complete texts; for the purposes of presenting a relatively complete picture of the field, writers of longer texts are represented by excerpts that can stand alone. Thus the anthology offers the resources for a complete course in shorter writing as well as providing a core text around which instructors can build by adding such works as *Wynema*, *Life Among the Piutes*, and *A Narrative of the Life of Mrs. Mary Jemison*.

The choice of time period encompassed by this collection ends, appropriately – given the political thrust of much of the writing included here – with a political rather than a literary moment: the granting of United States citizenship to include all of its Native American peoples. While this collection seeks to offer representative selections of individual authors, to say that it (or any other collection) is "representative" is, as my introduction explores, a task for future critical discussions of early Native American women's writing. This anthology does seek, however, to challenge traditional "mainstream" notions of what constitutes "literature," including political and historical writing alongside more familiarly "aesthetic" forms like romantic poetry, and representing in written forms texts that seem like oratory.

I hope that the final brief section, which incorporates selections by various authors, including children, young women from the Cherokee Female Seminary, and adults, will provide readers with a sense of the additional work that remains to be discovered and will inspire some to seek it out, extending further the literary conversation in which this anthology engages.

# Acknowledgments

Since I began work on *Native American Women Writers, c.1800-1924: An Anthology* in 1990, the recovery work in the field has expanded the available material dramatically, and the critical perspectives that have developed on earlier Native American women's literatures and cultures by both literary scholars and historians have helped provide me with a greater understanding of the collection's coherence at its completion. Particularly important has been work by Paula Gunn Allen, James Axtell, Gretchen Bataille, David Brumble, Dexter Fisher, Arnold Krupat, Daniel Littlefield, James Parins, Kenneth Roemer, A. LaVonne Brown Ruoff, Kathleen Sands, Cheryl Walker, and Andrew Wiget. Special thanks to Theda Perdue for making available the early Cherokee women's petitions. Without these scholars' groundbreaking work and that of many others in the field this collection would not have been finished without many additional years of effort.

I am grateful to my former home institution, the University of Hull, England, and its School of Arts and Department of American Studies for their support of this project. Various members of the Northeast Nineteenth-Century American Women Writers Study Group, many of whom are now part of the Society for the Study of American Women Writers, as well as the International Nineteenth-Century American Women Writers Research Group in the EC, have been helpful in ways both tangible and intangible. Again I would like to thank Westbrook College in Portland, Maine (now part of the University of New England) for honoring me with the Dorothy M. Healy Visiting Professorship for research; it provided me with the time and resources to advance this and other projects. I extend special thanks to Bobby Gray, the Librarian of the College, and the library staff, for work well above and beyond the call of duty. I would also like to thank the following college and university libraries, and their excellent staff members, for their resources and assistance: Albany, Arkansas, Bates, Brandeis, Colby, Cornell, Dartmouth, Duke, Georgia, Harvard, Hull, Massachusetts at Amherst, Massachusetts at Boston, Mount Holyoke, New Hampshire, North Carolina at Chapel Hill, North Carolina at Greensboro, Northeastern State, Tufts, Vermont, Virginia, Wake Forest, Wellesley, Westbrook, and Yale. The wonderful Interlibrary Loan Staff at the Walter Clinton Jackson Library of the University of North Carolina at Greensboro, especially Gaylor Callahan, deserve special mention for their patience and hard work. I am appreciative of the important assistance provided by the American Antiquarian Society, the Oklahoma Historical Society, the Nebraska Historical Society, Phillips Exeter Academy, the British Library, and the United States Library of Congress. Special thanks to the Minnesota Historical Society for permission to print work from the Gilbert L. and Frederick N. Wilson papers, which contain Gilbert L. Wilson's field notes recording the narratives of Buffalo Bird Woman, and to the American Museum of Natural History,

Department of Anthropology Archives, also for Buffalo Bird Woman. My most important resource, however, has been my home institution, the University of North Carolina at Greensboro, for providing generous research assistance, including Regular Faculty and Summer Excellence in Research Grants without which this volume would not have been possible; thanks to the staff in the Office of Research Services (especially Nelda French), to my former Department Head, Jim Evans, and to the Dean of the College of Arts and Sciences, Walter Beale, for their continuing assistance and support.

Over the years many students have served as a testing ground for these materials, including my 1991 Native American Literature senior and graduate seminar at Tufts University; but the members of my spring 1999 Native American Women Writers graduate seminar at UNCG were particularly helpful in enabling me to finalize the selections. This collection also owes a tremendous debt to my excellent graduate research assistants in the last several years – Mary-Robyn Adams, Greg Tredore, Anna Elkins, Cassie Gainer, Kelly Richardson, Katie Ryan, Joseph Thomas, and Laura Shearer – without whom it would not have been completed within this millennium. Special thanks to Steve Brandon for his meticulous research on Narcissa Owen, for composing the headnote and bibliography for her selection, and for helping with footnotes and cover art. Lydia Howard's ongoing assistance in many areas has been important to the completion of this work.

Finally, I thank my patient editor, Andrew McNeillie, my excellent desk editor, Juanita Bullough, and the editorial staff at Blackwell Publishers, who waited for the immense task of locating, ordering, and reviewing hundreds of texts to be completed.

The editor will donate her profits from the sale of this volume to support Native American educational purposes.

# Writing "The Red Woman's America":[1] An Introduction to Writing by Earlier Native American Women

"They account for it by the fact that I am a Redskin, but I am something else, too – I am a woman" (232). So begins Pauline Johnson's "As It Was in the Beginning," a thrilling and moving tale of love, betrayal, and power. This assertion by Johnson's protagonist, Esther, is one that resonates throughout the body of this literature, where gender and ethnicity sometimes mesh and at other times clash. Like her Old Testament counterpart, Esther becomes a kind of orphan when she leaves her family and Cree people to live with the putative Christian, Father Paul; like the biblical Esther, Johnson's heroine ultimately acknowledges her heritage, in an act that reaffirms its importance. But – having been labeled "savage" – Johnson's Esther rejects patriarchal European savagery and reaffirms her connection with her "pagan mother." By the end of the narrative, however, she remains haunted by her Christian training: "I dream nightly of the horrors of the white man's hell. Why did they teach me of it, only to fling me into it?"(236).

As Johnson's story underscores, perhaps the first problem encountered by both students and teachers of Native American literatures is one of definition. Who is a Native American? How can we define Native American literature? Is there a Native American women's literary tradition in the nineteenth and early twentieth centuries? Making pan-Indian (that is, cross-tribal) generalizations in such matters can be difficult and to do so means risking oversimplification, especially in the case of women who occupy intercultural positions.[2] On the other hand, to avoid such conceptualization merely because it is difficult and complex means to deny to Native American writers one kind of power and authority very much valued in mainstream United States culture: the power of having a coherent tradition. This introduction, then, seeks to articulate some answers to these questions.

## Native American Identity

The question of identity is one with which individuals and governments, both Native and non-Native, have struggled for many years. But before we can offer some responses, it is useful to outline certain

---

1 See Zitkala-Ša's poem, "The Red Man's America," below, 298.

2 James S. Olson and Raymond Wilson, *Native Americans in the Twentieth Century* (Urbana: Univ. of Illinois Press, 1982), 14.

features of the history of Native American cultures in what is now the United States. When European explorers arrived in North America in the late 1490s, they encountered not an empty continent but one peopled by diverse groups of tribal cultures dazzling in the variety of their language, religion, social and political organization, and means of livelihood. These first Americans numbered in the millions, and they spoke hundreds of different languages, often with many dialects within those languages; California alone contained nearly three hundred different tribes.[3] The conflicts that arose between them and Europeans emerged not only from the latter's trespass and appropriation of Indians' homelands, but also because of major cultural differences, including religion, economics, and self-definition. The Indians' polytheism or pantheism contrasted with Europeans' monotheism, especially with the latter's sense of dominion over the earth and its creatures; their social organization valued community well-being (as opposed to self-centered individualism), which was reflected in common ownership and use of land and other resources; and their sense of history and tradition revered place and regarded time as cyclical rather than as linear.

One source of cultural conflict is particularly significant for our purposes: the role of women in Indian and European societies. Again, given the diversity among tribes, such generalizations are crude, but we can say that Indian women were often more valued than their European counterparts, perhaps because they lived within communal cultural organizations where every member of the group contributed to its well-being. Many Indian cultures affirmed women's power, whether through their important role in political matters or via matrilineal and matrilocal kinship forms, as with the Seneca. Europeans regarded women's roles in Indian societies from ethnocentric perspectives that often misinterpreted these roles. For example, one stereotype that emerged from many Indian women's horticultural activities was that the men were lazy while the women were beasts of burden. Assuming that men should be farmers and do all the outdoor manual labor, such a perspective failed to account for the complementary roles of Indian men and women, as well as the respect accorded the women for their crucial contributions to community survival. Moreover, Indian women also were believed to possess important spiritual power to harm or heal, especially at times of menstruation and pregnancy, unavailable to their male counterparts.[4] Politically, too, Indian women were often more involved than their white counterparts; as the historian James Axtell observes, "It was with some astonishment that eastern tribes treating with colonial legislatures or councils met with no women" (142). What needs to be observed, finally, is the variety of gender arrangements within the various tribal groups, arrangements that influenced narratives in specific ways that I will attempt to explore briefly in individual headnotes.

As this historical sketch suggests, American Indian identity is extraordinarily complex and has varied over time and location. One answer to the question of definition is an individual's blood quantum.[5] In the texts collected here, this issue emerges both indirectly and directly. For example, Pauline Johnson writes with great love and admiration of both her Mohawk father and English mother, while Lucy Lowrey Hoyt Keys highlights the accomplishments of her Cherokee maternal grandfather. Narcissa Owen offers an extended tribal history of the Cherokees in her *Memoirs* – in effect both preserving that history and affirming her connection to it – and though much of her narrative focuses on her experiences as an affluent Southern woman, she affirms her own affiliation with the Cherokees and devotes a significant amount of her narrative to an account of working in the Cherokee Female Seminary. The limitations of the blood quantum definition, however, emerge in Mary Jemison's account of her origins in a Scotch-Irish immigrant family.

Jemison's situation leads to a second resource for identity – community opinion. Jemison herself

---

[3] Ibid.

[4] James Axtell, ed., *The Indian Peoples of Eastern America: A Documentary History of the Sexes* (New York: Oxford Univ. Press, 1981), 103–4, 138; 3.

[5] Kenneth M. Roemer, Introduction to *Native American Writers of the United States* (Detroit: Gale, 1997), xi–xii. Roemer cites several sources on this issue, highlighting, among them, the Osage writer Robert Allen Warrior's concern that an overemphasis on identity can be constraining to a more complex understanding of American Indian literatures. Roemer's introduction includes community opinion, commitment to tribe, and self-concept as important criteria of Native American identity; I am deeply indebted to his discussion of identity and the characteristics of Native American literatures for the direction of my own account. Roemer's essay also refers readers to a rich variety of sources.

underscores her adoption ("In the place of our brother she stands in our tribe") and her acceptance by the Seneca as a member of the tribe ("With care we will guard her from trouble; and may she be happy till her spirit shall leave us") (43). Similarly, although we might see Narcissa Owen as more white than Indian, her participation in the tribal community suggests her place as a Cherokee among the Cherokees in spite of her relatively small blood quantum and the fact that her father, not her mother, was Cherokee. On the other hand, even a fullblood like Zitkala-Ša could feel excluded by community opinion, symbolized by her own mother. After her sojourn in an eastern Quaker school and her acceptance of many white cultural norms, including dress and language, her mother, who wishes her to return permanently to the Sioux community, leaves her feeling excluded; as she concludes "The School Days of an Indian Girl," "In my mind I saw my mother far away on the Western plains, and she was holding a charge against me" (320).

As Zitkala-Ša's case demonstrates, education can be an important factor in determining identity. Although writers like Schoolcraft, Keys, Owen, Johnson, and Zitkala-Ša clearly considered themselves to be Indian, they were all, to a greater or lesser degree, acculturated into white society, sometimes, as Zitkala-Ša's "The School Days of an Indian Girl" describes, painfully and reluctantly, and other times, as Schoolcraft's multicultural education and work in both traditional European and Ojibwa genres suggests, without overt conflict. Callahan's *Wynema* offers another, positive view of the role of white education, indicating an implicit affirmation of her own experience in a privileged Muscogee family.

Education clearly influences what Kenneth Roemer calls "commitment and self-concept," another means of specifying Native American identity (xii). Zitkala-Ša's pieces establish clearly her alliances, as does her activism on behalf of American Indians, a position shared in different ways by Sarah Winnemucca, Susette LaFlesche, Pauline Johnson, and Ora Eddleman Reed. LaFlesche's introduction to the novel *Ploughed Under* articulates a sophisticated and passionate perspective on the "Indian question," as it explores the equally problematic treatment of Indians as noble savage or howling savage. LaFlesche's diagnosis of the Indian problem as one of white greed in the economic system surrounding the Indian Bureau and the reservation system, and her advocacy of citizenship and legal rights for Indians, opens out into an apocalyptic vision of America's future, if the foundation for that future is corruption, inequality, and inhumanity.

## Native American Literatures: Authorship, Aesthetics, and Politics

As the heading for this section suggests, the diversity of tribal identities necessitates our thinking plurally as well as singly about Native American literature(s). In some sense, the idea of "literature" is itself problematic in relation to tribal cultures based in oral traditions, because "literature" is by definition written language.[6] Several of the "writers" included here are actually speakers: Jemison, the Fox Indian woman, Buffalo Bird Woman, and Owl Woman. Many of the writers acknowledge the ostensible paradox of "oral literature" through their retelling of traditional narratives, whether they be Schoolcraft's Ojibwa origin stories, Zitkala-Ša's Sioux trickster tales, LaFlesche's "Omaha Legends and Tent-Stories," Anderson's "Nowíta, the Sweet Singer," or Johnson's *Legends of Vancouver*. Such oral forms emerge more indirectly in the context of the longer narratives by Winnemucca and Owen; in the reinvented trickster story of Reed, "Billy Bearclaws, Aid to Cupid" and her collection of "Indian Tales Between Pipes" for *Sturm's Statehood Magazine*; and in Jemison's account of the adoption ceremony, itself embedded in a larger oral narrative.

---

6 For an extensive discussion of Native American oral literatures, see the essays in Andrew Wiget, ed., *Dictionary of Native American Literature* (New York: Garland, 1994), 3–145.

Beyond orality in literature, another paradox for Native American authors occurs with the representation of the individual author. For cultures valuing community and authorizing communal voices, such individualism may be a negative value, in contrast to mainstream culture.[7] The oral narratives collected here represent one version of multiply-voiced literature; transcribed, edited, and sometimes translated by a white auditor, they provide examples of what Arnold Krupat has called "bicultural composite authorship."[8] In such cases, it may be very difficult to distinguish the white editor's voice from that of an Indian interlocutor, but sometimes we can do so by highlighting the cultural norms and traditions articulated in the narrative.[9] Though in different ways, many of the writers in this volume often elude or subvert norms of individual authorship. The incorporation of tribal history into Western "autobiography," as in the case of Jemison, Keys, Winnemucca, and Owen, for example, disperses the position of the author across a broader field. Another means of dispersal is the rejection of Western norms of structural "coherence" and cumulative organization. Hence, although Mary Jemison's narrative – and Buffalo Bird Woman's, in the version published by her editor Gilbert Wilson – follow linear and cumulative narrative and temporal structures, Narcissa Owen's meanders and jumps, sometimes moving – "abruptly" in Western terms – from tribal history to medicinal cures ("Cherokee Cure for Snake Bite") to personal story. We see this organizational "disruption" enacted in fictional form in Callahan's *Wynema*, which also crosses boundaries of "fiction" and "history" as it explores the fictional character of Wynema and represents such historical concerns as allotment and women's rights.[10]

In spite of these observations, Native American women authors of this period sometimes accepted individual authorship. Writers like Schoolcraft and Johnson, for example, take on the voice of the mainstream romantic or pre-modernist poet, and many of their poems are indistinguishable from those of their white contemporaries. Similarly, Callahan draws from the resources of the sentimental novel in *Wynema*, while Reed pursues modes of realism and regionalism familiar to the readers of the high-culture *Atlantic Monthly*. We need to be careful not to overread the project of cultural resistance in Native American women's writing, because many of the writers, such as Callahan and Owen, were not only themselves relatively assimilated into white culture, but they believed in assimilation as a goal for American Indians.

In considering the wide range of writing in this collection, then, we might do well to think of Native American women as translators of Indian cultures or as cultural mediators between mainstream and Indian cultures.[11] We can also regard them as advocates or spokespersons for Indian cultures. Sometimes an individual writer occupies both roles. For example, when Zitkala-Ša published her autobiographical narratives, "Impressions of an Indian Childhood," "The School Days of an Indian Girl," and "An Indian Teacher Among Indians," in the prestigious *Atlantic Monthly*, she was both articulating her resistance to mainstream culture and educating white readers about the struggles and transformations of her people. In her later role as secretary for the Society of American Indians, she acted more explicitly as an advocate for Native Americans, publishing informative and activist pieces in periodicals like the *American Indian Advocate* and the *American Indian Magazine*, and producing the exposé, *Oklahoma's Poor Rich Indians*.

---

7 See, for example, Paula Gunn Allen, *Introduction to Spider Woman's Granddaughters: Traditional Tales and Contemporary Writing by Native American Women* (Boston: Beacon Press, 1989), 5, 9.

8 Arnold Krupat, "The Indian Autobiography: Origins, Types, and Functions," *American Literature* 53 (1981): 24; see also Gretchen M. Bataille and Kathleen Mullen Sands, *American Indian Women: Telling Their Lives* (Lincoln: Univ. of Nebraska Press, 1984), 9.

9 For two important perspectives on this matter, see Arnold Krupat, *Ethnocriticism: Ethnography, History, Literature* (Berkeley: Univ. of California Press, 1992), 3–45; Susan Walsh, "'With Them Was My Home': Native American Autobiography and *A Narrative of the Life of Mrs. Mary Jemison*," *American Literature* 64:1 (1992): 49–70. In "We planted, tended and harvested our corn': Gender, Ethnicity, and Transculturation in *A Narrative of the Life of Mrs. Mary Jemison*," I argue that the image of corn, important to Seneca women's identity, structures Jemison's narrative – as indeed it did her life. Karen Oakes, *Women and Language: Women and the Language of Race and Ethnicity* 18:1 (1995): 45–51.

10 This genre hybridity occurs in the work of other, non-Indian, nineteenth-century American women writers; see, for example, Helen Hunt Jackson's *Ramona* (1884). For a discussion of genre hybridity, see Karen L. Kilcup, "'Essays of Invention': Transformations of Advice in Nineteenth-Century Women's Writing," in *Nineteenth-Century American Women Writers: A Critical Reader*, ed. Karen L. Kilcup (Malden, Mass. and Oxford: Blackwell, 1998), 184–205.

11 David Murray, *Forked Tongues: Speech, Writing, and Representation in North American Indian Texts* (Bloomington: Indiana Univ. Press, 1991).

In this connection, perhaps it is useful to raise the issue of "political" versus "literary" writing. For Native American women writers, even those educated in white institutions, this distinction was far less rigid than in mainstream culture either in their time or in our own. Although texts like the editorials by Zitkala-Ša and Reed are overtly political in that they critique the dominant culture and attempt to provoke activism, other more ostensibly "literary" texts like *Wynema* and the short fiction of Pauline Johnson, Zitkala-Ša, and Ora Eddleman Reed contain potent political messages. *Wynema* emphasizes the importance of what LaVonne Ruoff highlights as "justice for women and Indians,"[12] especially in the chapter "A Conservative," where Genevieve Weir's fiancé, Maurice Mauran, evinces what we would today call a racist and sexist perspective, causing Genevieve to reject him in favor of the more enlightened missionary, Gerald Keithly. Mauran not only has an "indifferent and slighting manner of speaking about religion and secular matters, temperance and her much-loved Indians," he also condescendingly tells her, "As for woman's rights, I don't want my little wife to bother her head about that, for it is immodest and unwomanly" (270). Later in the book, Callahan depicts the suffering of the Indians after the Wounded Knee massacre via the mainstream literary motif of the grieving widow.

Johnson fights the racism and sexism of mainstream culture even more directly than Callahan, perhaps because of the relatively higher status of women in Mohawk culture. As the passage cited at the beginning of this introduction suggests, in "As It Was in the Beginning" Johnson affirms the power of Indian women in the face of patriarchal norms enforced by Father Paul in his efforts to separate the Cree heroine, Esther, and his weak-willed white nephew, Laurence. In sharp contrast to Esther herself is the infantile Ida McIntosh, with her "baby face, her yellow hair, her whitish skin" (235). When Father Paul relies on stereotypes to dissuade Laurence from a marriage to Esther – he tells his nephew that "you can never tell what lurks in *a caged animal that has once been wild*" (234) – Johnson has Esther act, ironically, precisely according to those racist images. Similarly, Reed's "Aunt Mary's Christmas Dinner" assails stereotypes of the dark, ignorant, savage held by the heroine's adoptive family when she pretends to be a newly-arrived servant girl.

From the perspective of mainstream culture, perhaps the most "literary" of all genres is lyric poetry – although we need to be aware that genre is itself a Western construct and is most useful as a tool for understanding rather than as a categorical imperative.[13] The Native American women poets collected here manifest an array of perspectives and approaches to verse. Although Schoolcraft writes romantic poems like "Lines Written Under Severe Pain and Sickness" and "Lines Written Under Affliction" that are indistinguishable from those of her white American and European contemporaries, she also writes poetry that affirms the power of her Indian grandfather. Similarly, while Johnson's "Erie Waters" and "Low Tide at St. Andrews" only intimate her Mohawk ancestry, others, such as the exquisite "The Corn Husker," "The Indian Corn Planter," and "Lullaby of the Iroquois," mourn the losses of Iroquois culture as they affirm its continued presence and power. Zitkala-Ša's few surviving poems articulate a strongly political stance and express anger at whites' hypocrisy and cruelty; at the other end of the spectrum, Owl Woman's songs highlight the beauty of everyday life in ways that recall (though they transcend) modern imagist poetry;[14] with their emphasis on the connection between spiritual life and concrete objects, they affirm the powerful perspective of their "writer" and her role as a healer in Papago society.

At this point more needs to be said about the relationship between aesthetics and politics. In mainstream literary tradition, modernist literary critics disparaged the articulation of what they defined as "political" concerns, emphasizing the more "purely" beautiful. As Andrew Wiget has observed, "judgments of satisfaction [about the quality of a literary text] are intimately linked to the reader's prior literary experiences."[15] This fragmentation between art that is culturally engaged and art that is cultur-

[12] A. LaVonne Brown Ruoff, "Justice for Indians and Women: The Protest Fiction of Alice Callahan and Pauline Johnson," *World Literature Today* 66:2 (1992): 249–55. For a discussion of nineteenth-century Native American women's writing more broadly, see, for example, Ruoff, "Early Native American Women Authors: Jane Johnston Schoolcraft, Sarah Winnemucca, S. Alice Callahan, E. Pauline Johnson, and Zitkala-Ša," in Kilcup, 81–111.

[13] Allen, 2; see Wiget, 11.

[14] See Paula Bennett, Headnote for Owl Woman, *Nineteenth-Century American Women Poets: An Anthology* (Malden, Mass.: Blackwell, 1998), 358.

[15] Wiget, "Native American Oral Literatures: A Critical Orientation," in Wiget, 4.

ally detached has often hampered understanding of the complexity, power, and beauty of much "non-mainstream" writing – that is, writing by people of color and white women. In the case of Native American women writers, we can perceive a sophisticated and subtle kind of "double-voiced discourse" in much of their work. That is, rather than seeing their writing as lacking a coherent or unified perspective, we might more effectively understand their work in the way that Phillis Wheatley has recently been read: as speaking simultaneously to two audiences and from two sometimes conflicting perspectives.

One good example of this complicated discourse is the "Introductory" chapter of Callahan's *Wynema*. The opening lines suggest the framing of a mainstream sentimental novel: "In an obscure place, miles from the nearest trading point, in a tepee, dwelt the parents of our heroine when she first saw the light" (261). This paragraph invokes both a sentimental fictionality and an "objective" perspective akin to that of an anthropologist. The next paragraph assumes yet another stance: "Ah, happy, peaceable Indians! Here you may dream of the happy hunting-grounds beyond, little thinking of the rough, white hand that will soon shatter your dream and scatter the dreams" (261). The rhetorical transformation from the first paragraph to this one is so finely nuanced that we might miss it: the sentimental tone remains, but here it is coupled with a sympathetic voice of an insider that inaugurates an extended and ironic meditation on what has been lost. By framing her novel in this way, Callahan invokes two audiences – the ostensible, white audience whom she aims ultimately to engage toward activism on behalf of Native Americans, and a secondary, already sympathetic Indian audience with whom she shares a chronicle of loss and outrage. In some sense, the "bicultural composite authorship" of earlier texts transcribed by whites is transformed into an internalized bivocalization. Combining political and aesthetic ambitions, Callahan's complex use of voice resonates in other writers collected here, including Narcissa Owen, Ora Eddleman Reed, and Sarah Winnemucca.

Another element of aesthetic complexity in Native American women's writing emerges in its structure. Modernist critics and their successors have often diminished non-mainstream writing not only for its "incoherent" or "confusing" use of voice, but also for its "awkward" structure. Rather than imposing external standards upon this writing, however, we should consider its internally defined standards and ambitions. In this light, we might understand Winnemucca's "erratic" narrative – which, as it opens, moves quickly from personal history to tribal history to political narrative back to a traditional origin story – as an example of associative rather than linear narration. Punctuated by first-person interpolations ("I can imagine his feelings, for I have drank deeply from the same cup" [131]), her story acquires the status of a stream-of-consciousness composition style that combines aesthetic and political goals. Like those of Owen and Callahan, Winnemucca's narrative also exemplifies a quality that we might call "genre hybridity." Combined with an associative narrative structure, such hybridity, which may combine elements of oratory, myth, autobiography, and sentimental fiction (as we see in Winnemucca's text), is easily confused with "lack of coherence" or insufficient control by the author. Many readers of early Native American women writers may need to suspend ordinary reading practices that value "consistency" and "unity."

A few genres, however, are shaped by these authors in ways that emerge from oral traditions and, because they may be less familiar to some readers, require a brief discussion. For example, although oratory is a form common in Western tradition from the time of the Roman republic, Native Americans developed their own forms of oratory. In its most familiar manifestation, oratory means "speeches addressed to Euroamericans in defense of Indian life, property, and liberty."[16] Such speeches characteristically construct an argument on behalf of a community; while they may be aesthetically beautiful and powerful, they are fundamentally engaged in a political process. We see variations on this genre in the petitions of Nancy Ward and the early Cherokee women, as well as embedded in larger narratives like Winnemucca's. Other genres could be integrated into traditional oral practices as well. Because of its emphasis on the individual (as well as its written form), "autobiography, as it is generally understood in the West, did not traditionally exist as a genre of discourse among the indigenous peoples of the present-day United States."[17] Nevertheless, versions of the coup tale, a traditional kind of oral autobiography

[16] Donald Bahr, "Oratory," in Wiget, 107.

[17] David Brumble and Arnold Krupat, "Autobiography," in Wiget, 175.

that recounted an individual's (typically, a male's) special, defining deeds, and self-vindication narratives, which justified an individual's actions, emerge here in various places, including Mary Jemison's repeated admonitions that Indians acted cruelly only when provoked, and Winnemucca's chapter on "Wars and Their Causes." At the same time, both of these writers combined accounts of their personal experiences with those of the tribal community.

The narratives of Jemison, Keys, Owen, and Zitkala-Ša offer strong criticisms of mainstream United States culture; although they rely (in very different ways) on the Euroamerican genre of autobiography, at many moments they transform themselves into tribal histories. For example, Jemison is insistent in her references to "our people" and "our Indians," while Keys's and Owen's account of the Trail of Tears emerge as the most overtly activist portions of their narratives. Keys, for example, underlines the treachery of the US government and the particular suffering of the old people on the journey; she observes bluntly, "Every camping place was strewn with the graves of the dead" (86). Representing Native Americans more broadly, Zitkala-Ša's account of her childhood in an Indian boarding school contains perhaps the most scathing depictions of white cultural imperialism, as she tells about how she was dragged from under a bed to have her hair cut (like a coward), was forced to speak English and punished when she did not understand the language, and was insulted at an oratorical contest in college where she was publicly labeled a "squaw."

## Native American Women: Tracing Traditions

Literary tradition is customarily defined as a coherent, self-consciously intertextual grouping of literary texts. That is, we assume that writers need to be aware of each other and responsive, in some ways, to each other's work. But we can think of "tradition" in broader terms, where it does not depend on an "intraliterary dimension."[18] Instead, we can define a tradition as a group of texts that share concerns and perspectives and that react to a common pattern of historical, political, and cultural moments. In this context, we can begin to frame an understanding of these shared values. As I have outlined above, some of these values include an awareness of the importance of orality in Native American culture and an attempt to shape written texts to reflect that importance; and an emphasis on community well-being and communal history rather than a focus on an individual. The writers collected here also incorporate other important concerns and values that enable us to view them cohesively; for example, virtually all relate, directly or indirectly, to the problem of Native American survival. Much of the writing enters into the ongoing nineteenth-century discourse of "civilized" and "savage," with many writers contesting the affiliation of the former with European American and the latter with Indian.[19] The account below begins by tracing some of the recurrent themes in Native American women's writing and concludes by reflecting on the perspectives that they represent.

### Themes

A crucial subject for many American Indian women is religion, and especially the role of Christianity in transforming Indian culture. Mary Jemison, for example, highlights the detrimental consequences of Christian education: "the attempts which have been made to civilize and christianize [the Indians] by the white people, has constantly made them worse and worse; increased their vices, and robbed them of

18 Richard Brodhead, cited in Diane Lichtenstein, *Writing Their Nations: The Tradition of Nineteenth-Century American Jewish Women Writers* (Bloomington: Indiana Univ. Press, 1992), 2.

19 See Roy Harvey Pearce, *Savagism and Civilization* (Berkeley: Univ. of California Press, 1988) and Lucy Maddox, *Removals: Nineteenth-Century American Literature and the Politics of Indian Affairs* (New York: Oxford Univ. Press, 1991).

many of their virtues; and will ultimately produce their extermination" (47). Jemison may have been reacting in part to the leadership of the Seneca prophet Handsome Lake, who, at the end of the eighteenth century, articulated a critique of Christianity and urged the Iroquois to return to their traditional beliefs. Writing from a similar perspective in "The Devil" section of "The School Days of an Indian Girl," Zitkala-Ša describes the unchristian attitudes and violent behavior of the whites in the Quaker missionary school that she attended as a child: the teachers attempt to frighten the children into belief with terrifying accounts of "an insolent chieftain among the bad spirits" and cause Zitkala-Ša to have violent nightmares. Like Mary Jemison offering resistance to Christianization via her outspoken language, Zitkala-Ša also offers physical resistance even as a child: "Stealing into the room where a wall of shelves was filled with books, I drew forth The Stories of the Bible. With a broken slate pencil . . . I began by scratching out [the devil's] wicked eyes" (316). In addition, Zitkala-Ša overtly rejects Christianity in her essay "The Great Spirit."[20]

Not all of these writers offered resistance to Christianity; others found it an important means to connect with as well as to critique white society. Considering herself a Methodist,[21] Sarah Winnemucca uses Christianity like her predecessor William Apess: to underscore the inconsistencies between words and behavior. When the Paiutes' reservation agent gives one ton of flour to the Shoshones, she castigates him harshly: "'You come up here to show off before this [new agent]. Go and bring some flour to my people on Humboldt River, who are starving, the people over whom you are agent. For shame that you who talk three times a day to the Great Father in Spirit-land should act so to my people.' This man called himself a Christian too" (161). Slightly later, she appeals directly to the reader: "Oh, my dear good Christian people, how long are you going to stand by and see us suffer at your hands?" (162). Highlighting the spiritual beliefs of her tribe, she implies her own amalgamation of belief when she describes the healing practices of the tribe: "Our medicine man cures the sick by the laying on of hands, and we have doctresses as well as doctors. We believe that our doctors can communicate with holy spirits from heaven. We call heaven the Spirit Land" (135). This passage may intimate, as Winnemucca does elsewhere, the complementarity of gender roles and the valuing of women in Paiute culture. Less critical of Christianity are Lucy Lowrey Hoyt Keys and Alice Callahan. In the case of Callahan, we see an adaptation of Christianity to Indian culture and, as elsewhere, an amalgamation between two cultures. Such an amalgamation also emerges in the work of Annette Leevier, who apparently rejects the Catholicism of her French-born mother for a belief in the Great Spirit yet retains a Catholic priest as a spirit guide, along with such figures as her father and the famous chief Pontiac, who led a pan-Indian revolt against white expansion into Indian lands.

In addition to a concern about the role of Christianity in their respective cultures, all of the women writers collected here offer insight into women's roles and perspectives. In cultures that divided roles into complementary parts, it was appropriate for women to discuss their own contributions. As the narratives, poems, and stories below indicate, these roles varied according to tribal affiliation, location, and other factors. Nevertheless, many describe common features of women's lives, however different these may have been across cultures: coming of age, marriage, family life, the bearing and rearing of children, work, play, and religious practices. For example, Mary Jemison affirms the excellence of her first husband Sheninjee, describes the births and deaths of children, and depicts women working together; Lucy Keys discusses her children and husband, outlines her work (and play) in the Cherokee Female Seminary, and details her work for the Confederacy with other women; Ora Eddleman Reed depicts repeatedly the experiences of mixed-blood Indian women in contact with white society; and Sarah Winnemucca, the anonymous Fox woman, and Buffalo Bird Woman tell of girls' coming of age.

---

[20] For a discussion of whites' cultural imperialism via Indian schools, see Laura Wexler, "Tender Violence: Literary Eavesdropping, Domestic Fiction, and Educational Reform," in *The Culture of Sentiment: Race, Gender, and Sentimentality in Nineteenth-Century America* (New York: Oxford Univ. Press, 1992), 8–38. "The Great Spirit" was published earlier (in a slightly different form) in the *Atlantic Monthly* as "Why I Am a Pagan."

[21] Gae Whitney Canfield, *Sarah Winnemucca of the Northern Paiutes* (Norman: Univ. of Oklahoma Press, 1988), 158.

Perhaps the most compelling account of the intersection of gender and ethnicity is Winnemucca's description of white men's sexual predation toward Indian women, an issue that provides a consistent refrain throughout her narrative. In the first chapter, as part of her family travels to California with her grandfather to work for two wealthy white men, Winnemucca observes, "So my brothers took care of their horses and cows all winter, and they paid them well for their work. But, oh, what trouble we had for a while! The men whom my grandpa called his brothers would come into our camp and ask my mother to give our sister to them. They would come in at night, and we would all scream and cry; but that would not stop them. . . . My uncles and brothers would not dare to say a word, for fear they would be shot down" (142). The money the family earns costs them dearly; not only do they live in fear of the women's violation, but also of being murdered if they do not capitulate to their masters' power. Winnemucca reinforces this theme again later when she pointedly observes, "My people have been so unhappy for a long time they wish now to *disincrease*, instead of multiply. The mothers are afraid to have more children, for fear they shall have daughters, who are not safe even in their mother's presence" (147). At times using Christian discourse, Winnemucca again highlights the whites' unchristian behavior.

The position and roles of children in their respective cultures is an important concern for many of the writers. Winnemucca provides some of the most detailed accounts of children's place in Paiute society and the affection of parents and grandparents. She is forceful about several differences between white and Paiute culture, observing, for example, that "Indians do not whip their children" (139). In turn, while implying significant differences between white and Indian kinship and community structures, she emphasizes that the mutual affection of parents, children, and family members in general, and the respect with which children are treated, affect the culture more broadly: "Our children are very carefully taught to be good. . . . We are taught to love everybody. We don't need to be taught to love our fathers and mothers. We love them without being told to. Our tenth cousin is as near to us as our first cousin" (146). Again emphasizing the difference between "civilized" white culture, where females are devalued, and Paiute culture, she describes the Festival of Flowers that represents a coming-of-age ceremony for the girls. Winnemucca articulates the respect accorded the young women throughout this description – as when she observes that a young woman "is never forced by her parents to marry against her wishes" – as well as the complementarity of gender roles. Particularly striking is her account of a father's role in childcare; after the birth of a child, he assumes very particular responsibilities, and "If he does not do his part in the care of the child, he is considered an outcast" (148).

Like Winnemucca, LaFlesche depicts a system of child-rearing that emphasizes kind care and mutual responsibility. In "Nedawi," when the protagonist forgets her small brother who is left in her care, her mother does not punish her physically, but attempts, with the help of Nedawi's uncle, Two Crows, to convey the seriousness of her failure. Similarly, stories like Schoolcraft's "The Forsaken Brother" emphasize the disastrous results for whole tribes of a brother and sister's selfishness and lack of care for a weaker brother. As Zitkala-Ša's "The Soft-Hearted Sioux" and "The School Days of an Indian Girl" make evident, however, a child's care for his parents and a mother's ability to care for her daughter are compromised when white culture intervenes in traditional Indian life. The generosity of children and their understanding of the principle of family well-being emerges in Mabel Washbourne Anderson's "Joe Jamison's Sacrifice," while Pauline Johnson's "boy's stories" in *The Shagganappi* and Zitkala-Ša's *Old Indian Legends* reveal an investment in children's moral education.

Another subject that these writers repeatedly explore is the matter of alcohol abuse and temperance. Mary Jemison attributes the loss of three sons to alcohol abuse. Describing the death of her son Thomas at the hand of his brother, John, she asserts, "He fell a victim to the use of ardent spirits – a poison that will soon exterminate the Indian tribes in this part of the country, and leave their names without a root or branch" (55). Lucy Keys's tribal history echoes this theme, as she observes, "As early as 1808, prohibitory laws were made to prevent the introduction of intoxicants into the Nation, for, when the Annuities were to be paid, vicious whites were ready with Whiskey to give, or, sell to the Indians that they might obtain possession of their money; this nuisance became so prevalent as to make it an absolute necessity to the Nation to act in its own defence" (83). Pauline Johnson's autobiography describes how her father gave his life attempting to prevent the sale of alcohol to his people; she describes the influence of alcohol with passion and pain: "The black and subtle evil of the white man's firewater had commenced to touch with its poisonous finger the lives and lodges of his beloved people."[22]

The retention of land represents another important theme in American Indian cultural survival. Jemison tells of her struggle to retain a share of the traditional land of the Seneca, while detailing her sale or transferal of certain lands to whites, including her lawyer. Reading this account, one has the uneasy sense that she and the Seneca have been deprived of their land by grasping whites. Winnemucca's story repeatedly describes the uprooting of her people and her efforts to obtain for them a permanent homeland. One of the most noteworthy of such narratives about land is Zitkala-Ša's "Chipeta, Widow of Chief Ouray, with a Word about a Deal in Blankets," published in 1917 in the *American Indian Magazine*. In addition to discussing her concerns about peyote addiction, Zitkala-Ša describes the reward given to Chipeta for her and her husband's many years of loyal service to white settlers and obedience to the white government. While Zitkala-Ša at first imagines that the reward will be something like "a genuine guarantee of water rights to the Ute Indians, or the title to their 250,000 acres of grazing lands to be held intact for the future unallotted children, or a message from the Great White Father giving news of Federal action against the peyote drug," the actual gift is "a pair of trading store shawls" (336).

## Perspectives

One similarity that frames these accounts is important to observe: the relatively high status of virtually all of the women in this collection, in spite of their interstitial cultural position. For example, Jemison became a Seneca matron; Keys, Owen, Winnemucca, and Johnson were descendants of tribal leaders; Schoolcraft, Owen, LaFlesche, Callahan, and Zitkala-Ša were well educated; and Keys, Owen, Johnson, and Reed came from affluent families. Only the anonymous Fox woman, Buffalo Bird Woman, and Owl Woman lacked such putative advantages; but even the latter two enjoyed increased status by virtue of their age and experience. So in some sense, many of the voices here are atypical, representing a relatively high degree of acculturation or of cultural privilege. This privilege often emerges explicitly in the writers' accounts. Sarah Winnemucca, for example, uses her position to underscore the situation of the "ordinary" tribe member. In concluding her poignant description of how Indian mothers buried their children alive for fear that the whites would eat them, she appeals to the Christian feelings of her readers: "I was once buried alive; but my second burial shall be for ever, where no mother or father will come and dig me up. It shall not be with throbbing heart that I shall listen for coming footsteps. I shall be in the sweet rest of peace, – I, the chieftain's weary daughter" (134). Calling upon a European sentimental as well as religious discourse, Winnemucca invokes the leveling effect of death as she highlights the vulnerability not only of herself, but also of her people.

Another form of privilege emerges in the narratives of Owen and Keys. Owen, for example, indirectly mentions her family's wealth: "While the family were making the trip from Webbers Falls to [Beaties Prairie], in November, 1833, the celebrated display of a meteoric shower occurred and frightened all of our colored servants nearly to death. They thought the world was surely coming to an end" (97). In describing the unexpected death of her father, she recalls the grief of her "two colored nurses": "The distress of the colored nurses was so great and their demonstrations of sorrow alarmed me in such a way that the scene was vividly impressed on my memory, though I was only three years old at the time" (97). As her account later makes evident, these servants were slaves. Owen also relates an incident after the Civil War in which the "family pet," Uncle Humphrey, is hired as the gardener until he can find a better wage elsewhere. Like Owen's, Keys's family also held slaves. Describing her maternal grand-

---

[22] E. Pauline Johnson, "My Mother," in *The Moccasin Maker*, ed. A. LaVonne Brown Ruoff (Tucson: Univ. of Arizona Press, 1987), 64.

father, she observes, "When about twenty years old, George Lowrey was married to Lucy Benge, a Cherokee girl, also of Scottish descent[;] she, too, owned quite a considerable amount of property, as, slaves, horses, cattle &c." (82). Using a common stereotype, her account of a watermelon-stealing episode between a servant named Billy and Col. Lowrey highlights the status (though not the race) of the participants. In concluding her account of her grandfather, she writes: "The years brought increasing prosperity to Mr. Lowrey, and he became the owner of a large number of slaves" (82). More broadly, the presence in this collection of numerous Cherokee writers, such as Nancy Ward, Owen, Keys, Reed, and the various women represented in the selections from *Cherokee Rose Buds* and *A Wreath of Cherokee Rose Buds*, reminds us that Cherokee women early on enjoyed a greater degree of literacy in English than many of their counterparts in other tribes and that they also possessed positions of power, authority, and respect in their matrilineal and matrilocal culture.

Status emerges differently and less directly in such writers as Schoolcraft, Johnson, Zitkala-Ša, Callahan, and Reed. The composition of poems like "Resignation" and "Lines Written Under Affliction," essentially unmarked by ethnicity and echoing the norms of contemporary romantic poetry, situates Schoolcraft in the world of comfortable, genteel womanhood, even on the frontier. Although all of these writers focus on Native American culture as a theme, all write from a privileged and well-educated perspective indicated by "correct" English and participation in mainstream literary traditions. For example, Callahan draws upon the tradition of sentimental literature to depict an Indian girl's simultaneous passage to maturity and, not coincidentally, to "civilized" life, through the education of a white woman reformer, Genevieve Weir. Her account of the love affairs of both Genevieve and her Indian heroine, Wynema, invoke middle-class norms of romance and domesticity. Ora Eddleman Reed's push toward acculturation emerges not only in her short fiction depicting young Indian women who can "pass" as white, but also in her editorials affirming the civilized quality of life in Indian Territory.

These writers also use their education to instruct white readers about Native American cultures, to underline the values of those cultures, and to advocate social reforms. Reed and Zitkala-Ša provide the most direct examples. Reed's essays in *Twin Territories* and *Sturm's Oklahoma Magazine*, such as "Father of 90,000 Indians" and "The Choctaw People," both inform white readers and affirm Indian civility, while Zitkala-Ša's essays for both white and Indian readers offer evidence of her passionate commitment to the improvement of American Indians' lives. Zitkala-Ša also attempts to educate white readers about Indian loyalty – and indirectly, to condemn white indifference and racism – in her account of Indians' participation in World War I: "The red man, citizen or non-citizen of our United States, is a loyal son of America. Five thousand Indian men are in our army. Some have already spilled their life blood in the trenches. Others have won military medals 'Over There.' Indian women are courageously knitting sweaters, helmets and socks for our brave soldiers. . . . Notwithstanding the difficulties that arise from the complicated system of classifying the government's wards, the Indian is in the front ranks of American patriotism. For absolute loyalty to the Stars and Stripes, the Indian has no peer" (337).

In addition to highlighting an important traditional genre in this collection, Zitkala-Ša's oratorical skill suggests another important theme in much Native American women's literature: language.[23] Early in her narrative Mary Jemison discusses her mother's injunction for her to practice her English; later on Jemison tells us that her Seneca sisters "were diligent in teaching me their language; and to their great satisfaction I soon learned it so that I could understand it readily, and speak it fluently" (44). Winnemucca underscores the power of written language in her affirmation of her grandfather's "paper" which he tells her "can talk to all our white brothers, and our white sisters, and their children" (136). At the same time, however, she affirms the importance of the Paiutes' oral tradition in her accounts of origin stories, dreams, and oratories. Perhaps the most severe critic of all the writers included here is Zitkala-Ša, whose account (in "The School Days of an Indian Girl") of whites' brutality in the face of the Indian girls' lack of English provides a poignant and powerful reminder of the power relations embedded in the notion of

---

[23] Brian Swann and Arnold Krupat, Introduction to *Recovering the Word: Essays on Native American Literature* (Berkeley: Univ. of California Press, 1987), xi.

an official language. Like several of the writers, Callahan explores the significance to Indians of learning English so that they can survive in an increasingly white world.

As the preceding account suggests, survival is a central concern for Native American women writers. Their approaches to the problem vary – where some value the acquisition of English and the acceptance of Christianity as part of a broader process of acculturation, others resist these incursions into Native American culture and seek to preserve a domain that is distinctively Indian. Perhaps nowhere is this more evident than in the traditional narratives retold by many of the writers in this collection. From Schoolcraft's elaboration of "Moowis the Indian Coquette" to Zitkala-Ša's retelling of trickster stories, the women of this period valued and helped to preserve Native cultures. A part of this preservation lies not only in the literal retention of language itself, but in the acknowledgment of what Kenneth Roemer calls the "generative force of words" (xv). Language is not merely descriptive or representative of concrete "reality," but it initiates, creates. Ultimately, for many of these writers, speaking out offers both an opportunity to preserve the culture of their tribe and an expression of hope – even confidence – in the power of language to effect justice, challenging the United States to match its rhetoric with reality.

# Traditional Narratives and Songs

*Reflecting the power of and respect for women in Native American cultures, the selections collected here indicate the importance of traditional narratives, which perform a range of functions. "The Woman Who Fell from the Sky," for example, offers a version of the Earth Diver story found throughout North America; here, with the animals who save her life and enable her future, a woman creates a new world. Other pieces, like the narrative of Kana'tĭ and Selu, "The Huhu Gets Married" and "{The Moon}," help explain complementary gender roles and responsibilities in Cherokee society, along with natural phenomena that reflect normative cultural practices. "The Huhu Gets Married," for example, reflects the fact that Cherokee women were the permanent members of the household, while "{The Moon}" highlights an incest taboo and offers an explanation for the relative positions of the sun and the moon. "Nûñ'yunu'wĭ, The Stone Man" indicates the regard for the power of menstruating women, here employed to save the community. The Navajo story of Changing Woman and White Shell Woman is part of the much longer creation myth;[1] in this segment, they give birth to the heroic children of the Sun, who will eventually slay monsters threatening the people.*

*Such narratives provide us with a framework for understanding the work of individual writers. Cherokee women such as Narcissa Owen, Lucy Lowrey Hoyt Keys, and Ora Eddleman Reed emerged from a cultural background that valued strong women and their crucial contributions to the survival of tribal traditions, perhaps enabling these "modern" women to retell tribal history, to manage families in times of enormous cultural upheaval, and to successfully challenge the restrictions of mainstream society on women's roles. These traditional narratives also anticipate the recounting by individual women below of tribal origin stories (for example, Buffalo Bird Woman and Sarah Winnemucca), of admonitory stories that sought to regulate behavior (Schoolcraft, LaFlesche, Buffalo Bird Woman, and Zitkala-Ša), and of heroism or betrayal (Johnson, Anderson).*

*Like those below of Owl Woman, also collected by Frances Densmore, some of the songs included here suggest the continuous relationship between what Western tradition would call "spiritual life" and "everyday life," while others, such as the Pueblo songs, indicate the celebratory and initiatory qualities of music in Native American traditions. The exquisite images of many of these songs, many sung collectively, invite comparisons with imagist poetry as they invite readers unfamiliar with their perspectives to imagine a reinvented view of human experience.*

---

[1] In some versions of the story, it is Changing Woman who gives birth to both children (and White Corn Woman is one of her guises); the version below makes clear that both boys are children of the Sun rather than of the Sun and Water Sprinkler. Representing life and the power of creation, Changing Woman herself is a central figure in Navajo mythology. She is the daughter of First Man and First Woman, and all Earth Surface People come from her.

## BIBLIOGRAPHY

### Primary

Converse, Harriet Maxwell. "Myths and Legends of the New York State Iroquois." In *Education Department Bulletin* (ed. Arthur C. Parker) 437 (December 15, 1908): 33.
Densmore, Frances. *The American Indians and Their Music.* Woman's Press, 1926.
——. *Chippewa Music.* Bulletin 45. Smithsonian Institution Bureau of American Ethnology, 1910–13.
——. *Papago Music.* Bulletin 90. Smithsonian Institution Bureau of American Ethnology, 1929.
——. *Pawnee Music.* Bulletin 93. Smithsonian Institution Bureau of American Ethnology, 1929.
——. *Teton Sioux Music.* Bulletin 61. Smithsonian Institution Bureau of American Ethnology, 1918.
Fletcher, Alice, and Francis La Flesche. "The Omaha Tribe." *Twenty-Seventh Annual Report of the Bureau of American Ethnology. 1905–1906.* Smithsonian Institution, 1910.
Jenks, Albert Ernest. *Journal of American Folklore* 15 (1902): 33–5.
Matthews, Washington. *Navaho Legends.* Houghton Mifflin, 1897.
Mooney, James. *Myths of the Cherokees and Sacred Formulas of the Cherokees.* 1900; rpt. Elder, 1982.
Owen, Mary Alicia. *Folk-Lore of the Musquakie Indians of North America.* D. Nutt, 1904.

### Secondary

Austin, Mary. Introduction to *American Indian Poetry: An Anthology of Songs and Chants.* Ed. George W. Cronyn. Fawcett, 1991.
——. *The American Rhythm.* Harcourt, 1923.
Densmore, Frances. *The American Indians and Their Music.* Woman's Press, 1926.
Fletcher, Alice. "Indian Songs and Music." *Journal of American Folk-Lore* 11 (April–June, 1898): 85–104.
Hofman, Charles. *Frances Densmore and American Indian Music: A Memorial Volume.* Museum of the American Indian, 1968.
Kroeber, Karl. *Traditional American Indian Literatures: Texts and Interpretations.* Nebraska, 1981.
Krupat, Arnold. *Ethnocriticism: Ethnography, History, Literature.* California, 1989.
——. *The Voice in the Margin: Native American Literature and the Canon.* California, 1989.
Murray, David. *Forked Tongues: Speech, Writing, and Representation in North American Indian Texts.* Indiana, 1991.
Ramsey, Jarod. *Reading the Fire: Essays in the Traditional Indian Literatures of the Far West.* Nebraska, 1983.
Roemer, Kenneth, ed. *Native American Writers of the United States.* Gale, 1997.
Tedlock, Dennis. *The Spoken Word and the Work of Interpretation.* Pennsylvania, 1983.
Wiget, Andrew, ed. *Dictionary of Native American Literature.* Garland, 1994.

# Narratives

## From Converse, "Myths and Legends of the New York State Iroquois," (1908)

### [THE WOMAN WHO FELL FROM THE SKY] (IROQUOIS)

In the far away days of this floating island there grew one stately tree that branched beyond the range of vision. Perpetually laden with fruit and blossoms, the air was fragrant with its perfume, and the people gathered to its shade where councils were held.

One day the Great Ruler said to his people: "We will make a new place where another people may grow. Under our council tree is a great cloud sea which calls for our help. It is lonesome. It knows no rest and calls for light. We will talk to it. The roots of our council tree point to it and will show the way."

Having commanded that the tree be uprooted, the Great Ruler peered into the depths where the roots had guided, and summoning Ata-en-sic, who was with child, bade her look down. Ata-en-sic saw nothing, but the Great Ruler knew that the sea voice was calling, and bidding her carry its life, wrapped around her a great ray of light and sent her down to the cloud sea.

### Hah-nu-nah, the Turtle

Dazzled by the descending light enveloping Ata-en-sic, there was great consternation among the animals and birds inhabiting the cloud sea, and they counseled in alarm.

"If it falls it may destroy us," they cried.

"Where can it rest?" asked the Duck.

"Only the oeh-da (earth) can hold it," said the Beaver, "the oeh-da which lies at the bottom of our waters, and I will bring it." The Beaver went down but never returned. Then the Duck ventured, but soon its dead body floated to the surface.

Many of the divers had tried and failed when the Muskrat, knowing the way, volunteered to obtain it and soon returned bearing a small portion in his paw. "But it is heavy," said he, "and will grow fast. Who will bear it?"

The Turtle was willing, and the oeh-da was placed on his hard shell.

Having received a resting place for the light, the water birds, guided by its glow, flew upward, and receiving the woman on their widespread wings, bore her down to the Turtle's back.

And Hah-nu-nah, the Turtle, became the Earth Bearer. When he stirs, the seas rise in great waves, and when restless and violent, earthquakes yawn and devour.

## From *Myths of the Cherokee and Sacred Formulas of the Cherokees* (1900)

### KANA´TĬ AND SELU: THE ORIGIN OF GAME AND CORN (CHEROKEE)

Long years ago, soon after the world was made, a hunter and his wife lived at Pilot knob with their only child, a little boy. The father's name was Kana´tĭ (The Lucky Hunter), and his wife was called Selu (Corn). No matter when Kana´tĭ went into the wood, he never failed to bring back a load of game, which his wife would cut up and prepare, washing off the blood from the meat in the river near the house. The little boy used to play down by the river every day, and one morning the old people thought they heard laughing and talking in the bushes as though there were two children there. When the boy came home at night his parents asked him who had been playing with him all day. "He comes out of the water," said the boy, "and calls himself my elder brother." Then they knew that the strange boy had sprung from the blood of the game which Selu had washed off at the river's edge.

Every day when the little boy went out to play the other would join him, but as he always went back again into the water the old people never had a chance to see him. At last one evening Kana´tĭ said to his son, "Tomorrow, when the other boy comes to play, get him to wrestle with you, and when you have your arms around him hold on to him and call for us." The boy promised to do as he was told, so the next day as soon as his playmate appeared he challenged him to a wrestling match. The other agreed at once, but as soon as they had their arms around each other, Kana´tĭ's boy began to scream for his father. The old folks at once came running down, and as soon as the Wild Boy saw them he struggled to free himself and cried out, "Let me go; you threw me away!" but his brother held on until the parents reached the spot, when they seized the Wild Boy and took him home with them. They kept him in the house until they had tamed him, but he was always wild and artful in his disposition, and was the leader of his brother in every mischief. It was not long until the old people discovered that he had magic powers, and they called him I´năge-utăsûñ´hĭ (He-who-grew-up-wild).

Whenever Kana´tĭ went into the mountains he always brought back a fat buck or doe, or maybe a couple of turkeys. One day the Wild Boy said to his brother, "I wonder where our father gets all that game; let's follow him next time and find out." A few days afterward Kana´tĭ took a bow and some feathers in his hand and started off toward the west. The boys waited a little while and then went after him, keeping out of sight until they saw him go into a swamp where there were a great many of the small reeds that hunters use to make arrowshafts. Then the Wild Boy changed himself into a puff of bird's down, which the wind took up and carried until it alighted upon Kana´tĭ's shoulder just as he entered the swamp, but Kana´tĭ knew nothing about it. The old man cut reeds, fitted the feathers to them and made some arrows, and the Wild Boy – in his other shape – thought, "I wonder what those things are for?" When Kana´tĭ had his arrows finished he came out of the swamp and went on again. The wind blew the down from his shoulder, and it fell in the woods, when the Wild Boy took his right shape again and went back and told his brother what he had seen. Keeping out of sight of their father, they followed him up the mountain until he stopped at a certain place and lifted a large rock. At once there ran out a buck, which Kana´tĭ shot, and then lifting it upon his back he started for home again. "Oho!" exclaimed the boys, "he keeps all the deer shut up in that hole, and whenever he wants meat he just lets one out and kills it with those things he made in the swamp." They hurried and reached home before their father, who had the heavy deer to carry, and he never knew that they had followed.

A few days later the boys went back to the swamp, cut some reeds, and made seven arrows, and then started up the mountain to where their father kept the game. When they got to the place, they raised the rock and a deer came running out. Just as they drew back to shoot it, another came out, and then another and another, until the boys got confused and forgot what they were about. In those days all the deer had their tails hanging down like the other animals, but as a buck was running past the Wild Boy struck its tail with his arrow so that it pointed upward. The boys thought this good sport, and when the next one ran past the Wild Boy struck its tail so that it stood straight up, and his brother struck the next one so hard with his arrow that the deer's tail was almost curled over his back. The deer carries his tail this way ever since. The deer came running past until the last one had come out of the hole and escaped into the forest. Then came droves of raccoons, rabbits, and all the other four-footed animals – all but the bear, because there was no bear then. Last came great flocks of turkeys, pigeons, and partridges that darkened the air like a cloud and made such a noise with their wings that Kana´tĭ, sitting at home, heard the sound like distant thunder on the mountains and said to himself, "My bad boys have got into trouble; I must go and see what they are doing."

So he went up the mountain, and when he came to the place where they kept the game he found the two boys standing by the rock, and all the birds and animals were gone. Kana´tĭ was furious, but without saying a word he went down into the cave and kicked the covers off four jars in one corner, when out swarmed bedbugs, fleas, lice, and gnats, and got all over the boys. They screamed with pain and fright and tried to beat off the insects, but the thousands of vermin crawled over them and bit and stung them until both dropped down nearly dead. Kana´tĭ stood looking on until he thought they had been punished enough, when he knocked off the vermin and made the boys a talk. "Now, you rascals," said he, "you have always had plenty to eat and never had to work for it. Whenever you were hungry all I had to do was to come up here and get a deer or a turkey and bring it home for your mother to cook; but now you have let out all the animals, and after this when you want a deer to eat you will have to hunt all over the woods for it, and then maybe not find one. Go home now to your mother, while I see if I can find something to eat for supper."

When the boys got home again they were very tired and hungry and asked their mother for something to eat. "There is no meat," said Selu, "but wait a little while and I'll get you something." So she took a basket and started out to the storehouse. This storehouse was built upon poles high up from the ground, to keep it out of the reach of animals, and there was a ladder to climb up by, and one door, but no other opening. Every day when Selu got ready to cook the dinner she would go out to the storehouse with a basket and bring it back full of corn and beans. The boys had never been inside the storehouse, so wondered where all the corn and beans could come from, as the house was not a very large one; so as soon as Selu went out of the door the Wild Boy said to his brother, "Let's go and see what she does." They ran around and climbed up at the back of the storehouse and pulled out a piece of clay from between the logs, so that they could look in. There they saw Selu standing in the middle of the room with the basket in front of her on the floor. Leaning over the basket she rubbed her stomach – *so* – and the basket was half full of corn. Then she rubbed under her armpits – *so* – and the basket was full to the top with beans. The boys looked at each other and said, "This will never do; our mother is a witch. If we eat any of that it will poison us. We must kill her."

When the boys came back into the house, she knew their thought before they spoke. "So you are going to kill me?" said Selu. "Yes," said the boys, "you are a witch." "Well," said their mother, "when you have killed me, clear a large patch of ground in front of the house and drag my body seven times around the circle. Then drag me seven times over the ground inside the circle, and stay up all night and watch, and in the morning you will have plenty of corn." The boys killed her with their clubs, and cut off her head and put it up on the roof of the house with her face turned to the west, and told her to look for her husband. Then they set to work to clear the ground in front of the house, but instead of clearing the whole piece they cleared only seven little spots. This is why corn now grows only in a few places instead of over the whole world. They dragged the body of Selu around the circle, and wherever her blood fell on the ground the corn sprang up. But instead of dragging her body seven times across the ground they dragged it over only twice, which is the reason the Indians still work their crop but twice. The two brothers sat up and watched their corn all night, and in the morning it was full grown and ripe.

When Kana´tĭ came home at last, he looked around, but could not see Selu anywhere, and asked the boys where was their mother. "She was a witch, and we killed her," said the boys; "there is her head up there on top of the house." When he saw his wife's head on the roof, he was very angry, and said, "I won't stay with you any longer; I am going to the Wolf people."

## [THE MOON]

The Sun was a young woman and lived in the East, while her brother, the Moon, lived in the West. The girl had a lover who used to come every month in the dark of the moon to court her. He would come at night, and leave before daylight, and although she talked with him she could not see his face in the dark, and he would not tell her his name, until she was wondering all the time who it could be. At last she hit upon a plan to find out, so the next time he came, as they were sitting together in the dark of the âsĭ, she slyly dipped her hand into the cinders and ashes of the fireplace and rubbed it over his face, saying, "Your face is cold; you must have suffered from the wind," and pretending to be very sorry for him, but he did not know that she had ashes in her hand. After a while he left her and went away again.

The next night when the Moon came up in the sky his face was covered with spots, and then his sister knew he was the one who had been coming to see her. He was so much ashamed to have her know it that he kept as far away as he could at the other end of the sky all the night. Ever since he tries to keep a long way behind the Sun, and when he does sometimes have to come near her in the west he makes himself as thin as a ribbon so he can hardly be seen.

## NÛÑ´YUNU´WĬ, THE STONE MAN

This is what the old men told me when I was a boy.

Once when all the people of the settlement were out in the mountains on a great hunt one man who had gone on ahead climbed to the top of a high ridge and found a large river on the other side. While he was looking across he saw an old man walking about on the opposite ridge, with a cane that seemed to be made of some bright, shining rock. The hunter watched and saw that every little while the old man would point his cane in a certain direction, then draw it back and smell the end of it. At last he pointed it in the direction of the hunting camp on the other side of the mountain, and this time when he drew back the staff he sniffed it several times as if it smelled very good, and then started along the ridge straight for the camp. He moved very slowly, with the help of the cane, until he reached the end of the ridge, when he threw the cane out into the air and it became a bridge of shining rock stretching across the river. After he had crossed over upon the bridge it became a cane again, and the old man picked it up and started over the mountain toward the camp.

The hunter was frightened, and felt sure that it meant mischief, so he hurried on down the mountain and took the shortest trail back to the camp to get there before the old man. When he got there and told his story the medicine-man said the old man was a wicked cannibal monster called Nûñ´yunu´wĭ, "Dressed in Stone," who lived in that part of the country, and was always going about the mountains looking for some hunter to kill and eat. It was very hard to escape from him, because his stick guided him like a dog, and it was nearly as hard to kill him, because his whole skin was covered with a skin of solid rock. If he came he would kill and eat them all, and there was only one way to save themselves. He could not bear to look upon a menstrual woman, and if they could find seven menstrual women to stand on the path as he came along the sight would kill him.

So they asked all the women and found seven who were sick in that way, and with one of them it had just begun. By the order of the medicine-man they stripped themselves and stood along the path where the old man would come. Soon they heard Nûñ´yunu´wĭ coming through the woods, feeling his way with his stone cane. He came along the trail to where the first woman was standing, and as soon as he saw her he started and cried out: "*Yu!* my grandchild; you are in a very bad state!" He hurried past her, but in a moment he met the next woman, and cried out again: "*Yu!* my child; you are in a terrible way," and hurried past her, but now he was vomiting blood. He hurried on and met the third and the fourth and the fifth woman, but with each one that he saw his step grew weaker until when he came to the last one, with whom the sickness had just begun, the blood poured from his mouth and he fell down on the trail.

Then the medicine-man drove seven sourwood stakes through the body and pinned him to the ground, and when night came they piled great logs over him and set fire to them, and all the people gathered around to see. Nûñ´yunu´wĭ was a great ada´wehĭ and knew many secrets, and now as the fire came close to him he began to talk, and told them the medicine for all kinds of sickness. At midnight he began to sing, and sang the hunting songs for calling up the bear and the deer and all the animals of the woods and mountains. As the blaze grew hotter his voice sank low and lower, until at last when daylight came, the logs were a heap of white ashes and the voice was still.

Then the medicine-man told them to rake off the ashes, and where the body had lain they found only a large lump of red wâ´dĭ paint and a magic u´lûñsû´ti stone. He kept the stone for himself, and calling the people around him he painted them, on face and breast, with the red wâ´dĭ, and whatever each person prayed for while the painting was being done – whether for hunting success, for working skill, or for a long life – that gift was his.

## THE HUHU GETS MARRIED[2]

A widow who had an only daughter, but no son, found it very hard to make a living and was constantly urging upon the young woman that they ought to have a man in the family, who would be a good hunter and able to help in the field. One evening a stranger lover came courting to the house, and when the girl told him that she could marry only one who was a good worker, he declared that he was exactly that sort of man; so the girl talked to her mother, and on her advice they were married.

The next morning the widow gave her new son-in-law a hoe and sent him out to the cornfield. When breakfast was ready she went to call him, following a sound as of some one hoeing on stony soil, but when she came to the spot she found only a small circle of hoed ground and no sign of her son-in-law. Away over in the thicket she heard a huhu calling.

He did not come in for dinner, either, and when he returned home in the evening the old woman asked him where he had been all day. "Hard at work," said he. "But I didn't see you when I came to call you to breakfast." "I was down in the thicket cutting sticks to mark off the field," said he. "But why

[2] The huhu is the yellow mocking-bird. According to Mooney, "it is regarded as something supernatural, possibly on account of its imitative powers, and its heart is given to children to make them quick to learn" (285).

didn't you come in to dinner!" "I was too busy working," said he. So the old woman was satisfied, and they had their supper together.

Early next morning he started off with his hoe over his shoulder. When breakfast was ready the old woman went again to call him, but found no sign of him, only the hoe lying there and no work done. And away over in the thicket a huhu was calling, "*Sau-h! sau-h! sau-h! hu! hu! hu! hu! hu! hu! chi! chi! chi! – whew!*"

She went back to the house, and when at last he came home in the evening she asked him again what he had been doing all day. "Working hard," said he. "But you were not there when I came after you." "O, I just went over in the thicket a while to see some of my kinsfolk," said he. Then the old woman said, "I have lived here a long time and there is nothing living in the swamp but huhus. My daughter wants a husband that can work and not a lazy huhu; so you may go." And she drove him from the house.

## From Matthews, *Navaho Legends* (1897)

### [CHANGING WOMAN AND WHITE SHELL WOMAN] (NAVAJO)

The two divine sisters, Changing Woman[3] and White Shell Woman, were left on the mountain alone.

The women remained here four nights; on the fourth morning, Changing Woman said: "Younger Sister,[4] why should we remain here? Let us go to yonder high point and look around us." They went to the highest point of the mountain, and when they had been there several days, Changing Woman said: 'It is lonely here; we have no one to speak to but ourselves; we see nothing but that which rolls over our heads (the sun), and that which drops below us (a small dripping waterfall). I wonder if they can be people. I shall stay here and wait for the one in the morning, while you go down among the rocks and seek the other."

In the morning Changing Woman found a bare, flat rock and lay on it with her feet to the east, and the rising sun shone upon her. White Shell Woman went down where the dripping waters descended and allowed them to fall upon her. At noon the women met again on the mountain top and Changing Woman said to her sister: "It is sad to be so lonesome. How can we make people so that we may have others of our kind to talk to?" White Shell Woman answered: 'Think, Elder Sister; perhaps some days you may plan how this is to be done."

Four days after this conversation, White Shell Woman said: "Elder Sister, I feel something strange moving within me; what can it be?" and Changing Woman answered: "It is a child. It was for this that you lay under the waterfall. I feel, too, the motions of a child within me. It was for this that I let the sun shine upon me." Soon after the voice of the Talking God[5] was heard four times, as usual, and after the last call he and Water Sprinkler appeared. They came to prepare the women for their approaching delivery.

In four days they felt the commencing throes of labor, and one said to the other: 'I think my child is coming." She had scarcely spoken when the voice of the approaching god was heard, and soon the Talking God and Water Sprinkler were seen approaching. The former was the accoucheur[6] of Changing Woman, and the latter of White Shell Woman. To one woman a drag-rope of rainbow was given, to the other a drag-rope of sunbeam, and on these they pulled when in pain, as the Navaho woman now pulls on the rope. Changing Woman's child was born first. The Talking God took it aside and washed it. He was glad, and laughed and made ironical motions, as if he were cutting the baby in slices and throwing the slices away. They made for the children two baby-baskets, both alike; the foot-rests and the back battens were made of sunbeam, the hoods of rainbow, the side-strings of sheet lightning, and the lacing strips of zigzag lightning. One child they covered with the black cloud, and the other with the female rain.

---

3 Estsánatlehi; White Shell Woman: Yo*l*kaí Estsán.

4 *S*ite'*z*i.

5 *H*ast*s*eyal*t*i; Water Sprinkler: *Tó*'nenili.

6 Birthing assistant.

## From *Folk-Lore of the Musquakie Indians of North America* (1904)

### The Girl-with-Spots-on-Her-Face[7]

All of the girls went out to get plums. Some of the girls were going to get married. The girl-with-spots-on-her-face was going to marry soon. A band came along. It was an enemy's band of young men, and they chased the girls. Some girls ran and got killed, and some hid and got away home, and the girl-with-spots-on-her-face was one of the girls to get caught. The young braves took them home, and those girls belonged to those braves that took them home. The girls were mad, but they could not help themselves at all; but after a while the girl-with-spots-on-her-face, she could help them. She made medicine in the tent, when that brave that was her man she hated for a husband was gone out. One night she made that man sleep and all the people sleep, and she waked up those two girls that were taken with her. They killed those three men and no more, and she danced and sang with a corn-ear in her arm to keep those folks asleep; and they took many ponies and went back to their own folks. The folks were glad those girls got back; and the young man that was her young man before she was stolen fluted her again. But she told him: "Young man, stop that! I don't want you any more, because you did not come after me when I was a prisoner to that man I killed." So he stopped, and she would not have any man in that camp; and she could not get a man, till a big brave came from a tribe far off, and she said: "Yes, I will go with this man." So she went away, and it was a good thing for that tribe she went to. The other girls, they married their men they had in the first place to marry. They were not much of girls.

## From *Journal of American Folk-Lore* (1902)

### The Bear-Maiden:
### An Ojibwa Folk-Tale from Lac Courte Oreille Reservation, Wisconsin[8]

There was an old man and woman who had three daughters, two older ones, and a younger one who was a little bear. The father and mother got very old and could not work any longer, so the two older daughters started away to find work in order to support themselves. They did not want their little sister to go with them, so they left her at home.

After a time they looked around, and saw the little Bear running to overtake them. They took her back home and tied her to the door-posts of the wigwam, and again started away to find work; and again they heard something behind them, and saw the little Bear running toward them with the posts on her back. The sisters untied her from them and tied her to a large pine-tree. Then they continued on their journey. They heard a noise behind them once more, and turned around to find their younger sister, the little Bear, running to them with the pine-tree on her back. They did not want her to go with them, so they untied her from the pine-tree and fastened her to a huge rock, and continued on in search of work.

Soon they came to a wide river which they could not get across. As they sat there on the shore wondering how they could cross the river, they heard a noise coming toward them. They looked up and saw their younger sister running to them with the huge rock on her back. They untied the rock, threw it into the middle of the river, laid a pine-tree on it, and walked across. This time the little Bear went with them.

After a short journey they came to a wigwam where an old woman lived with her two daughters.

---

7 Collected by Mary Alicia Owen. Although she was adopted into the Fox tribe, Owen's accuracy as an ethnographer has been questioned; see Michelson's notes to "The Autobiography of a Fox Indian Woman," included below.

8 Collected by Albert Ernest Jenks. Jenks notes: "the 'Bear-Maiden' was told by old Pä-skin´´, an Ojibwa woman considerably more than one hundred years old" (35).

This old woman asked them where they were going. They told her that their parents were old, and that they were seeking work in order to support themselves. She invited them in, gave them all supper, and after supper the two older sisters and the two daughters of the old woman went to sleep in the same bed.

The old woman and the little Bear sat up, and the little Bear told many stories to the old woman. At last they both appeared to fall asleep. The little Bear pinched the old woman, and finding her asleep, went to the bed and changed the places of the four sleeping girls. She put the daughters of the old woman on the outside and her own sisters in the middle. Then she lay down as though asleep. After a short time the old woman awoke and pinched the little Bear to see whether she slept. She sharpened her knife and went to the bed and cut off the heads of the two girls at the outer edges of the bed. The old woman lay down and soon was sleeping. The little Bear awoke her sisters, and they all three crept away.

In the morning when the old woman got up and found that she had killed her two daughters, she was very angry. She jumped up into the sky, and tore down the sun and hid it in her wigwam, so that the little Bear and her sisters would get lost in the dark. They passed on and on, and at last met a man carrying a light. He said he was searching for the sun. They passed on, and soon came to a large village where all of the men were going around with lights. Their chief was sick because the sun had vanished.

He asked the little Bear whether she could bring back the sun. She said: "Yes, give me two handsful of maple-sugar and your oldest son." With the maple-sugar she went to the wigwam of the old woman, and, climbing up to the top, threw the sugar into the kettle of wild rice which the old woman was cooking. When the old woman tasted the rice she found it too sweet, so she went to get some water to put in the kettle, and the little Bear jumped down, ran into the wigwam, grabbed up the hidden sun, and threw it into the sky. When the little Bear returned to the village, she gave the oldest son of the chief to her oldest sister for a husband.

The old woman was angry, very angry, to find that the sun was again up in the sky, so she jumped up and tore down the moon. The good old chief again became sick because the nights were all dark. He asked the little Bear whether she could bring back the moon. She said: "Yes, if you give me two handsful of salt and your next oldest son." She took the salt, climbed on top of the wigwam of the old woman, and threw it into her boiling kettle. Again the old woman had to go away for water. The little Bear then ran into the wigwam, and, catching up the moon, tossed it into the sky. The little Bear returned to the village and gave the chief's second son to her other sister.

Again the old chief got sick, and he asked the little Bear whether she could get him his lost horse which was all covered with bells. She answered: "Yes, give me two handsful of maple-sugar and your youngest son." The little Bear went to the old woman's wigwam, and, doing as she had done before, she made the old woman go away for water. She then slipped into the wigwam and began taking the bells from the horse which was there. She led the horse outside, but she had neglected to take off one bell. The old woman heard the bell, and ran and caught the little Bear. She put the bells all back onto the horse, and put the little Bear into a bag and tied the bag to a limb of a tree. When this was done she went far away to get a large club with which to break the little Bear's neck.

While she was gone the little Bear bit a hole into the bag and got down. This time she took all of the bells from the horse, and then she caught all of the dogs and pet animals of the old woman, and put them and her dishes into the bag, and tied it to the limb. Pretty soon the old woman returned with her large club, and she began to beat the bag furiously. The little Bear could see from her hiding-place, and could hear the animals and hear the dishes breaking as the old woman struck the bag.

When the little Bear took the horse to the chief, he gave her his youngest son. They lived close to the other two brothers and sisters. The little Bear's husband would not sleep with her, so she became very angry, and told him to throw her into the fire. Her sisters heard the noise, and came in to see what the matter was. The young man told them what their sister had ordered him to do. When they went away he turned toward the fire, and a beautiful, very beautiful maiden sprang out from the flames. Then this beautiful maiden would not sleep with her husband.

# Songs

## From *Chippewa Music* (1910)[9]

### LOVE-CHARM SONGS[10]

#### No. 71 (a)

What are you saying to me?
I am arrayed like the roses
And beautiful as they

#### No. 72 (b)

I can charm the man
He is completely fascinated by me

#### No. 73 (c)

I can make that man bashful. I wonder what can be the matter that he is so bashful

## Social Songs on White Earth and Leech Lake Reservations

### LOVE SONGS

#### No. 135 "My Love Has Departed"[11]

A loon
I thought it was
But it was
My love's
Splashing oar

[9] Frances Densmore (see headnote for Owl Woman, below) collected these songs, published in the Smithsonian Institution's *Bureau of American Ethnology*, Bulletin 45. Her introduction notes, "The songs . . . in this paper were obtained during 1907, 1908, and 1909, from Chippewa Indians on the White Earth, Leech Lake, and Red Lake reservations in Minnesota, a few songs also being secured from a Chippewa living on the Bois Fort reservation in Minnesota . . . An interesting fact concerning Chippewa songs is that the melody is evidently considered more important than the words . . . [In the words], the idea is the important thing" (1, 2). Densmore goes on to note regional variations in the songs she recorded.

[10] Songs 71 to 73 are songs of the Mĭdé (Grand Medicine), which, according to Densmore's introduction, "is the native religion of the Chippewa. It teaches that long life is coincident with goodness, and that evil inevitably reacts on the offender. Its chief aim is to secure health and long life to its adherents, and music forms an essential part of every means used to that end" (13). Densmore's disparaging comments about the unnamed initial singer of the song – whom she persuaded to sing with great reluctance – are troubling (88–9). All four songs were later sung for recording by Na′waji′bigo′kwe (Woman Dwelling among the Rocks).

[11] Sung by Mrs. Mary English.

To Sault Ste. Marie
He has departed
My love
Has gone on before me
Never again
Can I see him

### No. 136 "Why Should I Be Jealous?"[12]

Why should
I, even I
Be jealous
Because of that bad boy?

### No. 137 "I Do Not Care For You Any More"[13]

I do not care for you any more
Some one else is in my thoughts

### No. 138 "Do Not Weep"

Do not weep
I am not going to die

### No. 139 "He Must Be Sorrowful"[14]

He must be very sorrowful
Since he so deceived and forsook me
During
My young days

### No. 140 "When I Think of Him"[15]

Although he said it
Still
I am filled with longing
When I think of him

## From *Music of Acoma, Isleta, Cochiti and Zuñi Pueblos* (1957)[16]

### No. 19 Mother's Song to a Baby (Acoma)

First, the little baby through the medicine man's prayers has been given life,
Here and there, with the medicine man's song.

---

12 Sung by Mrs. Mee. Densmore notes, "This song is not without its humorous side. It is said that in the old times an Indian maid would lie face down on the prairie for hours at a time singing this song, the words of which are so very independent and the music so forlorn. The song was as often sung by a young man, the words being appropriately changed" (151). Songs 139 and 140 may be sung by either a man or a woman, with the appropriate pronoun shifts.

13 Nos. 137 and 138 are sung by Ki´tcĭmak´wa ("Big Bear").

14 Sung by Ki´ose´wini´ni ("Good Hunter").

15 Sung by Henry Selkirk.

16 Frances Densmore (see headnote for Owl Woman, below) collected these songs, published in the Smithsonian Institution's *Bureau of American Ethnology*, Bulletin 165. The singers (often a group) are not identified.

For the baby the songs have been sung.
Next, the baby's mother,
With the songs of the rain gods she has cared for the little baby.
Here and there the mother with the cloud cradle,[17]
The little baby was cared for.
It was nice that the clouds came up like foam,
As if it was among those soft little clouds,
With this the baby was cared for.

## Winter Dance Songs (Acoma)

### No. 22 A Little Golden Calliste[18]

There in the eastern turquoise chamber
There this morning a baby golden calliste was born

### No. 25 The Rain Clouds Are Caring for the Little Corn Plants

Nicely, nicely, nicely, nicely, there away in the east,
The rain clouds are caring for the little corn plants as a mother takes care of her baby.

## Flower Dance Songs (Acoma)[19]

### No. 26 Opening Song of the Flower Dance

Butterfly, butterfly, butterfly, butterfly,
Oh look, see it hovering among the flowers,
It is like a baby trying to walk and not knowing how to go.
The clouds sprinkle down the rain.

## Corn-Grinding Songs (Isleta)[20]

### No. 41 The Coming of the Sun

Early this morning the coming of the sun,
For what purpose is it coming?
Perhaps for the cornmeal it is coming.
    Yonder in the west at Shiawibat[21]
    All Isleta maidens, what do you think?
    What do you say? Shall we sit and sing?
Early this morning the coming of the sun,
For what purpose is it coming?
Perhaps for the yellow dust from the corntassels[22] it is coming,
    Yonder in the west at Shiawibat,

---

[17] The "baby carrier," in which a mother carries her baby, is called a cloud cradle [Densmore's note].

[18] Eagle.

[19] According to Densmore, these songs are part of a dance performed each February or March "'as an invitation to the flowers to bloom again'" (34).

[20] Densmore notes that these songs were sung in the early morning as "the women at Isleta grind the corn for household use. They sing at their work, and if some of the men are near they may join in the singing" (60).

[21] "The native name of Isleta Pueblo is 'Shiewhibak'" [Densmore's note].

[22] Pollen.

People of Shiawibat, what do you think?
What do you say? Shall we sit and sing?
Early this morning the coming of the sun,
For what purpose is it coming?
Perhaps for sons and daughters of the people it is coming.
Yonder in the west,
People, what do you think?
What do you say? Shall we sit and sing?

## No. 42 The Sun and the Yellow Corn

Over in the east, in the lake of the rising sun[23]
Over straight in the east,
The sun and the yellow corn are coming to us.

Over in the east, in the lake of the rising sun,
Over straight in the east,
The sun and the yellow corn are coming among us.

## No. 43 The Sound of the Raingods

How pretty they are coming.
The raingods make a sound up above.
How pretty! How pretty! That is so.
That is why this year the raingods will travel,
How pretty! That is so.
That is why this year the rain will fall,
How pretty! That is so.

## No. 45 Song to a Bee

Flower-fly, how pretty you sound.
I am very lonely but you sound too far away.

---

[23] Ocean.

# Nancy Ward (Nan-ye-hi; Cherokee, c.1738–c.1822) and Cherokee Women

*Born at Chota, a "Peace Town," Nancy Ward is probably the most famous early Cherokee woman, occupying the elevated position of War Woman,*[1] *which she gained for joining a battle against the Creeks when her husband was killed. Having distinguished themselves in battle, such women were entitled to speak in council, to participate in ceremonies like the Eagle Dance, which memorialized earlier victories, and to decide the fate of war captives. Possessing both the traditional power of women and that of men made them extraordinary, to be both feared and admired. Like all women in matrilineal and matrilocal Cherokee society, Ward enjoyed considerable political power and authority, which was exercised according to the dictates of an individual's conscience but always with the community's best interests in mind; like some Cherokee women, Ward became an intermediary between her people and the United States. Meeting on two such occasions, in 1781 at Holston, in what is now northeastern Tennessee, and 1785 in Hopewell, South Carolina, with United States treaty commissioners, Ward used the rhetoric of motherhood to convey her desires and hopes for peaceful relations between the US government and Cherokee people. Underpinning her language was the esteem, prestige, and authority enjoyed by Cherokee women; rather than being a sentimental appeal to motherhood – which in white culture would have been an appeal to "influence" – her speeches attempt to establish a relationship of kinship, centered on women, fundamental in traditional Cherokee culture.*

*Ward's speeches to external authorities show one side of early Cherokee women's voices; another is the petition of a group of women – signed by thirteen, including Ward – to the Cherokee National Council in 1817. Drawing upon their traditional roles as mothers, agriculturalists, and keepers of the land, they forcefully argued on this occasion and again in 1818 against the sale of additional land to the US government and the allotment of land to individuals, both of which would have destroyed the communal social fabric and threatened the future of the Cherokee people. Although the women's efforts appear not to have been entirely successful (some land was ceded in 1817 and 1819), the council resisted allotment and ultimately affirmed that they would make no more cessions, prompting the US government to conspire with unauthorized representatives of the tribe to obtain the Treaty of New Echota in 1835, which exchanged the Cherokee homeland for land west of the Mississippi and agreed to the tribe's removal from their ancestral lands within two years. Many years later, even the progressive Cherokees Lucy Lowrey Hoyt Keys and Narcissa Owen recount with anger the abuses of the Trail of Tears during the winter of 1838–39, continuing a tradition of activism and protest that had begun much earlier.*

1 Ward is frequently referred to as the last Beloved Woman of the Cherokees. Perdue comments on the relationship between the titles "War Woman" and "Beloved Woman": "Some sources use the terms *War Woman* and *beloved woman* interchangeably, and they may have applied to the same women. But Cherokees distinguished between pre- and postmenopausal women, and evidence suggests that beloved women were elderly while War Women were of indeterminate age. War Women probably became "beloved" when they passed menopause" (39).

## BIBLIOGRAPHY


### Primary

*Nancy Ward*

Samuel Hazard[, ed]. *Pennsylvania Archives. Selected and Arranged from Original Documents in the Office of the Secretary of the Commonwealth, Conformably to Acts of the General Assembly, February 15, 1851, & March 1, 1852. By Commencing 1786.* Vol. XI. Philadelphia: Joseph Severns, 1855.

War Woman of Chota to the Treaty Commissioners, 23 Nov. 1785. *American State Papers*, Class 2: *Indian Affairs*. Gales and Seaton, 1832.

Williams, Samuel Cole. *Tennessee during the Revolutionary War*. Tennessee, 1974.

*Cherokee Women*

Brainerd Journal. June 30, 1818, Papers of the American Board of Commissioners for Foreign Missions. Houghton Library, Harvard University

Cyrus Kingsbury Journal. 13 February 1817. Papers of the American Board of Commissioners for Foreign Missions. Houghton Library, Harvard University.

Petition, *Cherokee Phoenix*, November 12, 1831.

Presidential Papers Microfilm: Andrew Jackson. Washington, DC, 1961. Vol. 44 (1817), Series 1, reel 22.

### Secondary

McClary, Ben Harris. "Nancy Ward: The Last Beloved Woman of the Cherokees." *Tennessee Historical Quarterly* 21 (1962): 352–64.

Smith, D. Ray. "Nancy Ward (1738–1822), Last Beloved Woman of the Cherokee." In *The Tennessee Encyclopedia of History & Culture*. Ed. Caroll Van West. Tennessee Historical Society and Rutledge Hill Press, 1998.

"Nancy Ward, c.1738–1824, Cherokee Tribal Leader." In *U X L® Biographies 2.0*. U X L, CD-ROM, Gale, 1996.

Perdue, Theda. *Cherokee Women: Gender and Culture Change, 1700–1835*. Nebraska, 1998.

Perdue, Theda, and Michael D. Green, eds. *The Cherokee Removal: A Brief History with Documents*. Bedford, 1995.

Williams, Samuel Cole. *Tennessee During the Revolutionary War*. Tennessee, 1974.


## [Speech to the US Treaty Commissioners] (Ward, 1781)

You know that women are always looked upon as nothing; but we are your mothers; you are our sons. Our cry is all for peace; let it continue. This peace must last forever. Let your women's sons be ours; our sons be yours. Let your women hear our words.[2]

---

[2] Colonel William Christian delivered the response: "Mothers: We have listened well to your talk; it is humane . . . No man can hear it without being moved by it. Such words and thoughts show the world that human nature is the same everywhere. Our women shall hear your words, and we know how they will feel and think of them. We are all descendants of the same woman. We will not quarrel with you, because you are our mothers. We will not meddle with your people if they will be still and quiet at home and let us live in peace" (cited in Williams, 201).

## [Speech to the US Treaty Commissioners] (Ward, 1785)

I am fond of hearing that there is a peace, and I hope you have now taken us by the hand in real friendship. I have a pipe and a little tobacco to give the commissioners to smoke in friendship. I look on you and the red people as my children. Your having determined on peace is most pleasing to me, for I have seen much trouble during the late war. I am old, but I hope yet to bear children, who will grow up and people our nation, as we are now to be under the protection of Congress, and shall have no more disturbance. – [A string, little old pipe, and some tobacco.]

The talk I have given, is from the young warriors I have raised in my town as well as myself. They rejoice that we have peace, and we hope the chain of friendship will never more be broke. – [A string of beads.]

## Cherokee Indian Women to President Franklin (1787)

Brother,

I am in hopes my Brothers & the Beloved men near the water side will heare from me. This day I filled the pipes that they smoaked in piece, and I am in hopes the smoake has Reached up to the skies above. I here send you a piece of the same Tobacco, and am in hopes you & your Beloved men will smoake it in Friendship – and I am glad in my heart that I am the mother of men that will smoak it in piece.

Brother,

I am in hopes if you Rightly consider it that woman is the mother of All – and that woman Does not pull Children out of Trees or Stumps nor out of old Logs, but out of their Bodies, so that they ought to mind what a woman says, and look upon her as a mother – and I have Taken the privelage to Speak to you as my own Children, & the same as if you had sucked my Breast – and I am in hopes you have a beloved woman amongst you who will help to put her Children Right if they do wrong, as I shall do the same – the great men have all promised to Keep the path clear & straight, as my Children shall Keep the path clear & white so that the Messengers shall go & come in safety Between us – the old people is never done Talking to their Children – which makes me say so much as I do. The Talk you sent to me was to talk to my Children, which I have done this day, and they all liked my Talk well, which I am in hopes you will heare from me Every now & then that I keep my Children in piece – tho' I am a woman giving you this Talk, I am in hopes that you and all the Beloved men in Congress will pay particular Attention to it, as I am Delivering it to you from the Bottom of my heart, that they will Lay this on the white stool in Congress, wishing them all well & success in all their undertakings – I hold fast the good Talk I Received from you my Brother, & thanks you kindly for your good Talks, & your presents, & the kind usage you gave to my son.

From KATTEUHA, The Beloved woman of Chota.[3]

---

[3] Accompanied by various gifts for "the Great Chiefs of the Cherokee Nation" and for "the Beloved Woman," the petition is signed by two other women, identified by the witnesses as Kaattahee (Corn Tassel) and Scolecutta (Haning Maw). Katteuha's identity is unclear. Because Nancy Ward was the only known Beloved Woman at this time, it is possible that the transcriber mistook her title, "Ghighau," for "Katteuha." Alternatively, "Katteuha" may refer to the national women's council, for whom, as Ghighau, Ward could have spoken.

## [Petition to the Cherokee National Council] (Cherokee Women and Ward, May 2, 1817)[4]

The Cherokee Ladys now being present at the meeting of the chiefs and warriors in council have thought it their duty as mothers to address their beloved chiefs and warriors now assembled.

Our beloved children and head men of the Cherokee Nation, we address you warriors in council. We have raised all of you on the land which we now have, which God gave us to inhabit and raise provisions. We know that our country has once been extensive, but by repeated sales has become circumscribed to a small track, and [we] never have thought it our duty to interfere in the disposition of it till now. If a father or mother was to sell all their lands which they had to depend on, which their children had to raise their living on, [it] would be indeed bad & [so would it be] to be removed to another country. We do not wish to go to an unknown country which we have understood some of our children wish to go [to] over the Mississippi, but this act of our children would be like destroying your mothers.

Your mothers, your sisters ask and beg of you not to part with any more of our lands. We say ours. You are our descendants; take pity on our request. But keep it for our growing children, for it was the good will of our creator to place us here, and you know our father, the great president,[5] will not allow his white children to take our country away. Only keep your hands off of paper talks for it is our own country. For [if] it was not, they would not ask you to put your hands to paper, for it would be impossible to remove us all. For as soon as one child is raised, we have others in our arms, for such is our situation & [they] will consider our circumstances.

Therefore, children, don't part with any of our lands but continue on it & enlarge your farms & cultivate and raise corn & cotton, and your mothers and sisters will make clothing for you which our father the president has recommended to us all. We don't charge any body for selling any lands, but we have heard such intentions of our children. But your talks become true at last & it was our desire to forwarn you all not to part with our lands.

Nancy Ward to her children: Warriors to take pity and listen to the talks of your sisters. Although I am very old yet [I] cannot but pity the situation in which you will here of their minds. I have great many grand children which I wish them to do well on our land.

## [Petition to the Cherokee National Council] (Cherokee Women and Ward, June 30, 1818)

Beloved Children,

We have called a meeting among ourselves to consult on the different points now before the council, relating to our national affairs. We have heard with painful feelings that the bounds of the land we now possess are to be drawn into very narrow limits. The land was given to us by the Great Spirit above as our common right, to raise our children upon, & to make support for our rising generations. We therefore humbly petition our beloved children, the head men & warriors, to hold out to the last in support of our common rights, as the Cherokee nation have been the first settlers of this land; we therefore claim the right of the soil.

We well remember that our country was formerly very extensive, but by repeated sales it has become circumscribed to the very narrow limits we have at present. Our Father the President advised us to become farmers, to manufacture our own clothes, & to have our children instructed. To this advice we have attended in every thing as far as we were able. Now the thought of us being compelled to remove

[4] This petition is signed by Nancy Ward and twelve other Cherokee women.

[5] James Monroe (1758–1838), fifth US president, 1817–25.

[to] the other side of the Mississippi is dreadful to us, because it appears to us that we, by this removal, shall be brought to a savage state again, for we have, by the endeavor of our Father the President, become too much enlightened to throw aside the privileges of a civilized life.

We therefore unanimously join in our meeting to hold our country in common as hitherto.

Some of our children have become Christians. We have missionary schools among us. We have heard the gospel in our nation. We have become civilized and enlightened, & are in hopes that in a few years our nation will be prepared for instruction in other branches of sciences & arts, which are both useful and necessary in civilized society.

There are some white men among us who have been raised in this country from their youth, are connected with us by marriage, & have considerable families, who are very active in encouraging the emigration of our nation. These ought to be our truest friends but prove our worst enemies. They seem to be only concerned how to increase their riches, but do not care what becomes of our Nation, nor even of their own wives and children.

## [Petition to the Cherokee National Council]
## (Cherokee Women, c. October, 1821; from the *Cherokee Phoenix*, 1831)

To the Committee and Council,

We the females, residing in Salequoree and Pine Log, believing that the present difficulties and embarrassments under which this nation is placed demands a full expression of the mind of every individual, on the subject of emigrating to Arkansas, would take upon ourselves to address you. Although it is not common for our sex to take part in public measures, we nevertheless feel justified in expressing our sentiments on any subject where our interest is as much at stake as any other part of the community.

We believe the present plan of the General Government to effect our removal West of the Mississippi, and thus obtain our lands for the use of the State of Georgia, to be highly oppressive, cruel and unjust. And we sincerely hope there is no consideration which can induce our citizens to forsake the land of our fathers of which they have been in possession from time immemorial, and thus compel us, against our will, to undergo the toils and difficulties of removing with our helpless families hundreds of miles to unhealthy and unproductive country. We hope therefore the Committee and Council will take into deep consideration our deplorable situation, and do everything in their power to avert such a state of things. And we trust by a prudent course their transactions with the General Government will enlist in our behalf the sympathies of the good people of the United States.

# Mary Jemison (Degiwene's, Two Falling Voices; Seneca, c.1743–1833)

*Born on the Atlantic crossing from Ireland in about 1743, Jemison settled with her Scotch-Irish parents, Thomas Jemison and Jane Erwin Jemison, on a farm in western Pennsylvania. When Jemison was about fifteen, a group of Shawnee Indians and French military forces captured her and her family, finally killing Jemison's parents, two brothers, and sister. The opening chapters of her narrative describe the hardships of the journey to the Fort Duquesne area, where she was adopted by two Seneca sisters to take the place of a brother who had been killed in war; such adoptions were a common practice not only for the Iroquois (of whom the Seneca were a member tribe) but for many Native American tribes. Becoming further integrated into the community after her marriages first, to a Delaware and, after his death, a Seneca man, she had several children. This fact, along with the respect and power accorded to Seneca women, probably cemented her decision to remain with the Indians when she had the opportunity to return to "civilized" society. Not uncommon, such a decision caused anxiety, if not consternation, in the supposedly "superior" culture.*

*Jemison's position as a Seneca matron in a matrilineal society meant that her powers included the ability to select and depose male members of war councils, to participate in tribal spiritual life, and to control property and family matters. We see her here focusing on matters most relevant to Seneca women's lives, including marriage, children, and family; the cultivation of the land; and, most poignantly, the deleterious consequences of contact with whites, including the introduction of "spiritous liquors" responsible for the violence in her own family. Reversing the stereotype of Indian women as beasts of burden, Jemison's narrative offers a striking comparison of Seneca women's horticultural duties with European American women's hard domestic labor. The story is structured in part by the seasons of corn growth, offering a cyclical pattern that counterpoints the linearity of the narrative emphasized or even imposed by the editor.*

*Jemison recounted her life story to this editor, the European American doctor James E. Seaver, when she was about 80 years old. Seaver's "Author's Preface" and "Author's Introduction" highlight the composite nature of the narrative, for we see him here acknowledging his editorial hand in matters such as organization and style. Seaver framed Jemison's story in the popular genre of the captivity narrative, a form of spiritual autobiography in which the captive depicts the trials of captivity and (at least in earlier incarnations) underscores God's power in enabling her or him to bear up under hardship and in effecting his or her release. Often lurid and violent, these narratives served in part to reinforce the superiority of "civilized" European Americans and the "savagery" of their Indian counterparts. Jemison's story escapes from the conventions of the captivity narrative, however, to emphasize the Indians' kindness, gentleness, and civility – often in contrast to white counterparts – and to explain the motivations behind their customs and behavior.*

*Living through a period of intense turmoil in American history – from the Revolutionary War to the War of*

*1812, Jemison offers the perspective of a woman who not only survived but prospered in her transcultural experience. "The White Woman of the Genessee" explicitly considers herself an Indian – as do the Seneca today, among whom live many of her descendants. Jemison provides a touchstone figure for matters of identity, and she has only recently begun to be recognized by scholars as a Native American. Because her narrative combines her voice and that of her white editor, reflecting the text's bicultural composite authorship, it continues to offer readers provocative questions about aesthetics, voice, authenticity, and assimilation.*

## BIBLIOGRAPHY


### Primary

*A Narrative of the Life of Mrs. Mary Jemison.* Ed. James E. Seaver. Syracuse, 1990.
*A Narrative of the Life of Mrs. Mary Jemison.* Ed. June Namias. Oklahoma, 1992.

### Secondary

Bataille, Gretchen M., and Kathleen Mullen Sands. *American Indian Women: Telling Their Lives.* Nebraska, 1984.

Kolodny, Annette. *The Land Before Her: Fantasy and Experience of the American Frontiers, 1630–1860.* North Carolina, 1984.

Namias, June. Introduction. *A Narrative of the Life of Mrs. Mary Jemison.* Oklahoma, 1992.

——. *White Captives: Gender and Ethnicity on the American Frontier.* North Carolina, 1993.

Oakes, Karen [Kilcup]. "'We Planted, Tended and Harvested Our Corn': Gender, Ethnicity, and Transculturation in *A Narrative of the Life of Mrs. Mary Jemison.*" *Women and Language* 18:1 (1995): 45–51.

Scheckel, Susan. *The Insistence of the Indian: Race and Nationalism in Nineteenth-Century American Literature.* Princeton, 1998.

VanDerBeets, Richard. *The Indian Captivity Narrative: An American Genre.* Univ. Press of America, 1984.

Walsh, Susan. "'With Them Was My Home": Native American Autobiography and *A Narrative of the Life of Mrs. Mary Jemison.*" *American Literature* 64:1 (1992): 49–70.


# From *A Narrative of the Life of Mrs. Mary Jemison* (1824)

## AUTHOR'S PREFACE
## [JAMES E. SEAVER]

That to biographical writings we are indebted for the greatest and best field in which to study mankind, or human nature, is a fact duly appreciated by a well-informed community. In them we can trace the effects of mental operations to their proper sources; and by comparing our own composition with that of those who have excelled in virtue, or with that of those who have been sunk in the lowest depths of folly and vice, we are enabled to select a plan of life that will at least afford self-satisfaction, and guide us through the world in paths of morality.

Without a knowledge of the lives of the vile and abandoned, we should be wholly incompetent to set an appropriate value upon the charms, the excellence and the worth of those principles which have produced the finest traits in the characters of the most virtuous.

Biography is a telescope of life, through which we can see the extremes and excesses of the varied properties of the human heart. Wisdom and folly, refinement and vulgarity, love and hatred, tenderness and cruelty, happiness and misery, piety and infidelity, commingled with every other cardinal virtue or vice, are to be seen on the variegated pages of the history of human events, and are eminently deserving the attention of those who would learn to walk in the "paths of peace."

The brazen statue and the sculptured marble, can commemorate the greatness of heroes, statesmen, philosophers, and blood-stained conquerors, who have risen to the zenith of human glory and popularity, under the influence of the mild sun of prosperity: but it is the faithful page of biography that transmits to future generations the poverty, pain, wrong, hunger, wretchedness and torment, and every nameless misery that has been endured by those who have lived in obscurity, and groped their lonely way through a long series of unpropitious events, with but little help besides the light of nature. While the gilded monument displays in brightest colors the vanity of pomp, and the emptiness of nominal greatness, the biographical page, that lives in every line, is giving lessons of fortitude in time of danger, patience in suffering, hope in distress, invention in necessity, and resignation to unavoidable evils. Here also may be learned, pity for the bereaved, benevolence for the destitute, and compassion for the helpless; and at the same time all the sympathies of the soul will be naturally excited to sigh at the unfavorable result, or to smile at the fortunate relief.

In the great inexplicable chain which forms the circle of human events, each individual link is placed on a level with the others, and performs an equal task; but, as the world is partial, it is the situation that attracts the attention of mankind, and excites the unfortunate vociferous eclat of elevation, that raises the pampered parasite to such an immense height in the scale of personal vanity, as, generally, to deprive him of respect, before he can return to a state of equilibrium with his fellows, or to the place whence he started.

Few great men have passed from the stage of action, who have not left in the history of their lives indelible marks of ambition or folly, which produced insurmountable reverses, and rendered the whole a mere caricature, that can be examined only with disgust and regret. Such pictures, however, are profitable, for "by others' faults wise men correct their own."

The following is a piece of biography, that shows what changes may be effected in the animal and mental constitution of man; what trials may be surmounted, what cruelties perpetrated, and what pain endured, when stern necessity holds the reins, and drives the car of fate.

As books of this kind are sought and read with avidity, especially by children, and are well calculated to excite their attention, inform their understanding, and improve them in the art of reading, the greatest care has been observed to render the style easy, the language comprehensive, and the description natural. Prolixity has been studiously avoided. The line of distinction between virtue and vice has been rendered distinctly visible; and chastity of expression and sentiment have received due attention. Strict fidelity has been observed in the composition: consequently, no circumstance has been intentionally exaggerated by the paintings of fancy, nor by fine flashes of rhetoric: neither has the picture been rendered more dull than the original. Without the aid of fiction, what was received as matter of fact, only has been recorded.

It will be observed that the subject of this narrative has arrived at least to the advanced age of eighty years; that she is destitute of education; and that her journey of life, throughout its texture, has been interwoven with troubles, which ordinarily are calculated to impair the faculties of the mind; and it will be remembered, that there are but few old people who can recollect with precision the circumstances of their lives, (particularly those circumstances which transpired after middle age.) If, therefore, any error shall be discovered in the narration in respect to time, it will be overlooked by the kind reader, or charitably placed to the narrator's account, and not imputed to neglect, or to the want of attention in the compiler.

The appendix is principally taken from the words of Mrs. Jemison's statements. Those parts which were not derived from her, are deserving equal credit, having been obtained from authentic sources.

For the accommodation of the reader, the work has been divided into chapters, and a copious table of contents affixed. The introduction will facilitate the understanding of what follows; and as it contains matter that could not be inserted with propriety in any other place, will be read with interest and satisfaction.

Having finished my undertaking, the subsequent pages are cheerfully submitted to the perusal and approbation or animadversion of a candid, generous and indulgent public.

At the same time it is fondly hoped that the lessons of distress that are pourtrayed, may have a direct tendency to increase our love of liberty; to enlarge our views of the blessings that are derived from our liberal institutions; and to excite in our breasts sentiments of devotion and gratitude to the great Author and finisher of our happiness.

*Pembroke, March 1, 1824*

## AUTHOR'S INTRODUCTION
## [JAMES E. SEAVER]

The Peace of 1783,[1] and the consequent cessation of Indian hostilities and barbarities, returned to their friends those prisoners, who had escaped the tomahawk, the gauntlet, and the savage fire, after their having spent many years in captivity, and restored harmony to society.

The stories of Indian cruelties which were common in the new settlements, and were calamitous realities previous to that propitious event; slumbered in the minds that had been constantly agitated by them, and were only roused occasionally, to become the fearful topic of the fireside.

It is presumed that at this time there are but few native Americans that have arrived to middle age, who cannot distinctly recollect of sitting in the chimney corner when children, all contracted with fear, and there listening to their parents or visitors, while they related stories of Indian conquests, and murders, that would make their flaxen hair nearly stand erect, and almost destroy the power of motion.

At the close of the Revolutionary war; all that part of the State of New York that lies west of Utica was uninhabited by white people, and few indeed had ever passed beyond Fort Stanwix, except when engaged in war against the Indians, who were numerous, and occupied a number of large towns between the Mohawk river and lake Erie. Sometime elapsed after this event, before the country about the lakes and on the Genesee river was visited, save by an occasional land speculator, or by defaulters who wished by retreating to what in those days was deemed almost the end of the earth, to escape the force of civil law.

At length, the richness and fertility of the soil excited emigration, and here and there a family settled down and commenced improvements in the country which had recently been the property of the aborigines. Those who settled near the Genesee river, soon became acquainted with "The White Woman," as Mrs. Jemison is called, whose history they anxiously sought, both as a matter of interest and curiosity. Frankness characterized her conduct, and without reserve she would readily gratify them by relating some of the most important periods of her life.

Although her bosom companion was an ancient Indian warrior, and notwithstanding her children and associates were all Indians, yet it was found that she possessed an uncommon share of hospitality, and that her friendship was well worth courting and preserving. Her house was the stranger's home; from her table the hungry were refreshed; – she made the naked as comfortable as her means would admit of; and in all her actions, discovered so much natural goodness of heart, that her admirers increased in proportion to the extension of her acquaintance, and she became celebrated as the friend of the distressed. She was the protectress of the homeless fugitive, and made welcome the weary wanderer. Many still live to commemorate her benevolence towards them, when prisoners during the war, and to ascribe their deliverance to the mediation of "The White Woman."

The settlements increased, and the whole country around her was inhabited by a rich and respectable people, principally from New-England, as much distinguished for their spirit of inquisitiveness as for their habits of industry and honesty, who had all heard from one source and another a part of her life in detached pieces, and had obtained an idea that the whole taken in connection would afford instruction and amusement.

Many gentlemen of respectability, felt anxious that her narrative might be laid before the public, with a view not only to perpetuate the remembrance of the atrocities of the savages in former times, but to preserve some historical facts which they supposed to be intimately connected with her life, and which otherwise must be lost.

Forty years had passed since the close of the Revolutionary war, and almost seventy years had seen Mrs. Jemison with the Indians, when Daniel W. Banister, Esq. at the instance of several gentlemen, and prompted by his own ambition to add something to the accumulating fund of useful knowledge, resolved, in the

---

[1] The Paris Peace Treaty of 1783 between Britain and the United States was a source of dispute for the Iroquois (including the Seneca), who claimed independent status. See Namias, 1992, 29–31.

autumn of 1823, to embrace that time, while she was capable of recollecting and reciting the scenes through which she had passed, to collect from herself, and to publish to the world, an accurate account of her life.

I was employed to collect the materials, and prepare the work for the press; and accordingly went to the house of Mrs. Jennet Whaley in the town of Castile, Genesee co. N.Y. in company with the publisher, who procured the interesting subject of the following narrative, to come to that place (a distance of four miles) and there repeat the story of her eventful life. She came on foot in company with Mr. Thomas Clute, whom she considers her protector, and tarried almost three days, which time was busily occupied in taking a sketch of her narrative as she recited it.

Her appearance was well calculated to excite a great degree of sympathy in a stranger, who had been partially informed of her origin, when comparing her present situation with what it probably would have been, had she been permitted to have remained with her friends, and to have enjoyed the blessings of civilization.

In stature she is very short, and considerably under the middle size, and stands tolerably erect, with her head bent forward, apparently from her having for a long time been accustomed to carrying heavy burdens in a strap placed across her forehead. Her complexion is very white for a woman of her age, and although the wrinkles of fourscore years are deeply indented in her cheeks, yet the crimson of youth is distinctly visible. Her eyes are light blue, a little faded by age, and naturally brilliant and sparkling. Her sight is quite dim, though she is able to perform her necessary labor without the assistance of glasses. Her cheek bones are high, and rather prominent, and her front teeth, in the lower jaw, are sound and good. When she looks up and is engaged in conversation her countenance is very expressive; but from her long residence with the Indians, she has acquired the habit of peeping from under eye-brows as they do with the head inclined downwards. Formerly her hair was of a light chestnut brown – it is now quite grey, a little curled, of middling length and tied in a bunch behind. She informed me that she had never worn a cap nor a comb.

She speaks English plainly and distinctly, with a little of the Irish emphasis, and has the use of words so well as to render herself intelligible on any subject with which she is acquainted. Her recollection and memory exceeded my expectation. It cannot be reasonably supposed, that a person of her age has kept the events of seventy years in so complete a chain as to be able to assign to each its proper time and place; she, however, made her recital with as few obvious mistakes as might be found in that of a person of fifty.

She walks with a quick step without a staff, and I was informed by Mr. Clute, that she could yet cross a stream on a log or pole as steadily as any other person.

Her passions are easily excited. At a number of periods in her narrative, tears trickled down her grief worn cheek, and at the same time a rising sigh would stop her utterance.

Industry is a virtue which she has uniformly practiced from the day of her adoption to the present. She pounds her samp, cooks for herself, gathers and chops wood, feeds her cattle and poultry, and performs other laborious services. Last season she planted, tended and gathered corn – in short, she is always busy.

Her dress at the time I saw her, was made and worn after the Indian fashion, and consisted of a shirt, short gown, petticoat, stockings, moccasins, a blanket and a bonnet. The shirt was of cotton and made at the top, as I was informed, like a man's without collar or sleeves – was open before and extended down about midway of the hips. – The petticoat was a piece of broadcloth with the list at the top and bottom and the ends sewed together. This was tied on by a string that was passed over it and around the waist, in such a manner as to let the bottom of the petticoat down half way between the knee and ankle and leave one-fourth of a yard at the top to be turned down over the string – the bottom of the shirt coming a little below, and on the outside of the top of the fold so as to leave the list and two or three inches of the cloth uncovered. The stockings, were of blue broadcloth, tied, or pinned on, which reached from the knees, into the mouth of the moccasins. – Around her toes only she had some rags, and over these her buckskin moccasins. Her gown was of undressed flannel, colored brown. It was made in old yankee style, with long sleeves, covered the top of the hips, and was tied before in two places with strings of deer skin. Over all this, she wore an Indian blanket. On her head she wore a piece of old brown woolen cloth made somewhat like a sun bonnet.

Such was the dress that this woman was contented to wear, and habit had rendered it convenient and comfortable. She wore it not as a matter of necessity, but from choice, for it will be seen in the sequel, that her property is sufficient to enable her to dress in the best fashion, and to allow her every comfort of life.

Her house, in which she lives, is 20 by 28 feet; built of square timber, with a shingled roof, and a framed stoop. In the centre of the house is a chimney of stones and sticks, in which there are two fire places. She has a good framed barn, 26 by 36, well filled, and owns a fine stock of cattle and horses. Besides the buildings above mentioned, she owns a number of houses that are occupied by tenants, who work her flats upon shares.

Her dwelling, is about one hundred rods north of the Great Slide, a curiosity that will be described in its proper place, on the west side of the Genesee river.

Mrs. Jemison, appeared sensible of her ignorance of the manners of the white people, and for that reason, was not familiar, except with those with whom she was intimately acquainted. In fact she was (to appearance) so jealous of her rights, or that she should say something that would be injurious to herself or family, that if Mr. Clute had not been present, we should have been unable to have obtained her history. She, however, soon became free and unembarrassed in her conversation, and spoke with a degree of mildness, candor and simplicity, that is calculated to remove all doubts as to the veracity of the speaker. The vices of the Indians, she appeared disposed not to aggravate, and seemed to take pride in extoling their virtues. A kind of family pride inclined her to withhold whatever would blot the character of her descendants, and perhaps induced her to keep back many things that would have been interesting.

For the life of her last husband, we are indebted to her cousin, Mr. George Jemison,[2] to whom she referred us for information on that subject generally. The thoughts of his deeds, probably chilled her old heart, and made her dread to rehearse them, and at the same time she well knew they were no secret, for she had frequently heard him relate the whole, not only to her cousin, but to others.

Before she left us she was very sociable, and she resumed her naturally pleasant countenance, enlivened with a smile.

Her neighbors speak of her as possessing one of the happiest tempers and dispositions, and give her the name of never having done a censurable act to their knowledge.

Her habits, are those of the Indians – she sleeps on skins without a bedstead, sits upon the floor or on a bench, and holds her victuals on her lap, or in her hands.

Her ideas of religion, correspond in every respect with those of the great mass of the Senecas. She applauds virtue, and despises vice. She believes in a future state, in which the good will be happy, and the bad miserable; and that the acquisition of that happiness, depends primarily upon human volition, and the consequent good deeds of the happy recipient of blessedness. The doctrines taught in the Christian religion, she is a stranger to.

Her daughters are said to be active and enterprising women, and her grandsons, who arrived to manhood, are considered able, decent and respectable men in their tribe.

Having in this cursory manner, introduced the subject of the following pages, I proceed to the narration of a life that has been viewed with attention, for a great number of years by a few, and which will be read by the public with the mixed sensations of pleasure and pain, and with interest, anxiety and satisfaction.

## CHAPTER 1 [PARENTS AND EARLY CHILDHOOD]

### Nativity of her Parents. – Their removal to America. – Her Birth. – Parents settle in Pennsylvania. – Omen of her Captivity.

Although I may have frequently heard the history of my ancestry, my recollection is too imperfect to enable me to trace it further back than to my father and mother, whom I have often heard mention the families from whence they originated, as having possessed wealth and honorable stations under the government of the country in which they resided.

On the account of the great length of time that has elapsed since I was separated from my parents and friends, and having heard the story of their nativity only in the days of my childhood, I am not able to state positively, which of the two countries, Ireland or Scotland, was the land of my parents' birth and

[2] The man who called himself George Jemison for economic gain was not in fact Mary's cousin; Seaver used his account to create the story of Hiokatoo, Jemison's second husband, that appeared in Chapter 11 of "her" narrative.

education. It, however, is my impression, that they were born and brought up in Ireland.

My Father's name was Thomas Jemison, and my mother's, before her marriage with him, was Jane Erwin. Their affection for each other was mutual, and of that happy kind which tends directly to sweeten the cup of life; to render connubial sorrows lighter; to assuage every discontentment; and to promote not only their own comfort, but that of all who come within the circle of their acquaintance. Of their happiness I recollect to have heard them speak; and the remembrance I yet retain of their mildness and perfect agreement in the government of their children, together with their mutual attention to our common education, manners, religious instruction and wants, renders it a fact in my mind, that they were ornaments to the married state, and examples of connubial love, worthy of imitation. After my remembrance, they were strict observers of religious duties; for it was the daily practice of my father, morning and evening, to attend, in his family, to the worship of God.

Resolved to leave the land of their nativity, they removed from their residence to a port in Ireland, where they lived but a short time before they set sail for this country, in the year 1742 or 3, on board the ship Mary William, bound to Philadelphia, in the state of Pennsylvania.

The intestine divisions, civil wars, and ecclesiastical rigidity and domination that prevailed in those days, were the causes of their leaving their mother country, to find a home in the American wilderness, under the mild and temperate government of the descendants of William Penn; where, without fear, they might worship God, and perform their usual avocations.

In Europe my parents had two sons and one daughter, whose names were John, Thomas and Betsey; with whom, after having put their effects on board, they embarked, leaving a large connexion of relatives and friends, under all those painful sensations, which are only felt when kindred souls give the parting hand and last farewell to those to whom they are endeared by every friendly tie.

In the course of their voyage I was born, to be the sport of fortune and almost an outcast to civil society; to stem the current of adversity through a long chain of vicissitudes, unsupported by the advice of tender parents, or the hand of an affectionate friend; and even without the enjoyment, from others, of any of those tender sympathies that are adapted to the sweetening of society, except such as naturally flow from uncultivated minds, that have been calloused by ferocity.

Excepting my birth, nothing remarkable occurred to my parents on their passage, and they were safely landed at Philadelphia. My father being fond of rural life, and having been bred to agricultural pursuits, soon left the city, and removed his family to the then frontier settlements of Pennsylvania, to a tract of excellent land lying on Marsh creek. At that place he cleared a large farm, and for seven or eight years enjoyed the fruits of his industry. Peace attended their labors; and they had nothing to alarm them, save the midnight howl of the prowling wolf, or the terrifying shriek of the ferocious panther, as they occasionally visited their improvements, to take a lamb or a calf to satisfy their hunger.

During this period my mother had two sons, between whose ages there was a difference of about three years: the oldest was named Matthew, and the other Robert.

Health presided on every countenance, and vigor and strength characterized every exertion. Our mansion was a little paradise. The morning of my childish, happy days, will ever stand fresh in my remembrance, notwithstanding the many severe trials through which I have passed, in arriving at my present situation, at so advanced an age. Even at this remote period, the recollection of my pleasant home at my father's, of my parents, of my brothers and sister, and of the manner in which I was deprived of them all at once, affects me so powerfully, that I am almost overwhelmed with grief, that is seemingly insupportable. Frequently I dream of those happy days: but, alas! they are gone: they have left me to be carried through a long life, dependent for the little pleasures of nearly seventy years, upon the tender mercies of the Indians! In the spring of 1752, and through the succeeding seasons, the stories of Indian barbarities inflicted upon the whites in those days, frequently excited in my parents the most serious alarm for our safety.

The next year the storm gathered faster; many murders were committed; and many captives were exposed to meet death in its most frightful form, by having their bodies stuck full of pine splinters, which were immediately set on fire, while their tormentors, exulting in their distress, would rejoice at their agony!

In 1754, an army for the protection of the settlers, and to drive back the French and Indians, was raised from the militia of the colonial governments, and placed (secondarily) under the command of Col. George Washington. In that army I had an uncle, whose name was John Jemison, who was killed at the battle at the Great Meadows, or Fort Necessity. His wife had died some time before this, and left a young child, which my mother nursed in the most tender manner, till its mother's sister took it away, a few months after my uncle's death. The French and Indians, after the surrender of Fort Necessity by Col. Washington, (which happened the same season, and soon after his victory over them at that place,) grew more and more terrible. The death of the whites, and plundering and burning their property, was apparently their only object: But as yet we had not heard the death-yell, nor seen the smoke of a dwelling that had been lit by an Indian's hand.

The return of a new-year's day found us unmolested; and though we knew that the enemy was at no great distance from us, my father concluded that he would continue to occupy his land another season; expecting (probably from the great exertions which the government was then making) that as soon as the troops could commence their operations in the spring, the enemy would be conquered and compelled to agree to a treaty of peace.

In the preceding autumn my father either moved to another part of his farm, or to another neighborhood, a short distance from our former abode. I well recollect moving, and that the barn that was on the place we moved to was built of logs, though the house was a good one.

The winter of 1754–5 was as mild as a common fall season, and the spring presented a pleasant seed time, and indicated a plenteous harvest. My father, with the assistance of his oldest sons, repaired his farm as usual, and was daily preparing the soil for the reception of the seed. His cattle and sheep were numerous, and according to the best idea of wealth that I can now form, he was wealthy.

But alas! how transitory are all human affairs! how fleeting are riches! how brittle the invisible thread on which all earthly comforts are suspended! Peace in a moment can take an immeasurable flight; health can lose its rosy cheeks; and life will vanish like a vapor at the appearance of the sun! In one fatal day our prospects were all blasted; and death, by cruel hands, inflicted upon almost the whole of the family.

On a pleasant day in the spring of 1755, when my father was sowing flax-seed, and my brothers driving the teams, I was sent to a neighbor's house, a distance of perhaps a mile, to procure a horse and return with it the next morning. I went as I was directed. I was out of the house in the beginning of the evening, and saw a sheet wide spread approaching towards me, in which I was caught (as I have ever since believed) and deprived of my senses! The family soon found me on the ground, almost lifeless, (as they said,) took me in, and made use of every remedy in their power for my recovery, but without effect till day-break, when my senses returned, and I soon found myself in good health, so that I went home with the horse very early in the morning.

The appearance of that sheet, I have ever considered as a forerunner of the melancholy catastrophe that so soon afterwards happened to our family: and my being caught in it, I believe, was ominous of my preservation from death at the time we were captured.

## CHAPTER 2 [EDUCATION; CAPTIVITY; MOTHER'S FAREWELL ADDRESS]

Her Education. – Captivity. – Journey to Fort Pitt. – Mother's Farewell Address. – Murder of her Family. – Preparation of the Scalps. – Indian Precautions. – Arrival at Fort Pitt, &c.

My education had received as much attention from my parents, as their situation in a new country would admit of. I had been at school some, where I learned to read in a book that was about half as large as a Bible; and in the Bible I had read a little. I had also learned the Catechism, which I used frequently to repeat to my parents, and every night, before I went to bed, I was obliged to stand up before my mother and repeat some words that I suppose was a prayer.

My reading, Catechism and prayers, I have long since forgotten; though for a number of the first years that I lived with the Indians, I repeated the prayers as often as I had an opportunity. After the revolutionary war, I remembered the names of some of the letters when I saw them; but have never read a word since I was taken prisoner. It is but a few years since a Missionary kindly gave me a Bible, which I am very fond of hearing my neighbors read to me, and should be pleased to learn to read it myself; but my sight has been for a number of years, so dim that I have not been able to distinguish one letter from another.

As I before observed, I got home with the horse very early in the morning, where I found a man that lived in our neighborhood, and his sister-in-law who had three children, one son and two daughters. I soon learned that they had come there to live a short time; but for what purpose I cannot say. The woman's husband, however, was at that time in Washington's army, fighting for his country; and as her brother-in-law had a house she had lived with him in his absence. Their names I have forgotten.

Immediately after I got home, the man took the horse to go to his house after a bag of grain, and took his gun in his hand for the purpose of killing game, if he should chance to see any. – Our family, as usual, was busily employed about their common business. Father was shaving an axe-helve at the side of the house; mother was making preparations for breakfast; – my two oldest brothers were at work near the barn; and the little ones, with myself, and the woman and her three children, were in the house.

Breakfast was not yet ready, when we were alarmed by the discharge of a number of guns, that seemed to be near. Mother and the woman before mentioned, almost fainted at the report, and every one trembled with fear. On opening the door, the man and horse lay dead near the house, having just been shot by the Indians.

I was afterwards informed, that the Indians discovered him at his own house with his gun, and pursued him to father's, where they shot him as I have related. They first secured my father, and then rushed into the house, and without the least resistance made prisoners of my mother, Robert, Matthew, Betsey, the woman and her three children, and myself, and then commenced plundering.

My two brothers, Thomas and John, being at the barn, escaped and went to Virginia, where my grandfather Erwin then lived, as I was informed by a Mr. Fields, who was at my house about the close of the revolutionary war.

The party that took us consisted of six Indians and four Frenchmen, who immediately commenced plundering, as I just observed, and took what they considered most valuable, consisting principally of bread, meal and meat. Having taken as much provision as they could carry, they set out with their prisoners in great haste, for fear of detection, and soon entered the woods. On our march that day, an Indian went behind us with a whip, with which he frequently lashed the children to make them keep up. In this manner we travelled till dark without a mouthful of food or a drop of water; although we had not eaten since the night before. Whenever the little children cried for water, the Indians would make them drink urine or go thirsty. At night they encamped in the woods without fire and without shelter, where we were watched with the greatest vigilance. Extremely fatigued, and very hungry, we were compelled to lie upon the ground supperless and without a drop of water to satisfy the cravings of our appetites. As in the day time, so the little ones were made to drink urine in the night if they cried for water. Fatigue alone brought us a little sleep for the refreshment of our weary limbs; and at the dawn of day we were again started on our march in the same order that we had proceeded on the day before. About sunrise we were halted, and the Indians gave us a full breakfast of provision that they had brought from my father's house. Each of us being very hungry, partook of this bounty of the Indians, except father, who was so much overcome with his situation – so much exhausted by anxiety and grief, that silent despair seemed fastened upon his countenance, and he could not be prevailed upon to refresh his sinking nature by the use of a morsel of food. Our repast being finished, we again resumed our march, and before noon passed a small fort that I heard my father say was called Fort Canagojigge.

That was the only time that I heard him speak from the time we were taken till we were finally separated the following night.

Towards evening we arrived at the border of a dark and dismal swamp, which was covered with small hemlocks, or some other evergreen, and other bushes, into which we were conducted; and having gone a short distance we stopped to encamp for the night.

Here we had some bread and meat for supper: but the dreariness of our situation, together with the uncertainty under which we all labored, as to our future destiny, almost deprived us of the sense of hunger, and destroyed our relish for food.

Mother, from the time we were taken, had manifested a great degree of fortitude, and encouraged us to support our troubles without complaining; and by her conversation seemed to make the distance and time shorter, and the way more smooth. But father lost all his ambition in the beginning of our trouble, and continued apparently lost to every care – absorbed in melancholy. Here, as before, she insisted on the necessity of our eating; and we obeyed her, but it was done with heavy hearts.

As soon as I had finished my supper, an Indian took off my shoes and stockings and put a pair of moccasins on my feet, which my mother observed; and believing that they would spare my life, even if they should destroy the other captives, addressed me as near as I can remember in the following words: –

"My dear little Mary, I fear that the time has arrived when we must be parted forever. Your life, my child, I think will be spared; but we shall probably be tomahawked here in this lonesome place by the Indians. O! how can I part with you my darling? What will become of my sweet little Mary? Oh! how can I think of your being continued in captivity without a hope of your being rescued? O that death had snatched you from my embraces in your infancy; the pain of parting then would have been pleasing to what it now is; and I should have seen the end of your troubles! – Alas, my dear! my heart bleeds at the thoughts of what awaits you; but, if you leave us, remember my child your own name, and the name of your father and mother. Be careful and not forget your English tongue. If you shall have an opportunity to get away from the Indians, don't try to escape; for if you do they will find and destroy you. Don't forget, my little daughter, the prayers that I have learned you – say them often; be a good child, and God will bless you. May God bless you my child, and make you comfortable and happy."

During this time, the Indians stripped the shoes and stockings from the little boy that belonged to the woman who was taken with us, and put moccasins on his feet, as they had done before on mine. I was crying. An Indian took the little boy and myself by the hand, to lead us off from the company, when my mother exclaimed, "Don't cry Mary – don't cry my child. God will bless you! Farewell – farewell!"

The Indian led us some distance into the bushes, or woods, and there lay down with us to spend the night. The recollection of parting with my tender mother kept me awake, while the tears constantly flowed from my eyes. A number of times in the night the little boy begged of me earnestly to run away with him and get clear of the Indians; but remembering the advice I had so lately received, and knowing the dangers to which we should be exposed, in travelling without a path and without a guide, through a wilderness unknown to us, I told him that I would not go, and persuaded him to lie still till morning.

Early the next morning the Indians and Frenchmen that we had left the night before, came to us; but our friends were left behind. It is impossible for any one to form a correct idea of what my feelings were at the sight of those savages, whom I supposed had murdered my parents and brothers, sister, and friends, and left them in the swamp to be devoured by wild beasts! But what could I do? A poor little defenseless girl; without the power or means of escaping; without a home to go to, even if I could be liberated; without a knowledge of the direction or distance to my former place of residence; and without a living friend to whom to fly for protection, I felt a kind of horror, anxiety, and dread, that, to me, seemed insupportable. I durst not cry – I durst not complain; and to inquire of them the fate of my friends (even if I could have mustered resolution) was beyond my ability, as I could not speak their language, nor they understand mine. My only relief was in silent stifled sobs.

My suspicions as to the fate of my parents proved too true; for soon after I left them they were killed and scalped, together with Robert, Matthew, Betsey, and the woman and her two children, and mangled in the most shocking manner.

Having given the little boy and myself some bread and meat for breakfast, they led us on as fast as we could travel, and one of them went behind and with a long staff, picked up all the grass and weeds that we trailed down by going over them. By taking that precaution they avoided detection; for each weed was so nicely placed in its natural position that no one would have suspected that we had passed that way. It is the custom of Indians when scouting, or on private expeditions, to step carefully and where no impression of their feet can be left – shunning wet or muddy ground. They seldom take hold of a bush or limb, and never break one; and by observing those precautions and that of setting up the weeds and grass which they necessary lop, they completely elude the sagacity of their pursuers, and escape that punishment which they are conscious they merit from the hand of justice.

After a hard day's march we encamped in a thicket, where the Indians made a shelter of boughs, and then built a good fire to warm and dry our benumbed limbs and clothing; for it had rained some through the day. Here we were again fed as before. When the Indians had finished their supper they took from their baggage a number of scalps and went about preparing them for the market, or to keep without spoiling, by straining them over small hoops which they prepared for that purpose, and then drying and scraping them by the fire. Having put the scalps, yet wet and bloody, upon the hoops, and stretched them to their full extent, they held them to the fire till they were partly dried and then with their knives commenced scraping off the flesh; and in that way they continued to work, alternately drying and scraping them, till they were dry and clean. That being done they combed the hair in the neatest manner, and then painted it and the edges of the scalps yet on the hoops, red. Those scalps I knew at the time must have been taken from our family by the color of the hair. My mother's hair was red; and I could easily distinguish my father's and the children's from each other. That sight was most appalling; yet, I was obliged to endure it without complaining.

In the course of the night they made me to understand that they should not have killed the family if the whites had not pursued them.

Mr. Fields, whom I have before mentioned, informed me that at the time we were taken, he lived in the vicinity of my father; and that on hearing of our captivity, the whole neighborhood turned out in pursuit of the enemy, and to deliver us if possible: but that their efforts were unavailing. They however pursued us to the dark swamp, where they found my father, his family and companions, stripped and mangled in the most inhuman manner: That from thence the march of the cruel monsters could not be traced in any direction; and that they returned to their homes with the melancholy tidings of our misfortunes, supposing that we had all shared in the massacre.

The next morning we went on; the Indian going behind us and setting up the weeds as on the day before. At night we encamped on the ground in the open air, without a shelter or fire.

In the morning we again set out early, and travelled as on the two former days, though the weather was extremely uncomfortable, from the continual falling of rain and snow.

At night the snow fell fast, and the Indians built a shelter of boughs, and a fire, when we rested tolerably dry through that and two succeeding nights.

When we stopped, and before the fire was kindled, I was so much fatigued from running, and so far benumbed by the wet and cold, that I expected that I must fail and die before I could get warm and comfortable. The fire, however, soon restored the circulation, and after I had taken my supper I felt so that I rested well through the night.

On account of the storm, we were two days at that place. On one of those days, a party consisting of six Indians who had been to the frontier settlements, came to where we were, and brought with them one prisoner, a young white man who was very tired and dejected. His name I have forgotten.

Misery certainly loves company. I was extremely glad to see him, though I knew from his appearance, that his situation was as deplorable as mine, and that he could afford me no kind of assistance. In the afternoon the Indians killed a deer, which they dressed, and then roasted it whole; which made them a full meal. We were each allowed a share of their venison, and some bread, so that we made a good meal also.

Having spent three nights and two days at that place, and the storm having ceased, early in the morning the whole company, consisting of twelve Indians, four Frenchmen, the young man, the little boy and myself, moved on at a moderate pace without an Indian behind us to deceive our pursuers.

In the afternoon we came in sight of Fort Pitt (as it is now called,) where we were halted while the Indians performed some customs upon their prisoners which they deemed necessary. That fort was then occupied by the French and Indians, and was called Fort Du Quesne. It stood at the junction of the Monongahela, which is said to signify, in some of the Indian languages, the Falling-in-Banks,[3] and the Alleghany[4] rivers, where the Ohio river begins to take its name. The word O-hi-o, signifies bloody.

At the place where we halted, the Indians combed the hair of the young man, the boy and myself, and then painted our faces and hair red, in the finest Indian style. We were then conducted into the fort, where we received a little bread, and were then shut up and left to tarry alone through the night.

---

[3] Navigator [Seaver's note].

[4] The word Allegheny, was derived from an ancient race of Indians called "Tallegawe." The Delaware Indians, instead of saying "Alleghenny," say "Allegawe," or "Allegawenink." Western Tour—p. 465 [Seaver's note].

## CHAPTER 3 [ADOPTION BY TWO SENECA SISTERS; FIRST MARRIAGE]

She is given to two Squaws. – Her Journey down the Ohio. – Passes a Shawanee town where white men had just been burnt. – Arrives at the Seneca town. – Her Reception. – She is adopted. – Ceremony of Adoption. – Indian Custom. – Address. – She receives a new name. – Her Employment. – Retains her own and learns the Seneca Language. – Situation of the Town, &c. – Indians go on a Hunting Tour to Sciota and take her with them. – Returns. – She is taken to Fort Pitt, and then hurried back by her Indian Sisters. – Her hopes of Liberty destroyed. – Second Tour to Sciota. – Returns to Wiishto, &c. – Arrival of Prisoners. – Priscilla Ramsay. – Her Chain. – Mary marries a Delaware. – Her Affection for him. – Birth and Death of her first Child. – Her Sickness and Recovery. – Birth of Thomas Jemison.

The night was spent in gloomy forebodings. What the result of our captivity would be, it was out of our power to determine or even imagine. – At times we could almost realize the approach of our masters to butcher and scalp us; – again we could nearly see the pile of wood kindled on which we were to be roasted; and then we would imagine ourselves at liberty: alone and defenseless in the forest, surrounded by wild beasts that were ready to devour us. The anxiety of our minds drove sleep from our eyelids; and it was with a dreadful hope and painful impatience that we waited for the morning to determine our fate.

The morning at length arrived, and our masters came early and let us out of the house, and gave the young man and boy to the French, who immediately took them away. Their fate I never learned; as I have not seen nor heard of them since.

I was now left alone in the fort, deprived of my former companions, and of every thing that was near or dear to me but life. But it was not long before I was in some measure relieved by the appearance of two pleasant looking squaws of the Seneca tribe, who came and examined me attentively for a short time, and then went out. After a few minutes absence they returned with my former masters, who gave me to them to dispose of as they pleased.

The Indians by whom I was taken were a party of Shawanees, if I remember right, that lived, when at home, a long distance down the Ohio.

My former Indian masters, and the two squaws, were soon ready to leave the fort, and accordingly embarked; the Indians in a large canoe, and the two squaws and myself in a small one, and went down the Ohio.

When we set off, an Indian in the forward canoe took the scalps of my former friends, strung them on a pole that he placed upon his shoulder, and in that manner carried them, standing in the stern of the canoe, directly before us as we sailed down the river, to the town where the two squaws resided.

On our way we passed a Shawanee town, where I saw a number of heads, arms, legs, and other fragments of the bodies of some white people who had just been burnt. The parts that remained were hanging on a pole which was supported at each end by a crotch stuck in the ground, and were roasted or burnt black as a coal. The fire was yet burning; and the whole appearances afforded a spectacle so shocking, that, even to this day, my blood almost curdles in my veins when I think of them!

At night we arrived at a small Seneca Indian town, at the mouth of a small river, that was called by the Indians, in the Seneca language, She-nan-jee,[5] where the two Squaws to whom I belonged resided. There we landed, and the Indians went on; which was the last I ever saw of them.

Having made fast to the shore, the Squaws left me in the canoe while they went to their wigwam or house in the town, and returned with a suit of Indian clothing, all new, and very clean and nice. My clothes, though whole and good when I was taken, were now torn in pieces, so that I was almost naked. They first undressed

[5] That town, according to the geographical description given by Mrs. Jemison, must have stood at the mouth of Indian Cross creek, which is about 76 miles by water, below Pittsburgh; or at the mouth of Indian Short creek, 87 miles below Pittsburgh, where the town of Warren now stands: But at which of those places I am unable to determine [Seaver's note].

me and threw my rags into the river; then washed me clean and dressed me in the new suit they had just brought, in complete Indian style; and then led me home and seated me in the center of their wigwam.

I had been in that situation but a few minutes, before all the Squaws in the town came in to see me. I was soon surrounded by them, and they immediately set up a most dismal howling, crying bitterly, and wringing their hands in all the agonies of grief for a deceased relative.

Their tears flowed freely, and they exhibited all the signs of real mourning. At the commencement of this scene, one of their number began, in a voice somewhat between speaking and singing, to recite some words to the following purport, and continued the recitation till the ceremony was ended; the company at the same time varying the appearance of their countenances, gestures and tone of voice, so as to correspond with the sentiments expressed by their leader:

"Oh our brother! Alas! He is dead – he has gone; he will never return! Friendless he died on the field of the slain, where his bones are yet lying unburied! Oh, who will not mourn his sad fate? No tears dropped around him; oh, no! No tears of his sisters were there! He fell in his prime, when his arm was most needed to keep us from danger! Alas! he has gone! and left us in sorrow, his loss to bewail: Oh where is his spirit? His spirit went naked, and hungry it wanders, and thirsty and wounded it groans to return! Oh helpless and wretched, our brother has gone! No blanket nor food to nourish and warm him; nor candles to light him, nor weapons of war: – Oh, none of those comforts had he! But well we remember his deeds! – The deer he could take on the chase! The panther shrunk back at the sight of his strength! His enemies fell at his feet! He was brave and courageous in war! As the fawn he was harmless: his friendship was ardent: his temper was gentle: his pity was great! Oh! our friend, our companion is dead! Our brother, our brother, alas! he is gone! But why do we grieve for his loss? In the strength of a warrior, undaunted he left us, to fight by the side of the Chiefs! His war-whoop was shrill! His rifle well aimed laid his enemies low: his tomahawk drank of their blood: and his knife flayed their scalps while yet covered with gore! And why do we mourn? Though he fell on the field of the slain, with glory he fell, and his spirit went up to the land of his fathers in war! Then why do we mourn? With transports of joy they received him, and fed him, and clothed him, and welcomed him there! Oh friends, he is happy; then dry up your tears! His spirit has seen our distress, and sent us a helper whom with pleasure we greet. Dickewamis has come: then let us receive her with joy! She is handsome and pleasant! Oh! she is our sister, and gladly we welcome her here. In the place of our brother she stands in our tribe. With care we will guard her from trouble; and may she be happy till her spirit shall leave us."

In the course of that ceremony, from mourning they became serene – joy sparkled in their countenances, and they seemed to rejoice over me as over a long lost child. I was made welcome amongst them as a sister to the two Squaws before mentioned, and was called Dickewamis; which being interpreted, signifies a pretty girl, a handsome girl, or a pleasant, good thing. That is the name by which I have ever since been called by the Indians.

I afterwards learned that the ceremony I at that time passed through, was that of adoption. The two squaws had lost a brother in Washington's war, sometime in the year before, and in consequence of his death went up to Fort Pitt, on the day on which I arrived there, in order to receive a prisoner or an enemy scalp, to supply their loss.

It is a custom of the Indians, when one of their number is slain or taken prisoner in battle, to give to the nearest relative to the dead or absent, a prisoner, if they have chanced to take one, and if not, to give him the scalp of an enemy. On the return of the Indians from conquest, which is always announced by peculiar shoutings, demonstrations of joy, and the exhibition of some trophy of victory, the mourners come forward and make their claims. If they receive a prisoner, it is at their option either to satiate their vengeance by taking his life in the most cruel manner they can conceive of; or, to receive and adopt him into the family, in the place of him whom they have lost. All the prisoners that are taken in battle and carried to the encampment or town by the Indians, are given to the bereaved families, till their number is made good. And unless the mourners have but just received the news of their bereavement, and are under the operation of paroxysm of grief, anger and revenge; or, unless the prisoner is very old, sickly, or homely, they generally save him, and treat him kindly. But if their mental wound is fresh, their loss so great that they deem it irreparable, or if their prisoner or prisoners do not meet their approbation, no torture, let it be ever so cruel, seems sufficient to make them satisfaction. It is family, and not national, sacrifices amongst the Indians, that has given them an indelible stamp as barbarians, and identified their character with the idea which is generally formed of unfeeling ferocity, and the most abandoned cruelty.

It was my happy lot to be accepted for adoption; and at the time of the ceremony I was received by the two squaws, to supply the place of their brother in the family; and I was ever considered and treated by them as a real sister, the same as though I had been born of their mother.

During my adoption, I sat motionless, nearly terrified to death at the appearance and actions of the company, expecting every moment to feel their vengeance, and suffer death on the spot. I was, however, happily disappointed, when at the close of the ceremony the company retired, and my sisters went about employing every means for my consolation and comfort.

Being now settled and provided with a home, I was employed in nursing the children, and doing light work about the house. Occasionally I was sent out with the Indian hunters, when they went but a short distance, to help them carry their game. My situation was easy; I had no particular hardships to endure. But still, the recollection of my parents, my brothers and sisters, my home, and my own captivity, destroyed my happiness, and made me constantly solitary, lonesome and gloomy.

My sisters would not allow me to speak English in their hearing; but remembering the charge that my dear mother gave me at the time I left her, whenever I chanced to be alone I made a business of repeating my prayer, catechism, or something I had learned in order that I might not forget my own language. By practicing in that way I retained it till I came to Genesee flats, where I soon became acquainted with English people with whom I have been almost daily in the habit of conversing.

My sisters were diligent in teaching me their language; and to their great satisfaction I soon learned so that I could understand it readily, and speak it fluently. I was very fortunate in falling into their hands; for they were kind good natured women; peaceable and mild in their dispositions; temperate and decent in their habits, and very tender and gentle towards me. I have great reason to respect them, though they have been dead a great number of years.

The town where they lived was pleasantly situated on the Ohio, at the mouth of the Shenanjee; the land produced good corn; the woods furnished a plenty of game, and the waters abounded with fish. Another river emptied itself into the Ohio, directly opposite the mouth of the Shenanjee. We spent the summer at that place, where we planted, hoed, and harvested a large crop of corn, of an excellent quality.

About the time of corn harvest, Fort Pitt was taken from the French by the English.[6]

The corn being harvested, the Indians took it on horses and in canoes, and proceeded down the Ohio, occasionally stopping to hunt a few days, till we arrived at the mouth of Sciota river; where they established their winter quarters, and continued hunting till the ensuing spring, in the adjacent wilderness. While at that place I went with the other children to assist the hunters to bring in their game. The forests on the Sciota were well stocked with elk, deer, and other large animals; and the marshes contained large numbers of beaver, muskrat, &c. which made excellent hunting for the Indians; who depended, for their meat, upon their success in taking elk and deer; and for ammunition and clothing, upon the beaver, muskrat, and other furs that they could take in addition to their peltry.

The season for hunting being passed, we all returned in the spring to the mouth of the river Shenanjee, to the houses and fields we had left in the fall before. There we again planted our corn, squashes, and beans, on the fields that we occupied the preceding summer.

About planting time, our Indians all went up to Fort Pitt, to make peace with the British, and took me with them.[7] We landed on the opposite side of the river from the fort, and encamped for the night.

---

[6] The above statement is apparently an error; and is to be attributed solely to the treachery of the old lady's memory; though she is confident that event took place at the time above mentioned. It is certain that Fort Pitt was not evacuated by the French and given up to the English, till sometime in November 1758. It is possible, however, that an armistice was agreed upon, and that for a time, between the spring of 1755 and 1758, both nations visited that post without fear of molestation. As the succeeding part of the narrative corresponds with the true historical chain of events, the public will overlook this circumstance, which appears unsupported by history [Seaver's note].

[7] History is silent as to any treaty having been made between the English, and the French and Indians, at that time; though it is possible that a truce was agreed on, and that the parties met for the purpose of concluding a treaty of peace [Seaver's note].

Early the next morning the Indians took me over to the fort to see the white people that were there. It was then that my heart bounded to be liberated from the Indians and to be restored to my friends and my country. The white people were surprised to see me with the Indians, enduring the hardships of a savage life, at so early an age, and with so delicate a constitution as I appeared to possess. They asked me my name; where and when I was taken – and appeared very much interested on my behalf. They were continuing their inquiries, when my sisters became alarmed, believing that I should be taken from them, hurried me into their canoe and recrossed the river – took their bread out of the fire and fled with me, without stopping, till they arrived at the river Shenanjee. So great was their fear of losing me, or of my being given up in the treaty, that they never once stopped rowing till they got home.

Shortly after we left the shore opposite the fort, as I was informed by one of my Indian brothers, the white people came over to take me back; but after considerable inquiry, and having made diligent search to find where I was hid, they returned with heavy hearts. Although I had then been with the Indians something over a year, and had become considerably habituated to their mode of living, and attached to my sisters, the sight of white people who could speak English inspired me with an unspeakable anxiety to go home with them, and share in the blessings of civilization. My sudden departure and escape from them, seemed like a second captivity, and for a long time I brooded the thoughts of my miserable situation with almost as much sorrow and dejection as I had done those of my first sufferings. Time, the destroyer of every affection, wore away my unpleasant feelings, and I became as contented as before.

We tended our cornfields through the summer; and after we had harvested the crop, we again went down the river to the hunting ground on the Sciota, where we spent the winter, as we had done the winter before.

Early in the spring we sailed up the Ohio river, to a place that the Indians called Wiishto,[8] where one river emptied into the Ohio on one side, and another on the other. At that place the Indians built a town, and we planted corn.

We lived three summers at Wiishto, and spent each winter on the Sciota.

The first summer of our living at Wiishto, a party of Delaware Indians came up the river, took up their residence, and lived in common with us. They brought five white prisoners with them, who by their conversation, made my situation much more agreeable, as they could all speak English. I have forgotten the names of all of them except one, which was Priscilla Ramsay. She was a very handsome, good natured girl, and was married soon after she came to Wiishto to Capt. Little Billy's uncle, who went with her on a visit to her friends in the states. Having tarried with them as long as she wished to, she returned with her husband to Can-a-ah-tua, where he died. She, after his death, married a white man by the name of Nettles, and now lives with him (if she is living) on Grand River, Upper Canada.

Not long after the Delawares came to live with us, at Wiishto, my sisters told me that I must go and live with one of them, whose name was She-nin-jee. Not daring to cross them, or disobey their commands, with a great degree of reluctance I went; and Sheninjee and I were married according to Indian custom.

Sheninjee was a noble man; large in stature; elegant in his appearance; generous in his conduct; courageous in war; a friend to peace, and a great lover of justice. He supported a degree of dignity far above his rank, and merited and received the confidence and friendship of all the tribes with whom he was acquainted. Yet, Sheninjee was an Indian. The idea of spending my days with him, at first seemed perfectly irreconcilable to my feelings: but his good nature, generosity, tenderness, and friendship towards me, soon gained my affection; and, strange as it may seem, I loved him! – To me he was ever kind in sickness, and always treated me with gentleness; in fact, he was an agreeable husband, and a comfortable companion. We lived happily together till the time of our final separation, which happened two or three years after our marriage, as I shall presently relate.

In the second summer of my living at Wiishto, I had a child at the time that the kernels of corn first appeared on the cob. When I was taken sick, Sheninjee was absent, and I was sent to a small shed, on the

[8] Wiishto I suppose was situated near the mouth of Indian Guyundat, 327 miles below Pittsburgh, and 73 above Big Sciota; or at the mouth of Swan creek, 307 miles below Pittsburgh [Seaver's note].

bank of the river, which was made of boughs, where I was obliged to stay till my husband returned. My two sisters, who were my only companions, attended me, and on the second day of my confinement my child was born; but it lived only two days. It was a girl: and notwithstanding the shortness of the time that I possessed it, it was a great grief to me to lose it.

After the birth of my child, I was very sick, but was not allowed to go into the house for two weeks; when, to my great joy, Sheninjee returned, and I was taken in and as comfortably provided for as our situation would admit of. My disease continued to increase for a number of days; and I became so far reduced that my recovery was despaired of by my friends, and I concluded that my troubles would soon be finished. At length, however, my complaint took a favorable turn, and by the time that the corn was ripe I was able to get about. I continued to gain my health, and in the fall was able to go to our winter quarters, on the Sciota, with the Indians.

From that time, nothing remarkable occurred to me till the fourth winter of my captivity, when I had a son born, while I was at Sciota: I had a quick recovery, and my child was healthy. To commemorate the name of my much lamented father, I called my son Thomas Jemison.

## CHAPTER 4 [WHITE AND INDIAN WOMEN; FAMILY LIFE]

She leaves Wiishto for Fort Pitt, in company with her Husband. – Her feelings on setting out. – Contrast between the labor of the white and Indian Women. – Deficiency of Arts amongst the Indians. – Their former Happiness. – Baneful effects of Civilization, and the introduction of ardent Spirits amongst them, &c. – Journey up the River. – Murder of three Traders by the Shawnees. – Her Husband stops at a Trading House. – Wantonness of the Shawnees. – Moves up the Sandusky. – Meets her Brother from Ge-nish-a-u. – Her Husband goes to Wiishto, and she sets out for Genishau in company with her Brothers. – They arrive at Sandusky. – Occurrences at that place. – Her Journey to Genishau, and Reception by Her Mother and Friends.

In the spring, when Thomas was three or four moons [months] old, we returned from Sciota to Wiishto, and soon after set out to go to Fort Pitt, to dispose of our fur and skins, that we had taken in the winter, and procure some necessary articles for the use of our family.

I had then been with the Indians four summers and four winters, and had become so far accustomed to their mode of living, habits and dispositions, that my anxiety to get away, to be set at liberty, and leave them, had almost subsided. With them was my home; my family was there, and there I had many friends to whom I was warmly attached in consideration of the favors, affection and friendship with which they had uniformly treated me, from the time of my adoption. Our labor was not severe; and that of one year was exactly similar, in almost every respect, to that of the others, without that endless variety that is to be observed in the common labor of the white people. Notwithstanding the Indian women have all the fuel and bread to procure, and the cooking to perform, their task is probably not harder than that of white women, who have those articles provided for them; and their cares certainly are not half as numerous, nor as great. In the summer season, we planted, tended and harvested our corn, and generally had all our children with us; but had no master to oversee or drive us, so that we could work as leisurely as we pleased. We had no ploughs on the Ohio; but performed the whole process of planting and hoeing with a small tool that resembled, in some respects, a hoe with a very short handle.

Our cooking consisted in pounding our corn into samp or hommany, boiling the hommany, making now and then a cake and baking it in the ashes, and in boiling or roasting our venison. As our cooking and eating utensils consisted of a hommany block and pestle, a small kettle, a knife or two, and a few vessels of bark or wood, it required but little time to keep them in order for use.

Spinning, weaving, sewing, stocking knitting, and the like, are arts which have never been practiced in the Indian tribes generally. After the revolutionary war, I learned to sew, so that I could make my own clothing after a poor fashion; but the other domestic arts I have been wholly ignorant of the application of, since my captivity. In the season of hunting, it was our business, in addition to our cooking, to bring home the game that was taken by the Indians, dress it, and carefully preserve the eatable meat, and prepare or dress the skins. Our clothing was fastened together with strings of deer skin, and tied on with the same.

In that manner we lived, without any of those jealousies, quarrels, and revengeful battles between families and individuals, which have been common in the Indian tribes since the introduction of ardent spirits amongst them.

The use of ardent spirits amongst the Indians and the attempts which have been made to civilize and christianize them by the white people, has constantly made them worse and worse; increased their vices, and robbed them of many of their virtues; and will ultimately produce their extermination. I have seen, in a number of instances, the effects of education upon some of our Indians, who were taken when young, from their families, and placed at school before they had had an opportunity to contract many Indian habits, and there kept till they arrived to manhood, but I have never seen one of those but what was an Indian in every respect after he returned. Indians must and will be Indians, in spite of all the means that can be used for their cultivation in the sciences and arts.

One thing only marred my happiness, while I lived with them on the Ohio; and that was the recollection that I had once had tender parents and a home that I loved. Aside from that consideration, or, if I had been taken in infancy, I should have been contented in my situation. Notwithstanding all that has been said against the Indians, in consequence of their cruelties to their enemies – cruelties that I have witnessed, and had abundant proof of – it is a fact that they are naturally kind, tender and peaceable towards their friends, and strictly honest; and that those cruelties have been practised, only upon their enemies, according to their idea of justice.

At the time we left Wiishto, it was impossible for me to suppress a sigh of regret on parting with those who had truly been my friends – with those whom I had every reason to respect. On account of a part of our family living at Genishau, we thought it doubtful whether we should return directly from Pittsburgh, or go from thence on a visit to see them.

Our company consisted of my husband, my two Indian brothers, my little son and myself. We embarked in a canoe that was large enough to contain ourselves and our effects, and proceeded on our voyage up the river.

Nothing remarkable occurred to us on our way, till we arrived at the mouth of a creek which Sheninjee and my brothers said was the outlet of Sandusky lake; where, as they said, two or three English traders in fur and skins had kept a trading house but a short time before, though they were then absent. We had passed the trading house but a short distance, when we met three white men floating down the river, with the appearance of having been recently murdered by the Indians. We supposed them to be the bodies of the traders, whose store we had passed the same day. Sheninjee being alarmed for fear of being apprehended as one of the murderers, if he should go on, resolved to put about immediately, and we accordingly returned to where the traders had lived, and there landed.

At the trading house we found a party of Shawnee Indians, who had taken a young white man prisoner, and had just begun to torture him for the sole purpose of gratifying their curiosity in exulting at his distress. They at first made him stand up, while they slowly pared his ears and split them into strings; they then made a number of slight incisions in his face; and then bound him upon the ground, rolled him in the dirt, and rubbed it in his wounds: some of them at the same time whipping him with small rods! The poor fellow cried for mercy and yelled most piteously.

The sight of his distress seemed too much for me to endure: I begged of them to desist – I entreated them with tears to release him. At length they attended to my intercessions, and set him at liberty. He was shockingly disfigured, bled profusely, and appeared to be in great pain; but as soon as he was liberated he made off in haste, which was the last I saw of him.

We soon learned that the same party of Shawnees had, but a few hours before, massacred the three white traders whom we saw in the river, and had plundered their store. We, however, were not molested by them, and after a short stay at that place, moved up the creek about forty miles to a Shawnee town, which the Indians called Gaw-gush-shaw-ga, (which being interpreted signifies a mask or a false face.) The creek that we went up was called Candusky.

It was now summer; and having tarried a few days at Gawgushshawga, we moved on up the creek to a place that was called Yis-kah-wa-na, (meaning in English open mouth.)

As I have before observed, the family to which I belonged was part of a tribe of Seneca Indians, who lived, at that time, at a place called Genishau, from the name of the tribe, that was situated on a river of the same name which is now called Genesee. The word Genishau signifies a shining, clear or open place. Those of us who lived on the Ohio, had frequently received invitations from those at Genishau, by one of my brothers, who usually went and returned every season, to come and live with them, and my two sisters had been gone almost two years.

While we were at Yiskahwana, my brother arrived there from Genishau, and insisted so strenuously upon our going home (as he called it) with him, that my two brothers concluded to go, and to take me with them.

By this time the summer was gone, and the time for harvesting corn had arrived. My brothers, for fear of the rainy season setting in early, thought it best to set out immediately that we might have good travelling. Sheninjee consented to have me go with my brothers; but concluded to go down the river himself with some fur and skins which he had on hand, spend the winter in hunting with his friends, and come to me in the spring following.

That was accordingly agreed upon, and he set out for Wiishto; and my three brothers and myself, with my little son on my back, at the same time set out for Genishau. We came on to Upper Sandusky, to an Indian town that we found deserted by its inhabitants, in consequence of their having recently murdered some English traders, who resided amongst them. That town was owned and had been occupied by Delaware Indians, who, when they left it, buried their provision in the earth, in order to preserve it from their enemies, or to have a supply for themselves if they should chance to return. My brothers understood the customs of the Indians when they were obliged to fly from their enemies; and suspecting that their corn at least must have been hid, made diligent search, and at length found a large quantity of it, together with beans, sugar and honey, so carefully buried that it was completely dry and as good as when they left it. As our stock of provision was scanty, we considered ourselves extremely fortunate in finding so seasonable a supply, with so little trouble. Having caught two or three horses, that we found there, and furnished ourselves with a good store of food, we travelled on till we came to the mouth of French Creek, where we hunted two days, and from thence came on to Conowongo Creek, where we were obliged to stay seven or ten days, in consequence of our horses having left us and straying into the woods. The horses, however, were found, and we again prepared to resume our journey. During our stay at that place the rain fell fast, and had raised the creek to such a height that it was seemingly impossible for us to cross it. A number of times we ventured in, but were compelled to return, barely escaping with our lives. At length we succeeded in swimming our horses and reached the opposite shore; though I but just escaped with my little boy from being drowned. From Sandusky the path that we travelled was crooked and obscure; but was tolerably well understood by my oldest brother, who had travelled it a number of times, when going to and returning from the Cherokee wars. The fall by this time was considerably advanced, and the rains, attended with cold winds, continued daily to increase the difficulties of travelling. From Conowongo we came to a place, called by the Indians Che-ua-shung-gau-tau, and from that to U-na-waum-gwa, (which means an eddy, not strong), where the early frosts had destroyed the corn so that the Indians were in danger of starving for the want of bread. Having rested ourselves two days at that place, we came on to Caneadea and stayed one day, and then continued our march till we arrived at Genishau. Genishau at that time was a large Seneca town, thickly inhabited, lying on Genesee river, opposite what is now called the Free Ferry, adjoining Fall-Brook, and about south west of the present village of Geneseo, the county seat for the county of Livingston, in the state of New-York.

Those only who have travelled on foot the distance of five or six hundred miles, through an almost pathless wilderness, can form an idea of the fatigue and sufferings that I endured on that journey. My clothing was thin and illy calculated to defend me from the continually drenching rains with which I was daily completely wet, and at night with nothing but my wet blanket to cover me, I had to sleep on the naked ground, and generally without a shelter, save such as nature had provided. In addition to all that, I had to carry my child, then about nine months old, every step of the journey on my back, or in my arms, and provide for his comfort and prevent his suffering, as far as my poverty of means would admit. Such was the fatigue that I sometimes felt, that I thought it impossible for me to go through, and I would almost abandon the idea of even trying to proceed. My brothers were attentive, and at length, as I have stated, we reached our place of destination, in good health, and without having experienced a day's sickness from the time we left Yiskahwana.

We were kindly received by my Indian mother and the other members of the family, who appeared to make me welcome; and my two sisters, whom I had not seen in two years, received me with every expression of love and friendship, and that they really felt what they expressed, I have never had the least reason to doubt. The warmth of their feelings, the kind reception which I met with, and the continued favors that I received at their hands, rivitted my affection for them so strongly that I am constrained to believe that I loved them as I should have loved my own sister had she lived, and I had been brought up with her.

## CHAPTER 6 {REVOLUTION; MORALS OF THE INDIANS}

Peace amongst the Indians. – Celebrations. – Worship. Exercises. – Business of the Tribes. – Former Happiness of the Indians in time of peace extolled. – Their Morals; Fidelity; Honesty; Chastity; Temperance. Indians called to German Flats. – Treaty with Americans. – They are sent for by the British Commissioners, and go to Oswego. – Promises made by those Commissioners. – Greatness of the King of England. Reward that was paid them for joining the British. They make a Treaty. – Bounty offered for Scalps. Return richly dressed and equipped. – In 1776 they kill a man at Cautega to provoke the Americans. Prisoners taken at Cherry Valley, brought Beard's Town; redeemed, &c. – Battle at Fort Stanwix. – Indians suffer a great loss. – Mourning at Beard's Town. – Mrs. Jemison's care of and services rendered to Butler and Brandt.

After the conclusion of the French war, our tribe had nothing to trouble it till the commencement of the Revolution. For twelve or fifteen years the use of the implements of war was not known, nor the war-whoop heard, save on days of festivity, when the achievements of former times were commemorated in a kind of mimic warfare, in which the chiefs and warriors displayed their prowess, and illustrated their former adroitness, by laying the ambuscade, surprizing their enemies, and performing many accurate manoeuvres with the tomahawk and scalping knife; thereby preserving and handing to their children, the theory of Indian warfare. During that period they also pertinaciously observed the religious rites of their progenitors, by attending with the most scrupulous exactness and a great degree of enthusiasm to the sacrifices, at particular times, to appease the anger of the evil deity, or to excite the commisseration and friendship of the Great Good Spirit, whom they adored with reverence, as the author, governor, supporter and disposer of every good thing of which they participated.

They also practised in various athletic games, such as running, wrestling, leaping, and playing ball, with a view that their bodies might be more supple, or rather that they might not become enervated, and that they might be enabled to make a proper selection of Chiefs for the councils of the nation and leaders for war.

While the Indians were thus engaged in their round of traditionary performances, with the addition of hunting, their women attended to agriculture, their families, and a few domestic concerns of small consequence, and attended with but little labor.

No people can live more happy than the Indians did in times of peace, before the introduction of spirituous liquors amongst them. Their lives were a continual round of pleasures. Their wants were few, and easily satisfied; and their cares were only for to-day; the bounds of their calculations for future comfort not extending to the incalculable uncertainties of to-morrow. If peace ever dwelt with men, it was in former times, in the recesses from war, amongst what are now termed barbarians. The moral character of the Indians was (if I may be allowed the expression) uncontaminated. Their fidelity was perfect, and became proverbial; they were strictly honest; they despised deception and falsehood; and chastity was held in high veneration, and a violation of it was considered sacrilege. They were temperate in their desires, moderate in their passions, and candid and honorable in the expression of their sentiments on every subject of importance.

Thus, at peace amongst themselves, and with the neighboring whites, though there were none at that time very near, our Indians lived quietly and peaceably at home, till a little before the breaking out of the revolutionary war, when they were sent for, together with the Chiefs and members of the Six Nations[9] generally, by the people of the States, to go to the German Flats, and there hold a general council, in order that the people of the states might ascertain, in good season, who they should esteem and treat as enemies, and who as friends, in the great war which was upon the point of breaking out between them and the King of England.

Our Indians obeyed the call, and the council was holden, at which the pipe of peace was smoked, and a treaty made, in which the Six Nations solemnly agreed that if a war should eventually break out, they would not take up arms on either side; but that they would observe a strict neutrality. With that the people of the states were satisfied, as they had not asked their assistance, nor did not wish it. The Indians returned to their homes well pleased that they could live on neutral ground, surrounded by the din of war, without being engaged in it.

About a year passed off, and we, as usual, were enjoying ourselves in the employments of peaceable times, when a messenger arrived from the British Commissioners, requesting all the Indians of our tribe to attend a general council which was soon to be held at Oswego. The council convened, and being opened, the British Commissioners informed the Chiefs that the object of calling a council of the Six Nations, was, to engage their assistance in subduing the rebels, the people of the states, who had risen up against the good King, their master, and were about to rob him of a great part of his possessions and wealth, and added that they would amply reward them for all their services.

The Chiefs then arose, and informed the Commissioners of the nature and extent of the treaty which they had entered into with the people of the states, the year before, and that they should not violate it by taking up the hatchet against them.

The Commissioners continued their entreaties without success, till they addressed their avarice, by telling our people that the people of the states were few in number, and easily subdued; and that on the account of their disobedience to the King, they justly merited all the punishment that it was possible for white men and Indians to inflict upon them; and added, that the King was rich and powerful, both in money and subjects: That his rum was as plenty as the water in lake Ontario: that his men were as numerous as the sands upon the lake shore: – and that the Indians, if they would assist in the war, and persevere in their friendship to the King, till it was closed, should never want for money or goods. Upon this the Chiefs concluded a treaty with the British Commissioners, in which they agreed to take up arms against the rebels, and continue in the service of his Majesty till they were subdued, in consideration of certain conditions which were stipulated in the treaty to be performed by the British government and its agents.

As soon as the treaty was finished, the Commissioners made a present to each Indian of a suit of clothes, a brass kettle, a gun and tomahawk, a scalping knife, a quantity of powder and lead, a piece of gold, and promised a bounty on every scalp that should be brought in. Thus richly clad and equipped, they returned home, after an absence of about two weeks, full of the fire of war, and anxious to encounter their enemies. Many of the kettles which the Indians received at that time are now in use on the Genesee Flats.

Hired to commit depredations upon the whites, who had given them no offence, they waited impatiently to commence their labor, till sometime in the spring of 1776, when a convenient opportunity offered for them to make an attack. At that time, a party of our Indians were at Cau-te-ga, who shot a man that was looking after his horse, for the sole purpose, as I was informed by my Indian brother, who was present, of commencing hostilities.

In May following, our Indians were in their first battle with the Americans; but at what place I am unable to determine. While they were absent at that time, my daughter Nancy was born.

[9] The constituent tribes of the Iroquois Confederacy: the Mohawk, Seneca, Oneida, Onondaga, Cayuga, and Tuscarora.

The same year, at Cherry Valley, our Indians took a woman and her three daughters prisoners, and brought them on, leaving one at Canandaigua, one at Honeoy, one at Cattaraugus, and one (the woman) at Little Beard's Town, where I resided. The woman told me that she and her daughters might have escaped, but that they expected the British army only, and therefore made no effort. Her husband and sons got away. Sometime having elapsed, they were redeemed at Fort Niagara by Col. Butler, who clothed them well and sent them home.

In the same expedition, Joseph Smith was taken prisoner at or near Cherry Valley, brought to Genesee, and detained till after the revolutionary war. He was then liberated, and the Indians made him a present, in company with Horatio Jones, of 6000 acres of land lying in the present town of Leicester, in the county of Livingston.

One of the girls just mentioned, was married to a British officer at Fort Niagara, by the name of Johnson, who at the time she was taken, took a gold ring from her finger, without any compliments or ceremonies. When he saw her at Niagara, he recognized her features, restored the ring that he had so impolitely borrowed, and courted and married her.

Previous to the battles at Fort Stanwix, the British sent for the Indians to come and see them whip the rebels; and, at the same time stated that they did not wish to have them fight, but wanted to have them just sit down, smoke their pipes, and look on. Our Indians went, to a man; but contrary to their expectation, instead of smoking and looking on, they were obliged to fight for their lives, and in the end of the battle were completely beaten, with a great loss in killed and wounded. Our Indians alone had thirty-six killed, and a great number wounded. Our town exhibited a scene of real sorrow and distress, when our warriors returned and recounted their misfortunes, and stated the real loss they had sustained in the engagement. The mourning was excessive, and was expressed by the most doleful yells, shrieks, and howlings, and by inimitable gesticulations.

During the revolution, my house was the home of Col's Butler and Brandt, whenever they chanced to come into our neighborhood as they passed to and from Fort Niagara, which was the seat of their military operations. Many and many a night I have pounded samp for them from sun-set till sun-rise, and furnished them with necessary provision and clean clothing for their journey.

## CHAPTER 9 [LANDOWNER]

Mrs. Jemison has liberty to go to her Friends. – Chooses to stay. – Her Reasons, &c. – Her Indian Brother makes provision for her Settlement. – He goes to Grand River and dies. – Her love for him, &c. – She is presented with the Gardow Reservation. – Is troubled by Speculators. – Description of the Soil, &c. of her Flats. – Indian notions of the ancient Inhabitants of this Country.

Soon after the close of the revolutionary war, my Indian brother, Kau-jises-tau-ge-au (which being interpreted signifies Black Coals), offered me my liberty, and told me that if it was my choice I might go to my friends.

My son, Thomas, was anxious that I should go; and offered to go with me and assist me on the journey, by taking care of the younger children, and providing food as we travelled through the wilderness. But the Chiefs of our tribe, suspecting from his appearance, actions, and a few warlike exploits, that Thomas would be a great warrior, or a good counsellor, refused to let him leave them on any account whatever.

To go myself, and leave him, was more than I felt able to do; for he had been kind to me, and was one on whom I placed great dependence. The Chiefs refusing to let him go, was one reason for my resolving to stay; but another, more powerful, if possible, was, that I had got a large family of Indian children, that I must take with me; and that if I should be so fortunate as to find my relatives, they would despise them, if not myself; and treat us as enemies; or, at least with a degree of cold indifference, which I thought I could not endure.

Accordingly, after I had duly considered the matter, I told my brother that it was my choice to stay and spend the remainder of my days with my Indian friends, and live with my family as I had heretofore done. He appeared well pleased with my resolution, and informed me, that as that was my choice, I should have a piece of land that I could call my own, where I could live unmolested, and have something at my decease to leave for the benefit of my children.

In a short time he made himself ready to go to Upper Canada; but before he left us, he told me that he would speak to some of the Chiefs at Buffalo, to attend the great Council, which he expected would convene in a few years at farthest, and convey to me such a tract of land as I should select. My brother left us, as he had proposed, and soon after died at Grand River.

Kaujisestaugeau, was an excellent man, and ever treated me with kindness. Perhaps no one of his tribe at any time exceeded him in natural mildness of temper, and warmth and tenderness of affection. If he had taken my life at the time when the avarice of the old King inclined him to procure my emancipation, it would have been done with a pure heart and from good motives. He loved his friends; and was generally beloved. During the time that I lived in the family with him, he never offered the most trifling abuse; on the contrary, his whole conduct towards me was strictly honorable. I mourned his loss as that of a tender brother, and shall recollect him through life with emotions of friendship and gratitude.

I lived undisturbed, without hearing a word on the subject of my land, till the great Council was held at Big Tree, in 1797, when Farmer's Brother, whose Indian name is Ho-na-ye-wus, sent for me to attend the council. When I got there, he told me that my brother had spoken to him to see that I had a piece of land reserved for my use; and that then was the time for me to receive it. – He requested that I would choose for myself and describe the bounds of a piece that would suit me. I accordingly told him the place of beginning, and then went round a tract that I judged would be sufficient for my purpose, (knowing that it would include the Gardow Flats,) by stating certain bounds with which I was acquainted.

When the Council was opened, and the business afforded a proper opportunity, Farmer's Brother presented my claim, and rehearsed the request of my brother. Red Jacket, whose Indian name is Sagu-yu-what-hah, which interpreted, is Keeper-awake, opposed me or my claim with all his influence and eloquence.[10] Farmer's Brother insisted upon the necessity, propriety and expediency of his proposition, and got the land granted. The deed was made and signed, securing to me the title to all the land I had described; under the same restrictions and regulations that other Indian lands are subject to.

That land has ever since been known by the name of the Gardow Tract.

Red Jacket not only opposed my claim at the Council, but he withheld my money two or three years, on the account of my lands having been granted without his consent. Parrish and Jones at length convinced him that it was the white people, and not the Indians who had given me the land, and compelled him to pay over all the money which he had retained on my account.

My land derived its name, Gardow, from a hill that is within its limits, which is called in the Seneca language Kautam. Kautam when interpreted signifies up and down, or down and up, and is applied to a hill that you will ascend and descend in passing it; or to a valley. It has been said that Gardow was the name of my husband Hiokatoo, and that my land derived its name from him; that however was a mistake, for the old man always considered Gardow a nickname, and was uniformly offended when called by it.

About three hundred acres of my land, when I first saw it, was open flats, lying on the Genesee River, which it is supposed was cleared by a race of inhabitants who preceded the first Indian settlements in this part of the country. The Indians are confident that many parts of this country were settled and for a number of years occupied by people of whom their fathers never had any tradition, as they never had seen them. Whence those people originated, and whither they went, I have never heard one of our oldest and wisest Indians pretend to guess. When I first came to Genishau, the bank of Fall Brook had just slid off and exposed a large number of human bones, which the Indians said were buried there long before their fathers ever saw the place; and that they did not know what kind of people they were. It however was and is believed by our people, that they were not Indians.

My flats were extremely fertile; but needed more labor than my daughters and myself were able to

[10] Red Jacket (c.1758–1830) was a famous Seneca chief; his birth-name was Otetiani, but he later took the name of Sagoyewatha. An articulate and powerful advocate for Native American autonomy and cultural preservation, he was an important negotiator for his tribe, not only within the Iroquois Confederacy, but also with the Europeans and later, the US government.

perform, to produce a sufficient quantity of grain and other necessary productions of the earth, for the consumption of our family. The land had lain uncultivated so long that it was thickly covered with weeds of almost every description. In order that we might live more easy, Mr. Parrish, with the consent of the chiefs, gave me liberty to lease or let my land to white people to till on shares. I accordingly let it out, and have continued to do so, which makes my task less burthensome, while at the same time I am more comfortably supplied with the means of support.

## CHAPTER 10 [SPIRITOUS LIQUORS AMONG THE SENECA; FRATRICIDE]

Happy situation of her Family. – Disagreement between her sons Thomas and John. – Her Advice to them, &c. – John kills Thomas. – Her Affliction. – Council. Decision of the Chiefs, &c. – Life of Thomas. – His Wives, Children, &c. – Cause of his Death, &c.

I have frequently heard it asserted by white people, and can truly say from my own experience, that the time at which parents take the most satisfaction and comfort with their families is when their children are young, incapable of providing for their own wants, and are about the fireside, where they can be daily observed and instructed.

Few mothers, perhaps, have had less trouble with their children during their minority than myself. In general, my children were friendly to each other, and it was very seldom that I knew them to have the least difference or quarrel: so far, indeed, were they from rendering themselves or me uncomfortable, that I considered myself happy – more so than commonly falls to the lot of parents, especially to women.

My happiness in this respect, however, was not without alloy; for my son Thomas, from some cause unknown to me, from the time he was a small lad, always called his brother John, a witch, which was the cause, as they grew towards manhood, of frequent and severe quarrels between them, and gave me much trouble and anxiety for their safety. After Thomas and John arrived to manhood, in addition to the former charge, John got two wives, with whom he lived till the time of his death. Although polygamy was tolerated in our tribe, Thomas considered it a violation of good and wholesome rules in society, and tending directly to destroy that friendly social intercourse and love, that ought to be the happy result of matrimony and chastity. Consequently, he frequently reprimanded John, by telling him that his conduct was beneath the dignity, and inconsistent with the principles of good Indians; indecent and unbecoming a gentleman; and, as he never could reconcile himself to it, he was frequently, almost constantly, when they were together, talking to him on the same subject. John always resented such reprimand, and reproof, with a great degree of passion, though they never quarrelled, unless Thomas was intoxicated.

In his fits of drunkenness, Thomas seemed to lose all his natural reason, and to conduct like a wild or crazy man, without regard to relatives, decency or propriety. At such times he often threatened to take my life for having raised a witch, (as he called John), and has gone so far as to raise his tomahawk to split my head. He, however, never struck me; but on John's account he struck Hiokatoo, and thereby excited in John a high degree of indignation, which was extinguished only by blood.

For a number of years their difficulties, and consequent unhappiness, continued and rather increased, continually exciting in my breast the most fearful apprehensions, and greatest anxiety for their safety. With tears in my eyes, I advised them to become reconciled to each other, and to be friendly; told them the consequences of their continuing to cherish so much malignity and malice, that it would end in their destruction, the disgrace of their families, and bring me down to the grave. No one can conceive of the constant trouble that I daily endured on their accounts – on the account of my two oldest sons, whom I loved equally, and with all the feelings and affection of a tender mother, stimulated by an anxious concern for their fate. Parents, mothers especially, will love their children, though ever so unkind and disobedient. Their eyes of compassion, of real sentimental affection, will be involuntarily extended after them, in their greatest excesses of iniquity; and those fine filaments of consanguinity, which gently entwine themselves around the heart where filial love and parental care is equal, will be lengthened, and enlarged to cords seemingly of sufficient strength to reach and reclaim the wanderer. I know that such exercises are frequently unavailing; but, notwithstanding their ultimate failure, it still remains true, and ever will, that the love of a parent for a disobedient child, will increase, and grow more and more ardent, so long as a hope of its reformation is capable of stimulating a disappointed breast.

My advice and expostulations with my sons were abortive; and year after year their disaffection for each other increased. At length, Thomas came to my house on the 1st day of July, 1811, in my absence, somewhat intoxicated, where he found John, with whom he immediately commenced a quarrel on their old subjects of difference. – John's anger became desperate. He caught Thomas by the hair of his head, dragged him out at the door and there killed him, by a blow which he gave him on the head with his tomahawk!

I returned soon after, and found my son lifeless at the door, on the spot where he was killed! No one can judge of my feelings on seeing this mournful spectacle; and what greatly added to my distress, was the fact that he had fallen by the murderous hand of his brother! I felt my situation unsupportable. Having passed through various scenes of trouble of the most cruel and trying kind, I had hoped to spend my few remaining days in quietude, and to die in peace, surrounded by my family. This fatal event, however, seemed to be a stream of woe poured into my cup of afflictions, filling it even to overflowing, and blasting all my prospects.

As soon as I had recovered a little from the shock which I felt at the sight of my departed son, and some of my neighbors had come in to assist in taking care of the corpse, I hired Shanks, an Indian, to go to Buffalo, and carry the sorrowful news of Thomas' death, to our friends at that place, and request the Chiefs to hold a Council, and dispose of John as they should think proper. Shanks set out on his errand immediately, and John, fearing that he should be apprehended and punished for the crime he had committed, at the same time went off towards Caneadea.

Thomas was decently interred in a style corresponding with his rank.

The Chiefs soon assembled in council on the trial of John, and after having seriously examined the matter according to their laws, justified his conduct, and acquitted him. They considered Thomas to have been the first transgressor, and that for the abuses which he had offered, he had merited from John the treatment that he had received.

John, on learning the decision of the council, returned to his family.

Thomas (except when intoxicated, which was not frequent,) was a kind and tender child, willing to assist me in my labor, and to remove every obstacle to my comfort. His natural abilities were said to be of a superior cast, and he soared above the trifling subjects of revenge, which are common amongst Indians, as being far beneath his attention. In his childish and boyish days, his natural turn was to practice in the art of war, though he despised the cruelties that the warriors inflicted upon their subjugated enemies. He was manly in his deportment, courageous and active; and commanded respect. Though he appeared well pleased with peace, he was cunning in Indian warfare, and succeeded to admiration in the execution of his plans.

At the age of fourteen or fifteen years, he went into the war with manly fortitude, armed with a tomahawk and scalping knife; and when he returned, brought one white man a prisoner, whom he had taken with his own hands, on the west branch of the Susquehannah river. It so happened, that as he was looking out for his enemies, he discovered two men boiling sap in the woods. He watched them unperceived, till dark when he advanced with a noiseless step to where they were standing, caught one of them before they were apprized of danger, and conducted him to the camp. He was well treated while a prisoner, and redeemed at the close of the war.

At the time Kaujisestaugeau gave me my liberty to go to my friends, Thomas was anxious to go with me; but as I have before observed, the Chiefs would not suffer him to leave them on the account of his courage and skill in war: expecting that they should need his assistance. He was a great Counsellor and a Chief when quite young; and in the last capacity, went two or three times to Philadelphia to assist in making treaties with the people of the states.

Thomas had four wives, by whom he had eight children. Jacob Jemison, his second son by his last wife, who is at this time twenty-seven or twenty-eight years of age, went to Dartmouth college, in the spring of 1816, for the purpose of receiving a good education, where it was said that he was an industrious scholar, and made great proficiency in the study of the different branches to which he attended. Having spent two years at that Institution, he returned in the winter of 1818, and is now at Buffalo; where I have understood that he contemplates commencing the study of medicine, as a profession.

Thomas, at the time he was killed, was a few moons over fifty-two years old, and John was forty-eight. As he was naturally good natured, and possessed a friendly disposition, he would not have come to so untimely an end, had it not been for his intemperance. He fell a victim to the use of ardent spirits – a poison that will soon exterminate the Indian tribes in this part of the country, and leave their names without a root or branch. The thought is melancholy; but no arguments, no examples, however persuasive or impressive, are sufficient to deter an Indian for an hour from taking the potent draught, which he knows at the time will derange his faculties, reduce him to a level with the beasts, or deprive him of life!

## Chapter 16 [Conclusion]

Conclusion. – Review of her Life. – Reflections on the loss of Liberty. – Care she took to preserve her Health. – Indians' abstemiousness in Drinking, after the French War. – Care of their Lives, &c. – General use of Spirits. – Her natural Strength. – Purchase of her first Cow. – Means by which she has been supplied with Food. – Suspicions of her having been a Witch. – Her Constancy. – Number of Children. – Number Living. – Their Residence. – Closing Reflection.

When I review my life, the privations that I have suffered, the hardships I have endured, the vicissitudes I have passed, and the complete revolution that I have experienced in my manner of living; when I consider my reduction from a civilized to a savage state, and the various steps by which that process has been effected, and that my life has been prolonged, and my health and reason spared, it seems a miracle that I am unable to account for, and is a tragical medley that I hope will never be repeated.

The bare loss of liberty is but a mere trifle when compared with the circumstances that necessarily attend, and are inseparably connected with it. It is the recollection of what we once were, of the friends, the home, and the pleasures that we have left or lost; the anticipation of misery, the appearance of wretchedness, the anxiety for freedom, the hope of release, the devising of means of escaping, and the vigilance with which we watch our keepers, that constitute the nauseous dregs of the bitter cup of slavery. I am sensible, however, that no one can pass from a state of freedom to that of slavery, and in the last situation rest perfectly contented; but as every one knows that great exertions of the mind tend directly to debilitate the body, it will appear obvious that we ought, when confined, to exert all our faculties to promote our present comfort, and let future days provide their own sacrifices. In regard to ourselves, just as we feel, we are.

For the preservation of my life to the present time I am indebted to an excellent constitution, with which I have been blessed in as great a degree as any other person. After I arrived to years of understanding, the care of my own health was one of my principal studies; and by avoiding exposures to wet and cold, by temperance in eating, abstaining from the use of spirits, and shunning the excesses to which I was frequently exposed, I effected my object beyond what I expected. I have never once been sick till within a year or two, only as I have related.

Spirits and tobacco I have never used, and I have never once attended an Indian frolic. When I was taken prisoner, and for sometime after that, spirits was not known; and when it was first introduced, it was in small quantities, and used only by the Indians; so that it was a long time before the Indian women begun to even taste it.

After the French war, for a number of years, it was the practice of the Indians of our tribe to send to Niagara and get two or three kegs of rum, (in all six or eight gallons,) and hold a frolic as long as it lasted. When the rum was brought to the town, all the Indians collected, and before a drop was drank, gave all their knives, tomahawks, guns, and other instruments of war, to one Indian, whose business it was to bury them in a private place, keep them concealed, and remain perfectly sober till the frolic was ended. Having thus divested themselves, they commenced drinking, and continued their frolic till every drop was consumed. If any of them became quarrelsome, or got to fighting, those who were sober enough bound them upon the ground, where they were obliged to lie till they got sober, and then were unbound. When the fumes of the spirits had left the company, the sober Indian returned to each the instruments with which they had entrusted him, and all went home satisfied. A frolic of that kind was held but once a year, and that at the time the Indians quit their hunting, and come in with their deer-skins.

In those frolics the women never participated. Soon after the revolutionary war, however, spirits became common in our tribe, and has been used indiscriminately by both sexes; though there are not so frequent instances of intoxication amongst the squaws as amongst the Indians.

To the introduction and use of that baneful article, which has made such devastation in our tribes, and threatens the extinction of our people, (the Indians,) I can with the greatest propriety impute the whole of my misfortune in losing my three sons. But as I have before observed, not even the love of life will restrain an Indian from sipping the poison that he knows will destroy him. The voice of nature, the rebukes of reason, the advice of parents, the expostulations of friends, and the numerous instances of sudden death, are all insufficient to reclaim an Indian, who has once experienced the exhilarating and inebriating effects of spirits, from seeking his grave in the bottom of his bottle!

My strength has been great for a woman of my size, otherwise I must long ago have died under the burdens which I was obliged to carry. I learned to carry loads on my back, in a strap placed across my forehead, soon after my captivity; and continue to carry in the same way. Upwards of thirty years ago, with the help of my young children, I backed all the boards that were used about my house from Allen's mill at the outlet of Silver Lake, a distance of five miles. I have planted, hoed, and harvested corn every season but one since I was taken prisoner. Even this present fall (1823) I have husked my corn and backed it into the house.

The first cow that I ever owned, I bought of a squaw sometime after the revolution. It had been stolen from the enemy. I had owned it but a few days when it fell into a hole, and almost died before we could get it out. After this, the squaw wanted to be recanted, but as I would not give up the cow, I gave her money enough to make, when added to the sum which I paid her at first, thirty-five dollars. Cows were plenty on the Ohio, when I lived there, and of good quality.

For provisions I have never suffered since I came upon the flats; nor have I ever been in debt to any other hands than my own for the plenty that I have shared.

My vices, that have been suspected, have been but few. It was believed for a long time, by some of our people, that I was a great witch; but they were unable to prove my guilt, and consequently I escaped the certain doom of those who are convicted of that crime, which, by Indians, is considered as heinous as murder. Some of my children had light brown hair, and tolerable fair skin, which used to make some say that I stole them; yet as I was ever conscious of my own constancy, I never thought that any one really believed that I was guilty of adultery.

I have been the mother of eight children; three of whom are now living, and I have at this time thirty-nine grand children, and fourteen great-grand children, all living in the neighborhood of Genesee River, and at Buffalo.

I live in my own house, and on my own land, with my youngest daughter, Polly, who is married to George Chongo, and has three children.

My daughter Nancy, who is married to Billy Green, lives about 80 rods south of my house, and has seven children.

My other daughter, Betsey, is married to John Green, has seven children, and resides 80 rods north of my house.

Thus situated in the midst of my children, I expect I shall soon leave the world, and make room for the rising generation. I feel the weight of years with which I am loaded, and am sensible of my daily failure in seeing, hearing and strength; but my only anxiety is for my family. If my family will live happily, and I can be exempted from trouble while I have to stay, I feel as though I could lay down in peace a life that has been checked in almost every hour, with troubles of deeper dye, than are commonly experienced by mortals.

# Jane Johnston Schoolcraft (Bame-wa-wa-ge-zhik-a-quay, Woman of the Stars Rushing Through the Sky; Ojibwe, 1800–1841)

*One of the most famous Indian women of her time, Schoolcraft was born in Sault Sainte Marie, Michigan, to John Johnston, a Scotch-Irish fur trader, and Ozha-guscoday-way-quay (Woman of the Green Valley) who, after her marriage to Johnston, took the English name of Susan. Susan's father was a renowned Ojibwe chief, Waub Ojeeg (White Fisher). While John Johnston taught his daughter European literary classics from his extensive library, her mother educated her and her siblings in Ojibwe language and traditions. Traveling with her father to places like Detroit, Quebec City, and Montreal, Jane also spent time in Ireland for additional schooling.*

*The young Jane Johnston met her future husband, the ethnographer and explorer Henry Rowe Schoolcraft, when he came in 1822 to the Sault as Upper Great Lakes Indian agent. He later acknowledged the central role of the Johnston family in advancing his research into Native American culture. A few years after Henry and Jane married, he began to publish* The Literary Voyager or Muzzeniegun, *a magazine that included myths, poetry, essays on Ojibwe history, and biographies. It was through her contributions to this journal under the pseudonyms "Leelinau" and "Rosa," as well as her Ojibwe name and her initials, that Jane acquired the reputation as the "northern Pocahontas," receiving visits from such admiring writers as Harriet Martineau and Anna Jameson.*

*The magazine was an outgrowth of a literary society founded by the Schoolcrafts composed of American and Canadian residents of Sault Sainte Marie and, although it was intended for local residents, it circulated in Detroit and New York City. Jane Schoolcraft's contributions to* The Literary Voyager *included traditional Indian tales of origin such as "The Origin of the Robin, An Oral Allegory," and "Origin of the Miscodeed, or the Maid of Taquimenon"; many of the tales were likely told to her by her mother. "The Forsaken Brother," like many traditional Native American narratives, emphasizes the importance of maintaining family responsibilities and connections, as opposed to following one's individual desires. Like her later counterparts Pauline Johnson and Zitkala-Ša, Jane recorded these stories both to preserve them for future generations and to build bridges of understanding between Indian and white cultures.*

*To contemporary readers much of her poetry seems to echo conventional romantic perspectives, themes, and aesthetic strategies; for example, "Lines to a Friend Asleep," "To Sisters on a Walk in the Garden," and "Resignation" parallel those by Euroamerican and British counterparts such as Lydia Sigourney, William Wordsworth, and Felicia Hemans. Some poems are influenced by her chronic ill health and attempts to find solace in religious faith, while others, like "Lines Written under Affliction" and "To My Ever Beloved and Lamented Son William Henry," reflecting her pain on the death of her young son William in 1826, participate in the tradition of child death poems, beginning in the United States with Anne Bradstreet and continuing with Sigourney and other of Schoolcraft's popular contemporaries. Perhaps her most interesting and important poems for today's readers are those depicting her powerful grandfather, Waub Ojeeg. In "Otagamiad" he affirms the need for the band to make war on its enemies to prevent enslavement; in "Invocation to My Maternal Grandfather on Hearing His Descent from Chippewa Ancestors Misrepresented," the author negates the rumor that her grandfather was a child taken from the tribe's enemies, the Sioux.*

*Her marriage to Henry often proved to be difficult for Jane, who wished to rear her children in the traditional close family atmosphere of the Ojibwe. Henry was often away on business trips and because of her own poor health Jane became addicted to laudanum. In 1838 Henry insisted on sending the children away to private schools, and his wife found herself unbearably lonely. Shortly after they settled in New York City in 1841, Henry traveled to England, and Jane died during his absence. Schoolcraft's production was relatively small but is important both for its participation in mainstream literary traditions and its contribution to the establishment of Native American literature.*

## BIBLIOGRAPHY


### Primary

Schoolcraft, Jane Johnston. Various pieces. In *The Literary Voyager or Muzzeniegun*. Ed. Philip P. Mason. Michigan State, 1962.

### Secondary

Bremer, Richard G. *Indian Agent and Wilderness Scholar: The Life of Henry Rowe Schoolcraft*. Central Michigan, 1987.

Parins, James W. "Jane Johnston Schoolcraft." In Kenneth M. Roemer, *Native American Writers of the United States*. Gale, 1997. 274–5.

Ruoff, A. LaVonne Brown. "Early Native American Women Authors: Jane Johnston Schoolcraft, Sarah Winnemucca, S. Alice Callahan, E. Pauline Johnson, and Zitkala-Ša." In *Nineteenth-Century American Women Writers: A Critical Reader*. Ed. Karen L. Kilcup. Blackwell, 1998. 81–111.

——. "Jane Johnston Schoolcraft." *Dictionary of Native American Literature*. Ed. Andrew Wiget. Garland, 1994. 295–7.

Schoolcraft, Henry. "To Our Correspondent, Leelinau." *Literary Voyager or Muzzeniegun*. 1 Dec. 1826.


# Poetry

## From *The Literary Voyager or Muzzeniegun*[1]

### RESIGNATION [1826]

How hard to teach the heart, opprest with grief,
Amid gay, worldly scenes, to find relief;
And the long cherish'd bliss we had in view.
To banish from the mind where first it grew!
But Faith, in time, can sweetly soothe the soul.
And Resignation hold a mild control;
The mind may then resume a proper tone,
And calmly think on hopes forever flown.

[1] "Muzzeniegun" is "a Chippewa word meaning a printed document or book" (Mason, xiv). The selections printed below were signed in various ways. "To My Ever Beloved and Lamented Son William Henry" was signed "Jane Schoolcraft," "Sonnet" was signed "J.S.," and "Otagamiad" was unsigned; all other poems were signed "Rosa" and the stories were signed "Leelinau."

## By an *Ojibway Female* Pen
## To Sisters on a Walk in the Garden, After a Shower [1826]

Come, sisters, come! The shower's past,
The garden walks are drying fast,
The Sun's bright beams are seen again,
And nought within, can now detain.
The rain drops tremble on the leaves,
Or drip expiring, from the eaves:
But soon the cool and balmy airs,
Shall dry the gems that sparkle there,
With whisp'ring breath shake ev'ry spray,
And scatter every cloud away.

Thus sisters! Shall the breeze of hope,
Through sorrow's clouds a vista ope;
Thus, shall affliction's surly blast,
By faith's bright calm be still'd at last;
Thus, pain and care,– the tear and sigh,
Be chased from every dewy eye;
And life's mix'd scene itself, but cease,
To show us realms of light and peace.

## Lines
## To a Friend Asleep [1827]

Awake my friend! the morning's fine,
Waste not in sleep the day divine,
Nature is clad in best array,
The woods, the fields, the flowers are gay; –
The sun is up, and speeds his march,
O'er heaven's high aerial arch,
His golden beams with lustre fall,
On lake and river, cot and hall; –
The dews are sparkling on each spray,
The birds are chirping sweet and gay,
The violet shows its beauteous head,
Within its narrow, figured bed; –
The air is pure, the earth bedight,
With trees and flowers, life and light,
All – all inspires a joyful gleam,
More pleasing than a fairy dream.
Awake! The sweet refreshing scene,
Invites us forth to tread the green,
With joyful hearts, and pious lays,
To join the glorious Maker's praise,
The wond'rous works – the paschal lamb,
The holy, high, and just I Am.

## LINES WRITTEN UNDER AFFLICTION [1827]

Ah! who, with a sensitive mind possest,
    Recalls the swift years that are gone,
Without mingled emotions – both bitter & blest,
    At the good & the ill he has known.

Or, how could a beautiful landscape please,
    If it showed us no feature but light?
'Tis the dark shades alone that give pleasure & ease,
    'Tis the unison of sombre and bright.

So wisely has God in his mercy ordain'd,
    That the bitterest cup he has cast,
Is mixed with a sweetness, which still is retain'd,
    To be drank and enjoyed at the last.

Thus feelings are chasten'd, & life is refin'd,
    By pangs that misfortunes convey,
To minds that have faith, & to bosoms resign'd,
    To bear – to forbear, and obey.

And tho' for a while, he condemns us in strife,
    To languish, and suffer, and die;
Yet the sunshine of promise – of hope & of life,
    Allures us to bliss in the sky.

## LINES WRITTEN UNDER SEVERE PAIN AND SICKNESS [1827]

Ah! why should I at fortune's lot repine,
Or fret myself against the will divine?
All men must go to death's deform'd embrace,
When here below they've run their destin'd race;
Oh! then on Thee, my Savior, I will trust,
For thou art good, as merciful and just, –
In Thee, with my whole heart I will confide,
And hope with Thee, forever to abide.
To Thee, my God, my heart & soul I raise,
And still thy holy, holy name I'll praise!
O! deign to give me wisdom, virtue, grace,
That I thy heavenly will may ever trace;
Teach me each duty always to fulfil,
And grant me resignation to Thy will,
And when Thy goodness wills that I should die,
This dream of life I'll leave without a sigh.

## OTAGAMIAD [1827]

In northern climes there liv'd a chief of fame,
LaPointé his dwelling, and Ojeeg his name,
Who oft in war had rais'd the battle cry,
And brav'd the rigors of an Arctic sky;

Nor less in peace those daring talents shone,
That rais'd him to his simple forest throne,
Alike endow'd with skill, such heaven's reward,
To wield the oaken sceptre, and to guard.
Now round his tent, the willing chieftains wait,
The gathering council, and the stern debate –
Hunters, & warriors circle round the green,
Age sits sedate, & youth fills up the scene,
While careful hands, with flint & steel prepare,
The sacred fire – the type of public care.

'Warriors and friends' – the chief of chiefs oppress'd,
With rising cares, his burning thoughts express'd.
'Long have our lands been hem'd around by foes,
Whose secret ire, no check or limit knows,
Whose public faith, so often pledg'd in vain,
'Twere base for freemen e'er to trust again.
Watch'd in their tracks our trusting hunters fall,
By ambush'd arrow, or avenging ball;
Our subtil foes lie hid in every pass,
Screen'd in the thicket, shelter'd in the grass,
They pierce our forests, & they cross our lines,
No treaty binds them, & no stream confines
And every spring that clothes the leafy plain,
We mourn our brethren, or our children slain.
Delay but swells our woes, as rivers wild,
Heap on their banks the earth they first despoil'd.
Oh chieftains! Listen to my warning voice,
War – war or slavery is our only choice.
No longer sit, with head & arms declined,
The charms of ease still ling'ring in the mind;
No longer hope, that justice will be given
If ye neglect the proper means of heaven:
Fear – and fear only, makes our foemen just
Or shun the path of conquest, rage or lust,
Nor think the lands we own, our sons shall share,
If we forget the noble rites of war.
Choose then with wisdom, nor by more delay,
Put off the great – the all important day.
Upon yourselves alone, your fate depends,
'Tis warlike acts that make a nation friends
'Tis warlike acts that prop a falling throne,
And makes peace, glory, empire, all our own.
Oh friends! Think deeply on my counsel – words
I sound no peaceful cry of summer birds!
No whispering dream of bliss without allay
Or idle strain of mute, inglorious joy
Let my bold voice arouse your slumb'ring hearts,
And answer warriors – with uplifted darts,
Thick crowding arrows, bristled o'er the plain,
And joyous warriors rais'd the battle strain.'

All but Camudwa,[2] join'd the shouting throng,
Camudwa, fam'd for eloquence of tongue
Whose breast resolv'd the coming strife with pain,
And peace still hop'd, by peaceful arts to gain.
'Friends' – he reply'd – 'our ruler's words are just,
Fear breeds respect and bridles rage or lust,
But in our haste, by rude and sudden hate,
To prop our own, or crush our neighbors' state
Valor itself, should not disdain the skill
By pliant speech, to gain our purpos'd will.
The foe may yet, be reason'd into right.
And if we fail in speech – we still may fight.
At least, one further effort, be our care,
I will myself, the daring message bear,
I give my body, to the mission free,
And if I fall, my country, 'tis for thee!
The wife and child, shall lisp my song of fame,
And all who value peace, repeat my name!'

''Tis well' – Baimwáwa[3] placidly replied,
'To cast our eyes, with care to either side,
Lest in our pride, to bring a rival low,
Our own fair fields shall fall beneath the foe.
Great is the stake, nor should we lightly yield,
Our ancient league by many a battle seal'd.
The deeds of other days before my eyes,
In all their friendship, love and faith arise,
When hand in hand with him we rov'd the wood,
Swept the long vale, or stem'd the boiling flood.
In the same war path, march'd with ready blade,
And liv'd, and fought, and triumph'd with his aid.
When the same tongue, express'd our joys and pains,
And the same blood ran freely thro' our veins?'

'Not we – not we' – in rage Keewaydin[4] spoke,
'Strong ties have sever'd, or old friendships broke,
Back on themselves the baseless charge must fall,
They sunder'd name, league, language, rites and all.
They, with our firm allies, the Gallic race,
First broke the league, by secret arts and base,
Then play'd the warrior – call'd our bands a clog,
And earn'd their proper title, Fox and Dog.
Next to the false Dacota gave the land,
And leagued in war, our own destruction plan'd.
Do any doubt the words I now advance,
Here is my breast' – he yelled & shook his lance.

---

2 A past sound [Henry Rowe Schoolcraft's note].

3 The passing thunder [Henry Rowe Schoolcraft's note].

4 The North Wind [Henry Rowe Schoolcraft's note].

'Rage' – interposed the sage Canowakeed,[5]
Ne'er prompted wit, or bid the council speed
For other aims, be here our highest end,
Such gentle aims as rivet friend to friend.
If harsher fires, in ardent bosoms glow,
At least restrain them, till we meet the foe,
Calm judgment here, demands the care of all,
For if we judge amiss, ourselves shall fall.
Beside, what boasts it, that ye here repeat,
The current tale of ancient scaith or heat,
Love, loss, or bicker, welcome or retort,
Once giv'n in earnest, or return'd sport
Or how, or when, this hapless feud arose,
That made our firmest friends, our firmest foes.
That so it is, by causes new or old,
There are no strangers present, to be told,
Each for himself, both knows & feels & sees,
The growing evils of a heartless peace,
And the sole question, of this high debate,
Is – shall we longer suffer – longer wait,
Or, with heroic will, for strife prepare,
And try the hazard of a gen'ral war!'

## Invocation
## To My Maternal Grandfather
## On Hearing His Descent from Chippewa Ancestors
## Misrepresented [1827]

Rise bravest chief! of the mark of the noble deer,
With eagle glance,
Resume thy lance,
And wield again thy warlike spear!
The foes of thy line,
With coward design,
Have dar'd, with black envy, to garble the truth,
And stain, with a falsehood, thy valorous youth.

They say, when a child, thou wert ta'en from the Sioux,
And with impotent aim,
To lessen thy fame
Thy warlike lineage basely abuse,
For they know that our band,
Tread a far distant land,
And thou noble chieftain! art nerveless and dead,
Thy bow all unstrung, and thy proud spirit fled.

Can the sports of thy youth, or thy deeds ever fade?
Or those ever forget,

[5] He Who Takes After the Wind [Henry Rowe Schoolcraft's note].

Who are mortal men yet,
The scenes where so bravely thou'st lifted the blade,
Who have fought by thy side,
And remember thy pride,
When rushing to battle, with valor and ire,
Thou saw'st the fell foes of thy nation expire.

Can the warrior forget how sublimely you rose?
Like a star in the west,
When the sun's sunk to rest,
That shines in bright splendor to dazzle our foes;
Thy arm and thy yell,
Once the tale could repel
Which slander invented, and minions detail,
And still shall thy actions refute the false tale.

Rest thou, noblest chief! in thy dark house of clay,
Thy deeds and thy name,
Thy child's child shall proclaim,
And make the dark forests resound with the lay;
Though thy spirit has fled,
To the hills of the dead,
Yet thy name shall be held in my heart's warmest care,
And cherish'd, till valor and love be no more.

## SONNET [1827]

The voice of reason bids me dry my tears,
But nature frail, still struggles with that voice;
Back to my mind that placid form appears
Lifeless, – he seemed to live and to rejoice,
As in the arms of death he meekly lay.
Oh, Cherub Babe! thy mother mourns thy loss,
Tho' thou hast op'd thine eyes in endless day;
And nought, on earth, can chase away my grief
But Faith – pleading the merits of the Cross,
And Him, whose promise gives a sure relief.

## TO MY EVER BELOVED AND LAMENTED SON WILLIAM HENRY [1827]

"Who was it nestled on my breast,
"And on my cheek sweet kisses prest"
And in whose smile I felt so blest?
Sweet Willy.

Who hail'd my form as home I stept,
And in my arms so eager leapt,
And to my bosom joyous crept?
My Willy.

Who was it, wiped my tearful eye,
And kiss'd away the coming sigh,
And smiling bid me say "good boy"?
Sweet Willy.

Who was it, looked divinely fair,
Whilst lisping sweet the evening pray'r,
Guileless and free from earthly care?
My Willy.

Where is that voice attuned to love,
That bid me say "my darling dove"?
But oh! that soul has flown above.
Sweet Willy.

Whither has fled the rose's hue?
The lilly's whiteness blending grew,
Upon thy cheek – so fair to view.
My Willy.

Oft have I gazed with rapt delight,
Upon those eyes that sparkled bright,
Emitting beams of joy and light!
Sweet Willy.

Oft have I kiss'd that forehead high,
Like polished marble to the eye,
And blessing, breathed an anxious sigh.
For Willy.

My son! Thy coral lips are pale,
Can I believe the heart-sick tale,
That I, thy loss must ever wail?
My Willy.

The clouds in darkness seem to low'r,
The storm has past with awful pow'r,
And nipt my tender, beauteous flow'r!
Sweet Willy.

But soon my spirit will be free,
And I my lovely son shall see,
For God, I know, did this decree.
My Willy.

# Traditional Narratives

## THE ORIGIN OF THE ROBIN
## AN ORAL ALLEGORY [1827]

Spiritual gifts, are sought by the Chippewas through fasting. An old man had an only son, a fine promising lad, who had come to that age which is thought by the Chippewas to be most proper to make the long and final fast, that is to secure through life a guardian spirit, on whom future prosperity or adversity is to depend, and who forms and establishes the character of the faster to great or ignoble deeds.

This old man was ambitious that his son should surpass all others in whatever was deemed most wise and great amongst his tribe. And to fulfill his wishes, he thought it necessary that his son must fast a much longer time than any of those persons known for their great power or wisdom, whose fame he envied.

He therefore directed his son to prepare with great ceremony, for the important event. After he had been in the sweating lodge and bath several times, he ordered him to lie down upon a clean mat, in the little lodge expressly prepared for him, telling him, at the same time to bear himself like a man, and that at the expiration of twelve days, he should receive food, and the blessing of his father.

The lad carefully observed this injunction, laying with his face covered with perfect composure, awaiting those happy visitations which were to seal his good or ill fortune. His father visited him every morning to encourage him to perseverance, expatiating at full length on the renown and honor that would attend him through life, if he accomplished the full term prescribed. To these admonitions the boy never answered, but lay without the least sign of unwillingness till the ninth day, when he addressed his father – "My father, my dreams are ominous of evil! May I break my fast now, and at a more propitious time, make a new fast?" The father answered – "My son, you know not what you ask! If you get up now, all your glory will depart. Wait patiently a little longer. You have but three days yet to accomplish what I desire. You know, it is for your own good."

The son assented, and covering himself closer, he lay till the eleventh day, when he repeated his request to his father. The same answer was given him, by the old man, adding, that then next day he would himself prepare his first meal, and bring it to him. The boy remained silent, but lay like a skeleton. No one would have known he was living but by the gentle heaving of his breast.

The next morning the father, elated at having gained his end, prepared a repast for his son, and hastened to set it before him. On coming to the door, he was surprized to see his son talking to himself. He stooped to listen, and looking through a small aperture, was more astonished when he beheld his son painted with vermilion on his breast, and in the act of finishing his work by laying on the paint as far as his hand could reach on his shoulder, saying at the same time: – "My father has ruined me, as a man; he would not listen to my request; he will now be the loser. I shall be forever happy in my new state, for I have been obedient to my parent; he alone will be the sufferer; for the Spirit is a just one, though not propitious to me. He has shown me pity, and now I must go."

At that moment the old man broke in, exclaiming, "My son! my son! do not leave me!" But his son with the quickness of a bird had flown up to the top of the lodge, and perched on the highest pole, a beautiful robin red-breast. He looked down on his father with pity beaming in his eyes, and told him, that he should always love to be near men's dwellings, that he should always be seen happy and contented by the constant cheerfulness and pleasure he would display, that he would still cheer his father by his songs, which would be some consolation to him for the loss of the glory he had expected; and that, although no longer a man, he should ever be the harbinger of peace and joy to the human race.

## MOOWIS
## THE INDIAN COQUETTE[6]
## A CHIPPEWA LEGEND [1827]

There was a village full of Indians, and a noted belle or *muh-muh daw go qua* was living there. A noted beau or *muh muh daw go, ninnie* was there also. He and another young man went to court this young woman, and laid down beside her, when she scratched the face of the handsome beau. He went home and would not rise till the family prepared to depart, and he would not then arise. They then left him, as he felt ashamed to be seen even by his own relations. It was winter, and the young man, his rival, who was his cousin, tried all he could to persuade him to go with the family, for it was now winter, but to no purpose, till the whole village had decamped and had gone away. He then rose and gathered all the bits of clothing, and ornaments of beads and other things, that had been left. He then made a coat and leggins of the same, nicely trimmed with the beads, and the suit was fine and complete. After making a pair of moccasins, nicely trimmed, he also made a bow and arrows. He then collected the dirt of the village, and filled the garments he had made, so as to appear as a man, and put the bow and arrows in his hands, and it came to life. He then desired the dirt image to follow him to the camp of those who had left him, who thinking him dead by this time, were surprized to see him. One of the neighbors took in the dirt-man and entertained him. The belle saw them come and immediately fell in love with him. The family that took him in made a large fire to warm him, as it was winter. The image said to one of the children, "sit between me and the fire, it is too hot," and the child did so, but all smelt the dirt. Some said, "some one has trod on, and brought in dirt." The master of the family said to the child sitting in front of the guest, "get away from before our guest, you keep the heat from him." The boy answered saying, "he told me to sit between him and the fire." In the meantime, the belle wished the stranger would visit her. The image went to his master, and they went out to different lodges, the image going as directed to the belle's. Towards morning, the image said to the young woman (as he had succeeded) "I must now go away," but she said, "I will go with you." He said "it is too far." She answered, "it is not so far but that I can go with you." He first went to the lodge where he was entertained, and then to his master, and told him of all that had happened, and that he was going off with her. The young man thought it a pity that she had treated him so, and how sadly she would be punished. They went off, she following behind. He left her a great way behind, but she continued to follow him. When the sun rose high, she found one of his mittens and picked it up, but to her astonishment, found it full of dirt. She, however took it and wiped it, and going on further, she found the other mitten in the same condition. She thought, "fie! ! why does he do so," thinking he dirtied in them. She kept finding different articles of his dress, on the way all day, in the same condition. He kept ahead of her till towards evening, when the snow was like water, having melted by the heat of the day. No signs of her husband appearing, after having collected all the cloths that held him together, she began to cry, not knowing where to go, as their track was lost, on account of the snow's melting. She kept crying *Moowis* has led me astray, and she kept singing and crying Moowis nin ge won e win ig, ne won e win ig.

## THE FORSAKEN BROTHER
## A CHIPPEWA TALE [1827]

It was a fine summer evening; the sun was scarcely an hour high, – its departing rays beamed through the foliage of the tall, stately elms, that skirted the little green knoll, on which a solitary Indian lodge stood. The deep silence that reigned in this sequestered and romantic spot, seemed to most of the inmates of that lonely hut, like the long sleep of death, that was now evidently fast sealing the eyes of the

[6] When Schoolcraft's husband Henry later published this legend elsewhere, he commented on the warning it offered Indian girls, like their white counterparts, on the evils of vanity. The highly derogative term "Moowis" derives from the term for filth or excrement. See Mason, 176–7 n. 79.

head of this poor family. His low breathing was answered by the sighs of his disconsolate wife and their children. Two of the latter were almost grown up, one was yet a mere child. These were the only human beings near the dying man. The door of the lodge was thrown open to admit the refreshing breeze of the lake, on the banks of which it stood; and as the cool air fanned the head of the poor man, he felt a momentary return of strength, and raising himself a little, he thus addressed his weeping family. "I leave you – thou, who hast been my partner in life, but you will not stay long to suffer in this world. But oh! my children, my poor children! you have just commenced life, and mark me, unkindness, and ingratitude, and every wickedness is the scene before you. I left my kindred and my tribe, because I found what I have just warned you of. I have contented myself with the company of your mother and yourselves, for many years, and you will find my motives for separating from the haunts of men, were solicitude and anxiety to preserve you from the bad examples you would inevitably have followed. But I shall die content, if you, my children promise me, to cherish each other, and on no account to forsake your youngest brother, of him I give you both particular charge." The man became exhausted – "My daughter! Never forsake your little brother. My son, never forsake your little brother." "Never, never!" they both exclaimed. "Never – never!" repeated the father and expired.

The poor man died happy, because he thought his commands would be obeyed. The sun sank below the trees, and left a golden sky behind, which the family were wont to admire, but no one heeded it now. The lodge that was so still an hour before, was now filled with low and unavailing lamentations. Time wore heavily away – five long moons had passed and the sixth was nearly full, when the mother also died. In her last moments she pressed the fulfillment of their promise to their departed father. They readily renewed their promise, because they were yet free from any selfish motive. The winter passed away, and the beauties of spring cheered the drooping spirits of the bereft little family. The girl, being the eldest, dictated to her brothers, and seemed to feel a tender and sisterly affection for the youngest, who was rather sickly and delicate. The other boy soon showed symptoms of restlessness, and addressed the sister as follows. "My sister, are we always to live as if there were no other human beings in the world. Must I deprive myself the pleasure of associating with my own kind? I shall seek the villages of men; I have determined, and you cannot prevent me." The girl replied, "My brother, I do not say no, to what you desire, we were not prohibited, the society of our fellow mortals, but we were told to cherish each other, and that we should [do] nothing independent of each other – that neither pleasure nor pain ought ever to separate us, particularly from our helpless brother. If we follow our separate gratifications, it will surely make us forget *him* whom we are alike bound to support." The young man made no answer, but taking his bow and arrows left the lodge, and never returned.

Many moons had come and gone, after the young man's departure, and still the girl administered to the wants of her younger brother. At length, however, she began to weary of her solitude, and of her charge. Years, which added to her strength and capability of directing the affairs of the household, also brought with them the desire of society, and made her solitude irksome. But in meditating a change of life, she thought only for herself, and cruelly sought to abandon her little brother, as her elder brother had done before.

One day after she had collected all the provisions she had set apart for emergencies, and brought a quantity of wood to the door, she said to her brother, "My brother, you must not stray far from the lodge. I am going to seek our brother: I shall soon be back." Then taking her bundle, she set off, in search of habitations. She soon found them, and was so much taken up with the pleasures and amusements of society, that all affection for her brother was obliterated. She accepted a proposal of marriage, and after that, never thought more of the helpless relative she had abandoned.

In the meantime the elder brother had also married, and settled on the shores of the same lake, which contained the bones of his parents, and the abode of his forsaken brother.

As soon as the little boy had eaten all the food left by his sister, he was obliged to pick berries and dig up roots. Winter came on, and the poor child was exposed to all its rigors. He was obliged to quit the lodge in search of food, without a shelter. Sometimes he passed the night in clefts of old trees, and ate the refuge meats of the wolves. The latter soon became his only resource, and he became so fearless of these animals, that he would sit close to them whilst they devoured their prey, and the animals seemed to pity his condition, and would always leave something. Thus he lived, as it were, on the bounty of fierce wolves until spring. As soon as the lake was free from ice, he followed his new found friends and companions to the shore. It happened his brother was fishing in a canoe in the lake, a considerable distance out, when he thought he heard the cry of a child, and wondered how any could exist on so bleak a part of the shore. He listened again more attentively, and distinctly heard the cry repeated. He made for shore as quickly as possible, and as he approached land, discovered and recognized his little brother, and heard him singing in a plaintive voice –

*Neesya, neesya, shyegwuh gushuh!*
*Ween ne myeengunish!*
*ne myeengunish!*
My brother, my brother,
I am now turning into a Wolf! –
I am turning into a Wolf.

At the termination of his song, he howled like a Wolf, and the young man was still more astonished when, on getting nearer shore, he perceived his poor brother half turned into that animal. He however, leapt on shore and strove to catch him in his arms, and soothingly said – "My brother, my brother, come to me." But the boy eluded his grasp, and fled, still singing as he fled – "I am turning into a Wolf – I am turning into a Wolf," and howling in the intervals.

The elder brother, conscience struck, and feeling his brotherly affection returning with redoubled force, exclaimed in great anguish, "My brother, my brother, come to me." But the nearer he approached the child, the more rapidly his transformation went on, until he changed into a perfect wolf, – still singing and howling, and naming his brother and sister alternately in his song, as he fled into the woods, until his change was complete. At last he said, "I am a Wolf," and bounded out of sight.

The young man felt the bitterness of remorse all his days, and the sister, when she heard of the fate of the little boy whom she had so cruelly left, and whom both she and her brother had solemnly promised to foster and protect, wept bitterly; and never ceased to mourn until she died.

## ORIGIN OF THE MISCODEED[7] OR THE MAID OF TAQUIMENON [1827]

The daughter of Ma Mongazida, was the pride of her parents, and their only child. Beauty sat upon her lips, and life and animation marked all her motions. Fourteen summers had witnessed the growth of her stature, and the unfolding of her charms, and each spring, as it came around, had beheld her, in her happy simplicity, revelling amid the wild flowers of her native valley. There was no valley so sweet as the valley of Taquimenon [Tahquamenon]. There, she listened to the earliest notes of the wild birds, who returned from the south, to enliven the forests after the repose of winter; and there, also, she had prepared her bower of branches, and fasted to obtain a guardian spirit, to conduct her through life, according to the belief and customs of her people. Sweet valley of the Taquimenon, thou didst bless her with the charms of thy fragrance, causing the most profound sensations of pleasure. There, she first beheld that little angel, who in the shape of a small white bird, of purest plumage, assumed to be her guardian spirit, in cot and wood, through sun and storm, for the remainder of her days. Happy were her slumbers in this delightful visitation, and happy her awakening, as she hasted back, with fawn-like fleetness, to her parents' lodge, with one more charm – one more pleasing recollection – one more tie to bind her fancy and her heart to the sweet valley of the Taquimenon. Beautiful valley of soft repose! there, she had first learned to know the sweet face of nature, and seen the river leap & laugh in foam, form the rocks, and then pursue its sylvan course through the green leafed forest. Sweet enthusiast of nature! wild gazer of the woods! There, too, were the sacred graves of her forefathers, and there, she hoped, when the Great Spirit should summon her to depart, her friends would lay her simply bark-enchased body, under the shady foliage in a spot she loved.

---

7 Claytonia Virginia [Henry Rowe Schoolcraft's note].

It was early in the Strawberry Moon.[8] The white coat of winter was remembered for its having lingered on many spots, which were secluded from the sun's influence. But the flowers of the forest were now in bloom, and the birds had re-visited the valley. There was a soft and balmy air, and life and animation seemed to be newly bestowed upon the whole face of the earth. The robin and the mamaitwa came back to sing, and the murmuring of waters, in the little glens and by-vallies, rose, like pleasing music on the ear, and denoted the time for the opening of buds, and the springing of flowers. Never, had the scene appeared more attractive to her eye. "Oh," she exclaimed, "that it were ever spring! that I could ever live and revel in the wild beauties of my native valley – the sweet valley of the Taquimenon."

But while all nature rejoiced, there was a deep gloom gathering over the brows of Ma Mongazida.[9] Whispers of the sign of an enemy on the lofty shores of the Pictured Rocks, had reached his ears. He thought of the haughty air of the audacious tribe of the Outagamies, who, but a few moons before, invaded the country, and had been baffled in their design. He thought of the bitter feuds of the border bands, yet pleased himself in his own seclusion far from the war path of the enemy, where, for the space of fifteen winters, there had not a hostile footprint been seen. While he lay on his couch, pondering on these things, sleep ensued, and he fancied himself to be the leader of a hostile band, who broke from the ambush, at the earliest dawn, and carried death and desolation to a slumbering village. Shocked at the catastrophe, he awoke. The dream alarmed him. He remembered that birds of ill omen had crossed his path, the day before.

"Had it been my enemies, the Dacotahs," said he to his wife, "I should have feared no evil, but to dream of raising the war club against the Outagamies my own blood kindred, and with whom we have been long in peace, bodes me sure disaster. Some hostile foot is, even now, on the track. Some evil bird has flown over my lodge. I will no longer abide here. Had I sons to stand by my side, most freely would I meet the foe; but, single-handed, with no one but thee, to bury me, if I am slain, and my tender Miscodeed to witness my fall, and become their prey, it were madness to abide. And this day, even before the sun is at the zenith, will I quit the peaceful valley I love – the sweet valley of the Taquimenon."

In haste, they took their morning's meal, and made their preparations to leave a scene, so loved and cherished, but loved and cherished by none, more than the gentle and enthusiastic Miscodeed. She was indeed a precious wild flower. But while they yet sat around their lodge-fire, the instinctive sagacity of that trusty friend of the Red Hunter, the household dog, betokened approaching evil, at first, by restlessness and low murmurs, and then breaking into a loud bark, as he flew out of the door. It was a daring war party of the treacherous Mendawakantons[10] from the Mississippi. A volley of arrows followed, piercing the thin barks, which hung, like tapestry, around the lodge, and sealing in death at the same instant, the lips of both father and mother. "Oh, bird of my dreams," cried Miscodeed, "my beautiful white wing! – my angel of promise! Save me from the hands of my cruel enemies." So saying, she sunk, lifeless to the ground.

With loud yells and rapid footsteps the foe entered. Conspicuous, in front, stood the eldest son of a warrior, who had been killed by the Chippewas in the great battle of the falls of the river St. Croix. His brows were painted red, and his spear poised. But the work of death was soon finished. There lay, motionless, the husband and the wife alike beyond the influence of hope or fear, hate or harm. But no other human form appeared, and the eye of the savage leader rolled in disappointment around, as he viewed the spot where Miscodeed, his meditated victim, had sunk into the earth. A small and beautiful white bird, was seen to fly from the top of the lodge. It was the guardian spirit of Miscodeed. The knife and the tomahawk were cheated of their prey – her guardian angel had saved her from being the slave of her enemy.

But the sanguinary rites of war were quickly performed; the scalps of the hunter and his wife, were torn away, and with hurry & fear, the enemy was soon on his way to his native land. When the friends of the slaughtered family, visited the silent lodge, where welcome had so often greeted them, all they saw on the ground where the maid of Taquimenon had fallen, was a modest little white flower, bordered with pink border which was at once destined to be her emblem.

---

8 June [Henry Rowe Schoolcraft's note].

9 Means: print of the Loon's foot [Henry Rowe Schoolcraft's note]. Ma Mongazida was Jane Johnston Schoolcraft's maternal great-grandfather, the father of Waub Ojeeg.

10 A branch of the Dakota Sioux.

# Lucy Lowrey Hoyt Keys (Wahnenauhi, Over-There-They-Just-Arrived-With-It; Cherokee, 1831–1912)

*Born in Willstown, Alabama, Keys was a member of a distinguished Cherokee family. We know more about her maternal grandfather, Major George Lowrey, who figures largely in her narrative of Cherokee history, than we do about the author herself, who attended the Cherokee Female Seminary, graduating in 1855 as part of its first class of 12 students. Part of what Kilpatrick calls the "planter class of mixbloods," she belonged to an affluent, acculturated, and educated family that apparently adhered to many of the strictures of white Southern society, including the use of English as a first language and the acceptance of Christianity as its religion. Her account is valuable for many reasons, not least for its discussion of Sequoyah's and her grandfather's roles in Cherokee history. Although she does not mention the fact, the latter contributed at least a part of the translation of the Four Gospels published in the* Cherokee Phoenix *in 1829. Wahnenauhi married Monroe Calvin Keys sometime after his graduation from the Cherokee Male Seminary; Monroe fought for the Confederacy in the Civil War. During this time Keys and her children lived in the Choctaw Nation, where she taught school. In the early 1870s, the family moved to Pheasant Hill, near Vinita, Oklahoma, where her husband died in 1875. Disabled after a bad fall 25 years before her death, Keys died in 1912.*

*Keys appears to have written her manuscript sometime in 1889, for in September of that year she sent a copy to the Bureau of (American) Ethnology, with a request that it be examined and that "if of value to you, remit what you consider an equivalent." The Bureau purchased the manuscript in November for $10. However acculturated she may have been, her vivid account of the Trail of Tears offers an insider's view of that tragic journey, while her descriptions of food and clothing seek to preserve a changing way of life. Noteworthy by its absence here is an acknowledgment of the status and power of women in the Cherokees' traditionally matrilineal and matrilocal culture. One other feature of her account is especially interesting – the incorporation of oral stories into the larger narrative. Strikingly, for a Christian woman, she emphasizes the plurality of the divine spirit in her creation myth, which combines a brief version of an Earth Diver story with a more detailed account of the origins of various foods, as well as gender roles in their acquisition. Keys's narrative offers today's readers an important tribal and personal history, fascinating for its complex perspective and aesthetic strategies.*

BIBLIOGRAPHY

## Primary

"The Wahnenauhi Manuscript." Ed. Jack Frederick Kilpatrick. [1889] Bureau of American Ethnology, Anthropological Papers 77 (1966): 179–213.

## Secondary

Bataille, Gretchen M., and Kathleen Mullen Sands. *American Indian Women: Telling Their Lives*. Nebraska, 1984.

Mihesuah, Devon A. *Cultivating the Rose Buds: The Education of Women at the Cherokee Female Seminary, 1851–1909*. Illinois, 1993.

Mooney, James. *Myths of the Cherokee and Sacred Formulas of the Cherokees*. 1900; rpt. Elder, 1982.

Perdue, Theda. *Cherokee Women: Gender and Culture Change, 1700–1835*. Nebraska, 1998.

——. *Nations Remembered: An Oral History of the Five Civilized Tribes, 1865–1907*. Greenwood, 1980.

——. *Slavery and the Evolution of Cherokee Society, 1540–1866*. Tennessee, 1979.

Sattler, Richard A., "Women's Status among the Muskogee and Cherokee." In Laura F. Klein and Lillian A. Ackerman, eds. *Women and Power in Native North America*. Oklahoma, 1995.

# Historical Sketches of the Cherokees, Together with Some of Their Customs, Traditions, and Superstitions (1889)

Fifty years ago, if someone had undertaken to write a History of the Cherokee Nation, he would have done so with some hope of success.[1]

At that time Traditions were learned and remembered by those who regarded it worth while to preserve from oblivion the Origin and Customs of the Tribe. I know of only one person who attempted the task of preparing such a work, Major George Lowrey, who was, for many years, a prominent member of the nation, and well-versed in Cherokee Lore.[2]

The Manuscript was written in the Cherokee Language, and is supposed to have been destroyed during the Civil War of the United States.

The following Sketches and Incidents are given as I remember to have heard them of older persons; and I trust they will be acceptable to those interested in Indian History.

When the English first came to America, a large tribe of Indians, calling themselves the Ke-too-wha, occupied the South Eastern portion of North America; The Country now comprizing the states of Virginia, Pennsylvania,[3] North and South Carolina, Tennessee, Alabama, and Georgia.

Very little is known of them, only as Tradition comes to us.

They have always considered themselves the largest and most powerful Tribe on the Eastern side of the Continent, and have been so acknowledged by the other Tribes.

Holding this place of Supremacy made them selfconfident and independent. In disposition they were friendly and generous, though always reserved before strangers. Fearless in danger, intrepid and daring when occasion required, they were slow to take offence at fancied injuries or insults.

They were always on friendly terms with the Delawares, by whom they were called Ke-too-whah-kee. So highly were they esteemed that, at one time, a Ketoo-wha was chosen and served as Chief of the Delaware Tribe.[4]

The Whites first met with these Indians in one of their towns, on the bank of a small stream, which they named Cherry Creek, from the number of Cherry trees which grew there; the people they called, the "Cherry Creek Indians." This name, by gradual variations, came to be Cherok, then, Cherokee, as it now

[1] Keys refers to the removal era

[2] See Mooney for further discussion of the history of the Cherokees, and on Lowrey (115, 135).

[3] Kentucky, portions of which the Cherokee claimed, was possibly intended [Kilpatrick's note].

[4] Documentation exists for proving that the Cherokee and Delaware came into conflict within the historic period; we have not discovered documentation for Wahnenauhi's statement to the effect that a Cherokee served as a Delaware chief [Kilpatrick's note].

is. The Tribe, becoming familiar with their White Brothers, finally renounced their original name, Ke-too-wha, and adopted that of "Cherokee," by themselves pronounced "Dtsah-lah-gee."[5]

There were several different Dialects used in the Language of the Cherokees.

In explaining the cause of this, we have recourse only to Tradition:

This tells us that in the "long time ago" there were several Tribes conquered and adopted or "naturalized" by the Ke-too-wha, they retained their own Idiom of Speech, or, used a brogue in trying to learn the Language of their Conquerers.[6] This Story is the generally approved explanation of the difference in the Language of the Cherokees. One dialect is the "Pipestem," another the "Overhill," in this the most noticeable peculiarity is the prominent sound of *R* instead of "L," there being no "R" in the pure Cherokee. The Cherokee Tribe was divided into seven Clans, or, Families. There are some interesting facts in regard to the operation and influence of Clanship.

If any one was killed, either by accident, or with malicious intention, his death must be revenged by members of his own Clan.

When the murderer could not be found, a Substitute might be taken from his Clan. The Chief Town of the Nation was the only place of saf[e]ty for the Slayer, should he succeed in reaching this Refuge, he must remain in it until after the Annual Green Corn Dance.

He was then at liberty to leave, his life being no longer in danger.

The marriage of persons belonging to the same Clan, and of the father's Clan was strictly forbidden; and also marriage was prohibited between relatives by blood. Capital punishment was the penalty for breaking this Law.

Clan-kin was held most sacred.

The mother was the Head of the Family, and the children were called by the name of her Clan. Affectionate regard for kindred was cherished; and old persons were treated with great respect and tenderly cared for. Persons, who had at any time, especially distinguished themselves by deeds of Courage or Bravery were highly esteemed, we give an illustration –

Once, a town was surprised by a band of enemies, and the Chief killed: His wife, whose name was "Cuh-tah-la-tah," on seeing her husband fall, immediately snatched up his hatchet, shouting, "Hi-lu-ki! Hi-lu-ki!" (Kill! Kill!) rushed forward on the invaders, striking down all who opposed her.

Her bravery so inspired the discouraged warriors with fresh Courage that they hurried on to the fight and gained a complete victory. Many instances could be quoted, of brave deeds and victories won by Cherokee Patriots.

The Cherokees believed in one God, whom they called "Oo-na-hlah-nau-hi," meaning "Maker of all Things," and "Cah-luh-luh-ti-a-hi," or, "The One who lives above." They acknowledged Him as their Friend, and believed that He made every thing, and possessed unlimited Power.

They also believed in an Evil Spirit, called in their language, "Skee-nah"; to his malicious influence they attributed all trouble, calamity, and sickness.[7]

They believed in Familiar Spirits, Witch-craft and Conjurors. Witches were supposed to be able to do much harm, both to persons and to property. They received their power from the familiar spirits, who were emissaries of the Evil one. The more easily to affect their plans, witches were thought, sometimes to assume the form of birds or beasts.

Conjurors were doctors who, besides curing deseases, were thought to have power to counteract the evil doings of Witches, and even to destroy the witches themselves, without ever going near, or, seeing them.

If a person was suddenly taken with a new or uncommon desease, a Conjuror was immediately summoned by the friends of the afflicted one. He first examined the patient, looking intently at him, and asking questions about him.

---

[5] Along with conservative Cherokees at the time, Kilpatrick disputes this derivation and offers an alternative.

[6] Cherokees themselves are quite aware that certain words, especially specific proper names, in common usage are of foreign origin [Kilpatrick's note].

[7] There is no universal evil spirit, corresponding to Satan, in Cherokee theology [Kilpatrick's note].

He then made tea of some kind of roots, giving the sick one to drink, and bathing his face and limbs with it. He then had recourse to incantations, blowing his breath on the patient, making manipulations over his body and all the time muttering or speaking in a low tone as if conversing with some one.[8]

In cases of severe pain, the Conjuror procured bark from a particular kind of tree, and burned it to coals, then after warming his hands over the fire, would press them tightly to the pain, then rub them briskly over the fire. After performing this operation several times, quite often the patient recovered.

If this treatment proved unsuccessful then some one suspected of being a witch was accused as the cause of the trouble.

Various methods, at different times, were resorted to, to find out and punish the offender. One way was, to make a picture representing the accused and shoot it. If the person died soon after, that fact was proof conclusive of his guilt.[9]

Many medicinal plants and roots were known and used by the people in common deseases. The bark of the Birch Tree was considered a specific for Cancer and malignant ulcers. A leaden-colored, oval-shaped stone, thought to be solidified lightning, as it was dug from near the roots of a lightning-struck tree, was a cure for Rheumatism.

I think the Cherokees were not more superstitious than some Civilized Nations.

A few birds and some wild animals were said to be messengers of evil tidings.[10]

There is a Legend of a large serpent, called the "Ground snake," being the color of the ground was said to betoken death to the one who saw it; if it appeared to several persons a National Calamity was apprehended.

A buzzard feather placed over the door prevented the witches from entering their cabins.[11]

The Cherokees had many Traditions. Some are interesting, some appear simply foolish, but hold some hidden meaning; others sound strangely familiar, and are so like the Bible stories that Christian mothers tell their little children, as to make one say, "Where, or, how did they obtain them?" Such is the one about the Boy who was swallowed by a fish.

The Cherokee Story is, that the boy was sent on an errand by his father, and not wishing to go, he ran away to the river. After playing in the sand for a short time, some boys of his acquaintance came by in a canoe, who invited him to join them. Glad of the opportunity to get away, he went with them, but had no sooner got in than the canoe began to tip and rock most unaccountably. The boys became very much frightened, and in the confusion the bad boy fell into the water and was immediately swallowed by a large fish. After lying there for some time he became very hungry, and on looking around he saw the fish's liver hanging over his head. Thinking it was dried meat, he tried to cut off a piece with a mussle shell that he had been playing with and which he still held in his hand. The operation sickened the fish and it vomited the boy.

The story of how the world was made is this, – Observe that in the telling of the Creation, the plural number "They" is used for the Creator.

It is said, They took a turtle and covered its back with mud. This grew larger and continued to increase until it became quite a large island.

They then made a man and a woman, and led them around the edge of the island. On arriving at the starting place, They planted some corn and then told the man and the woman to go around in the way they had been led, this they did; returning, they found the corn up and growing nicely.

They were then told to continue the circuit; each trip consumed more time, at last the corn was ripe and ready for use. Then fire was wanted.

[8] Wahnenauhi . . . [here] confused specific curing procedures with general [Kilpatrick's note].

[9] This is not one of the standard techniques employed by the [healer] in "working against" someone who is molesting his patient [Kilpatrick's note].

[10] Kilpatrick notes that Wahnenauhi does not report examples of animals commonly regarded as good luck by the Cherokee.

[11] Kilpatrick disputes this specific detail, affirming the use of buzzard feathers to ward off disease and as a more general watcher of the house. He also corrects various small factual details not noted here.

The animals were called together, and the question asked, "Who will go and bring fire?" The 'possum first came forward and offered to go; he was sent, but returned without it; he had tried to carry it with his tail, but had that member so scorched and burned that he made a failure. They then sent the buzzard, he, too, failed, returning with his head and neck badly burned. A little spider then said, "I will go and get fire," upon which the beasts and birds raised an uproar, ridiculing the spider, but not one was willing to undertake the hazardous journey, and the spider was allowed to go. She made a little bowl of mud and placing it on her back started, spinning a thread as she traced her way over the water. On arriving at the fire, she carefully placed some coals in her cup and returned crossing safely on the bridge which she had spun.

Another story is told of how sin came into the world. A man and woman brought up a large family of children in comfort and plenty, with very little trouble about providing food for them. Every morning the father went forth and very soon returned bringing with him a deer, or, turky or some other animal or fowl. At the same time the mother went out and soon returned with a large basket filled with ears of corn which she shelled and pounded in a mortar, thus making meal for bread.

When the children grew up, seeing with what apparent ease food was provided for them, they talked to each other about it, wondering that they never saw such things as their parents brought in.

At last one proposed to watch when their parents went out and follow them.

Accordingly next morning the plan was carried out. Those who followed the father, at a short distance from the cabin, saw him stop and turn over a large stone that appeared to be carelessly leaned against another.

On looking closely they saw an entrance to a large Cave and in it were many different kinds of animals and birds, such as their father had sometimes brought in for food. The man standing at the entrance called a deer, which was lying at some distance and back of some other animals, it rose immediately, as it heard the call, and came close up to him.

He picked it up, closed the mouth of the cave and returned, not once seeming to suspect what his sons had done.

When the old man was fairly out of sight, his sons, rejoicing how they had outwitted him, left their hiding place, and went to the cave, saying, they would show the old folks that they too could bring in some thing. They moved the stone away – though it was very heavy, and they were obliged to use their united strength.

When the cave was opened, the animals, instead of waiting to be picked up, all made a rush for the entrance, and leaping past the frightened and bewildered boys, scattered in all directions and disappeared in the wilderness, while the guilty offenders could do nothing but gaze in stupefied amazement as they saw them escape. There were animals of all kinds, large and small – Buffaloes, deer, elks, antelopes, raccoons and squirrels; even catamounts and panthers, wolves and foxes, and many others, all fleeing together; at the same time birds of every kind were seen emerging from the opening, all in the same wild confusion as the quadrupeds: – Turkeys, geese, swans, ducks, quails, eagles, hawks and owls.

Those who followed the mother, saw her enter a small cabin, which they had never seen before, and close the door.

The culprits found a small crack through which they could peer.

They saw the woman place a basket on the ground, and standing over it shook herself vigourously, jumping up and down when lo! and behold! large ears of corn began to fall into the basket. When it was well filled she took it up, and placing it on her head came out, fastened the door and prepared their breakfast as usual. When the meal was finished in silence, the man spoke to his children, telling them that he was aware of what they had done, that now he must die, and they would be obliged to provide for themselves, he made bows and arrows for them, then sent them to hunt for the animals that they had turned loose.

Then the mother told them that, as they had found out her secret, she could do nothing more for them, that she would die, and they must drag her body around over the ground, that where ever her body was dragged, corn would come up, of this they were to make their bread. She told them that they must always save some for seed and plant every year.

I have heard a story about the "Little People," or "Children."[12] "Nuh-na-yie" is the Cherokee name for them. It was said that in old times they were very numerous; they were inoffensive, and would often help any persons whom they found in distress, especially children who were lost, if a child were found, the Nuh-na-yie would appoint several of their number to take care of it and supply it with food until it could be restored to its parents or friends. For this reason they [were] very much loved by the Indians who took great care not to offend them, but for all that something happened by which the Nun-na-yie felt themselves very much insulted, and for which they determined to leave. The Indians were aware of their intention, and exerted all their arts of persuasion to induce them to remain, but without success. There was nothing for them to do but to see the last of them. There was an arm of the sea which the Little People were to cross.

The Indians assembled on the bank near the place of crossing, looking at them sadly as they passed: on they went into the water, the Indians watching all the time until on the opposite side they disappeared in what seemed to be the mouth of a large cave in the margin of the water. Nothing more was ever heard of them. In appearance, the little people were described as being wellformed, not more than two feet tall, with an abundance of long black hair almost trailing on the ground. It was said that they were very fond of music.

The drum seemed to be their favorite musical instrument, it was used on all occasions; when on a journey they marched to the sound of the drum.

It was often heard by the Indians, before the Nuh-na-yie went away, sometimes in the mountains, or, in lonely situations far from human habitations. Sometimes in the night folks were awakened by the sound of a drum very near their cabins, then it was said that the Nuh-na-yie were about, and on going to their work in the early morning, as gathering in their corn, or, clearing off land for a new field, sometimes they were greatly surprised by finding it all finished up, corn all gathered and put away, or, ground made ready for planting, trees and brush all taken off and put up around the sides, making a fence much better than they themselves would have done.

In early times, the clothing of the Cherokees was made entirely of the skins of animals which they killed in hunting.[13] The Cherokee women became quite skilful in making clothes for their families, when very young, girls were instructed in the art of preparing material for, and making clothing. After dressing, the skins were rubbed and polished until they were very smooth and soft, often nicely ornamented, by painting in different colors; for paint, or dye, the juices of plants were used. The men wore a turban on their heads, their other clothing consisted of a hunting-shirt, leggins and moccasins, all deeply fringed.

The hunting-shirt was worn wrapped tightly around and folded over the chest, fastened with a belt around the waist.

Belts in later years, came to be very much prized, being worn as an ornament.

They were made of bright colored worsted yarn interwoven with white beads, and were several yards in length, so as to fold many times around the body, they were tied at the left side, the ends, ornamented with tassels, hung nearly to the knees. Garters, made to match the belt were tied over the leggins below the knees, the tasseled ends left dangling.

The women wore a skirt and short jacket, with leggins and moccasins, the jacket was fastened in front with silver broaches, the skirt was fringed and either plaited or embroidered with beads, and the moccasins were trimmed with beads, in many colors. Their hair, they combed smooth and close, then folded into a club at the back of the head, and tied very tight with a piece of dried eel-skin, which was said to make the hair grow long.

The men, in cutting their hair, always left the lock growing on the crown of the head, this was braided and hung down the back. It was called a "coo-tlah."

Both sexes were fond of wearing ornaments. Some wore broad bands of silver on the arms above the elbows, and on the wrists and ankles, they wore rings on their fingers, and in the nose, and ears; I

---

12 Wahnenauhi means what might be called "elf" or "sprite," a being who lives forever.

13 According to Kilpatrick, the early Cherokees also used vegetable fibers and featherwork.

have seen old men with holes made in their ears from the lower edge to the very top; I never saw them wear more than two pair of ear-rings at one time. They liked very much to wear beads around their necks.[14]

Their dwellings were sometimes made by bending down saplings and tying the tops together and filling in between with poles tied with bark and interwoven with cane or withes, and a space left open for a door, also a small opening near the top for smoke to escape.

For winter sleeping room, the saplings were bent quite low, making the hut not more than four or five feet high in the centre; after finishing off as the other, it was thickly daubed on the outside with mud, leaving only a small opening near the ground, large enough for a man to creep through; a large fire, of bark and dry sticks, was made, and when burned up, the ashes and embers were taken out, and two persons crawled in, and, with turkey wings, fanned out all the smoke, and closed the entrance by hanging a skin over it.

This hut was called a "hothouse" and it was sometimes used to steam a sick person in. This is the way it was done, – The hot-house being made ready, the invalid was given as much cold water as he could drink, then taken in and left upon the ground until he was in a profuse perspiration, when he was taken out and plunged into a cold water bath.

In their intercourse with all, except most intimate friends, the Cherokees were reserved and independant, though very hospitable and often generous; they preferred to give favors rather than to ask them.

All Indians were called by them, "Yuh-wi-yah-i" which means, "The real People," others were designated by their color, as white people, were "Yuh-wi-na-kah" and black people, "Yuh-wi-kuh-hna-ka."

As before mentioned the Cherokees were given to hospitality; on rude side-boards, in their camps or cabins, prepared food was always kept, and any persons coming in, were at liberty to help themselves, food was always offered to visitors or strangers stopping, and a refusal to partake of it was considered an insult.

The women made bowls and cooking vessels of clay, and the men made spoons and bowls of wood, and spoons of buffalo horn, which were really pretty, as they were capable of being highly polished.

The women and girls prepared the food as is customary with other nations. The principal dish, "Con-nau-ha-nah,"[15] was made of Corn, Cuh-whe-si-ta was meal made of parched corn, and was used when on a journey, the hungry and weary traveler on arriving at a spring of water, alights and taking his bag of Cuh-whe-si-ta, puts a few spoonfuls into a cup which he carries for the purpose, mixes it with water and drinks it down, the requirements of Nature are satisfied – and the traveler goes on his way as much refreshed as when he began his journey in the early morning. The Cherokees also used a drink called "Con-nau-su-kah," it was made of grapes which were boiled, strained and sweetened with maple sugar or honey. Corn was beaten in a mortar to make meal for bread, walnuts, chestnuts, and hickory-nuts were often used in cooking, so were different kinds of berries, of which the huckle-berry was the favorite.

The men provided meat, and when game was plentiful, there was no lack of such food.

Boys were taught when very young, to shoot with bow and arrows, to hunt and to fish. Wrestling, foot-racing, ball-playing and corn-stalk-shooting were continually practiced, not only as a pastime, but as a necessary exercise.

Before starting on an expedition, or, engaging in a contest of any kind, they were obliged to take medicine, scratch and bathe, the scratching was done with a small instrument having six points, some said the points were rattle-snake teeth, but the one I saw was made of a half dozen pins fastened together with two pieces of wood or bone.

This practice was strictly observed by ball-players when preparing for a "big play" – it was thought to make them brave and strong. And, before the Annual Festival of the Green Corn Dance,[16] which lasted

[14] Wahnenauhi's statements as to early nineteenth-century Cherokee dress are strongly supported by the brushes of [famous painters] Francis Parsons, George Caitlin, and John Mix Stanley. Throughout this whole passage there is some confusion of dress at the time of contact with what the author saw in her childhood. The scalplock, for example, she may never have seen [Kilpatrick's note].

[15] A hominy prepared with lye leached from green hardwood ash [Kilpatrick's note].

[16] The Green Corn Ceremony was a major celebration held in July or August when corn became edible; see Perdue, 1998, 25–7.

seven days, all must be scratched, none might partake of the feast unless he had performed this operation; after this Festival, green corn and all other vegetables were freely eaten.

At the Stomp Dances,[17] terrapin shells enclosing pebbles, were worn, fastened to the ankles, by the dancing women.

When the English came to America they were peaceably received by the Cherokees, who presented them with food in token of their good will. 1730[18] is the earliest recorded date of a Treaty being made by the Cherokees with the English; in 1755[19] they ceded territory to the British Colonists, and permitted them to build forts. Prior to any treaty, a band of Cherokees utterly rejecting proposals of Peace, used all their powers of eloquence to prevent the Tribe from making a treaty.

They said that the Foreigners would get possession of a little now, then a little more and would not be satisfied until they had taken all the land, and there would be nothing left for the Indians.

Finding their efforts were unsuccessful, they determined to abandon the Tribe, going far away into the Wilderness, crossing the "Ummie Aquah,"[20] and on to the "Cuh-too-sa Aqua,"[21] they would find a Country for themselves, where the "Yuh-wi-na-kah" could not follow. Possessed by this one wild idea – to retreat from the neighborhood of the Whites, – deaf to the passionate entreaties of their friends, they made hurried preparations for their departure.

Although the greater part of the Tribe was very unwilling to have them leave, yet, finding their efforts to persuade them to remain, were unsuccessful, they assisted them in making preparations for the journey: some furnished "pack ponies," while others loaded them with "Cuh-whe-si, tah," "Cuh-nuh-tsi,"[22] dried venison and other things. They were led by the Chief, "Yuhwi-oo-skah-si-ti."

For many weeks communications were kept up between the two divisions, by "runners," who were sent from either side to enquire of their welfare, or to take messages.

A company, each member selected for their courage and perseverance, were sent to assist the travelers in crossing the "Big River." After this all intercourse between the two parties was ended, and no more was heard of the wanderers. In the course of time the run-away band was forgotten, or, remembered as only an old tale which no one believes.

A long time afterwards, some adventurous hunters met with a band of Indians who spoke the Cherokee Language and lived as the Cherokees did before they had learned any thing of civilized life.

These Indians were found at the Eastern side of the Rocky Mountains. They were supposed to be the lost Band.

After the Wanderers left, the remainder of the Tribe continued friendly with the Whites, trading with them and learning much that was useful to them; but alas! they also learned much that was bad, the vices of civilization, the worst for the Indians being drinking and gambling, but soon as the evil tendencies of these practices were known the Chiefs and Headmen made exertions to suppress them.

It is an established principle with the Cherokees, in common with all Indians, that Air, Water and Land is the free gift of the Creator to all men, and when Land is traded it is always understood that only the right to use it is meant.

Soon after the English began to settle in America, the Cherokees were persuaded, for a compensation, to relinquish the Northern part of their Domain. By this arrangement, they were forced into more narrow limits.

The Creeks were their Southern neighbors. Peace between these two Tribes was continually disturbed by feuds and war. This state of affairs was caused by a misunderstanding about their Boundary.

Each Tribe was accused of encroaching on the hunting grounds of the other. These disturbances were continued until Cherokee and Creek were names considered antagonistic almost by nature. As late as

---

17 Not widely shared with outsiders, Stomp Dances were (and are) celebratory dances forming part of a larger community gathering that affirms and preserves traditional culture. Occurring at night, the songs accompanying the dancing can focus on subjects ranging from love and friendship to animals and humorous stories.

18 This was the Treaty of Nequassee, negotiated by Sir Alexander Cuming [Kilpatrick's note].

19 This was the Treaty of Saluda, negotiated by Gov. James Glen of South Carolina [Kilpatrick's note].

20 "Big Water," or the Mississippi River.

21 The Rocky Mountains.

22 *Ga:nvtsi* the Cherokee consider to be their national dish. It is a soup made of hominy and crushed hickory nuts [Kilpatrick's note].

1813 the two Nations were yet enemies. The Cherokees and Choctaws assisted the United States, under command of General Jackson, in the famous Creek War.

The decisive battle was fought at the Horse shoe Bend in the Tennessee River, it was the most terrible battle with the Indians, of which we have an account, it is said, that the river for several miles ran red with blood. But it was not until 1821[23] that a Treaty of Peace was finally made by the Cherokees and Creeks. It was modified in 1822, '23, by which the question of "Boundary Line" was decided, and, "forever hereafter was acknowledged by both Nations to be permanent."

Members of either Tribe living within the boundaries of the other, were permitted to become Citizens of that Nation, if they chose to do so.

About other matters, the most liberal provisions were made.

The obligations of this Treaty have never been broken, and as a consequence these two Nations are still at peace.

During the time of the Colonization of North America, by the Whites a number of English and Scotchmen came to the Cherokee Nation on trading expeditions, and on becoming acquainted with the people, soon found themselves so much pleased that they persuaded the Cherokees to adopt them and give them wives.

Most of these men became very much interested in the welfare of the Indians, and tried to make their home-life more pleasant and comfortable.

An Englishman, named Edward Graves,[24] who had married "Lah-to-tau-yie," sent to England for a spinning wheel, cards and cotton, and taught his wife to card and spin, he then made a loom, and taught her how to weave, and make clothing for herself and children. Lah-to-tau-yie learned the art very easily, for she was interested in the work, and wished to please her husband by dressing herself and children neatly. Edward Graves was a Christian and told his wife and children about God and the Savior, Jesus Christ and taught them to pray.

Lah-to-tau-yie received this good news of salvation with a glad heart. She said, she knew about the great Being who made every thing, but she had never heard of the Savior. She told the Story to all her neighbors and relatives, and many of them became Christians, quite often many of them would meet in her cabin for prayer. Lah-to-tau-yie is supposed to be the first Cherokee converted to Christ. Her children all became Christians, and many of her descendants are now living, and honor the profession by consistent living.

The first Treaty with the United States was made in 1785,[25] by which land was again given up and Boundary lines confirmed. Owing to the encroachments of white settlers, and the miserable wars with the Carolinas, in 1791,[26] and '98[27] still more land was ceded away.

By this time many of the people had become disgusted and dissatisfied with so much "Treating for Land" and their thoughts, instinctivly, turning west, they soon decided, in that direction to seek for themselves a future home.

Adventurous persons then started out on prospecting tours, going as far as the Arkansas River.

The first Company who returned gave wonderful accounts of the Good Country at the "far West," they had found plenty of water, good timber, rich soil for farming, and game in abundance: immense herds of Buffalo, deer and antelopes, flocks of wild turkeys, geese and ducks, and the waters teeming with fish of all kinds. A veritable paradise, go they must.

George Lowrey was the son of Charles Lowrey, a Scotch trader, who had married a Cherokee woman named Tah-nie, and had settled in the Cherokee Nation. George was the oldest of several children, and was born about the year 1770 at Tah-skeegee, a place on the bank of the Tennessee River.[28]

He grew up as most other Indian lads of his time, but was very observant and selfreliant; when he was

[23] This was the Treaty of Indian Spring, January 8, 1821 [Kilpatrick's note].

[24] According to Kilpatrick, this identification appears to be inaccurate.

[25] The Treaty of Hopewell, November 28, 1785 [Kilpatrick's note].

[26] The Treaty of Holston, July 2, 1791 [Kilpatrick's note].

[27] The Treaty of Tellico, October 2, 1798 [Kilpatrick's note].

[28] According to several sources, Wahnenauhi seems to have some details wrong here; George Lowrey's father was also named George, and he was the second son. See Kilpatrick, 196 n.57.

ten or twelve years old he had the misfortune to lose his father; he was killed and robbed while crossing the Mountains in Tennessee, with pack-mules.

George Guess, or "Se-quoh-yah," as he was usually called, and John Leach, his cousins, and about the same age as himself, were his constant companions, and the Trio grew up together intimate friends.

Once, when about seventeen years old, while out on a hunting expedition, with several others of the Tribe, they met with a Company of white hunters; this accidental meeting proved to be quite an important, as well as a very pleasing incident to the Indians, as it was the means of changing the life-purpose of at least two of them.

Lowrey was the only one of his party who spoke the English Language and this he did very imperfectly.

One of the white men who gave his name as "Dickey," by his affability, quite won the Indians from their natural reserve and diffidence, and had a very interesting conversation with Lowrey, the leader of his party.

The whites and Indians camped near each other, ate and smoked together, and spent several hours in pleasant intercourse.

Dickey persuaded them to tell him many curious incidents relating to Indian habits and customs, while he gave them some ideas of civilized life.

He had with him a small book which he showed and explained to them; Lowrey acting as Interpreter for both parties – the Indians were filled with astonishment at the new and interesting things they had learned; and soon after separating with the white hunters they decided to return home. For the first time in their lives, Lowrey and Sequoyah felt an intense and longing desire for improvement; they had had a glimpse of a better way of life, and they determined to reach it.

From this time their careless, wild life lost all attractions for them; they were often taunted and ridiculed for their changes of deportment; their friends tried to cheer and enliven them by persuading them to attend the ball-plays and dances, by making them many valuable presents, and in other ways showing kindness to them.

Out of regard to their friends and kindred, they still attended the gatherings of the people, as, Green Corn Dances, Foot-races, and Ball-plays. They were dissatisfied, inattentive and listless. They both embraced every opportunity of learning the "white man's ways."

Indeed many of their relatives and other friends were persuaded by them and followed their example, they began to build better houses, make larger fields and gather around them cattle, horses, and hogs.

Many years passed bringing changes to all, and much improvement to the Cherokees.

Sequoyah often wandered away alone avoiding every one, at such times he was absent for hours, no one knew where. One day, a hunter on his way home, in passing Sequoyah's cabin, and seeing his wife at the door, called to her and said that he had seen Sequoyah in the woods, seated on the ground, playing like a child with pieces of wood that he had chopped from a tree. That he spoke to him but could not attract his attention, he was so intent at his play. After this he was often seen in this way; always making odd little marks, sometimes on rocks, using paint rocks as pencils, and sometimes, with his knife cutting them on wood.

After trying for a long time to divert his attention from these "Worse than childish ways" his wife and other friends left him alone to do as he pleased. From being very indignant, they became very much alarmed about him; they knew not what to think.

Some said, he was crazy, but that was impossible, for who ever heard of a crazy Indian?

They then decided that he was in communication with the Spirits, and for this reason many of his friends neglected him and refused to have any thing to do with him.[29] He endured with seeming indifference the neglect of friends, and the annoying sarcasm of opponents.

In all this time Sequoyah had been industrious and prudent, had gathered some property around

29 The basis for the antagonism toward Sequoyah's experiments was the fear that he was practicing sorcery [Kilpatrick's note].

him, and neglected nothing that would bring comfort to his family, endearing himself to them by kind attention to their simple wants; and by his proverbial hospitality and conciliating manners, enlarging the circle of his friends. Sequoyah did not speak the English language, and understood only a few words, of which he could make but little use; though he had seen but few books, he had learned something about them, and how distant friends could communicate with each other by writing. He was convinced that if a written language was beneficial to one people, it would be equally so to another so he determined to make this for his people, the Cherokees. Once the resolution formed it was never given up.

Many years Sequoyah dreamed, studied and worked until success crowned his efforts: and he presented to his people a methodically arranged alphabetical language, containing the eighty six syllables of which the Cherokee language is composed. He first taught the Alphabet to his little daughter, a girl of about ten years old, afterwards he persuaded a few of his friends to learn it.

However, it was not received with favor by the people generally, until after many experiments, it was proved beyond a doubt that Sequoyah had indeed devised a wonderful invention. He sent a letter to some friends, who had removed to the Arkansas Territory, and on receiving a reply, all doubts were forever banished.

Nearly every member of the Tribe became interested in the new movement, and learned the letters and to read and write.

Sequoyah now became a most popular man, and was respected, as almost superhuman; for he was regarded as a great benefactor of his Nation.

Valuable presents were given to him by the Chiefs and men of influence, and a sum of money, out of the National Treasury was paid to him, in consideration of his inestimable service.[30]

Afterward, a pension, to be paid out of the Public Treasury, was settled on him for life, to be continued to his wife after his death.

George Lowrey spent his time very differently from Sequoyah, being generally engaged in more active Public Life.

However, they continued to be firm friends, and Lowrey was one of the first to recognize the great advantages which would come to his people by the use of the native Alphabet, and used his influence to have them learn it, speaking enthusiastically of it on all occasions.

He embraced every opportunity of learning the Customs of Civilization.

Being a very fluent speaker, he often talked to his people about these things; urging them to forsake their careless, disorderly life, and try to improve their condition, by learning from and imitating the whites who had settled near them, many of whom were wealthy and refined people, to whom Lowrey was a steadfast friend. It was his earnest endeavor continually to improve his own mind, and his outward circumstance, always, by precept and example, trying to induce others to do the same.

It was customary with the Cherokees to name a person for, either some fancied resemblance, for something said or done, or some trait of Character: On account of Lowrey's peculiar Characteristics, his friends sometimes called him "Ah-gee-hli," which word means "Rising" or "Aspiring." And the name so appropriately chosen, that from this time, in Cherokee, he was spoken of as "Dtsah-tsi Ah-gee-hli," "Dtsah-tsi," meaning George.

In early manhood, George Lowrey distinguished himself by important services rendered, both to his own people and to the United States.

He was employed, at one time, by General Washington, to convey to the French in Canada, a secret message of great importance.

Most of the way lay through an unbroken Wilderness, inhabited only by hostile Tribes.

As the greatest caution and skill were necessary; to ensure the success of the undertaking, he made the journey on foot. Accompanied only by Billy, a colored slave; one other Indian began the journey with him, but on account of the hard-ships to be encountered, his resolution failed, and he returned.

---

30 The General Council of the Cherokee Nation presented a medal to Sequoyah in 1825. The United States Government promised him $500.00 in the Treaty of 1828 with the Western Cherokees. He never received the full amount [Kilpatrick's note].

The success gained by means of this perilous journey, won for Lowrey, Washington's warmest approval and esteem; and the greatest confidence and regard of his people.

In 1791, George Lowrey was chosen one of a Delegation sent to Washington City, to solicit payment of the Annuity which had been promised in the Treaty of 1785, and had not been paid. This expidition met with a favorable issue, and the payment was made in the following year.

When about twenty years old, George Lowrey was married to Lucy Benge, a Cherokee girl, also of Scottish descent; she, too, owned quite a considerable amount of property, as, slaves, horses, cattle &c. It was customary, in those times, for a young Indian man, contemplating marriage, first to prepare a dwelling place, making it as comfortable as he knew how; then the consent of the girl must be obtained, as also that of her mother, after which, at a time previously agreed upon, the girl accompanied him to his home and became his wife.

Thus it was that Mr. and Mrs. Lowrey began their wedded life.

They were truly devoted to each other, and up to old age treated each other with the greatest respect and kindness. Their children, in after years, in speaking of their parents, were heard to remark, "Never a hard word passed between them, and they never had a misunderstanding."

Mrs. Lowrey was very industrious, and kept every thing around her in beautiful order.

She also learned to spin and weave, and took great delight in making clothing for her family, in making quilts, in embroidery and other fancy work.

She was very skilful in making the beaded belts, so highly prized by the Cherokee braves and warriors.

She and "Wuttie," the wife of John Lowrey, George's younger brother, so improved and embellished these belts, that they generally sold for twenty five dollars apiece.

In sickness, being unwilling to trust the members of her family to native doctors and conjurers, Mrs. Lowrey attained great skill in the use of medicinal roots and herbs, especially in cases of the bite or sting of reptiles or poisonous insects.

The years brought increasing prosperity to Mr. Lowrey, and he became the owner of a large number of slaves, over whom, as a reward for his faithful services, Billy was advanced to the position of overseer, which station he occupied as long as he lived.

One instance only of Billy failing the confidence reposed in him is known.

Mr. Lowrey had a large piece of ground cleared, broken up and planted with watermelons,[31] he had it fenced with picketts, a strong gate made, fastened with a lock with two keys, one of which he gave to Billy, reserving the other himself.

When the melons began to ripen, one morning, Mr. Lowrey went in to get a melon that he had selected the evening before; to his great surprise it was gone, however he said nothing about it: but when the same thing happened again, and yet another time he decided that it was time for him to investigate. Accordingly, when evening came, he concealed himself just outside the gate and waited.

Pretty soon Billy came to the gate and opening it walked in, carefully closing and locking it. He soon came out with a large melon under his arm.

His master, leaving his place of concealment, met him, saying, "Ah! Billy, I find it no harm watch honest man!" To cover his confusion, Billy handed the melon to his master trying to pretend that he had gathered it for him: it was haughtily refused, with the words, "no, I got key, I able to get my own melon." Nothing more was said of the affair, and no more melons mysteriously disappeared.[32]

Mr. and Mrs. Lowrey were the parents of six children, three sons and three daughters, all of whom grew up, and worthily filled respectable places in the Nation, Mr. Lowrey was very anxious that their children should be educated in the English Language, for this purpose a white man was employed to teach them.

[31] Even among themselves the Cherokees' predilection for watermelons is proverbial [Kilpatrick's note].

[32] This vignette is one of the few authentic glimpses available to us of the relationship of the Cherokee planter class to its slaves [Kilpatrick's note].

That the children might make more rapid progress, the teacher was required to live with the family while teaching. A small cabin was builded in a pleasant locality near the dwelling house, and fitted up for a school house. Mr. Lowrey paid the teacher a liberal salary, expecting in return their best work. He invited some of his neighbors to send their children to his school, which privilege they gladly accepted. After trying three or four men, at different times, and not being pleased with their manner of educating, he gave up this plan, and sent the older children to a distinguished school near Nashville, Tenn.

About the year 1803, Mr. and Mrs. Gambold, Moravian Missionaries, came to the Cherokees, who received them joyfully.

Arrangements were immediately made by the Chiefs and Headmen to select a suitable locality for a Mission Station. A school was soon put into operation, and Hicks, Ross, Lowrey[33] and many other influential men immediately availed themselves of the privilege of sending their children to a Christian School. In 1804, Presbyterian Missionaries were sent to the Cherokee Nation, and in a short time several Mission Stations were located in different parts of the Nation, Schools were established and Churches organized. But many of the people still adhered to the old ways, would have nothing to do with the Missionaries, and ignored all their efforts made for educating and civilizing the Indians.

At their dances and ball-plays, whiskey was brought in and freely used; very often the gatherings were broken up by drunken quarrels, and sometimes by brutal murder.

However, the most influential persons, who were followed by the greater part of the Nation, anxious to secure educational advantages for their children, made great exertions to assist the Missionaries in building houses, and providing things necessary for their comfort while working among them.

In 1817 the Station at Brainerd was begun and the school put into successful operation.[34] And in a few years several other Mission Stations were established, and the schools well attended and prosperous. The Baptist and Methodist also had Mission Stations among the Cherokees. As a Nation, they were now prepared to receive the Gospel, brought to them by the Missionaries.

Many were converted, among others, Hicks, who was then Principal Chief, Lowrey and his wife, Rising-fawn, Sleeping Rabit, Mr. John Brown, the father of Catherine[35] and David of whom so much was written at the time by the Missionaries, and a great many more. The Missionaries were greatly loved by the Cherokees, who had by this time received such an impetus towards Christianity and Civilization that it was impossible for them to return to barbarism.

Some years before all this, the Chiefs, Headmen and Warriors, had met together in Council and agreed, for the general good of the Nation, to make a more united Form of Government; instead of each Clan working for its own, they chose one Principal Chief, an Assistant and a Council, consisting, at first of thirteen members, upon whom devolved all the business of the Nation, as making laws, appointing officers, &c. They immediately organized Companies, called Regulators, or, Lighthorse whose duty it was to suppress theft and robbery, and to protect the peace. This Legislative Body made laws, as they saw needful, for the protection and improvement of the Nation. As early as 1808, prohibitory laws were made to prevent the introduction of intoxicants into the Nation, for, when the Annuities were to be paid, vicious whites were ready with Whiskey to give, or, sell to the Indians that they might obtain possession of their money; this nuisance became so prevalent as to make it an absolute necessity to the Nation to act in its own defence. Although the law could not wholly eradicate the evil, it proved a wholesome check to the flood of intemperance and, with amendments, has continued in force in the Cherokee nation to this time. Black Fox was Principal Chief at that time.

---

33 Charles Hicks (1767–1827), Assistant Principal Chief (1817–27), Principal Chief for 13 days prior to his death; John Ross (1790–1866), Principal Chief (1827–66) [Kilpatrick's note].

34 Founded by the American Board of Commissioners for Foreign Missions, this Tennessee mission also included a gristmill and workshops for vocational education.

35 See Perdue, 1998, 169–70; Rufus Anderson, *Memoirs of Catherine Brown, a Christian Indian of the Cherokee Nation*, Armstrong and Crocker and Brewster, 1825.

About the same time, laws against poligamy were enacted.

The first Public use made of Sequoyah's Alphabet was to print the Gospel of Mathew, and a Collection of Hymns in the Cherokee Language.[36] – In 1828 Public Schools were established by the Council, to be supported by the National Government.

Educational exercises conducted in both Cherokee and English languages.

Two years previously measures were taken by the National Council to have published at the National expense, a News Paper, devoted to the Interest of the Indian People.

This paper, called "The Cherokee Phenix," printed in both languages, continued to be published until the removal of the Tribe, West of the Mississippi.[37] In History, little is said of this event, so laden with loss and suffering to the Cherokee Indians.

It is only what has been repeated many times since, in the case of other Indian Tribes.

If the Cherokees could have been united and acted under one Leader, they might have escaped much of the trouble and loss by which they were overtaken. The dissatisfaction, already mentioned as existing in the Nation, on account of selling land to the aggressive whites continued, and no wonder, for no less than sixteen treaties were made with the United States, each one requiring land to be given up, and likewise, each one promising to protect the Cherokees in their homes.

Companies of Emigrants were very frequently seen, on their way to the "Far West." Reluctant, indeed, they were to leave their loved homes, and the "graves of their Dead." Love of peace urged them on. And they believed that only by seeking a new Country, they could build up permanent homes for their children. Sequoyah, whose English name was George Guess, went with that division of his people who emigrated prior to the "Treaty of 1834–35"[38] and continued to be one of their leading men. Aaron Price, for quite a number of years, was Principal Chief of the "Western Cherokees," who after the Union were called, "Old Settlers." After Price, John Jolly was chosen Principal Chief and filled the office acceptably to his people. Black Coat and Col. Walter Webber were elected Second and Third Chiefs; the three Chiefs were invested with equal authority and received the same Salary, – one hundred dollars each.

The Western Cherokees manifested the same zeal in improvement, in civilization, and educational advantages as before their emigration. The difference of climate was a severe tax on their health, and many of them died.

Besides this, they were obliged to be always on their guard, on account of the Osages, who were continually committing depredations, as driving away their horses and cattle, &c.

All this led to long and troublesome wars with the Osages. The difficulty was eventually settled by a Treaty with the United States, and the lines of boundary between the two Nations decided. In a few years the Western Settlers began to be very prosperous; and were very much pleased with their change. During all this time, the majority of the Tribe continued in their homes, looking to their Chiefs for advice and protection.

The Chiefs and Headmen relied on the good faith of the Government of the United States, who had in the Treaty guaranteed to them their Country for ever, using the expression, "As long as grass grows, and water runs."

In no case had the Cherokees signed away their inheritance.

The declarations of the Government, and of the Indian Agents, had been always directed to one point, – that was, to satisfy the Cherokees that the Government would deal justly and fairly with the Indians, and would perform all its engagements to secure to them the permanent possession of their Country.

---

[36] The Cherokee hymnal, first issued at New Echota in 1829, is still in use after having gone through many editions. It is largely the work of the brilliant fullblood Cherokee scholar, Elias Boudinot (1802–39), and Rev. Samuel Worcester [Kilpatrick's note].

[37] The Cherokee Phoenix was founded in 1828; it was suppressed by Georgia in 1834. Elias Boudinot was its first editor. Although bilingual, it was in one sense the first newspaper in an American Indian language [Kilpatrick's note]. The "removal" in this paragraph refers to the infamous forced march west, the Trail of Tears. Although some of the dates and minor details of the account of Georgia's and the federal government's treachery are incorrect, the outline is basically accurate.

[38] Treaty of New Echota, December 29, 1835 [Kilpatrick's note].

They had been constantly urged to become farmers, to educate their children, and to form a regular Government for themselves. And all this they had done. – In 1826 this opinion was written by a Missionary, a faithful friend of the Cherokees, –

"It is now too late to talk of the impracticability of Indian civilization.

"Strangers who pass through the Nation now, and who had passed through it several years ago, are often heard to express their astonishment at the change which has taken place." –

"The mass of the people in their dress, houses, furniture, agricultural implements, manner of cultivating the soil, raising stock, providing for their families and in their estimate of the value of an education, would not suffer by a comparison with the whites in the neighboring settlements."

The mass of the people had practically embraced Christianity.

Intemperance had been checked – some, notoriously intemperate, had been reformed.

Owing partly to political disturbances, the encouraging aspect of the Nation became clouded with confusion and depression. The Public men manifested much firmness and dignity of character, and remained steadfast friends to the moral and intellectual elevation of their people; and advised them to remain at home, quietly attending to their usual business of farming and taking care of their stock.

They firmly believed that the United States would fulfill its treaty obligations, and protect them in their homes.

Since 1819 the Cherokees had refused to sell any more land.

Gold had been found in some parts of the Nation, and this fact, by exciting the cupidity of the Whites, had brought to a crisis the circumstances which resulted in the removal.

In 1827, Georgia assumed an arrogant attitude towards the Cherokees, declaring that they had no title to the land, only that of occupancy, determinable at the pleasure of Georgia, that *she* had a perfect title by right of discovery, to all the land within her chartered limits, that the United States were bound to extinguish the Indian title.

In 1828 Georgia extended her laws over the Cherokees. Their Government was hindered in its operations, their laws counteracted, and some of their citizens imprisoned, the missionaries were forbidden to preach to them, and on their non-compliance, were shamefully treated and imprisoned in the penitentiary. The Cherokees appealed for protection, to the President of the United States, who informed them that he had no constitutional power to protect them.

They then petitioned Congress, and while their Petition was pending, a Bill was introduced into Congress for the purpose of enabling them to remove west of the Mississippi; the Bill for the removal was passed, and preparations were immediately begun to have it enforced.

To give some show of law to this deed of violence, a Sham Treaty was made with a few irresponsible Cherokees, who, for love of money, accepted a bribe, and immediately left for the Western Country.

Meanwhile, many acts of lawlessness were perpetrated on the Cherokees, horses and cattle were driven away, hogs were taken without the consent of the owners, murders were committed, and the friends of the slain were powerless to bring the offenders to justice.

Even the graves of the dead were not safe, but were opened in order to obtain the treasures supposed to be buried with them.

The Headmen and Chiefs called the people together for the purpose of deciding what course to pursue as the best means of protection.

Many eloquent speeches were made, but nothing was decided; A few spoke of resistance, that was evidently so unavailing, – it would only be self-destruction; and to the helpless wives and innocent children, more suffering and distress.

This was a critical time for the Cherokee Nation, its very existence was threatened, and all was to be determined by the Chiefs now in Council. How this great responsibility pressed upon them! perish or remove! it might be, – remove *and* perish! a long journey through the Wilderness, – could the little ones endure? and how about the sick? the old people and infirm, could they possibly endure the long tedious journey; Should they leave?

This had been the home of their Ancestors from time out of mind.

Every thing they held dear on the earth was here, *must* they leave?

The graves of their kindred forsaken by them would be desecrated by the hand of the White Man! The very air seemed filled with an under-current of inexpressible sadness and regret.

They could almost hear the reproaches and wailings of the dear dead they were leaving.

How must these Chiefs decide for their people? No wonder it seemed that Despair in its thickest blackness had settled down and enfolded in gloom this assemblage of brave and true-hearted Patriots.

But no time could they spend in regrets and forboding, although their own hearts were torn with grief, throwing aside their private troubles, they set themselves to the task of preparing the people for the inevitable journey. A Delegation was appointed and authorized to make arrangements with Major General Scott for Supplies required for the Removal.

For convenience in protecting, providing for and distributing to, so large a Body of people, they were divided into Companies, or, Detachments, as they were called, each provided with a Captain, whose duties were to attend to the necessities of all in his particular Detachment.

Some of the Cherokees, remained in their homes, and determined not to leave.

For these soldiers were sent, by Georgia, and they were gathered up and driven, at the point of the bayonet, into camp with the others. They were not allowed to take any of their household stuff, but were compelled to leave as they were, with only the clothes which they had on. One old, very old man, asked the soldiers to allow him time to pray once more, with his family in the dear old home, before he left it forever. The answer was, with a brutal oath, "No! no time for prayers. Go!" at the same time giving him a rude push towards the door.[39]

In many instances, the families of settlers were at hand, and as the Indians were evicted, the whites entered, taking full possession of every thing left.

It is useless to attempt to describe the long, wearisome passage of these exiled Indians.

The journey had but just begun when sickness attacked them.

Many of the old people, already enfeebled by age, were unable to endure the fatigue and hardships of the way, and sank unresistingly.

Every camping place was strewn with the graves of the dead.

Not one family was exempted from the tax of the Death-Angel. It was estimated, on reaching their destination, that fully two-thirds of the number that began the journey fell by the way. Many more died after their arrival.[40]

As the emigrants arrived too late in the Season for planting, an Appropriation was made for their subsistance during that year.

Some of the Missionaries, true and beloved friends of the Cherokees, went with them and shared with them the trials and hardships by the way; others followed them very soon.

Forever revered be their memory for that Act of Sympathetic Mercy!

At the time of the Removal, Mr. John Ross was Principal Chief, and Maj. George Lowrey, Assistant Principal Chief.

Both had occupied these Stations for several years, having been repeatedly elected by the People.

As soon as practicable after the arrival of the Emigrants a Convention of all the people was held in order to form a union between the two Divisions.

George Lowrey was chosen President of the Eastern Cherokees, and Sequoyah, George Guess President of the Western.

By an Act of this Assembly, the two parties agreed to form themselves into one Body.

A system of Government was matured, adapted to their changed condition, providing equally for the protection of all in the enjoyment of their rights. An Instrument was modeled, considered and approved by the respective Chiefs; John Ross, Principal Chief of the Eastern Cherokees; and John Looney, Acting Principal Chief of the Western Cherokees, and signed by a great number of Old Settlers

[39] Wahnenauhi may have witnessed this scene [Kilpatrick's note].

[40] Approximately 4,000 Cherokees perished in the course of the removal [Kilpatrick's note]. Some contemporary historians place the figure much higher than this.

and Late Emigrants. The long journey from the Old Home to the New had caused much suffering and Loss.

The people, however, were not wholly disheartened; – Friends and kindred welcomed and sympathized with them, the Missionaries were still with them, their leading men were earnestly interested in their welfare and advancement, and in a few years Prosperity again smiled upon them. However, success did not come to them without great effort on their part.

Besides the usual difficulties, incident to the Settlers of a new Country, the Cherokees were harrassed by internal strife; Party feeling ran high. Several men, accused of being implicated in the loss of their old home, were killed at the instigation of a Secret Organization, formed by a few who felt themselves called to avenge the wrongs of their people.[41] Anarchy almost prevailed.

Had it not been that the Almighty had designs of mercy for the People, and in His Providence placed at the Head of Government wise and good men, the Nation would then undoubtedly have been destroyed.

A Constitution for the Government of the Cherokee Nation was framed, and established subject to amendments by the National Council. This Constitution stands an advantageous comparison with that of the United States.

In 1828, the proceeds of a Sale of Land was vested in a permanent School Fund; and the interest divided between the two Branches of the Cherokee Family.

After the Reunion, as payment was made for the Lands east of the Mississippi, a part of the money was added to the original School Fund; more Public Schools were established, and also two High Schools were located near Tahlequah, the Capital of the Nation.

Provisions were made for an Orphan Asylum, which, later on was firmly established, and has since continued in a prosperous condition. Besides these schools, an Asylum for the Blind and other unfortunates was founded, and is maintained by a National Fund appropriated to that purpose.

The barbarous practice of punishment by Public Whipping has been long ago abolished, and confinement in Prison substituted.

In closing these imperfect sketches, the reader will be interested to know of the last days of the two men of whom I have made most prominent mention.

On account of Sequoyah's declining health, he was advised to travel.

He had thought much of the Legend of the Rockey Mountain Cherokees, and the hope of satisfying his curiosity with regard to this myth made him anxious to take a westward trip; he was also very desirous of seeing and exploring the western outlet belonging to the Cherokees. These inducements led to his decision.

On the early spring of 1842, he, with about twelve attendants, two of whom were his sons, set out on the journey.

Not caring to be needlessly burdened the Company carried with them only a small amount of provision, expecting to supply their immediate wants by killing the wild game with which they supposed the Country to abound. For this purpose they were provided with a sufficient stock of ammunition.

By traveling slowly, examining the nature and appearance of the Country as they passed along, stopping to camp or hunt whenever it suited Sequoyah to do so, the time passed pleasantly and swiftly. Sequoyah's strength returned, and his health improved so rapidly that strong hopes were entertained of his permanent recovery.

His pet idea of visiting the Rockey Mountains seemed about to be fulfilled, and all rejoiced in the apparent success of their journey.

Almost suddenly, the features of the Country changed, water became scarce, and what there was, very bad. Game was hard to find, and the Company was obliged often to make forced marches in order to obtain water and shelter, while on account of having no food, some of the men must continually hunt

[41] This refers to the June 22, 1839, assassination of Elias Boudinot, Major Ridge, and John Ridge, leaders of the faction that had advocated removal [Kilpatrick's note].

the game which seemed to have eluded them. Sequoyah, supposing this arid land to be only a narrow strip that could be crossed in a very short time, persuaded his companions to persevere in their course, still hoping to gain his wish of reaching the Rockies.

Not strong enough to endure the fatigue and privations to which he was subjected, Sequoyah's new-found health gave way, and he gave orders to turn and retrace their steps; his strength now failed so rapidly that he was unable to travel, he gave up all hope of recovery, but wished to get home before he died. He became so reduced, they could make only short distances with him, often they were obliged to stop in very unfavorable conditions.

In all his journey, he had busied himself with writing descriptions of the country through which they passed; this he continued to do, at intervals, as his strength allowed.

Coming to a Cave, Sequoyah thought he might gain strength by resting here for a few days; they remained at this place perhaps a week, the men going every day to hunt, always leaving one of their number to take care of him.

One morning he sent them all off. On their return in the evening, he was gone, but had left a skin hanging at the entrance of the Cave.

On this he had written directions for them to follow him to a certain place, indicated in the directions.

They immediately set out but failed to find him until the next evening, they found him dead, the appearance of the body showed that he had been dead for several hours.

The time being the heat of summer, it was impossible to take him home.

Carrying the body far back into the Cave, and placing his writing with him, they wrapped it in skins as securely as they could.

They marked the place so that it would without difficulty be found, and then set out on their return.

Immediately on their arrival, preparations were made and a Company organized and sent with the men to convey the remains home. They did not find even the place where they had left him. Thus Sequoyah, the Indian who most deserves the respect and gratitude of his people, sleeps in his last resting-place with no Monument to mark the spot.

Every true-hearted Cherokee will ever hold his Memory dear, and will speak with pride of their gifted Brother.

All men, whatever their Nationality, whether friend or foe to the Indian, will acknowledge the wonderful genius of Sequoyah, he who gave to his people their written Language.

George Lowrey continued to be a ruling spirit among his people – their trusted Friend and Adviser. He rejoiced with his people in the peace and security which assured prosperity to them; and in the steady progress they had made toward Civilization.

His own individual peace was soon to be disturbed by a great sorrow.

He was called home from the National Council by the sickness of his wife, whose death occured in October the 20th 1846.

Five years later Lowrey was declared too old to perform the duties of a Chief, and a younger man was placed in the office so long and ably filled by him.

Old, very old he was – his formerly erect frame bowed with the weight of years, yet he possessed all his native energy of mind. Declining to retire from Active Service, he was assigned an office in the Executive Committee; a position of high trust.[42]

Death found him at his post, faithfully discharging the duties of his office. He was compelled, by his own sickness, to leave the Council.

Six years after his wife's death: – October 20th 1852, George Lowrey entered into that "Rest" prepared for the people of God.

His remains were followed to their last resting place, in the Cemetary at Tahlequah, by a multitude.

Besides his immediate relatives and friends, there marched in the long procession, all the Members of

[42] In the government of the Cherokee Nation, the Executive Committee corresponded somewhat to the Cabinet of the President of the United States [Kilpatrick's note].

the National Council, headed by the Chiefs and the two remaining members of the Executive Committee, the Students from both Seminaries, Free Masons, Sons of Temperance and many other persons.[43]

All appeared to realize that "A Great man had fallen!"

As a fitting close to this Sketch, I will give a quotation from the Monument which marks his grave.

> "Erected
> by order of the
> National Council."
> "He filled the duties of every office well,
> An Honest man –
> A Spotless Patriot –
> A Devoted Christian."

[43] George Lowrey was probably a Freemason . . . Lucy Lowrey Hoyt would appear to have been a student at the Cherokee Female Seminary at the time of her grandfather's death [Kilpatrick's note].

# Narcissa Owen (Cherokee, 1831–1911)

*Owen was born on October 3, 1831 at Webber's Falls, Arkansas Indian Territory, to Thomas and Martha Warton Chisholm. Her father was a leader of the Old Settlers (that is, those who had moved to Arkansas Territory prior to Cherokee removal). Narcissa was the fourth of six children, three boys and three girls. Her family were wealthy, well-educated, slave-owning farmers. Hence, even after her father's death in November 1843, she was able to attend school – at Old Dwight Mission School; Mose Daniel's School; the college for young ladies in New Albany, Indiana; then Miss Sawyer's Female Academy in Fayetteville, Arkansas. Following her graduation from Miss Sawyer's, Narcissa taught music there for a year, then was offered the position of music teacher at the Masonic High School in Jonesboro, Tennessee. While at Jonesboro, she met Robert Lathem Owen, who worked as a surveyor during the construction of the Virginia and Tennessee Railroad. They began their happy marriage on October 4, 1853.*

*Prior to finally settling in Robert's native Lynchburg, Virginia, the family lived in Rogersville, Tennessee, then at Tazewell and Evan's Bridge, Virginia, on the Clinch River. In 1860, Robert was elected president of the Virginia and Tennessee Railroad and later received a commission of colonel in the Confederate Army. While Robert managed the railroad during the war, Narcissa raised two sons, William and Robert; oversaw the family home, Point of Honor; and helped supervise over five hundred women in the production of uniforms and hospital supplies. Those who supervised this war work were in charge of distributing materials and collecting finished work from the wives and daughters of poorer soldiers. When production of such war supplies was no longer needed, Narcissa solicited monies from other financially secure women around Lynchburg to ensure that the poorer women were cared for.*

*After the war Robert continued to work with the railroad until 1867, when he resigned, entering politics for two years in the Virginia Senate. Suffering financially, the family left Lynchburg in 1870 and purchased a farm on the Elizabeth River near Norfolk. After Robert's death in 1873, Narcissa would never remarry. Left with two sons to raise and in a state of near financial ruin, Narcissa sold what was left of the family's land, managing to ensure that both sons received excellent educations, with William Otway Owen attending the Virginia Military Institute before receiving a medical degree from the University of Virginia, and Robert Lathem Owen, Jr. graduating as valedictorian of his class from Washington and Lee University. In 1880 Narcissa received an appointment to teach in the Cherokee Female Seminary in Talequah, Oklahoma, and she and Robert Jr. moved to the Cherokee Nation. Narcissa taught at the Seminary for almost four years, while her son worked as principal teacher at the Orphan Asylum and edited and published the* Indian Chieftain, *a daily newspaper, before beginning to practice law. In 1885, Robert Jr. became the United States Indian Agent for the Five Civilized Tribes and moved to Muskogee.*[1] *Narcissa managed Robert's home until 1889 when he married.*

[1] Robert Jr.'s reputation among traditional Native Americans is mixed at best, for he worked tirelessly for individual ownership of tribal lands and may have profited from this stance on allotment.

*Narcissa's lifetime interest in art was renewed following a visit to Fort Spokane in Washington Territory in 1835. She painted landscapes and miniatures, and went on to display her work at the Louisiana Exposition of 1904, where she was presented with a diploma and a medal. Her later years were split between her home, Monticello, on the Little Caney River in Cherokee Territory, and Washington, DC, where she lived with Robert after he became one of Oklahoma's first senators. During her stays in Washington, she maintained an art studio. She died at the age of 80 and is buried with her husband in the Sprint Hill Cemetery in Lynchburg.*

*Written and published late in her life, her autobiography represents a fascinating amalgamation of genres, including tribal history, advice writing, and sketch. Pursuing an accretive rather than a linear narrative organization, Owen's voice shifts tone and stance frequently, incorporating humor as well as delight, and anger as well as appreciation. She clearly loved her husband and was proud both of her children and of her own independence. Representing herself as a version of the "Indian Princess," like Sarah Winnemucca and Pauline Johnson she conjured up white stereotypes of American Indian women while she simultaneously deconstructed them, asserting her status as both an educated, privileged lady and a strong Cherokee woman. Some of the most interesting parts of her narrative relate to her personal experiences – saving two young women from drowning, resisting the advances of a drunken man while out horseback riding, and conspiring with one of her ex-slaves to foil robbers. These experiences, combined with the tales she relates of her time at the Seminary, reveal her to be a witty, energetic, and independent woman capable, like Mary Jemison, of meeting many challenges. Even though, from a traditional – matrilineal – standpoint, Owen was not Cherokee, her narrative bears witness both to the changing and diverse roles of affluent Cherokee women late in the nineteenth century and the ways in which many claimed the power of their predecessors.*

Stephen Brandon with Karen Kilcup

## BIBLIOGRAPHY


### Primary

*Memoirs of Narcissa Owen: 1831–1907*. Washington, DC: n.p., 1907. Rpt. Owensboro, Kentucky: McDowell, 1979. Rpt. Siloam Springs, Arkansas: Simon Sage, 1983.

### Secondary

Garrett, Steven. "Review of *Memoirs of Narcissa Owen: 1831–1907*." *Chronicles of Oklahoma* 63 (Spring 1985): 102.

Mihesuah, Devon A. *Cultivating the Rose Buds: The Education of Women at the Cherokee Female Seminary, 1851–1909*. Illinois, 1993.

Mooney, James. *Myths of the Cherokee and Sacred Formulas of the Cherokees*. 1900. Rpt. Charles and Randy Elder, 1982.

Obituaries of Robert L. Owen, Jr. *New York Times*, 20 July 1947. *Washington Post*, 19 July 1947. *Lynchburg News*, 20 July 1947.

Perdue, Theda. *Cherokee Women: Gender and Culture Change, 1700–1835*. Nebraska, 1998.

Reed, Mrs. Ora Eddleman. "Great Work of an Indian." *Sturm's Oklahoma Magazine* 2:6 (1906): 7–9.

Shaffer, Janet. "Narcissa and Robert Owen: The Point of Honor Years." *Virginia Magazine of History and Biography* 89 (1981): 153–69.

Snelling, Lois. "Review of *Memoirs of Narcissa Owen: 1831–1907*." *Arkansas Historical Quarterly* 40 (Spring 1981): 80–1.

# From *Memoirs of Narcissa Owen: 1831–1907* (1907)

## FROM CHAPTER 1: SOME OLD CHEROKEE LEGENDS AND BELIEFS

### [The Founding of the Cherokee Nation]

The Cherokee Nation was founded by seven brothers, who came from the east so long ago that all traces of the date of their coming has faded from the memory of their descendants; but by the law of their clans their names have been handed down through the mothers of the people. The mothers were the historians of the seven clans, and, like the Arabs, their narrations came down from time immemorial by word of mouth alone, until such time as the people began to have a written history, or about the time of the death of the last hereditary chief, Thomas Chisholm, in 1834, before the eastern Cherokees emigrated to the west.

The names of the founders of the Cherokee Nation are as follows:[2]

Long Hair (Arni Kilawhi),
Blind Savannah,
The Painter (Arni Waut),
The Deer,
The Wolf,
The Acorn,
The Holly.

The seven brothers lived together in great love and harmony, being devotedly attached to each other. Their home life was to them like an Eden, until their children and grandchildren grew to be men and women. Then new interests began to conflict in many ways that were unexpected and undesirable. The heart of each mother went out in love to her own children. Her sympathies were enlisted in behalf of those of her own house, and who were the treasures of her own heart. When the seven mothers, with the same blind devotion to their descendants, undertook to champion and defend them from the encroachments of any and all those whose interests were at variance, naturally a rough current was given to the stream of love which had for generations glided along in unbroken peace.

These seven brothers, seeing the conflict between their wives and children, decided the wisest thing to be done by them was to separate. They then held a council and made laws for the government of their families.

In compensation for this decision, the first law that they made was to meet annually at their old home. They next decided that the head of all the clans should be Long Hair (Ar-ni-ki-law-hi), who would at these annual meetings settle all difficulties arising among the people. Each clan was to be governed by the eldest or best male member. Whenever there was more than one inheritor of the chief's office, the mothers, with the head men of each clan, made a selection of the one thought to be most worthy of the inherited right of being head chief.

Children belonging to the same clan must never, under penalty of death, intermarry. They were the same to each other as brothers and sisters, and it was known that fatal diseases came from such intermarriages. In that case it was better that the parents should be put to death than for the young and innocent to be born to such an inheritance.

The true descent of a chief should never be in doubt. The succession of the office of chief must and

---

[2] These clan names represent a variation on those listed by Perdue (42) and Mooney (212–13) Details of the early part of Owen's account are not always reliable; nevertheless, her narrative makes apparent the important role of women in Cherokee culture. Her naming of her father as the last hereditary chief of the Cherokees represents a complex interpretation of Cherokee systems of authority; her goal seems to be to underscore for white readers her status as a Cherokee "princess."

shall be descended from the mother's side of the family. All clan names must follow the clan of the mother. In this way there was no doubt of the true descent of all the seven clans, from the days of the seven brothers down to the last hereditary chief.

Stealing shall be punished by cutting off an ear; a second offense, both ears; the third offense, the end of the nose must pay the penalty, making it impossible for a thief to conceal his character.

A murderer must be executed by the nearest of kin of the person slain, and in the same way in which he had committed murder, and among the seven clans killing was murder, whether accident or intention.

The bones of the dead were all to be brought to these annual meetings, but only those who had been dead a year or more could be brought. These bones were to be placed in a mound, and the women and children brought earth in baskets to cover them. This is supposed to be the beginning of the mound-building among the Cherokees. Twenty-one miles southeast of Fort Gains, Georgia, is a mound seventy feet high, six hundred feet in circumference, covered with trees five hundred years old. "A sixty-foot shaft exposed human bones five feet in depth, thoroughly decayed." (1847, book by Dr. Woodruff, page 151.)

As stated above, the continual quarrels among the women and children of the devoted brothers made it imperative to make the above laws and to separate the clans. But the great grief of the brothers was in a measure compensated by the annual meetings of the council of the seven clans. They met to establish justice and peace, to promote the instruction of the young people, and to keep up friendly intercourse and the intermarriages of their children as well as placing in the sacred mound the bones of all their dead, or, as it is expressed in the Cherokee language, "those who have passed to other lands." Too soon after the separation they met enemies, and had to reunite for self-defense. In that union, however, many of their old quarrels were forgotten, and peace reigned, to the great pleasure of the seven old brothers.

Years afterward, when all the dear old grandfathers had passed on to other lands and their bones were resting in the sacred mound, their successors, having been brought up under wise counselors, made the people happy and industrious by teaching them how to provide food and home for their families. Thus they lived until A. D. 1585, when Sir Walter Raleigh visited North America and incidentally visited the Cherokees, and found them to be small farmers, cultivating some food products which he considered worthy of cultivation by the English people, chiefly tobacco, corn, and beans, and white, or so-called "Irish," potatoes. It would have been pre-eminently proper to have named that tuber "Cherokee potato," as it was the original food of the Cherokee Indians, as it afterwards became the food of the Irish.

In giving the history of Cherokee families it is almost impossible to tell their connection, on account of the absence of family surnames. The clan names are the nearest approach they have to anything like the English surname. Until 1700 the Cherokee people never had any other names than the inherited clan names of their mothers (except personal names, which were often changed, but clan names never). The changing of the names of the men – for instance, the sons of Chief Caulunna from Ka-la-nah to Sow-we-noo-ky (Shawnee), and from Chic-sa-te-hee to Bushyhead – makes it almost impossible to trace any family beyond the memory of the living. [. . .][3]

## A Cherokee Rheumatism Cure

Take a piece of the root of the trumpet vine about five or six inches long, and with a knife scrape the bark carefully into a cup of water, and have a little thin muslin bag, and when the bark of the root is all scraped off, pour it into the bag, and you have a poultice to apply to the pain. Save the water in which the bark has been scraped for moistening the poultice a second or third time, if needed. Keep the poultice on fifteen or twenty minutes at a time. The effect is very peculiar. It gives a sensation like prickly heat, and it is a rubefacient. It will relieve any ordinary rheumatic pain.

---

[3] The variations on Cherokee names are huge; see Mooney, 523, 531, for some variations on those listed here. See also Perdue, 82. Here the narrative continues to trace Cherokee history, speculating on connections between the Cherokees and the Powhatans before returning to the selections that follow.

## Cherokee Cure for Snake Bite

Take the leaves of a farm weed known as the cockle-bur, enough to make a poultice, and simmer them over a fire until sufficiently pliant to make a poultice; then apply them to the wound. Take of the water that they were boiled in, about half a teacupful, as a drink.

My sister Jane was cured of the bite of a diamond rattlesnake, and of a ground rattlesnake, and the third time she was cured of the bite of the spider. I myself gathered the leaves for her, and made the poultice under her directions, and gave her the water to drink, and though she was quite sick from the poison, she was relieved almost immediately.

When sister Jane (Mrs. Jane Bruton, of Muldrow)[4] was a little girl and running barefoot, she was out walking in the woods along a path one day, when a diamond rattlesnake struck at her. She continued on her way, but had only gone a little way when, from the shock, she fell in a faint. She then knew that she had been badly bitten by the snake, and as soon as she recovered consciousness she went home, and mother engaged the Indian doctor to cure her. He used the above remedy. In that way she learned how to take care of herself. Years afterwards, when she was a rather elderly woman, she went out into her garden to see if she didn't have some new potatoes large enough to eat. In examining the rows of growing potatoes she noticed in a good many places that the earth had cracked open. Presuming that a potato had cracked it, she put her hand into one of the openings to see if she couldn't get hold of the potato. In doing so she felt that something had pricked her finger, but thought perhaps it was a brier or splinter buried in the earth. She looked at her hand and failed to see anything, so she put it back into the hole. This time she made no mistake about something having pierced her finger. She pulled out her hand, and there hung a little ground rattlesnake from her finger, ten or twelve inches long. She immediately tried her remedy, and had no further trouble from the bite.

In the case of the spider bite, that happened in the night, when she couldn't see what did it. The next day her hand swelled up and troubled her some, when she was going to Muskogee to meet me. She found that I had gone to Ogeechee, where my other sister (Mrs. Em. Breedlove) lived, and she took the train and came on to sister Em's home, but by the time she reached there was quite sick. Then she knew, from the appearance of her hand and the way she felt, that she must have been bitten by one of the poisonous spiders that infest the country. So I went out and gathered some cockle-bur leaves and made the poultice, giving her the half cup of tea, when she was relieved.

### FROM CHAPTER II: THE FIRST MIGRATION TO THE INDIAN TERRITORY

## [US Government Treachery and the Trail of Tears]

In the early years of 1800 the hereditary rulers of the Cherokees, realizing that they were not to be permitted to continue their old form of government, began to consider how they might save themselves and their own self-government from the encroachments of the whites. In 1817 they made a treaty, and in 1819 the Old Settlers, or "Western Cherokees," my grandfather, John D. Chisholm, being one of the leaders, made a treaty and moved west, settling on the Spadra and Arkansas Rivers, where they made farms and homes for themselves and cabins for their slaves, most of the first settlers being well-to-do slave-owners.

My mother told me that while the folks were making this move to the west, on one occasion a large party of them came by way of an old-fashioned, noisy, high-pressure steamboat, which could be heard for miles away. A considerable number of mountain men, who had never seen such a boat, hearing the noise, concluded that it was some strange monster. So, getting their guns, they went out in a body to the river, determined on war to the knife, when they were amazed to find instead a boat full of their own countrymen.

In 1819 the whole Cherokee population had been estimated at 15,000, one-third of them being west of

[4] Oklahoma.

the Mississippi, but over one hundred years before that time they had been estimated to have 50,000 warriors. In 1825 the census of the Eastern Nation showed: Native Cherokees, 13,563; white men intermarried with the nation, 147; white women married into the nation, 73; negro slaves, 1,277.[5] The people had large herds of cattle, horses, hogs, and sheep, with large crops of every staple. Simultaneously with the decrees establishing a national press in the Cherokee language (Sequoyah's invention), the Cherokee Nation, in general convention of delegates held for the purpose at New Echota, July 25, 1827, adopted a national constitution based on their distinct and independent nationality. John Ross was president of the convention which framed the constitution. Charles R. Hicks, a Moravian convert and at that time the most influential man in the nation, was elected the Principal Chief, and Ross was the assistant. As has been shown in this narrative, the Cherokees had an old code of laws, fixed by the seven clans, from the earliest days of that race of men, and all the clans met once a year to be given a true understanding of those laws.

The old Cherokee laws were better for that early people than those of today. Their fixed laws were best suited to them. The Ross party wanted to make a new set of laws, and the project received the warm encouragement of President Jefferson.[6] It was with the understanding that the two parties – the Old Settlers and the Eastern Cherokees – were to be reunited as one nation, that the western emigration was first officially recognized a few years later. Immediately upon the return of the delegates from Washington, the Cherokees drew up their first brief written code of laws, modeled according to the friendly suggestion of Jefferson.

The Cherokees, however, with their independent self-government, were a thorn in the flesh to the people of the State of Georgia, and during President Jackson's administration things came to a climax, and, contrary to the pledges of the U. S. Government to them, Georgia decided to get rid of the Cherokees. When the Government found that it either had to sacrifice the Cherokees or use military force against the Georgians, they decided to compel the Cherokees to move west.

In 1698 the French estimate of the population of the Cherokees was 50,000 warriors. The Jesuit priest, Priber,[7] who made his home with them, was Secretary of State for the Chief and had a very fair knowledge of the facts as given by the French historians. As soon as the English knew of the French report, efforts were made to gain the Cherokee friendship. The treaty of 1730[8] was the result. Then began the encroachments of the colonists on the Indians, and they continued until the Cherokees were driven from their native land at the point of the bayonet. There were two scourges of smallpox and seven years or more of war against them; but at the end of that time the population is shown to be only 15,000, including all classes of citizens.

In 1835 President Jackson sent Rev. J. W. Schermerhorn to negotiate a treaty with the Eastern Cherokees; he submitted a form of treaty to them in October, 1835, which they unanimously rejected. In December, 1835, Schermerhorn called a mass meeting, unauthorized by the Cherokee law and unattended by the Cherokee people, except a very small number induced to come by promises. On December 31, 1835, Schermerhorn secured the signatures of a number of Cherokee citizens, inducing them to sign this pretended treaty under which the land east of the Mississippi River was sold to the United States for five millions of dollars, to be invested in various ways.[9] The Cherokee lands amounted to nearly eight million acres and were valued at that time at about $20,000,000.

The Cherokees protested against this pretended treaty vigorously, but to their great astonishment, although they presented a petition to the United States Senate signed by over 16,000 Cherokee

---

[5] For census figures at various periods of Cherokee history, see Mooney 34, 123, 125, 155.

[6] Jefferson believed that the Cherokees could be assimilated into the mainstream of US culture, which meant, of course, the transformation of their matrilineal traditions in which women were the agriculturalists into a patriarchal system of male farmers. See Perdue. Owen appears to be echoing Mooney's account of Jefferson's encouragement of the Cherokees (see Mooney, 113).

[7] Acting as an agent of the French, the Jesuit priest, Christian Priber, came to live with the Cherokees in 1736 (Mooney, 36–7).

[8] In the Treaty of Nequassee, negotiated by English representative Sir Alexander Cuming, the Cherokees allied themselves with the British.

[9] The Treaty of New Echota was signed on December 29, 1835; as Owen suggests, the US government achieved this treaty via an abuse of power. The most prominent signatories were Major John Ridge and Elias Boudinot, the former editor of the *Cherokee Phoenix*. Mooney remarks, "Neither John Ross nor any one of the officers of the Cherokee Nation was present or represented" (125).

names, urging the defeat of this pretended treaty, it was nevertheless ratified by the Senate, on the theory that the removal of the Cherokees was the only way to protect them from the violence of Georgia. Georgia had already passed laws very injurious and harmful to the Cherokees. Indeed, Georgia's laws were ruinous, imprisoning even missionaries who preached the gospel, and forbidding a Cherokee his right to appear as a witness in case of life and death. The unfortunate men who Schermerhorn induced to sign this treaty were afterwards ostracized by the Cherokees and a number of them assassinated.

A large part of the $5,000,000 agreed to be paid by this treaty (1835) was diverted by the United States for the expense of officials, and not paid per capita, as promised. In 1900 my son, Robert L. Owen, of Muskogee, Indian Territory, was engaged to collect this balance, and after a legal battle of six years, involving various acts of Congress, resolutions of Senate and House of Representatives, and hearings in committees of Congress, in the executive departments, and in the courts, he obtained a judgment in the Supreme Court of the United States for the balance due, which, with interest from 1838, amounted to about $5,000,000. The record of this case can be seen in the Congressional Library, in a volume he filed there, under the heading of Eastern Cherokees *vs.* United States.

Both the North and the South had been parties to the treaties made with the Cherokees, and the South was just as much pledged to those treaties as the North. If Georgia had been made at that time to respect the Federal treaties with the Cherokees, the Confederate war would never have sacrificed its millions of money and men. No wonder God permitted that war. The United States Government and its people, North and South, had need to be taught to see the truth of God's word, "With what measure ye mete, it shall be measured to you again."[10] Both North and South paid in blood and treasure for the cruelty and inhumanity and bad faith shown to the Cherokees in their removal from Georgia to the present Cherokee country. There was a decision of the Supreme Court in favor of the Cherokees by John Marshall, Chief Justice of the Supreme Court of the United States,[11] and Jackson said, "John Marshall has given his opinion, and now I would like to see him execute it." Jackson had little love, I think, for the Cherokees, and was willing to take the side of the Georgians.

The transportation of those people to the west was the most cruel piece of business you can imagine. The people were all running around from house to house, telling the news to each other, about how they were going to be picked up and taken by force and carried away, and the soldiers were ordered to capture them anywhere they found them, and take them to the camps, where they were concentrated. A wife might be taken to one of those places, a husband to another, and the children to a third, making the most cruel separation of families; and, as the detachments did not all go together, families were often separated so far that they never met again.

Hildebrand's detachment, at the end of the journey, stopped on my mother's homestead, near Beattie's Prairie; and these people, being transplanted from a warm climate, and having to live in open tents in January and to suffer the blizzards of that country in the winter, died in hosts. There were between fifty and a hundred of them buried in my father's graveyard, at Chisholm's Spring, a mile west of Maysville, Arkansas.[12]

## FROM CHAPTER III: CONCERNING MY FATHER, THOMAS CHISHOLM, AND PRESIDENT THOMAS JEFFERSON

### [My Father]

My father spoke the French and Cherokee languages as well as English. He was an energetic business man and had a very nice home in the old Cherokee Nation, about twenty miles east of Huntsville,

---

10 A variation of Matthew 7:2, Mark 4:24, and Luke 6:38.

11 Marshall (1755–1835) was Chief Justice from 1801 to 1835. The historic decision that he wrote in favor of the Cherokee land claims was ignored by Andrew Jackson.

12 Both Maysville (which is a contemporary town) and "Beattie's Prairie" were in the northwest corner of the state. Owen misspells Batie Prairie, named for the first known [white] settler on the Arkansas prairie.

Alabama; but when it was thought best to move west he walked out and left everything standing, and his property was taken possession of by the white settlers. The United States Government promised to pay my father for his improvements, but never a dollar has been received, and it still owes about $3,000 for them. My father went, with a large number of his people, to the lands located near Spadre, the name of a creek where the great coal mines are, on the Arkansas River, and I suppose not very far from Roseville, Arkansas. He was there until the time the Government let the Old Settler Cherokees have the present Territory, 1828.

Not far from Roseville, Arkansas, my maternal grandfather, William Wharton, lived, and one Christmas, while Thomas Chisholm had gone to the Old Nation on some business, grandfather insisted on my mother bringing her children and coming over the river to spend the holidays with him and their grandmother. While she was there with her father and mother her house was robbed and burned. That was the most fortunate Christmas she ever experienced; if she had been at home she would have been killed. She said that the cellar under her house had had a large quantity of sweet potatoes stored in it, and that when she went back, there was the largest roast of sweet potatoes that ever was known, but she was only thankful that it was her potatoes instead of herself and children that got the roasting. It was supposed that this deed was done by some cut-throat movers who were passing through the country. When my father returned from the Old Nation mother had already built a new house, and was ready to receive him.

Mother told me that when she moved from lower Arkansas to the present country, at Webbers Falls, about 1828, there was a really beautiful fall, nearly or quite across the whole of the Arkansas River, about three or four feet in height. The June rise of 1833 came with such terrific force and such a quantity of water that the falls were entirely buried in sand, and the flooding of the country made it very unhealthy there afterwards.

When the surveyors ran the line between the State of Arkansas and the Indian territory my father had accompanied the corps of engineers, had become well acquainted with the country, and found at Maysville a section beautifully watered, with the finest springs in the world. On account of the health of the region he concluded to move his family to Beaties Prairie. While the family were making the trip from Webbers Falls to that country, in November, 1833, the celebrated display of a meteoric shower occurred and frightened all of our colored servants nearly to death. They thought the world was surely coming to an end. Afterwards I remember hearing the colored people tell how the falling stars seemed to be coming right down on their heads, and then, much to their surprise, they would fall in the far distance, "The Lord only knows where."

The next November father went to council on the Illinois River, near where Tahlequah now stands, and was taken ill with typhoid fever. Mother, hearing of it, went for him and brought him home, but too late to be of any service to him. He died that same month, in the year 1834. During his illness, in order to give him quiet, mother had sent two colored nurses out with myself and little brother, when a messenger notified us of father's death.

The distress of the colored nurses was so great and their demonstrations of sorrow alarmed me in such a way that the scene was vividly impressed on my memory, though I was only three years old at that time.

At the graveyard, at the close of the funeral, the coffin was opened for the friends to have a last look, and I noticed that my mother and sister Jane were weeping, but my ignorance of death prevented me from appreciating the cause of their sorrow, though the whole scene filled my little heart with awe and was vividly impressed on my mind forever. They took me to see my father's face, and, though so young, I remember every peculiarity of his expression.

After our bereavement we were all scattered. My two brothers and sister Jane were sent to Dwight Mission school, at that time the best and only school, where the children had a home as well as instructions. For a while I was too young to go, but two years later my sister took me with her.

My mother used to tell me of my father's position as chief, and on one occasion, when she showed me my father's Jefferson medal, she said, "This," holding the medal in her hand, "was given to him in recognition of his being the king of his people," teaching me to have great respect and reverence for his memory.

## The Jefferson Medal

About March 4, 1808, President Thomas Jefferson gave a silver Peace and Friendship medal to Thomas Chisholm, he being the hereditary war chief of the Cherokees. Mr. Jefferson wished to promote friendship and peace with the Cherokees. My brother, Albert Finney Chisholm, inherited the above-mentioned medal, which was about four inches in diameter. In 1862, at Fort Gibson, Indian Territory, A. F. Chisholm died, and the medal disappeared from among his effects, and was not regained until March 28, 1905. A friend of my brother, Bluford W. Alberty, told me that a man who was present at the time of my brother's death appropriated this medal, and, attaching a brass ring to it by using soft solder, used it as a dangling ornament to his belt.

Nothing more was heard of it by the family until I saw the article in the *Evening Star* which had been copied from the *Kansas City Journal*. I recognized the description as being that of the medal of my father, and immediately opened a correspondence with the writer (Mr. E. Fancher of Snyder, Oklahoma). He had been out in the Wichita Mountains prospecting, when his dog chased a rabbit into a small hole in the mountain side, which, when examined, proved to be the mouth of a cavern, stones having been used to close the opening from the inside. When Mr. Fancher entered the cavern and made an investigation, he found the bones of a man, with an old flint-lock gun lying near him, three or four bars of lead, with a melting ladle for the manufacture of bullets, a frying pan, an old stone pipe – a rough Indian-looking affair – and the rust-eaten remains of what had been an iron or steel buckle, which had belonged to the man's belt. When the pieces of the buckle had been removed, underneath them, covered with rust, was found my father's Jefferson medal. All appearances indicated that these remains of the past had been resting there for at least forty years – just about the time that the medal had been lost. From the appearance of the medal, the rust had been burned into it, perhaps by leaves and prairie grasses being blown into the cavern during prairie fires.

After a year of correspondence, Mr. Fancher became convinced that we were the legitimate owners of the medal, and expressed it to my sister, Mrs. N. B. Breedlove, who recognized it on sight, having been accustomed to seeing it in her early childhood. She showed it to the Rev. W. A. Duncan, who knew my brother and knew about the Chisholm medal. He thought the medal must be mine, and sister Em felt sure of it: said she knew it the moment she looked at it. She expressed it to me at Caney, Kansas, and the instant I looked at it the days of my childhood were present and mother was again showing me my dead father's medal and teaching me to love and honor his memory as an hereditary ruler of his people and a noble father. Mrs. Breedlove being my half-sister (Judge William Wilson's daughter), the medal came by hereditary right to me.

## FROM CHAPTER IV: SOME RECOLLECTIONS OF MY EARLY LIFE

## [My Education; Desperate Characters Infesting the Western Country]

In 1829 old Dwight Mission, a Presbyterian mission school, that had been established in Arkansas, was moved to Kidron post-office, on Sallisaw Creek, in the Cherokee Nation. The Rev. and Mrs. Cephas Washburn, Mr. and Mrs. James Orr, Mr. and Mrs. Asa Hitchcock, Mr. and Mrs. Jacob Hitchcock, Miss Stetson, Miss Esther Smith, Miss Emeline Bradshaw (afterwards Mrs. Dr. Dodge, of Little Rock, Arkansas), and Miss Thrall composed the school faculty. They had many buildings there, with farms and gardens. The school for the boys was used as a church, and Dr. Washburn had his private home, as did all the other gentlemen and ladies who had charge of the school. Miss Stetson was the head of the young ladies' school department and home.

Here is where, about 1836, I had my first lesson in art; however, not from any of my teachers. I drew on my slate what I thought was a beautiful lady, giving her a low neck and short-sleeved dress, with lovely white neck and arms, when I was discovered neglecting my duty and made to stand up in the floor and hold my slate to show the school girls how idle I had been. Though my first efforts were so much denounced and I was punished, the art spirit remains in me to this day. Speaking of art reminds me that

I am not the only artist from old Dwight Mission. Dr. Washburn had three sons. The eldest, Woodward, may have had many talents, but I do not remember him very well; but the two younger brothers were talented. Henry Washburn was a poet of merit and Edward was a beautiful artist, and in the last few months the Sturm Magazine, of Oklahoma City, had a complimentary article in reference to his talents and some of his compositions.

My first lessons in knitting were given me at this school, Olivia Bushyhead and myself were knitting on the same pair of socks, and we were given a task of so many rounds to knit. We were not equal to the demands made on our industry and we were punished by not being permitted to go to our supper, down at the general dining hall. We naughty children were distressed at being left without our supper, but later we felt as if the good Lord had taken care of us, for while all of the girls and teachers were down at the dining hall refreshing themselves on hominy and milk, Jacob Bushyhead, Olivia's father, came, bringing us apples and cake; so that while the others ate their simple meal, we were faring sumptuously.

Possibly in this day we would have a management that would be superior to that early time, but the school did a great deal of good and many of the best families in the nation belong to the boys and girls educated at that institution. Later I went to what we called an old-field country school with puncheon seats (about 1840); had to walk a mile or two to and from the school being taught by an Irishman. One of his rules in the spelling classes was that the pupil who stood at the head of the spelling class had to keep the ferrule in his hand, and if any of the pupils missed a word he had to hold out the palm of his hand while the head of the class walked down and gave him a stroke with this ruler. The consequence was that the pupils were always trying to get even with the head of the class. This teacher used to be very lenient during the playtime, but the minute he said "Boo-o-ks!" we were in terror of having to balance accounts for every neglected duty. During 1883 or '84, when I was teaching at the Female Seminary at Tahlequah, I went one day to the insane asylum, and one of the inmates there recognized me and said, "Don't you remember that school at Mose Daniel's where you and I used to go to school together near Beatties Prairie? I burned up that schoolhouse to see the big fire."

The Beatties Prairie home country was beautifully watered by clear, flinty springs and streams running through it. There is where I had to walk a mile and a half to the Irishman's school that I mentioned, and there was the Mose Daniel school, which crazy John Daniel told me over forty years afterward he had burned down "just to see the beautiful fire." One of the sources of pleasure of my childhood was pulverizing the soft white stones (tripoli) out of which so many of these springs ran, making basins for the water and pretty play places for our dolls and "make-believe" housekeeping. Another pleasure was going on trips in search of the hazel-nuts and plums, the woods being full of them. It was a great country for summer grapes, much like the cultivated variety of Concord.

After the emigration from the Old Nation (1838), there was a band of desperate characters infesting the western country. One cold, glittering moonlight Christmas night (1845), three of these men had been to Maysville and gotten their usual amount of intoxicants, and they reached my sister's house about 12 or 1 o'clock at night. My sister Jane, thinking they were negroes who had come to entice the men on the place away to a dance, went out on the porch to prohibit them from interfering with the colored men, when she saw them lower two guns at her. She jumped inside her door and barred it, and where they shot at her there were marks of fourteen slugs on the floor of the porch. The men told her who they were, and then she knew that her only safety was in flight. She was alone, with the exception of a colored nurse and her two little girls, Mary and Alice Lynde. The colored nurse taking Alice and sister taking the older child in her arms, they began to make their escape from the house, since the men were already beating on the doors and windows with sticks of heavy cord-wood, determined to get in. She sent the nurse ahead and she, following, in some mysterious way caught her clothes on the latch of the door, tearing them all down the back and slamming the door shut with great violence. The robbers heard the door slam and ran around the house to come in. Finding the door shut, they presumed she was inside. They immediately proceeded to hunt her, and went into a closet under the stairway, where there was a large pile of soiled clothes ready for the wash. Sister heard the men cursing her, for they thought they had found her hid under the clothes. She didn't wait to hear any more, but ran through the thick orchard, which concealed her from sight, and made her escape to a neighbor's.

She didn't realize at the time that she was hurt, the excitement was so great, but as soon as she got into the house and took her seat, somebody noticed that something was on the floor, and it was discovered that her feet were bleeding at a frightful rate, making her unable to wear her shoes for three months.

It seems that these men had heard that Mr. Lynde had been on a collecting tour. He was the sutler at Fort Wayne.[13] They imagined that they would get a good lot of money. However, the only money in the house was in sister's dress pocket, and in rummaging the house they had thrown that dress out into the yard. Everything in the house had been thoroughly searched for the money they had expected to find.

They brought in wood from the porch and built up a big fire in an open fireplace and pushed the bed up in front of it. Bringing a grindstone that was out in the yard where the negro men sharpened their axes, they had ground their knives and hatchets inside my sister's bed-room before this big fire, making themselves comfortable. Granny Jenny heard the shots and waked up all the women and children in her house, and made them take their bed-clothes and go and hide in the brush, saying, "Miss Jane done killed or gone, so hurry and hide yourselves."

People used to be in terror of their lives from these desperate characters, and we were always looking out for them. I learned to hate the singing of the katydids and the grasshoppers and the other noisy insects at night that prevented us from hearing the approach of the intruders. One night at my mother's place, about the same year (1845), two drunken men rode up in front of the house and began firing. Fortunately there were a lot of men at home – my brothers and stepfather – and when the marauders found that the women and children were protected they made hot haste away. Our men pursued them, but did not overtake them. My remembrance of this period of my life is not of a character to give steady nerves to man or woman.

## FROM CHAPTER V: MEMORIES OF CLINCH RIVER AND LYNCHBURG

### Life on Clinch River, at Evan's Bridge

While he [Colonel Owen] was running the survey from Asheville to Cumberland Gap we lived for a while at Tazewell, a little mountain town and county-seat. The hotel being small, whenever court time came everybody occupying certain rooms had to move. (Those rooms were said to be lawyer Such-an-one's room and lawyer Another-one's room, and no one could keep them when court was in session.) I happened to be one of the unfortunates and had to get out, and as I didn't wish to sleep on the floor or be inconvenienced I suggested to Colonel Owen that I had noticed a very pleasant place down at Evan's Bridge, on Clinch River. There was a kind of country boarding-house there, and I found Mr. and Mrs. Hamilton Evans very pleasant people. They had four daughters and a son. The girls all had been educated at Salem, North Carolina, and it occurred to me that with a nice piano in the house and so many nice girls, I would rather live in the country than in town; so the corps of engineers moved down to Evans' Bridge, as it was called, with Colonel Owen when he gave up the rooms in Tazewell, and we made our home there as long as they were surveying the railroad.

This home was a pleasant kind of wild, romantic place, with the river making a wide, grand circle around it. It was most picturesque, being very secluded, four or five miles from other settlements, and when we had visitors it was usual for them to stay always two or three days.

On one occasion when the engineers were at home, and we had two or three visiting young ladies, the party concluded that they would go bathing at a deep place in the river called the Cat-hole, where the water was very deep, though so limpid that ledges of stone could be seen almost across the river, and the girls who couldn't swim went wading out on these ledges in most dangerous-looking places. None of the party could swim except myself, and when they were all ready to start on their bathing expedition they sent for me to join them, but I excused myself, preferring to stay at home with Colonel Owen, who was a kind of visitor, only coming home to write up the engineer's notes and to put the books and profiles in order. Very soon after the girls had gone on the bathing trip Colonel Owen concluded to go

[13] A sutler was a merchant who followed an army and sold provisions to the soldiers.

fishing. I preferred to go swimming. In that way I at once put on my bathing suit and followed the girls to the above-mentioned Cat-hole, only stopping on the bank of the river long enough to drop the suit that I was going to wear home, following two of the girls that were wading across the river. I followed, swimming, and as I did so, when about twenty feet from them, I noticed that Eliza Evans was going up and down in the water, and then I saw her catch hold of her sister Lucy, who at once went up and down likewise.

I then saw they were in water over their heads, and I hurried to them, and as Lucy came up I saw that she was terribly frightened, and I said, "Don't be alarmed; I am coming," and then she reached her hand to me as far as she could tip. I felt for the depth of the water, and I found it up to my mouth, but, fortunately for me and them, I extended my hand as far as possible and our fingers tipped and our hands clinched. Then their weight drew me over to them, in twelve feet of water. With only one hand to swim and two well-grown girls suspended from the other, I did the most vigorous swimming that woman ever did before or since. I suppose that I was sinking with them, but I had gotten back on the ledge of rocks where they had been wading, one of my feet touching the stone, and I proceeded to stand up at once, and found the water up to my arm pits. Then, with the assistance of Lucy, who hadn't been under for the third time, we managed to hold Eliza up until she could catch her breath. As soon as I had caught hold of the girls I called to those on the bank who were watching us. Realizing that we were in the grip of death, I said, "We are all gone!" but I kept my free hand making heavy swimming strokes, and we were glad enough to wade back to the shore. With this experience ended our river bathing.

Realizing how the mother of the young ladies would be distressed over the incident, we all pledged ourselves not to tell at the house how near we were to being drowned, but of course the excitement and the expression of our faces gave Mrs. Evans a clue that she followed up, when she soon had the whole story out of them. I had gone to my room on the upper floor to dress when I heard the little old lady coming up the steps in a most excited manner. As she entered my room she exclaimed, "Mrs. Owen, I know you are an angel! I know you are an angel!"

She was a good Presbyterian, and believed in predestination. My following the girls did seem as if it was most providential. If I had been one instant later in reaching them they surely would have been drowned. I tried to cheer up the old lady, and laughed and told her that I thought she had rather a bad angel to help her.

This occurred when my son, Robert L. Owen, Jr., was an infant of six months. If I had been drowned that day, Colonel Owen would have been left with two babes to care for, because when I held out my hand to those girls I had but one idea, and that was to save their lives. If I had stopped to reason that I had a six-months' old infant at home, I would have had to draw a line between a mother's love and duty to strangers. I guess it is a good thing that there are times in our lives when emergencies arise that we have but one thought, and that an unreasoning impulse, as in this instance, to save life.

Evan's Bridge was one of the most pleasant homes I ever had. We had parties there – just the corps of engineer and the young ladies of the house, with two or three young ladies of the neighborhood. We would all play on the piano for each other to dance, and many a concert and many a dance we had in that pleasant social circle four miles from any neighbor. I considered it one of the most fortunate moves I ever made to be located there in preference to the village.

All of us had our riding horses, and on one occasion Lucy, one of the girls that I saved from drowning, and a neighbor, Lizzie Shultz, who had been visiting us, started out riding, and Lucy and I were going to accompany Lizzie home. When we had gone about a mile and a half we met a party of movers, with two or three white-covered wagons, the kind that we call out West "prairie schooners." There were a number of women and four or five men in the party, along with their cattle and horses, and each and all of them seemed to think that they had some right to enter into conversation with us as we passed. One man seemed to be drunk. After going beyond them some distance I spoke to Lucy Evans, and said to her I thought we ought to go back, that I would be afraid to pass those people if it were a little later; so we turned about, after going pretty near home with Lizzie.

As we came up to these people they were in the act of shooting some kind of game in a tree. I spoke to the man and asked him if he wouldn't be good enough to allow us to pass before he shot, as our horses were a little wild and I was afraid for him to shoot. He said, "You've no business to ride such fine horses. I'd like to trade with you." We laughed at the kind of drunken joke of the man, and all of the women had some remark to make about our horses. So we passed them, and just as we thought we had gotten a safe distance beyond them, we looked back and one of those impudent fellows had gotten on a riding horse and was in full pursuit of us. Lucy turned deadly pale, and I thought she was going to faint, and just as the man rode up I said to her, "Don't be frightened; I am not afraid."

The man said he had come to ride with us. His impertinence made me so angry that I shook my riding whip in his face and gave him peremptory orders to march on. He saw how angry I was, and I don't know but that he thought I had a pistol. We were going through a very narrow gorge, with just enough room for the road, with mountains on both sides of us, and there was no getting away from him. I guess that fellow never had such positive orders to move on before in his life. He obeyed, but muttered as he did so. We were glad to know we were not far from the bridge, and as soon as the man came in sight of it he took the road down the river to a fording place, and we went on over the bridge home, the house being in full view. The man then knew that we had some one to defend us and asked no more of our company.

The winter after this occasion was frightfully cold, and though the Clinch River was a very rapid stream it was frozen over. Finally there came a sudden warm spell and heavy rains with it, breaking up all at once the ice on the river, making it look like a live body that went floating and rolling outward, turning over and over, like the wheels of some great vessel, and came near wearing away the bridge piers. It was the most magnificent ice display I ever witnessed. There was a terrific force expressed in the rushing onward of the moving mass. There was no show of the water, only the mad rush of the crushed and broken river of ice. A more awe-inspiring sight could hardly be imagined.

## Making Confederate Uniforms

During the first year of the war there was a large encampment of soldiers near Lynchburg, recruits for the Confederacy. They had enlisted down in Georgia, Alabama, and Tennessee, and had been mustered into service dressed just as they were, in their rough mountain and farm clothes. So the Lynchburg ladies, five hundred strong, banded together to try and provide uniforms as well as hospital supplies for them. The Confederate Government provided us with large quantities of bonsack gray, from the mills above Lynchburg, for the uniforms and piles of white goods for the other supplies. We met in the large hall of the old Masonic Building and worked like beavers. We gave out a great deal of the work to the wives and daughters of the poorer soldiers around Lynchburg so as to help them to provide the necessities of life. It soon became one of my duties to give out this sewing and to receive it again from the women who did the work. I would count it in, and then give them an order on the treasurer for whatever was due them.

We made quantities of clothing, and were, of course, very proud of our work. But I will never forget the morning after our first company had been equipped with uniforms. Their captain marched them to drill in front of my house, to show off the new uniforms. They marched up and down with the sleeves of their gray shirts flapping about five inches over their hands. They were ordered to ground arms, and stood waving their sleeves like the arms of windmills. There was nothing for us to do but to have all the shirts returned to the hall and proceed to shorten the sleeves. This uniforming continued as long as the Confederate Government needed such volunteer assistance, for gradually they took charge of such things themselves, and by degrees the ladies retired from taking an active part in the work.

But we still had the wives and children of the soldiers of Lynchburg on our hands, and a few of the ladies made it their duty, as well as their pleasure, to look after the welfare of these people as best we could. Mrs. Kirkpatrick, the mother of Hon. Thomas Kirkpatrick, who afterward succeeded my husband as State Senator from the Eleventh District of Virginia, and myself, were the last two to resign our services. There was no longer any work to be obtained for these women, but friends of the cause contributed money for their help. This money was turned over to me, and I in turn put it in the hands of one of our local grocery men; so when the women came to me in distress I could write them an order for whatever they needed that could be obtained at his store. We had before this time given up the large hall, and toward the last we met in a room on Church street, opposite the Arlington Hotel. Finally Mrs.

Kirkpatrick came to me and said, "Mrs. Owen, I believe that you can do all that is necessary to be done now." So we gave up the room, and I had the women come to my home until the end of the war, and we endeavored to render them every assistance in our power and in the power of other friends.

Immediately after this, when Lee surrendered, there was a large class of persons who were desperately poor, and, disregarding all conditions and defying law, helped themselves wherever they could to the Confederate commissaries.

One morning Wirt Roberson, our dining-room man, said; "Mars Robert, I would like some market money." "Look on the sofa and you will find some in my pants' pocket." "But they are not here, sir." In the search they were found, with both pockets rifled, Colonel Owen's valuable railroad watch gone, his coat in one place, his vest in another, and his pants in a third. By that time we were thoroughly aroused. Then I recalled having heard the noise of an opening window, when some one must have entered our room. Knowing that Colonel Owen was a restless man, often getting up in the night and reading his sleepless hours away, I had taken the noise as being made by him, and I had asked in a dreamy voice, "Did you open the window to let in the morning light?" The noise made by the invaders must have prevented their hearing me and braining both Colonel Owen and myself. But we both slept soundly through the time of the robbery.

Not long after this affair (1866) I was walking one day in my garden when I discovered a set of holes bored through a plank in the back of my smoke-house, which was full of nice bacon and other provisions. I called Uncle Humphrey Shelton (an old family pet of Colonel Owen's). The old man looked and said, "Miss Ciss, robbers done that last night. About the time they were boring these holes they must have been frightened away by Dr. and Mrs. Owen coming from the party." We agreed to play a trick on the thieves. Every piece of meat was packed away in a large store-room, leaving the smoke-house entirely empty, but well locked, and James Waller, instead of the police, was set to watch the results and to frighten and run the thieves away.

The morning came and the plank had been torn away and an entrance made, only to find themselves cheated out of their booty. James's house was on a line with the smoke-house and only 8 or 10 feet away. The thieves consisted of seven men, good stout fellows, as James reported. First one came on the garden side of his house, then the second on the other side, until the seven found themselves in the empty smoke-house. James concluded not to meet them in the dark, and to take daylight to acquaint the household with the result of his guardianship. Though he did not choose to meet them, since he knew he would be overpowered, he enjoyed the prank played on them by Uncle Humphrey and "Miss Ciss."

Uncle Humphrey was a good old Baptist preacher for forty years, and after the war Colonel Owen gave him a home with us until the night he died of apoplexy. One of his grandsons came rushing into our room the night he died to hurry Colonel Owen to him, saying. *"De witches is done ridin' him, suh!"* On going to his room Colonel Owen found the old man dead, but before burial he paid twenty dollars to have a crayon likeness made of him by Mr. Fisher, an artist of Lynchburg. That sketch is now in the possession of Major W. O. Owen, U.S.A.

After the Confederate war, when the North and South had kissed and made friends, our colored brothers began to look around and wonder how the new order of things was going to work. Uncle Humphrey Shelton retired because of age; Westley Lucas, and his half-brother, James Waller, all had at various times in their lives been office men for old Dr. William Owen and Dr. W. Otway Owen, of Lynchburg, Virginia, and incidentally had been gardeners and care-takers of the teams of the doctors whenever they came home from their rounds of drives among their patients in the country or city.

For years Uncle Humphrey had been associated in Colonel Owen's mind with childhood, when Humphrey's wife was the family cook. They were both most kindly remembered for their faithfulness to the children and home duties. The cook had long ago gone to her reward in the land of spirits, but Uncle Humphrey remained to teach and preach to his colored friends, and was a family pet, bossing the garden and grounds at his own free will. James Waller was the gardener, and, knowing Uncle Humphrey had the inside track to the family heart, sent him to me to inquire what kind of arrangements, under the new order of labor, we would make. "Well, Uncle Humphrey there is no need for James to get his information second hand; send him to me, and I will be glad to talk over the situation with him." When he made his appearance I said, "Whatever will be right as wages for a gardener, I am willing to give you;

but your wife and children I have always taken care of, in sickness and health, giving them their board and clothes and a comfortable home. You and Milly talk things over, and see if you think you can do better. When you have concluded what to do, let me know your decision."

A few days later they had rented a house and came to bid me good-bye. They were going to house-keeping. When they came I said, "James, what have you to do?" "Oh, nothing, mum; nothin." "But," I said, "man, that is not the way to do. You have a wife and children to support now, and you must have work to make a living for yourself and them. Don't you think you had better keep my garden until you can find work which will pay you better?" "That's a fact, Miss Ciss," he said, after putting his hands to his head and thinking a while. "Yes, ma'am, I will work the garden and do the best I can." For one year he remained with me in this capacity. At the end of this time I gave him a letter of recommendation, which proved to be a good thing for himself and family, getting him a position with the railroad, which he kept till he died. He was a good man and a true Christian.

While in a boarding-house in Lynchburg with Mr. and Mrs. Abram Biggers, one cold morning at breakfast time there was a very bright coal fire, and their eldest daughter stood before it warming herself. Incidentally, her dress became overheated, and as she suddenly turned before the glowing coals her skirt touched them and immediately went up ablaze. I was the first to see her, and made a rush for her, and was successful in smothering the fire; but though I had been successful in saving her from being burned, I had burned my own hands badly. Fortunately for myself a servant entered with a pitcher of ice water just at the instant I needed it most. Running both hands down into the ice water seemed to take the fire from my burns, and prevented my hands from being seriously injured.

## The King Story

During the Confederate war an employee of the Virginia and Tennessee Railroad (a Mr. King) bought of Judge Daniel, father of Senator J. W. Daniel, a small-one-roomed cottage and lot, and had paid nearly all the purchase-money except one hundred dollars when he died, leaving a wife, two small boys, and a little girl about four or five years.

The King cottage was near the front gate of my home (Point of Honor), on Daniel Hill. Jack King and his brother used often to be in the rock battles among the Daniel Hill boys, and in that way the King family became known to me in rather an unpleasant manner, though after all they were not as bad as some other boys on the hill, and with their widowed mother and little sister, they had my sympathy. Finally Mrs. King was taken very ill with typhoid fever and hysteria, and the children were all too young to do anything for their own support. The good neighbors all around, who knew she was ill, in charity took care of the children and sat up at night, caring for the sick. Mrs. King was ill for nine weeks, and all the good neighbors were worn out with the care of the poor woman and her children.

It occurred to me to hire a girl to stay all the time with Mrs. King, and I found an orphan girl, Bettie, from Amherst Heights, who was so ignorant that she had never heard of such a personage as Jesus Christ. There I found a little more missionary work to do. Bettie was all right under instructions, so between the neighbors, Bettie and myself doing faithful work, our invalid got well enough to resume home and motherly duties. When Mrs. King was first taken ill with the fever she had a fine suit of rich brown hair, which I knew would be ruined in a long spell of fever, and would be bad for her comfort; so, without consulting any one in regard to the matter, I cut it all off, only leaving the entire suit about one inch long all over her head. I knew how to make the long hair into braids or switches, so while I was cutting her hair I carefully kept each lock straight and in order, and when I saw her comfortable I carried her hair home with me and made it into two fine braids, selling them for fifty dollars each in Confederate money.

In the last of her illness she became rigid, and for thirty-six hours she remained as stiff as a corpse, and of course I thought she must die. Father McGuirk came to see her while in that condition. Of course he thought as I did – that she must soon die. That was late Saturday evening, and he said that Sunday morning his duties at church would prevent his coming to give her the last rites of the church and we both thought it would be better, as there seemed no hope of her recovery, to do so at once. Then he proceeded to give her extreme unction, and left me with the dying patient. I looked up on the hill and saw Dr. William Otway Owen on his way home. I called for him and got a last prescription for my patient (blisters for her wrists and ankles). I then left her for the night with the neighbors, with directions what to do for her. In the early morning I returned, expecting to see a corpse, and was greeted by her in this wise, "Good morning, Mrs. Owen," in a clear tone of voice. She seemed quite refreshed by her long rigid sleep.

She soon recovered from her illness. Then I talked business with her. In early girlhood she had been a factory girl in New England, and I advised her to go to Judge Daniel, to whom was due one hundred dollars. I then gave her the hundred dollars *made by the sale of her own hair,* and told her to get the deed to her house and leave the godfather of her children to collect the rent for her, and to return to the New England factories, where she could get work, and to send all her children to the public schools. She did just as I suggested to her, and ten years later she returned to Lynchburg. Dora King was then a young woman, and she and her mother came to call on me, and Mrs. King presented me with a box of a dozen spools of gorgeous-colored silk thread as a token of her gratitude, just like the true Irish heart in her. Jack and his brother were then young men and Dora was a young lady.

## FROM CHAPTER VI: THE AUTHOR AS MOTHER AND TEACHER – VICISSITUDES

### [Return to the Cherokee Nation; Seminary Experiences]

I then considered the matter of going to the Cherokee Nation, of which I was a citizen. Col. Wm. Penn Adair, whom Robert had met in Washington, suggested that he go to the Cherokee Nation, and I encouraged him to do so, because he was entitled to citizenship there and my kinspeople were there.

In 1879 I went with him to pay a visit to my relations, and while there I asked a position of the Board of Education in the Cherokee Female Seminary. My niece, Lelia Breedlove, who had been given a position in the school, insisted that I had been appointed, but I had received no official notice of it, and, as I felt that I couldn't afford to hold my hands, after spending the summer with my kinspeople, I went back to Virginia and resumed my class in Lynchburg.

Lelia had been so positive of my having been appointed that I concluded the polite thing to do was write a note to the Board of Education, telling them what I had heard, and explain to them how I couldn't afford to be idle – was compelled to work – but if they had really given me the appointment I would be glad to return to the Nation to live. The next year, in 1880, I returned and the Board of Education sent me my appointment, which I was very glad to receive.

Some of my Seminary experiences I will relate. Many of them are better forgotten, but the world has gone on, and as a nation I think my people have become much wiser and have had wholesome experiences in governmental matters.

One morning at the seminary some one came into my music-room and told me that Florence Fowler, one of my pupils, had had a chill. I supposed that it was the ordinary chills that we had in that country, which are usual with what we call chills and fever. I was very busy all day teaching, but when night came Lelia Breedlove, my niece, who was also a teacher, and I went to see Florence. We found her seriously ill with pneumonia in both lungs and the doctor four miles away.

She was delirious with fever, and we concluded to try and use a remedy that had been recommended to my sister in a case of pneumonia, "the potato poultice." The next thing to do was to get the materials required, these being potatoes and earth. There was a terrible storm and everything was covered with sleet, and it was very cold outside. The question was, how could we get any earth to put into our poultice. Lelia went down into the Seminary store-room and found a quart of white potatoes, while I looked around, thinking what I could do, being determined to get the needed earth. In my search I found a flower-pot in one of the windows, which had belonged to one of the school-girls. The plant was dry and dead, so I proceeded to get my earth out of the pot. Then Lelia boiled the potatoes in a tin wash-basin on her stove, after which we mashed them, using a sufficient quantity of the boiling water to cream them nicely. Then, I mixed in the dry earth, and we had prepared a thin bag of cheese-cloth large enough to cover the whole chest of our patient; so we put on the poultice, covering her up to the very throat in it, as hot as she could bear it.

We got it on about nine o'clock, and then sat with her till midnight, when her fever had gone down entirely and she went to sleep, resting quietly until about seven o'clock the next morning, when one of the girls came for me in great haste. Florence had commenced to expectorate, and one of her roommates handed her a large white wash-bowl, and when I reached the room she was expectorating a bloody mucous, which had frightened her terribly. When I came in I felt alarmed for her myself, but I could not afford to let her see how I felt; so I said to her, "Last night both your lungs were terribly inflamed, so go ahead now and clean them out and get rid of all this phlegm; then you'll be all right." My assurances satisfied her and relieved her of the alarm she had been suffering. After a few hours she was thoroughly relieved, and felt so well that she wanted to get up and dress herself. I refused to allow her to do so, because I thought it would be very imprudent, as she might take more cold. But the next morning she was up and dressed at an early hour, and the fourth day afterwards she took her Christmas holiday by going thirty miles in an open wagon, and was not troubled any more with that cold.

We had many funny experiences. We were four miles from our doctor and the sick nurse, Aunt Cynthia Mayes, used to laugh and say that I was her "first assistant." One night one of the girls, while half asleep, thought she would get through a window into an upper hallway. Instead of that she climbed out of her window into an open porch, falling about 16 feet and dislocating both her shoulder and her hip. The sick nurse sent for me at once and I discovered that the girl's shoulder was out of joint and proceeded to replace it.

I suppose I was a careless "assistant." I didn't investigate her injuries enough to find out that the hip was also injured, and when the doctor came he didn't seem to be any wiser than myself, and left the dislocated hip-joint, which resulted in making her a cripple for life.

My second experience was going on a picnic with fifteen or twenty of the girls in wagons, and while going down a steep, rocky hill, the driver going at break-neck speed the wagon bounced over a big stone, pitching one of the girls, who was sitting in a chair, out, and the wheel ran over her shoulders, breaking her collar-bone on both sides. The doctor being so far away, I had to set the girl's bones and to sit on the ground for an hour, holding them in place, until the doctor reached us and bandaged the patient.

On another occasion one of the girls cut her foot on a piece of glass across the main joint of the big toe, and, as usual, I was sent for, being the "Auntie" of the establishment and the "assistant" sick nurse and expected to do all kinds of things. I proceeded to get my needle and thread, and, without the use of any antiseptic or anything but the clean needle and thread, put in a number of stitches. Fortunately the result was entirely satisfactory.

I found that not only the girls used to call on the "Auntie" of the school, but on the first day of April, 1881, all the girls determined they would play a big April-fool trick on the principal; so before breakfast about two-thirds of the school ran away going on a kind of picnic trip without permission. Then the principal sent for me in great tribulation, to ask what on earth she should do, as she couldn't think of expelling two-thirds of the school. "Why," said I, "that's all right. This is Friday and you haven't girls enough to keep school today. Just let Miss James and myself take charge of the remaining girls and you give them a holiday for today. Tomorrow, being Saturday, ring your school bell at the regular hour and make them all go to school for the day. Don't give any indications of your knowledge of their having played truant, nor any information as to what you are going to do tomorrow."

So Miss James and I got a quantity of lunch for the girls, and then we went down on the little stream near Mr. George Murrell's place, and the girls had a wild, free day of it, gathering wild onions and such wild flowers as were out at that time. I took the onions which the girls had gathered and went to one of the neighbors and bought eggs, having the onions cooked, which have here a delicate, delicious flavor, and served them with scrambled eggs. All seemed to have a very nice dinner of it, and the novelty of the thing seemed more refreshing than any dessert that could have been served up at the school. By three o'clock in the afternoon they were all pretty well tired and more than willing to return to school. None of the teachers took any notice of what had happened. Nothing was said to any of the girls, and they couldn't imagine what was in store for them. They thought things were not going exactly in the usual way and were perfectly amazed the next morning when the school bell rang and they had to go to school on Saturday and take their share of April fooling. As far as I personally know, this was the last April-fool prank of the Seminary girls.

The Cherokees have a large school fund, bearing 5 percent interest, which is used to support the schools. The seminaries are supported by this income, which belongs to all the people, and the male and female seminaries, as these schools are called, took care of one hundred children, free of charge, furnishing them not only their tuition and books, but their board and clothes as well. The money, belonging to all alike was not so much of a charity as it seems at first sight, the recipients being part owners of the fund. These children were called primaries; all others paid their board.

For some reason, in the winter of 1882–83 the Council decided to let out the boarding and clothing of these children by contract, but the result wasn't quite as satisfactory as the teachers and boarders wished, and I used to keep in my private room what I called "my kitchen," which was a manufactured seat, to all intents and purposes, but inside of it were kept pies, bread and butter, etc., and there was a set of girls who knew all about this establishment and would come up for dessert after their meals. Aunt Eliza Alberty would furnish us with these delicacies for our kind of sub-rosa dining-room annex, where the initiated could come and get refreshed. One year of the contract satisfied not only the National Council, but all the people as well. After that year we went back to the original way of paying for everything needed for a comfortable home. [. . . ]

I was at the Seminary four and one-half years and had many experiences – good, bad, and indifferent. One of the things that happened was caused by some person thinking I had an over-amount of self-esteem. In my absence they had gone into my music-room and had written in a bold hand on the blackboard: "Nothing among women shows a lack of knowledge like thinking she hath it." So I wrote my reply underneath in equally as bold a hand: "Nothing among *men* or women is so contemptible as a sneak." Having only a suspicion as to who the writer was, I went to Mr. Reese, who was in charge of the culinary department, and told him that while I was at church on Sunday some one had gone into my teaching-room and had written on the blackboard, and that my answer was there waiting for them, knowing he would surely tell the writer. The answer was about as effective as the remedy used for stopping the April-fool business. The blackboard in my room had no more words of wisdom placed there for my benefit.

One of the amusing incidents was as follows: Some of the girls standing at the front gate, which was some distance away from the building, about dusk, saw little Eliza Wilson and Jennie Breedlove playing dolls at the front garret window, and, knowing that the garret was not used for the school, they concluded at once that witches were there, and so reported to Mrs. Breedlove, the matron. A search was then made of the garret, and of course nothing was found. I then went into the room where the witches were supposed to be and gave as near as I could a dying yell of a supposed witch. That voice sent all the witch-hunters screaming downstairs. When they found I had only made sport of their witch story and had the laugh against them, that was the end of the faith in witches. I assured them that the dying cry that they heard was that of the last Cherokee "spook," as I had swallowed it. If an Indian hates anything more than to be laughed at, I have yet to find out what it is.

## A New Variety of Burglar

In the Cherokee Nation, when summer comes, at night it is the usual thing to leave every door open, only putting chairs in the doors to keep out the family dogs. My kinswoman, who for many years had a country home near Muldrow, Indian Territory, was used to leaving her doors open at night to get the cool air. Always in the Indian Country that custom worked very well, but later she and her husband, John, bought a home in Fort Smith, Arkansas, where they could have better school advantages for their family. John still kept his business home at Muldrow, and the trains he was accustomed to come home on were always midnight affairs. Mrs. John, as usual, left her doors open for the cool air. She heard a slight noise one night and said, "Is that you John?" "Yes honey," was the reply, and, a most unusual thing, the supposed John walked up to the bed and gave her a kiss. Calling her "Honey" was not her John's mode of salutation, and the kiss brought a frightened, hysterical scream. The burglar vanished, the scream brought the family from above. The hysterics increased, Mrs. John screaming, *"Water! Water! Wet Water!"* as reported by her brother. That kiss had to be washed off in hot haste. When the true John arrived, a few minutes later, it was found that Mr. Burglar had been upstairs and emptied all the pockets and taken such jewels as pleased his fancy. The Fort Smith burglar is a new specimen of that profession. If you want a demonstration of affection, he is your man. [. . .]

The Muskogee fairs were one of our pastimes. At one of them I happened to be a kind of queen bee of the women's department. Among the exhibits from the extreme west of the Territory was an Indian man's beaded suit (leggings, shirt, and moccasins). While paying the prize money to the owner, I asked the Indians if they knew the difference between the whites and the Indians in the matter of their dress? When no one answered I told them that it was this: A white man would work himself to death to make his wife look pretty, while an Indian woman would do the same thing, and in addition nearly put her eyes out with this beadwork to make her husband outshine all the other fellows. It is said that Indians do not laugh, but that is certainly a mistake.

## FROM CHAPTER IX: BEING A MISCELLANEOUS CHAPTER CONCERNING MANY PERSONS AND THINGS

### from Home at the Metropolitan

In the first of my home life at the Metropolitan Hotel,[14] when Mr. William Selden was the proprietor, I enjoyed seeing a number of presidential parades on Pennsylvania Avenue, Cleveland, Harrison, and McKinley being among the number. When any favorite would pass, an immense concourse of onlookers would set up a yell of appreciation, and when Fitzhugh Lee passed on horseback there was a greater explosion of joy than when the new President passed in review. Evidently the crowd was largely Southern, and Fitzhugh was honored as a representative of the family of Gen. Robert E. Lee. At least that seemed to be the opinion of all who were near me and enjoying the grand procession of the most noted men of our forty-five States.

From the Riggs House I saw Theodore Roosevelt and the notables of the day with him in the last presidential procession. A new feature of the procession was the introduction of Indians, representing the wild tribes from the Western plains and Oklahoma. Decidedly the most artistically dressed American figures were the four Indian chiefs on horseback, dressed in their native costume, with their heads bedecked with their gorgeous war bonnets. These Indians seemed to form a body-guard for the President, following so closely in his wake. Artistically speaking, they were picturesque beyond expression.

### from Some Family Data

[...] I have referred to my connections to show how broad they have been, although I was a Cherokee citizen by blood and was born and reared among the Cherokees. The Cherokees are in like manner connected with families all over the United States [. . . .] I have always felt a pride in my father's people, the Cherokees – in their mental capability, in their natural nobility, in their great courage and resolution, in their native generosity and integrity, and in their patriotism. They are a warm and generous hearted people.

While I have deplored the aggressions on the Cherokees, yet it seems to be the providence of God that they should have been merged into the full citizenship of the new State to be, and I fully expect to see them prove entirely equal to the demands of the new conditions. Any failure on their part to do so would be a great grief to me and a disappointment.

### from Some Things I Have Enjoyed

In bringing these memoirs to a close I recall with gratitude the great number of good friends I have enjoyed and of whom I should like to have given a sketch, had the narrow limit of this memoir permitted.

---

[14] In Lynchburg, Virginia.

I have always delighted in plant life, and have at various times had the pleasure of fine vegetable and flower gardens, which I personally conducted, especially at my home, "Point of Honor," in Lynchburg, and at Monticello, in Indian Territory. Raising chickens and turkeys and other fowl has also been a great pleasure to me, in which I have indulged my fancy whenever conditions were at all favorable.

My greatest pleasure, perhaps, has been music, enjoying playing the piano especially, and the guitar, and I have always loved to sing, still retaining my voice to an extent that is very unusual to one of my age. When I was young I delighted in dancing, being very light on my feet and loving a good time.

In oil painting and in miniatures I have found great interest and entertainment, as well as in sketching in water colors, and still indulge in this agreeable pastime.

When I was younger and had stronger eyesight, I enjoyed embroidering in colors, which was quite like painting with the needle, but I have long since given this up.

Public affairs always have had an interest for me, and I still enjoy reading the public press and knowing what is going on: but that which has been of the greatest interest and pleasure of all to me has been those good friends, relatives, and kinspeople, and especially young people, with whom my life has been thrown. I still love the company of young people.

When I grew up it was fashionable to serve wine and spirits but since I was eighteen years of age I have been a total abstainer, teaching my sons by example, but above all by vigorous precept. I recall showing to my boys while they were young revolting individual cases of the imbecility and degradation of drunkenness, so that they grew up with a proper knowledge of the insidious danger of alcohol.

The beauty of natural scenery in the wonderful forms and colors with which our good Lord has adorned the earth and sky has been a source of the greatest enjoyment to me, and especially at my country place, Monticello, on Caney River, in the Cherokee Nation, where the views have given me endless pleasure.

# Buffalo Bird Woman (Waheenee, Maxídiwiac; Hidatsa, c.1839–1932)

*Born around 1839 in a North Dakota village by the mouth of the Knife River, "three years after the smallpox winter,"an epidemic among Native Americans from Alaska to the Pueblos that killed over half the Hidatsas, Buffalo Bird Woman was a traditionalist who lived through a time of enormous upheaval for her people. Her mother, Weahtee, who died when Buffalo Bird Woman was six, was one of four wives of her father, Small Ankle. Because the wives were sisters, her aunts were like mothers; her close family included her grandmother, Turtle, who cared for her after her mother's death.*

*In 1845 the Hidatsa and affiliated Mandan tribes moved upstream to Like-a-Fish-hook Village on the Missouri River. When she was sixteen Buffalo Bird Woman and her half-sister married Magpie, and the three lived in the women's lodge, a customary practice among the matrilineal and usually matrilocal Hidatsa. Shortly after Magpie's death from tuberculosis, she married Son of a Star, and, at the age of thirty, had Tskaka-sakis, or Goodbird, her only child. Her son became an important mediator when, beginning in 1906, Buffalo Bird Woman was interviewed by ethnographer and minister Gilbert L. Wilson over the next twelve years at the Fort Berthold reservation in north-central North Dakota. A progressive Christian who could speak several languages including English, Edward Goodbird translated his mother's Hidatsa narratives for Wilson, who compiled his field notes in* Waheenee: An Indian Girl's Story Told by Herself to Gilbert L. Wilson *(1921) and* Agriculture of the Hidatsa Indians: An Indian Interpretation *(1917), as well as Goodbird's autobiography. The first of these volumes was written for children as well as adults and organizes the meandering subject matter of the original interviews for a Western audience. Although Wilson's perspective can be ethnocentric, his sympathy for his subject, developed over a relationship of many years, is evident, and he affirms in his 1917 volume, "May the Indian woman's story of her toil be a plea for our better appreciation of her race."*

*The narratives collected here reflect Buffalo Bird Woman's traditional perspective, parallel to that of the Fox woman autobiographer, while they often echo the attention to women's experiences found in different forms in the other writers in this collection. Although behavioral standards before marriage were strict, as we see in "Corn Songs" and "A Daughter's Training," the freedom of Hidatsa women relative to their white counterparts is evident in her accounts of women's ability to divorce. We also learn of childbearing and childrearing practices, courtship customs, and punishments. Perhaps most engaging to contemporary readers are her narratives about the trickster Itsikamahidish, which reveal her sense of humor; like the Iktomi tales retold by Zitkala-Ša, these stories about the foolish, greedy, gluttonous trickster were intended in part to teach a youthful audience about proper behavior. Readers may sense that her careful attention to details relating to Hidatsa customs and beliefs reflects her attempt to help preserve an earlier version of what she regarded as a rapidly transforming culture, as her remarks on "Indian Life in Former days Compared with the Present Life" poignantly highlight.*

## BIBLIOGRAPHY


### Primary

Bowers, Alfred W. *Hidatsa Social and Ceremonial Organization.* Nebraska, 1992.
Goodbird, Edward. *Goodbird the Indian: His Story, Told by Himself to Gilbert L. Wilson.* Revell, 1914.
Wilson, Gilbert. Diaries, Notebooks, and Reports, undated and 1905–1929. Minnesota Historical Society.
Wilson, Gilbert L. *Agriculture of the Hidatsa Indians: An Indian Interpretation.* University of Minnesota Studies in the Social Sciences, no. 9, 1917.
——. *Buffalo Bird Woman's Garden: Agriculture of the Hidatsa Indians.* Minnesota Historical Society, 1987.
——. *Waheenee: An Indian Girl's Story Told by Herself to Gilbert L. Wilson.* Nebraska, 1987.

### Secondary

Babcock, Barbara, and Jay Cox. "The Native American Trickster." In *Dictionary of Native American Literature.* Ed. Andrew Wiget. Garland, 1994. 98–105.
Bataille, Gretchen M., and Kathleen Mullen Sands. *American Indian Women: Telling Their Lives.* Nebraska, 1984.
——. "Women's Autobiography." In *Dictionary of Native American Literature.* Ed. Andrew Wiget. Garland, 1994. 187–92.
Colasurdo, Christine. "'Tell Me a Woman's Story': The Question of Gender in the Construction of *Waheenee*, Pretty-Shield, and Papago Woman." *American Indian Quarterly* 21:3 (1998): 385–97.
Gilman, Carolyn, and Mary Jane Schneider. *The Way to Independence.* Minnesota Historical Society, 1987.
Jersen, Joan M. *With These Hands: Women Working the Land.* Feminist Press, 1981.
Wilson, Norma C. "Buffalo Bird Woman." In *Native American Women: A Biographical Dictionary.* Ed. Gretchen M. Bataille. Garland, 1993.


# Autobiography, As Told to Gilbert L. Wilson, From Field Notes by Wilson, 1906–1929

## ORIGIN OF THE HIDATSAS (VOL. 13, 1913)[1]

It is hard to know just how my people came to Knife River but I will tell the story as I heard it myself from my father and some others.

My people lived under Devil's Lake. They came up to the ground by a vine root. I do not know who found the vine. The people kept coming up until a woman quae praegnans erat[2] and therefore heavy, attempted to climb the root and broke it. Those of the tribe who had not yet climbed are still beneath the lake in the old home.

Goodbird Interrupting: "Our Hidatsa tale is just like that of the Mandans excepting that the tribes came from different places. The Hidatsas came from Devil's Lake and the Mandans from the mouth of the Mississippi from under the ocean, as the stories tell."

Buffalo Woman Resuming: I do not know whether our country under Devil's Lake had a sun and moon and stars or not. And I do not know whether they planted fields underneath or not.

[1] The volume numbers after the title of each selection refer to the Minnesota Historical Society's listing.

[2] Who was pregnant. The insertion of the Latin phrase here reflects Wilson's understanding that sexuality and women's bodies were sensitive subjects in European American culture. See the Fox Woman's discussion, and Kilpatrick's response to it below (278, 280, 283).

When the people came out of Devil's Lake they built villages near by. We know this not only from the tales told in my tribe, but because the sites of these old villages are there yet. My father, when going on war parties, had occasion to stop at this lake and he found three of those old sites there yet. My father Small Ankle, also said that a part of our tribe are still there under the lake, because the drums in their villages could sometimes be heard, the sound coming up through the water. Afterwards, the Sioux came to this lake and lived there and they said the same thing, that they could hear drums under the water.

At this time our people did not raise any corn or squashes but as we have heard in old tales, they did have gardens in their villages beside Devil's Lake. In these gardens they raised what we Indians call wild potatoes – a kind of artichoke, I think, which grows along in the bottom land beside the Missouri. There also grows here a kind of wild bean. These beans do not appear on the vine above ground, but an inch or two under the soil. These two vegetables were cultivated in the Devil's Lake villages as we hear from old times. We do not cultivate them now but we do gather these wild potatoes and ground beans and eat them.

The seeds for these ground beans and wild potatoes or artichokes were brought up from under Devil's Lake at the time that the people ascended up to this earth. Whether they had gardens underneath the water or not, I do not know. I only know that the story says the Hidatsas brought the seeds of both these vegetables from under the water. The story does not say how these beans and artichokes spread over this world.

I have said that the Hidatsas had gardens of these two vegetables in their villages at Devil's Lake. I think these gardens must have been small. I know that whenever we moved to a new place to build a village, our gardens were quite small at first. We always made them down in the woods and gradually worked them bigger and bigger.

The Hidatsas had already heard of the Missouri River before Itsikamahidish told them of it. A war party I think of about ten men had once come to the Missouri River. Looking across, they saw a village of Indians on the other side. Each party however, was afraid to cross for fear that the others might be enemies.

It was in the autumn and the Missouri River was quite low so that an arrow could be shot from shore to shore. Some of the Mandans took ears of corn and broke off pieces with the grain upon it. These pieces they parched in the fire with the grain still on the cob. They then stuck the pieces upon the points of arrows and shot them across the river to the Hidatsas, which as I say could be done because the river was running low. They called out to the Hidatsas to eat. Whether they did this in the sign language, or by words, I do not know; but the word for eat is the same in both Mandan and Hidatsa.

The members of the war party ate the pieces of parched ears and liked the taste of the new food. We still parch corn on the cob as was done by the Mandans at this time. A ripe ear is stuck on the end of a stick and held over a bed of coals. Such parched corn is eaten by young people who have good teeth but not by us elders.

The members of the war party returned home and told the rest of the tribe what they had seen. "We have found another people on the Missouri who have a strange kind of grain which we ate and it was good." However, the rest of the tribe were not very much interested. They made no effort to visit the Mandans, some of them fearing that they might be enemies.

However, a number of years afterwards, another war party of Hidatsas came to the Missouri River and crossed to visit the Mandans near Bird Beak Hill. The Mandans broke an ear of corn and gave a piece to the Hidatsas for seed. It was a yellow ear. I do not know how many were in this second war party nor how they crossed the river. Probably they crossed in bull boats brought over by the Mandans. There were many boats in both tribes in old times, two or three in each lodge, for there were many buffaloes then.

The Mandans must have lived at Bird Beak Hill for a long time.

Ká-ħo-hĕ was chief of the Mandans at this time. The name means, Corn-stalk-moving-in-the-wind. I do not know whether it was he or other members of the tribe who gave the Hidatsas the ear of corn, but the Hidatsas as I have said, took the seed home to their villages and soon everybody was planting yellow corn.

I think my tribe must have gotten our other garden seeds, beans, squash, sun flower seed, and the other varieties of corn besides the yellow, at subsequent times. But there is no story about how this was done, so far as I know.

I do not know when our people quit planting ground beans and wild artichokes but the ground beans were hard to dig and the villagers liked the new kind of beans better.

While my people still lived at Devil's Lake Itsikamahidish visited them and said, "I will lead you to a better place, on the Missouri River, and you shall be called the Missouri River People." As he promised, Itsikamahidish led the tribe to a bluff on the east side of the Missouri, opposite the mouth of Knife River. Here he rested his foot on a big stone. The stone yielded like soft mud so that a track was left upon it the shape of Itsikamahidish's foot. This stone is there yet I think, for my father once saw it.

"There!" said Itsikamahidish, pointing opposite to the other side of the Missouri. "There shall be your village. You will grow up like red willows, so numerous will you become." The Hidatsas crossed the Missouri and built a village on the south side of the Knife River and increased rapidly, as Itsikamahidish said they would. Red willows grow very quickly. When the waters go down and leave an exposed sand bar, it is soon covered with these shoots of a kind of red willow, but they are not kinnikinick.

There were three villages in all at the Knife River of our tribe. Each of these villages was one people and spoke a dialect of its own. The Hidatsa people used the waters of the Knife River as their village was a mile or a mile and a half from the Missouri. But I am sure they must sometimes have used the Missouri waters.

The Awaȟáwi were the people nearest the Missouri at the mouth of Knife River. The Awatiȟá liked buffalo fish and so buffalo fish is called Awatiȟá-ita-múa to this day.

The three villages were about a mile and a half apart[.]

Our next move was to Fort Berthold, or Like-a-fish-hook village. We never counted the winter village as a village as we considered our winter camp very much as a hunting camp. I was born in the Awatiȟá village and therefore belong to that tribe. My father Small Ankle, was an Awaȟáwi, but my husband Son-of-a-star, and my grandfather Big Cloud, were Hidatsas. I was taken to old Fort Berthold when I was four years old at the time that my tribe removed thither. As I have said, the dialects of the three tribes differed a little bit and there is a story that quarrels sometimes arose through misunderstanding of one another's language.

## Birth and Childhood (vol. 9, 1910)

When suffering took hold on a woman and she was about to become a mother, she took medicine. She was soon delivered, without a great deal of pain. Different ones in our tribe knew different medicines that they sold to others. These medicines given a woman in labor were not always the same. I know one kind myself, but I do not happen to have any of it on hand just now. It is called . . . big medicine. It is a plant that grows in the timber and is about five feet high. This medicine is used by us for almost everything.

As you have just said of white people, we also know that the easiest birth was when a woman was about twenty years old. I was thirty when my only child, Goodbird, was born; and I suffered greatly.

Accidents sometimes happened at birth. The woman was sometimes torn, or the womb or womb parts might become inverted, – come out I mean, protrude. We sometimes remedied this by having the woman sit on her heel and press upward on the parts and force them back into place.

When a birth was expected, we of course got ready for it in the earth lodge. Two sticks or posts were driven into the earth floor, about three feet high and about two and a half feet apart, at the place the bed was to be. This bed we made of dry grass which we fetched in for the purpose and covered with a buffalo robe. The bed was four or six inches thick and the woman knelt on it, grasping the two posts in her hands; she did this to support herself.

A buffalo calf skin was ready to receive the babe when it was born. It was placed all ready for the child and was always a tanned skin.

We have a story that Itsikamahidiś spoke once to his wife, "Wife, when I kill a buffalo, as soon as I skin it, the hide will be all ready to wear, shall it not, – or what do you think?"

"No," answered his wife, "we women would have too easy a time; I want to work!"

"All right," said Itsikamahidiś, "Be it so! The hide shall be useless until it is tanned – and it shall be a woman's work to tan it."

That is why we Hidatsa women could not use a buffalo hide until it was tanned, – not even for a bed for the new babe!

The birth was easier when the feet of the child appeared first. If the head appeared first, the pain was more severe.

We believed also that birth was harder, when the mother lay down, tho some did this. But when this was done, the mother was likely to be torn.

There were women in the tribe that acted as mid-wives. When a woman knew she was to be a mother, she notified one of these midwives when to expect to be called. When the pains began, the midwife was summoned and hurried to the scene. One duty of this midwife was to straighten the child's head. A new-born child's head is soft, and for this reason often appeared out of proportion; it was for example, too long, or flat, or pushed in on one side, or the like. With her palms the midwife kneaded the child's head to normal shape, or the deformity, we thought, would continue thru life.

During the birth, men and children were put out of the earth lodge. Besides the midwife, there might be one or two other women present, assisting her.

There might also be a medicine man present, for if the family could, they often sent for one. This medicine man sang mystery songs, and might even give medicine to the woman in labor. Songs and medicine were both designed to influence a normal birth. The medicine man bought the right to his profession, from others who owned it. There were several ceremonies that we believed aided women in labor, the River ceremony, the Corn ceremony, the Buffaloes' ceremony, the Wolves' ceremony, were among these.

Those present at the birth talked only in whispers and everything was kept as quiet as possible. Quiet was also enjoined for ten days after the birth.

If the mother died at birth bed, some relative who happened to be suckling a babe, took the little orphan. A pony was a common gift for such a favor. [. . .]

## How Maxídiwiac Got Her Name (vol. 16, 1914)

I was born down at Knife River in the Five Villages. My people had had the small pox so that they still speak of it as the small pox year. My birth was three years after the small pox year. I was born in an earth lodge.

I was first named when I was ten days old. My grandmother called Nothing-but-water "brother"; and he was asked to name me. He named me "Good Way." By this he meant that he hoped that I would go thru life by a good way, – that I would be good all my days, would not be quarrelsome, would not steal, would not do evil, and would have good fortune all my life.

But as a babe I proved rather sickly, and my father, to get me over my sickness, decided to give me a new name, and called me Maxídiwiac, or Buffalo Bird Woman. Wia or mia, in Hidatsa means woman; and Maxídi means cowbird, or buffalo bird, as this little brown-black bird is called in the buffalo country. I do not know why my father chose this name to give me. Perhaps he had a dream or vision; he never told me.

My father, Small Ankle, however, looked upon the birds as his protecting gods.

My grandmother's mother was living when I was a child. I called her "grandmother," and she took a good deal of care of me. Her name was A-tá-kic, meaning Soft White Corn.

I slept with Atákic, for she took me to bed with her. Once she told me this story:

"One day the small pox appeared in the Five Villages. Many people died. My sister had married into the Hidatsa band; and she died of the small pox. My husband also died, and I also took the small pox. I had a little baby, very small, not able to walk yet, only creep. I was very sick with the small pox. I had sores all over my body, and the inside of my throat was very sore, and I was very thirsty.

There was no water in the lodge, and carrying my child as I could, I crept down to the river to drink. I drank of the water, and then fell dead.[3] My little child played by the river, paddling its hands in the water. I do not know how long I was dead. When I came to again, I picked up my child, put it on my back, and managed to return home.

---

[3] Fainted [Wilson's note].

I got well of the small pox after a time. One day, after I had gotten well, my father called my dead sister's husband to the lodge. He came, and my father said to me, "My daughter, this is your husband. Your sister is dead, and your husband is dead. This man will now take care of you!" My new husband's name was It-si-dí-ci-dic, or Yellow Horse. The word can also be translated Yellow Elk, but we recognized his name to mean, Yellow Horse.

Itsidícidic wept as my father said these words.

It was customary for a man to marry his dead wife's sister. The father of the dead wife would love his son-in-law and would want to have him remain in the family.

Itsidícidic had had the small pox and had died of it. They had carried him out of the village and buried him on a hill. They wrapped him in an old tent skin, for there was no time to make a scaffold. They piled some logs over him to keep off the wolves.

In the night the people heard some one calling, "I have waked up! Come for me!" The voice came from the burying ground. The people, "That is a ghost! It is a very dangerous spirit!" And they feared to go.

Now the voice was but Itsidícidic's, who had come to and wanted to leave his grave. He called to some of the people by name.

At last some very brave young men went out to his burial place. "Are you alive again?" they called.

"Yes. I have waked up," the voice answered.

The young men went to the grave and unbound Itsidicidic. And because he was too weak to walk, they carried him to the village.

But as they started off with him, he cried, "Wait! Get my horse. They gave me a calico colored horse in ghost land. I tied him to one of those logs on my grave." The young men looked, but they could not find the horse.

Afterwards, the Crows came to our tribe to trade, and I[4] bought a calico mare from them for some corn. That mare had many colts and they were calico colored like her self. Everybody in the village knew this, and they said "Itsidicidic's vision has come true."

That same small pox year there was a woman also who died and visited the ghost village. They gave her, in that ghost village, a bundle of dried meat cut into strips. She came alive again and said to the people, "I have some dried meat that I wrapped up in strips in the ghost village. It is here under my robe under my arm." She opened her robe, and sure enough there was the dried meat. But it was very old, and was white, as if it had been exposed a long time to the air.

The people wanted to see what that meat from the ghost village was like; so they boiled it, and tried to eat it but it was not good at all. They then gave it to the dogs, but the dogs would not eat it."

Atákic was a very old woman. One night she died in her bed. We found her the next morning, dead.

## A DAUGHTER'S TRAINING (VOL. 18, 1915)

A mother began to teach her daughter household duties at about the age of thirteen. The girl was taught to chop wood, hoe in the garden and embroider bead work. My mother said to me:

"We are a family who have not one bad woman in it so you must try and not be bad."

She meant that I should obey my parents and marry only as my parents wished and I never met young men at night or smiled at them.

My grandfather, Big Cloud talked to me very often.

"My granddaughter," he would say, "try to be good and you will grow up to be a good woman. Obey your parents and remember what I say. You must not quarrel nor steal. You must not answer bad words."

After I was married my father said to me:

"My daughter, you are married, you must stay home and try to be a good worker; you will sometimes not want to do your work; you will think it is too hard but stand up, go forward and see if you can not do it any way."

---

4 That is, Atákic.

Now all these things that I have told you how I cook and mix foods my mother did not teach me. These things I learn[ed] myself as I saw my mother do them many times.

## CORN SONGS (VOL. 18, 1915)

We had many songs that were sung by the watchers on their stages in the corn field, or by the women hoing in their gardens. Here are two of them:

"All of that one's age have gone on a war party.
They are seeking to win honor marks,
On the north side of the river (Missouri).
They keep awake all night;
Like wolves, they do not sleep!
But this man, here, said, 'You elk woman, you stay here,
(By me) and I will not go away on a warparty!'
And that elk woman never moved (to go to him)!"

By "elk woman" is meant "sweetheart," but the term is not a very dignified one, and was used rather as a teasing word. The song is sung as upbraiding a young man who whispered to some young woman he loved, that he would rather stay by her side than go on a war party; but as the song says, she would not go to him, doubtless because she felt contempt for his sloth.

I have told you what is a band cousin, or clan cousin; and that a clan cousin had the right of taunting another clan cousin without fear of its being resented. He or she might even taunt with words or jests that under any other circumstances, or in the mouth of any but a clan cousin, would have provoked a fight.

Also I have told you that it was our custom, when a wife left her husband to go to live with another man, that her husband let her go. This did not mean that he had no right to call her back, if he cared to do so. In old times, if a woman left her husband for another, and her husband sent for her to come back to him, she could not refuse. If she did, her new husband would say, "Go back; he is your husband!" But for a husband thus to call back his deserting wife, was counted among us to be shameful thing, even while we recognized that he had the right if he chose to exercise it.

Now there was a young man once who had two sweethearts. One of these was a clan cousin, but the young man married the sweetheart who was not a clan cousin. Afterwards, another man stole his wife from him. Instead of letting her go, as a man of strong heart should do, the husband sent a friend to her and called her back to him. After this, he no longer went on war parties, because he feared the young men would taunt him for what he had done.

Now his clan cousin had not forgotten that the young man had not married her, but had taken her rival. Hence the song, which is supposed to be in the clan cousin's mouth:

Our word for band cousin is ma-kú-tsa-ti.

"I think that clan cousin of mine hears the pines when
The wind blows thru them *sh-sh-sh*!
I think he hears them as he sleeps, sh-sh-sh!
And when I think of this, I never sleep, thinking, thinking all the night!

"My heart, I will tell you what you love to do!
It is to take your wife back from that man!
That you think is your best day! You care for naught else!
You do not love any thing else at all!"

The words of the first stanza of the song are spoken sarcastically. The girl taunts the young man who stays at home with his recalled wife, instead of being off on a war party.

Very few men in our tribe ever called back a wife who had deserted for another man.

The allusion to the pines, is to the enemy's country, where pines grow, and where the young man should have been with his fellow warriors.

## Goodbird is Nearly Drowned (vol. 18, 1915)[5]

At the mouth of the Little Missouri River, we came very near having a fatal accident. When we left our winter camp in the west, grass was growing and the snow had disappeared from the ground, but now as we came down the Missouri a snow storm came up. It was terribly windy and as we rounded the bend at the Little Missouri River the water became very rough and the waves made our boats see-saw up and down, in a way that frightened us all.

The storm had come up very suddenly. Of course, we turned and rode towards shore, both myself and my husband using our paddles vigorously. In paddling a bull boat, the usual way when a husband and wife crossed the river is for the wife to kneel in the front and paddle, while the husband sits in the tail of the boat to balance it. But coming down the Missouri with a load in tow, was quite another matter and both my husband and I used paddles, sitting side by side in the boat. Now when the storm came up we turned toward shore, using our paddles in this manner, one on either side of the boat.

Suddenly, my husband stopped paddling and leaned over the side of the boat. He leaned over so far that I was nearly pitched over upon his side. A bull boat is a tub-like craft, rather clumsy, and is easily upset. My husband leaned over so far that the edge of the boat came clear down on his stomach.

Then I saw what was the matter. My baby Goodbird had fallen into the water, and my husband had just caught him and was taking him into our boat.

I have already explained that the boat which my husband and myself paddled had two others in tow, each of them loaded with hides and meat, and that in the middle boat, the one immediately behind ours, was Flies Low, my younger brother, holding my infant son Goodbird. It was customary when a small child cried and wept, to loosen his cradle bundle.

After my husband drew the child up into the boat, I saw that Goodbird's cradle clothes had been so treated. Probably the child had become restless and Flies Low had loosened his clothes a little to give the little babe room to move his limbs. This loosening of the cradle wrappings had made them buoyant so that the baby had floated on the water and my husband was able to rescue him.

## Punishment of Children, of Adults; Ideas of Crime (vol. 10, 1911)

To punish children we scolded them; and usually this was sufficient. But if a boy was persistently bad to his parents or made himself objectionable, crying all the time and refusing to stop, because he wanted something; or if the child was obdurate or disobeyed or got saucy, the parents might call in one of the same band and say, "Brother, take your bad (band) brother down to the river and throw him in!"

This the other would pretend to do, frightening the child who would cry out, "Don't, I will be good!"

"Are you sure?" would be asked him.

"Yes I am sure!"

"Well, don't do it again; for the next time I will drown you." And the child would be let go.

Or the member of the band called in might thrust the bad boy's head in a bucket of water; or if it was winter, take him out and throw him in a snow bank and kick snow over him. Or he might take an arrow and say, "You bad boy, I will cut thru your skin with this arrow!" Thus scaring the boy.

Some parents punished by striking the child with the hand, or pushing him down on the floor. Many of the meaner families of the tribe even whipped with sticks. But the better families did not like to do this, and loved their children.

---

[5] This event occurs while the family is participating in a buffalo hunt.

A boy that was punished too often was apt to get reckless and not listen to his parents. But that was not a good way to train a child. It was better to talk with him and be patient, and tell him to be good.

Some mean families punished their children so often that they spoiled them.

Girls were punished as were boys, by calling in a band sister, or even an elder sister in the same family.

In our village were living three different tribes. The boys of the different tribes were apt to quarrel and fights were of almost daily occurrence.

Our Indian boys did not fight with their fists, but clawed with their fingers, kicked and pulled hair, threw one another down or threw stones.

Ordinarily, parents did not bother themselves much in these children's quarrels. Sometimes two families would have a difference about children, but the affair seldom got beyond words.

Even when boys threw stones, parents did not interfere, unless a boy was struck by a stone so as to draw blood. If this happened, the parents of the wounded boy would go to the parents of the boy that threw the stone, and ask pay, which would be given.

We did not think it right for men to get jealous and fight about women. In old times, if one fought over a woman, no matter how many honor marks or how brave he might be, we talked against him severely.

I never heard of but two men who fought over women.

One was named Lone Buffalo. His wife ran away with two young men; the three went up the river.

Lone Buffalo gave chase and overtook them at White Earth river. The two young men were sitting eating. Their ponies were grazing. Lone Buffalo shot the ponies with his gun and took his wife back.

Our people thought this very wrong. The whole tribe talked against Lone Buffalo.

His band spoke against him a great deal. He was often made to hear remarks made against him.

Another man was named His-hand-has-no-fore-finger. One night he came upon his wife lying outside of his earth lodge with a young man. His-hand-has-no-fore-finger got his hatchet and went out to kill his wife. But she dodged the blow and the hatchet hit the young man she lay with in the shoulder, hurting him severely.

All the people talked against His-hand-has-no-fore-finger. They said, "He should be ashamed of himself!"

If a man fought with another and killed him, the brothers and relatives of the slain man got angry and wanted to kill the murderer.

Then the members of some one of the dance societies in the village would make a collection of valuable things, a horse etc., and fill a pipe and come to the relatives. "Here," they would say," take these presents and obey this pipe! Be peaceable!"

We thought that if the pipe were not obeyed, then ill-luck would follow those who refused. They were almost certain to obey the pipe.

Always we tried to prevent the slaying of the murderer.

If a man went out and shot a buffalo before the others of the village, the soldier society, the Black Mouths, made it very hard for him.

A man was not permitted to hunt buffaloes by himself. If he did so and was found out, the soldiers got ready their arrows and knives and went to the offender's lodge. They broke his gun, cut up all his meat and threw it to dogs, and whipped him with sticks or with their bows; they shot all his dogs and if he had a tent, they cut it up. As they went to punish him, they sang songs against him.

In my life, I have known four men so punished.

Of the songs which the Black Mouths sang as they went to punish an offending hunter, one had as I remember, these words:

"How many want to die? Let them die!"

### June Berry (vol. 20, 1916)

June berries are much used on this reservation, even now; and the wood we thought very useful in old times. In fact we called the tree itself, mída̭ káti, real tree, genuine tree, because we thought the wood the best of the forest.

June berry wood is hard, and we used it in making wooden pins to stake out green hides to dry, and for tent pins. It was the usual wood for making arrow shafts; being tough and unyielding, we used it for anything for which we required hard wood.

June berries were gathered when ripe, to be dried and stored away for winter. The berries differed a good deal on the various trees. Some trees bore very sweet berries, others those less sweet; and some bore large berries, some small berries. And besides these were white June berries, of which I will speak later.

We gathered June berries, either picking them off the tree by hand, or we broke off a laden branch and beat it with a stick, thus knocking the berries off upon a skin.

Picking June berries was woman's work, but the men helped break the branches. A husband would break branches and bear them to his wife, who took charge of them thereafter.

The picking season lasted about the month of July – the berries ripened the very last of June and lasted about thru the next month. In this time I used to go out picking June berries about two or three times; but they were very plentiful some years, and a single picking might be enough. [. . .]

I used to go June berrying with my husband; or before I was married, with my girl friends. Or a young woman might go with her love boy-sweetheart, who helped her. They worked together, but there were others working within sight of them. We did not all go in a big party however.

We went early in the morning, while it was cool. We would gather, each woman one or two calf skin bags full.

It was as I have said, a common thing for a young man to help his sweetheart pick June berries. A young man might send word to his sweetheart by some female relative of his own saying, "That young man says that when you want to go for June berries, he wants to go along with you!" Or else he watched when she came out of the lodge to start berrying; for it was not our custom for a young man to talk openly with a young woman.

Sometimes a young man who went out thus to help his sweetheart talked with her as they worked. But very often they worked in silence. Young people who did talk with each other always had marriage in mind.

A young man who sent word to his sweetheart would not wait and walk with her to the berry grounds, but would go on ahead and wait in the woods for her to come. A young man who would go to the girl's lodge and talk openly with her we thought was something like a fool; and if he did such a thing, the girl would get mad at him.

When a party of pickers went out together, the men usually walked together, by themselves.

Always a man carried a gun with him, or some weapon. Enemies might be lurking in the woods – indeed that is why the men went. Also there were grizzlies about, and they were dangerous. For these reasons the women were glad to have the men along, and always felt safer if they were.

The pickers ate a breakfast in the lodge, before they went. They took no lunch with them for they expected to return soon after noon.

When a couple were working, either a man and his wife or a maiden and her sweetheart, the man kept his gun lying at his feet as he worked.

Of course a young man gave all his attention to his sweetheart, so far as did work.

Once I was out picking June berries with Pink Blossom. A young man named Old Bear wanted to get after Pink Blossom, but she refused to encourage him, tho he persisted. Old Bear made a big pocket in his robe under his arm – as Indians do by folding the robe – and filled it full of berries he picked and emptied them in Pink Blossom's sack. But she was angry and threw them out. She did not want him to pay her attention.

The pickers went home a little after noon. When it was time to go, the women bore off the berry sacks, never the men; but first the women put sweet-leaf plants or ash branches, or other leafy branches over their backs, so that the juice that oozed out of the sacks might not soil their garments. The mouths of the sacks were tied shut, and sacks were carried like wood, – packed on the back.

If the woman was accompanied by her husband, he went home with her, walking before her Indian fashion, or if they wanted to talk, he walked at her side, either on the right or left. But a young man did not walk home with his sweetheart. As soon as the berries were picked, the young man went off by another road. He did not follow her or watch her with his eyes. The young woman did not even bother to thank him, I think.

## COURTSHIP AND MARRIAGE (VOL. 9, 1910/1912)[6]

Marriage by purchase, we called "buying a woman." It was done as follows.

Perhaps a man and his wife had a daughter old enough to marry. A young man in the village sees and admires her. He asks his mother or father to go and see the girl's parents about it. One of these goes and says, "We put all your kindness before you, that you remember it! We have a son who wishes to marry your daughter. We know she belongs to a good family. As for ourselves, we know we are poor. But we want to appeal to your kindness in this matter. Remember your son you have lost, your daughter that has died! Remember, and pity us, and help us! We are poor, humble!"

If the girl's parents did not want to accept the young man, they would say, "No, our daughter is too young!" or they would make some other excuse.

But if the offer was acceptable to them, they would say, "That is very good! We are poor; and we see that you want to help us with presents. We are glad. We shall be glad to have our daughter enter your family!"

The young man's parent would then go back and get ready the gifts that were to be given to the parents of the girl. These were sometimes very valuable, – a war bonnet or eagle hat as we called it, a gun, and a pony, or two ponies, four ponies; even as high as ten ponies have been paid for a girl. If the groom's parents do not have the necessary amount of gifts, their relatives help them and collect gifts for them.

On the morning of the wedding day the parents of the young man brought the gifts to the lodge of the girl's parents, tying the ponies just outside of the earth lodge. Toward evening, the girl went to the young man's lodge, or to his parents' lodge since he usually lived with his parents, with the feast and the return gifts. Ponies were given, or other gifts, and her parents were often helped by their relatives also, just as the young man's parents had been helped by their relatives. Two women would leave the girl's lodge with a long pole borne between them on which were strung the pots with the wedding feast. Often, the girl herself walked before the two women, leading a fine pony, sometimes with a war bonnet on, – gifts these, to her future husband. Sometimes the feast pots were carried on the arms of the bearers, instead of on a pole. The two bearers were ordinarily relatives of the girl.

The feast would be of dried meat cut up, boiled, and bone grease poured over it; and of boiled pounded corn.

The guests to the feast were invited by the young man's parents. Friends of both parties were invited, but especially the members of the young man's band. Among his band members the young man's parents went inviting as many as they could; but the members of the young woman's band were not invited as were those of the young man's.

Each of the guests was expected to bring a present, – a robe, dress, leggings, painted robe, calico, or the like. These gifts were all for the bride.

Most of the guests were women, but there would be some men. The women sat on one side, the men on the other.

As a rule the feast was served to the guests by young men, or by some one who had been invited to do so.

As each guest arrived he deposited the gift he had brought; but some guests would not bring any gift, but were welcomed just the same. One might not be able to afford a gift, but was invited nevertheless.

It did not take long for the feast to be served and eaten. When it was over, the guests, men and women, got up and left. The bride and the young man's parents were now in the lodge, but the young man was out in the village. The parents of the bride now came and gathered together all the gifts brought for the bride by the guests. The bride now divided them among her relatives, and her parents

---

[6] Wilson's notes indicate a collection date of August 1912; I have given the Minnesota Historical Society's identification in parentheses.

took the gifts home to distribute them. But the bride was careful to retain for her own use what she needed; generosity, however, was admired and encouraged.

The bride remained in her father-in-law's lodge. When the guests and her parents had gone home, the bridegroom himself came home.

When a young man bought his wife his friends often laughed and said to him, "You bought your wife! No woman would have you. You are ugly!" And the young man would get red in the face, and feel shame.

But when women would laugh at the bride who had been bought, she would retort, "Yes, I was bought. But you want some man to run after you. But I was bought. I was handsome. I was married in the earth lodge!"

For this reason, very few women were bought.

But there was another way to get married. A young man got old enough to begin to take note of a girl and see that she was industrious. He would watch her and if she was about of the same age and, when he looked at her, and she smiled back at him and kind of laughed, he would begin to feel that she had an interest in him. This might go on for a long time before she would come to him; but by these signs, he knew that she favored him, and she knew that he admired her. Perhaps the girl at last gave him some sign or secret encouragement, and he would come to her and talk with her, and touch her, and come to see her often. And by and by they would get married.

He would come by night to meet his sweetheart. He might try for a long time before she would consent to come to him.

Eighteen years of age was thought to be a suitable marriageable age.

A girl did not always yield at once, as I have said. Sometimes a young man admired a girl greatly, but she did not care much for him. He would then go and get someone to go and talk with her; but she would refuse to listen. He would send someone else; again she would refuse. Again he would send someone who was near to her, – some young man or young woman, her near friend or relative to talk for him and plead his cause. At the end, the girl sometimes yielded.

Often there was reason why the girl was in no hurry to yield. The man perhaps had already married, and wanted to discard his former wife. Then that good girl would say, "I do not want that man. It will be only a short time until he will want to leave me too!"

The kind of a man who left his wife often, frequently found it hard to get a wife. Often he would have to give a horse, or two horses, or three, or four, or five, to get her, because she would say, "You will tire of me soon, and want to put me away; but if you do, at least I want to be able to say I have some property!"

Both old men and young men used both these forms of marriage that I have described, marriage by purchase, and marriage by just going to the man's lodge.

Some women did not care for the men, and did not marry at all. Others were fond of men and kept going from one to another; just kept going to the next one.

A good woman did not yield readily, but made her courtship a long one. If a girl permitted a man to put his arm around her, the other women talked against her and said to her, "He is not your husband! What you do is a shame."

A woman that liked to be married, often let a man put his arm around her.

The ways of you white men, I think, must differ from ours. When you court a girl, you take her out to walk with you, or to drive, and I think you must put your arm around her. But I do not know. I do not know white men's ways. I was never in a white village, nor off this reservation.

There was yet another way to marry. A man's wife may have died; but the man may have a reputation for being a good hunter, a good worker, and industrious. The parents of some girl might give their daughter to him, even if the girl did not care for the man. The parents did this because they knew the man would give their daughter a good home, good protection and pleasant words; and that he would treat her just like a daughter. That the girl might object, made no difference.

Then, too, the girl's parents might have another reason for marrying her in this fashion. She may have given signs of becoming a bad woman, perhaps; or at least the parents may have feared this, and rather than risk letting her become such, they would decide to give her to a husband.

Some women were not good; such a woman would get after a young man, only to leave him soon and go after another. Women were not all alike. Some were good, some were bad, and others were just fair, neither good nor bad.

Ordinarily, when a girl married by just going home with a young man, her parents were expecting it, and made no objection. But sometimes they scolded her.

In those days the government did not have laws for us to follow. All the people then did as they thought good. In later days the government has made laws for us so that our marriage customs have changed.

When a woman had an illegitimate babe, she would tell who the babe's father was. He did not have to marry the woman if he did not want to; the people would merely call the child the daughter or son "of so and so," for everyone would learn the father's name. The woman would be called a bad woman. Usually the man would not marry the mother of his illegitimate child, and had no high regard for her.[7]

## HONOR MARKS OF WOMEN (VOL. 11, 1912)

We Hidatsa women had a kind of honor mark, for industry, something like the honor marks the men had for striking the enemy.

If a girl was a worker and tanned hundreds of hides her aunt might give her an honor mark. My aunt Sage gave me such, a maípsukaśa or woman's belt. These were broad as a man's suspender and worked in beads, sometimes blue, sometimes with a cross design. One could not purchase or make such a belt; it had to be given.

For working a quill decorated tent, a bracelet was given; for making a quill embroidered robe, a ring.

There were no other honor marks for industry, but these three.

## CHILDREN'S TALES (VOL. 10, 1911)

There were a great many stories that we told to children for their amusement and children were very fond of hearing them. Following is a good example of such stories. We call it,

Itsikamahidish and Grease.

Itsikamahidish was once roaming about looking for food. He was very hungry and willing to eat almost anything he could find. Very happy he was to see an earth lodge ahead of him. He went to the door of the lodge and entered. A man sat within making arrows. He had a pile of shafts lying beside him and was gluing feathers on them. The man was short of stature and with thick broad body.

Itsikamahidish stood, not knowing just what to say to the man, but at last ventured, "My elder brother bade me ask you for some arrow sticks!"

"Good!" said the man. He arose, went to one side of the room and came back with his arms full of buffalo entrails boiled and dried, that had been hanging there.

Itsikamahidish was glad indeed to receive them. He went out of the lodge, sat down and ate the entrails all up.

He went about with a comfortable stomach after this but was curious to know who it was that had given him his feast. He met a man going over the prairie and stopped him. "In that earth lodge that stands yonder, – who is that short, thick man who sits within?"

"His name is Grease," answered the other.

"I am glad you have told me," Itsikamahidish said. He was growing hungry again.

He returned to the earth lodge and found Grease still gluing on feathers to his shafts. Itsikamahidish stood and said, "My elder brother sends me to ask you for some sand-paper!" This sand paper we made

---

[7] Note added by Goodbird: We know that in old times when a man having a marriageable daughter, had also a very fine horse, sometimes a selfish man having also a son, would urge that son to marry that girl; he did this so that the girl's father would return to him a gift of that handsome horse. But this was a very selfish thing to do, and no good man would do it.

in old times from powdered flint. We spread glue over a piece of skin and sprinkled the powdered flint over it. We used the sandpaper to smooth arrow shafts.

Grease arose as before and took down the fat fleshy covering of a buffalo paunch and gave it to Itsikamahidish. "There is your sand paper," he said.

Itsikamahidish went without and ate the paunch covering as he had the entrails.

He went roaming about again but soon grew hungry and returned again to the earth lodge. "My elder brother sends me to ask you for your arrow polisher."

These arrow polishers we made in old times from the boney process that arose from the vertebra of a buffalo's neck. The process was pierced with a hole to push the shaft thru. Less often polishers were made from buffalo ribs.

Grease arose and fetched the lower intestine of a buffalo, fat and ready cooked, and gave to Itsikamahidish. The latter went out and ate it; he went about again, feeling good now with a full stomach.

All this time Grease sat in his lodge industriously making arrows.

A fourth time Itsikamahidish entered the earth lodge and said, "Grease, my elder brother sends me to ask you for some arrow grease." In old times it was customary for arrow shafts to be greased or oiled before they were feathered; and they were oiled again if shot into a buffalo and drawn out.

"Very well," said Grease, "Come and take a mouthful out of my left shoulder!"

Itsikamahidish came behind Grease and opened his coyote mouth and took a big bite, – nearly the whole of the other's shoulder. Grease looked around behind him and saw by his mouth that it was Itsikamahidish. This frightened him for he knew Itsikamahidish for a trickster.

Grease ran out of the lodge and fled, with Itsikamahidish in hot pursuit. The first now turned into what he really was, a buffalo bladder filled with grease and went bumping on over the prairie. Itsikamahidish kept up his pursuit, often nearly overtaking the other. Grease rolled at last into a water hole.

Itsikamahidish ran swiftly around the water hole. He saw that bone grease was arising out of the bladder, yellow, and floating on the water. Soon it covered the water.

Itsikamahidish thought how he could skim the grease off the water, for he was now hungry as ever. "I will cut off my tail," he said to himself; "and with it sop up the grease from the top of the water." He came close to the water's edge and cut off his tail with his knife. But when he reached out with the tail to sop up the grease, the grease all turned blue and disappeared.

"Wow!" groaned Itsikamahidish, "I know just how that happened. It is my deceiving (adopted) brother that did that, Spotted Tail the raccoon. He has skimmed off the grease with his hairy paws and eaten it. I am left without even a tail!"

Itsikamahidish mourned greatly that he had no tail. "I fear I shall never find another tail like that one of mine!" he said. He went about weeping.

A fox came by. "How would my tail suit you?" he asked. "You may have it if you will."

"No," said Itsikamahidish," that is not like my fine tail!"

An old wolf was sitting not far away. His tail was long and bushy. "How would you like my tail?" he called.

Itsikamahidish looked. "That is a fine tail. I like it!" he cried. So the old wolf gave it him.

That is why coyotes have long bushy tails like wolves.

Stories such as the foregoing we told to children not of tenderest years, – to children, say, of six or seven years of age, or a little older. Following is another story of this class. [. . .]

Itsikamahidish and the Prairie Chickens.

One day Itsikamahidish was wandering about when he came upon a prairie chicken's nest with many young ones in it. When he touched the nest every one of the young ones opened its mouth supposing one of their parents had come to feed them. Itsikamahidish urinated into the mouth of one and dunged into the mouth of another. He thought it great fun to mock the young chickens thus.

He went on a little way, stopped and looking back began to sing: [. . .]

Grouse young I urinated in mouth, I dunged in mouth, cluck-cluck, cluck-cluck!

And as he sang he danced.

One of the young chickens cried after him, "Look out! My mother and father always inspire fear in others!"

Itsikamahidish went on and came to a river. He went along its bank. In his path, one of the old parent chickens had hidden; and as Itsikamahidish came near and nearly stepped on the prairie chicken, the latter flew up with a great *wh-i-rr – putt*! Itsikamahidish leaped back.

The beavers had been cutting down small trees on the bank and the stump of one of the trees, gnawed sharp, stood near by. Itsikamahidish came down on the stump and was run thru the body by the sharp point.

There was a beaver den under the bank. A young beaver came out and saw the man hanging on the stump with his feet swinging clear of the ground.

The beaver called out to one of his fellows, "O Yellow One, some one hangs on the point of your sharp weapon!" And he plumped back onto the water.

A second time the young beaver came out and called out, "Yellow One, someone is hanging on your sharp stick. Come out and see him! What traveller hereabouts can he be?" And he dived again into the water.

The big Yellow beaver came out and looked and cried. "Oh, that is my man brother!"

Itsikamahidish now began to chant aloud,

"All your family come out here and doctor me!
All your family come out here and doctor me!"

All the beavers came out. They gnawed down the stump and took the sick man into their lodge, in the dam that they had built in the river. One of them went out and cut down a sapling and peeled off the bark.

They doctored him there until he was much better. Then he said, "Sisters, make me a staff to walk with."

One went out and cut down a sapling and skinned off the bark.

"That is not such as I want," said Itsikamahidish. "I want one that is heavier and with a head or knob at one end."

One of the beavers went out and brought in a stick with a great knob at one end.

"That is what I want," cried Itsikamahidish.

A young beaver woman took sick. "I will doctor her," cried Itsikamahidish.

"Do so," said all the others.

Itsikamahidish took his stick. The beaver lay down on her back. Itsikamahidish pushed on her belly with the big end of his stick as we Indians do with the doctoring stick that we call a stomach pusher, and that we use in cases of constipation. Itsikamahidish pushed so hard that he burst the beaver's liver.

As he pushed Itsikamahidish sang this mystery song: [. . .]

Some one must die he will die
One must hang, he will hang.
Your tail near by part I eat.
I wait long.

That is, If one is to die, he will die. If one is to hang (in a burial tree) he will hang. I am going to eat the part (haunch) near your tail. I have waited long (for it).

Itsikamahidish also sang another mystery song: [. . .]

Young beaver your feet's sides earth press flatly.
Your eyes small Your tail near part I eat
I wait long.

This means, Young beaver the sides of your feet press the ground. Your eyes are small. I am going to eat the part near your tail. I have waited for it long.

The sick beaver woman cried out, "Oh, brother, your song sounds dangerous!"

"No," answered Itsikamahidish, "With this song I cure any sickness!"

Soon the young beaver died.

"Sisters," said Itsikamahidish, "let us think how we shall dispose of the body. If we bury her in a tree, ravens will eat her eyes. If we bury her in the ground, beetles will tear out her eyes. Let us tie some logs together, lay her thereon and float her down the river." All the beaver women agreed.

Itsikamahidish tied some logs together into a raft, laid the body on them and pushed the raft out into the current.

"I will go across yonder to that point of land and weep as she passes by," said Itsikamahidish. "Then I will come back."

He hastened across to the point of land on the further side of a bend in the river where the body must pass. Here he wailed loudly, "My young little sister beaver! My heart!" And he wept.

But as the raft came in sight he sprang into the water and with the head of his walking stick he hooked the raft and pulled it to shore.

He made a fire, dressed the beaver, roasted and ate the flesh.

A little winter bird came flying about crying, "Tsi-ka-dēē-dēē-dēē! Brother give me some!"

"No," he cried, "this is not food for children!"

"Then I shall go and tell the young beaver's mother!" cried the winter bird.

Away the bird flew, and having come to the dam, cried aloud: "That deceiver is eating your little daughter. He has made a fire and won't give me any of the meat. Therefore I tell you!"

"Oh, we will kill that man," cried all the beavers and they ran and got their digging sticks.

They started off for the place where he was eating. But he knew the winter bird had told of him; so he hasted and ate up all the beaver and rubbed white clay on his mouth and face and ran thru rose bushes and scratched himself on the legs and arms as if he were suffering greatly.

The beavers went on to meet Itsikamahidish. "We believe what the little bird told us," they said and they wept. But when they saw Itsikamahidish they said, "Behold our brother, how he suffers!" And they went home again.

When Itsikamahidish returned he said, "It is not well for me to stay here much longer. You beaver families, you have lost your little sister; and I also have lost a son; his name was Yellow Bars. Enemies killed him. Let us go on a war party against our enemies and cure our sorrow!"

He looked toward the north. "See the smoke! It is of enemies! There also is where my son was slain!"

The beavers looked toward the north, and sure enough they saw the smoke – of a prairie fire! "Let us go!" They all cried, "Let us go to war!"

Itsikamahidish offered his pipe to the turtles. The turtle lighted the pipe (thus accepting the invitation to go on the war party).

The party started north. When they were far in the hills, Itsikamahidish thought, "Now I will kill all in this party and have plenty of meat to eat!"

A spotted gopher came out and stood by his hole. "Friend," said Itsikamahidish, "I invite you to go with me on this war party. Enemies have killed my son Spotted Ears. Look toward the north. You will see smoke from their fires!"

The gopher said to himself, "This is the Deceiver. He tries to trick me!" and he ran into his hole. In a moment he ran out again and looking to the north, saw smoke. Then he believed.

Itsikamahidish held out his pipe to him. The gopher opened his mouth to smoke. Itsikamahidish pushed the stem and pressed the gopher against the side of his hole, killing him.

"Friend," called out Itsikamahidish, "will you not smoke?" But the gopher was dead.

With his stick, used now as a club, Itsikamahidish sprang upon the beavers and slew them one after another.

But the turtle went right on. Itsikamahidish hit him, and hit him, but made no impression on the turtle, who coming to a pond walked right into the water.

The turtle put out his head and called back at Itsikamahidish, "You will have to drink kneeling down on your hands and putting your lips to the water."

Itsikamahidish was thirsty and wanted to drink but he would not put down his lips for fear of the turtle's words. He looked about for a reed or a buffalo horn with which to drink the water. But he found none.

He went on a little way and found a pool of water lying in a hollow of a flat rock. "The turtle is not here," he thought. "I can now drink in safety." He stooped to drink. The turtle seized him by the upper lip, holding him fast.

The same little winter bird now came flying about in evident joy and singing, "Ná-sȧ-sȧ," Don't bite hard! The turtle loosened his hold, but did not let go. The bird sang, "Ná-ski-skid, Bite hard!" The turtle did so. So the two worried Itsikamahidish for some time. At last the bird flew away with a flirt, calling, "Ki-da-kip!" Bite it off!" The turtle bit off the coyote's lip.

Itsikamahidish took clay and plastered it over his upper lip. "It hurts me," he groaned. But he went back and cut up the beavers, making a great pile of meat.

## STORY OF ITSIKAMAHIDISH AND THE WILD POTATO (VOL. 16, 1914)

Once Itsikamahidish was wandering around after a heavy rain. In a coulee in the woods, he found a place where the rain had washed down the earth of the embankment on either side, washing out at the same time a number of wild potato roots; these roots were lying in the bottom of the coulee.

"Ha," thought the chief, – Itsikamahidish was Coyote chief, – "I shall eat now and be full!" and he smiled for he was hungry.

He spoke to one of the roots. "Who are you, Wild Potato?"

"You already know me; have you not just called me Potato?" asked the root.

"Always every chief has two names; what is your other name?" asked Itsikamahidish.

"I have no other; I am just Potato," the wild potato answered.

"Oh, yes you have. Tell it to me!" said Itsikamahidish.

The potato got mad at this. "Yes, I have another name," he said sarcastically. It is "When-a-man-emits-gas-he-goes-up-high."

"Good!" said Itsikamahidish. "That is a fine name!" and he sat down and ate and ate till he filled up his stomach. Then he went away.

After a while he emitted gas, and he shook a little as he did so. "Good!" he laughed.

In a little time he emitted gas a second time. "Good, good," he cried. But again he shook. "I must look fine! I must look fine!" he cried. "I will go and call on my sweet heart. She will be proud of me."

He dressed and painted and even trimmed his hair a little.

Again he emitted gas, and this time he leaped up a little. Still delighted, he ran around among his friends and showed them what strange new thing he could do. But now every time he emitted gas he leaped higher and higher. He got scared. He leaped to the height of the trees, and even higher. Now when he came down he was nearly killed with the fall.

He seized hold of trees and held on when he emitted gas, but the trees were torn out by the roots. He tried to retain the gas in his stomach but could not.

He went about crying out, "Who can keep me from leaping when I emit gas?"

The broom brush (or buck brush) cried out, "What is the matter with you, Itsikamahidish?"

Itsikamahidish took out his pipe and gave it to the broom brush to smoke. "I want to find what thing is the strongest in all the world," he said. "I want it to hold me. When I take hold of rocks or trees and emit gas, I tear them all out by the roots!"

"All right," said the broom brush, "take hold of me. I am strong!"

"I want to emit gas now," said Itsikamahidish, "what shall I do?"

"Seize me with both hands," cried the broom brush. Itsikamahidish did so. When he emitted gas his legs flew up in the air, but he was not precipitated upward himself. All day long he remained by the bush. Every time he gassed, his legs flew upward, but he saved himself from flying upward by holding to the broom brush.

At the end of the day the Indians found him lying there. Itsikamahidish's legs and the lower parts of his body were all swelled up and he was a very sick man.

And that is the end of the story.

Thus you see that wild potatoes cause one to emit gas. If you eat many of them, either raw or cooked, they will cause your body to swell up and you to emit gas, just as happened to Itsikamahidish.

## HOW THE PRAIRIE CHICKEN WAS MADE (VOL. 18, 1915)

The two Elders, Itsikamahidic and One Man, made the earth and the world, and last of all, the birds, all kinds. They had finished, and had said to the birds, "Get ready to fly to that tree, to make your nests." This tree stood solitary, by itself, on the bank of the Missouri.

The birds were nearly ready to start, when a bird ran forward, with just one feather; the feather had pretty bars on it. "Here," he cried, "I am the tsistska, or prairie chicken. I want to be made into a bird!" This being was of course a spirit, and he wanted to be made into a bird, with a bird's body.

"We are nearly ready to start," said one of the elders. "Therefore hasten, – and here, everybody, give something of yours to make this bird a body!"

Men and animals and all kinds of created things were around the elders, for they had created them. A spirit of fun took possession of the company. And each one began to offer something of his own to make the prairie chicken's body, – something that would appear ridiculous.

"I will give one of my claws for his beak," cried the beaver.

A man drew back the prepuce of his penis, exposing the head. "Here, he cried, "take my penis for the bird's head!" This the elders did, fixing the beaver's claw on the end, for the beak.

"I will be the prairie chicken's eye," called the little black bug that lives in the ground. So the prairie chicken now had an eye.

"And here," said the owl, "take one of my soft feathers and put it on his head, for a crest!" This also they did. And now that the new bird's head was provided for, they built together the body.

First came the breast. "Here," said a woman, "take this for his breast." And she pointed on her body to the mons veneris, the swelling out place just above a woman's secret parts, and over the forward part of the pelvic bone. This was made into the bird's breast.

Above a prairie chicken's eye is a yellow place. Said the baby, "Take my dung and paint a yellow spot over each of the bird's eyes."

When bones that are partly decayed are boiled for bone grease, the oil floats on the top of the water in the pot in globules, making the surface of the water appear spotted. Some one, perhaps seeing some bone grease on the ground, cried out, "Put this grease on his back." They did so, and now a prairie chicken's back is spotted, like bone grease on the top of the water in which it is boiled.

The vine cried out, "I will give myself to make his guts." The elders took the vine and filled the inside of the bird's body.

"Let him have a leg just like mine," said the owl, offering his own leg for the purpose. The elders gave the owl's leg, down to the feet, covered the whole way with short feathers! For in a prairie chicken the leg is feathered down to the toes, like an owl's.

"Give the new bird wings," somebody cried.

"Take my paws for his wings," said the grizzly bear, a big one. And now a prairie chicken's wings are bent just like a bear's paws.[8]

"Some one give him feet," they cried.

"I will give the feet," said the little worm. And the prairie chicken has toes and foot the color and appearance of a little worm.

"Now somebody give him claws," cried the people.

"I will be claws for him," cried the sunflower seed. And sure enough the prairie chicken has claws like sunflower seed to this day.

"The bird has no tail yet," laughed the people. "Somebody furnish him one."

---

8 The Hidatsas do not admit that a black bear is a true bear [Wilson's note].

"I will give him my tail," said the rattle snake.

And now, when the prairie chickens dance in the spring you can hear their tails rattle a quarter of a mile away.

## INDIAN LIFE IN FORMER DAYS COMPARED WITH THE PRESENT LIFE (VOL. 22, 1918)

In old times, and even when I was young, it was hard for us to get tools; and house building of any kind was hard work. Now we can build a house of any shape we wish, and tools are easy to get. In this respect our new way of living is better than the old.

On the other hand, we had plenty to eat and wear then, abundance of meat and fur robes and tanned skins. We did not have to buy food with money, and the new food that white men have brought us, and their diseases, cause our people to die. In olden days we did not thus die.

Neither do I like white men's laws. I do not understand them nor know how to make them rule my life.

I think also that it is a very hard thing for us to have to let our children be taken from us and sent away to school where we cannot see them.

# Sarah Winnemucca
# (Thocmetony, Shell Flower; Paiute, c.1844–1891)

*The daughter of a respected Paiute leader, Sarah Winnemucca was born about 1844 near Humboldt Lake in what is now northwestern Nevada. Winnemucca became a well-known activist for Indian rights in the late nineteenth century. Primarily self-educated, becoming fluent in three Indian languages as well as English and Spanish, Winnemucca spent periods of her youth among whites, briefly attending a white school during one of her periods of residence in southern California. She lived during a period of extreme upheaval and hardship, for white settlers appeared in increasing numbers on traditional Northern Paiute lands in present-day western Nevada, northern California and southeastern Oregon. Assuming the place of tribal interpreter, Winnemucca was a courageous intermediary between US military leaders, government agents, other tribes, and her own people, facing daunting personal hardship and danger in service to her community.*

Life Among the Piutes: Their Wrongs and Claims, *her wide-ranging major publication, describes such events as the first encounters of Paiutes with whites; the Bannock Indian War of 1878; and the achievement of her father's dream, the creation of a reservation in 1889 on some of the Paiutes' ancestral lands. Complex in both content and form, combining elements of history, autobiography, myth, sentimental appeal, humor, adventure, political tract, and oratory, Winnemucca's remarkable story grips the reader with its intensity and fast pace. Describing her diverse experience as a translator for the US Army, an advocate for the Paiutes in Washington, an accomplished and powerful stage performer on both coasts, and an innovative school reformer and teacher, the volume also seeks to teach white readers about the beliefs and experiences of her people. Like Alice Callahan, Winnemucca delineates a peaceful and civilized tribe deserving whites' generosity and understanding. Willing to risk her livelihood and even her life, she gives outspoken testimony against the wrongs committed by reservation agents, whose corruption, greed, and indifference to suffering outraged not only Sarah but many sympathetic observers. She also exposes how governmental representatives and elected officials attempted to prevent her from lecturing and garnering support for her cause.*

*Many contemporary readers may be surprised by her praise of the US Army, whose commanding officers often proved to be much more honorable and humane than government-appointed reservation agents, who were sometimes only putative Christians. These agents draw some of Winnemucca's most intense scorn and severest criticism, for they not only profited from government supplies intended for the Indians, but they regularly permitted the Indians in their care to freeze and starve to death. Her fiery stance, which contributed to the controversy that she often provoked, inspired her to tell one agent that "hell is full of just such Christians as you are."*

*Negotiating between two worlds was never easy, and Winnemucca was often placed in an unstable and uncomfortable position with her own people by the false promises of white officials as well as by her willingness to participate in some of the policies of assimilation. Her gender also caused her difficulties; like many women reformers of her time of any ethnicity, she suffered from the claim that she was promiscuous. In view of the prevalent and unrelenting sexual abuse of Indian women by white men, this charge against her was intensely ironic. At least two of the wars that Sarah describes were sparked by such abuse; in the case of the Pyramid Lake War of 1860, two traders kidnapped and concealed two girls of about twelve years old, and when their father discovered them "lying on a little bed with their mouth tied up with rags," members of the tribe killed the perpetrators. Engendering a similar response in the reader, Sarah's outrage is palpable when she reports local whites' version of the incident: "The bloodthirsty savages had murdered two innocent, hard-working, industrious, kind-hearted settlers."*

*Later in her life, frustrated and disappointed with the government's false promises and the corruption of its agents, Winnemucca decided that she could best serve her people by opening an Indian-run school. With the support of formidable Boston reformer, Elizabeth Palmer Peabody, and her sister Mary Mann (also the editor of* Life Among the Piutes*), Sarah founded, managed, and taught at the Peabody Indian School for nearly four years. Her school not only practiced bilingualism, it also affirmed Paiute values and traditions, in sharp contrast to government-run schools and missionary institutions like the one described by Zitkala-Ša. Winnemucca died young, and in her last few years, she suffered from ill health brought on by long-term physical hardship in her varying roles, as well as from the emotional stresses due to her last marriage to Lewis Hopkins, a drinker and gambler. Participating in the traditions of Indian women's autobiography and social activism, Winnemucca offers a touchstone voice in the latter part of the nineteenth century.*


## BIBLIOGRAPHY

### Primary

Winnemucca, Sarah. *Life Among the Piutes: Their Wrongs and Claims*. Ed. Mrs. Horace Mann. Boston and New York: privately printed, 1883. Rpt. Chalfant, 1969; Nevada, 1994.

### Secondary

Canfield, Gae Whitney. *Sarah Winnemucca of the Northern Paiutes*. Oklahoma, 1983.

Georgi-Findlay, Brigitte. "The Frontiers of Native American Women's Writing: Sarah Winnemucca's *Life among the Piutes*." In *New Voices in Native American Literary Criticism*. Ed. Arnold Krupat. Smithsonian, 1993. 222–52.

Lape, Noreen Groover. "I would rather be with my people, but not to live with them as they live": Cultural Liminality and Double Consciousness in Sarah Winnemucca Hopkins's *Life Among the Piutes: Their Wrongs and Claims*. *American Indian Quarterly* 22:3 (1998): 259–79.

Lukens, Margo. "Her 'Wrongs and Claims': Sarah Winnemucca's Strategic Narrative of Abuse." *Wicazo Sa Review* 13:1 (1998): 93–108.

Ruoff, A. LaVonne Brown. "Three Nineteenth-Century American Indian Autobiographers." In Ruoff, A. LaVonne Brown and Jerry W. Ward, eds. *Redefining American Literary History*. New York : MLA, 1990. 251–69.

——. "Early Native American Women Authors: Jane Johnston Schoolcraft, Sarah Winnemucca, S. Alice Callahan, E. Pauline Johnson, and Zitkala-Ša." In *Nineteenth-Century American Women Writers: A Critical Reader*. Ed. Karen L. Kilcup. Blackwell, 1998. 81–111.

Sands, Kathleen Mullen. "Indian Women's Personal Narrative: Voices Past and Present." In Culley, Margo, ed. *American Women's Autobiography: Fea(s)ts of Memory*. Wisconsin, 1992. 268–94.

Strange, William C. "Story, Take Me Home: Instances of Resonance in Sarah Winnemucca Hopkins' Life Among the Piutes." In Schirer, Thomas E., ed. *Entering the 90s: The North American Experience: Proceedings from the Native American Studies Conference at Lake Superior University, October 27–28, 1989*. Lake Superior UP, 1991. 184–94.

Walker, Cheryl. "Sarah Winnemucca's Mediations." *Indian Nation: Native American Literature and Nineteenth-Century Nationalisms*. Duke, 1997. 139–63.

# From *Life Among the Piutes* (1883)

## EDITOR'S PREFACE

My editing has consisted in copying the original manuscript in correct orthography and punctuation, with occasional emendations by the author, of a book which is an heroic act on the part of the writer. Mrs. Hopkins came to the East from the Pacific coast with the courageous purpose of telling in detail to the mass of our people, "extenuating nothing and setting down naught in malice," the story of her people's trials. Finding that in extemporaneous speech she could only speak at one time of a few points, she determined to write out the most important part of what she wished to say. In fighting with her literary deficiencies she loses some of the fervid eloquence which her extraordinary colloquial command of the English language enables her to utter, but I am confident that no one would desire that her own original words should be altered. It is the first outbreak of the American Indian in human literature, and has a single aim – *to tell the truth* as it lies in the heart and mind of a true patriot, and one whose knowledge of the two races gives her an opportunity of comparing them justly. At this moment, when the United States seem waking up to their duty to the original possessors of our immense territory, it is of the first importance to hear what only an Indian and an Indian woman can tell. To tell it was her own deep impulse, and the dying charge given her by her father, the truly parental chief of his beloved tribe.

M. M. [Mary Mann]

## CHAPTER I: FIRST MEETING OF PIUTES AND WHITES

I was born somewhere near 1844, but am not sure of the precise time. I was a very small child when the first white people came into our country. They came like a lion, yes, like a roaring lion, and have continued so ever since, and I have never forgotten their first coming. My people were scattered at that time over nearly all the territory now known as Nevada. My grandfather was chief of the entire Piute nation, and was camped near Humboldt Lake, with a small portion of his tribe, when a party travelling eastward from California was seen coming. When the news was brought to my grandfather, he asked what they looked like? When told that they had hair on their faces, and were white, he jumped up and clasped his hands together, and cried aloud, –

"My white brothers, – my long-looked for white brothers have come at last!"

He immediately gathered some of his leading men, and went to the place where the party had gone into camp. Arriving near them, he was commanded to halt in a manner that was readily understood without an interpreter. Grandpa at once made signs of friendship by throwing down his robe and throwing up his arms to show them he had no weapons; but in vain, – they kept him at a distance. He knew not what to do. He had expected so much pleasure in welcoming his white brothers to the best in the land, that after looking at them sorrowfully for a little while, he came away quite unhappy. But he would not give them up so easily. He took some of his most trustworthy men and followed them day after day, camping near them at night, and travelling in sight of them by day, hoping in this way to gain their confidence. But he was disappointed, poor dear old soul!

I can imagine his feelings, for I have drank deeply from the same cup. When I think of my past life, and the bitter trials I have endured, I can scarcely believe I live, and yet I do; and, with the help of Him who notes the sparrow's fall, I mean to fight for my down-trodden race while life lasts.

Seeing they would not trust him, my grandfather left them, saying, "Perhaps they will come again next year." Then he summoned his whole people, and told them this tradition: –

"In the beginning of the world there were only four, two girls and two boys. Our forefather and mother were only two, and we are their children. You all know that a great while ago there was a happy family in this world. One girl and one boy were dark and the others were white. For a time they got along together without quarrelling, but soon they disagreed, and there was trouble. They were cross to one another and fought, and our parents were very much grieved. They prayed that their children might learn better, but it did not do any good; and afterwards the whole household was made so unhappy that the father and mother saw that they must separate their children; and then our father took the dark boy and girl, and the white boy and girl, and asked them, 'Why are you so cruel to each other?' They hung down their heads, and would not speak. They were ashamed. He said to them, 'Have I not been kind to you all, and given you everything your hearts wished for? You do not have to hunt and kill your own game to live upon. You see, my dear children, I have power to call whatsoever kind of game we want to eat; and I also have the power to separate my dear children, if they are not good to each other.' So he separated his children by a word. He said, 'Depart from each other, you cruel children; – go across the mighty ocean and do not seek each other's lives.'

"So the light girl and boy disappeared by that one word, and their parents saw them no more, and they were grieved, although they knew their children were happy. And by-and-by the dark children grew into a large nation; and we believe it is the one we belong to, and that the nation that sprung from the white children will some time send some one to meet us and heal all the old trouble. Now the white people we saw a few days ago must certainly be our white brothers, and I want to welcome them. I want to love them as I love all of you. But they would not let me; they were afraid. But they will come again, and I want you one and all to promise that, should I not live to welcome them myself, you will not hurt a hair on their heads, but welcome them as I tried to do."

How good of him to try and heal the wound, and how vain were his efforts! My people had never seen a white man, and yet they existed, and were a strong race. The people promised as he wished, and they all went back to their work.

The next year came a great emigration, and camped near Humboldt Lake. The name of the man in charge of the trains was Captain Johnson, and they stayed three days to rest their horses, as they had a long journey before them without water. During their stay my grandfather and some of his people called upon them, and they all shook hands, and when our white brothers were going away they gave my grandfather a white tin plate. Oh, what a time they had over that beautiful gift, – it was so bright! They say that after they left, my grandfather called for all his people to come together, and he then showed them the beautiful gift which he had received from his white brothers. Everybody was so pleased; nothing like it was ever seen in our country before. My grandfather thought so much of it that he bored holes in it and fastened it on his head and wore it as his hat. He held it in as much admiration as my white sisters hold their diamond rings or a sealskin jacket. So that winter they talked of nothing but their white brothers. The following spring there came great news down the Humboldt River, saying that there were some more of the white brothers coming, and there was something among them that was burning all in a blaze. My grandfather asked them what it was like. They told him it looked like a man; it had legs and hands and a head, but the head had quit burning, and it was left quite black. There was the greatest excitement among my people everywhere about the men in a blazing fire. They were excited because they did not know there were any people in the world but the two, – that is, the Indians and the whites; they thought that was all of us in the beginning of the world, and, of course, we did not know where the others had come from, and we don't know yet. Ha! ha! oh, what a laughable thing that was! It was two negroes wearing red shirts!

The third year more emigrants came, and that summer Captain Fremont, who is now General Fremont.

My grandfather met him, and they were soon friends. They met just where the railroad crosses Truckee River, now called Wadsworth, Nevada. Captain Fremont gave my grandfather the name of Captain Truckee, and he also called the river after him. Truckee is an Indian word, it means *all right*, or *very well.* A party of twelve of my people went to California with Captain Fremont. I do not know just how long they were gone.

During the time my grandfather was away in California, where he staid till after the Mexican war, there was a girl-baby born in our family. I can just remember it. It must have been in spring, because everything was green. I was away playing with some other children when my mother called me to come to her. So I ran to her. She then asked me to sit down, which I did. She then handed me some beautiful beads, and asked me if I would like to buy something with them. I said: –

"Yes, mother, – some pine nuts."

My mother said: –

"Would you like something else you can love and play with? Would you like to have a little sister?" I said, –

"Yes, dear mother, a little, little sister; not like my sister Mary, for she won't let me play with her. She leaves me and goes with big girls to play;" and then my mother wanted to know if I would give my pretty beads for the little sister.

Just then the baby let out such a cry it frightened me; and I jumped up and cried so that my mother took me in her arms, and said it was a little sister for me, and not to be afraid. This is all I can remember about it.

When my grandfather went to California he helped Captain Fremont fight the Mexicans. When he came back he told the people what a beautiful country California was. Only eleven returned home, one having died on the way back.

They spoke to their people in the English language, which was very strange to them all.

Captain Truckee, my grandfather, was very proud of it, indeed. They all brought guns with them. My grandfather would sit down with us for hours, and would say over and over again, "Goodee gun, goodee, goodee gun, heap shoot." They also brought some of the soldiers' clothes with all their brass buttons, and my people were very much astonished to see the clothes, and all that time they were peaceable toward their white brothers. They had learned to love them, and they hoped more of them would come. Then my people were less barbarous than they are nowadays.

That same fall, after my grandfather came home, he told my father to take charge of his people and hold the tribe, as he was going back to California with as many of his people as he could get to go with him. So my father took his place as Chief of the Piutes, and had it as long as he lived. Then my grandfather started back to California again with about thirty families. That same fall, very late, the emigrants kept coming. It was this time that our white brothers first came amongst us. They could not get over the mountains, so they had to live with us. It was on Carson River, where the great Carson City stands now. You call my people bloodseeking. My people did not seek to kill them, nor did they steal their horses, – no, no, far from it. During the winter my people helped them. They gave them such as they had to eat. They did not hold out their hands and say: –

"You can't have anything to eat unless you pay me." No, – no such word was used by us savages at that time; and the persons I am speaking of are living yet; they could speak for us if they choose to do so.

The following spring, before my grandfather returned home, there was a great excitement among my people on account of fearful news coming from different tribes, that the people whom they called their white brothers were killing everybody that came in their way, and all the Indian tribes had gone into the mountains to save their lives. So my father told all his people to go into the mountains and hunt and lay up food for the coming winter. Then we all went into the mountains. There was a fearful story they told us children. Our mothers told us that the whites were killing everybody and eating them. So we were all afraid of them. Every dust that we could see blowing in the valleys we would say it was the white people. In the late fall my father told his people to go to the rivers and fish, and we all went to Humboldt River, and the women went to work gathering wild seed, which they grind between the rocks. The stones are round, big enough to hold in the hands. The women did this when they got back, and when they had gathered all they could they put it in one place and covered it with grass, and then over the grass mud. After it is covered it looks like an Indian wigwam.

Oh, what a fright we all got one morning to hear some white people were coming. Every one ran as best they could. My poor mother was left with my little sister and me. Oh, I never can forget it. My poor mother was carrying my little sister on her back, and trying to make me run; but I was so frightened I could not move my feet, and while my poor mother was trying to get me along my aunt overtook us, and she said to my mother: "Let us bury our girls, or we shall all be killed and eaten up." So they went to work and buried us, and told us if we heard any noise not to cry out, for if we did they would surely kill us and eat us. So our mothers buried me and my cousin, planted sage bushes over our faces to keep the sun from burning them, and there we were left all day.

Oh, can any one imagine my feelings *buried alive*, thinking every minute that I was to be unburied and eaten up by the people that my grandfather loved so much? With my heart throbbing, and not daring to breathe, we lay there all day. It seemed that the night would never come. Thanks be to God! the night came at last. Oh, how I cried and said: "Oh, father, have you forgotten me? Are you never coming for me?" I cried so I thought my very heartstrings would break.

At last we heard some whispering. We did not dare to whisper to each other, so we lay still. I could hear their footsteps coming nearer and nearer. I thought my heart was coming right out of my mouth. Then I heard my mother say, "'T is right here!" Oh, can any one in this world ever imagine what were my feelings when I was dug up by my poor mother and father? My cousin and I were once more happy in our mothers' and fathers' care, and we were taken to where all the rest were.

I was once buried alive; but my second burial shall be for ever, where no father or mother will come and dig me up. It shall not be with throbbing heart that I shall listen for coming footsteps. I shall be in the sweet rest of peace, – I, the chieftain's weary daughter.

Well, while we were in the mountains hiding, the people that my grandfather called our white brothers came along to where our winter supplies were. They set everything we had left on fire. It was a fearful sight. It was all we had for the winter, and it was all burnt during that night. My father took some of his men during the night to try and save some of it, but they could not; it had burnt down before they got there.

These were the last white men that came along that fall. My people talked fearfully that winter about those they called our white brothers. My people said they had something like awful thunder and lightning, and with that they killed everything that came in their way.

This whole band of white people perished in the mountains, for it was too late to cross them. We could have saved them, only my people were afraid of them. We never knew who they were, or where they came from. So, poor things, they must have suffered fearfully, for they all starved there. The snow was too deep.

Early in the following spring, my father told all his people to go to the mountains, for there would be a great emigration that summer. He told them he had had a wonderful dream, and wanted to tell them all about it.

He said, "Within ten days come together at the sink of Carson, and I will tell you my dream."

The sub-chiefs went everywhere to tell their people what my father had told them to say; and when the time came we all went to the sink of Carson.

Just about noon, while we were on the way, a great many of our men came to meet us, all on their horses. Oh, what a beautiful song they sang for my father as they came near us! We passed them, and they followed us, and as we came near to the encampment, every man, woman, and child were out looking for us. They had a place all ready for us. Oh, how happy everybody was! One could hear laughter everywhere, and songs were sung by happy women and children.

My father stood up and told his people to be merry and happy for five days. It is a rule among our people always to have five days to settle anything. My father told them to dance at night, and that the men should hunt rabbits and fish, and some were to have games of football, or any kind of sport or playthings they wished, and the women could do the same, as they had nothing else to do. My people were so happy during the five days, – the women ran races, and the men ran races on foot and on horses.

My father got up very early one morning, and told his people the time had come, – that we could no longer be happy as of old, as the white people we called our brothers had brought a great trouble and sorrow among us already. He went on and said, –

"These white people must be a great nation, as they have houses that move. It is wonderful to see them move along. I fear we will suffer greatly by their coming to our country; they come for no good to us, although my father said they were our brothers, but they do not seem to think we are like them. What do you all think about it? Maybe I am wrong. My dear children, there is something telling me that I am not wrong, because I am sure they have minds like us, and think as we do; and I know that they were doing wrong when they set fire to our winter supplies. They surely knew it was our food."

And this was the first wrong done to us by our white brothers.

Now comes the end of our merrymaking.

Then my father told his people his fearful dream, as he called it. He said, –

"I dreamt this same thing three nights, – the very same. I saw the greatest emigration that has yet been through our country. I looked North and South and East and West, and saw nothing but dust, and

I heard a great weeping. I saw women crying, and I also saw my men shot down by the white people. They were killing my people with something that made a great noise like thunder and lightning, and I saw the blood streaming from the mouths of my men that lay all around me. I saw it as if it was real. Oh, my dear children! You may all think it is only a dream, – nevertheless, I feel that it will come to pass. And to avoid bloodshed, we must all go to the mountains during the summer, or till my father comes back from California. He will then tell us what to do. Let us keep away from the emigrant roads and stay in the mountains all summer. There are to be a great many pine-nuts this summer, and we can lay up great supplies for the coming winter, and if the emigrants don't come too early, we can take a run down and fish for a month, and lay up dried fish. I know we can dry a great many in a month, and young men can go into the valleys on hunting excursions, and kill as many rabbits as they can. In that way we can live in the mountains all summer and all winter too."

So ended my father's dream. During that day one could see old women getting together talking over what they had heard my father say. They said, –

"It is true what our great chief has said, for it was shown to him by a higher power. It is not a dream. Oh, it surely will come to pass. We shall no longer be a happy people, as we now are; we shall no longer go here and there as of old; we shall no longer build our big fires as a signal to our friends, for we shall always be afraid of being seen by those bad people."

"Surely they don't eat people?"

"Yes, they do eat people, because they ate each other up in the mountains last winter."

This was the talk among the old women during the day.

"Oh, how grieved we are! Oh, where will it end?"

That evening one of our doctors called for a council, and all the men gathered together in the council-tent to hear what their medicine man had to say, for we all believe our doctor is greater than any human being living. We do not call him a medicine man because he gives medicine to the sick, as your doctors do. Our medicine man cures the sick by the laying on of hands, and we have doctresses as well as doctors. We believe that our doctors can communicate with holy spirits from heaven. We call heaven the Spirit Land.

Well, when all the men get together, of course there must be smoking the first thing. After the pipe has passed round five times to the right, it stops, and then he tells them to sing five songs. He is the leader in the song-singing. He sings heavenly songs, and he says he is singing with the angels. It is hard to describe these songs. They are all different, and he says the angels sing them to him.

Our doctors never sing war-songs, except at a war-dance, as they never go themselves on the war-path. While they were singing the last song, he said, –

"Now I am going into a trance. While I am in the trance you must smoke just as you did before; not a word must be spoken while I am in the trance."

About fifteen minutes after the smoking was over, he began to make a noise as if he was crying a great way off. The noise came nearer and nearer, until he breathed, and after he came to, he kept on crying. And then he prophesied, and told the people that my father's dream was true in one sense of the word, – that is, "Our people will not all die at the hands of our white brothers. They will kill a great many with their guns, but they will bring among us a fearful disease that will cause us to die by hundreds."

We all wept, for we believed this word came from heaven.

So ended our feast, and every family went to its own home in the pine-nut mountains, and remained there till the pine-nuts were ripe. They ripen about the last of June.

Late in that fall, there came news that my grandfather was on his way home. Then my father took a great many of his men and went to meet his father, and there came back a runner, saying, that all our people must come together. It was said that my grandfather was bringing bad news. All our people came to receive their chieftain; all the old and young men and their wives went to meet him. One evening there came a man, saying that all the women who had little children should go to a high mountain. They wanted them to go because they brought white men's guns, and they made such a fearful noise, it might even kill some of the little children. My grandfather had lost one of his men while he was away.

So all the women that had little children went. My mother was among the rest; and every time the guns were heard by us, the children would scream. I thought, for one that my heart would surely break.

So some of the women went down from the mountain and told them not to shoot any more, or their children would die with fright. When our mothers brought us down to our homes the nearer we came to the camp, the more I cried, –

"Oh, mother, mother, don't take us there!" I fought my mother, – I bit her. Then my father came, and took me in his arms and carried me to the camp. I put my head in his bosom, and would not look up for a long time. I heard my grandfather say, –

"So the young lady is ashamed because her sweetheart has come to see her. Come, dearest, that won't do after I have had such a hard time to come to see my sweetheart, that she should be ashamed to look at me."

Then he called my two brothers to him, and said to them, "Are you glad to see me?" And my brothers both told him that they were glad to see him. Then my grandfather said to them, –

"See that young lady; she does not love her sweetheart any more, does she? Well, I shall not live if she does not come and tell me she loves me. I shall take that gun, and I shall kill myself."

That made me worse than ever, and I screamed and cried so hard that my mother had to take me away. So they kept weeping for the little one three or four days. I did not make up with my grandfather for a long time. He sat day after day, and night after night, telling his people about his white brothers. He told them that the whites were really their brothers, that they were very kind to everybody, especially to children; that they were always ready to give something to children. He told them what beautiful things their white brothers had, – what beautiful clothes they wore, and about the big houses that go on the mighty ocean, and travel faster than any horse in the world. His people asked him how big they were. "Well, as big as that hill you see there, and as high as the mountain over us."

"Oh, that is not possible, – it would sink, surely."

"It is every word truth, and that is nothing to what I am going to tell you. Our white brothers are a mighty nation, and have more wonderful things than that. They have a gun that can shoot a ball bigger than my head, that can go as far off as that mountain you see over there."

The mountain he spoke of at that time was about twenty miles across from where we were. People opened their eyes when my grandfather told of the many battles they had with the Mexicans, and about their killing so many of the Mexicans, and taking their big city away from them, and how mighty they were. These wonderful things were talked about all winter long. The funniest thing was that he would sing some of the soldier's roll-calls, and the air to the Star-spangled Banner, which everybody learned during the winter.

He then showed us a more wonderful thing than all the others that he had brought. It was a paper, which he said could talk to him. He took it out and he would talk to it, and talk with it. He said, "This can talk to all our white brothers, and our white sisters, and their children. Our white brothers are beautiful, and our white sisters are beautiful, and their children are beautiful! He also said the paper can travel like the wind, and it can go and talk with their fathers and brothers and sisters, and come back to tell what they are doing, and whether they are well or sick."

After my grandfather told us this, our doctors and doctresses said, –

"If they can do this wonderful thing, they are not truly human, but pure spirits. None but heavenly spirits can do such wonderful things. We can communicate with the spirits, yet we cannot do wonderful things like them. Oh, our great chieftain, we are afraid your white brothers will yet make your people's hearts bleed. You see if they don't; for we can see it. Their blood is all around us, and the dead are lying all about us, and we cannot escape it. It will come. Then you will say our doctors and doctresses did know. Dance, sing, play, it will do no good; we cannot drive it away. They have already done the mischief, while you were away."

But this did not go far with my grandfather. He kept talking to his people about the good white people, and told them all to get ready to go with him to California the following spring.

Very late that fall, my grandfather and my father and a great many more went down to the Humboldt River to fish. They brought back a great many fish, which we were very glad to get; for none of our people had been down to fish the whole summer.

When they came back, they brought us more news. They said there were some white people living at the Humboldt sink. They were the first ones my father had seen face to face. He said they were not like "humans." They were more like owls than any thing else. They had hair on their faces, and had white eyes, and looked beautiful.[1]

I tell you we children had to be very good, indeed, during the winter; for we were told that if we were not good they would come and eat us up. We remained there all winter; the next spring the emigrants came as usual, and my father and grandfather and uncles, and many more went down on the Humboldt River on fishing excursions. While they were thus fishing, their white brothers came upon them and fired on them, and killed one of my uncles, and wounded another. Nine more were wounded, and five died afterwards. My other uncle got well again, and is living yet. Oh, that was a fearful thing, indeed!

After all these things had happened, my grandfather still stood up for his white brothers.

Our people had council after council, to get my grandfather to give his consent that they should go and kill those white men who were at the sink of Humboldt. No; they could do nothing of the kind while he lived. He told his people that his word was more to him than his son's life, or any one else's life either.

"Dear children," he said, "think of your own words to me; – you promised. You want me to say to you, Go and kill those that are at the sink of Humboldt. After your promise, how dare you to ask me to let your hearts be stained with the blood of those who are innocent of the deed that has been done to us by others? Is not my dear beloved son laid alongside of your dead, and you say I stand up for their lives. Yes, it is very hard, indeed; but, nevertheless, I know and you know that those men who live at the sink are not the ones that killed our men."

While my grandfather was talking, he wept, and men, women, and children, were all weeping. One could hardly hear him talking.

After he was through talking, came the saddest part. The widow of my uncle who was killed, and my mother and father all had long hair. They cut off their hair, and also cut long gashes in their arms and legs, and they were all bleeding as if they would die with the loss of blood. This continued for several days, for this is the way we mourn for our dead. When the woman's husband dies, she is first to cut off her hair, and then she braids it and puts it across his breast; then his mother and sisters, his father and brothers and all his kinsfolk cut their hair. The widow is to remain unmarried until her hair is the same length as before, and her face is not to be washed all that time, and she is to use no kind of paint, nor to make any merriment with other women until the day is set for her to do so by her father-in-law, or if she has no father-in-law, by her mother-in-law, and then she is at liberty to go where she pleases. The widower is at liberty when his wife dies; but he mourns for her in the same way, by cutting his hair off.

It was late that fall when my grandfather prevailed with his people to go with him to California. It was this time that my mother accompanied him. Everything had been got ready to start on our journey. My dear father was to be left behind. How my poor mother begged to stay with her husband! But my grandfather told her that she could come back in the spring to see her husband; so we started for California, leaving my poor papa behind. All my kinsfolk went with us but one aunt and her children.

The first night found us camped at the sink of Carson, and the second night we camped on Carson River. The third day, as we were travelling along the river, some of our men who were ahead, came back and said there were some of our white brothers' houses ahead of us. So my grandfather told us all to stop where we were while he went to see them. He was not gone long, and when he came back he brought some hard bread which they gave him. He told us that was their food, and he gave us all some to taste. That was the first I ever tasted.

Then my grandfather once more told his people that his paper talked for him, and he said, –

"Just as long as I live and have that paper which my white brothers' great chieftain has given me, I shall stand by them, come what will." He held the paper up towards heaven and kissed it, as if it was really a person. "Oh, if I should lose this," he said, "we shall all be lost. So, children, get your horses ready, and we will go on, and we will camp with them to-night, or by them, for I have a sweetheart along who is dying for fear of my white brothers." He meant me; for I was always crying and hiding under somebody's robes, for we had no blankets then.

1 When asked to explain this, she said, "Oh, their eyes were blue, and they had long beards." – Editor [Mary Mann's note].

Well, we went on; but we did not camp with them, because my poor mother and brothers and sisters told my grandfather that I was sick with crying for fright, and for him not to camp too close to them. The women were speaking two words for themselves and one for me, for they were just as afraid as I was. I had seen my brother Natchez crying when the men came back, and said there were white men ahead of us. So my grandfather did as my mother wished him to do, and we went on by them; but I did not know it, as I had my head covered while we were passing their camp. I was riding behind my older brother, and we went on and camped quite a long way from them that night.

So we travelled on to California, but did not see any more of our white brothers till we got to the head of Carson River, about fifteen miles above where great Carson City now stands.

"Now give me the baby." It was my baby-sister that grandpa took from my mother, and I peeped from under my mother's fur, and I saw some one take my little sister. Then I cried out, –

"Oh, my sister! Don't let them take her away."

And once more my poor grandfather told his people that his white brothers and sisters were very kind to children. I stopped crying, and looked at them again. Then I saw them give my brother and sister something white. My mother asked her father what it was, and he said it was *Pe-har-be,* which means sugar. Just then one of the women came to my mother with some in her hand, and grandpa said: –

"Take it, my child."

Then I held out my hand without looking. That was the first gift I ever got from a white person, which made my heart very glad.

When they went away, my grandfather called me to him, and said I must not be afraid of the white people, for they are very good. I told him that they looked so very bad I could not help it.

We travelled with them at that time two days, and the third day we all camped together where some white people were living in large white houses. My grandpa went to one of the houses, and when he came back he said his white brothers wanted him to come and get some beef and hard bread. So he took four men with him to get it, and they gave him four boxes of hard bread and a whole side of beef, and the next morning we got our horses ready to go on again. There was some kind of a fight, – that is, the captain of the train was whipping negroes who were driving his team. That made my poor grandfather feel very badly. He went to the captain, and told him he would not travel with him. He came back and said to his people that he would not travel with his white brothers any farther. We travelled two days without seeing any more of my grandfather's white brothers. At last we came to a very large encampment of white people, and they ran out of their wagons, or wood-houses, as we called them, and gathered round us. I was riding behind my brother. I was so afraid, I told him to put his robe over me, but he did not do so. I scratched him and bit him on his back, and then my poor grandfather rode up to the tents where they were, and he was asked to stay there all night with them. After grandpa had talked awhile, he said to his people that he would camp with his brothers. So he did. Oh, what nice things we all got from my grandpa's white brothers! Our men got red shirts, and our women got calico for dresses. Oh, what a pretty dress my sister got! I did not get anything, because I hid all the time. I was hiding under some robes. No one knew where I was. After all the white people were gone, I heard my poor mother cry out: –

"Oh, where is my little girl? Oh, father, can it be that the white people have carried her away? Oh, father, go and find her, – go, go, and find her!" And I also heard my brothers and sister cry. Yet I said nothing, because they had not called me to get some of the pretty things. When they began to cry, I began crawling out, and then my grandfather scolded me, and told me that his brothers loved good children, but not bad ones like me. How I did cry, and wished that I had staid at home with my father! I went to sleep crying.

I did not forget what had happened. There was a house near where we camped. My grandfather went down to the house with some of his men, and pretty soon we saw them coming back. They were carrying large boxes, and we were all looking at them. My mother said there were two white men coming with them.

"Oh, mother, what shall I do? Hide me!"

I just danced round like a wild one, which I was. I was behind my mother. When they were coming nearer, I heard my grandpa say, –

"Make a place for them to sit down."

Just then, I peeped round my mother to see them. I gave one scream, and said, –

"Oh, mother, the owls!"

I only saw their big white eyes, and I thought their faces were all hair. My mother said, –

"I wish you would send your brothers away, for my child will die."

I imagined I could see their big white eyes all night long. They were the first ones I had ever seen in my life.

We went on the next day, and passed some more of our white brothers' houses, as we called their wagons at that time. We camped on the Sanvada mountains and spent the night. My grandfather said everything that was good about the white people to me. At last we were camped upon the summit, and it snowed very hard all night, and in the morning my grandfather told his people to hurry and get their horses, and travel on, for fear we might get snowed into the mountains. That night we overtook some emigrants who were camped there to rest their oxen. This time I watched my grandfather to see what he would do. He said, "I am going to show them my rag friend again." As he rode up to one of their tents, three white men came out to him; then they took him to a large tent. Quite a number of white men came out to him. I saw him take out the paper he called his rag friend and give it to one of the men who stood looking at it; then he looked up and came toward him and held out his hand to my grandfather, and then the rest of the white men did the same all round. Then the little children and the women did the same, and I saw the little ones running to their tents and back again with something in their hands, and they were giving it to each man. The next morning I could not eat, and said to my mother, –

"Let us go back to father – let us not go with grandpa, for he is bad." My poor mother said, "We can't go alone; we would all be killed if we go, for we have no rag friend as father has. And dear, you must be good, and grandpa will love you just as well as ever. You must do what he tells you to do."

Oh, how badly I did feel! I held my two hands over my face, and was crying as if my heart would break.

"My dear, don't cry; here comes grandpa."

I heard him say, –

"Well, well, is my sweetheart never going to stop crying? Come, dear, I have something for my baby; come and see what it is."

So I went to him with my head down, not because I was afraid he would whip me, – no – no, for Indians do not whip their children. Oh, how happy I was when he told me he would give me something very beautiful. It was a little cup, and it made me very glad, indeed; and he told me it was to drink water out of, not to wear. He said, –

"I am going to tell you what I did with a beautiful gift I received from my white brothers. It was of the same kind, only it was flat and round, and it was as bright as your cup is now."

He said to his wife, "Give me my bright hat"; and she did so.

"You see I used to wear it on my head, because my white brother did not tell me what it was for." Then he began to laugh, and he laughed so long! then he stopped and said, "it was not to wear, but to eat out of, and I have made myself a fool by wearing it as a hat. Oh, how my brothers did laugh at me because I wore it at our first fight with Mexicans in Mexico. Now, dearest children, I do not want you to think my brothers laughed at me to make fun of me; no – no – it was because I wore the tin plate for a hat, that's all."

He also said they had much prettier things than this to eat out of. He went on and told us never to take anything belonging to them or lying outside of his white brothers' houses. "They hang their clothes out of doors after washing them; but they are not thrown away, and for fear some of you might think so and take them, I tell you about it. Therefore, never take anything unless they give it to you; then they will love you."

So I kept thinking over what he said to me about the good white people, and saying to myself, "I will make friends with them when we come into California."

When we came to Sacramento valley (it is a very beautiful valley), my grandfather said to his people that a great many of his white brothers were there, and he knew a great many of them; but we would not go there, – we would go on to Stockton. There he had a very good brother, who had a very big house, made of red stone; it was so high that it would tire any one to go up to some of the rooms. My uncle, my mother's brother, asked him how many rooms were up there? My grandpa said, –

"We have to climb up three times to get to the top." They all laughed, as much as to say my grandpa lied. He said, "You will not laugh when I show you what wonderful things my white brothers can do. I will tell you something more wonderful than that. My brother has a big house that runs on the river, and it whistles and makes a beautiful noise, and it has a bell on it which makes a beautiful noise also." My uncle asked again how big it was.

"Oh, you will see for yourself; we will get there to-morrow night. We will stop there ten days, and you can see for yourselves, and then you will know, my brothers, that what I have told you is true."

After travelling all day we went into camp for the night. We had been there but a little while, and there came a great many men on horseback, and camped near us. I ran to my mother and said I was sleepy, and wanted to go to bed. I did so because I did not want to see them, and I knew grandpa would have them come to see us. I heard him say he was going to see them. I lay down quietly for a little while, and then got up and looked round to see if my brother was going too. There was no one but my mother and little sister. They had all gone to see them.

"Lie down, dear," my mother said.

I did so, but I did not sleep for a long time, for I was thinking about the house that runs on the water. I wondered what it was like. I kept saying to myself, "Oh, I wish it was to-morrow now." I heard mother say, –

"They are coming." Pretty soon I heard grandpa say, "They are not my brothers." Mother said, "Who are they?"

"They are what my brothers call Mexicans. They are the people we fought; if they knew who I was they would kill me, but they shall not know. I am not going to show them my rag friend, for fear my rag friend will tell of me."

Oh my! oh my! That made me worse than ever. I cried, so that one could have heard my poor heart beat. Oh, how I wished I was back with my father again! All the children were not afraid of the white people – only me. My brothers would go everywhere with grandpa. I would not have been so afraid of them if I had not been told by my own father and grandmamma that the white people would kill little children and eat them.

Everything was all right, and the next day we went on our journey, and after a whole day's journey we came within a mile of the town. The sun was almost down when grandpa stopped and said, –

"Now, one and all, listen as you go on. You will hear the water-house bell ring."

So we did, and pretty soon we heard the prettiest noise we had ever heard in all our life-time. It became dark before we got to the town, but we could see something like stars away ahead of us. Oh, how I wished I had staid with my father in our own country. I cried out, saying, –

"Oh, mother, I am so afraid. I cannot go to the white people. They are so much like the owls with their big white eyes. I cannot make friends with them."

I kept crying until we came nearer the town, and camped for the night. My grandpa said to his men, –

"Unsaddle your horses while I go and see my friend."

He came back in a few moments, and said: –

"Turn your horses into the corral, and now we will go to bed without making any fire."

So we did, and I for one was glad. But although very tired I could not sleep, for grandpa kept telling us that at daybreak we would hear the water-house's whistle. The next morning my mother waked me, and I got up and looked round me. I found no one but mother.

"Oh, where is sister, mother?"

"Oh, she has gone with the rest to see the water-house."

"Mother, did you hear it whistle?"

"Yes, we all heard it, and it made such a fearful noise! The one that whistled has gone on. But another came in just like it, and made just such a noise. Your brother was here awhile ago. He said the water-house had many looking-glasses all round it, and when it came in it was so tired, it breathed so hard, it made us almost deaf."

"Say, mother, let us go and see."

But mother said, –

"No, your brother said there were so many white people that one can hardly get along. We will wait until your grandpa comes, and hear what they all say. A'n't you hungry, my child?"

I said, "Yes."

"Your brother brought something that tastes like sugar."

It was cake, and I ate so much it made me sick.

I was sick all day and night, and the next day I had the chills. Oh, I was very, very sick; my poor mother thought I would die. I heard her say to grandpa one day, –

"The sugar-bread was poisoned which your white brother gave us to eat, and it has made my poor little girl so sick that I am afraid she will die." My poor mother and brothers and sisters were crying; mother had me in her arms. My grandpa came and took me in his arms and said to me, –

"Open your eyes, dear, and see your grandpa!" I did as he told me, because I had not forgotten what mother had said to me, to do whatever he told me to do, and then he would love me. The reason I had not opened my eyes was because my head ached so badly that it hurt me so I shut them again. My poor mother cried the more, and all our people gathered around us and began to cry. My mother said to grandpa, –

"Can there be anything done for her?"

"Dear daughter," he said, "I am sorry you have such bad hearts against my white brothers. I have eaten some sugar-bread, and so have you, and all the rest of us, and we did not get sick. Dear daughter, you should have blessed the strange food before you gave it to your child to eat; maybe this is why she is sick."

It is a law among us that all strange food is blessed before eaten, and also clothing of any kind that is given to us by any one, Indians or white people, must be blessed before worn. So all my people came together and prayed over me, but it was all in vain. I do not know how long I was sick, but very long. I was indeed poisoned, not by the bread I had eaten, but by poison oak. My face swelled so that I could not see for a long time, but I could hear everything. At last some one came that had a voice like an angel. I really thought it must be an angel, for I had been taught by my father that an angel comes to watch the sick one and take the soul to the spirit land. I kept thinking it must be so, and I learned words from the angel (as I thought it). I could not see, for my eyes were swollen shut. These were the words, "Poor little girl, it is too bad!" It was said so often by the pretty sweet voice, I would say it over and over when I was suffering so badly, and would cry out, "Poor little girl, it is too bad!" At last I began to get well, and I could hear my grandpa say the same words.

Then I began to see a little, and the first thing I asked my mother, was, "What was the angel saying to me?" Oh, how frightened my poor mother was! She cried out, –

"Oh, father, come here! My little girl is talking to the angels, – she is dying."

My sister and brothers ran to her, crying, and for the first time since I was sick I cried out, "Oh, don't, don't cry! I am getting well, – indeed I am. Stop crying, and give me something to eat. I was only asking you what the angel meant by saying 'Poor little girl, it is too bad!'"

"Oh," says grandpa, "it is the good white woman; I mean my white sister, who comes here to see you. She has made you well. She put some medicine on your face, and has made you see. Ain't you glad to see?"

"I said, "Can I see her now?"

"Yes, she will come pretty soon; she comes every day to see you."

Then my mother came with something for me to eat, but I said, "Wait, grandpa, tell me more about the good woman."

He said, "My dear child, she is truly an angel, and she has come every day to see you. You will love her, I know."

"Dear grandpa, will she come pretty soon? I want to see her."

Grandpa said, "I will go and get her. You won't be afraid, will you?"

So my grandpa went. I tried my best to eat, but I could not, it was so hard.

My sister said, "They are coming."

I said, "Mother, fix my eyes so I can see the angel. Has it wings, mother?"

Mother said, "You will see for yourself."

Just then they came, and grandpa said, "Here she is." The first thing she did she put her beautiful white hand on my forehead. I looked at her; she was, indeed, a beautiful angel. She said the same words as before. I asked my grandpa what she was saying. Then he told me what she meant by it. I began to get well very fast, and this sweet angel came every day and brought me something nice to eat; and oh, what pretty dresses she brought me. When she brought the dresses she talked to my grandpa a long time, and she cried, and after she went away he said to my mother, –

"The dresses which my white sister gave my child were her dead child's clothes, so they should be burned." I began to cry, because I did not want them burned. He said to me, –

"Don't cry, my child; you will get nicer ones than these if you learn to love my white sister."

Of course the clothes were burned, and after I got well my grandpa took great delight in taking us all to see his white brothers and sisters, and I knew what he meant when he said "my little girls;" I knew he meant me and sister, and he also would say "my little boys," when he was talking about my brothers.

He would say, pointing to my brother, "my Natchez;"[2] he always said this. So the white people called one of my brothers Natchez, and he has had that name to this day.

So I came to love the white people. We left Stockton and went on farther to a place called San Joaquin River. It took us only one day to go there. We only crossed that river at that time.

One of my grandpa's friends was named Scott, and the other Bonsal. After we got there, his friend killed beef for him and his people. We stayed there some time. Then grandpa told us that he had taken charge of Mr. Scott's cattle and horses, and he was going to take them all up to the mountains to take care of them for his brothers. He wanted my uncles and their families and my mother and her two sons and three daughters to stay where they were; that is, he told his dear daughter that he wanted her two sons to take care of a few horses and cows that would be left. My mother began to cry, and said, –

"Oh, father, don't leave us here! My children might get sick, and there would be no one to speak for us; or something else might happen." He again said, "I don't think my brothers will do anything that is wrong to you and your children." Then my mother asked my grandfather if he would take my sister with him. My poor mother felt that her daughter was unsafe, for she was young and very good-looking.

"I would like to take her along," he said, "but I want her to learn how to work and cook. Scott and Bonsal say they will take the very best care of you and the children. It is not as if I was going to leave you here really alone; your brothers will be with you." So we staid. Two men owned the ferry, and they had a great deal of money. So my brothers took care of their horses and cows all winter, and they paid them well for their work. But, oh, what trouble we had for a while! The men whom my grandpa called his brothers would come into our camp and ask my mother to give our sister to them. They would come in at night, and we would all scream and cry; but that would not stop them. My sister, and mother, and my uncles all cried and said, "Oh, why did we come? Oh, we shall surely all be killed some night." My uncles and brothers would not dare to say a word, for fear they would be shot down. So we used to go away every night after dark and hide, and come back to our camp every morning. One night we were getting ready to go, and there came five men. The fire was out; we could see two men come into the tent and shut off the postles outside. My uncles and my brothers made such a noise! I don't know what happened; when I woke I asked my mother if they had killed my sister. She said, "We are all safe here. Don't cry."

"Where are we, mother?"

"We are in a boarding-house."

"Are my uncles killed?"

"No, dear, they are all near here too."

I said, "Sister, where are you? I want to come to you."

She said, "Come on."

I laid down, but I could not sleep. I could hear my poor sister's heart beat. Early the next morning we

---

2 Natchez means boy [Mary Mann's note].

got up and went down stairs, for it was upstairs where we slept. There were a great many in the room. When we came down, my mother said, "We will go outside."

My sister said, "There is no outlet to the house. We can't get out."

Mother looked round and said, "No, we cannot get out." I as usual began to cry. My poor sister! I ran to her, I saw tears in her eyes. I heard some one speak close to my mother. I looked round and saw Mr. Scott holding the door open. Mother said, "Children, come."

He went out with us and pointed to our camp, and shook his head, and motioned to mother to go into a little house where they were cooking. He took my hand in his, and said the same words that I had learned, "Poor little girl." I could see by his looks that he pitied me, so I was not afraid of him. We went in and sat down on the floor. Oh, what pretty things met my eyes. I was looking all round the room, and I saw beautiful white cups, and every beautiful thing on something high and long, and around it some things that were red.

I said to my sister, "Do you know what those are?" for she had been to the house before with my brothers. She said, "That high thing is what they use when eating, and the white cups are what they drink hot water from, and the red things you see is what they sit upon when they are eating." There was one now near us, and I thought if I could sit upon it I should be so happy! I said to my mother, "Can I sit on that one?" She said, "No, they would whip you." I did not say any more, but sat looking at the beautiful red chair. By-and-by the white woman went out, and I wished in my heart I could go and sit upon it while she was gone. Then she came in with her little child in her arms. As she came in she went right to the very chair I wanted to sit in so badly, and set her child in it. I looked up to my mother, and said, "Will she get a whipping?"

"No, dear, it belongs to her father."

So I said no more. Pretty soon a man came in. She said something to him, and he went out, and in a little while they all came in and sat round that high thing, as I called it. That was the table. It was all very strange to me, and they were drinking the hot water as they ate. I thought it was indeed hot water. After they got through, they all went out again, but Mr. Scott staid and talked to the woman and the man a long time. Then the woman fixed five places and the men went out and brought in my brothers, and kept talking to them. My brother said, "Come and sit here, and you, sister, sit there." But as soon as I sat down in the beautiful chair I began to look at the pretty picture on the back of the chair. "Dear, sit nice and eat, or the white woman will whip you," my mother said. I was quiet, but did not eat much. I tasted the black hot water; I did not like it. It was coffee that we called hot water. After we had done, brother said, "Mother, come outside; I want to talk to you." So we all went out. Brother said, "Mother, Mr. Scott wants us all to stay here. He says you and sister are to wash dishes, and learn all kinds of work. We are to stay here all the time and sleep upstairs, and the white woman is going to teach my sister how to sew. I think, dear mother, we had better stay, because grandpa said so, and our father Scott will take good care of us. He is going up into the mountains to see how grandpa is getting along, and he says he will take my uncles with him." All the time brother was talking, my mother and sister were crying. I did not cry, for I wanted to stay so that I could sit in the beautiful red chairs. Mother said, –

"Dear son, you know if we stay here sister will be taken from us by the bad white man. I would rather see her die than see her heart full of fear every night."

"Yes, dear mother, we love our dear sister, and if you say so we will go to papa."

"Yes, dear son, let us go and tell him what his white brothers are doing to us."

"Then I will go and tell Mr. Scott we want to go to our papa." He was gone some time, and at last came back.

"Mother," he says, "we can't go, – that is, brother and I must stay; – but you and sister can go if you wish to."

"Oh no, my dear children, how can I go and leave you here? Oh, how can that bad man keep you from going? You are not his children. How dare he say you cannot go with your mother? He is not your father; he is nothing but a bad white man, and he dares to say you cannot go. Your own father did not say you should not come with me. Oh, had my dear husband said those words I would not have been here to-day, and see my dear children suffer from day to day. Oh, if your father only knew how his children were suffering, I know he would kill that white man who tried to take your sister. I cannot see for my life why my father calls them his white brothers. They are not people; they have no thought, no mind, no love. They are beasts, or they would know I, a lone woman, am here with them. They tried to take my girl from me and abuse her before my eyes and yours too, and oh, you must go too."

"Oh, mother, here he comes!"

My mother got up. She held out her two hands to him, and cried out, –

"Oh, good father, don't keep my children from me. If you have a heart in you, give them back to me. Let me take them to their good father, where they can be cared for."

We all cried to see our poor mother pleading for us. Mother held on to him until he gave some signs of letting her sons go with her; then he nodded his head, – they might go. My poor mother's crying was turned into joy, and we were all glad. The wagon was got ready, – we were to ride in it. Oh, how I jumped about because I was going to ride in it! I ran up to sister, and said, –

"Ain't you glad we are going to ride in that beautiful red house?" I called it house. My sister said, –

"Not I, dear sister, for I hate everything that belongs to the white dogs. I would rather walk all the way; oh, I hate them so badly!"

When everything was got ready, we got into the red house, as we called the wagon. I soon got tired of riding in the red house and went to sleep. Nothing happened during the day, and after awhile mother told us not to say a word about why we left, for grandpa might get mad with us. So we got to our people, and grandpa ran out to meet us. We were all glad to see him. The white man staid all night, and went home the next day. After he left us my grandpa called my brothers to him.

"Now, my dear little boys, I have something to tell you that will make you happy. Our good father (he did not say my white brother, but he said our good father) has left something with me to give you, and he also told me that he had given you some money for your work. He says you are all good boys, and he likes you very much; and he told me to give you three horses apiece, which makes six in all, and he wants you and your brother to go back and to go on with the same work, and he will pay you well for it. He is to come back in three days; then if you want to go with him you can."

Brother said, "Will mother and sisters go too?"

"No, they will stay with me." My brothers were so happy over their horses.

Now, my dear reader, there is no word so endearing as the word father, and that is why we call all good people father or mother; no matter who it is, – negro, white man, or Indian, and the same with the women. Grandpa talked to my mother a long time, but I did not hear what he said to her, as I went off to play with the other children. But the first thing I knew the white man came and staid four days. Then all the horses were got up, and he saw them all, and the cattle also. I could see my poor mother and sister crying now and then, but I did not know what for. So one morning the man was going away, and I saw mother getting my brothers' horses ready too. I ran to my mother, and said, "Mother, what makes you cry so?" Grandpa was talking to her. He said, "They will not be hurt; they will have quite a number of horses by the time we are ready to go back to our home again."

I knew then that my brothers were going back with this man. Oh, then I began to cry, and said everything that was bad to them. I threw myself down upon the ground.

"Oh, brothers, I will never see them any more. They will kill them, I know. Oh, you naughty, naughty grandpa, you want my poor brothers to be killed by the bad men. You don't know what they do to us. Oh, mother, run, – bring them back again!"

Oh, how we missed our brothers for a long time. We did not see them for a long time, but the men came now and then. They never brought my brothers with them. After they went away, grandpa would come in with his rag friend in hand and say to mother, "My friend here says my boys are all right, not sick."

My mother said, "Father, why can you not have them come and see us sometimes?"

"Dear daughter, we will get ready to go home. It is time now that the snow is off the mountains. In ten days more we will go, and we will get the children as we go by."

Oh, how happy everybody was! Everybody was singing here and there, getting beautiful dresses made, and before we started we had a thanksgiving dance. The day we were to start we partook of the first gathering of food for that summer. So that morning everybody prayed, and sang songs, and danced, and ate before starting. It was all so nice, and everybody was so happy because they were going to see their dear country and the dear ones at home. Grandpa took all the horses belonging to the white men. After we got home the horses were put into the corral for all night, and the two white men counted their horses the next morning. They gave my grandpa eight horses for his work, and two or three horses each to some of the people. To my two brothers they gave sixteen horses and some money, and after we all got our horses, grandpa said to his people, –

"Now, my children, you see that what I have told you about my white brothers is true. You see we have not worked very much, and they have given us all horses. Don't you see they are good people?"

All that time, neither my uncles nor my mother had told what the white men did while we were left all alone.

So the day was set for starting. It was to be in five days. We had been there three days when we saw the very men who were so bad to us. Yes, they were talking to grandpa. Mother said to sister, –

"They are talking about us. You see they are looking this way."

Sister said, "Oh, mother, I hope grandpa will not do such a wicked thing as to give me to those bad men."

Oh, how my heart beat! I saw grandpa shake his head, and he looked mad with them. He came away and left them standing there. From that day my grandma took my sister under her care, and we got along nicely.

Then we started for our home, and after travelling some time we arrived at the head of Carson River. There we met some of our people, and they told us some very bad news, indeed, which made us all cry. They said almost all the tribe had died off, and if one of a family got sick it was a sure thing that the whole family would die. He said the white men had poisoned the Humboldt River, and our people had drank the water and died off. Grandpa said, –

"Is my son dead?"

"No, he has been in the mountains all the time, and all who have been there are all right."

The men said a great many of our relations had died off.

We staid there all night, and the next day our hair was all cut off. My sister and my mother had such beautiful hair!

So grandpa said to the man, –

"Go and tell our people we are coming. Send them to each other, and tell my son to come to meet us."

So we went on our journey, and after travelling three days more we came to a place called Genoa, on the west side of Carson River, at the very place where I had first seen a white man.[3] A saw-mill and a grist-mill were there, and five more houses. We camped in the very same place where we did before. We staid there a long time waiting for my father to come to meet us. At last my cousin rode into our camp one evening, and said my father was coming with many of his people. We heard them as they came nearer and nearer; they were all crying, and then we cried too, and as they got off their horses they fell into each other's arms, like so many little children, and cried as if their hearts would break, and told what they had suffered since we went away, and how our people had died off. As soon as one would get sick he would drink water and die right off. Every one of them was in mourning also, and they talked over the sad things which had happened to them during the time we were away. One and all said that the river must have been poisoned by the white people, because that they had prayed, and our spirit-doctors had tried to cure the sick; they too died while they were trying to cure them. After they had told grandpa all, he got angry and said –

"My dear children, I am heartily sorry to hear your sad story; but I cannot and will not believe my white brothers would do such a thing. Oh, my dear children, do not think so badly of our white fathers, for if they had poisoned the river, why, my dear children, they too would have died when they drank of the water. It is this, my dear children, it must be some fearful disease or sickness unknown to us, and

3 In the foothills of the Sierra Nevadas, Genoa was the first permanent white settlement in the state, founded c.1849 as Mormon Station.

therefore, my dear children, don't blame our brothers. The whole tribe have called me their father, and I have loved you all as my dear children, and those who have died are happy in the Spirit-land, though we mourn their loss here on earth. I know my grandchildren and daughters and brothers are in that happy bright Spirit-land, and I shall soon see them there. Some of you may live a long time yet, and don't let your hearts work against your white fathers; if you do, you will not get along. You see they are already here in our land; here they are all along the river, and we must let our brothers live with us. We cannot tell them to go away. I know your good hearts. I know you won't say *kill them.* Surely you all know that they are human. Their lives are just as dear to them as ours to us. It is a very sad thing indeed to have to lose so many of our dear ones; but maybe it was to be. We can do nothing but mourn for their loss." He went on to say, –

"My dear children, you all know the tradition says: 'Weep not for your dead; but sing and be joyful, for the soul is happy in the Spirit-land.' But it is natural for man or woman to weep, because it relieves our hearts to weep together, and we all feel better afterwards."

Every one hung their heads while grandpa talked on. Now and then one could hear some of them cry out, just as the Methodists cry out at their meetings; and grandpa said a great many beautiful things to his people. He talked so long, I for one wished he would stop, so I could go and throw myself into my father's arms, and tell him what the white people were. At last he stopped, and we all ran to our father and threw our arms around his neck, and cried for joy; and then mother came with little sister. Papa took her in his arms, and mother put her hand in his bosom, and we all wept together, because mother had lost two sisters, and their husbands, and all their children but one girl; and thus passed away the day. Grandpa had gone off during our meeting with father, and prayer was offered, and every one washed their face, and were waiting for something else. Pretty soon grandpa came, and said: "This is my friend," holding up his paper in his hand. "Does it look as if it could talk and ask for anything? Yet it does. It can ask for something to eat for me and my people. Yet, it is nothing but a rag. Oh, wonderful things my white brothers can do. I have taken it down to them, and it has asked for sacks of flour for us to eat. Come, we will go and get them." So the men went down and got the flour. Grandpa took his son down to see the white men, and by-and-by we saw them coming back. They had given my father a red blanket and a red shirt.

## Chapter II: Domestic and Social Moralities

Our children are very carefully taught to be good. Their parents tell them stories, traditions of old times, even of the first mother of the human race; and love stories, stories of giants, and fables; and when they ask if these last stories are true, they answer, "Oh, it is only coyote," which means that they are make-believe stories. Coyote is the name of a mean, crafty little animal, half wolf, half dog, and stands for everything low. It is the greatest term of reproach one Indian has for another. Indians do not swear, – they have no words for swearing till they learn them of white men. The worst they call each is bad or coyote; but they are very sincere with one another, and if they think each other in the wrong they say so.

We are taught to love everybody. We don't need to be taught to love our fathers and mothers. We love them without being told to. Our tenth cousin is as near to us as our first cousin; and we don't marry into our relations. Our young women are not allowed to talk to any young man that is not their cousin, except at the festive dances, when both are dressed in their best clothes, adorned with beads, feathers or shells, and stand alternately in the ring and take hold of hands. These are very pleasant occasions to all the young people.

Many years ago, when my people were happier than they are now, they used to celebrate the Festival of Flowers in the spring. I have been to three of them only in the course of my life.

Oh, with what eagerness we girls used to watch every spring for the time when we could meet with our hearts' delight, the young men, whom in civilized life you call beaux. We would all go in company to see if the flowers we were named for were yet in bloom, for almost all the girls are named for flowers. We talked about them in our wigwams, as if we were the flowers, saying, "Oh, I saw myself to-day in full bloom!" We would talk all the evening in this way in our families with such delight, and such beautiful thoughts of the happy day when we should meet with those who admired us and would help us to sing our flower-songs which we made up as we sang. But we were always sorry for those that were not named after some flower, because we knew they could not join in the flower-songs like ourselves, who were named for flowers of all kinds.[4]

At last one evening came a beautiful voice, which made every girl's heart throb with happiness. It was the chief, and every one hushed to hear what he said to-day.

"My dear daughters, we are told that you have seen yourselves in the hills and in the valleys, in full bloom. Five days from to-day your festival day will come. I know every young man's heart stops beating while I am talking. I know how it was with me many years ago. I used to wish the Flower Festival would come every day. Dear young men and young women, you are saying, 'Why put it off five days?' But you all know that is our rule. It gives you time to think, and to show your sweetheart your flower."

All the girls who have flower-names dance along together, and those who have not go together also. Our fathers and mothers and grandfathers and grandmothers make a place for us where we can dance. Each one gathers the flower she is named for, and then all weave them into wreaths and crowns and scarfs, and dress up in them.

Some girls are named for rocks and are called rock-girls, and they find some pretty rocks which they carry; each one such a rock as she is named for, or whatever she is named for. If she cannot, she can take a branch of sage-brush, or a bunch of rye-grass, which have no flower.

They all go marching along, each girl in turn singing of herself; but she is not a girl any more, – she is a flower singing. She sings of herself, and her sweetheart, dancing along by her side, helps her sing the song she makes.

I will repeat what we say of ourselves. "I, Sarah Winnemucca, am a shell-flower, such as I wear on my dress. My name is Thocmetony. I am so beautiful! Who will come and dance with me while I am so beautiful? Oh, come and be happy with me! I shall be beautiful while the earth lasts. Somebody will always admire me; and who will come and be happy with me in the Spirit-land? I shall be beautiful forever there. Yes, I shall be more beautiful than my shell-flower, my Thocmetony! Then, come, oh come, and dance and be happy with me!" The young men sing with us as they dance beside us.

Our parents are waiting for us somewhere to welcome us home. And then we praise the sage-brush and the rye-grass that have no flower, and the pretty rocks that some are named for; and then we present our beautiful flowers to these companions who could carry none. And so all are happy; and that closes the beautiful day.

My people have been so unhappy for a long time they wish now to *disincrease*, instead of multiply. The mothers are afraid to have more children, for fear they shall have daughters, who are not safe even in their mother's presence.

The grandmothers have the special care of the daughters just before and after they come to womanhood. The girls are not allowed to get married until they have come to womanhood; and that period is recognized as a very sacred thing, and is the subject of a festival, and has peculiar customs. The young woman is set apart under the care of two of her friends, somewhat older, and a little wigwam, called a teepee, just big enough for the three, is made for them, to which they retire. She goes through certain labors which are thought to be strengthening, and these last twenty-five days. Every day, three times a day, she must gather, and pile up as high as she can, five stacks of wood. This makes fifteen stacks a day. At the end of every five days the attendants take her to a river to bathe. She fasts from all flesh-meat during these twenty-five days, and continues to do this for five days in every month all her life. At the end of the twenty-five days she returns to the family lodge, and gives all her clothing to her attendants in payment for their care. Sometimes the wardrobe is quite extensive.

It is thus publicly known that there is another marriageable woman, and any young man interested in her, or wishing to form an alliance, comes forward. But the courting is very different from the courting

4 Indian children are named from some passing circumstance; as, for instance, one of Mrs. Hopkins' brothers was named Black-eye, because when a very small child, sitting in a sister's lap, who had beautiful black eyes, he said, "What beautiful black eyes you have!" If they observed the flight of a bird, or an animal, in short, anything striking that became associated with them, that would be their appellation [Mary Mann's note].

of the white people. He never speaks to her, or visits the family, but endeavors to attract her attention by showing his horsemanship, etc. As he knows that she sleeps next to her grandmother in the lodge, he enters in full dress after the family has retired for the night, and seats himself at her feet. If she is not awake, her grandmother wakes her. He does not speak to either young woman or grandmother, but when the young woman wishes him to go away, she rises and goes and lies down by the side of her mother. He then leaves as silently as he came in. This goes on sometimes for a year or longer, if the young woman has not made up her mind. She is never forced by her parents to marry against her wishes. When she knows her own mind, she makes a confidant of her grandmother, and then the young man is summoned by the father of the girl, who asks him in her presence, if he really loves his daughter, and reminds him, if he says he does, of all the duties of a husband. He then asks his daughter the same question, and sets before her minutely all her duties. And these duties are not slight. She is to dress the game, prepare the food, clean the buckskins, make his moccasins, dress his hair, bring all the wood, – in short, do all the household work. She promises to "be himself," and she fulfils her promise. Then he is invited to a feast and all his relatives with him. But after the betrothal, a teepee is erected for the presents that pour in from both sides.

At the wedding feast, all the food is prepared in baskets. The young woman sits by the young man, and hands him the basket of food prepared for him with her own hands. He does not take it with his right hand; but seizes her wrist, and takes it with the left hand. This constitutes the marriage ceremony, and the father pronounces them man and wife. They go to a wigwam of their own, where they live till the first child is born. This event also is celebrated. Both father and mother fast from all flesh, and the father goes through the labor of piling the wood for twenty-five days, and assumes all his wife's household work during that time. If he does not do his part in the care of the child, he is considered an outcast. Every five days his child's basket is changed for a new one, and the five are all carefully put away at the end of the days, the last one containing the navel-string, carefully wrapped up, and all are put up into a tree, and the child put into a new and ornamented basket. All this respect shown to the mother and child makes the parents feel their responsibility, and makes the tie between parents and children very strong. The young mothers often get together and exchange their experiences about the attentions of their husbands; and inquire of each other if the fathers did their duty to their children, and were careful of their wives' health. When they are married they give away all the clothing they have ever worn, and dress themselves anew. The poor people have the same ceremonies, but do not make a feast of it, for want of means.

Our boys are introduced to manhood by their hunting of deer and mountain-sheep. Before they are fifteen or sixteen, they hunt only small game, like rabbits, hares, fowls, etc. They never eat what they kill themselves, but only what their father or elder brothers kill. When a boy becomes strong enough to use larger bows made of sinew, and arrows that are ornamented with eagle-feathers, for the first time, he kills game that is large, a deer or an antelope, or a mountain-sheep. Then he brings home the hide, and his father cuts it into a long coil which is wound into a loop, and the boy takes his quiver and throws it on his back as if he was going on a hunt, and takes his bow and arrows in his hand. Then his father throws the loop over him, and he jumps through it. This he does five times. Now for the first time he eats the flesh of the animal he has killed, and from that time he eats whatever he kills but he has always been faithful to his parents' command not to eat what he has killed before. He can now do whatever he likes, for now he is a man, and no longer considered a boy. If there is a war he can go to it; but the Piutes, and other tribes west of the Rocky Mountains, are not fond of going to war. I never saw a war-dance but once. It is always the whites that begin the wars, for their own selfish purposes. The government does not take care to send the good men; there are a plenty who would take pains to see and understand the chiefs and learn their characters, and their good will to the whites. But the whites have not waited to find out how good the Indians were, and what ideas they had of God, just like those of Jesus, who called him Father, just as my people do, and told men to do to others as they would be done by, just as my people teach their children to do. My people teach their children never to make fun of any one, no matter how they look. If you see your brother or sister doing something wrong, look away, or go away from them. If you make fun of bad persons, you make yourself beneath them. Be kind to all, both poor and rich, and feed all that come to your wigwam, and your name can be spoken of by every one far and near. In this way you will make many friends for yourself. Be kind both to bad and good, for you don't know your own heart. This is the way my people teach their children. It was handed down from father to son for many generations. I never in my life saw our children rude as I have seen white children and grown people in the streets.[5]

The chief's tent is the largest tent, and it is the council-tent, where every one goes who wants advice. In the evenings the head men go there to discuss everything, for the chiefs do not rule like tyrants; they discuss everything with their people, as a father would in his family. Often they sit up all night. They discuss the doings of all, if they need to be advised. If a boy is not doing well they talk that over, and if the women are interested they can share in the talks. If there is not room enough inside, they all go out of doors, and make a great circle. The men are in the inner circle, for there would be too much smoke for the women inside. The men never talk without smoking first. The women sit behind them in another circle, and if the children wish to hear, they can be there too. The women know as much as the men do, and their advice is often asked. We have a republic as well as you. The council-tent is our Congress, and anybody can speak who has anything to say, women and all. They are always interested in what their husbands are doing and thinking about. And they take some part even in the wars. They are always near at hand when fighting is going on, ready to snatch their husbands up and carry them off if wounded or killed. One splendid woman that my brother Lee married after his first wife died, went out into the battle-field after her uncle was killed, and went into the front ranks and cheered the men on. Her uncle's horse was dressed in a splendid robe made of eagles' feathers and she snatched it off and swung it in the face of the enemy, who always carry off everything they find, as much as to say, "You can't have that – I have it safe"; and she staid and took her uncle's place, as brave as any of the men. It means something when the women promise their fathers to make their husbands *themselves.* They faithfully keep with them in all the dangers they can share. They not only take care of their children together, but they do everything together; and when they grow blind, which I am sorry to say is very common, for the smoke they live in destroys their eyes at last, they take sweet care of one another. Marriage is a sweet thing when people love each other. If women could go into your Congress I think justice would soon be done to the Indians. I can't tell about all Indians; but I know my own people are kind to everybody that does not do them harm; but they will not be imposed upon, and when people are too bad they rise up and resist them. This seems to me all right. It is different from being revengeful. There is nothing cruel about our people. They never scalped a human being.

---

5 In one of her lectures Mrs. Hopkins spoke of other refinements and manners that the Indian mother teaches her children; and it is worthy the imitation of the whites. Such manners in the children account for their behavior to each other in manhood, their self-respect, and their respect for each other. The Indian children really get education in heart and mind, such as we are beginning to give now to ours for the first time. They are taught a great deal about nature; how to observe the habits of plants and animals. It is not unlikely that when something like a human communication is established between the Indians and whites, it may prove a fair exchange, and the knowledge of nature which has accumulated, for we know not how long, may enrich our early education as much as reading and writing will enrich theirs. The fact that the Indian children are not taught English, makes the provision for education made by our government nugatory. Salaries are paid teachers year after year, who sit in the school-rooms (as Mrs. Hopkins says) and read dime novels, and the children play round, and learn nothing from them, except some few hymns *by rote,* which when visitors come they sing, without understanding one word of it. It is not for the advantage of the agents to civilize and teach the Indians. And by means of necessary interpreters there is constant mutual misunderstanding. Indians are made to sign papers that have very different contents from what they are told. The late William B. Ogden, of Chicago, who has always maintained that the Indians ought to have citizens' rights, and be represented in Congress, founding his opinion on his life-long knowledge of the high-toned morality of Indians who wore blankets, said to my sister in 1853, that it was the stereotyped lie of the fur-traders (whose interest it was) that they could not be civilized; and the late Lewis Cass was their attorney, writing in the North American Review about it, for his fortune came largely through the fur-interests. We know from H. H.'s "Century of Dishonor," that from the beginning the Christian bigots who peopled America looked upon the Indians as heathen, to be dealt with as Moses commanded Joshua to deal with the heathen of Syria, who "passed their children through the fire to Moloch," and the services of whose temples were as licentious as they were cruel. Thus Christendom missed the moral reformation it might have had, if they had become acquainted with the noble Five Nations, and others whom they have exterminated. But, "it is never too late to mend," as at last, the country is beginning to see [Mary Mann's note]. *A Century of Dishonor* (1881) was written by Helen Hunt Jackson as a protest to the US Congress against the federal government's treatment of Native Americans. Moloch (or Molech) has traditionally been understood as a deity to whom children were burned in sacrifice. See 2 Kings 23:10; Jer. 32:35.

The chiefs do not live in idleness. They work with their people, and they are always poor for the following reason. It is the custom with my people to be very hospitable. When people visit them in their tents, they always set before them the best food they have, and if there is not enough for themselves they go without.

The chief's tent is the one always looked for when visitors come, and sometimes many come the same day. But they are all well received. I have often felt sorry for my brother, who is now the chief, when I saw him go without food for this reason. He would say, "We will wait and eat afterwards what is left." Perhaps little would be left, and when the agents did not give supplies and rations, he would have to go hungry.

At the council, one is always appointed to repeat at the time everything that is said on both sides, so that there may be no misunderstanding, and one person at least is present from every lodge, and after it is over, he goes and repeats what is decided upon at the door of the lodge, so all may be understood. For there is never any quarrelling in the tribe, only friendly counsels. The sub-chiefs are appointed by the great chief for special duties. There is no quarrelling about that, for neither sub-chief or great chief has any salary. It is this which makes the tribe so united and attached to each other, and makes it so dreadful to be parted. They would rather all die at once than be parted. They believe that in the Spirit-land those that die still watch over those that are living. When I was a child in California, I heard the Methodist minister say that everybody that did wrong was burned in hell forever. I was so frightened it made me very sick. He said the blessed ones in heaven looked down and saw their friends burning and could not help them. I wanted to be unborn, and cried so that my mother and the others told me it was not so, that it was only here that people did wrong and were in the hell that it made, and that those that were in the Spirit-land saw us here and were sorry for us. But we should go to them when we died, where there was never any wrongdoing, and so no hell. That is our religion.

My people capture antelopes by charming them, but only some of the people are charmers. My father was one of them, and once I went with him on an antelope hunt.

The antelopes move in herds in the winter, and as late in the spring as April. At this time there was said to be a large herd in a certain place, and my father told all his people to come together in ten days to go with him in his hunt. He told them to bring their wives with them, but no small children. When they came, at the end of ten days, he chose two men, who he said were to be his messengers to the antelopes. They were to have two large torches made of sage-brush bark, and after he had found a place for his camp, he marked out a circle around which the wigwams were to be placed, putting his own in the middle of the western side, and leaving an opening directly opposite in the middle of the eastern side, which was towards the antelopes.

The people who were with him in the camp then made another circle to the east of the one where their wigwams were, and made six mounds of sage-brush and stones on the sides of it, with a space of a hundred yards or more from one mound to the next one, but with no fence between the mounds. These mounds were made high, so that they could be seen from far off.

The women and boys and old men who were in the camp, and who were working on the mounds, were told to be very careful not to drop anything and not to stumble over a sage-brush root, or a stone, or anything, and not to have any accident, but to do everything perfectly and to keep thinking about the antelopes all the time, and not to let their thoughts go away to anything else. It took five days to charm the antelopes, and if anybody had an accident he must tell of it.

Every morning early, when the bright morning star could be seen, the people sat around the opening to the circle, with my father sitting in the middle of the opening, and my father lighted his pipe and passed it to his right, and the pipe went round the circle five times. And at night they did the same thing.

After they had smoked the pipe, my father took a kind of drum, which is used in this charming, and made music with it. This is the only kind of musical instrument which my people have, and it is only used for this antelope-charming. It is made of a hide of some large animal, stuffed with grass, so as to make it sound hollow, and then wound around tightly from one end to the other with a cord as large as my finger. One end of this instrument is large, and it tapers down to the other end, which is small, so that it makes a different sound on the different parts. My father took a stick and rubbed this stick from one end of the instrument to the other, making a penetrating, vibrating sound, that could be heard afar off, and he sang, and all his people sang with him.

After that the two men who were messengers went out to see the antelopes. They carried their torches in their right hands, and one of them carried a pipe in his left hand. They started from my father's wigwam and went straight across the camp to the opening; then they crossed, and one went around the second circle to the right and the other went to the left, till they met on the other side of the circle. Then they crossed again, and one went round the herd of antelopes one way and the other went round the other way, but they did not let the antelopes see them. When they met on the other side of the herd of antelopes, they stopped and smoked the pipe, and then they crossed, and each man came back on the track of the other to the camp, and told my father what they saw and what the antelopes were doing.

This was done every day for five days, and after the first day all the men and women and boys followed the messengers, and went around the circle they were to enter. On the fifth day the antelopes were charmed, and the whole herd followed the tracks of my people and entered the circle where the mounds were, coming in at the entrance, bowing and tossing their heads, and looking sleepy and under a powerful spell. They ran round and round inside the circle just as if there was a fence all around it and they could not get out, and they staid there until my people had killed every one. But if anybody had dropped anything, or had stumbled and had not told about it, then when the antelopes came to the place where he had done that, they threw off the spell and rushed wildly out of the circle at that place.

My brother can charm horses in the same way.

The Indian children amuse themselves a great deal by modelling in mud. They make herds of animals, which are modelled exceedingly well, and after setting them up, shoot at them with their little bows and arrows. They also string beads of different colors and show natural good taste.

## CHAPTER III: WARS AND THEIR CAUSES

I will now stop writing about myself and family and tribe customs, and tell about the wars, and the causes of the wars. I will jump over about six years. My sister and I were living at this time in Genoa with Major Ormsbey's family, who took us as playmates for their little girl. While with them we learned the English language very fast, for they were very kind to us. This was in the year 1858, I think; I am not sure. In that year our white brothers had their houses all along Carson River. There were twenty-one houses there in our country. I know all the names of the people that lived in them. One man who was on the upper part of Carson River was Mr. Olds; the next man by the name of Palmer had a family. The third one, by the name of Job, also had a family. Another family was named Walters; another man, whose name was Dr. Daggett, had no family; nor had the next one, whose name was Van Sickle. The next one had more than one family; he had two wives, and his name was Thornton. The man who lived in the next house had still more wives. There were two brothers; one had three wives, and the other five. Their name was Reuse. The next man was named Nott, and had no family. The next house had three brothers, named Sides, with no families. The next was named Gilbert, and had no family. The next was named Alridge, and had a family. Then came our friend, Major Ormsbey. Next came Adams and brothers, who had no wives. Then Jones and family, Miller and family; Brown, with no family; Elsey, with no family; Mr. Ellis and family; Williams brothers, no family; Mr. Cole and family; Mr. Black and family at Humboldt Lake. All these white people were loved by my people; we lived there together, and were as happy as could be. There was no stealing, no one lost their cattle or horses; my people had not learned to steal. We lived that way in peace for another year; our white brothers gave my people guns for their horses in the way of trading; yet my people never said, "We want you to give us something for our land." Now, there were a great many of our white brothers everywhere through our country, and mines or farms here and there. The Mormons came in a great many wagons and settled down in Carson Valley, where now stands the great Carson City, as it is called. The following year,

1859, we were yet living with Major Ormsbey, and mother and father were down at Pyramid Lake with all our people, so sister and I were all alone there with our dear good friend, Major Ormsbey.

Late that fall there happened a very sad thing, indeed. A white man who was dearly beloved by my people started for California to get provisions for the winter, as they all did every winter. Mr. McMullen took a great deal of money to lay in large supplies, for they had a store about thirty miles down Carson River. Two of them, MacWilliams and McMullen, went off the same night, and camped in the mountains. Some one came in the night and killed them both, and after they had shot them with guns or pistols, they placed arrows in the wounds to make it appear as if Indians had killed them. The next day news came in that Indians had killed John McMullen. They were asked how they knew that Indians had killed him, and they answered, –

"We know, because it was done with arrows."

That same afternoon thirty men went to get the dead bodies of the two men. They brought them in, and the arrows too. Of course everybody said it was the Indians that killed them. My brother, Natchez, and our cousin, who was called young Winnemucca, and one hundred others were sent for. In two days' time they came. My brother was then peace-chief. Major Ormsbey asked if he knew what tribe of Indians those arrows belonged to. My cousin told his white brothers the arrows belonged to the Washoes.[6] So our good father Major Ormsbey said to my brother, –

"Will you help us to get the Washoe chief to come in and give up the men who killed the two white men?" My brothers said they would help to find the men that killed poor John McMullen. So that evening my people had what they call a war-dance, the first one I had ever seen. A great many white men and women came to see them, and Lizzie Ormsbey kept saying, "Where is Natchez?" He was dressed up so we did not know him. The white people staid until it was all over, and when it was all over the Major called his men and said, –

"We will sing the Star-spangled Banner."

It was not a bit like the way my grandfather used to sing it, and that was the first time I had heard it sung by the white people.

My cousin was the war-chief. He sent five men to bring in the Washoe chief. The next morning they came in with about ten Washoes. As soon as they came in the white men gathered round them. Major Ormsbey showed the arrows, and asked them if they knew them. The Washoe chief, who is called Jam, said, "You ask me if these are my people's arrows. I say yes." Major Ormsbey said, –

"That is enough." He said to my brother Natchez, –

"Tell Captain Jam that his people have killed two men, and he must bring the men and all the money, and they shall not be hurt, and all will be right." The Washoe chief said, –

"I know my people have not killed the men, because none of my men have been away; we are all at Pine-nut Valley, and I do not know what to think of the sad thing that has happened."

"But here are your arrows, and you cannot say anything," said my cousin, the war-chief. "We will give you ten days to bring the men who killed our two white brothers, and if you do not we shall have to fight you, for they have been so kind to us all. Who could have the heart to kill them? Now go and bring in the men."

Poor, poor Washoes, they went away with very sad hearts. After they left brother talked with all his men, and asked them what they thought about it. They all said it was very strange, indeed; time would tell whether they killed them or not. Six days after, the Washoe chief came in with three prisoners. One of the prisoners had a wife, the other two had none, but their mothers came with them. The white men gathered round them and put handcuffs on them to lock them up in a small house for the night. Next morning all the white people came to see them. Some said, "Hang the red devils right off," and the white boys threw stones at them, and used most shameful language to them. At about three o'clock in the afternoon came thirty-one white men, all with guns on their shoulders, and as they marched along my brother and cousin ran to meet them. One Washoe woman began to scream, "Oh, they have come to

6 The Washoes were a neighboring tribe whose territory extended from Honey Lake in northeast California near the Nevada border to Mono Lake in California and Walker Lake in Nevada. They sometimes intermarried with the Paiutes.

kill them !" How they did cry ! One could hear the poor things miles away. My brother went to them and told them not to cry.

"Oh, dear chieftain, they did not kill the white men, – indeed they did not. They have not been away from our camp for over a month. None of our men were away, and our chief has given these three young men because they have no fathers." One of the young girls said, –

"You who are the mighty chieftain, save my poor brother, for he is all mother and I have to hunt for us. Oh, believe us. He is as innocent as you are. Oh, tell your white brothers that what we tell you is true as the sun rises and sets;" and one woman ran to my cousin, the war-chief, and threw herself down at his feet and cried out, "Oh, you are going to have my poor husband killed. We were married this winter, and I have been with him constantly since we were married. Oh, Good Spirit, come ! Oh, come into the hearts of this people. Oh, whisper in their hearts that they may not kill my poor husband ! Oh, good chief, talk for him. Our cruel chief has given my husband to you because he is afraid that all of us will be killed by you," and she raised up her head and said to the Washoe chief, "You have given my innocent blood to save your people." Then my brother said to the Washoes, "These white men have come to take the three Washoe men who killed John McMullen and MacWilliams to California to put them in jail."

Just then one of the women cried out, "Look there, they have taken them out. See, they are taking them away." We were all looking after them, and before brother got near them the three prisoners broke and ran. Of course they were shot. Two were wounded, and the third ran back with his hands up. But all of them died.

Oh, such a scene I never thought I should see! At daybreak all the Washoes ran to where they were killed. The wife of the young man threw herself down on his dead body. Such weeping was enough to make the very mountains weep to see them. They would take the dead bodies in their arms, and they were all bloody themselves. I ran to Mrs. Ormsbey crying. I thought my poor heart would break. I said to her, "I believe those Washoe women. They say their men are all innocent. They say they were not away from their camp for a long time, and how could they have been the men that killed the white men?" I told her all I had heard the women say, and I said I believed them. Mrs. Ormsbey said, –

"How came the Washoe arrows there? and the chief himself has brought them to us, and my husband knows what he is doing."

I ran back to see what they were going to do with the dead bodies, as I had heard my people say that the Washoes were like the Digger Indians, who burn their dead.[7] When I got there the Washoe chief was talking to my brother. I did not know what he said before I came, but I know from what I heard that he had been making confession. He said, pointing down to the men that were innocently killed, –

"It is true what the women say, – it is I who have killed them. Their blood is on my hands. I know their spirits will haunt me, and give me bad luck while I live."

This was what the Washoe chief said to my brother. The one that was wounded also died, and the sister and the mother it was dreadful to see. The mother cried out, –

"Oh, may the Good Spirit send the same curse upon you ! You may all live to see the day when you will suffer at the hands of your white brothers, as you call them." She said to her girl, –

"My child, you have no brother now, – no one to love you, no one to come with game and say, 'Here, sister, here is game for you.' You are left all alone. Oh, my sweet son, – gone, gone !"

This was the first trouble the poor Washoes had with white people, and the only one they ever did have with them.

So the day passed away, and the two dead Washoes were taken away, and their bodies were burned. That is their custom. The other was taken to California. My poor little sister made herself sick she cried so much that day.

Two days afterwards Major Ormsbey sent his men home; so he did my cousin, who is called young Winnemucca, and brother staid longer for us, because we had been with Major Ormsbey a long time, and we could talk very well. My poor little sister was so very sick it was two weeks before we could go to

7 Certain bands of the Bannock and Shoshone Indians were called "Digger" because they used hard sticks to dig for food. Some of the Western Shoshone were most closely associated with the burning of their dead.

our mother. When we got home it was winter. There was so much snow that we staid in the mountains where now stands the great city called Virginia City. It was then our Pine-nut mountains. Some time during the winter the Washoe chief came and told us that the white men who killed McMullen and MacWilliams were caught. My brother Natchez said, –

"Oh, have they been caught ?" "Yes, that is what Major Ormsbey said; so did all the others." The Washoe chief went on and said, "I have come to ask you to pay me for the loss of the two men. The white men have brought back the other men, and they say that they have hung two men." My brother told the Washoe chief that his people had nothing to do with what the white people had done. "It is you who ought to pay the poor mother and sister and wife of your own tribe, because you gave them up yourself, therefore you must not blame us. We only did our duty, and we all know that the white men did nothing to us, and we did no more than what they would do for us." Next day my brother went to see for himself. He gave the Washoe chief a horse to go with him, for the poor Washoes had never owned a horse in their lives. Ten men went with my brother.

## Chapter IV: Captain Truckee's Death

My grandfather was very sick at that time. My brother was away two days and my grandfather was very low, so they had to send to him to come back. As soon as he came, word was sent everywhere that their mighty chief was dying. In two days' time we could see the signal-fires of death on every mountain-top. My brother came back and told his people that it was true that their own white brothers had killed the men for their money. The way they were found out was this: They were playing cards for the money, and one of the men lost his. There were five of them. They were almost fighting about the money, and two men who were out hunting heard them, and went near enough to hear all. One of the men went to town to bring some one to arrest them, and the other staid to watch them. The one that lost his money said: –

"If you won't give me back my money I will tell of you. Are you going to give me back my money or not?"

They all swore at him, and told him if he did not stop talking they would shoot him. Then the sheriffs came and took them and all the money they had. Two of the men told how they got the Washoe arrows and placed them in the wounds, as if the Indians had killed them. This is what brother told his people; he said, "This is what our white brothers told me to say to you."

Our people gathered from far and near, for my poor, poor grandpa was going very fast. His beloved people were watching him. It was the most solemn thing that I ever saw, before or since. Now he sent for a dear beloved white brother of his, named Snyder. My brother went for him. When he came my poor, dear grandfather called him to his bedside and said to him: –

"I am now going to die. I have always loved you as if you were my dear son; and one thing I want you to do for me."

He said to my father: "Raise me up; I want to see my children."

My father raised him up, and while he was looking around him his eyes fell on me and my sisters. He just looked at us, and he said to the white man: –

"You see there are my two little girls and there is my big girl, and there are my two boys. They are my sons' children, and the two little girls I want you to take to California, to Mr. Bonsal and Mr. Scott. They will send them to school to 'the sisters,' at San José. Tell them this is my last request to them. I shall soon die. I shall never see them in person; they have promised to teach my two little girls when they become large enough." He looked up and said, "Will you promise to do this for me ?"

The white man took my grandfather's hand and promised to do as he asked. My grandfather then bade him good-by, and said, "I want to talk to my own people." When he was gone he looked at my father and told him what he must do, as he was to be head chief of the Piute nation. He cautioned him to be a good father, as he had always been, and, after talking awhile, he broke down. We all cried. He remained in that way all night and every one watched him. Next morning about ten o'clock, a great many of our people came. The doctor was called to lay hands on him, and try to bring him to; but all efforts were in vain, so nothing could be done but watch him, which was done all day. Night came on, and still the watch was kept up. At midnight, which was told by the seven stars reaching the same place the sun reaches at midday, he turned and twisted without opening his eyes. The doctor said, "He is dying – he will open his eyes in a minute." Ten minutes passed, when he opened his eyes in his usual bright and beautiful way, and his first words were: –

"Son, where are you? Come and raise me up – let me sit up."

My father raised him up. Then he called mother, saying: –

"Bring all the children." Mother awoke my sister. I was not asleep, small as I was. I lay awake, watching for fear he would die while I was asleep. We gathered around him. He looked around to see if there were any others but his family present. He saw the white man, the same one that had promised to take care of his little girls. He pointed to his feet when we gathered round him and motioned for him to cover them and he did so. Then he said: –

"I've only a minute to spare. I'm so tired; I shall soon be happy. Now, son, I hope you will live to see as much as I have, and to know as much as I do. And if you live as I have you will some day come to me. Do your duty as I have done to your people and to your white brothers." He paused, closed his eyes, and stretched out. My poor mother, thinking he was dead, threw herself upon his bosom, but was aroused by the doctor's saying, "Hold on, – the spirit has not left the body." My mother rose up, and of course, all of us were crying, "Poor grandpa ! Poor grandpa !" Then he recovered himself again, and, opening his eyes, said:

"Don't throw away my white rag-friend; place it on my breast when you bury me." He then looked at his wife as if he wanted to say something, but his voice failed. Then the doctor said, "He has spoken his last words, he has given his last look, his spirit is gone; watch his lips, – he will speak as he enters the Spirit-land"; and so he did, at least he seemed to. His lips moved as if he was whispering. We were then told by the doctor that he was in heaven, and we all knew he was. No one who knew him would doubt it. But how can I describe the scene that followed? Some of you, dear reader, can imagine. Every one threw themselves upon his body, and their cries could be heard for many a mile. I crept up to him. I could hardly believe he would never speak to me again. I knelt beside him, and took his dear old face in my hands, and looked at him quite a while. I could not speak. I felt the world growing cold; everything seemed dark. The great light had gone out. I had father, mother, brothers, and sisters; it seemed I would rather lose all of them than my poor grandpa. I was only a simple child, yet I knew what a great man he was. I mean great in principle. I knew how necessary it was for our good that he should live. I think if he had put out his hands and asked me to go with him, I would gladly have folded myself in his arms. And now, after long years of toil and trouble, I think if our great Father had seen fit to call me with him, I could have died with a better opinion of the world.

In regard to the doctor's saying, "He will speak as he enters the Spirit-land," I wish to say it is the belief of my people that the spirit speaks as it goes in. They say if a child has a mother or a father in the Spirit-land, he will cry as his soul enters.

Such a scene I never had seen before. Everybody would take his dead body in their arms and weep. Poor papa kept his body two days. Now came the burial. Every thing he had was put into the grave with him. His body was put into blankets when it was ready to be put into the grave, and after he was buried, six of his horses were killed. Now, my dear readers, I do not want you to think that we do this thing because we think the dead use what we put in; or, if we kill horses at any one's death that they will use them in the Spirit-land. No, no; but it is the last respect we pay our dead.

In the spring of 1860, my sister and I were taken to San José, California. Brother Natchez and five other men went with us. On our arrival we were placed in the "Sisters' School" by Mr. Bonsal and Mr. Scott. We were only there a little while, say three weeks, when complaints were made to the sisters by wealthy parents about Indians being in school with their children. The sisters then wrote to our friends to come and take us away, and so they did, – at least, Mr. Scott did. He kept us a week, and sent word to brother Natchez to come for us, but no one could come, and he sent word for Mr. Scott to put us on the stage and send us back. We arrived at home all right, and shortly after, the war of 1860 began in this way: –

Two little girls about twelve years old went out in the woods to dig roots, and did not come back, and so their parents went in search of them, and not finding them, all my people who were there came to their help, and very thoroughly searched, and found trails which led up to the house of two traders named Williams, on Carson River, near by the Indian camp. But these men said they had not seen the children, and told my people to come into the house and search it; and this they did, as they thought, thoroughly. After a few days they sorrowfully gave up all search, and their relations had nearly given them up for dead, when one morning an Indian rode up to the cabin of the Williamses. In those days the settlers did not hesitate to sell us guns and ammunition whenever we could buy, so these brothers proposed to buy the Indian's horse as soon as he rode up. They offered him a gun, five cans of powder, five boxes of caps, five bars of lead, and after some talk the trade was made. The men took the horse, put him in the stable and closed the door, then went into the house to give him the gun, etc. They gave him the gun, powder, and caps, but would not give him the lead, and because he would not take a part, he gave back what he had taken from them, and went out to the barn to take his horse. Then they set their dog upon him. When bitten by the dog he began halloing, and to his surprise he heard children's voices answer him, and he knew at once it was the lost children. He made for his camp as fast as he could, and told what had happened, and what he had heard. Brother Natchez and others went straight to the cabin of the Williams brothers. The father demanded the children. They denied having them, and after talking quite awhile denied it again, when all at once the brother of the children knocked one of the Williamses down with his gun, and raised his gun to strike the other, but before he could do so, one of the Williams brothers stooped down and raised a trap-door, on which he had been standing. This was a surprise to my people, who had never seen anything of the kind. The father first peeped down, but could see nothing; then he went down and found his children lying on a little bed with their mouths tied up with rags. He tore the rags away and brought them up. When my people saw their condition, they at once killed both brothers and set fire to the house. Three days after the news was spread as usual. "The bloodthirsty savages had murdered two innocent, hard-working, industrious, kind-hearted settlers;" and word was sent to California for some army soldiers to demand the murderers of the Williamses. As no army soldiers were there just then, Major Ormsbey collected one hundred and sixty volunteers, and came up, and without asking or listening to any explanation demanded the men. But my people would not give them up, and when the volunteers fired on my people, they flew to arms to defend the father and brother, as any human beings would do in such a case, and ought to do. And so the war began. It lasted about three months, and after a few precious ones of my people, and at least a hundred white men had been killed (amongst them our dear friend, Major Ormsbey, who had been so hasty), a peace was made. My brother had tried to save Major Ormsbey's life. He met him in the fight, and as he was ahead of the other Indians, Major Ormsbey threw down his arms, and implored him not to kill him. There was not a moment to be lost. My brother said, –

"Drop down as if dead when I shoot, and I will fire over you;" but in the hurry and agitation he still stood pleading, and was killed by another man's shot.

Some other friends of my brother, Judge Broomfield and servant, and a Spaniard lived in a small cabin about twelve miles off. They were not fighting against us, and my brother defended their lives and risked his own. He stood at their cabin door, and beat back the assailants with a club, and succeeded in driving them off. But my uncle and cousins were so angry with him for saving white men's lives that they whipped him with a horsewhip. We all knew my uncle loved us. He was always kind to us; but I never could love him again as I had done after he whipped my brother, – my noble, patient brother, who bore his uncle no ill-will, but was satisfied that he had saved the lives of his friends.

Brave deeds don't always get rewarded in this world.

There was another occasion when my brother saved the life of his friend, Mr. Seth Cook, of San Francisco, and of six others; but as I do not remember all the particulars I will not attempt to relate it. Mr. Cook had often given my brother valuable assistance, and he is still living, and can tell the story of his escape from death himself.

The regular troops at last reached the ground, and after fighting a little while raised a flag of truce, which was responded to by my brother, and peace was made, and a treaty giving the Pyramid Lake Reservation to my people. I have no way of telling any of the particulars. The reservation was given to us in 1860, and we were to get large supplies as long as we were peaceful; but though there were thirteen agents there in the course of twenty-three years, I never knew of any issue after that first year.

Among the traditions of our people is one of a small tribe of barbarians who used to live along the Humboldt River. It was many hundred years ago. They used to waylay my people and kill and eat them. They would dig large holes in our trails at night, and if any of our people travelled at night, which they did, for they were afraid of these barbarous people, they would oftentimes fall into these holes. That tribe would even eat their own dead – yes, they would even come and dig up our dead after they were buried, and would carry them off and eat them. Now and then they would come and make war on my people. They would fight, and as fast as they killed one another on either side, the women would carry off those who were killed. My people say they were very brave. When they were fighting they would jump up in the air after the arrows that went over their heads, and shoot the same arrows back again. My people took some of them into their families, but they could not make them like themselves. So at last they made war on them. This war lasted a long time. Their number was about twenty-six hundred (2600). The war lasted some three years. My people killed them in great numbers, and what few were left went into the thick bush. My people set the bush on fire. This was right above Humboldt Lake. Then they went to work and made tuly or bulrush boats, and went into Humboldt Lake. They could not live there very long without fire. They were nearly starving. My people were watching them all round the lake, and would kill them as fast as they would come on land. At last one night they all landed on the east side of the lake, and went into a cave near the mountains. It was a most horrible place, for my people watched at the mouth of the cave, and would kill them as they came out to get water. My people would ask them if they would be like us, and not eat people like coyotes or beasts. They talked the same language, but they would not give up. At last my people were tired, and they went to work and gathered wood, and began to fill up the mouth of the cave. Then the poor fools began to pull the wood inside till the cave was full. At last my people set it on fire at the same time they cried out to them, "Will you give up and be like men, and not eat people like beasts ? Say quick – we will put out the fire." No answer came from them. My people said they thought the cave must be very deep or far into the mountain. They had never seen the cave nor known it was there until then. They called out to them as loud as they could, "Will you give up? Say so, or you will all die." But no answer came. Then they all left the place. In ten days some went back to see if the fire had gone out. They went back to my third or fifth great-grandfather and told him they must all be dead, there was such a horrible smell. This tribe was called people-eaters, and after my people had killed them all, the people round us called us *Say-do-carah.* It means conqueror; it also means "enemy." I do not know how we came by the name of Piutes. It is not an Indian word. I think it is misinterpreted. Sometimes we are called Pine-nut eaters, for we are the only tribe that lives in the country where Pine-nuts grow. My people say that the tribe we exterminated had reddish hair. I have some of their hair, which has been handed down from father to son. I have a dress which has been in our family a great many years, trimmed with this reddish hair. I am going to wear it some time when I lecture. It is called the mourning dress, and no one has such a dress but my family.

## CHAPTER V: RESERVATION OF PYRAMID AND MUDDY LAKES

This reservation, given in 1860, was at first sixty miles long and fifteen wide. The line is where the railroad now crosses the river, and it takes in two beautiful lakes, one called Pyramid Lake, and the one on the eastern side, Muddy Lake. No white people lived there at the time it was given us. We Piutes have always lived on the river, because out of those two lakes we caught beautiful mountain trout, weighing from two to twenty-five pounds each, which would give us a good income if we had it all, as at first. Since the railroad ran through in 1867, the white people have taken all the best part of the reservation from us, and one of the lakes also.

The first work that my people did on the reservation was to dig a ditch, to put up a grist-mill and saw-mill. Commencing where the railroad now crosses at Wadsworth, they dug about a mile; but the saw-mill and grist-mill were never seen or heard of by my people, though the printed report in the United States statutes, which my husband found lately in the Boston Athenaeum, says twenty-five thousand dollars was appropriated to build them. Where did it go? The report says these mills were sold for the benefit of the Indians who were to be paid in lumber for houses, but no stick of lumber have they ever received. My people do not own any timber land now. The white people are using the ditch which my people made to irrigate their land. This is the way we are treated by our white brothers. Is it that the government is cheated by its own agents who make these reports?

In 1864–5 there was a governor by the name of Nye. There were no whites living on the reservation at that time, and there was not any agent as yet. My people were living there and fishing, as they had always done. Some white men came down from Virginia City to fish. My people went up to Carson City to tell Governor Nye that some white men were fishing on their reservation. He sent down some soldiers to drive them away. Mr. Nye is the only governor who ever helped my people, – I mean that protected them when they called on him in this way.

In 1865 we had another trouble with our white brothers. It was early in the spring, and we were then living at Dayton, Nevada, when a company of soldiers came through the place and stopped and spoke to some of my people, and said, "You have been stealing cattle from the white people at Harney Lake." They said also that they would kill everything that came in their way, men, women, and children. The captain's name was Wells. The place where they were going to is about three hundred miles away. The days after they left were very sad hours, indeed. Oh, dear readers, these soldiers had gone only sixty miles away to Muddy Lake, where my people were then living and fishing, and doing nothing to any one. The soldiers rode up to their encampment and fired into it, and killed almost all the people that were there. Oh, it is a fearful thing to tell, but it must be told. Yes, it must be told by me. It was all old men, women and children that were killed; for my father had all the young men with him, at the sink of Carson on a hunting excursion, or they would have been killed too. After the soldiers had killed all but some little children and babies still tied up in their baskets, the soldiers took them also, and set the camp on fire and threw them into the flames to see them burn alive. I had one baby brother killed there. My sister jumped on father's best horse and ran away. As she ran, the soldiers ran after her; but, thanks be to the Good Father in the Spirit-land, my dear sister got away. This almost killed my poor papa. Yet my people kept peaceful.

That same summer another of my men was killed on the reservation. His name was Truckee John. He was an uncle of mine, and was killed by a man named Flamens, who claimed to have had a brother killed in the war of 1860, but of course that had nothing to do with my uncle. About two weeks after this, two white men were killed over at Walker Lake by some of my people, and of course soldiers were sent for from California, and a great many companies came. They went after my people all over Nevada. Reports were made everywhere throughout the whole country by the white settlers, that the red devils were killing their cattle, and by this lying of the white settlers the trail began which is marked by the blood of my people from hill to hill and from valley to valley. The soldiers followed after my people in this way for one year, and the Queen's River Piutes were brought into Fort Churchill, Nevada, and in that campaign poor General McDermit was killed. These reports were only made by those white settlers so that they could sell their grain, which they could not get rid of in any other way. The only way the cattle-men and farmers get to make money is to start an Indian war, so that the troops may come and buy their beef, cattle, horses, and grain. The settlers get fat by it.

During this time my poor mother and sister died, and we were left all alone, with only father. The two Indians were taken who had killed the two white men over at Walker Lake. It was said they killed those two white men because the soldiers had killed their fathers at Muddy Lake, but they had no right to say so. They had no proof.

I will tell you the doings of the agents in that agency. The first six who came I did not know. In 1866, after my poor mother and sister Mary died, I came down from Virginia City to live with my brother Natchez, while there were some white men living on the agency. They had a great many cattle on the reservation at the time. My people did not know how to work as yet. The agent was living there, and had a store of dry goods which he sold to my people. I staid with my brother all winter, and got along very poorly, for we had nothing to eat half of the time. Sometimes we would go to the agent's house and he would get my sister-in law to wash some clothes, and then he would give us some flour to take home.

In the month of May the agent sold an Indian man some powder. He crossed the river, when he was met by one of the agent's men, who shot him dead on the spot, because he had the powder. My brother and I did not know what to do. All our people were wild with excitement. Brother and I thought he did wrong to sell the powder to one of our men, knowing it was against the law. Our people said they would go and kill him.

Brother said to me, "What shall we do?" I said, "We will go and tell them all to go away this very night." So we put saddles on our horses, and away we went to tell the agent what our people had said. The river was very high; when crossing it my horse fell down in the river, and I got very wet. Brother jumped off his horse, and helped me on again. We went up to the house, and I said to him, –

"Mr. Newgent, go away, quick! My people are coming here to kill all of you, and tell all who are on the river to go too, for they will surely come and kill them all." He said, "I am not afraid of them, – they will be glad to stop before they do anything. We have a good many guns." He called to his men, saying, "Get your guns ready; we will show the damned red devils how to fight." Brother said again to him, "We would like to have you go; please do not get us into any more trouble." He told my brother and me to go away. We did so. As soon as we got to our home, my brother got all his people together, and told them to get ten young men and go and watch the crossing of the river, and if any one tried to cross, to catch him. "If there is more than one kill them if you can; by so doing we will save ourselves, for you know if we allowed our people to kill the white men we should all be killed here. It is better that we should kill some of our own men than to be all killed here."

About midnight my brother called his people together again. They all came running. Brother said to them, "I had a dream, and it is true that our people who were coming to kill the agent and his men are not going to kill them, but they are going to the Deep Wells, and the deed is already done." The place he spoke of is about thirty miles from the place where we were then, near Virginia City, Nevada. He said, "I see only one dead; one is not dead, but he will die. I see a great many horses taken by them. It is only a dream, but nevertheless, it is true. Get your horses; we will go after them. We must do it or we will all be in trouble."

So brother took thirty of his men to go and head them off, if they could. After he went away, I heard one of the men say, "I wonder if what our chief said is true!" Just then some one was seen coming. He gave an alarm of danger at hand. Every one jumped to their guns. I jumped on a horse, barebacked, to go and meet him, and my men did likewise. When we met him my first word was, "What is it?" He said, "We shall all die this very day." "Why?" said I. "Oh, somebody has killed a white man and another is almost dead." "Where are they?" said I. "At the Deep Wells." One of the men said, " Did you see them?" He said, "Yes, and that is not all; our agent has gone to get soldiers to come and kill us all." I said, "Where did you see him?" "Half way to the soldiers."

Just then we heard another alarm. We all turned our heads towards the noise. We saw another of our men coming as if he was running for his dear life. We all ran to meet him. He too said, "We shall all be killed." He told the same thing about one dead man and one almost dead. So we returned to the camp again.

The sub-chief sent out spies to watch and come in to tell us in time to meet our enemies. In this way passed the day. Newgent, our agent, had left his house at daybreak to go to the fort to see some of the officers there. He rode up to the house, got off his horse, and went in to tell them about the trouble he had on the agency. A fearful thing met his eyes. One man was really dead, and the other almost dead. He asked what was the matter. The man answered, "Three Indians came here last night and shot us, and they thought they had killed both of us. They have taken all our things away, and they swore at us in good English language that the agent had their brother killed." Poor man, he did not know that he was talking to the very devil that had made all the trouble. Very late that evening, two of our men came as before. They brought me a letter; these were the words –

"Miss Sarah Winnemucca, – Your agent tells us very bad things about your people's killing two of our men. I want you and your brother Natchez to meet me at your place to-night. I want to talk to you and your brother.

Signed, Captain Jerome,

*Company M, 8th Cavalry."*

It took me some time to read it, as I was very poor, indeed, at reading writing; and I assure you, my dear readers, I am not much better now. After reading it four or more times, I knew what it said. I did not know what to do, as brother had not returned. I had no ink to write with. My people all gathered round me waiting for me to tell them something. I did not say anything. They could not wait any longer. They asked me what the paper said. I said, "The soldiers are coming; the officer wants me and my brother to see them at our place." At that time, brother and I had a place on the reservation.

They said, "Oh, it is too bad that he went off this morning; you and he might be the means of saving us. Can you speak to them on paper?"

I said, "I have nothing to write with. I have no ink. I have no pen."

They said, "Oh, take a stick, – take anything. Until you talk on that paper we will not believe you can talk on paper."

I said, "Make me a stick with a sharp point, and bring me some fish's blood." They did as I told them, and then I wrote, saying, –

"Hon. Sir, – My brother is not here. I am looking for him every minute. We will go as soon as he comes in. If he comes to-night, we will come some time during the night. Yours,

S. W."

I sent the same man back with the letter. He had not been gone long when my brother came in with his men. Everybody ran to him and told him his dream had come true. Some of the men who were with brother said, "We knew it was true before we got here. We saw the horses' tracks, so it is nothing strange to us." Then I told him that the agent had a company of soldiers waiting for him and me at our place. Brother asked when Newgent went for them. "Early in the morning," I guessed, "and your dream, dear brother, was true. Mr. Coffman and his man are killed." "Oh, sister, do not fool with your brother."

I said, "Indeed, indeed, it is so." Everybody cried out, "It is every word of it true."

"Get us fresh horses," said he, "and we will go and see them. Wife, get me something to eat before I go. I want twenty men to go with me and my sister. Dear sister, did you send them word that we would come as soon as I came home?" "Yes brother." We were soon on the road to see the soldiers. We went like the wind, never stopping until we got there. The officer met us. I told him everything from the first beginning of the trouble. I told him that the agent sold some powder to an Indian, and that his own men had killed the Indian. I told him how brother and I went to him and asked him and his men to go away, as we had heard that our people were going to kill him. I told him that he talked bad to brother and me, because we went to tell him of it. I told this to the officer right before the agent. The agent did not have anything to say, and then the officer asked my brother what he knew about it, and if he had seen anything during that day. He asked: –

"How many head of horses do you think they have?" "I don't know – a good many." "Well, how many do you think?" "Maybe sixty, or more."

I think the officer did not speak to the agent while we were there. We did not stay long, because I was afraid of the soldiers, although the officer asked us to stop all night. I said, "Brother, we will go back." The officer said, "We will come down to-morrow, and have another talk with your sister." So off we went.

Many of our people did not sleep that night. Brother called all his people together at one place. He told them the soldiers were their friends, and not to be afraid of them, because if they had come to fight with them they would have brought more with them. He told our people there were only a few. So we watched for their coming the next morning. At last they came, and camped alongside of brother's camp. The first thing he did was to tell us not to be afraid. If we wanted protection the officer would send for his company to come down from Carochel. We said our people were very much afraid of the soldiers. He asked us what we had to eat. We told him we had nothing just then, but we hoped the fish would soon run up the river, so that we might catch some. He saw that we had nothing at all. He said he would go up to the Fort and tell the commanding officer about us. So he took two men with him, and left the rest with us. Two days afterwards a soldier came in and told brother that the captain had three wagons of provisions for him and his people. Oh, how glad we were, for we were very poorly off for want of something to eat. That was the first provision I had ever seen issued to my people! The agent came to the officer, and said, "If you want to issue beef to the Indians, I have some cattle I can sell you." The officer told him "to be off." Five days after, five soldiers came down from the Fort with a letter for the captain. After he read the letter, he called brother and me to him, and said: –

"I have got a letter from the commanding officer at the Fort, asking me if your father is here with you." Brother told him he had not been with us for a long time. I was crying, and I told him father had not been in since the soldiers killed my little brother. I told him that he sent word to us some six months ago that he had gone to live in the mountains, and to die there. I was crying all the while I was talking to him. My people were frightened; they did not know what I was saying. Our men gathered all round us. They asked brother what was the matter. He told them what the officer said to me.

"Sarah, don't cry, you and your brother shall go with me, and we will get your father here. If he will come in he will be cared for by the officers of the army. The commanding officer says you are to go with me to Camp McDermitt, and you can get your father and all your people to come into the army post, where you can be fed. Now, if you will go, we will start by the first of July. Brother asked me what I thought about it. "Dear brother," I said, "I will do whatever you say. If you say so, we will go and get our father if we can. We can try it." Brother told all to his people. Some said: –

"Maybe they will kill him. You and your sister know what liars the white people are, and if you go and get him and he is killed by the soldiers, his blood will be on you." Brother said –

"I believe what the officers say, and if father comes in they will take good care of us." They said, "Well, it is your father, and you two know best what to do. If anything happens to him, you will have no one to blame but yourselves." Brother said, "What has my father done to the white people that they should harm him? Because white people are bad that is no reason why the soldiers should be bad, too."

(Brother and my people always say "the white people," just as if the soldiers were not white, too.) So we told the captain that we would go with him.

Now, dear readers, this is the way all the Indian agents get rich. The first thing they do is to start a store; the next thing is to take in cattle men, and cattle men pay the agent one dollar a head. In this way they get rich very soon, so that they can have their gold-headed canes, with their names engraved on them. The one I am now speaking of is only a sub-agent. He told me the head agent was living in Carson City, and he paid him fifteen hundred dollars a year for the use of the reservation. Yet, he has fine horses and cattle and sheep, and is very rich. The sub-agent was a minister; his name was Balcom. He did not stay very long, because a man named Batemann hired some Indians to go and scare him away from the reservation, that he might take his place. The leader of these Indians was named Dave. He was interpreter at the Pyramid Lake Reservation. So Batemann got the minister away, and then he got rich in the same way.

While Batemann was agent, I was asked to act as interpreter to the Shoshones by a man called Captain Dodge, agent for the Shoshone Indians. He was going to issue clothing to them at a place called Battle Mountain. My brother Natchez went all about to summon the people there. I told Colonel Dodge all about our agent at Pyramid Lake Reservation. He said he would go to see him, which he did. It took three days for the people to come up. Oh, such an issue! It was enough to make a doll laugh. A family numbering eight persons got two blankets, three shirts, no dress-goods. Some got a fishhook and line; some got one and a half yards of flannel, blue and red; the largest issue was to families that camped together, numbering twenty-three persons: four blankets, three pieces of red flannel, and some of blue, three shirts, three hooks and lines, two kettles. It was the saddest affair I ever saw. There were ready-made clothes of all kinds, hats, shoes, and shawls, and farming utensils of all kinds. Bales upon bales of clothing were sent away to Salt Lake City. After the issue, the things were all to be put into one place. Holy songs were offered up to the Great Spirit Father. The things were blessed before they were to be worn, and all the young men put the blankets round them and danced. In the morning some of the men went round with only one leg dressed in flannel, which made all the white people laugh. At this issue our agent, Mr. Batemann, gave the Shoshones one ton of flour before this new agent, which made me very angry, and I talked to him before Colonel Dodge. I said, "You come up here to show off before this man. Go and bring some flour to my people on Humboldt River, who are starving, the people over whom you are agent. For shame that you who talk three times a day to the Great Father in Spirit-land should act so to my people." This man called himself a Christian, too.

Then came another agent by the name of Spencer. He was a better one than we had ever had. He issued some blankets to some old men and women and blind people, and gave brother some pieces of land to work upon. He then gave my people wagons, – about ten altogether; and he had his daughter brought as a teacher, at the rate of fifty dollars a month. But he soon died, and then came our present agent. He was not married at the time, but he very soon learned that there was money to be made, so he went back and got married. Of course he put his wife in as teacher. Mr. MacMasters, for that is his name, has his own method of making my people divide the produce. If they raise five sacks of grain, they give one sack for the Big Father in Washington; if they have only three sacks, they still have to send one. Every fourth load of hay goes to the Big Father at Washington, yet he does not give my people the seed. The head-farmer, who is called Mushrush, never shows my people how to work. This is why they said, "Why does the Big Father want us to pay him when he does not give us the seed? We have to pay for the seed ourselves." Both the agent and farmer told my people they would have to pay it or the Big Father would take away their wagons. So my people talked it over and said, "We will pay it." Later they got up a paper, which the agent and the farmer wanted my people to sign. The sub-chief would not put his hand to the pen. He said to the agent, –

"I have been working for so many years, and I have never received anything as yet. You say it is supplies you are sending me and my people; but I am sick and tired of lies, and I won't sign any paper." Of course our agent, Mr. MacMasters, told him to leave the reservation. His wagon was taken from him. At this my people sent me down to San Francisco to tell the commanding officer. I did so. I gave Gen. McDowell a full account of the doings, and he reported him to the authorities. The following spring my poor brother Natchez went to the agent and asked him to help him to a plough, and to give him a set of harness. He told my brother to go away. "You and your sister," he said, "talk about me all the time. I don't want you and your sister here." At this my poor brother got angry and said to him, "This is my reservation, not yours. I am going to stay here just as long as I like. My poor father and I never got so much as an old rag from any agent that ever came here." At this our minister got angry, and telegraphed to the soldiers to come and take brother and carry him to the Acotrass Islands. He wrote a letter, saying all my people wanted him to send my brother away where they could never see him any more. After he had written it, he called up all the head men of our people, and told them he had written to their father in Washington for good clothing for them, and wished them to sign the paper. Of course, they did not know any better; they put their names to the paper, and signed their chief away! So the soldiers came and took brother to San Francisco, Cal. Brother was only there a little while when two white men whose lives he had saved went and took him out and sent him home, and wrote to our minister agent. Of course I knew not what was in the letter.

Dear reader, I must tell a little more about my poor people, and what we suffer at the hands of our white brothers. Since the war of 1860 there have been one hundred and three (103) of my people murdered, and our reservations taken from us; and yet we, who are called blood-seeking savages, are keeping our promises to the government. Oh, my dear good Christian people, how long are you going to stand by and see us suffer at your hands? Oh, dear friends, you are wrong when you say it will take two or three generations to civilize my people. No! I say it will not take that long if you will only take interest in teaching us; and, on the other hand, we shall never be civilized in the way you wish us to be if you keep on sending us such agents as have been sent to us year after year, who do nothing but fill their pockets, and the pockets of their wives and sisters, who are always put in as teachers, and paid from fifty to sixty dollars per month, and yet they do not teach. The farmer is generally his cousin, his pay is nine hundred dollars ($900) a year, and his brother is a clerk. I do not know his name. The blacksmith and carpenter have from five hundred to eleven hundred dollars per year. I got this from their own statements. I saw a discharged agent while I was on my way here, who told me all the agents had to pay so much to the Secretary of the Interior, who had to make up what he paid to the agents. This I know to be a true confession, or the Secretary of the Interior and all the government officers would see into the doings of these Christian agents. Year after year they have been told of their wrong-doings by different tribes of Indians. Yet it goes on, just the same as if they did not know it.

When I went to Carson City in 1870, to see about my people's affairs, I was sent by the officials from one to another. At last we went to San Francisco to see General Schofield, and he sent me back to see Senator Jones. So brother and I went to where he was living in Gold Hill. I told him how my people were treated by the agents. He said, "I will see to it." He then put into my hands twenty dollars, which I took gratefully, for we were always poor, and brother and I went away. I have never seen or heard from him since.

I can give you one example to show how easily the Indians are influenced by those they respect and believe in. In 1868 many of my people were at Camp C. F. Smith,[8] taking care of themselves, but under many difficulties, and very destitute. There was no game in that region of any kind, except now and then a hare. They had no land to cultivate, but were living upon anything they could do or gather. Some citizens wrote to Col. McElroy, who was at that time commanding officer at Camp McDermitt, that the Indians were starving, and they were afraid there might be some outbreak, or depredations, and asking him to have them taken to his post. I was interpreter at Camp McDermitt at that time. Five hundred of my people, men, women and children, were already there. There were four hundred at Camp C. F. Smith. Col. McElroy asked me how many companies of soldiers it would take to escort them. I told him none; that he and I could escort them, or my brother Lee and I. He could not believe me at first; but I told him I knew my people, and he and I, with one servant, went for them.

I went into council with my people. My brother Lee, who was there, and I sat up all night talking with them, and telling them what we wished them to do. We Indians never try to rule our people without explaining everything to them. When they understand and consent, we have no more trouble.

Some of the interpreters are very ignorant, and don't understand English enough to know all that is said. This often makes trouble. Then I am sorry to say these Indian interpreters, who are often half-breeds, easily get corrupted, and can be hired by the agents to do or say anything. I know this, for some of them are my relatives. My people are very reasonable and want to understand everything, and be sure that there is fair play.

For one thing, they said they had so many children they would find it hard to carry them sixty-five miles. Did I think Col. McElroy would let them have some wagons? I said I would ask him. He said "yes;" and he furnished fifteen wagons, which transported the women and children comfortably in two days, and the men had their horses. The recruits who were watching the buildings at Camp C. F. Smith (for there was not a large force there) furnished rations for the two days, and Col. McElroy was to replenish them from Camp McDermitt.

There were now nine hundred in all at Camp McDermitt. Every head of a family was furnished with a good tent of the requisite size for his family, such tents as are used by the soldiers; and every morning, at five o'clock, rations for the day were issued. A pound and a half of meat was given to every grown person, and good bread, – for they actually baked good bread for them, – and once a month coffee, rice, sugar, salt, pepper, and beans were issued. Each woman came to me every day with her basket, and her number on a tag, fastened to a leather thong tied round her neck, and told the size of her family and took what she needed from me; and everything was recorded, for that is the way things are done in soldiers' camps. Every one had enough. My father was with us at that time. He told my people in council one day that he thought it was an imposition to be living entirely on the soldier-fathers, when we could do something to support ourselves. He wanted them to go on hunting excursions in the summer, and bring in dried venison, rabbits, and what other game they could find; and the women to go out and gather grass-seed, and dig roots and do what they could toward the supplies of the next winter. I told Col. McElroy what my father had said to his people, and he told them to go to the sutler's store and get what ammunition they wanted and bring him the record of it, and he would see that it was paid for. My father knew that the army gave this support for the Indians as prisoners out of its own supplies. My people had enough, I said; they had more than enough, and by being prudent about their rations they could save and sell enough to get calicoes and other necessary things for the women and children; for these things are not found in army supplies. It is this generosity and this kind care and order and discipline that make me like the care of the army for my people.

Col. McElroy belonged to Company M, Eighth Cavalry. He had my people in charge three years, and

8 In Oregon, about 25 miles northwest of Fort McDermit.

was then ordered to New Mexico; but before he could go, he died in San Francisco. He was the first officer I ever worked for as interpreter.

Can you wonder, dear readers, that I like to have my people taken care of by the army? It is said that I am working in the interest of the army, and as if they wanted all this care. It is not so; but they know more about the Indians than any citizens do, and are always friendly. Nobody really knows Indians who cheat them and treat them badly. They may be very peace-loving people, but that would make saints sin. They are the most sociable people in the world in their own camps; but they are shut up to white people, because they are so often wronged by them.

I remained at Camp McDermitt after Col. McElroy's death. They thought it best to buy a large herd of cattle for beef for the soldiers and my people, and for a time they hired some of the Indians for herdsmen; but this proved too expensive, and they were discharged from that service, which was given to some soldiers. One night the whole herd was stolen and driven off. The greatest search was made for them, but all in vain. It seemed as if they had vanished. But at last, the commanding officer thought the Indians, who knew how to track a trail, would do better at such business than white men, who do not know how to find a trail of anything. My brother Lee was staying with me then, and he and five other men undertook to find the cattle. They were gone five days, and at the end of the time came back and said they were found. They had traced them to a deep cañon, and they were driven by one single man. One man had stolen and driven away all those cattle. My people had come back to get soldiers to go with them to capture him. So he was arrested, and brought back to the post with all the cattle. It was truly comical to think of it. I was very glad my people were successful, for it would surely have been believed that some Indians, if not mine, had driven those cattle off.

The last time sister and I were on a visit to our people at our old home, just before I was married, we stopped with a white lady named Nichols, at Wadsworth, Nevada, on Pyramid Lake Reservation, the head-farmer named Mushrush, and the sub-agent at Walker River Reservation in Nevada. Some one tried to break through our bedroom door, and my sister cried out to them, saying, "Get away from that door or I will shoot!" At my sister's words they went away. The name of the sub-agent is Louis Veviers, who has been with my people about eight years. All my people call him dog, because there is nothing too bad for him to say to them. After I was married, I went to let my people see my husband. While we were there we staid with my brother Tom. On New Year's evening we heard a great noise coming towards the house. They were trying to make a noise like my people who had just lost a son, and were crying. They were mocking them as they came on. There were four men, – the doctor, the carpenter, the blacksmith, and one of their friends. My brother's wife gave them some pine-nuts. By-and-by one of them gave my husband a bottle of fire-water, and asked him to pass it round. My husband replied, "Pass it round yourselves." They said, "Give some to your brother-in-law." My husband said, "Give it to him yourself." This is the kind of people, dear reader, that the government sends to teach us at Pyramid Lake Reservation.

My people wanted to cut the hay, but they were not allowed to sell it until within five years. My cousin, Captain Bill, and his brother, had borrowed some seed by promising to divide the wheat after harvest, which they did; and then the farmer, who never showed them how to sow their grain, came to Bill, and said, "You must pay me for the use of the government land." "What for?" said Bill. "Well, that's what the Big Father in Washington says." Then Bill said, "Take it all." After Mr. Mushrush took his unjust share, my poor cousin had only three sacks left for himself. Our present agent made my people give every third sack of grain, and the same of everything else. Every third load of hay is given. My people asked why, as he had not given them seed for planting, nor did the farmer help them. They did not see why they should pay so much, but the agent told them that was the order from Washington. They refused to pay it. The agent told them they must pay it or he would take their wagons away. They went home to talk it over that night. However, Jim, the sub-chief, told his people that the white men had been stealing from them for a long time, "and now I am going to steal from them this very night. I am going to have my family hide away half of my grain. I have sixty sacks of wheat and twenty-six of potatoes. As for the hay-cart I don't care. What do you think of me for talking so to you? I see I can't keep up with the white people. They think it right to steal all they can while they are with us. And I am going to do another thing; I am going to quit signing any paper, for I don't know what I have been signing all these twenty-two years." My cousin Captain Bill, and his brother, said, "We will keep all our grain, and if he wants the wagon he can take it." Then all the rest of the men said, "We will do the same as our chief, and what is left he can have." Some of them said, "We have only a little, and what shall we do?" The next morning they went to the agent's house to see if he had changed his mind, but he told them that was the law. Bill told him that he might go and get his wagon. "I bought my seed and paid my own money for it, and you did not help me." The agent replied, "If you won't do what the government orders, you must leave the reservation." Jim, the sub-chief, said, "You may take all I have, leave my people theirs, and I will go away into the mountains, and there I will live and die." But the agent would not hear to it, and they all had to pay their share. My brother Tom said, "If we don't pay it we shall have to leave the reservation."

The agent thought it necessary to make a show of some kind, and this is the way he did it. There are unprincipled men in all tribes, as I suppose there are among all people, and the agent found one for his work. He is known as "Captain Dave." His Indian name is Numana. The plan made and carried out was this: Captain Dave was furnished with money, and appointed captain of police, a useless office, for Indians could not arrest either an Indian or a white man. They really were nothing but private servants to the agent. But this was promised to Captain Dave, provided he and six others would go to San Francisco, and do what the agent wanted them to do.

They were furnished with a drawing of a bridge that had been built, and told to go to the newspaper offices in San Francisco, and say beautiful things of the agent and his men. Every reasonable person will see by reading this paper, which was published in a newspaper, that the most intelligent Indian could not have given such a description of a bridge without he had been furnished with a memorandum of it: –

"Captain Dave and the Reservation. – Numana, better known as Captain Dave, one of the leading men of the Piute nation, called on us yesterday, and showed us several papers, among which was a letter of recommendation from Governor Kinkead, and an appointment from the Indian Commissioner as captain of the Indian police at Pyramid Reservation. Dave is a very intelligent Indian, and gave us the following facts connected with the Piutes and their doings: He and his body-guard of six Piutes have just returned from a trip to San Francisco, where they spent the holidays pleasantly. He had in his possession a very good cut of the bridge at the reservation and its dimensions, which are, length one hundred and sixty-five feet, width twenty feet, height fifteen feet above low-water mark. A flume crossing the river on the bridge which carries the water from their irrigating ditch on the east side of the river to the other measures as follows: length twelve hundred feet, width six feet, height above ground on trestle eight to fifteen feet. He showed us by a rough sketch the course of the river at the reservation, the position of the dam, and the route of the ditch, which is not finished as yet. The dam is so constructed as to allow a channel (whereby the fish can run up) about ten feet wide and three or four feet deep. From the head of the ditch to the bridge is about one and a quarter miles, from the bridge to the Reservation House, about two miles. The ditch, when completed, will measure four miles and will irrigate a large area of land. The Indians are not working now, but are devoting their time to fishing. Agent McMasters is well-liked by the Indians, and he has a system of dealing with them which they fully understand and appreciate. Mrs. McMasters has charge of the school, and teaches some thirty Indian children, many of them being apt scholars, and all seeming to like to attend school.

"Mr. Mushrush, the farmer, is giving perfect satisfaction, showing the Indians how to work, and doesn't simply order, but takes a hand himself, which Dave says pleases them.

"They intend to farm on a larger scale next year than at any time before. Mr. McMasters' method in dividing the produce is stated by Captain Dave to be in this way. The Indian raises five sacks of grain, he retains four, and gives the government one. If he has four loads of hay he gives one of them to the government. This is given by the Indians to help feed the government stock, which is kept at work hauling stone, lumber, wood, etc., etc. Dave is very desirous of having the Piutes in all parts of Nevada notified to come to the reservation, and help build it up. He claims that in one year's time they will have room and work for them, and they can come there and build a home. He is also very anxious that the whiskey traffic among them be stopped, and to that end asks that the officers in every town will see that a drunken Indian be punished as severely as possibly. This, he claims, is a terrible curse among them, and is gaining ground."

No newspaper in San Francisco would publish this statement, and they were obliged to have it done in Reno, Nevada, in a paper the civilized world knows nothing of. I will only speak now of the character of "Captain Dave." I said Mr. Batemann hired an Indian to frighten Mr. Balcom away. That Indian was this very "Captain Dave." I have known him many years, and have always been ashamed of him as a Piute. Twenty years ago I knew him to blow a young girl's brains out because she refused to marry him, and his behavior ever since has been in keeping with that. It is no secret among my people that he exposes his wife to bad white men for money. He is not a "leading man." No man can be a leading man among Indians, unless he is honorable and brave. Dave is neither. On the contrary, he has no character whatever, and could always be hired to do a wicked thing. He is my own cousin.

Mr. Mushrush, the farmer spoken of in the printed article, does all his farming *in the bar-room at Wadsworth.* We have a store at this agency kept by Mr. Eugene Griswold. He is the man who always gets the beef contracts. It may be in another man's name sometimes, but it is all the same.

It has always been a mystery to me what this beef contract is for. If they mean it for a license to sell beef, why don't they say so? I defy them to find a man, woman, or child outside their ring who has ever received a pound of meat of any kind from them. I have a brother who lives on the agency, and he has never got an ounce of meat that he has not paid for. The contractors, Griswold, McMasters, etc., really keep a butcher's shop, but call it a beef contract. Those that have money can come up and buy. Those that have none stand back and cry, often with hunger.

All this refers to the Pyramid Lake Agency. The contractors call it the "Nevada Agency."

Brother and I started for Camp McDermitt, Nevada, at the time set, along with company M, First Cavalry. It took us twenty-eight days to reach Camp McDermitt. Nothing happened during our journey. We reached the camp late in the evening. Brother and I did not see anybody until the next day. After we had something to eat in the morning the commanding officer, Major Seward, sent for us to come to his office. We did so. He was a very nice man. He said to brother, "Are you tired?" Brother said, "Not much. I guess my sister is." He said to me, "You find it pretty hard travelling, don't you." I answered, "It is pretty hard, it is so very warm." He said to my brother Natchez, "Do you think you can find your father, or don't you think you can get him and his people to come to this place? I would like to have him come, so he can be taken care of. He is too old to be out in this bad country. If Gen. Crook should find him and his people, he might make him some trouble. The white settlers are talking very badly through the whole country, and they have sent for Gen. Crook to come and kill all the Indians that are not on some reservation. I am afraid to have your father out there. Natchez, if you can bring him in, I will feed him and his people, and will give them clothes, such as the soldiers wear. I will be his friend and fight for him if he and his people are good." I said, "Colonel, my good papa has never done anything unkind to the white people yet, and the soldiers came to Muddy Lake and killed a great many of our people there without our doing any bad thing to them. They killed my little brother. This is what drove my poor papa away; we have not seen him for two years." Brother then said, "Yes, colonel, it is too bad the way the white people say all the time that Indians are bad, and that they have bad hearts, and that their hearts are very black. Colonel, if you will give me your heart and hand, I will go and try to get my father to come to you."

"Yes, Natchez, I will do everything I have told you. I will send one company of cavalry with you. Your sister can stay here, and talk for those that are already here. She shall be my interpreter, and I will pay her sixty-five dollars per month, and I will pay you five dollars a day while you are away."

Brother said, "Colonel, I don't want to have any soldiers go with me. I will go all alone, because my people will think I have brought soldiers to fight them. For fear they will think so, I will go alone. I will find my father sooner by going alone; for I will make the son's signal-fire as I go along, and my father will know it is I who is coming to see him (the signal-fires are like so many telegraphs of many kinds and orders), and he will come to meet me. And colonel, you will take good care of my sister. See that no soldiers talk to her, and colonel, I want you to give me a paper to tell the white people I meet who I am, so they will not kill me. You know, colonel, the white men like to kill us Indians."

The colonel said, "All right, Natchez, I will give you a paper."

So the talk ended. My brother was to go in the morning. The colonel said, "We will go now and see the prisoners. I have twenty-five Queen's River Piutes here already." As we walked along he said, –

"They are very good Indians. They are always ready to do whatever I tell them to do that is in the line of work. You will see that I have given them such clothes as I give my soldiers, but the women and children I can't do much for, because the government does not give me anything for them. But we will see what can be done for them after your father comes in, and when your sister gets rested, she may be able to do something for them." We got to the camp at last. They all ran out of their tents to see us. The men ran to brother, saying, "My brother, oh, my brother!" They threw their arms round him, calling him many endearing words. Then they would throw their robes down on the ground for him to sit upon. They had not said a word to me until my brother told them I was his sister. Then they held out their hands to me, saying, "Our sister, we are glad to see you too. Oh, how kind of you to come and see us so far away." Then the women came to me crying, and said the same, "Our sister, we are glad to see you. Oh, how kind of you to come and see us so far away." It is the way we savages do when we meet each other; we cry with joy and gladness. We told the officer to go, – we would come back soon. We would be ready at seven o'clock. Our people said many beautiful things about their black-clothes fathers. They should have said blue-clothes. They said, "We are getting plenty to eat, and we men get nice clothes to wear, and we do very little work for the clothes. All the work we do is only child's play. We would do more if they would only ask us to. We are as happy as we can be." Brother said, "I am so glad, my people, to hear you say so, because I was going to leave my poor sister here all alone with the soldiers. I was afraid they might abuse her." Then some of the women said to me, "Oh, dear, you can stay with us; we will make you a nice place." I said, "Oh, brother, why can't I stay here with our own people? I will be so happy here with the girls."

"Oh, yes! Stay here with us, we will have such a good time."

Brother told them he was going to see his father, and try to get him to come and live there with them.

They all said, "How nice that will be!"

Some of the old men said, "Oh, if he could only forget the wrong that the white men did to him. But of course he cannot forget it. Oh, it is hard how the white people are treating us. We cannot help it, we have to stand it like a little mouse under a cat's paws. They like to see us suffer, and they laugh at us when we weep; but our soldier-fathers are good; we will go with you to get your father. We can tell him how kind the soldiers are to us."

While the talk was going on, a soldier came and said that the commanding officer wanted us. Brother told the commanding officer he wanted five men to go with him in the morning. I was afraid. I said to brother, "Can't I stay here while you go and see what he wants with us?" He went up. It was lunch time. After lunch brother told the commanding officer that he had heard something good about him and his men. He answered, 'I am glad of it." Brother told him he would take five men with him to speak for him. "I think I shall have no trouble," he said, "in getting my father to come." The officer said, "All right, Natchez; you want six horses, then." So next morning very early they started out and left me alone. I felt so badly, and I cried so much, that my eyes were all swelled up. I could not eat anything. After my brother had gone, I went to the commanding officer, and said, "Colonel, I am here all alone with so many men, I am afraid. I want your protection. I want you to protect me against your soldiers, and I want you to protect my people also; that is, I want you to give your orders to your soldiers not to go to my people's camp at any time, and also issue the same order to the citizens." Accordingly the order was issued, and posted here and there, and the result was that we lived in peace. Soon after this my brother found and persuaded my father and four hundred and ninety of my people to come into Camp McDermitt. On their arrival they were kindly received by the commanding officer. Clothing such as the soldiers wear was given to them, and rations were also issued, – good bread, coffee, sugar, salt, pepper, pork, beef, and beans. So we lived quietly for two years. One night a man named Joe Lindsey crawled into our camp. It was reported by one of my men to the commanding officer, who had him arrested and confined that night, and the next day he was released with the understanding that he would leave the reservation. Nothing of importance occurred for three weeks, when a soldier who had been fishing, and having drank more than was good for him, staggered through our camp, and although he troubled no one he was corrected and tied up by the thumbs all day, and then placed in the guard-house all night. I tell this to show what is done to any one who violates the orders given by officers of the army. The following winter the man Lindsey came back with the express purpose of killing the Indian who reported him. He met him in the post-traders' store. There were several white men in the store at the time. The Indian could not understand English, so did not know that they were planning to kill him. After some talk, Lindsey said, "I'll bet the whiskey for the crowd that I can shoot his eye out." Some one took the bet, and without any more delay, he turned round and shot him just below the eye. He then coolly pulled out his knife and scalped him and put the scalp in his pocket, got on the stage and went to Winnemucca, eighty-five miles; then went from saloon to saloon calling for drinks, and offering to pay for them with a scalp of a good Indian – a dead one. His partner put the body of the unfortunate Indian in the trader's buggy, and tried to hide it; but the beautiful white snow was too pure to hide the cowardly deed. His blood could be seen for miles and miles, and so we tracked them and brought the body back; and such a time as I had to keep my people quiet! Early the next morning the warriors assembled, determined to begin a war to the death. I talked and reasoned for hours, and at last persuaded them to go to their camps. Every effort was made by the commanding officer, Major Seward, to bring those "hard-working, honest, and kind-hearted settlers" to trial, but in vain. All that could be done was done. Their den was broken up, and shortly after this very gang had the audacity to put in a bill of damages against the government, because the commanding officer had their cabin torn down and moved away.

# Susette LaFlesche [Tibbles] (Inshta Theamba, Bright Eyes; Omaha, 1854–1903)

*LaFlesche was born into a prominent, affluent, and acculturated Omaha family. Her half-French and half-Ponca father, Joseph (Insta Maza or "Iron Eye"), was the last recognized chief of the Omaha tribe, while her mother, Mary Gale (Hinnuagsnun, or "the One Woman"), was also mixed-blood, being Omaha and white. Although she was brought up to cherish her Indian heritage, her father, who favored assimilation, provided a strong influence, not only ensuring that his children received excellent educations in both white and Omaha cultural traditions, but also bringing white education to the reservation. Attending the mission school until it closed in 1869, she traveled from her home in Nebraska to New Jersey to enroll in the Elizabeth Institute for Young Ladies in 1872. An excellent student, she nevertheless struggled to find employment as a teacher upon her return to the reservation after graduation in 1875.*

*LaFlesche became involved in Indian politics when the neighboring Poncas were removed against their will to Indian Territory; their chief, Standing Bear, was arrested when he led a group of his people back to their traditional homeland. These events sparked LaFlesche to become an ardent and effective advocate for the Poncas and for Indian rights more generally, and she joined an eastern tour with Standing Bear and others as an orator, speaking to reform-minded groups from Chicago to Boston and eventually testifying in 1880 before the US Senate on Ponca removal. This tour not only made her famous, it gave her the opportunity to meet such well-known writers as Henry Wadsworth Longfellow and Helen Hunt Jackson, who would in 1881 publish* A Century of Dishonor *about the United States's shameful treament of Indians. After the wife of the tour organizer, Thomas Tibbles, died, he and LaFlesche married, and she continued to pursue her activist agenda both in the United States and in England and Scotland during an 1887 lecture tour with her husband. The pair also witnessed the events leading up to and the massacre at Wounded Knee. Apart from these travels, LaFlesche spent the rest of her life on or near the Omaha reservation.*

*LaFlesche's published work includes newspaper columns from the* Omaha World Herald *and her husband's* The Independent. *She also wrote the powerful introductions to William Justin Harsha's 1881 Indian reform novel,* Ploughed Under: The Story of an Indian Chief, *and to Tibbles's* The Ponca Chiefs. *Offering another model of intercultural collaboration than that of Mary Jemison – her husband supplied the footnotes for her "Omaha Legends and Tent Stories" – her works in children's periodicals such as those reprinted here from the children's magazines,* St. Nicholas *and* Wide Awake, *sought to educate white readers about Indian culture. Like its counterpart in Sarah Winnemucca's nonfiction narrative of "Domestic and Social Moralities," "Nedawi" contains quiet messages about proper gender relations, while the narrative of "The Babes in the Woods," like Schoolcraft's "The Forsaken Brother," highlights the necessity of family and community responsibility for one another. Such an ethic of responsibility was clearly part of LaFlesche's own life. In her testimony before the US Senate, she faced powerful senators including Henry Dawes of Massachusetts, the architect of the General Allotment Act of 1887 (as well as a member of the Committee on Indian Affairs during the 47th to 52nd Congresses and from 1893 to 1903 the Chairman of a commission created to administer the affairs of the Five Civilized Tribes), and John Tyler Morgan, an Alabama Democrat who supported segregation for blacks but sometimes proved a surprising ally to Native Americans. LaFlesche's testimony reveals a strong-minded woman who could not be silenced by authority; at one rather heated point in the hearing, when Morgan attempts to make her define the term "civilized," she responds, "I do not know what you mean by civilized." With her sister, Susan, who became the first Indian woman medical doctor, and her brother, Francis, who became a noted ethnologist, LaFlesche was a gifted speaker and a lifelong advocate for Indian rights.*

BIBLIOGRAPHY

## Primary

"An Indian Woman's Letter." *The Southern Workman*, April 1879.
Introduction to *Ploughed Under: The Story of an Indian Chief.* By William Justin Harsha. Fords, Howard, and Hulbert, 1881.
Introduction to *The Ponca Chiefs*. By Thomas H. Tibbles. Lockwood, Brooks, 1880.
Letter to *St. Nicholas*. *St. Nicholas* (September 1880): 918.
"Nedawi." *St. Nicholas*. January 1881.
"Omaha Legends and Tent Stories." *Wide Awake*, June 1883.
Senate testimony. "Removal of the Ponca Indians." 13 February 1880.

## Secondary

Clark, Jerry E., and Martha Ellen Webb. "Susette and Susan LaFlesche: Reformer and Missionary." In *Being and Becoming Indian: Biographical Studies of North American Frontiers*. Ed. James A. Clifton. Dorsey, 1989. 137–50.
Green, Norma Kidd. *Iron Eye's Family: The Children of Joseph LaFlesche.* Johnsen, 1969.
LaFlesche Family Papers. Nebraska State Historical Society, Lincoln.
Parins, James W. "Susette LaFlesche Tibbles." In *Native American Women: A Biographical Dictionary*. Ed. Gretchen M. Bataille. Garland, 1993.
Wilson, Dorothy Clarke. *Bright Eyes: The Story of Susette LaFlesche, An Omaha Indian*. McGraw-Hill, 1974.

# AN INDIAN WOMAN'S LETTER (*THE SOUTHERN WORKMAN*, APRIL, 1879)

The following is an extract from a letter from an Indian woman, a teacher among the Omaha Indians, to some friends in Philadelphia. The original is exceedingly well done and could not easily be surpassed by an educated white woman.

After an interesting account of a Christmas tree supplied by the friends to whom she was writing, she says:

"Yonder is a man in a faded blanket with nothing striking about him but his tall and vigorous form. He has killed many enemies in battle. He is ever ready, at the risk of his life, to defend the weak and helpless. He never hesitates to rebuke the vices of his people even though he bring down their anger on his head; and yet underneath that stern exterior is as true and loving a heart as ever beat. When a little grandson of his died, 'he wept and would not be comforted.' I have singled him out from the rest because I know him so well, and not because he is the only one. There are others like him, more or less, and when I see them I think to myself, if they have become what they are, amid all their disadvantages, what would they not be with the religion of Christ to help them? Oh! you do not know how hard the work is out here. They have lost all confidence in your people. The good that Christ's followers can do is counteracted by the behavior of your government toward them. They look on the white people as all alike. How can they believe in the good will and good faith among you when your Government, pretending good faith and good will, and pretending to ratify it by solemn treaties, breaks them at pleasure, taking their lands from them and driving them hither and thither? Some of the more intelligent among them have thrown aside their own customs as foolish, but refuse to have anything to do with the white man's religion. They have said to me, 'The white men speak fair words to us, but they treat us as dogs, and we have not a spot we can call our own or where we feel safe.' Wa-ja-pa, one of my father's band, once said to a minister at my house, 'We Indians *know* there is a God. We have always known it. He made us and gave us this land. We pray to Him in our hearts always, and not outwardly, as you do. We pray to Him when we lie down at night and when we rise in the morning. We pray to Him to bless us in whatever we do, whether it be in our daily rounds or when we go forth to battle. He has power to send us good or evil, and it is right, for we are His. But as for this book you talk about so much, and God's son, whom you say came into this world, we know nothing of them. Our ancestors never told us about them, and many of us do not care to have anything to do with your religion.'

"I am coming more and more to the conclusion that the surest and almost the only way of reaching the parent is through the children. Almost the only comforts they have in their lives consists in their children. For them they are willing to lay aside their arms and take up the plow and mower, all unused as they are to labor. For them they are willing to pass over injuries, lest the wrath of the government be aroused and their children slain. For the sake of their children they are willing to break up their nationality, their tribal relations, and all that they hold dear, to become citizens. Said one man to me, 'I wish that I had had the advantages in my youth which you have. I could then have had a chance to become something other than I am, and could have helped my people; I am now helpless and ignorant, but I shall die content if my children after me live better than I have done.'"

## LETTER TO *ST. NICHOLAS* (1880)

DEAR ST. NICHOLAS: I do not know whether you allow "savages" in your "Letter-Box," but my two younger sisters seeming to have no doubt whatever on the subject, Rosalie and I have concluded not to let them get ahead of us; besides, nothing is ever complete unless "we four" are all "in it." As my little brother Mitchell (who, by the way, considers himself the most important member of the family) is unable to write for himself, I will attempt to do it for him. He is six years old, – so old that he constitutes himself our protector on all occasions.

He tries to re-assure mother by telling her that he will keep all the Sioux and Winnebagoes away from us. He can speak only a few sentences in English, although he chatters fast enough in Omaha, our own language. He admires the white people immensely. He said to me once:

"Sister, don't you like the white people? I do."

"I don't know," said I; "why should I?"

"Oh, because they know how to do everything."

He is rather afraid of them, though, when he sees a good many of them together. The members of the "Joint Indian Commission" were out here a short time ago visiting the different tribes, and they called on us for a few minutes. While we were all busy entertaining and being entertained by them, we forgot Mitchell entirely. A gentleman – one of the employés of the Indian Reserve – came to the kitchen where Mitchell was and asked him if the Major (the agent of a Reserve is often called "Major" by Reserve people) was in the front room.

"No," said Mitchell.

"Then please go and tell the Major that I want to see him," said the gentleman.

"Oh, no," said Mitchell, "I can't."

"Why not?"

"Oh! I can't; there are too many white men in there for me."

When our visitors had gone away, we found Mitchell standing by the dining-room window, with the tears rolling down his face, while he shook from head to foot with fright. I never knew him to be afraid of anything except white men, especially when he saw a good many of them together.

When he was three years old, he began riding horseback. When he was four years old, he rode alone to a neighbor's, nearly a mile off, although the road led over steep bluffs near the Missouri River. Now, he can get off and on a horse without any help whatever. We often see little Indian boys younger than he riding out alone on the prairie, hunting horses with perhaps an older brother. Mitchell can go in among a number of horses standing close together, and bring out any one of them without making any confusion or getting hurt.

## FROM TESTIMONY BEFORE THE US SENATE ON THE REMOVAL OF THE PONCA INDIANS (1880)

While we were there [on the Ponca reservation near Arkansas City, Kansas] about fifty men, women, and children had gone to visit the Cheyenne tribe; they had been invited to go there. They had been told that if they would come the Cheyennes would give them ponies. Nearly all the Poncas' horses were gone – had died, or been stolen by the white people. What ponies they had were almost starved. They had to keep them tied within a few yards of our tents; and even then they would be stolen by white men and negroes. They had asked the agent, again and again, to let them go on a visit to the Cheyennes, and get the ponies which the Cheyennes had promised them. But the agent refused to let them go. They said the agent was a very domineering sort of a man; and that if the Indians did not obey, he would take measures to see that they did. Finally they stole away, and went down to visit the Cheyennes. As soon as they were gone, the agent sent orders to the commander at Fort Reno for troops to bring them back. . . .

[When Standing Bear and his group left the Ponca reservation in Indian Territory,] the Omahas invited them to come and stay on the reserve. . . . They did not know whether Standing Bear would accept the invitation or not. We next heard that Standing Bear had come to our reserve. The Omahas held a council with the agent, and wanted him to give Standing Bear land, and let him come into the tribe as one of us; and let his family come to live with us as a part of the Omaha tribe. We said we were all formerly one people, the same as brothers. The agent said he would not give any advice in the case; that Standing Bear could go on or come to the reserve just as he chose. Then we heard that Standing Bear was coming; and then he did come. He had been there about two weeks, when, one Sunday morning, one of my sisters looked out of the window and said that some soldiers had come. We knew, of course, that they had come to arrest Standing Bear. All the Omahas were very much excited, and gathered around the agency and the blacksmith shop. Standing Bear and the others who had left the Indian Territory with him had camped over beyond a hill where we could not see the camp. Men kept coming to us and telling us, and my brother heard that Lieutenant Carpenter with a lot of soldiers had gone into tents, and that the government had sent them to call Standing Bear and his men back to the Indian Territory. By and by the white soldiers came to Standing Bear's camp to take them. There was one man who was sick, lying down on the ground in a tent; he tried to jump up and get to his gun; then he drew his knife; then the soldiers handcuffed him; they put him in irons and took him down near the blacksmith shop, where they were camping; my brother was there nearly all night with him. They had him tied. The next morning, early, he was shaking with the chills. He was so sick he could not eat his breakfast; but they kept him handcuffed, and the soldiers staid there guarding him with a bayonet. Standing Bear went and talked with him, and said it was of no use to resist; they had committed no crime, had done no wrong, but the government was strong and they were powerless and could not resist. The next morning the soldiers started off with them; we were standing by the door and saw the whole company file past, as the soldiers were taking Standing Bear and his companions down to the

Indian Territory. The Omahas felt very bad; but they could not even go and shake hands with them. . . .

I would like to say that when I was down at the Ponca Agency, in the Indian Territory, the white people there at the agency tried to make out that the Poncas did not suffer any; that they were getting acclimated and now had come to like the land, and all that. I was talking with a trader at the agency there. He brought my father and me up in a buggy to take the cars at Wichita. He said the agent was a very severe man – disposed to be very severe to the Indians; but he thought he was trying to do the best he could for the tribe. If Standing Bear had staid there, he said, he thought he would be satisfied now; he said the agent had issued wagons and reapers and mowers to the Indians, and was building them homes, and all that. After finishing our talk on such subjects we went to talking of other things, books and poetry and music and such things. Among the rest we happened to get talking about the climate of the different States, and comparing that of the Indian Territory with that of other places, "And," said he, "do you know the Poncas have suffered terribly? A great many of them have been sick, and have had nothing to protect them but a canvas tent." This he said without intending to tell me anything. . . . [When I visited in May, the Poncas] had six little shanties, I do not think as large as this room. They were made of rough, unplaned boards, with knot-holes in them; they had two doors and two windows, but no up-stairs, no stoves, no bedsteads in them. The school-house was not finished. The agent's house was very handsomely built and finished off. There was a trader's store there and a blacksmith's shop. The Indians told me that they wanted to work for themselves, but they had no horses. The agent hired a man to come from Arkansas City to plow a little piece of ground. The Indians wanted to do it themselves and get the pay that white man would get. They said they would ask his permission to haul things from Arkansas City that the government issued to them; but the agent refused, and he hired white men to do it. . . .

I will tell you what I heard said by some Indians of the Santee tribe. The Santees are more civilized than the Omaha tribe. The Santee tribe have their boarding-school and churches and a great deal of property; they have a paper, published in their own language – now I forget whether it is the Santee or the Yankton tribe that publishes the paper; the editors are Indians; they have native ministers, and all that. Three of these Santee Sioux came to my father's house last winter and staid some time; they took dinner at my house. They told my father that there was a bill before Congress by which the white people were trying to take their land from them and send them to another piece of land. They said they would be quiet until the last moment; but when worse came to worse they would fight rather than leave. And the Omahas have always been afraid, as far back as I can remember, that the government would take their lands away from them. When the land of the Poncas was taken from them, the inspector, or whoever it was, told the Poncas – when they spoke of having relatives among the Omahas, and asked to be allowed to remain with them, and all live together as the same tribe – that the Omahas would be taken down to the Territory too, very soon, so they need not object to staying there. That scared the Omahas, and the Omahas, at every council I have been in, have asked for titles to lands. I have often heard Indians say, "What is the use of doing anything? If I make a fine farm and build me a good house, and fix up everything comfortable and nice, the government will take it away and some white man will get the benefit of it. What is the use of my doing anything?" I have heard Indians say that again and again.

I was surprised to find that the white settlers around the reserve opposed the Poncas being taken away, and that they thought it was an outrage. I was surprised, because I heard that the white settlers hated the Indians and wanted to get their lands. . . . One of the reasons the Poncas gave the inspector – one of the reasons why they did not wish to move to the Indian Territory – was that the people down there were all wild Indians, dirty, with hair uncombed; and if the Poncas went down there and lived with them, they would get to be just like them. And the Omahas say that they would rather live surrounded by white people, so as to become like them; while, if they were surrounded only by Indians, they would stay where they are, and not become civilized.

I want to say a word about the Pawnees. They asked us to do something for their help, if it ever came so that we could. They were taken from their own lands, in Nebraska, four years ago. They were taken down to the Indian Territory, where they became sick and died at an alarming rate. When my father and

I were down there, they told me that in one band, which consisted of a hundred families when they first went down there, eighty families were entirely extinct. The others are dying all the time. And the condition of things is not growing any better. . . .

## INTRODUCTION TO *THE PONCA CHIEFS*, BY THOMAS H. TIBBLES (1880)

This little book is only a simple narration of facts concerning some of my people. Many of the transactions recorded in it came under my own observation, my uncle, White Swan, being one of the chiefs who underwent so much suffering after being left in the Indian Territory.

Wrongs more terrible than those related here have been practised on others of my people, but they have had no writer to make them known.

I wish for the sake of my race, that I could introduce this little book into every home in this land, because in these homes lies the power to remedy the evil shown forth in these pages. The people are the power which move the magistrates who administer the laws.

It is a little thing, a simple thing, which my people ask of a nation whose watchword is liberty; but it is endless in its consequences. They ask for their liberty, and law is liberty. "We did not know of these wrongs," say the magistrates. Is not that only the cry of "Am I my brother's keeper?" For years the petitions of my people have gone up unnoticed, unheeded by all but their Creator, and now at last a man of your race has arisen, who has shown faith enough in humanity to arouse the nation from the sin of its indifference. Thank God, it was only indifference, and not hatred, which withheld from an oppressed and unfortunate race, justice and mercy.

May those who read this story, when they think of the countless happy homes which cover this continent, give help to a homeless race, who have no spot on earth they can call their own.

## NEDAWI (AN INDIAN STORY FROM REAL LIFE) (*ST. NICHOLAS*, JANUARY, 1881)

"Nedawi!" called her mother, "take your little brother while I go with your sister for some wood." Nedawi ran into the tent, bringing back her little red blanket, but the brown-faced, roly-poly baby, who had been having a comfortable nap in spite of being all the while tied straight to his board, woke with a merry crow just as the mother was about to attach him, board and all, to Nedawi's neck. So he was taken from the board instead, and, after he had kicked in happy freedom for a moment, Nedawi stood in front of her mother, who placed Habazhu on the little girl's back, and drew the blanket over him, leaving his arms free. She next put into his hand a little hollow gourd, filled with seeds, which served as a rattle; Nedawi held both ends of the blanket tightly in front of her, and was then ready to walk around with the little man.

Where should she go? Yonder was a group of young girls playing a game of konci or dice. The dice were five plum-seeds, scorched black, and had little stars and quarter-moons instead of numbers. She went over and stood by the group, gently rocking herself from side to side, pretty much as white children do when reciting the multiplication table. The girls would toss up the wooden bowl, letting it drop with a gentle thud on the pillow beneath, the falling dice making a pleasant clatter which the baby liked to hear. The stakes were a little heap of beads, rings, and bracelets. The laughter and exclamations of the girls, as some successful toss brought down the dice three stars and two quarter-moons (the highest throw), made Nedawi wish that she, too, were a young girl, and could win and wear all those pretty things. How gay she would look! Just then, the little glittering heap caught baby's eye. He tried to wriggle out of the blanket to get to it, but Nedawi held tight. Then he set up a yell. Nedawi walked away very reluctantly, because she wanted to stay and see who would win. She went to her mother's tent, but found it deserted. Her father and brothers had gone to the chase. A herd of buffalo had been seen that morning, and all the men in the tribe had gone, and would not be back till night. Her mother, her sister, and the women of the household had gone to the river for wood and water. The tent looked enticingly cool, with the sides turned up to let the breeze sweep through, and the straw mats and soft robes seemed to invite her to lie down on them and dream the afternoon away, as she was too apt to do. She did not yield to the temptation, however, for she knew Mother would not like it, but walked over to her cousin Metai's tent. She found her cousin "keeping house" with a number of little girls, and stood to watch them while they put up little tents, just large enough to hold one or two girls.

"Nedawi, come and play," said Metai. "You can make the fire and cook. I'll ask Mother for something to cook."

"But what shall I do with Habazhu?" said Nedawi.

"I'll tell you. Put him in my tent, and make believe he's our little old grandfather."

Forthwith he was transferred from Nedawi's back to the little tent. But Habazhu had a decided objection to staying in the dark little place, where he could not see anything, and crept out of the door on his hands and knees. Nedawi collected a little heap of sticks, all ready for the fire, and went off to get a fire-brand to light it with. While she was gone, Habazhu crawled up to a bowl of water which stood by the intended fire-place, and began dabbling in it with his chubby little hands, splashing the water all over the sticks prepared for the fire. Then he thought he would like a drink. He tried to lift the bowl in both hands, but only succeeded in spilling the water over himself and the fire-place.

When Nedawi returned, she stood aghast; then, throwing down the brand, she took her little brother by the shoulders and, I am sorry to say, shook him violently, jerked him up, and dumped him down by the door of the little tent from which he had crawled. "You bad little boy!" she said. " It's too bad that I have to take care of you when I want to play."

You see, she was no more perfect than any little white girl who gets into a temper now and then. The baby's lip quivered, and he began to cry. Metai said to Nedawi: "I think it's real mean for you to shake him, when he doesn't know any better."

Metai picked up Baby and tried to comfort him. She kissed him over and over, and talked to him in baby language. Nedawi's conscience, if the little savage could be said to have any, was troubling her. She loved her baby brother dearly, even though she did get out of patience with him now and then.

"I'll put a clean little shirt on him and pack him again," said she, suddenly. Then she took off his little wet shirt, wrung it out, and spread it on the tall grass to dry in the sun. Then she went home, and, going to a pretty painted skin in which her mother kept his clothes, she selected the red shirt, which she thought was the prettiest. She was in such a hurry, however, that she forgot to close and tie up the skin again, and she carelessly left his clean shirts lying around as she had laid them out. When Baby was on her back again, she walked around with him, giving directions and overseeing the other girls at their play, determined to do that rather than nothing.

The other children were good-natured, and took her ordering as gracefully as they could. Metai made the fire in a new place, and then went to ask her mother to give her something to cook. Her mother gave her a piece of dried buffalo meat, as hard as a chip and as brittle as glass. Metai broke it up into small pieces, and put the pieces into a little tin pail of water, which she hung over the fire. "Now," she said, "when the meat is cooked and the soup is made, I will call you all to a feast, and Habazhu shall be the chief."

They all laughed. But alas for human calculations! During the last few minutes, a shy little girl, with soft, wistful black eyes, had been watching them from a little distance. She had on a faded, shabby blanket and a ragged dress.

"Metai," said Nedawi, "let's ask that girl to play with us; she looks so lonesome."

"Well," said Metai, doubtfully, "I don't care; but my mother said she didn't want me to play with ragged little girls."

"My father says we must be kind to poor little girls, and help them all we can; so I'm going to play with her if you don't," said Nedawi, loftily.

Although Metai was the hostess, Nedawi was the leading spirit, and had her own way, as usual.

She walked up to the little creature and said, "Come and play with us, if you want to." The little girl's eyes brightened, and she laughed. Then she suddenly drew from under her blanket a pretty bark basket, filled with the most delicious red and yellow plums. "My brother picked them in the woods, and I give them to you," was all she said. Nedawi managed to free one hand, and took the offering with an exclamation of delight, which drew the other girls quickly around. Instead of saying "Oh! Oh!" as you would have said, they cried "Hin! Hin!" which expressed their feeling quite as well, perhaps.

"Let us have them for our feast," said Metai, taking them.

Little Indian children are taught to share everything with one another, so it did not seem strange to Nedawi to have her gift looked on as common property. But, while the attention of the little group had been concentrated on the matter in hand, a party of mischievous boys, passing by, caught sight of the little tents and the tin pail hanging over the fire. Simultaneously, they set up a war-whoop and, dashing into the deserted camp, they sent the tent-poles scattering right and left, and snatching up whatever they could lay hands on, including the tin pail and its contents, they retreated. The little girls, startled by the sudden raid on their property, looked up. Rage possessed their little souls. Giving shrieks of anger, they started in pursuit. What did Nedawi do? She forgot plums, baby, and everything. The ends of the blanket slipped from her grasp, and she darted forward like an arrow after her companions.

Finding the chase hopeless, the little girls came to a stand-still, and some of them began to cry. The boys had stopped, too; and seeing the tears flow, being good-hearted boys in spite of their mischief, they surrendered at discretion. They threw back the articles they had taken, not daring to come near. They did not consider it manly for big boys like themselves to strike or hurt little girls, even though they delighted in teasing them, and they knew from experience that they would be at the mercy of the offended party if they went near enough to be touched. The boy who had the dinner brought the little pail which had contained it as near as he dared, and setting it down ran away.

"You have spilt all our soup. There's hardly any of it left. You bad boys!" said one of the girls.

They crowded around with lamentations over their lost dinner. The boys began to feel remorseful.

"Let's go into the woods and get them some plums to make up for it."

"Say, girls, hand us your pail, and we'll fill it up with plums for you."

So the affair was settled.

But, meanwhile, what became of the baby left so unceremoniously in the tall grass? First he opened his black eyes wide at this style of treatment. He was not used to it. Before he had time, however, to make up his mind whether to laugh or cry, his mother came to the rescue. She had just come home and thrown the wood off her back, when she caught sight of Nedawi dropping him. She ran to pick him up, and finding him unhurt, kissed him over and over. Some of the neighbors had run up to see what was the matter. She said to them:

"I never did see such a thoughtless, heedless child as my Nedawi. She really has 'no ears.' I don't know what in the world will ever become of her. When something new interests her, she forgets everything else. It was just like her to act in this way."

Then they all laughed, and one of them said:

"Never mind – she will grow wiser as she grows older," after which consoling remark they went away to their own tents.

It was of no use to call Nedawi back. She was too far off.

Habazhu was given over to the care of the nurse, who had just returned from her visit. An hour or two after, Nedawi came home.

"Mother!" she exclaimed, as she saw her mother frying bread for supper, "I am so hungry. Can I have some of that bread?"

"Where is your little brother?" was the unexpected reply.

Nedawi started. Where had she left him? She tried to think.

"Why, Mother, the last I remember I was packing him, and – and oh, Mother! you know where he is. Please tell me."

"When you find him and bring him back to me, perhaps I shall forgive you," was the cold reply.

This was dreadful. Her mother had never treated her in that way before. She burst into tears and started out to find Habazhu, crying all the way. She knew that her mother knew where baby was, or she would not have taken it so coolly; and she knew also that her mother expected her to bring him home. As she went stumbling along through the grass, she felt herself seized and held in somebody's strong arms, and a great, round, voice said:

"What's the matter with my little niece? Have all her friends deserted her that she is wailing like this? Or has her little dog died? I thought Nedawi was a brave little woman."

It was her uncle Two Crows. She managed to tell him, through her sobs, the whole story. She knew, if she told him herself, he would not laugh at her about it, for he would sympathize in her troubles, though he was a great tease. When she ceased, he said to her: "Well, your mother wants you to be more careful next time, I suppose; by the way, I think I saw a little boy who looked very much like Habazhu, in my tent."

Sure enough, she found him there with his nurse. When she got home with them, she found her mother, – her own dear self, – and, after giving her a big hug, she sat quietly down by the fire, resolved to be very good in the future. She did not sit long, however, for soon a neighing of horses, and the running of girls and children through the camp to meet the hunters, proclaimed their return. All was bustle and gladness throughout the camp. There had been a successful chase, and the led horses were laden with buffalo meat. These horses were led by the young girls to the tents to be unpacked, while the boys took the hunting-horses to water and tether in the grass. Fathers, as they dismounted, took their little children in their arms, tired as they were. Nedawi was as happy as any in the camp, for her seventeen-year-old brother, White Hawk, had killed his first buffalo, and had declared that the skin should become Nedawi's robe, as soon as it was tanned and painted.

What a pleasant evening that was to Nedawi when the whole family sat around a great fire, roasting the huge buffalo ribs, and she played with her little brother Habazhu, stopping now and then to listen to the adventures of the day, which her father and brothers were relating! The scene was truly a delightful one, the camp-fires lighting up the pleasant family groups here and there, as the flames rose and fell. The bit of prairie where the tribe had camped had a clear little stream running through it, with shadowy hills around, while over all hung the clear, star-lit sky. It seemed as if nature were trying to protect the poor waifs of humanity clustered in that spot. Nedawi felt the beauty of the scene, and was just thinking of nestling down by her father to enjoy it dreamily, when her brothers called for a dance. The little drum was brought forth, and Nedawi danced to its accompaniment and her brothers' singing. She danced gravely, as became a little maiden whose duty it was to entertain the family circle. While she was dancing, a little boy, about her own age, was seen hovering near. He would appear, and, when spoken to, would disappear in the tall, thick grass.

It was Mischief, a playmate of Nedawi's. Everybody called him "Mischief," because mischief appeared in every action of his. It shone from his eyes and played all over his face.

"You little plague," said White Hawk; "what do you want?"

For answer, the "little plague" turned a somersault just out of White Hawk's reach. When the singing was resumed, Mischief crept quietly up behind White Hawk, and, keeping just within the shadow, mimicked Nedawi's grave dancing, and he looked so funny that Nedawi suddenly laughed, which was precisely Mischief's object. But before he could get out of reach, as he intended, Thunder, Nedawi's other brother, who had been having an eye on him, clutched tight hold of him, and Mischief was landed in front of the fire-place, in full view of the whole family. "Now," said Thunder, "you are my prisoner. You stay there and dance with Nedawi." Mischief knew there was no escape, so he submitted with a good grace. He went through all sorts of antics, shaking his fists in the air, twirling suddenly around and putting his head close to the ground, keeping time with the accompaniment through it all.

Nedawi danced staidly on, now and then frowning at him; but she knew of old that he was irrepressible. When Nedawi sat down, he threw into her lap a little dark something and was off like a shot, yelling at the top of his voice, either in triumph at his recent achievements or as a practice for future war-whoops.

"Nedawi, what is it?" said her mother.

Nedawi took it to the fire, when the something proved to be a poor little bird.

"I thought he had something in his hand when he was shaking his fist in the air," said Nedawi's sister, Nazainza, laughing.

"Poor little thing!" said Nedawi; "it is almost dead."

She put its bill into the water, and tenderly tried to make it drink. The water seemed to revive it somewhat.

"I'll wrap it up in something warm," said Nedawi, "and may be it will sing in the morning."

"Let me see it," said Nedawi's father.

Nedawi carried it to him.

"Don't you feel sorry for it, daughter?"

"Yes, Father," she answered.

"Then take it to the tall grass, yonder, and put it down where no one will step on it, and, as you put it down, say: 'God, I give you back your little bird. As I pity it, pity me.'"

"And will God take care of it?" said Nedawi, reverently, and opening her black eyes wide at the thought.

"Yes," said her father.

"Well, I will do as you say," said Nedawi, and she walked slowly out of the tent.

Then she took it over to the tall, thick grass, and making a nice, cozy little nest for it, left it there, saying just what her father had told her to say. When she came back, she said:

"Father, I said it."

"That was right, little daughter," and Nedawi was happy at her father's commendation.

Nedawi always slept with her grandmother and sister, exactly in the middle of the circle formed by the wigwam, with her feet to the fire-place. That place in the tent was always her grandmother's place, just as the right-hand side of the tent was her father's and mother's, and the left-hand her brothers'. There never was any confusion. The tribe was divided into bands, and every band was composed of several families. Each band had its chief, and the whole tribe was ruled by the head-chief, who was Nedawi's father. He had his own particular band besides. Every tent had its own place in the band, and every band had its own particular place in the great circle forming the camp. Each chief was a representative, in council, of the men composing his band, while over all was the head-chief. The executive power was vested in the "soldiers' lodge," and when decisions were arrived at in council, it was the duty of its soldiers to execute all its orders, and punish all violations of the tribal laws. The office of "town-crier" was held by several old men, whose duty it was "to cry out" through the camp the announcements of councils, invitations to feasts, and to give notice of anything in which the whole tribe were called on to take part.

Well, before Nedawi went to sleep this evening, she hugged her grandmother, and said to her:

"Please tell me a story."

"I cannot, because it is summer. In the winter I will tell you stories."

"Why not in summer?" said Nedawi.

"Because, when people tell stories and legends in summer, the snakes come around to listen. You don't want any snakes to come near us to-night, do you?"

"But," said Nedawi, "I have not seen any snakes for the longest times, and if you tell it right softly they won't hear you."

"Nedawi," said her mother, " don't bother your grandmother. She is tired and wants to sleep."

Thereupon Grandmother's heart felt sorry for her pet, and she said to Nedawi:

"Well, if you will keep still and go right to sleep when I am through, I will tell you how the turkeys came to have red eyelids.

"Once upon a time, there was an old woman living all alone with her grandson, Rabbit. He was noted for his cunning and for his tricks, which he played on every one. One day, the old woman said to him, 'Grandson, I am hungry for some meat.' Then the boy took his bow and arrows, and in the evening he came home with a deer on his shoulders, which he threw at her feet, and said, 'Will that satisfy you?' She said, 'Yes, grandson.' They lived on that meat several days, and, when it was gone, she said to him again, 'Grandson, I am hungry for some meat.' This time he went without his bow and arrows, but he took a bag with him. When he got into the woods, he called all the turkeys together. They gathered around him, and he said to them: 'I am going to sing to you, while you shut your eyes and dance. If one of you opens his eyes while I am singing, his eyelids shall turn red.' Then they all stood in a row, shut their eyes, as he had told them, and began to dance, and this is the song he sang to them while they danced:

> "'Ha! wadamba thike
> Inshta zhida, inshta zhida
> Imba theonda,
> Imba theonda.'

[The literal translation is:

> "Ho! he who peeps
> Red eyes, red eyes,
> Flap your wings,
> Flap your wings."]

"Now, while they were dancing away, with their eyes shut, the boy took them, one by one, and put them into his bag. But the last one in the row began to think it very strange that his companions made no noise, so he gave one peep, screamed in his fright, 'They are making 'way with us!' and flew away. The boy took his bag of turkeys home to his grandmother, but ever after that the turkeys had red eyelids."

Nedawi gave a sigh of satisfaction when the story was finished, and would have asked for more, but just then her brothers came in from a dance they had been attending in some neighbor's tent. She knew her lullaby time had come. Her brothers always sang before they slept either love or dancing songs, beating time on their breasts, the regular beats making a sort of accompaniment for the singing. Nedawi loved best of all to hear her father's war-songs, for he had a musical voice, and few were the evenings when she had gone to sleep without hearing a lullaby from her father or brothers. Among the Indians, it is the fathers who sing instead of the mothers. Women sing only on state occasions, when the tribe have a great dance, or at something of the sort. Mothers "croon" the babies to sleep, instead of singing.

Gradually the singing ceased, and the brothers slept as well as Nedawi, and quiet reigned over the whole camp.

## INTRODUCTION TO *PLOUGHED UNDER: THE STORY OF AN INDIAN CHIEF, TOLD BY HIMSELF*, BY WILLIAM JUSTIN HARSHA (1881)

The white people have tried to solve the "Indian Question" by commencing with the proposition that the Indian is different from all other human beings.

With some he is a peculiar being, surrounded by a halo of romance, who has to be set apart on a reservation as something sacred, who has to be fed, clothed, and taken care of by a guardian or agent, by whom he is not to be allowed to come into contact with his conquerors lest it might degrade him; his conquerors being a people who hold their civilization above that of all others on the earth, because of their perfect freedom and liberty. "The contact of peoples is the best of all education." And this the ward is denied.

With others again he is a savage, a sort of monster without any heart or soul or mind, but whose whole being is full of hatred, ferocity, and blood-thirstiness. They suppose him to have no family affections, no love for his home, none of the sensitive feelings that all other human beings presumably have. This class demand his extermination.

Under the shelter of the conflicting laws imposed by these two extreme views, the clever operators of the Indian Ring – not caring what he is, but looking on him for what he has, and the opportunities he affords, as legitimate prey – pounce on him and use him as a means of obtaining contracts, removals, land speculations, and appropriations which are to be stolen. They tear him from his home, disregarding all the rights of his manhood.

Allow an Indian to suggest that the solution of the vexed "Indian Question" is *Citizenship*, with all its attending duties and responsibilities, as well as the privileges of protection under the law, by which the Indian could appeal to the courts, when deprived of life, liberty, or property, as every citizen can, and would be allowed the opportunity to make something of himself, in common with every other citizen. If it were not for the lands which the Indian holds, he would have been a citizen long before the negro; and in this respect his lands have been a curse to him rather than a blessing. But for them, he would have been insignificant in the eyes of this powerful and wealthy nation, and allowed to live in peace and quietness, without attracting the birds of prey forever hovering over the helpless; then his citizenship would have protected him, as it does any other ordinary human being. As a "ward," or extraordinary being, if he is accused of committing a crime, this serves as a pretext of war for his extermination, and his father, mother, sister, brother, wife, or people are involved in one common ruin; while if he were simply a citizen, he would be individually arrested by the sheriff, and tried in court, and protected in his innocence or convicted and punished in his guilt. The Indian, as a "ward," or extraordinary being, affords employment to about ten thousand employés in the Indian Bureau, with all the salaries attached, as well as innumerable contractors, freighters, and land speculators. He requires also, periodically, immense appropriations to move him from place to place. Imagine a company of Irish immigrants requiring from Congress an appropriation to move them from one part of the country to another! No wonder that the powers-that-be refuse to recognize the Indian as an ordinary human being, but insist that he be taken care of and "protected" by the decisions of the Indian Bureau. In this "land of freedom and liberty" an Indian has to get the permission of an agent before he can either step off his reservation or allow any civilization to enter it; and this, under heavy penalty for disobedience. In this land, where the boast is made that all men are "equal before the law," the Indian cannot sue in the courts for his life, liberty, or property, because, forsooth, the Indian is not a "person," as the learned attorney employed by a Secretary of the Interior argued for five hours, when an Indian appealed to the writ of *habeas corpus* for his liberty.

The key to this complicated problem is, simply: To recognize the Indian as a person and a citizen, give him a title to his lands, and place him within the jurisdiction of the courts, *as an individual*. It is absurd for a great government like this to say that it cannot manage a little handful of helpless people, who are but as an atom in the mass of fifty millions of people, unless they treat them as "wards."

No, the Indian is not an extraordinary being; he is of the race of man, and, like others, is the creature of his surroundings. If you would know something of what he is, of how his spirit and his disposition are affected by his circumstances, read the record of life – its loves and hates – here set forth. As the hero of this story says, "If those of our race who have been slain by the white man should spring up from the sod as trees, there would be one broad moaning forest from the great river to the sea." The incidents of this tale are based upon easily authenticated facts – most of them, indeed, being matters of official record. The lines are not too deep nor the colors too strong. It would be impossible to exaggerate the sufferings imposed upon my people by the cruel greed of their plunderers. As the author has so graphically described, the huge plough of the "Indian system" has run for a hundred years, beam deep, turning down into the darkness of the earth every hope and aspiration which we have cherished. The sod is rich with the blood of human beings of both races. What sort of a harvest, think you, will it yield in the future to the nation whose hand has guided this plough?

## Omaha Legends and Tent-Stories (*Wide Awake*, June, 1883)

To the readers of Wide Awake: These legends, a few of which I have translated, are nearly the same in every tribe – a little varied, it is true – but substantially the same, which shows, I think, that they are of common origin.

These which I have translated, are as told by the Omaha tribe. I have written them down just as they were told to me by my father, mother and grandmother, only of course I have translated them into English.

I wish I could have written the music of the songs. I think they are beautiful. I have heard some of your finest singers, but nothing I ever heard from them has touched me so profoundly as the singing of the Indians. The tears fill my eyes as I listen to their wild, weird singing, and I can never seem to tell myself why.

Among the Omahas, and I suppose in all the tribes, there are men and women, who, though they are not professional story tellers, yet as they can tell stories and legends so much better than any one else, are often invited by families to come visiting for the sole purpose of story-telling. The best story-teller that I know of in the tribe is "Onidabi." Last winter our family took a four days' journey, and with us travelled this man. Evening after evening we gathered round the fire to hear him tell stories, the tent so full that it could not hold another person, and we laughed till the tears came as he told story after story in rapid succession, with such inimitable gestures and changes of tone, that it would have been a study for any of your most accomplished elocutionists, and one by which they might have profited. Any one standing outside the tent and not knowing what was going on within, would have declared that he heard a conversation carried on by several people, when in reality it was only one person speaking, so perfectly did he imitate the tones of old men, women and children. He did not have to say of his characters, "the old man said this, the young warrior this," or "the little boy said this," but we knew at once by the tone of his voice, who was speaking. When we went to bed at night we would be as tired from laughing as though we had been hard at work all day.

My mother told me that one of the stories I have written out, was told her by an old man when she was a little child, and that it was her delight after coaxing her mother to get a nice supper, to go to the old man's tent and invite him to supper. When he came she would wait on him herself, and when he had finished eating, she would say: "Grandfather, please tell me a story!" The old man would pretend to be very reluctant at first, for the pleasure of having her coax him, and then he would comply with story after story from those strange legends, while she listened with rapt attention, until my grandmother bade her get ready for bed.

I never read any of your "Mother Goose Rhymes" until I was grown up, and I used to be inclined to feel sorry sometimes that I had missed them in my childhood; but if I had known them, I should probably have never known the nursery stories of my own people, and so I am satisfied.

My grandmother tells exactly the same old stories and sings the same queer little songs to my sister's children that she used to sing to us when we were babies, and only yesterday when I asked her to tell me a story, she laughed at me, and made up a funny little song which she sang to her great grandson, aged six months, telling him about his big auntie who wanted to be told a story as though she were a baby like him.

How often I have fallen asleep when a child, with my arms tight around my grandmother's neck, while she told me a story, only I did not fall asleep till the story was finished. When thinking of those old days – so happy and free, when we slept night after night in a tent on the wide trackless prairie, with nothing but the skies above us and the earth beneath; with nothing to make us afraid; not even knowing that we were not civilized, or were ordered to be by the government; not even knowing that there were such beings as white men; happy in our freedom and our love for each other – I often wonder if there is anything in your civilization which will make good to us what we have lost. I sometimes think not, unless it be the wider, fuller knowledge of God and his Word. But I am straying from my subject. Thinking of these legends brought back the old days so vividly. I wish I could gather up all the old legends and nursery songs so that they could live after we were dead, but some of them are so fragmentary and nonsensical that I hesitate.

In reading these legends, I hope my readers will try to imagine themselves in a tent, with the firelight flaming up now and then, throwing weird effects of light and shadow on the eager listening faces, and seeming to sympathize and keep pace with the story; and how we have had only these legends and stories in place of your science and literature. After all, that is only what your forefathers had before the days of books, and perhaps remembering that will make your thoughts more charitable toward a people having no literature.

These legends have never been published, with the exception of one which was published in The Critic. I have taken them down fresh from the lips of my father, mother and grandmother. I suppose legends something like them have been published from time to time by people from other tribes. These are Omaha legends.

Bright Eyes.

## I.—The Babes in the Woods.

Once on a time,[1] there stood a tent all alone by itself in the woods, and in it lived a man, his wife, and their two children, a little girl and boy. One morning he combed his wife's hair[2] carefully, braided it, painted red the parting of her hair, and painted red her cheeks. Then he started out to hunt all day.

He killed a deer and brought it home with him at night. When he saw his wife he saw that her hair, which he had combed so smoothly on starting out, had become all rumpled, and was in a sad state, while nearly all the paint had been rubbed off her cheeks. He wondered at it, but made no comment.

The next day he combed his wife's hair as usual and started out again. When he came home at night with more game, he noticed again that her hair was rumpled and the paint gone. Still he kept silent. On the third day, the same things occurred as on the two preceding days. On the fourth morning,[3] the man said to himself, I wonder what the meaning of all this is? After he had combed her hair he started out apparently to hunt as before, but when he had gone a little way he turned back and hid near the tent, in order to find out what his wife did that disordered her hair so. After a while his wife came out of the tent, and walked away through the woods. He followed her, concealing himself as he went, lest she should turn and see him.

Of a sudden a bear came out from the thick undergrowth, and going up to her, took her head in his two great paws and commenced to pat it from side to side as though it were a ball. Too frightened to stop to think that his wife, finding the bear harmless, might have been amusing herself with it in his absences, he raised his bow and shot at the bear, but the arrow struck her as well as the bear, and killed her. When he saw her lying there dead, he realized what he had done, and was horror-struck.

"No one must ever know what I have done," he said to himself.

On his starting out he had taken some meat, for his noonday meal, and this he hurriedly cut into strips, convenient for eating, and hung on the branches of a tree, near where the body of his dead wife lay. Then he went back to his tent where his two motherless children were at play. He said to them: "You know that oak-tree, where your mother took you once? On it you will find hanging some meat which I have placed there for you to eat."

The little girl who was older than her brother, took him by the hand and started for the tree. When they reached the tree, they found the meat hanging from the branches as their father had said, but just as they were about to eat it, the little girl caught sight of her mother's body.

"Oh! brother," she said, "father has killed our mother."

Then they dropped the meat and went back to the tent, but it was empty. Their father had deserted them. The girl said: "Oh! brother, our father has left us, and we will follow his footsteps."

---

1 *Agsthe*, the word with which Indian legends begin, "one time," or "once on a time," just like the English phrase [Tibbles's note].

2 In many tribes the men always comb their wives' hair and braid it. They use for this purpose a brush made of small twigs of stiff grass [Tibbles's note].

3 The number "four" is a sacred number among Indians. In their religious legends things are always repeated four times. It is also used as an indefinite [Tibbles's note].

Then they followed his footsteps hand-in-hand, until they came to a great camp full of people. And the people of the place said to each other: "Whence come these children all alone?" and they said to the children, "Why are you come and what are you doing here all alone?" And the girl answered: "We are following our father's footsteps. Did you see him pass this way?" And they said to the children, "He passed by here yesterday, and there are his footsteps beyond."

Then the children travelled on again, hand-in-hand, following their father's footsteps until they came to another great camp. Here the people asked them the same questions as had been asked them in the first camp, and they made the same answers as before. And they passed on again until they came to the third great camp, and the same questions and answers were given as before. The children passed on until they came to a fourth great camp.

Then the people of this camp said to each other: "Whence come these children, and why are they all alone?" And they said to the children:

"Why are you come, and why are you travelling alone by yourselves?"

The girl answered as before:

"We are following our father's footsteps. Did you see him pass this way?"

Then the people said to each other:

"The man who came yesterday alone must be their father whom they are seeking."

Then they brought the father before the children and said to him:

"Are these your children?"

The father said:

"Take those children away out of my sight; I hate them, for they killed their mother, and I left them to get rid of them. Send them away!"

Then the people said to the children:

"Your father says that you are bad children. Go away from here! We do not want you."

Then the children went hand-in-hand away from the camp, and they came to a little tent that stood by itself, far off from the main camp. An old woman who was living all alone, came to the tent door and saw the two children standing near, and she said to them:

"Oh! grandchildren, I am glad to see you, but what are you doing here all alone?"

Then the children told her all their story, and how the people of the camps had told them to go away, because they were so bad.

The old woman said, "Come in and sit down here!" And she gave them the guests' place[4] in the middle of the tent, and gave them something to eat; and after they had eaten, she spread a robe on the ground for them, and they went to sleep.

Now near the camp was a great body of water, so wide that they could not see the farther shore. While the children were asleep, the father said to the people:

"Those children are monsters. If the tribe stay here, I am afraid they will harm some of the people. Come and let us go to the other side of this big water, where they cannot reach us!"

All the people believed him, and they got ready to start, but before they started, they took glue-sticks[5] and stuck the children's eyelids together while they were asleep, to keep them from following. Then they ordered the old woman not to awaken the children, but to get ready to go with them. The old woman after they had gone out, gathered together a quantity of provisions, dug a pit near the sleeping children, and, filling it with the provisions, covered it with grass and earth, then followed the tribe as they crossed the water. When the people were all gone across the water, the little boy awoke first. He tried to open his eyes and could not, and he called out:

"Oh! sister, I cannot open my eyes."

4 The place reserved for guests in an Indian tent, is opposite the place of entrance. Those to whom they wish to show respect or honor are invited to sit there [Tibbles's note].

5 In every Indian tent in the old time, there were always "glue sticks." The glue is generally made from parts of the turtle. A stick about two feet long, is put into it as it cools, and slowly turned around until it sticks fast, in shape like an egg. The glue is used to fasten the feathers on the arrows, and for other purposes. To use it, they only have to dip the stick in warm water [Tibbles's note].

She said, "Neither can I open my eyes."

As they lay there a mouse ran once across them and back again, and they said nothing. Then the mouse ran across them and back again. This time the little girl said:

"Oh! you hateful mouse, why have you no pity on us when we are so helpless? You run over us in this way as though you were mocking us."

The mouse answered: "I wanted to help you get your eyes open. Why do you scold me?"

"Oh! grandmother,"[6] the girl exclaimed, "have pity on us and open our eyes, but first of all open my little brother's eyes!"

Then the mouse rubbed the little boy's eyes with its little paws, and they opened.

"Oh! I can see now, sister," cried the little boy.

Then the mouse performed the same office for the girl's eyes. The children thanked the mouse, and the little girl said:

"Grandmother, for this kind help which you have given us, you shall have ever hereafter for your food the underground beans."[7]

This is how the ground-mice came to store the under-ground beans for their winter food.

When the mouse had gone away, the girl and the boy went toward the camp to find the old woman. The tents were all gone, and not a human being was in sight. They saw the broad trail which led to the water, and the girl said to her brother:

"Let us follow this trail to the water; perhaps the old woman has not crossed yet, and we may find her."

When they reached the water, they could see no one, but they heard from afar off a voice calling. It was the voice of the old woman, and it said:

"Under the ground where I slept. Under the ground where I slept."

Over and over again were these words repeated. The girl stood thinking. Of a sudden she exclaimed:

"Oh! I know. Our grandmother must have left something in the tent for us."

They went back to the tent and looked on the ground where the old woman had slept. When they had found the pit, they ate the provisions which the old woman had left there for them.

The two children lived alone in this place for a long time.

When the boy was almost grown up, he said to his sister:

"Sister, can't you make me a bow and some arrows?"

His sister answered: "Yes, brother. Let us go to the deserted camp and see if we cannot find a broken knife."[8]

When they had hunted and found a broken knife, they also found pieces of sinew[9] with which to make the cord for the bow, and feathers with which to wing the arrows.

---

6 I know of nothing which is so understood by all classes of whites, as the Indian habit of saying "Father," "Grandfather," "Grandmother," etc. It is simply a title of respect, and means, when used in this way, nothing more than "Sir," or "Madam." They never say "*Great* Father" when speaking of the President, as the interpreters always render it, but "Grand Father."

Indian relationship is extended to very remote degrees, and is regulated by such complicated laws that it takes long and severe study to understand it. The following gives only a mere idea of its complexity:

First cousins are called uncles and aunts. A son of a nephew is called grandson. A great uncle on the female side is called uncle. A great uncle on the male side is called grandfather. A third cousin on the female side is a nephew or niece to the second cousin on the male side, and grandson to the fourth cousin on the same side. A step-nephew to an uncle, is a son-in-law to that uncle and all his children, grandchildren and great grandchildren, and brother-in-law to the children, grandchildren and great grandchildren of his wife's mother and all the children, grandchildren and great grandchildren of his wife's aunts. A man marrying into a family is grandfather to the children of his wife's brother to the latest generation. The first child of a wife's brother is her son or daughter, the others, grandchildren and so on, *ad infinitum*. So they always address each other by their relationship title; names are seldom heard [Tibbles's note].

7 There is a bean, very much like the common butter bean, which grows under ground. These the field mice gather in great quantities and store in holes in the ground. The Indians get bushels of them by robbing these stores, very much after the same fashion that we take honey from the bees [Tibbles's note].

8 Indians used originally for knives, sharp flint-stone which was fastened with thongs to a handle of wood. The knife part often fell out and was lost [Tibbles's note].

9 This is the Indian thread. It is taken from each side of the backbone of the buffalo, elk, deer, antelope, and horse. That taken from the deer is the best. It is hung up, dried, and then torn into threads. These are twisted together for bow strings and for other purposes where a small, stout cord is needed [Tibbles's note].

On the morning after the bow and the arrows were finished, the boy said:

"Sister, I shall go out hunting to-day!"

His sister gave him his bow and arrows, and he started out. On this first day of his hunt he killed a little speckled bird.

Toward evening, his sister, sitting alone in the tent, heard his voice singing in the distance, and this was the song he sang as he travelled homewards:[10]

Sister, sister, I have killed
A little speckled thing.
Sister, I have killed it.
Sister, I have killed it.

His sister went gladly out to meet him, and when she saw what it was he held, she said gayly, "Oh! brother, this little speckled thing you have killed is called a woodpecker, but it is not good to eat." And she was proud to think he had been so successful.

The next day the brother went out to hunt again, and this time he killed a turkey.

Toward evening his sister heard again his voice in the distance, and this was the song he sang:

Sister, sister, I have killed
Something with long legs.
Sister, I have killed it,
Sister, I have killed it.

Then his sister ran out to meet him, and when she saw what he held in his hand, she was very proud, and she said:

"Oh! brother, this that you have killed is called a turkey, and it is very good to eat."

Next day the brother went out hunting again, and this time he killed a deer. As he walked homeward he sang:

Sister, sister, I have killed
Something large and swift,
And its tail is very short.
Sister, I have killed it.

When his sister heard his voice she ran out to meet him, and when she saw what he was carrying, she clapped her hands and said:

"Oh! brother, brother, this that you have killed is called a deer, and it is very good to eat."

Then they took the deer and cut it up. She took the meat and sliced it into great, broad, thin slices, and made a scaffolding and hung it up to dry for future use.

On the fourth day the brother went out again to hunt; this time he killed a bear. And the song which he sang as he came homeward was the fourth and last of all the songs he sang:

Sister, sister, I have killed
Something large and black,
Sister, I have killed it.
Sister, I have killed it.

[10] The tune to which this is sung is exceedingly pretty and the Indians never tire of hearing its repetition. The words in the original are very musical. The third verse, which is introduced a little further on in the story, is the easiest to write in our English alphabet.

"Tangaho, tangaha adaden,
Seinda chaskati roin,
Ta athetho, tangaha,
Ta athetho, tangaha."

His sister ran to meet him, and when she saw what he carried, she said:

"Oh! brother, this black thing that you have killed is called a bear."

Then after they had cut it up, she tried out the fat and made a great quantity of oil from the bear.

And after this fourth day her brother killed of all the animals and birds that were good to eat, and brought them home to her, and she dried and put away for use great quantities of meat. She also pounded buffalo meat and marrow. And she took ten great buffalo robes and tanned them thin and sewed them together with an awl and sinew, and made a very large tent in which she and her brother lived comfortably.

When they had accumulated numberless packs of provisions, the tribe who had deserted them and gone across the water, came back in a starving condition. Many of their number had died of starvation in the land across the water. The girl, now grown into a fine young woman, and the boy into as fine a young man as one would ever wish to see, went down to the bank of the water to watch the people as they continued landing all day in their canoes. And when they had nearly all landed, the young man said to the people:

"I have a proposal to make to you which you can accept or not as you please. You can come back here and live with us in this land and I will give you all you want to eat and save you from starving. But it can only be on the condition that you will not allow my father, who so cruelly deserted us, to come back here. I hear that he has married again. Let him stay with his wife in the land to which he carried you, but let him not come back here. Then, and only then, will we keep you."

The people were starving, and assented to his proposal, and the young man and his sister opened all their stores to the people and fed them.

And the young woman took the old woman who had helped them in their need, into their tent, and cared for her tenderly all the remaining years of her life. And the young man and woman became prominent members of the tribe, and lived happily ever after.

# Annette Leevier (Ojibwe, 1856–?)

*Born in Quebec in 1856 to a French Catholic mother and an Ojibwe–Mohawk father, Annette Leevier received a convent education beginning at the age of three and subsequently became a nun. She affirms that her paternal grandfather, Big Sun, was a Mohawk, while her grandmother, Princess Laconquinne, was Ojibwe. At present little is known of Leevier's life beyond what she relates in her narrative, where we learn that her mother died during Leevier's stay in the Montreal convent school. In her absence, her father remarried, and when Leevier visited her family as a young woman, she discovered that she was unwelcome. This discovery impelled her move to a convent in New York, where she fell in love with a priest who soon afterward died. Leevier was a spiritualist and visionary who believed in mediumistic communication, and her dead lover became one of the many spirit guides who would direct her actions, ultimately leading her to leave the convent, reject Christianity, and move to the Walpole Island (Ontario) Indian reservation. Her account details her healing powers and benevolent work in various locations in the United States and Canada.*

*While Leevier's experiences may seem outlandish to many of today's readers, her Western contemporaries probably understood her in the context of the popular and controversial spiritualist movement that attracted the interest (and sometimes scorn) of people all over the United States, Canada, and Europe, including such writers as Nathaniel Hawthorne, Harriet Beecher Stowe, Herman Melville, Elizabeth Stuart Phelps, Sarah Orne Jewett, Celia Thaxter, W. B. Yeats, Henry James, and William Dean Howells. Beginning in 1848 and enjoying surges of intensified popularity in the decades of the 1850s, 1870s, and 1880s, spiritualism was from its inception closely affiliated with movements for social justice and cultural amelioration, including abolition, woman suffrage, temperance, and women's health. Often associated (problematically for many nineteenth-century people) with "free love," it enabled for many a liberating view of religion, holding that individuals – including women – could have direct access to divine truth via spirit communication, a belief sometimes more comfortable for Catholics than for mainstream Protestants. Leevier's capacities as a spiritualist and mediumistic healer, and her accounts of visions, would also have seemed unexceptional in the context of Native American cultures, where women – including Owl Woman – acted as doctors, and spirit guides and vision quests were an important part of normal life experience. Like other tribes, the Ojibwe believed in the continuity between what many Westerners would have seen as separate "spirit" and "ordinary" worlds. When Leevier went to Walpole Island, there had been an Anglican mission presence firmly established since 1846 – in spite of years of Ojibwe resistance to both Catholicism and Anglicanism – but she affirms her own intention to follow the religion of the Great Spirit.*

*A story of adventure and excitement, Leevier's narrative reveals her ability to imagine for herself a powerful bicultural identity that drew strength from every element of her personal history. Recalling the spiritual narratives of earlier African American women like "Old Elizabeth" and the Shaker eldress and visionary, Rebecca Cox Jackson,*

*Leevier's narrative represents a fascinating amalgamation of spiritual narrative, sentimental poetry, and coup tale. Like writers such as Owen and Winnemucca, Leevier offers readers a fecund generic hybridity that distinguishes her writing from that of many European American counterparts and challenges readers unaccustomed to nonlinear forms of expression to understand experience differently.*

## BIBLIOGRAPHY


### Primary

*Psychic Experiences of an Indian Princess, daughter of Chief Tommyhawk*. Austin, 1920.

### Secondary

Braude, Ann. *Radical Spirits: Spiritualism and Women's Rights in Nineteenth-Century America*. Beacon, 1989.

Goldfarb, Russell M. and Clare R. Goldfarb. *Spiritualism and Nineteenth-Century Letters*. Fairleigh Dickinson, 1978.

Humez, Jean McMahon, ed. *Gifts of Power: The Writings of Rebecca Cox Jackson, Black Visionary, Shaker Eldress*. Massachusetts, 1981.

Kerr, Howard. *Mediums, and Spirit-Rappers, and Roaring Radicals: Spiritualism in American Literature, 1850–1900*. Illinois, 1972.

Lépicier, Alexis Henri Marie, Cardinal. *The Unseen World: An Exposition of Catholic Theology in Reference to Modern Spiritism*. Kegan Paul, Trench, Trübner, 1906. Sheed, 1929.

Murphy, Lucy Eldersveld, and Wendy Hamand Venet, ed. *Midwestern Women: Work, Community, and Leadership at the Crossroads*. Indiana, 1997.

Thurston, Herbert. *The Church and Spiritualism*. Bruce, 1933.


# *Psychic Experiences of an Indian Princess, Daughter of Chief Tommyhawk* (1920)

### TO SITTING BULL – THE SIOUX BRAVE

Oh, Sitting Bull, to you I say
        Come close to me and always stay;
That I may know you're ever near,
        And knowing it I'll never fear.
Let your judgment and wisdom rule
        In me – an ever ready tool –
To give your dictates to mankind
        That men the light may ever find.

Oh, Brave, in all your pow'r and might,
        Come unto me both day and night,
And in your power let me stand
        An instrument shaped to your hand.
That through your power I may find
        The means of helping all mankind,
To ope my way by voice and pen
        For blessing to my fellow men.

## Foreword.

Since facts, no matter how prepared, clothed, or presented, are the stepping stones and guiding stars to truth, light, and vision, this work presented in the following pages is but a stepping stone for those who may desire to grasp, or those who are grasping – the spiritual principles linking the past and the present in a homogeneous ascendancy to that wonderful future and supreme hope – life after death.

The work is incorporated as an autobiography consisting of two parts, the first dealing with events in my life while in the convent, and the second, with experiences as a medium and healer. No notoriety is expected, or inflated statements recorded; but, a presentation of the truths – heretofore tabooed and retarded by the hands of opposition and prejudice – which have occurred as personal incidents or achievements in my life.

An apology is necessary to the reader for not recording a more detailed account of my life. Owing to the circumstances of my early life – living within the perpetual darkness of convent walls – days, months, and years passed in a monotonous procession, marked here and there with incidents unforgetable, which are stated in the work.

If the reader has any antipathy toward Spiritualism and challenges the veracity of the statements in this work, I would be pleased in every instance to give the names and addresses of the anonymous persons mentioned. The reason for preserving and withholding the name is simply a question of deference. People concerned – if living – might object to the use of their names, hence, I have taken the alternative of merely telling the incident but reserving the right of supplying the correct names.

Lastly, Spiritualism withholds nothing – and emphatically demands the truth and nothing but the truth – hence, if this work attracts and causes some sensible-minded individuals to see the light where darkness has heretofore existed, and furthermore causes them to enter circles – the doorway to spiritual unfoldment and knowledge – in pursuit of further enlightenment, the effort spent in preparing this work will be well compensated.

## PART I

From the available but vague and scattered family records handed down by word of mouth, or through the memory of recitals of glorious deeds and suffering hardships, I am able to give but a brief sketch of my ancestry. But brief as it is, I value it for that reason the more. My grand parents were in America and took part in the early wars between the English and French settlers of Quebec – now a Canadian province.

My grandfather on my father's side was known as Big Sun of the Pontiac branch of the Mohawk tribe; Pontiac being a very prominent figure in the very early Indian Wars for possessions of lands.[1] My grandmother was known as Princess Laconquinne of the Ojibwah tribe of Indians.

The mother side of the house came from Bordeaux, France. My grandparents – leaving France because of the Revolution – sought temporary refuge in America until peace had been restored. While in the midst of preparations prior to returning to their native land, fire broke out in their home and destroyed all their earthly possessions. This made it necessary for them to remain on this side. They never saw their native land again in the material life.

Father was born in Quebec in 1836, and was called Sunnie, because he was born in the early morning about sunrise. He was of the Ojibwah tribe of Indians. This was due to frequent intermarriages of the Ojibwahs with the Mohawks – his father being a Mohawk. His education was purely Indian, being specially well versed in the use of herbs. As he grew older he became such a scrapper that he was nicknamed Chief Tommyhawk – after a famous predecessor.

---

1 Allied with the French, Pontiac (Ottawa, c.1720–69) helped defeat British General Braddock in 1755. He ultimately sought to create a Pan-Indian confederacy that would prevent Europeans from encroaching on Indian lands, leading a "rebellion" from 1763 to 1764. An Ojibwa woman ultimately betrayed him to the British.

He lived amongst the Ojibwahs until he fell in love with a young French girl. This brought trouble, because the parents did not approve of the pact. Leaving their homes, the young couple eloped and were married in the Roman faith – my mother being a good Catholic, but my father being a believer in the Great Spirit, never entered a church in his life.

I first saw daylight in Quebec, being born, as I was told later, with a hazy veil over my face, regarded at that time as a sign of wisdom. I was also possessed of spiritual powers, being born with such an intensely sensitive organization that I responded to the necessities of the time and became an instrument in the hands of higher intelligences long before I fully realized my gifts, and much longer before I was able to fully reason the why and how of them. Often rappings were heard in my presence in the evening, and mother had to awaken me to quiet the spirits. These were the cause of mother's interference, and caused the suppression of all my efforts in telling people interesting things.

As a consequence, I received a Convent education. At three years of age I was put into the hands of the Sisters of the small community Convent, to be raised and taught religion. When of proper school age, I was sent to Notre Dame in Montreal, at which place mother had arranged and paid for my tuition and care, until I was prepared to become a matron or a nurse or take the veil. Choosing the latter when the time arrived for a decision, I took the white veil. It was a sane course to take – as I thought at the time – for my mother had departed from the material life and my father had married again.

After a time I became restless, nervous and in general, feeling ill, besides being very anxious to know more about my new mother. Receiving permission, I paid a visit to my father's home. It took but a short time to learn the bitter truth – that I was not wanted. Knowing that the time had come for a change to other scenes and conditions, I went to bed in that house for the last time during the visit.

While in bed I felt myself taken out of the body and seemingly made to float through the atmosphere and space. I know not how long I remained in this condition, but on my return to the body I sought father. After a long talk and argument, it was decided that I would either have to return to whence I came or go to New York.

Choosing the latter, arrangements were made whereby I was transferred to New York to another Convent to work out my own salvation. One afternoon – the day preceding the anniversary of my birth – I again seemed to be taken out of the body. This time I spent the afternoon – as we call it – in visiting another planet to witness what you would term "Life after Death." Not being quite able to understand these transitions, they became a source of worryment to me, more so on this particular day.

My duties now became varied between matron, nurse, and housekeeper, and through all this my first love affair developed and progressed. My greatest earth hope and lover was a priest, but as we were not allowed to speak, we enjoyed communication in its elemental form. During a sickness which proved fatal to him, I became his nurse in company with an associate – the rule being that we must always work in pairs under such conditions. While on his deathbed, he promised faithfully to return to me. Being mediumistic, he believed in spirit return.

As time passed I became restless and worried, for my lover had not returned to me as he had promised. I had hoped for greater changes, and had looked forward to frequent visits from him from the spirit side. But to think of entering into a new year without him was perplexing to me. My whole soul cried out to him, and I prayed for him to hasten the time when I could come to him.

Early in the afternoon of a hot summer day – the 4th of July – I heard the beautiful strains of the Rosary. Following this a great change seemed to come over me, a drowsiness and a longing to get to my cell and lie down. As I came to my door on the way to carrying out my desire, I saw a misty, shadowy form standing outside my cell, apparently awaiting me. I crossed the sill, turned and locked the doors and laid down on the couch.

The physical senses became dormant almost immediately, and a sinking sensation ensued, followed by the casting off of physical limitations – a tearing sensation at first – causing a sudden expanding feeling, bringing joyousness and the new thought of freedom. The freedom of mind brought on the intense desire for knowledge. With avidity the mind had adjusted itself as a finely, sensitively attuned instrument, to respond to the thoughts of spiritual beings – to hear, see, and learn that which only higher spiritual intelligence can accomplish and teach.

The door quickly opened and someone stepped into the room. Moving hurriedly to the side of the couch, and reaching out his hand he demanded that I go with him. Casting my eyes up, I recognized him – the object of all my affections – the one to whom my heart had been crying out. My prayers seemingly were answered. He said, "Come, as I desire to keep my promise."

He did not appear to me just as he had been in the body. His face had undergone such decided changes – appearing so much brighter than I had been familiar with – that I could scarcely look at him. A long loose robe covered his body. He did not appear to walk on the floor, but to tread on air. When I arose and took his hand neither of us seemed to walk but to glide onward and upward. On looking back, I saw my own body lying on the couch apparently in slumber, but in reality awaiting my return.

We seemed to rise through ceiling and roof out into the air, in line with and over the great cross on the spire. Looking down, we could see a wonderful panorama of the city and its people – a criss-cross myriad of finely woven webs of street intersections, blended and mingled with the glittering sun rays merrily ricochetting from New York's water boundaries. Soon this was lost to view, for we traveled inconceivably fast.

Looking about, I became aware of the fact that we were nearing what appeared to be another plane or planetary sphere. I asked, "What do you call that place?" His answer wafted to me like the soothing murmur of a zephyr, "Home of your Soul." Looking, I first saw a most beautiful river. On crossing this water, it appeared to be more white than blue and so tranquil and placid that not a ripple could be seen anywhere. Beyond this a tropical country scene unfolded itself to our view. This view made me think that this entire plane had been carpeted with an over-abundance of grasses and flowers – the grasses appearing a greenish blue color. Tropical ferns seemed to abide everywhere. Oh, it was beautiful and delectable to behold. Everything we looked at appeared possessed with a diamond lustre, but in reality only the brilliance of dew drops. Stars and colors were prominent and intermingled at all points. The fragrance was inspiring and odoriferous. There was nothing of a harsh nature to be seen, everything being of that harmony one would expect to find in our spirit or eternal home. There was nothing to greet my ears but the soft murmur of voices linked with that beauty and sweetness which can only come from a heavenly sphere.

After allowing me time to view this heavenly condition, we sailed on and came onto a view of a beautiful city. I can give but a faint idea of the construction of the same. No tall buildings were visible; all evidently of a uniform order. These abodes – for such they obviously were – were strangely fashioned with no roofs and of one color – white.

One in particular that I was attracted to was an exception in magnificence and splendor, and unusually large compared to those in the vicinity. As we approached there appeared to be a large veranda covered with flowers and vines of every description; but no steps to any part of this house were discernable. We came closer. I could see no one but could hear the rapturous strains of music and soft, cooing murmur of voices within. As we listened, it seemed as if elaborate preparations were being made for some special ceremony. Some one came to the door and said, "Come, for the feast is ready." It evidently had been prepared for me.

I seemed to feel the presence of relatives and friends within, especially that of mother. I started to go in but my guide checked me, saying, "You must not enter there, for I have orders to take you on with me." As I turned it seemed to me that my loved ones felt my presence, for a great desire came over me to stay. You can readily know how I felt when I was told that I could not stay with them. To relieve the condition they did not come into view. I asked of the guide what it meant, and he replied, "If I allow you to go in there I could not get you back." He was right, for had I met and seen mother he never could have persuaded me to leave. I would have sacrificed all in my power to have stayed there.

I worried and grieved very much because I could not have my own way, but he knew better than I. My soul's desire was to go to mother or to keep him – my guide – with me, but my time had not come for that end. My mission on earth had not been completed. If I remain true to my trust and my spirit appointments and work diligently, I shall receive my reward in the future. When the time comes he will return for me and then there will be no more separation.

Allowing me another view of the big city, he turned me on our homeward journey. We stopped nowhere, having overstayed our time at the one particular place. Slowly we floated back toward our own earth plane. On our way, I seemed to be returning to a dark prison or vault. On approaching closer to our earth the din of noises and confusion, the rumble of traffic greeted our ears – at first but faint but increasing in crescendo until it became a veritable profaneness. It was a hard task to reconcile myself to the consequences and the accompanying feeling. I could but recall the following words: –

"Weary of earth and ladened with care
I looked toward heaven and longed to be there."

Being in bondage and trying to repent that great, quiet under-way of living, and at the same time trying to worship God, a fearful chill came over me and seemed to repulse me completely. I felt I could not enter my house of flesh. Before entering my cell, I pleaded earnestly to return with him. He only allowed me to wrestle with him, but I clung so tight to his robe that he came in with me and waited until I had regained my earthly consciousness, giving me the charge that we both should know the truth, and that he would soon come and take me on another flight or soul excursion. To my surprise, I found that I had just enough time to attend to my duties, having been out of my body for five hours from one o'clock until six o'clock.

After that flight or soul excursion, I have never felt as though I belonged to this earth or plane, always wanting to turn away from here and go home, for it is the home I'm preparing for myself on this material plane. In a message sent me sometime later through another medium, he said, "Marie, I am awaiting you over on the golden shore where parting comes to us no more, where eternal happiness awaits us. Safe with me, for I love you best of all; you are my choice and I rejoice; then, in our happy home never more to roam alone you will become my loving wife. H.T."

Several months later I was shocked to hear the sad news that father was dying. Receiving permission from my superiors, I returned home for the last time. He lingered but a few days. During his dying moments I stood at the foot of the bed, and as if in a dream I saw father leave his body, rise into the air, transform and come back to earth as a spirit being.

At the funeral while the prayers were being said, a knocking was heard. The neighbor friend next to me tip-toed to the front door, but saw no one. Again the knocking was heard. This time the woman went to the back door, but again found no one. I never spoke a word, thinking to quiet the spirit in that way. That it was the spirit of my father, making a noisy protestation against the prayers being offered over his dead body – he not being a church member, but a believer in the Great Spirit and spirit return – is true without a shadow of a doubt. After the funeral, I could hear him meandering about with that same old dragging, shuffling step. At one time noises were heard emanating from father's former bedroom. On investigation no one was seen, but I soon understood for I remembered that a "strong-box," covered with metal sheeting, in which father kept all his valuables and important documents, was in the room. He had evidently been knocking against this sheeting. The reason I did not enter the rooms frequented much by him was that it was only a signal for him to begin his knocking. My sojourn in this room was of the shortest possible duration, soon returning to New York again to resume my former duties.

At another time while sitting under a tree in the Convent in meditation, I heard music. It seemed to be above me in the tree, of a weird, far-away tone quality. I looked up but saw no one. I knew no singing was allowed at that hour, yet it came louder with the rustle of the leaves, so clear, so strong. I knew in an instant it was no earthly music, for I felt as though no earthly voice could render such sweet song as that, as on my ears these gracious tidings fell, "Believe and confess – thou shalt be loose from all."

I then looked up. Laying aside my Rosary that I always had carried and had placed such confidence in, I began to rejoice with the heavenly hosts. As I did so, I heard the most delightful string music sounding like that of a harp. It increased in volume until it reached a tremendous climax point, and then I recognized that hymn of hymns – "Rock of Ages." In full melody it seemed to vibrate through all things in my surroundings. I did not recognize any of the voices as belonging to any one I knew who had crossed the divide. In a little while the strains of music left me, taking with them my longing to follow and my lingering gaze. I saw nothing; I could only hear these words, "Blessed is he who believes but does not see."

Before entering the house, I read the II. Samuel 22:2, "The Lord is my rock and my fortress." Then I arose perfectly content and went in, realizing we walk by faith and not by sight. I was so content that I took only what the spirit world gave me, feeling sure sight would come later. The environment and unconscious sway of influence these intelligencies had over me made it impossible for me to question what the ultimate result of it all would be.

I did not get back out of doors again in a long time to visit that beloved spot under the tree. Having overstayed my time that evening, I had to undergo a light punishment. I sat a watch in my own room and sang. While singing, "Jerusalem, Hark, the Angels Sing" – to my surprise came the music on the harp as an accompaniment. A few moments later all left and there came a reaction and calm. Being disgusted and discouraged with the turn of events, I had had enough experience inside of those walls, and should lay plans for my escape.

A nun sat in her prison cell
Doomed all the days of her life,
And her thoughts went out to the beautiful world,
"Will I never be free from this strife?"

A songster sat on the window ledge
And the poor girl's heart was stirred;
"Just follow me," it seemed to urge,
To the Convent sang the bird.

I became so useful in my life as a Sister that I was trusted with a visiting list so often that I was practically privileged to go about wherever I pleased in New York. I not only went where they sent me, but also where I was not expected to go – listening all of the time to my spirit guides, and going wherever they took me. I – Indian-like – desired to roam from one scene to another, appearing sometimes at places where I had no business being. There seemed a condition surrounding me, such that I never tried to avoid anything I came in contact with. No matter where I went I could always see or feel Big Chief – my father – close to me watching that no harm befell me, and I never felt any uneasiness. Many times as I wandered on in deep thought, I would hear his voice calling me to take care and give attention.

I frequently came in contact with poor, down-trodden men and women, who would appeal to me for help and financial assistance. Very often I gave up half of what I had previously collected from patrons on my visiting lists. Many times I went to the homes of the poor and the criminal, and what I saw would make me heartsick. In some I found intoxicated men and women so low down and degraded that there seemed to be no possible help for them; in others all stages and descriptions of diseases were present; while in others crime and filth were the outstanding features. Many of these people were out of the daily prescribed route, but that made no difference to me; I did all the good I possibly could.

One day I passed by a large prison. On looking up I saw Big Chief standing, looking at me, and he said, "Here is work for you to do." "But how can I get in?" I asked. The next day, as I passed the same prison, I saw a poor, care-worn woman who stooped and asked for prayers, also begging me to say a prayer for her son who was incarcerated within. I was only too glad and willing, and availed myself of the opportunity.

Following the poor mother, we were allowed admittance. I talked to the son and prayed for him and bade him read a small Bible which I left, and which he took with him to Sing Sing prison. Having an opportunity to follow up the career of this young man, I later learned that the seed I had planted had yielded fruit.

I did not think it wise to tell my superiors what work I was doing. By doing this I had better opportunities to carry out my plans. There was a great longing in my breast to see Coney Island – New York's amusement park – by night, for I had heard so much about it.

Making my plans accordingly, I walked out the back door one evening and down the garden to the wall. Under my arm was a box with a rope in it. At the wall whom should I see but Big Chief – my guide. Below him I saw notches in the brick wall by means of which I was soon over the wall. On the other side

I found a good thorough-fare for making my way without attracting the attention of anyone, to the home of a friend of mine with whom my escape had been prearranged. In a short time I was properly attired and my friend and I set out for the park. How I enjoyed that lark no one knows but myself. I came face to face with many I knew but they, seeing me in civilian clothes, did not recognize me.

I was forced to spend the night with my friend, as it was not feasible to attempt to return at such a late hour. Coming back early enough in the morning, I passed through the Church saying my prayers. When asked where I had been I replied, "Out on a little mission." The Mother Superior thought different and started in to box my ears, but this was one of the times I would not submit. Reaching out, I tore the veil from her head and she just barely escaped with her life, for I was so furiously angry that I was tempted to throw her over the railing and down the stairs. The sentence and punishment meted out to me was the maximum imposed for such offences.

On my way to my cell for punishment I was met by the cook who stealthily handed me a lunch, for she knew I would get nothing all day. This I secreted until I had been locked in. Then I took time to eat and enjoy a small chicken, and amongst other things a flask of wine.

While eating, a shadow passed through the door and there before me stood Big Chief. He flashed a spirit light about the cell so that I could see where I was. He showed me a vision of the assassination of President McKinley; several war views, one of them fought under palm trees, while in the other red-coated soldiers were engaged; an earthquake; and a stream of roaring water predicting floods. He knelt beside me and pleaded with me to leave the place we were in and to trust myself to his guidance, for he would take care of me. Then a vision of mother came – weeping because she had left me in such bondage.

I vowed to follow Big Chief and confide in the Great Spirit. Going to the door – with my guide – I found it unlocked. I went about my duties as if nothing had happened, trusting all the time in my guide. When my superiors saw this they hurriedly made arrangements for my transfer to Philadelphia.

Thinking to get rid of me, I was sent from Philadelphia to Newport News, Va., where an epidemic of yellow fever was raging. But all to no avail, for I took up my duties as a nurse and gave what succor I was capable of, without being protected in any way from the disease. I realized later what danger I had submitted myself to, but only received greater faith in my guides. When my work at this place had been completed, I was sent back to Philadelphia to assume my new duties there.

I found quite a few mediums among the priests and nuns. On recollection, I don't wonder at the above statement. For what is more desirable for spiritual unfoldment and attraction to the Great Beyond than to be shut in from the noise of the busy world, surrounded by flowers, music and incense and of necessity – concentration on devotion. Unconsciously or subconsciously the gateway is opened, bringing joy for the discovery of the newly found truth but disappointment for the environments and servitude chained to them during their physical life.

Psychic phenomena were demonstrated daily. The Sister Superior often interrupted my associate Sister and me while we were enjoying thought transference with both the living and the dead – for no other reason than she herself was psychic and knew of our pastime. Of one particular instance I remember where the spirit of my lover – the priest – brought me thoughts from a priest in Cleveland who was to figure prominently in subsequent events. While this side of the experience was roses, the thorns presented themselves in as much as we had to be guarded in both active and subconscious thoughts, and in our actions, lest the psychic Mother Superior get acquainted with everything about and between us.

I had been ailing three weeks with a rheumatic attack which affected my left limb, when an interesting incident occurred. Coming down the stairs very early one morning to prepare the lights for early mass, I felt weak and faint, making it necessary for me to support myself on the railing. Suddenly a crescent about two feet wide appeared at my feet. I stepped onto it with my left foot and immediately a light flared up. Frightened, I ran up the stairs and down by another, to perform my duties; but the ailment had left me. Several years later the spirit of Moonbeam – came to me with a light and a crescent, and I then realized that Moonbeam had cured me of my rheumatic attack.

About this time I began to listen to my spirit friend in his effort to have me give up this bondage and go out into the world to see and do what I could. After due consideration of all things concerned and connected with my proposed flight, I told the Sisters. This created quite an excitement amongst them. They threatened, scolded, cajoled and promised, but all to no purpose, for I had had a glimpse of what was in store for me, and determined that my relations with them must cease. They sent urgent messages to the heads in Montreal, but this made no impression on me. The orders from Montreal were to hold me to the vows I had taken, and promised me a better home for the money my mother paid for my tuition and care.

Fortifying myself against all or any possible conditions that might arise – knowing that an authority from Montreal would likely arrive any time – I went quietly into the last prayers of my career as a nun – one night. While kneeling before a life-sized crucifix, and all sincere in my devotions, I heard a great crash, and instantly following this, Big Chief appeared before me, accompanied by the spirits of my mother and of two Sisters I had known in life. They stood side by side until I had finished and then they faced about and in single file passed through the door. By impulse I followed them out. As we passed the door, I went into the Church proper where I saluted and paid my respects to the fourteen stations of the Cross – representing Christ on his way to Calvary; also paying my best and most loving tribute to the Madonna for a special prayer in my behalf. When the great outer doors closed behind me, freedom was mine.

At that moment the thought came, "What shall I do?" The exultation, the new air, the quickened, unknown heartbeat, the desire to shout to all the world the news of my freedom – all descended upon me so quickly that I was completely confounded. While I was pondering and thinking over how I had previously arranged my plans, a bird twittered and finally broke into a song. It seemed to be a message of love and encouragement to me; it seemed as if the birds were even interested in my case.

Recovering my mental equilibrium, I hurried to my friend's home – the one who had escorted me on the Coney Island escapade. After a hurried explanation and consultation, she gave me some civilian clothes to wear on my flight. Further cautioning and urging her to keep my flight from the priests' ears, I departed, feeling somewhat easier in the acquired attire.

Having some means I went to the station and purchased a ticket for Cleveland, Ohio. At this place I found old friends and neighbors of my father's who were sympathetic with me in my flight and with whom I rejoiced in my newly acquired freedom. For a whole day I remained indoors still wary lest I be apprehended.

The following day we started on a shopping tour to outfit a wardrobe for myself. While busily engaged in talking and viewing the sights while passing from one store to another, I espied a priest coming towards us. In passing, our eyes met, and I knew I had been recognized through the medium of higher intelligences, and by means of powers acquired through unfoldment and environments – as referred to previously. I acquainted my friend with the news, at the same time telling her I would journey to another point.

That night I took a boat to Detroit. In the morning I hunted for a desirable room – finding one, about noon time. The relaxation, the cold, cheerless four walls surrounding enclosure and the future outlook made me despondent. There I was – unwelcomed – a fugitive in the eyes of the world – trembling, nervous, blue, downhearted. Do you wonder, gentle reader, at my condition? My thoughts were as nervous as I physically was. They agitated me in a comparison of the past – the quiet life – with the then present – dodging, unhonored, unrespected career. In this brooding state of mind I passed the whole of the afternoon.

In the evening, I lay down all worn out. I immediately became aware of the fact that I was not alone. I closed my eyes and instantly saw the shepherd – my priest – standing close by saying that he had given up his life for his sheep. He had his crook in his hand and two small lambs in his arms. He came so close that he touched me, saying, "It is the songs you sing and the smiles you wear that makes the sunshine glow; also, may every morning seem to say there is something happy on the way." Jumping to my feet in a dazed condition, I cried, "I am ready – take me now." I had not stopped to think; this I realized when I had recovered fully. I knew I was not ready, for there were many things not yet accomplished. My mission on earth really just had its beginning. But before I had arrived at a worthy end I could not expect the longed for journey across the divide to join my loved ones. To Jesus I said, "My sorrow sets too deep for this life to look for peace and happiness from anyone but you. Human sympathy is too shallow as a rule, so I must look higher and say,

'Thou does't remember,
Midst all the glories of Thy Throne –
The sorrows of humanity,
For they were once Thine own.' "

In the morning restlessness returned to me. I later received a visit from Big Chief who bade me follow him. My destination under his guidance was Walpole Island – the Indian Reserve.[2] While there I sent word to the Mother Superior at Philadelphia and the priest in Cleveland that I had sought refuge among my ancestors' people, and had further denounced all creeds and joined the Great Spirit worshippers. Also, during my stay, I attracted the Spirit of Pontiac – the great Indian warrior and trailer.

The following day I retraced my route to Detroit again. On returning to my place I found that I was not alone, for the Spirit of Pontiac was my companion. He came to me as a shepherd to watch over me, as I was one of his lambs, and to teach me to trust in him.

He took my soul on a journey to develop within me the desires of my spirit loved ones for my education that was to fit me for my lifework. He showed me the great peaceful river; he took me a long distance over green fields and towns and finally stopped at a large, beautiful fountain where he bade me drink. At another stop he invited me to a great feast. Oh, what joy there seemed to be among the people over the return of Big Chief Tommyhawk with a brother from earth life who was to remain with them. I could not see him – Tommyhawk – but I felt his presence. This feast appeared to take place in the open and under the protection of a hill.

We then visited with Princess Laconquinne, my grandmother on my father's side – who sat at the entrance of a magnificent white palace. She evidently was mistress of the place, which apparently was a haven for mothers. I was then piloted through a long dark valley. A light was visible in the distance, at first a dim ray, but brightening as we neared the end. At the end I was met by my spirit guide and returned to the body. As evidence of their faith and watchfulness, I received the following poem.

There's a fair Indian maid
    Whose duties are laid,
On the banks of a beautiful river.
With her guides, their lives never sever.

Her duties are plain
    As they sweep through the brain,
Their love for her so exceeding,
    Revealing to her their presence so near
As they touch her when gently kneeling.

The Physical plain oft causes a pain
    When absence is felt when she wanders,
But oh, what joys
When she hears from her boys,
For she feels they are always about her.

These brave Indian boys
    Were always her joy
When oft on the trail they did wander,
    Ever mindful of her and the pleasure she seeks,
Ever watchful that love will surround her.

Her desires for good
    Are all understood
By the braves that give her power;
    Make her life very dear, with their presence so near,
And always on watch to defend her.

2 In the delta of the St. Clair River in south Ontario.

Entering on the second phase of my career – which appears to be a reincarnation to do worldly good – have myself wondered and marveled – on retrospection – at the absolute power of the unseen forces. My lifework had been cut out for me; chiseled, irremovable on the marble pillars of accomplishment. My guides – the spirits of the known and unknown to me in this material life – being parties to the conspiracy to effect my escape, gave birth to the desire within my mind – nursing it in characteristic fashion until the psychological moment had arrived for the smouldering in my breast to break out into a seething flame. The turn of events which made my freedom possible is but another instance of their handiwork. Once free, I was further directed on my course. I do not lament; I only wonder and try to surmise what I will be called upon to do next; I am ready, at all times under all conditions.

Being prepared and ready to do the bidding of my spirit guides, I failed to keep as accurate and as detailed an account of my later life as would be necessary for a work of this type. Consequently, the work under this part is not recorded in a chronological sequence, but under headings of the various topics such as Healing, Trailing, etc., which gives in a synopsized form, an account of my experiences and accomplishments. Even the various cities and towns – there being so many – are not mentioned in detail. I belong to various state organizations, but I always undertook volunteer work, never waiting to be called upon by the associations. Arriving at one destination and completing my mission, I was either invited or guided to another – usually within a short radius. Using one of these places as a headquarter, I worked out from the same – in this manner covering quite an extensive territory. I've made no commercial issue of my talents, just taking and receiving remuneration with my traveling expenses plus my upkeep.

My guides, who have striven to render invaluable aid to alleviate some of the perplexities of the material life, are all Indians with the exception of two – my mother and H.T., the priest.

H.T., my priest, is my personal comforter and guide, helping me at all times and teaching me of his world and what I have to look forward to in the future life.

Mother – is the receptive guardian – the gatekeeper for all spirits who desire to communicate with me.

Tommyhawk – my father – for self-protection and for those I ask of him to battle for. In true Indian style, he comes accompanied by his six dogs which have materialized in a materializing circle.

Sitting Bull[3] – Tommyhawk's companion at times.

Princess Laconquinne – my grandmother on my father's side – for message work.

Two Indian children – who help in circle work.

Moonbeam – my Indian medicine-man who helps me in my healing.

Pontiac – the trailer and locator for the hidden or the lost.

Of these guides, the first three mentioned were known to me in earth life, while the remaining were attracted at some previous time. I can depend on my Indian guides not to give false or misleading statements because in earth life an Indian despises the man with a crooked tongue. Further, they do not throw the condition of their passing out of this material life over me. Examples of what they have accomplished through me and my talents are given under the following articles:

## Healing

In a peculiar yet simple and logical manner my success as a healer can be comprehended. My father was known among the Indians for his knowledge of herbs and the manner of compounding simple remedies – crude in most ways, yet common-sense, practical Nature in themselves. These necessary prerequisites in physical structure and properties were mine. My hands are soft, cushiony, and warm, allowing the vital magnetism to be directed outward, drawing the blood with it. Then thru psychometrical work I am able to locate the center and base of ailments, making it possible in many cases to do away with all experimenting.

In my work in this branch, I have learned fundamental points which – if the doctors would follow more closely – would compensate both doctor and patient. Of the greatest importance is the diverting of

---

3 Sioux, c.1830–90. A renowned warrior – known for his defeat of George Armstrong Custer in the 1876 Battle of Little Big Horn—and spiritual leader of the Lakotas, he was also the principal negotiator of the 1868 Fort Laramie Treaty aimed at protecting Lakota land rights against the depredations of the federal government.

the patient's mind from the ailment. This accomplished, I gently touch the afflicted parts and with low words of assurance offer suggestions, but being tactful to have the patients follow me throughout all. For some I pray and have them pray. Where music is advisable I have it played or sung. But of all, I take greatest care to await impressions to do the healing – not at any time but only when encouraged and aided by my spirit guides.

While traveling from Detroit to Sandusky, Ohio, in answer to a call from a circle and to help the resident members to the best of my ability, the spirit of Moonbeam – the Indian medicine-man – appeared before me. He informed me that there was work to be done and that he would be with me throughout the entire period.

He was right. On appearing on the rostrum, I found that I could not go on with the scheduled message work. Going down into the audience, I walked down the aisle and was guided to a certain woman whose name I don't know. I felt my arm; there was a pain. "I hurt myself by falling out through the doorway with a washtub," I told her. Much to her surprise and chagrin, I took her arm and gently massaged it. My statements were correct, for she admitted that she had hurt herself in the manner stated. Being a poor woman who washed for a living, I was heartily pleased with my work and thanked my guides.

At another time while there, I undertook to cure a case without personal contact with the party. I stood on the rostrum and in answer to my guides said, "There is a certain party by name of Henry – a lawyer – who has an injured wrist and whose father also tells me that he is skeptical about our work." The man's wife raised her hand and verified my statements. "He hurt his wrist while out on a hunting trip and while carrying a gun," I continued. They also acknowledged that. I told him to remove his wrist band and give me a good thought. I rubbed and treated my own wrist and prayed for him, knowing that the spirit of his father was doing likewise with his. I was informed later by his wife that he had never worn the wrist band again and that his views on the subject had been revised considerably.

By means of massaging and the prayer cure a crippled woman was somewhat relieved. She had been unable to walk without the aid of a crutch for three years, and the last five months preceding the treatments she had been in bed. After three treatments a relaxation of the muscles was effected and since then the woman has been able to walk with the aid of a cane.

People are skeptical of such versions as stated above. In Columbus, in a circle, a doctor – receptive to a certain extent but still a doubter – brought in a paper on a difficult medical case where exact diagnosis was lacking. By means of psychometrical reading, I was able to locate the exact center and base of the ailment. He became very enthusiastic and wanted to know why he, with all his university training and technical knowledge, had to be told by one who had no diploma, nor had seen the patient. Then he became acquainted with the fact that everyone is psychic – some very much more so than others. The requirement to develop the hidden powers within ourselves to attend circles and try to unfold. This power is but dormant in some people, and like a stiffened member of the body, needs exercise, it needs but attention and patience. The doctor became an enthusiastic member of the circles I held during the year I was there.

## Trailing

In my work under this heading, my guide, Pontiac, figures conspicuously. While working – recuperating from the exhaustion brought on from the healing cases – Pontiac came to me and said, "Tell your neighbor that her son is not lost. Tell her to go to Coldwater, Michigan; visit a man there by the name of Ames who runs a barber shop, and he will tell her where to find her son Les." This I did and she became highly excited, for she said that she had been awaiting an opportunity to ask if I could help her in locating her "lost boy." Following my instructions, she brought the "boy" back home with her shortly before Christmas and was able to enjoy the first happy Yuletide in the twelve years of his absence.

Another lady hearing of the above by means of some devious channel, as news of this character travels, came to see me about her son. Pontiac told her through me that her son had gone never to return home to settle down. He further added that she should go home and call on the Great Spirit every day until he brought the son to her from Huntington, Indiana. During the interval preceding the young man's return, I sat under the sunflowers – at the back of my lodging – at twilight, and kept in touch with the spirits of the young man's actions. At the end of three weeks, the prodigal son returned for a visit to his home in Freemont, Ohio.

Shortly after this, while at Amherst, Ohio, a man from Republic, Ohio, came to see me. Before he had made the object of his visit known to me, Pontiac told me to say, "Your mother has the money, that's why you no find. Go to your home in country; go to spring house where you keep milk; look down deep in mud under water-trough, and in a cream jar you will find 500 wampams ($500)." He did so, and found the amount as stated. The father and mother of this man had quarreled. Following the disagreement, the mother had hid the money but had died before telling her son where to find it.

In a case of this kind, locating treasure is permissible. But I have emphatically nothing whatever to do with seeking or helping others to locate treasures that were acquired unlawfully and then hidden. The spirit condition guarding the treasure is anything but satisfactory. Should the treasure be found, the visitation of bad luck, failures, and apprehension will soon deprive the finder of his ill-gotten fortune. Death is a very common gain reaped by such treasure hunters.

A case of this character was enacted in the vicinity of where I was staying, Pontiac explaining to me the cause of it all. Four young men had stolen some money, and in their flight, one of their number was killed by pursuers. The money was buried by the remaining three in a thick woods. One night one of the three attempted to crawl up and get his share of the booty. He was shot and killed by one of the others who happened to be lying there unknown to the first man. A clear instance of the earth-bound spirit of the first killed wreaking havoc on the other three by causing one of their number to die the death he did.

Pontiac guides me clearly enough in such cases. His work is only to do good for humanity. The instances as stated give but a few examples of the work he had helped perform to relieve a few of the many aching hearts.

## Titanic Prophecy

Three days before the Titanic went down to its watery grave,[4] I had a vision of the disaster, but did not get it clear enough to distinguish a ship, nor the place of the accident. The evening of the fatal night, while sitting by myself I felt a feeling of unrest and weariness coming over me. Giving way to my feeling I prepared to retire, but before I was even comfortably settled, I saw a shadow cross my eyes. Looking up, I saw Big Chief and a Hindoo member of his band.

They talked together for a few moments, and immediately after their conversation I felt myself drawn toward them. It seemed as if we were floating above the ocean. Looking off into space, we could see what appeared to be a large floating palace. As we approached, it seemed to take on all the colors of the rainbow – a picturesque object. When we came closer to it, its appearance changed to that of a large, beautiful butterfly – a winged personification of gayiety and supremacy. It sped on and we watched. Suddenly it seemed to disappear between two walls of ice and snow – we lost it. On coming to my senses, I was wet from sweat, cold, and frozen from the effects. Several mornings following, the world received the news of the great marine disaster.

## Soul Flight

Following shortly after the Titanic premonition, the spirit of Tommyhawk – my father – came to me. "It is time to take another flight to the ethereal planes," he told me. Having no control over my physical body when in his hands, I could but obey his instructions. In a few minutes I felt my soul leave the body and we went up until I became hopelessly lost.

At this time I seemed to hear father speak to me; he bade me look. As I looked in the indicated direction, the most beautiful castles came into view. On approaching and entering the doorway, we were enveloped by the inky black which seemed to hang on every side. The corridor was with apparently no sidewalls. On the far end we met with the extreme opposite; a flood of glistening sunshine greeted us.

The view afforded at this juncture was delectable to behold. Within a magnificent wigwam, sat Prin-

4 The *Titanic* sank on April 15, 1912.

cess Laconquinne, my father's mother. On seeing father and me, she gave us a great welcome and took me inside of the wigwam. When we went in I was astonished at the transformation, for instead of seeing the interior of a wigwam, as I had expected, I found that I was within a spacious, awe-inspiring palace. Within, forest flowers and fruits abounded, while without, a placid stream flowed gently on – a picture of love and peace, purity and wisdom. We walked or floated side by side for what seemed like hours until she halted and bade me eat of the fruit which appeared to be cherries; but they were very large and juicy.

While eating she pointed off into the distance and said, "There is the Happy Hunting Ground of the Indians." There seemed to be no end to the hosts of people on the banks of the river. All were busy on missions of import, coming, going, making visits, always smiling; always on the watch for the arrival of some loved one from the earth plane who had not come as yet; always clothed in such garb as would easily be recognized by those just coming over the divide. In place of the customary war implements, they all carried musical instruments of various kinds, together with flags and other ornamental trimmings. While looking on this ostentatious display, music of the sweetest harmony seemed to surround us.

I turned my eyes toward the river, which was full of brightly painted canoes, going and coming. I asked Princess Laconquinne what was going on and why all these people seemed to be preparing for some royal event. As we talked a canoe came into sight; as it approached it looked as if it had turned into a beautiful palace floating in the ethereal air, fully decorated with flags and feathers of all kinds and variegated colors. As it approached the shores someone said it had the soul of one who had just departed from the material life. I thought of the joy of the meeting, but could not see or hear what was taking place about the newly arrived soul. I expressed a desire to come home in the same manner, but Princess Laconquinne told me that was only used for spirit purposes. She then led me back to where Tommyhawk was patiently waiting for me. He in turn guided me back to my body. As I watched, I saw him step into his canoe and while gliding away heard his voice singing so sweetly, "Yes, we'll gather at the water that leads to the Happy Hunting Ground."

## Waiting

Loved ones are waiting yonder,
   Over the Crystal Sea.
Oft do we hear their voices,
   Calling to you and me.
Oft do we see their shadows
   Oft hear the still small voice
Making our hearts feel lighter,
   Making our Souls rejoice.

Oft do we hear their music,
   Music of heavenly strain,
Naught but a voice from Heaven,
   Could sound that glad refrain.
Soon they will come and take me,
   To that dear Home on High
Where all is bright and happy
   And sweet welcome Bye and Bye.

Zimran[5] is lingering near you,
   Filling your soul with love,
Teaching the path of duty
   Leading to joys above.

5 The name of one of the sons of Abraham and Keturah; see Genesis 25:2. Though the Bible says little about Zimran, his name appears to mean "singer"; hence, Leevier may merely be suggesting the idea of "holy singer."

Oft, yes, oft do we grieve him
When heed we not his voice,
But if we do his bidding
Then does his soul rejoice

Angels all robed in beauty
Stand near the open door;
Oh, will you bid them enter,
Cheering us more and more.
Stars from their home are shining
Over each path of woe,
Trying to lead us upward,
Pointing the way to go.
Dear Ones, why tarry longer?
Choose the right path today;
Let your face beam with gladness
For those across the way.
Zimran is calling down to you
And He will bring the key,
In all His truth and grandeur,
Unlocking the Mystery.

## Tiffin Prophecy

While resting one evening in my room by myself, prior to holding a circle Big Chief came to me looking sad. He vanished from my view and another form came into view, that of the warning spirit. He stood before me clothed all in white, a trumpet in hand, a sword laid across his breast, and very angry – his face very expressive. I arose trembling. I saw great bodies of water gushing in torrents; I saw houses, people, and animals floating by. I fainted and lay in this condition for some time.

Recovering my senses, I called my class around me and made the prophecy that Tiffin, Ohio[6] would be under water within a short time. When the Mayor heard of the prophecy, he notified me that Tiffin tolerated no such folly and that I either had to leave the town or be subject to arrest. I sat down to look matters straight in the face; I surely had not expected such a reception from the city officials. It was discouraging – but just for a moment to know the truth – but have the populace decrying your statements as false, nonsensical and undesirable. While pondering as to my future course, Pontiac and Captain John Smith appeared before me. They held a jury trial over me – the jury consisting of the unseen forces. The verdict was in my favor; I remained in Tiffin until a few days before the flood. Knowing my vision was to be fulfilled, I went over to Fostoria, Ohio. The great Angel went with me and drawing his sword he divided the city so that I knew where to seek refuge from the impending danger.

The flood came – the flood of 1913 – that damaged or sideswiped every city, town and hamlet that bordered on a stream or river in the Ohio River basin. On returning to Tiffin – after the flood had reached its crest and had begun to recede – I found that six bridges had been swept away and ruin and devastation left in its wake. As I stood on the banks of the river, my messenger – the bird – came to me and sang a slow mournful song which spoke louder to me than a human voice.

Searching parties were busy seeking the bodies of all persons reported missing. They were successful in finding all with the exception of one – a Mr. Axline. Big Chief and Pontiac both came to the rescue and searching parties following my instructions were able to locate and recover the body. This was

6 At the end of March, 1913, heavy rains caused the neighboring Sandusky River to rise 24 feet above normal, causing a million dollars of property damage and the loss of about 20 lives.

another triumph for me – the people having begun to believe a little when my prophecy on the flood had been fulfilled. To cap the climax, I told a woman – who had been made a widow through the flood – where to find her husband's gold watch.

Later on I made another prophecy that Tiffin would be somewhat damaged by a severe storm in the fall of that same year. To my gratification, the news was received by the people in a totally different manner from that which the flood prophecy had been treated.

Following my prophecies, I received further evidences from spirit friends who are at work at all times in connection with the human race, ever ready to send forth their messages of love to us. These were received on various occasions while quietly sitting – with my eyes closed – about twilight time. The name given at the end of each message is that of the spirit who transmitted the message to you through me and my guides. At the command of Princess Laconquinne to write, I received the following:

"Working out our own salvation,
Firm and patient day by day,
Clearing thorns from each one's pathway
Keeping enemies at bay,
No one far or near is slighted.
Drop a line to each one here,
Never let one go unnoticed
Banish every doubt and Fear."
– Martin Luther.

"While gazing in the great beyond
And asking if my friends are there,
The answer come and lo! anon
There comes a music on the air."
– Longfellow.

"Nothing pleases better
Than to soothe the suff'ring one.
Let them know the Learned Healer
Still on earth can appear."
– Alice Bennette, Cleveland.

"It's only one more day, tonight,
A message to you I did write,
Courage loved one you are right,
Remove the cross out of your sight;
This spirit world is what we see
They took the cross away from me."
– Martin Luther.

"There came to me a guiding star,
It fell to floor. It came I know not where;
I looked it o'er, 'twas made with care,
A lov'd one's hand had placed it there.
A star in your crown you have won,
You have toiled for Christ from sun to sun;
There's no reward on earth for this,
The Master does not pay in gold."
– Abraham Lincoln

"Beyond the pearly gates I stand,
 A manuscript in my left hand;
What e'er you do both right and wrong
 I'll weight it out and put it down.

Your judgment comes just once a year,
 In this same month when you were born
You'll realize if you have passed
 And entered in a better class.

Your teacher is the Master, dear.
 His life you've taught without a fear,
Those little ones brought near to Him
 And older ones with faith in Him."

Being near to my birthday, when I received the above anonymous spirit manifestation, I was greatly alarmed for the reason that no spirit name was given. This is regarded by mediums as an upbraiding for some wrong we may have committed or the omen that we would be censured even to the point of having the Holy Spirit send the summons to cross the Great Divide.

## Tribute from Chief Tommyhawk

Muche heape Good Man too
 Gave my country for His sake.
All I do for Great Spirit too,
 Fighting battles for all of you;
We are warriors brave and bold,
 We have no fear for our souls,
We know Him who gave us birth,
 He'll take care of all on earth.
No more our quarrels do we fight,
 Only your earth plots to make right.
Muche heape spirits bright,
 Draped in feathers all in white.
Robes white too, our faces fair,
 Are blessings sent to you so rare
By Sitting Bull your comforter.
 Our wigwam doors are open wide
And he is constant by your side;
 I never leave you now alone
Until this long life's battle's won."

## Obsession and Spirit Conditions

Why I never married can be again attributed to the unseen forces. On becoming a nun, I was married to the cross and to those sacred vows. After laying aside the sacred veil and after those massive doors had closed me out into the noise contaminated world to go at will, the cross haunted me. Naturally enough, many times I sat and pondered over my escape, and thought of the cold convent life. To be all alone in this world was enough to bring on moroseness; to be compelled to learn the ways of the wicked at such a late period in life was distasteful; to think of being forced to make my living, to make my new acquaintances, to learn·to travel, was distracting. Taken in all, the predicament I found myself in – without the aid of the superior beings – was unenviable. But trusting to my spirit guides, they blazed the trail for my journey in life up to the present, and have made the life that looks barren to the uninformed bystander as pleasant as they have seen fit and necessary.

But the idea dawned on me to have an earth companion as well as a soul mate. It was embarrassing to me to have to wander onward over this earth's surface without a protector and a guide. Again I felt the result of being shut in from the world. What must I do? That was my problem. I had enough admirers through the work I've accomplished to choose from. Was it up to me to make the initiative? Well, I made my individual attempts to fulfill my desires, but my guides were instrumental in frustrating my plans.

My first selection was a gentleman who had been an altar server in a Catholic Church. We were acquainted, and as far as I could comprehend certainly loved one another. Our plans for our future were maturing. We were to join another church of my designation, and also to have a happy, comfortable home. But before the climax of our simple love affair was attained, we had a disagreement one evening. As lovers generally do, we began to spat. Suddenly a light appeared in the doorway – peculiar, shimmering, and similar to that of a small gas flame. It came between us and then faded away. We both observed this phenomenon; we could spat no more. He asked an explanation of me, but I was too dazed at the time and offered none. He left me but we were never the same lovers after this visit from the spirit who protected me – there being no one on this earth to do it. Later my guide simply told me that my suitor and I could never have agreed, so I had to forget.

Another gentleman with whom I became great friends was in the navy of this country. I found great pleasure in his company until the day the crisis came. I knew it and felt it. I went with him to visit on the battleship Delaware – before it had been officially accepted. On going down the stairs while on the warship, I saw my spirit guide standing at the foot of the stairs. Then I knew the worst would come. Right enough, we disagreed over an insignificant topic before we left the ship and never made up again.

In another and last instance, the gentleman was a brother of one of my most intimate lady friends. We three spent many a happy time together, and I felt sure my spirit guide wouldn't interfere between us. But finally the long awaited day arrived. While we were walking the Boardwalk of Atlantic City, I met my spirit and knew the end was near. Later on he went to work with the engineer corps on the Panama Canal. Since the time of his departure I have heard but once from him.

I was disappointed at the outcome of my love affairs, but thought over the reason behind these failures. I found that the spirit of the priest – my lover while in the convent and my conductor on the soul flight – had obsessed me, and had been the guiding influence. It was not his desire to have me become married. He had previously promised me that after I had fulfilled my share of work allotted to me, I would find happiness with him across the Great Divide. As further evidence from him to urge me onward, I received a poem from him, counselling me to obey the heavenly voice.

## Obsession

Obsession has given me unlimited food for thought. The subject is so large, so expansive and engrossing that volumes upon it could be written. But in the short space allotted in this work, it is hoped that the statements and references will cause the reader to desire more knowledge of same.

No one who is obsessed by a good spirit can go into bad company or commit evil; it won't allow you to. It's easy to attract a good spirit if we understand spirit return and obey the laws set forth by those who are capable of doing so. Unless the gateway – the inclination to resist with the indomitable strength of higher thoughts and aspirations the influences of a lower nature – is open, such influences of a lower nature cannot enter as obsessing forces. That's why I wish everyone would concentrate; we are all psychic; not only the mediums but everyone. Thoughts are things – living things – therefore give out your best thoughts toward everyone and nothing but good comes back to you. By doing so we cannot attract an evil spirit wandering around on earth – commonly called the devil – who may have left the body under peculiar circumstances, and who may induce others to do likewise.

Have you ever stopped to think that through obsession a cause can be found for innumerable crimes committed, for the hosts of suicides and maniacs? The organization of the obsessing force must be similar to that of the obedient obsessed being. Realizing this and knowing that a spirit enters the spirit world just as it left this, there must be an innumerable host of low, uneducated, and evil spirits about.

Hence if the obsessed party offers a deficiency of will power – weakness in control of their individuality – the gateway is open for an evil spirit of a harmonious organization – with that of the obsessed to enter. The ensuing result is a heartbreaking chapter of evil for which inevitable retribution must be received.

Think of those who give themselves to drink. One drinking man came to me while I was in Sandusky, Ohio, to ask me to help him. I said to him, "You have the spirit control of a man who passed out while intoxicated." "Yes, I know it," he replied. "We were both out fishing some twelve years ago in Sandusky Bay and became drunk. The result was that the boat capsized and he drowned. In going down the last time he yelled, 'I hope you drown.' Since that time I've been a drunkard. Whenever the thought of that drowning man comes to me I have to go in and drink. Furthermore, I neglect my family and their suffering makes me feel wretched when I'm sober."

I told him how to "brace up" – how it was possible to throw off his spirit condition. I had him come often; I prayed for him and gave him a prayer that he had at hand and repeated at any time the desire for his former debauchery seized him. I impressed on his mind the necessity of concentration on keeping straight – the fact that he still possessed will power and that he had to trust in it. In following up this man's case, I found that in obeying instructions, his home life had as a result been revolutionized – from a heart-broken to a happy state of existence.

Many spirits in similar instances of souls transient have obsessed the living person to live out the time they should have lived in their own house of flesh. In the above example, the spirit of the drinking partner had been back here on earth using this man's body just the same as if the body had been its own.

Spirit enlightenment of "earthbound" spirits can be accomplished by having them enter a circle. The spirit of Stanford White was in this terrible plight until I brought it to light. This spirit followed me for a long time, but didn't try to obsess me because he was too busy guarding Harry K. Thaw – his murderer – and keeping him in prison.[7] I was holding a séance in Columbus, Ohio, when the spirit took hold of me. I was under control and tried to fight; I was so angry that I had to be held tight by those earnest sitters until the strife was over, and the spirit of his mother had joined him. Then came calm. Then he said, "Now that I'm with mother I cling no more to this earth. My desire is to get away if I can and Harry K. Thaw can go free." This was before Thaw's freedom for the sitters made note of the message and watched the newspapers. Within a short time – less than a year – Thaw's escape was announced and at this writing he is still a free man. The spirit of White has returned many times to thank me for uniting his spirit with his mother's. Had this spirit not been enlightened, it may have wandered on earth until it had attracted some weaker person and had made them die as he did.

Those gunmen of New York – who paid the penalty with their lives in the electric chair – also came in spirit, asking prayers, so that they, too, might get away from this earth – having passed out before their time had arrived. But such is in our life. The spirit missionaries, the spirit friends, and loved ones are incessantly helping those terribly hypnotized "earthbound" spirits from their lowly cycles on the upward path to the love that is ultimately awaiting them.

No wonder enmity and war never cease – whether individual, family, commercial, state, or international – once a start is made. There are more spirits fighting than human beings in any strife. As an instance, while conducting a circle in Cleveland a short time after Señor Huerta's – the former Mexican President[8] – demise from earth life, the spirit of my guide Pontiac came and told me that Huerta was busy at the time fighting for and aiding that faction that had been his while he was Dictator.

If people knew what they were made for they wouldn't cause so many heartaches of others. But they don't understand the life they live and pass out to the Great Divide without knowing why and where they are going.

Honor those whose words or deeds  
Thus help us in our daily needs;

7 Stanford White was an architect murdered in the summer of 1906 by famous socialite Harry K. Thaw over White's affair with Thaw's beautiful wife, Evelyn Nesbit.

8 Victoriano Huerta (1854–1916) was president of Mexico from October 1913 to July 1915, a time of constitutional crisis.

And by their loving overflow
Raise us from whate'er is low.

## Conclusion

In summing up the story of my life, the question in my mind, dear reader, is not that of the past, present and future of myself, but for you and your future. I have been educated by my guides to prepare myself for the future – the real life and to know that the purpose of the physical body is the evolution of the spirit. In all history we find record of where our departed loved ones say to us, "If I only could have known of the beauties of what was in store for me, how I would have made greater effort to be more prepared for what was to come." So you can see, my friends, that even as we are, they do not forget to send us a knowledge of what their surroundings are. Every effort of theirs is only for our betterment, trying in their way to guide us not only to a better knowledge of our own lives and conditions, but also of theirs. If nature should forget to produce her part where would we, as a people, be in a short time? But as you know, all things are provided for, and if we do not get what we want, it may be because our spirit loved ones do not think it best for us to have it. The trials of this life are only the purifying crucible we must pass through to make us understand our condition, and when all seems darkness and gloom, we are only coming to the purer light and condition of our real life.

And, if those we mourn as dead, live and love us beyond the shadows, we should not be content with bare facts; the more thoroughly we are convinced, the more eagerly should we avail ourselves of every opportunity to converse and receive messages. Through messages, they teach us that after death there is an immortal state, blissful, enjoyable for those who have led a good life on this earth, but dark, gloomy, abysmal for those whose lives were stained.

Are you going to live a true life, or are you going to live a life of mockery? Will you live for Truth and Knowledge, or will you live a false life in the face of all sacred Truths and Principles as laid down? Will you live for a future life, or will you only live for the present? Will you live for our fellow man and woman, or will you live for mere selfish gain, ignoring all pretenses to goodness only to find after years of fad and fashion your life laid bare on the rotten shore of discord and discontent? Your answer and the faithful toil of abiding by your choice – dear reader – seals for you the future fate which all must meet, each one for himself. The Keeper can't be bribed. He doesn't pay or receive with gold but with Love.

Believe in the Golden Rule, "Whatsoever ye would that others should do unto you, do ye also unto them." Analyze your own character, and know you are above reproach, then practise the above and your lives will be in the care of the higher spirit powers. Don't give up in despair; remember that they will help you when you need help, providing you are deserving of it. In closing, I hope this small publication and others that will follow will touch some heart that is looking for peace and comfort from the spirit side and help guide them in some manner so that all will be found in the knowledge of a happy future and belief in the Great Spirit.

Sometime not far in the future
Where the evening shadows play,
You'll watch the beautiful sunset
And the power of sin fade away.

And as you sit in the twilight
Dreaming of youthful hours,
The angels will come from heaven
And strew your path with flowers.

But soon the glorious sunrise
Will illuminate your soul,
And angels will come from heaven
To gather you into the fold.

# E. Pauline Johnson (Tekahionwake, Double Wampum; Mohawk, 1861–1913)

*Like her counterparts Narcissa Owen and Alice Callahan, Emily Pauline Johnson enjoyed a privileged upbringing. Born at Chiefswood, her family's spacious home on the Grand River Reservation of the Six Nations, near Brantford, Ontario, Johnson was educated in English literary traditions, and especially in the English Romantics, by her mother, Emily Susanna Howells. Her father, George Henry Martin Johnson, was a well-known chief of the Mohawks who spent his life in service to his people, serving as a mediator between Mohawks and whites and attempting to prevent the illegal trade in alcohol on the reservation. George was also a talented orator, like his own father, John "Smoke" Johnson (Sakayengwaraton, "Disappearing Mist"), who was a hero in the War of 1812 and an important formative influence on Pauline.*

*After her father's death in 1884, probably as the result of injuries incurred many years earlier from a gang of alcohol traffickers, Johnson's life changed radically. She, her mother, and her sister could no longer afford to remain at Chiefswood and, like many nineteenth-century women writers, Johnson turned to writing for income. Her upbringing as a genteel middle-class woman, combined with her oratorical talents, became useful when she developed a career as a platform performer in Canada, the United States, and abroad, beginning in 1892. Performing the Indian portion of her program in a fringed buckskin dress that she had designed, Johnson, like Sarah Winnemucca and Zitkala-Ša, took advantage of white audiences' desire for the exotic, becoming "The Mohawk Princess" and calling upon the image of the noble savage. The second half of Johnson's program counteracted cultural stereotypes, as she appeared in an evening gown. This ability to cross cultures was something of which Johnson was very proud, and it served her well in her travel in London society in 1894 and throughout her life.*

*Although stage performances proved to be the most reliable source of income, poetry was a valued part of her work. In 1895 she published* The White Wampum, *a collection of thirty-six poems that ranged widely in subject and form, including both traditionally romantic works, dramatic Indian poems, and pre-modern nature lyrics. The selections included here reflect the diversity of this collection,* Canadian Born (1903), *and* Flint and Feather (1912), *which brought together work from the first two volumes with later materials. Like Zitkala-Ša and Ora Eddleman Reed, Johnson wrote effectively in many genres. "As It Was in the Beginning" translates into fictional terms the clash often occurring between white and Indian cultures; Johnson shows the hypocrisy of so-called Christians as she gives us a complex and resonant portrait of Esther's movement from "savage" to "civilized" and back due to the "savage" betrayal of her white, Christian mentor, Father Paul. "The Envoy Extraordinary" shows Johnson's playful side, while her boy's stories reveal her ability to write adventure stories, twenty-one of which were later collected in* The Shagganappi (1913), *that combine strong moral messages with ethnographic materials on several tribes. Betrayal and constancy are repeated themes that emerge in both her adult and "children's" fiction, perhaps in part because of her broken engagement in 1898 to Charles Robert Lumley*

*Drayton, whose parents opposed his marriage to a mixed-blood woman performer. This disappointment, combined with the loss of her mother in 1898 and the advantage taken by her manager, Charles Wuerz, made these years around the turn of the century difficult, as she continued to tour and perform in the United States, Canada, and London.*

*Among her most interesting works are her stories collected in* Legends of Vancouver (1911), *which interpret narratives gathered from several sources, but principally from a Squamish man, Chief Joe Capilano, whom she met in London in 1906. Revealing a poetic style and creating an intimacy between reader and writer, these stories are among her most compelling. One of the writers in this anthology who has received the most critical attention, Johnson's work combines elements of sentimentalism, romance, nature writing, adventure writing, and protest fiction in complex ways that we are still in the process of understanding. Johnson retired from performing in 1908; settling in Vancouver, she continued to write and publish. After a battle with cancer, she died there in 1913.*

## Bibliography


### Primary

*Canadian Born*. Morang, 1903.
*Flint and Feather*. Musson, 1912.
*Legends of Vancouver*. McClelland, 1911.
*The Moccasin Maker*. Ryerson, 1913. Rpt. Arizona, 1987, ed. Ruoff.
*The Shagganappi*. Briggs, 1913.

### Secondary

Gerson, Carole. " 'The Most Canadian of All Canadian Poets': Pauline Johnson and the Construction of a National Identity." *Canadian Literature* 158 (1998): 90–107.

Hoefel, Roseanne. "Writing, Performance, Activism: Zitkala-Ša and Pauline Johnson." In *Native American Women in Literature and Culture*. Ed. Susan Castillo and Victor M. P. Da Rosa. Fernando Pessoa, 1997.

Keller, Betty. *Pauline: A Biography of Pauline Johnson*. Douglas & McIntyre, 1981.

Lyon, George W. "Pauline Johnson: A Reconsideration." *Studies in Canadian Literature/Etudes en Littérature Canadienne* 15:2 (1990): 136–59.

Payne, James Robert. "E. Pauline Johnson." In *Native American Women: A Biographical Dictionary*. Ed. Gretchen Bataille. Garland, 1993.

Ruoff, A. LaVonne Brown. "E. Pauline Johnson (Tekahionwake)." In *Dictionary of Literary Biography*. Vol. 175. Ed. Kenneth M. Roemer. Gale, 1997. 131–6.

——. "Early Native American Women Authors: Jane Johnston Schoolcraft, Sarah Winnemucca, S. Alice Callahan, E. Pauline Johnson, and Zitkala-Ša." In *Nineteenth-Century American Women Writers: A Critical Reader*. Ed. Karen L. Kilcup. Blackwell, 1998. 81–111.

——. "Justice for Indians and Women: The Protest Fiction of Alice Callahan and Pauline Johnson." *World Literature Today* 66:2 (1992): 249–55.

Van Steen, Marcus, ed. *Pauline Johnson: Her Life and Work*. Hodder and Stoughton, 1965.

# Poetry

## From *Flint and Feather* (1912)

### CANADA

(Acrostic)

Crown of her, young Vancouver; crest of her, old Quebec;
Atlantic and far Pacific sweeping her, keel to deck.
North of her, ice and arctics; southward a rival's stealth;
Aloft, her Empire's pennant; below, her nation's wealth.
Daughter of men and markets, bearing within her hold,
Appraised at highest value, cargoes of grain and gold.

### THE CATTLE THIEF

They were coming across the prairie, they were galloping hard and fast;
For the eyes of those desperate riders had sighted their man at last –
Sighted him off to Eastward, where the Cree encampment lay,
Where the cotton woods fringed the river, miles and miles away.
Mistake him? Never! Mistake him? the famous Eagle Chief!
That terror to all the settlers, that desperate Cattle Thief –
That monstrous, fearless Indian, who lorded it over the plain,
Who thieved and raided, and scouted, who rode like a hurricane!
But they've tracked him across the prairie; they've followed him hard and fast;
For those desperate English settlers have sighted their man at last.

Up they wheeled to the tepees, all their British blood aflame,
Bent on bullets and bloodshed, bent on bringing down their game;
But they searched in vain for the Cattle Thief: that lion had left his lair,
And they cursed like a troop of demons – for the women alone were there.
"The sneaking Indian coward," they hissed; "he hides while yet he can;
He'll come in the night for the cattle, but he's scared to face a *man*."
"Never!" and up from the cotton woods rang the voice of Eagle Chief;
And right out into the open stepped, unarmed, the Cattle Thief.
Was that the game they had coveted? Scarce fifty years had rolled
Over that fleshless, hungry frame, starved to the bone and old;
Over that wrinkled, tawny skin, unfed by the warmth of blood.
Over those hungry, hollow eyes that glared for the sight of food.

He turned, like a hunted lion, "I know not fear," said he;
And the words outleapt from his shrunken lips in the language of the Cree.
"I'll fight you, white-skins, one by one, till I kill you *all*," he said;
But the threat was scarcely uttered, ere a dozen balls of lead
Whizzed through the air about him like a shower of metal rain,
And the gaunt old Indian Cattle Thief dropped dead on the open plain.
And that band of cursing settlers gave one triumphant yell,

And rushed like a pack of demons on the body that writhed and fell.
"Cut the fiend up into inches, throw his carcass on the plain;
Let the wolves eat the cursed Indian, he'd have treated us the same."
A dozen hands responded, a dozen knives gleamed high,
But the first stroke was arrested by a woman's strange, wild cry.
And out into the open, with a courage past belief,
She dashed, and spread her blanket o'er the corpse of the Cattle Thief;
And the words outleapt from her shrunken lips in the language of the Cree,
If you mean to touch that body, you must cut your way through *me*."
And that band of cursing settlers dropped backward one by one,
For they knew that an Indian woman roused, was a woman to let alone.
And then she raved in a frenzy that they scarcely understood,
Raved of the wrongs she had suffered since her earliest babyhood:
"Stand back, stand back, you white-skins, touch that dead man to your shame;
You have stolen my father's spirit, but his body I only claim.
You have killed him, but you shall not dare to touch him now he's dead.
You have cursed, and called him a Cattle Thief, though you robbed him first of bread –
Robbed him and robbed my people – look there, at that shrunken face,
Starved with hunger, we owe to you and your race.
What have you left to us of land, what have you left of game,
What have you brought but evil, and curses since you came?
How have you paid us for our game? how paid us for our land?
By a *book*, to save our souls from the sins *you* brought in your other hand.
Go back with your new religion, we never have understood
Your robbing an Indian's *body*, and mocking his *soul* with food.
Go back with your new religion, and find – if find you can –
The *honest* man you have ever made from out a *starving* man.
You say your cattle are not ours, your meat is not our meat;
When *you* pay for the land you live in, *we'll* pay for the meat we eat.
Give back our land and our country, give back our herds of game;
Give back the furs and the forests that were ours before you came;
Give back the peace and the plenty. Then come with your new belief,
And blame, if you dare, the hunger that *drove* him to be a thief."

## The Corn Husker

Hard by the Indian lodges, where the bush
  Breaks in a clearing, through ill-fashioned fields,
She comes to labour, when the first still hush
  Of autumn follows large and recent yields.

Age in her fingers, hunger in her face,
  Her shoulders stooped with weight of work and years,
But rich in tawny colouring of her race,
  She comes a-field to strip the purple ears.

And all her thoughts are with the days gone by,
  Ere might's injustice banished from their lands
Her people, that to-day unheeded lie,
  Like the dead husks that rustle through her hands.

## Erie Waters

A dash of yellow sand,
Wind-scattered and sun-tanned;
Some waves that curl and cream along the margin of the strand;
And, creeping close to these
Long shores that lounge at ease,
Old Erie rocks and ripples to a fresh sou'-western breeze.

A sky of blue and grey;
Some stormy clouds that play
At scurrying up with ragged edge, then laughing blow away,
Just leaving in their trail
Some snatches of a gale;
To whistling summer winds we lift a single daring sail.

O! wind so sweet and swift,
O! danger-freighted gift
Bestowed on Erie with her waves that foam and fall and lift,
We laugh in your wild face,
And break into a race
With flying clouds and tossing gulls that weave and interlace.

## The Idlers

The sun's red pulses beat,
Full prodigal of heat,
Full lavish of its lustre unrepressed;
But we have drifted far
From where his kisses are,
And in this landward-lying shade we let our paddles rest.

The river, deep and still,
The maple-mantled hill,
The little yellow beach whereon we lie,
The puffs of heated breeze,
All sweetly whisper – These
Are days that only come in a Canadian July.

So, silently we two
Lounge in our still canoe,
Nor fate, nor fortune matters to us now:
So long as we alone
May call this dream our own,
The breeze may die, the sail may droop, we care not when or how.

Against the thwart, near by,
Inactively, you lie,
And all too near my arm your temple bends,
Your indolently crude,
Abandoned attitude,
Is one of ease and art, in which a perfect languor blends.

Your costume, loose and light,
Leaves unconcealed your might
Of muscle, half suspected, half defined;
And falling well aside,
Your vesture opens wide,
Above your splendid sunburnt throat that pulses unconfined.

With easy unreserve,
Across the gunwale's curve,
Your arm superb is lying, brown and bare;
Your hand just touches mine
With import firm and fine,
(I kiss the very wind that blows about your tumbled hair).

Ah! Dear, I am unwise
In echoing your eyes
Whene'er they leave their far-off gaze, and turn
To melt and blur my sight;
For every other light
Is servile to your cloud-grey eyes, wherein cloud shadows burn.

But once the silence breaks,
But once your ardour wakes
To works that humanized this lotus-land;
So perfect and complete
Those burning words and sweet,
So perfect is the single kiss your lips lay on my hand.

The paddles lie disused,
The fitful breeze abused,
Has dropped to slumber, with no after-blow;
And hearts will pay the cost,
For you and I have lost
More than the homeward blowing wind that died an hour ago.

## In the Shadows

I am sailing to the leeward,
Where the current runs to seaward
        Soft and slow,
Where the sleeping river grasses
Brush my paddle as it passes
        To and fro.

On the shore the heat is shaking
All the golden sands awaking
        In the cove;
And the quaint sand-piper, winging
O'er the shallows, ceases singing
        When I move.

On the water's idle pillow
Sleeps the overhanging willow,
    Green and cool;
Where the rushes lift their burnished
Oval heads from out the tarnished
    Emerald pool.

Where the very silence slumbers,
Water lilies grow in numbers,
    Pure and pale;
All the morning they have rested,
Amber crowned, and pearly crested,
    Fair and frail.

Here, impossible romances,
Indefinable sweet fancies,
    Cluster round;
But they do not mar the sweetness
Of this still September fleetness
    With a sound.

I can scarce discern the meeting
Of the shore and stream retreating,
    So remote;
For the laggard river, dozing,
Only wakes from its reposing
    Where I float.

Where the river mists are rising,
All the foliage baptizing
    With their spray;
There the sun gleams far and faintly,
With a shadow soft and saintly,
    In its ray.

And the perfume of some burning
Far-off brushwood, ever turning
    To exhale
All its smoky fragrance dying,
In the arms of evening lying,
    Where I sail.

My canoe is growing lazy,
In the atmosphere so hazy,
    While I dream;
Half in slumber I am guiding,
Eastward indistinctly gliding
    Down the stream.

## The Indian Corn Planter

He needs must leave the trapping and the chase,
For mating game his arrows ne'er despoil,
And from the hunter's heaven turn his face,
To wring some promise from the dormant soil.

He needs must leave the lodge that wintered him,
The enervating fires, the blanket bed –
The women's dulcet voices, for the grim
Realities of labouring for bread.

So goes he forth beneath the planter's moon
With sack of seed that pledges large increase,
His simple pagan faith knows night and noon,
Heat, cold, seedtime and harvest shall not cease.

And yielding to his needs, this honest sod,
Brown as the hand that tills it, moist with rain,
Teeming with ripe fulfilment, true as God,
With fostering richness, mothers every grain.

## Joe

### An Etching

A meadow brown; across the yonder edge
A zigzag fence is ambling; here a wedge
Of underbrush has cleft its course in twain,
Till where beyond it staggers up again;
The long, grey rails stretch in a broken line
Their ragged length of rough, split forest pine,
And in their zigzag tottering have reeled
In drunken efforts to enclose the field,
Which carries on its breast, September born,
A patch of rustling, yellow, Indian corn.
Beyond its shriveled tassels, perched upon
The topmost rail, sits Joe, the settler's son,
A little semi-savage boy of nine.
Now dozing in the warmth of Nature's wine,
His face the sun has tampered with, and wrought,
By heated kisses, mischief, and has brought
Some vagrant freckles, while from here and there
A few wild locks of vagabond brown hair
Escape the old straw hat the sun looks through,
And blinks to meet his Irish eyes of blue.
Barefooted, innocent of coat or vest,
His grey checked shirt unbuttoned at his chest,
Both hardy hands within their usual nest–
His breeches pockets – so, he waits to rest
His little fingers, somewhat tired and worn,
That all day long were husking Indian corn.

His drowsy lids snap at some trivial sound,
With lazy yawns he slips towards the ground,
Then with an idle whistle lifts his load
And shambles home along the country road
That stretches on, fringed out with stumps and weeds,
And finally unto the backwoods leads,
Where forests wait with giant trunk and bough
The axe of pioneer, the settler's plough.

## Low Tide at St. Andrews

(New Brunswick)

The long red flats stretch open to the sky,
Breathing their moisture on the August air.
The seaweeds cling with flesh-like fingers where
The rocks give shelter that the sands deny;
And wrapped in all her summer harmonies
St. Andrews sleeps beside her sleeping seas.

The far-off shores swim blue and indistinct,
Like half-lost memories of some old dream.
The listless waves that catch each sunny gleam
Are idling up the waterways land-linked,
And, yellowing along the harbour's breast,
The light is leaping shoreward from the west,

And naked-footed children, tripping down,
Light with young laughter, daily come at eve
To gather dulse and sea clams and then heave
Their loads, returning laden to the town,
Leaving a strange grey silence when they go, –
The silence of the sands when tides are low.

## Lullaby of the Iroquois

Little brown baby-bird, lapped in your nest
          Wrapped in your nest,
          Strapped in your nest,
Your straight little cradle-board rocks you to rest;
          Its hands are your nest;
          Its bands are your nest;
It swings from the down-bending branch of the oak;
You watch the camp flame, and the curling grey smoke;
But, oh, for your pretty black eyes sleep is best, –
Little brown baby of mine, go to rest.

Little brown baby-bird swinging to sleep,
          Winging to sleep,
          Singing to sleep,
Your wonder-black eyes that so wide open keep,

Shielding their sleep,
Unyielding to sleep,
The heron is homing, the plover is still,
The night-owl calls from his haunt on the hill,
Afar the fox barks, afar the stars peep, –
Little brown baby of mine, go to sleep.

## MARSHLANDS

A thin wet sky, that yellows at the rim,
And meets with sun-lost lip the marsh's brim.

The pools low-lying, dank with moss and mould,
Glint through their mildews like large cups of gold.

Among the wild rice in the still lagoon,
In monotone the lizard shrills his tune.

The wild goose, homing, seeks a sheltering,
Where rushes grow, and oozing lichens cling.

Late cranes with heavy wing, and lazy flight,
Sail up the silence with the nearing night.

And like a spirit, swathed in some soft veil,
Steals twilight and its shadows o'er the swale,

Hushed lie the sedges, and the vapours creep,
Thick, grey and humid, while the marshes sleep.

## PENSEROSO

Soulless is all humanity to me
To-night. My keenest longing is to be
Alone, alone with God's grey earth that seems
Pulse of my pulse and consort of my dreams.

To-night my soul desires no fellowship,
Or fellow-being; crave I but to slip
Thro' space on space, till flesh no more can bind,
And I may quit for aye my fellow kind.

Let me but feel athwart my cheek the last
Of whipping wind, but hear the torrent dash
Adown the mountain steep, 'twere more my choice
Than touch of human hand, than human voice.

Let me but wander on the shore night-stilled,
Drinking its darkness till my soul is filled;
The breathing of the salt sea on my hair,
My outstretched hands but grasping empty air.

Let me but feel the pulse of Nature's soul
Athrob on mine, let seas and thunders roll
O'er night and me; sands whirl; winds, waters beat;
For God's grey earth has no cheap counterfeit.

## The Quill Worker

Plains, plains, and the prairie land which the sunlight floods and fills,
To the North the open country, southward the Cyprus Hills;
Never a bit of woodland, never a rill that flows,
Only a stretch of cactus beds, and the wild, sweet prairie rose;
Never a habitation, save where in the far south-west
A solitary teepee lifts its solitary crest,
Where Neykia in the doorway, crouched in the red sunshine,
Broiders her buckskin mantle with the quills of the porcupine.

Neykia, the Sioux chief's daughter, she with the foot that flies,
She with the hair of midnight and the wondrous midnight eyes,
She with the deft brown fingers, she with the soft, slow smile,
She with the voice of velvet and the thoughts that dream the while –
"Whence come the vague to-morrows? Where do the yesters fly?
What is beyond the border of the prairie and the sky?
Does the maid in the Land of Morning sit in the red sunshine,
Broidering her buckskin mantle with the quills of the porcupine?"

So Neykia, in the westland, wonders and works away,
Far from the fret and folly of the "Land of Waking Day."
And many the pale-faced trader who stops at the teepee door
For a smile from the sweet, shy worker, and a sigh when the hour is o'er.
For they know of a young red hunter who oftentimes has stayed
To rest and smoke with her father, tho' his eyes were on the maid;
And the moons will not be many ere she in the red sunshine
Will broider his buckskin mantle with the quills of the porcupine.

## Shadow River

### Muskoka

A stream of tender gladness,
Of filmy sun, and opal tinted skies;
Of warm midsummer air that lightly lies
In mystic rings,
Where softly swings
The music of a thousand wings
That almost tones to sadness.

Midway 'twixt earth and heaven,
A bubble in the pearly air, I seem
To float upon the sapphire floor, a dream
Of clouds of snow,
Above, below,
Drift with my drifting, dim and slow,
As twilight drifts to even.

The little fern-leaf, bending
Upon the brink, its green reflection greets,
And kisses soft the shadow that it meets
With touch so fine,
The border line
The keenest vision can't define;
So perfect is the blending.

The far, fir trees that cover
The brownish hills with needles green and gold,
The arching elms o'erhead, vinegrown and old,
Repictured are
Beneath me far,
Where not a ripple moves to mar
Shades underneath, or over.

Mine is the undertone;
The beauty, strength, and power of the land
Will never stir or bend at my command;
But all the shade
Is marred or made,
If I but dip my paddle blade;
And it is mine alone.

O! pathless world of seeming!
O! pathless life of mine whose deep ideal
Is more my own than ever was the real.
For others Fame
And Love's red flame,
And yellow gold: I only claim
The shadows and the dreaming.

## Thistle-Down

Beyond a ridge of pine with russet tips
The west lifts to the sun her longing lips,

Her blushes stain with gold and garnet dye
The shore, the river and the wide far sky;

Like floods of wine the waters filter through
The reeds that brush our indolent canoe.

I beach the bow where sands in shadows lie;
You hold my hand a space, then speak good-bye.

Upwinds your pathway through the yellow plumes
Of goldenrod, profuse in August blooms

And o'er its tossing sprays you toss a kiss;
A moment more, and I see only this –

The idle paddle you so lately held,
The empty bow your pliant wrist propelled,

Some thistles purpling into violet,
Their blossoms with a thousand thorns afret,

And like a cobweb, shadowy and grey,
Far floats their down – far drifts my dream away.

## Under Canvas

### In Muskoka

Lichens of green and grey on every side;
And green and grey the rocks beneath our feet;
Above our heads the canvas stretching wide;
And over all, enchantment rare and sweet.

Fair Rosseau slumbers in an atmosphere
That kisses her to passionless soft dreams.
O! joy of living we have found thee here,
And life lacks nothing, so complete it seems.

The velvet air, stirred by some elfin wings,
Comes swinging up the waters and then stills
Its voice so low that floating by it sings
Like distant harps among the distant hills.

Across the lake the rugged islands lie,
Fir-crowned and grim; and further in the view
Some shadows seeming swung 'twixt cloud and sky,
Are countless shores, a symphony of blue.

Some northern sorceress, when day is done,
Hovers where cliffs uplift their gaunt grey steeps,
Bewitching to vermilion Rosseau's sun,
That in a liquid mass of rubies sleeps.

The scent of burning leaves, the camp-fire's blaze,
The great logs cracking in the brilliant flame,
The groups grotesque, on which the firelight plays,
Are pictures which Muskoka twilights frame.

And Night, star-crested, wanders up the mere
With opiates for idleness to quaff,
And while she ministers, far off I hear
The owl's uncanny cry, the wind loon's laugh.

## The Wolf

Like a grey shadow lurking in the light,
He ventures forth along the edge of night;

With silent foot he scouts the coulie's rim
And scents the carrion awaiting him.
His savage eyeballs lurid with a flare
Seen but in unfed beasts which leave their lair
To wrangle with their fellows for a meal
Of bones ill-covered. Sets he forth to steal,
To search and snarl and forage hungrily;
A worthless prairie vagabond is he.
Luckless the settler's heifer which astray
Falls to his fangs and violence a prey;
Useless her blatant calling when his teeth
Are fast upon her quivering flank – beneath
His fell voracity she falls and dies
With inarticulate and piteous cries,
Unheard, unheeded in the barren waste,
To be devoured with savage greed and haste.
Up the horizon once again he prowls
And far across its desolation howls;
Sneaking and satisfied his lair he gains
And leaves her bones to bleach upon the plains.

## WOLVERINE

"Yes, sir, it's quite a story, though you won't believe it's true,
But such things happened often when I lived beyond the Soo."
And the trapper tilted back his chair and filled his pipe anew.

"I ain't thought of it neither fer this many 'n many a day,
Although it used to haunt me in the years that's slid away,
The years I spent a-trappin' for the good old Hudson's Bay.

"Wild? You bet, 'twas wild then, an' few an far between
The squatters' shacks, for whites was scarce as furs when things is green,
An' only reds an' 'Hudson's' men was all the folk I seen.

"No. Them old Indyans ain't so bad, not if you treat 'em square.
Why, I lived in amongst 'em all the winters I was there,
An' I never lost a copper, an' I never lost a hair.

"But I'd have lost my life the time that you've heard tell about:
I don't think I'd be settin' here, but dead beyond a doubt,
If that there Indyan 'Wolverine' jest hadn't helped me out.

"'Twas freshet time, 'way back, as long as sixty-six or eight,
An' I was comin' to the Post that year a kind of late,
For beaver had been plentiful, and trappin' had been great.

"One day I had been settin' traps along a bit of wood,
An' night was catchin' up to me jest faster 'an it should,
When all at once I heard a sound that curdled up my blood.

"It was the howl of famished wolves – I didn't stop to think
But jest lit out across for home as quick as you could wink,
But when I reached the river's edge I brought up at the brink.

"That mornin' I had crossed the stream straight on a sheet of ice
An' now, God help me! There it was, churned up an' cracked to dice,
The flood went boiling past – I stood like one shut in a vice.

"No way ahead, no path aback, trapped like a rat ashore,
With naught but death to follow, and with naught but dead afore;
The howl of hungry wolves aback – ahead, the torrent's roar.

"An' then – a voice, an Indyan voice, that called out clear and clean,
'Take Indyan's horse, I run like deer, wolf can't catch Wolverine.'
I says, 'Thank Heaven.' There stood the chief I'd nicknamed Wolverine.

"I lept on that there horse, an' then jest like a coward fled,
An' left that Indyan standin' there alone, as good as dead,
With the wolves a-howlin' at his back, the swollen stream ahead.

"I don't know how them Indyans dodge from death the way they do,
You won't believe it, sir, but what I'm tellin' you is true,
But that there chap was 'round next day as sound as me or you.

"He came to get his horse, but not a cent he'd take from me.
Yes, sir, you're right, the Indyans now ain't like they used to be;
We've got 'em sharpened up a bit an' *now* they'll take a fee.

"No, sir, you're wrong, they ain't no 'dogs.' I'm not through tellin' yet;
You'll take that name right back again, or else jest out you get!
You'll take that name right back when you hear all this yarn, I bet.

"It happened that same autumn, when some Whites was comin' in,
I heard the old Red River carts a-kickin' up a din,
So I went over to their camp to see an English skin.

"They said, 'They'd had an awful scare from Injuns,' an' they swore
That savages had come around the very night before
A-brandishing their tomahawks an' painted up for war.

"But when their plucky Englishmen had put a bit of lead
Right through the heart of one of them, an' rolled him over, dead,
The other cowards said that they had come on peace instead.

" 'That they (the Whites) had lost some stores, from off their little pack,
An' that the Red they peppered dead had followed up their track,
Because he'd found the packages an' came *to give them back.'*

" 'Oh!' they said, 'they were quite sorry, but it wasn't like as if
They had killed a decent Whiteman by mistake or in a tiff,
It was only some old Injun dog that lay there stark an' stiff.'

"I said, 'You are the meanest dogs that ever yet I seen,'
Then I rolled the body over as it lay out on the green;
I peered into the face – My God! 'twas poor old Wolverine."

## From *American Canoe Club Year Book* (1893)

### THE PORTAGE

Now for a careful beach atween the towering
    Grey rocks a'yawn like tombs,
Aft lies the lake, blurred by our paddle's scouring,
    Forward the Portage looms,
        Beyond the fastnesses, a river creeping,
        Then – rapids leaping.

Now for a bracing up of stalwart shoulders
    And now a load to lift;
An uphill tramp through tangled briars and boulders,
    The irksome weight to shift,
        And through it all, the far incessant calling
        Of waters falling.

What of the heat? the toil? the sun's red glaring?
    The blistered fingers, too?
What of the muscles teased and strained in bearing
    The fearless fleet canoe?
        Brief is the labour, then the wild sweet laughter
        Of rapids after.

# Fiction and Prose Nonfiction

## From *The Moccasin Maker* (1913)

### CATHARINE OF THE "CROW'S NEST"

The great transcontinental railway had been in running order for years before the managers thereof decided to build a second line across the Rocky Mountains. But "passes" are few and far between in those gigantic fastnesses, and the fearless explorers, followed by the equally fearless surveyors, were many a toilsome month conquering the heights, depths and dangers of the "Crow's Nest Pass."

Eastward stretched the gloriously fertile plains of southern "Sunny Alberta," westward lay the limpid blue of the vast and indescribably beautiful Kootenay Lakes, but between these two arose a barrier of miles and miles of granite and stone and rock, over and through which a railway must be constructed. Tunnels, bridges, grades must be bored, built and blasted out. It was the work of science, endurance and indomitable courage. The summers in the cañons were seething hot, the winters in the mountains perishingly cold, with apparently inexhaustible snow clouds circling forever about the rugged peaks – snows in which many a good, honest laborer was lost until the eagles and vultures came with the April thaws, and wheeled slowly above the pulseless sleeper, if indeed the wolves and mountain lions had permitted him to lie thus long unmolested. Those were rough and rugged days, through which equally rough and rugged men served and suffered to find foundations whereon to lay those two threads of steel that now cling like a cobweb to the walls of the wonderful "gap" known as Crow's Nest Pass.

Work progressed steadily, and before winter set in construction camps were built far into "the gap," the furthermost one being close to the base of a majestic mountain, which was also named "The Crow's Nest." It arose beyond the camp with almost overwhelming immensity. Dense forests of Douglas fir and bull pines shouldered their way up one-third of its height, but above the timber line the shaggy, bald rock reared itself thousands of feet skyward, desolate, austere and deserted by all living things; not even the sure-footed mountain goat travelled up those frowning, precipitous heights; no bird rested its wing in that frozen altitude. The mountain arose, distinct, alone, isolated, the most imperial monarch of all that regal Pass.

The construction gang called it "Old Baldy," for after working some months around its base, it began to grow into their lives. Not so, however, with the head engineer from Montreal, who regarded it always with baleful eye, and half laughingly, half seriously, called it his "Jonah."

"Not a thing has gone right since we worked in sight of that old monster" he was heard to say frequently; and it did seem as if there were some truth in it. There had been deaths, accidents and illness among the men. Once, owing to transportation difficulties, the rations were short for days, and the men were in rebellious spirit in consequence. Twice whiskey had been smuggled in, to the utter demoralization of the camp; and one morning, as a last straw, "Cookee" had nearly severed his left hand from his arm with a meat axe. Young Wingate, the head engineer, and Mr. Brown, the foreman, took counsel together. For the three meals of that day they tried three different men out of the gang as "cookees." No one could eat the atrocious food they manufactured. Then Brown bethought himself. "There's an Indian woman living up the cañon that can cook like a French chef," he announced, after a day of unspeakable gnawing beneath his belt. "How about getting her? I've tasted pork and beans at her shack, and flapjacks, and – "

"Get her! get her!" clamored Wingate. "Even if she poisons us, it's better than starving. I'll ride over to-night and offer her big wages."

"How about her staying here?" asked Brown. "The boys are pretty rough and lawless at times, you know."

"Get the axe men to build her a good, roomy shack – the best logs in the place. We'll give her a lock and key for it, and you, Brown, report the very first incivility to her that you hear of," said Wingate, crisply.

That evening Mr. Wingate himself rode over to the cañon; it was a good mile, and the trail was rough in the extreme. He did not dismount when he reached the lonely log lodge, but rapping on the door with the butt of his quirt, he awaited its opening. There was some slight stirring about inside before this occurred; then the door slowly opened, and she stood before him – a rather tall woman, clad in buckskin garments, with a rug made of coyote skins about her shoulders; she wore the beaded leggings and moccasins of her race, and her hair, jet black, hung in ragged plaits about her dark face, from which mournful eyes looked out at the young Montrealer.

Yes, she would go for the wages he offered, she said in halting English; she would come to-morrow at daybreak; she would cook their breakfast.

"Better come to-night," he urged. "The men get down the grade to work very early; breakfast must be on time."

"I be on time," she replied. "I sleep here this night, every night. I not sleep in camp."

Then he told her of the shack he had ordered, and that was even now being built.

She shook her head. "I sleep here every night," she reiterated.

Wingate had met many Indians in his time, so dropped the subject, knowing well that persuasion or argument would be utterly useless.

"All right," he said; " you must do as you like; only remember, an early breakfast to-morrow."

"I 'member," she replied.

He had ridden some twenty yards, when he turned to call back: "Oh, what's your name, please?"

"Catharine," she answered, simply.

"Thank you," he said, and, touching his hat lightly, rode down towards the cañon. Just as he was dipping over its rim he looked back. She was still standing in the doorway, and above and about her were the purple shadows, the awful solitude, of Crow's Nest Mountain.

* * *

Catharine had been cooking at the camp for weeks. The meals were good, the men respected her, and she went her way to and from her shack at the cañon as regularly as the world went around. The autumn slipped by, and the nipping frosts of early winter and the depths of early snows were already daily occurrences. The big group of solid log shacks that formed the construction camp were all made weather-tight against the long mountain winter. Trails were beginning to be blocked, streams to freeze, and "Old Baldy" already wore a canopy of snow that reached down to the timber line.

"Catharine," spoke young Wingate, one morning, when the clouds hung low and a soft snow fell, packing heavily on the selfsame snows of the previous night, "you had better make up your mind to occupy the shack here. You won't be able to go to your home much longer now at night; it gets dark so early, and the snows are too heavy."

"I go home at night," she repeated.

"But you can't all winter," he exclaimed. "If there was one single horse we could spare from the grade work, I'd see you got it for your journeys, but there isn't. We're terribly short now; every animal in the Pass is overworked as it is. You'd better not try going home any more."

"I go home at night," she repeated.

Wingate frowned impatiently; then in afterthought he smiled. "All right, Catharine," he said, "but I warn you. You'll have a search-party out after you some dark morning, and you know it won't be pleasant to be lost in the snows up that cañon."

"But I go home, night-time," she persisted, and that ended the controversy.

But the catastrophe he predicted was inevitable. Morning after morning he would open the door of the shack he occupied with the other officials, and, looking up the white wastes through the gray-blue dawn, he would watch the distances with an anxiety that meant more than a consideration for his breakfast. The woman interested him. She was so silent, so capable, so stubborn. What was behind all this strength of character? What had given that depth of mournfulness to her eyes? Often he had surprised her watching him, with an odd longing in her face; it was something of the expression he could remember his mother wore when she looked at him long, long ago. It was a vague, haunting look that always brought back the one great tragedy of his life – a tragedy he was even now working night and day at his chosen profession to obliterate from his memory, lest he should be forever unmanned – forever a prey to melancholy.

He was still a young man, but when little more than a boy he had married, and for two years was transcendently happy. Then came the cry of "Kootenay Gold" ringing throughout Canada – of the untold wealth of Kootenay mines. Like thousands of others he followed the beckoning of that yellow finger, taking his young wife and baby daughter West with him. The little town of Nelson, crouching on its beautiful hills, its feet laved by the waters of Kootenay Lake, was then in its first robust, active infancy. Here he settled, going out alone on long prospecting expeditions; sometimes he was away a week, sometimes a month, with the lure of the gold forever in his veins, but the laughter of his child, the love of his wife, forever in his heart. Then – the day of that awful home-coming! For three weeks the fascination of searching for the golden pay-streak had held him in the mountains. No one could find him when it happened, and now all they could tell him was the story of an upturned canoe found drifting on the lake, of a woman's light summer shawl caught in the thwarts, of a child's little silken bonnet washed ashore.[1] The great-hearted men of the West had done their utmost in the search that followed. Miners, missionaries, prospectors, Indians, settlers, gamblers, outlaws, had one and all turned out, for they liked

[1] Fact [Johnson's note].

young Wingate, and they adored his loving wife and dainty child. But the search was useless. The wild shores of Kootenay Lake alone held the secret of their resting-place.

Young Wingate faced the East once more. There was but one thing to do with his life – work, *work,* WORK; and the harder, the more difficult, that work, the better. It was this very difficulty that made the engineering on the Crow's Nest Pass so attractive to him. So here he was building grades, blasting tunnels, with Catharine's mournful eyes following him daily, as if she divined something of that long-ago sorrow that had shadowed his almost boyish life.

He liked the woman, and his liking quickened his eye to her hardships, his ear to the hint of lagging weariness in her footsteps; so he was the first to notice it the morning she stumped into the cook-house, her feet bound up in furs, her face drawn in agony.

"Catharine," he exclaimed, "your feet have been frozen!"

She looked like a culprit, but answered: "Not much; I get lose in storm las' night."

"I thought this would happen," he said, indignantly. "After this you sleep here."

"I sleep home," she said, doggedly.

"I won't have it," he declared. "I'll cook for the men myself first."

"Allight," she replied. "You cookee; I go home – me."

That night there was a terrible storm. The wind howled down the throat of the Pass, and the snow fell like bales of sheep's wool, blanketing the trails and drifting into the railroad cuts until they attained their original level. But after she had cooked supper Catharine started for home as usual. The only unusual thing about it was that the next morning she did not return. It was Sunday, the men's day "off." Wingate ate no breakfast, but after swallowing some strong tea he turned to the foreman. "Mr. Brown, will you come with me to try and hunt up Catharine?" he asked.

"Yes, if we can get beyond the door," assented Brown. "But I doubt if we can make the cañon, sir."

"We'll have a try at it, anyway," said the young engineer. "I almost doubt myself if she made it last night."

"She's a stubborn woman," commented Brown.

"And has her own reasons for it, I suppose," replied Wingate. "But that has nothing to do with her being lost or frozen. If something had not happened I'm sure she would have come to-day, notwithstanding I scolded her yesterday, and told her I'd rather cook myself than let her run such risks. How will we go, Mr. Brown; horses or snowshoes?"

"Shoes," said the foreman decidedly. "That snow'll be above the middle of the biggest horse in the outfit."

So they set forth on their tramp up the slopes, peering right and left as they went for any indication of the absent woman. Wingate's old grief was knocking at his heart once more. A woman lost in the appalling vastness of this great Western land was entering into his life again. It took them a full hour to go that mile, although both were experts on the shoes, but as they reached the rim of the cañon they were rewarded by seeing a thin blue streak of smoke curling up from her lodge "chimney." Wingate sat down in the snows weakly. The relief had unmanned him.

"I didn't know how much I cared," he said, "until I knew she was safe. She looks at me as my mother used to; her eyes are like mother's, and I loved my mother."

It was a simple, direct speech, but Brown caught its pathos.

"She's a good woman," he blurted out, as they trudged along towards the shack. They knocked on the door. There was no reply. Then just as Wingate suggested forcing it in case she were ill and lying helpless within, a long, low call from the edge of the cañon startled them. They turned and had not followed the direction from which the sound came more than a few yards when they met her coming towards them on snowshoes; in her arms she bore a few faggots, and her face, though smileless, was very welcoming.

She opened the door, bidding them enter. It was quite warm inside, and the air of simple comfort derived from crude benches, tables and shelves, assured them that she had not suffered. Near the fire was drawn a rough home-built couch, and on it lay in heaped disorder a pile of gray blankets. As the two men warmed their hands at the grateful blaze, the blankets stirred. Then a small hand crept out and a small arm tossed the covers a little aside.

*"Catharine,"* exclaimed Wingate, "have you a child here?"

"Yes," she said simply.

"How long is it that you have had it here?" he demanded.

"Since before I work at your camp," she replied.

"Whew!" said the foreman, "I now understand why she came home nights."

"To think I never guessed it!" murmured Wingate. Then to Catharine: "Why didn't you bring it into camp and keep it there day and night with you, instead of taking these dangerous tramps night and morning?"

"It is a girl child," she answered.

"Well what of it?" he asked impatiently.

"Your camp no place for girl child," she replied, looking directly at him. "Your men they rough, they get whisky sometimes. They fight. They speak bad words, what you call *swear.* I not want her hear that. I not want her see whisky man."

"Oh, Brown!" said Wingate, turning to his companion. "What a reproach! What a reproach! Here our gang is – the vanguard of the highest civilization, but unfit for association with a little Indian child!"

Brown stood speechless, although in his rough, honest mind he was going over a list of those very "swears" she objected to, but they were mentally directed at the whole outfit of his ruffianly construction gang. He was silently swearing at them for their own shortcomings in that very thing.

The child on the couch stirred again. This time the firelight fell full across the little arm. Wingate stared at it, then his eyes widened. He looked at the woman then back at the bare arm. It was the arm of a *white* child.

"Catharine, was your husband *white?"* he asked, in a voice that betrayed anxiety.

"I got no husban'," she replied, somewhat defiantly.

"Then – " he began, but his voice faltered.

She came and stood between him and the couch. Something of the look of a she-panther came into her face, her figure, her attitude. Her eyes lost their mournfulness and blazed a black-red at him. Her whole body seemed ready to spring.

"You not touch the girl child!" she half snarled. "I not let you touch her; she *mine,* though I have no husban'!"

"I don't want to touch her, Catharine," he said gently, trying to pacify her. "Believe me, I don't want to touch her."

The woman's whole being changed. A thousand mother-lights gleamed from her eyes, a thousand measures of mother-love stormed at her heart. She stepped close, very close to him and laid her small brown hand on his, then drawing him nearer to her said: "Yes you *do* want to touch her; you not speak truth when you say 'no.' You *do* want to touch her!" With a rapid movement she flung back the blankets, then slipping her bare arm about him she bent his form until he was looking straight into the child's face – a face the living miniature of his own! His eyes, his hair, his small kindly mouth, his fair, perfect skin. He staggered erect.

"Catharine! what does it mean? What does it mean?" he cried hoarsely.

*"Your child – "* she half questioned, half affirmed.

"Mine? Mine?" he called, without human understanding in his voice. "Oh, Catharine! Where did you get her?"

"The shores of Kootenay Lake," she answered.

"Was – was – she *alone?"* he cried.

The woman looked away, slowly shaking her head, and her voice was very gentle as she replied: "No, she alive a little, but *the other,* whose arms 'round her, she not alive; my people, the Kootenay Indians, and I – we – we bury that other."

For a moment there was a speaking silence, then young Wingate, with the blessed realization that half his world had been saved for him, flung himself on his knees, and, with his arms locked about the little girl, was calling:

"Margie! Margie! Papa's little Margie girl! Do you remember papa? Oh, Margie! Do you? Do you?"

Something dawned in the child's eyes – something akin to a far-off memory. For a moment she looked wonderingly at him, then put her hand up to his forehead and gently pulled a lock of his fair hair that always curled there – an old trick of hers. Then she looked down at his vest pocket, slowly pulled out his watch and held it to her ear. The next minute her arms slipped round his neck.

"Papa," she said, "papa been away from Margie a long time."

Young Wingate was sobbing. He had not noticed that the big, rough foreman had gone out of the shack with tear-dimmed eyes, and had quietly closed the door behind him.

*   *   *

It was evening before Wingate got all the story from Catharine, for she was slow of speech, and found it hard to explain her feelings. But Brown, who had returned alone to the camp in the morning, now came back, packing an immense bundle of all the tinned delicacies he could find, which, truth to tell, were few. He knew some words of Kootenay, and led Catharine on to reveal the strange history that sounded like some tale from fairyland. It appeared that the reason Catharine did not attempt to go to the camp that morning was that Margie was not well, so she would not leave her, but in her heart of hearts she knew young Wingate would come searching to her lodge. She loved the child as only an Indian woman can love an adopted child. She longed for him to come when she found Margie was ill, yet dreaded that coming from the depths of her soul. She dreaded the hour he would see the child and take it away. For the moment she looked upon his face, the night he rode over to engage her to cook, months ago, she had known he was Margie's father. The little thing was the perfect mirror of him, and Catharine's strange wild heart rejoiced to find him, yet hid the child from him for very fear of losing it out of her own life.

After finding it almost dead in its dead mother's arms on the shore, the Indians had given it to Catharine for the reason that she could speak some English. They were only a passing band of Kootenays, and as they journeyed on and on, week in and week out, they finally came to Crow's Nest Mountain. Here the child fell ill, so they built Catharine a log shack, and left her with plenty of food, sufficient to last until the railway gang had worked that far up the Pass, when more food would be available. When she had finished the strange history, Wingate looked at her long and lovingly.

"Catharine," he said, "you were almost going to fight me once to-day. You stood between the couch and me like a panther. What changed you so that you led me to my baby girl yourself?"

"I make one last fight to keep her," she said, haltingly. "She mine so long, I want her; I want her till I die. Then I think many times I see your face at camp. It look like sky when sun does not shine – all cloud, no smile, no laugh. I know you think of your baby then. Then I watch you many times. Then after while my heart is sick for you, like you are my own boy, like I am your own mother. I hate see no sun in your face. I think I not good mother to you; if I was good mother I would give you your child; make the sun come in your face. To-day I make last fight to keep the child. She's mine so long, I want her till I die. Then somet'ing in my heart say, 'He's like son to you, as if he your own boy; make him glad – happy. Oh, ver' glad! Be like his own mother. Find him his baby.'"

"Bless the mother heart of her!" growled the big foreman, frowning to keep his face from twitching.

It was twilight when they mounted the horses one of the men had brought up for them to ride home on, Wingate with his treasure-child hugged tightly in his arms. Words were powerless to thank the woman who had saved half his world for him. His voice choked when he tried, but she understood, and her woman's heart was very, very full.

Just as they reached the rim of the cañon Wingate turned and looked back. His arms tightened about little Margie as his eyes rested on Catharine – as once before she was standing in the doorway, alone; alone, and above and about her were the purple shadows, the awful solitude of Crow's Nest Mountain.

"Brown!" he called. "Hold on, Brown! *I can't do it! I can't leave her like that!"*

He wheeled his horse about and, plunging back through the snow, rode again to her door. Her eyes radiated as she looked at him. Years had been wiped from his face since the morning. He was a laughing boy once more.

"You are right," he said, "I cannot keep my little girl in that rough camp. You said it was no place for a girl child. You are right. I will send her into Calgary until my survey is over. Catharine, will you go with her, take care of her, nurse her, guard her for me? You said I was as your own son; will you be that good mother to me that you want to be? Will you do this for your white boy?"

He had never seen her smile before. A moment ago her heart had been breaking, but now she knew with a great gladness that she was not only going to keep and care for Margie, but that this laughing boy would be as a son to her for all time. No wonder that Catharine of the Crow's Nest smiled!

## THE ENVOY EXTRAORDINARY

There had been a great deal of trouble in the Norris family, and for weeks old Bill Norris had gone about scowling as blackly as a thundercloud, speaking to no one but his wife and daughter, and oftentimes muttering inaudible things that, however, had the tone of invective; and accompanied, as these mutterings were, with a menacing shake of his burly head, old Bill finally grew to be an acquaintance few desired.

Mrs. Norris showed equal, though not similar, signs of mental disturbance; for, womanlike, she clothed her worry in placidity and silence. Her kindly face became drawn and lined; she laughed less frequently. She never went "neighboring" or "buggy-riding' with old Bill now. But the trim farmhouse was just as spotless, just as beautifully kept, the cooking just as wholesome and homelike, the linen as white, the garden as green, the chickens as fat, the geese as noisy, as in the days when her eyes were less grave and her lips unknown to sighs. And what was it all about but the simple matter of a marriage – Sam's marriage? Sam, the big, genial, curly-headed only son of the house of Norris, who saw fit to take unto himself as a life partner tiny, delicate, college-bred Della Kennedy, who taught school over on the Sixth Concession, and knew more about making muslin shirtwaists than cooking for the threshers, could quote from all the mental and moral philosophers, could wrestle with French and Latin verbs, and had memorized half the things Tennyson and Emerson had ever written, but could not milk a cow or churn up a week's supply of butter if the executioner stood ready with his axe to chop off her pretty yellow mop of a head in case she failed. How old Billy stormed when Sam started "keeping company" with her!

"Nice young goslin' fer you to be a-goin' with !" he scowled when Sam would betake himself towards the red gate every evening after chores were done. "Nice gal fer you to bring home to help yer mother; all she'll do is to play May Queen and have the hull lot of us a-trottin' to wait on her. You'll marry a farmer's gal, *I* say, one that's brung up like yerself and yer mother and me, or I tell yer yer shan't have one consarned acre of this place. I'll leave the hull farm to yer sister Jane's man. *She* married somethin' like – decent, stiddy, hard-working man is Sid Sampson, and *he'll* git what land I have to leave."

"I quite know that, dad," Sam blazed forth, irritably; "so does he. That's what he married Janie for – the whole township knows that. He's never given her a kind word, or a holiday, or a new dress, since they were married – eight years. She slaves and toils, and he rich as any man need be; owns three farms already, money in the bank, cattle, horses – everything. But look at Janie; she looks as old as mother. I pity *his* son, if he ever has one. Thank heaven, Janie has no children!"

"Come, come, father – Sam !" a patient voice would interrupt, and Mrs. Norris would appear at the door, vainly endeavoring to make peace. "I'll own up to both of you I'd sooner have a farmer's daughter for mine-in-law than Della Kennedy. But, father, he ain't married yet, and – "

"Ain't married, eh?" blurted in old Bill. "But he's a-goin' to marry her. But I'll tell you both right here, she'll never set foot in my house, ner I in her'n. Sam ken keep her, but what on, I don't know. He gits right out of this here farm the day he marries her, and he don't come back, not while I'm a-livin'."

It was all this that made old Billy Norris morose, and Mrs. Norris silent and patient and laughless, for Sam married the despised "gosling" right at harvest time, when hands were so scarce that farmers wrangled and fought, day in and day out, to get one single man to go into the field.

This was Sam's golden opportunity. His father's fields stood yellow with ripening grain to be cut on the morrow, but he deliberately hired himself out to a neighbor, where he would get good wages to start a little home with; for, farmer-like, old Billy Norris never paid his son wages. Sam was supposed to work for nothing but his clothes and board as reward, and a possible slice of the farm when the old man died, while a good harvest hand gets board and high wages, to boot. This then was the hour to strike, and the morning the grain stood ready for the reaper Sam paused at the outside kitchen door at sunrise.

"Mother," he said, "I've got to have her. I'm going to marry her to-day, and to-morrow start working for Mr. Willson, who will pay me enough to keep a wife. I'm sorry, mother, but – well, I've got to have her. Some day you'll know her, and you'll love her, I know you will; and if there's ever any children – "

But Mrs. Norris had clutched him by the arm. "Sammy," she whispered, "your father will be raging mad at your going, and harvest hands so scarce. I *know* he'll never let me go near you, never. But if there's ever any children, Sammy, you just come for your mother, and I'll go to you and her *without* his letting."

Then with one of the all too few kisses that are ever given or received in a farmhouse life, she let him go. The storm burst at breakfast time when Sam did not appear, and the poor mother tried to explain his absence, as only a mother will. Old Billy waxed suspicious, then jumped at facts. The marriage was bad enough, but this being left in the lurch at the eleventh hour, his son's valuable help transferred from the home farm to Mr. Willson's, with whom he always quarreled in church, road, and political matters, was too much.

"But, father, you never paid him wages," ventured the mother.

"Wages? Wages to one's own son, that one has raised and fed and shod from the cradle? Wages, when he knowed he'd come in fer part of the farm when I'd done with it? Who in consarnation ever gives their son wages?"

"But, father, you told him if he married her he was never to have the farm – that you'd leave it to Sid, that he was to get right off the day he married her."

"An' Sid'll get it – bet yer life he will – fer I ain't got no son no more. A sneakin' hulk that leaves me with my wheat standin' an' goes over to help that Methodist of a Willson is no son of mine. I ain't never had a son, and you ain't, neither; remember that, Marthy – don't you ever let me ketch you goin' a-near them. We're done with Sam an' his missus. You jes' make a note of that." And old Billy flung out to his fields like a general whose forces had fled.

It was but a tiny, two-room shack, away up in the back lots, that Sam was able to get for Della, but no wayfarer ever passed up the side road but they heard her clear, young voice singing like a thrush; no one ever met Sam but he ceased whistling only to greet them. He proved invaluable to Mr. Willson, for after the harvest was in and the threshing over, there was the root crop and the apple crop, and eventually Mr. Willson hired him for the entire year. Della, to the surprise of the neighborhood, kept on with her school until Christmas.

"She's teachin' instid of keepin' Sam's house, jes' to git money fer finery, you bet!" sneered old Billy. But he never knew that every copper for the extra term was put carefully away, and was paid out for a whole year's rent in advance on a gray little two-room house, and paid by a very proud little yellow-haired bride. She had insisted upon this before her marriage, for she laughingly said, "No wife ever gets her way afterwards."

"I'm not good at butter-making, Sam," she said, "but I *can* make money teaching, and for this first year *I* pay the rent." And she did.

And the sweet, brief year swung on through its seasons, until one brown September morning the faint cry of a little human lamb floated through the open window of the small gray house on the back lots. Sam did not go to Willson's to work that day, but stayed at home, playing the part of a big, joyful, clumsy nurse, his roughened hands gentle and loving, his big rugged heart bursting with happiness. It was twilight, and the gray shadows were creeping into the bare little room, touching with feathery fingers a tangled mop of yellow curls that aureoled a pillowed head that was not now filled with thoughts of Tennyson and Emerson and frilly muslin shirtwaists. That pretty head held but two realities – Sammy, whistling robin-like as he made tea in the kitchen, and the little human lamb hugged up on her arm.

But suddenly the whistling ceased, and Sammy's voice, thrilling with joy, exclaimed:

"Oh, mother!"

"Mrs. Willson sent word to me. Your father's gone to the village, and I ran away, Sammy boy," whispered Mrs. Norris, eagerly. "I just ran away. Where's Della and – the baby?"

"In here, mother, and – bless you for coming!" said the big fellow, stepping softly towards the bedroom. But his mother was there before him, her arms slipping tenderly about the two small beings on the bed.

"It wasn't my fault, daughter," she said, tremulously.

"I know it," faintly smiled Della. "Just these last few hours I know I'd stand by this baby boy of mine here until the Judgment Day, and so I now know it must have nearly broken your heart not to stand by Sammy."

"Well, grandmother!" laughed Sam, "what do you think of the new Norris?"

"Grandmother?" gasped Mrs. Norris. "Why, Sammy, *am* I a *grandmother?* Grandmother to this little sweetheart?" And the proud old arms lifted the wee "new Norris" right up from its mother's arms, and every tiny toe and finger was kissed and crooned over, while Sam shyly winked at Della and managed to whisper, "You'll see, girl, that dad will come around now; but he can just keep out of *our house.* There are two of us that can be harsh. I'm not going to come at *his* first whistle."

Della smiled to herself, but said nothing. Much wisdom had come to her within the last year, within the last day – wisdom not acquired within the covers of books, nor yet beneath college roofs, and one truth she had mastered long ago – that

"To help and to heal a sorrow
Love and silence are always best."

But late that night, when Martha Norris returned home, another storm broke above her hapless head. Old Billy sat on the kitchen steps waiting for her, frowning, scowling, muttering. "Where have you been?" he demanded, glaring at her, although some inner instinct told him what her answer would be.

"I've been to Sammy's," she said, in a peculiarly still voice, "and I'm going again to-morrow." Then with shoulders more erect and eyes calmer than they had been for many months, she continued: "And I'm going again the next day, and the next. Billy, you and I've got a grandson – a splendid, fair, strong boy, and – "

"What!" snapped old Billy. "A grandson! I got a grandson, an' no person told me afore? Not even that there sneak Sam, cuss him! He always was too consarned mean to live. A grandson? I'm a-goin' over termorrer, sure's I'm alive."

"No use for you to go, Billy," said Mrs. Norris, with marvellous diplomacy for such a simple, unworldly farmer's wife to suddenly acquire. "Sammy wouldn't let you set foot on his place. He wouldn't let you put an eye or a finger on that precious baby – not for the whole earth."

"What! Not *me*, the little chap's *grandfather*?" blurted old Billy in a rage. "I'm a-goin' to see that baby, that's all there is to it. I tell yer, I'm a-goin'."

"No use, father; you'll only make things worse," sighed Sam's mother, plaintively; but in her heart laughter gurgled like a spring. To the gift of diplomacy Mrs. Norris was fast adding the art of being an actress. "If you go there Sam'll set the dog on you. I *know* he will, from the way he was talking," she concluded.

"Oh! got a *dog*, have they? Well, I bet they've got no *cow*," sneered Billy. Then after a meaning pause: "I say, Marthy, *have* they got a cow?"

"No," replied Mrs. Norris, shortly.

*"No cow*, an' a sick woman and a baby – *my* grandchild – in the house? Now ain't that jes' like that sneak Sam? They'll jes' kill that baby atween them, they're that igner'nt. Hev they got enny milk fer them two babbling kids, Della an' the baby – my grandchild?"

"No!" snapped Mrs. Norris, while through her mind echoed some terrifying lines she had heard as a child:

"All liars dwell with him in hell,
And many more who cursed and swore."

"An' there's that young Shorthorn of ours, Marthy. Couldn't we spare her ?" he asked with a pathetic eagerness. "We've got eight other cows to milk. Can't we spare her? If you think Sam'll set the dog on *me,* I'll have her drive over in the mornin'. Jim'll take her."

"I don't think it's any use, Bill; but you can try it," remarked Mrs. Norris, her soul singing within her like a celestial choir.

* * *

"Where are you driving that cow to?" yelled Sam from the kitchen door, at sunrise the following morning. "Take her out of there! You're driving her into my yard, right over my cabbages."

But Jim, the Norris' hired man, only grinned, and proceeding with his driving, yelled back: "Cow's yourn, Sam. Yer old man sent it – a present to yer missus and the babby."

"You take and drive that cow back again!" roared Sam. "And tell my dad I won't have hide nor hair of her on my place."

Back went the cow.

"Didn't I tell you?" mourned Mrs. Norris. "Sam's that stubborn and contrary. It's no use, Billy; he just doesn't care for his poor old father nor mother any more."

"By the jumping Jiminy Christmas! I'll *make* him care !" thundered old Billy. "I'm a-goin' ter see that grandchild of mine." Then followed a long silence.

"I say, Marthy, how are they fixed in the house?" he questioned, after many moments of apparently brown study.

"Pretty poor," answered Sam's mother, truthfully this time.

"Got a decent stove, an' bed, an' the like?" he finally asked.

"Stove seems to cook all right, but the bed looks just like straw tick – not much good, I'd say," responded Mrs. Norris, drearily.

*"A straw tick!"* fairly yelled old Billy. "A straw tick fer my grandson ter sleep on? Jim, you fetch that there cow here, right ter the side door."

"What are you going to do?" asked Martha, anxiously.

"I'll show yer!" blurted old Billy. And going to his own room, he dragged off all the pretty patchwork quilts above his neatly-made bed, grabbed up the voluminous feather-bed, staggered with it in his arms down the hall, through the side door, and flung it on to the back of the astonished cow.

" Now you, Jim, drive that there cow over to Sam's, and if you dare bring her back agin, I'll hide yer with the flail till yer can't stand up."

"Me drive that lookin' circus over to Sam's?" sneered Jim. "I'll quit yer place first. Yer kin do it yerself;" and the hired man turned on his lordly heel and slouched over to the barn.

"That'll be the best way, Billy," urged Sam's mother. "Do it yourself."

"I'll do it, too," old Billy growled. "I ain't afraid of no dog on four legs. Git on there, bossy! Git on, I say!" and the ridiculous cavalcade started forth.

For a moment Martha Norris watched the receding figure through blinding tears. "Oh, Sammy, I'm going to have you back again! I'm going to have my boy once more!" she half sobbed. Then sitting down on the doorsill, she laughed like a schoolgirl until the cow with her extraordinary burden, and old Billy in her wake, disappeared up the road.[2]

From the pillow, pretty Della could just see out of the low window, and her wide young eyes grew wider with amazement as the gate swung open and the "circus," as Jim called it, entered.

"Sammy!" she called, "Sammy! For goodness sake, what's that coming into our yard?"

Instantly Sam was at the door.

"Well, if that don't beat anything I ever saw!" he exclaimed. Then "like mother, like son," he, too, sat down on the doorsill and laughed as only youth and health and joy can laugh, for, heading straight for the door was the fat young Shorthorn, saddled with an enormous featherbed, and plodding at her heels was old Billy Norris, grinning sheepishly.

It took just three seconds for the hands of father and son to meet. "How's my gal an' my grandson?" asked the old farmer, excitedly.

"Bully, just bully, both of them!" smiled Sam, proudly. Then more seriously, "Ah, dad, you old tornado, you! Here you fired thunder at us for a whole year, pretty near broke my mother's heart, and made my boy's little mother old before she ought to be. But you've quit storming now, dad. I know it from the look of you."

---

2 This incident actually occurred on an Ontario farm within the circle of the author's acquaintance. [Johnson's note]

"Quit forever, Sam," replied old Billy, "fer these mother-wimmen don't never thrive where there's rough weather, somehow. They're all fer peace. They're worse than King Edward an' Teddy Roosevelt fer patchin' up rows, an' if they can't do it no other way, they jes' hike along with a baby, sort o' treaty of peace like. Yes, I guess I thundered some; but, Sam, boy, there ain't a deal of harm in thunder – but *lightnin'*, now that's the worst, but I once heard a feller say that feathers was non-conductive." Then with a sly smile, "An' Sam, you'd better hustle an' git the gal an' the baby on ter this here feather-bed, or they may be in danger of gittin' struck, fer there's no tellin' but I may jes' start an' storm thunder an' *lightnin'* this time."

## AS IT WAS IN THE BEGINNING

They account for it by the fact that I am a Redskin, but I am something else, too – I am a woman.

I remember the first time I saw him. He came up the trail with some Hudson's Bay trappers, and they stopped at the door of my father's tepee. He seemed even then, fourteen years ago, an old man; his hair seemed just as thin and white, his hands just as trembling and fleshless as they were a month since, when I saw him for what I pray his God is the last time.

My father sat in the tepee, polishing buffalo horns and smoking; my mother, wrapped in her blanket, crouched over her quill-work, on the buffalo-skin at his side; I was lounging at the doorway, idling, watching, as I always watched, the thin, distant line of sky and prairie; wondering, as I always wondered, what lay beyond it. Then he came, this gentle old man with his white hair and thin, pale face. He wore a long black coat, which I now know was the sign of his office, and he carried a black leather-covered book, which, in all the years I have known him, I have never seen him without.

The trappers explained to my father who he was, the Great Teacher, the heart's Medicine Man, the "Blackcoat" we had heard of, who brought peace where there was war, and the magic of whose black book brought greater things than all the Happy Hunting Grounds of our ancestors.

He told us many things that day, for he could speak the Cree tongue, and my father listened, and listened, and when at last they left us, my father said for him to come and sit within the tepee again.

He came, all the time he came, and my father welcomed him, but my mother always sat in silence at work with the quills; my mother never liked the Great "Blackcoat."

His stories fascinated me. I used to listen intently to the tale of the strange new place he called "heaven," of the gold crown, of the white dress, of the great music; and then he would tell of that other strange place – hell. My father and I hated it; we feared it, we dreamt of it, we trembled at it. Oh, if the "Blackcoat" would only cease to talk of it! Now I know he saw its effect upon us, and he used it as a whip to lash us into his new religion, but even then my mother must have known, for each time he left the tepee she would watch him going slowly away across the prairie; then when he was disappearing into the far horizon she would laugh scornfully and say:

"If the white man made this Blackcoat's hell, let him go to it. It is for the man who found it first. No hell for Indians, just Happy Hunting Grounds. Blackcoat can't scare me."

And then, after weeks had passed, one day as he stood at the tepee door he laid his white, old hand on my head and said to my father: "Give me this little girl, chief. Let me take her to the mission school; let me keep her, and teach her of the great God and His eternal heaven. She will grow to be a noble woman, and return perhaps to bring her people to the Christ." My mother's eyes snapped. "No," she said. It was the first word she ever spoke to the "Blackcoat." My father sat and smoked. At the end of a half-hour he said:

"I am an old man, Blackcoat. I shall not leave the God of my fathers. I like not your strange God's ways – all of them. I like not His two new places for me when I am dead. Take the child Blackcoat, and save her from hell."

* * *

The first grief of my life was when we reached the mission. They took my buckskin dress off, saying I was now a little Christian girl and must dress like all the white people at the mission. Oh, how I hated that stiff new calico dress and those leather shoes. But, little as I was, I said nothing, only thought of the time when I should be grown, and do as my mother did, and wear the buckskins and the blanket.

My next serious grief was when I began to speak the English, that they forbade me to use any Cree words whatever. The rule of the school was that any child heard using its native tongue must get a slight punishment. I never understood it, I cannot understand it now, why the use of my dear Cree tongue could be a matter for correction or an action deserving punishment.

She was strict, the matron of the school, but only justly so, for she had a heart and a face like her brother's, the "Blackcoat." I had long since ceased to call him that. The trappers at the post called him "St. Paul," because, they told me, of his self-sacrificing life, his kindly deeds, his rarely beautiful old face; so I, too, called him "St. Paul," though oftener "Father Paul," though he never liked the latter title, for he was a Protestant. But as I was his pet, his darling of the whole school, he let me speak of him as I would, knowing it was but my heart speaking in love. His sister was a widow, and mother to a laughing yellow-haired little boy of about my own age, who was my constant playmate and who taught me much of English in his own childish way. I used to be fond of this child, just as I was fond of his mother and of his uncle, my "Father Paul," but as my girlhood passed away, as womanhood came upon me, I got strangely wearied of them all; I longed, oh, God, how I longed for the old wild life! It came with my womanhood, with my years.

What mattered it to me now that they had taught me all their ways? – their tricks of dress, their reading, their writing, their books. What mattered it that "Father Paul" loved me, that the traders at the post called me pretty, that I was a pet of all, from the factor to the poorest trapper in the service? I wanted my own people, my own old life, my blood called out for it, but they always said I must not return to my father's tepee. I heard them talk amongst themselves of keeping me away from pagan influences; they told each other that if I returned to the prairies, the tepees, I would degenerate, slip back to paganism, as other girls had done; marry, perhaps, with a pagan – and all their years of labor and teaching would be lost.

I said nothing, but I waited. And then one night the feeling overcame me. I was in the Hudson's Bay store when an Indian came in from the north with a large pack of buckskin. As they unrolled it a dash of its insinuating odor filled the store. I went over and leaned above the skins a second, then buried my face in them, swallowing, drinking the fragrance of them, that went to my head like wine. Oh, the wild wonder of that wood-smoked tan, the subtilty of it, the untamed smell of it! I drank it into my lungs, my innermost being was saturated with it, till my mind reeled and my heart seemed twisted with a physical agony. My childhood recollections rushed upon me, devoured me. I left the store in a strange, calm frenzy, and going rapidly to the mission house I confronted my Father Paul and demanded to be allowed to go "home," if only for a day. He received the request with the same refusal and the same gentle sigh that I had so often been greeted with, but *this* time the desire, the smoke-tan, the heart-ache, never lessened.

Night after night I would steal away by myself and go to the border of the village to watch the sun set in the foothills, to gaze at the far line of sky and prairie, to long and long for my father's lodge. And Laurence – always Laurence – my fair-haired, laughing, child playmate, would come calling and calling for me: "Esther, where are you? We miss you; come in, Esther, come in with me." And if I did not turn at once to him and follow, he would come and place his strong hands on my shoulders and laugh into my eyes and say, "Truant, truant, Esther; can't *we* make you happy?"

My old child playmate had vanished years ago. He was a tall, slender young man now, handsome as a young chief, but with laughing blue eyes, and always those yellow curls about his temples. He was my solace in my half-exile, my comrade, my brother, until one night it was, "Esther, Esther, can't *I* make you happy?"

I did not answer him; only looked out across the plains and thought of the tepees. He came close, close. He locked his arms about me, and with my face pressed up to his throat he stood silent. I felt the blood from my heart sweep to my very finger-tips. I loved him. O God, how I loved him! In a wild, blind instant it all came, just because he held me so and was whispering brokenly, "Don't leave me, don't leave me, Esther; *my* Esther, my child-love, my playmate, my girl-comrade, my little Cree sweet-heart, will you go away to your people, or stay, stay for me, for my arms, as I have you now?"

No more, no more the tepees; no more the wild stretch of prairie, the intoxicating fragrance of the smoke-tanned buckskin; no more the bed of buffalo hide, the soft, silent moccasin; no more the dark faces of my people, the dulcet cadence of the sweet Cree tongue – only this man, this fair, proud, tender man who held me in his arms, in his heart. My soul prayed his great white God, in that moment, that he let me have only this. It was twilight when we re-entered the mission gate. We were both excited, feverish. Father Paul was reading evening prayers in the large room beyond the hallway; his soft, saint-like voice stole beyond the doors, like a benediction upon us. I went noiselessly upstairs to my own room and sat there undisturbed for hours.

The clock downstairs struck one, startling me from my dreams of happiness, and at the same moment a flash of light attracted me. My room was in an angle of the building, and my window looked almost directly down into those of Father Paul's study, into which at that instant he was entering, carrying a lamp. "Why, Laurence," I heard him exclaim, "what are you doing here? I thought, my boy, you were in bed hours ago."

"No, uncle, not in bed, but in dreamland," replied Laurence, arising from the window, where evidently he, too, had spent the night hours as I had done.

Father Paul fumbled about a moment, found his large black book, which for once he seemed to have got separated from, and was turning to leave, when the curious circumstance of Laurence being there at so unusual an hour seemed to strike him anew. "Better go to sleep, my son," he said simply, then added curiously, "Has anything occurred to keep you up?"

Then Laurence spoke: "No, uncle, only – only, I'm happy, that's all."

Father Paul stood irresolute. Then: "It is – ?"

"Esther," said Laurence quietly, but he was at the old man's side, his hand was on the bent old shoulder, his eyes proud and appealing.

Father Paul set the lamp on the table, but, as usual, one hand held that black book, the great text of his life. His face was paler than I had ever seen it – graver.

"Tell me of it," he requested.

I leaned far out of my window and watched them both. I listened with my very heart, for Laurence was telling him of me, of his love, of the new-found joy of that night.

"You have said nothing of marriage to her?" asked Father Paul.

"Well – no; but she surely understands that – "

"Did you speak of *marriage*?" repeated Father Paul, with a harsh ring in his voice that was new to me.

"No, uncle, but – "

"Very well, then; very well."

There was a brief silence. Laurence stood staring at the old man as though he were a stranger; he watched him push a large chair up to the table, slowly seat himself; then mechanically following his movements, he dropped on to a lounge. The old man's head bent low, but his eyes were bright and strangely fascinating. He began:

"Laurence, my boy, your future is the dearest thing to me of all earthly interests. Why, you *can't* marry this girl – no, no, sit, sit until I have finished," he added, with raised voice, as Laurence sprang up, remonstrating. "I have long since decided that you marry well; for instance, the Hudson's Bay factor's daughter."

Laurence broke into a fresh, rollicking laugh. "What, uncle," he said, "little Ida McIntosh? Marry that little yellow-haired fluff ball, that kitten, that pretty little dolly?"

"Stop," said Father Paul. Then with a low, soft persuasiveness, "She is *white*, Laurence."

My lover started. "Why, uncle, what do you mean?" he faltered.

"Only this, my son: poor Esther comes of uncertain blood; would it do for you – the missionary's nephew, and adopted son, you might say – to marry the daughter of a pagan Indian? Her mother is hopelessly uncivilized; her father has a dash of French somewhere – half-breed, you know, my boy, half-breed." Then, with still lower tone and half-shut, crafty eyes, he added: "The blood is a bad, bad mixture, *you* know that; you know, too, that I am very fond of the girl, poor dear Esther. I have tried to separate her from evil pagan influences; she is the daughter of the church; I want her to have no other parent; but you never can tell what lurks in *a caged animal that has once been wild*. My whole heart is with the Indian people, my son; my whole heart, my whole life, has been devoted to bringing them to Christ, *but it is a different thing to marry with one of them.*"

His small old eyes were riveted on Laurence like a hawk's on a rat. My heart lay like ice in my bosom.

Laurence, speechless and white, stared at him breathlessly.

"Go away somewhere," the old man was urging; "to Winnipeg, Toronto, Montreal; forget her, then come back to Ida McIntosh. A union of the church and the Hudson's Bay will mean great things, and may ultimately result in my life's ambition, the civilization of this entire tribe, that we have worked so long to bring to God."

I listened, sitting like one frozen. Could those words have been uttered by my venerable teacher, by him whom I revered as I would one of the saints in his own black book? Ah, there was no mistaking it. My white father, my life-long friend who pretended to love me, to care for my happiness, was urging the man I worshipped to forget me, to marry with the factor's daughter – because of what? Of my red skin; my good, old, honest pagan mother; my confiding French-Indian father. In a second all the care, the hollow love he had given me since my childhood, were as things that never existed. I hated that old mission priest as I hated his white man's hell. I hated his long, white hair; I hated his thin, white hands; I hated his body, his soul, his voice, his black book – oh, how I hated the very atmosphere of him.

Laurence sat motionless, his face buried in his hands, but the old man continued, "No, no; not the child of that pagan mother; you can't trust her, my son. What would you do with a wife who might any day break from you to return to her prairies and her buckskins? *You can't trust her.*" His eyes grew smaller, more glittering, more fascinating then, and leaning with an odd secret sort of movement toward Laurence, he almost whispered, "Think of her silent ways, her noiseless step; the girl glides about like an apparition; her quick fingers, her wild longings – I don't know why, but with all my fondness for her, she reminds me sometimes of a strange – *snake.*"

Laurence shuddered, lifted his face, and said hoarsely: "You're right, uncle; perhaps I'd better not; I'll go away, I'll forget her, and then – well, then – yes, you are right, it *is* a different thing to marry one of them." The old man arose. His feeble fingers still clasped his black book; his soft white hair clung about his forehead like that of an Apostle; his eyes lost their peering, crafty expression; his bent shoulders resumed the dignity of a minister of the living God; he was the picture of what the traders called him – "St. Paul."

"Good-night, son," he said.

"Good-night, uncle, and thank you for bringing me to myself."

They were the last words I ever heard uttered by either that old arch-fiend or his weak, miserable kinsman. Father Paul turned and left the room. I watched his withered hand – the hand I had so often felt resting on my head in holy benedictions – clasp the door-knob, turn it slowly, then, with bowed head and his pale face wrapped in thought, he left the room – left it with the mad venom of my hate pursuing him like the very Evil One he taught me of.

What were his years of kindness and care now? What did I care for his God, his heaven, his hell? He had robbed me of my native faith, of my parents, of my people, of this last, this life of love that would have made a great, good woman of me. God! how I hated him!

I crept to the closet in my dark little room. I felt for a bundle I had not looked at for years – yes, it was there, the buckskin dress I had worn as a little child when they brought me to the mission. I tucked it under my arm and descended the stairs noiselessly. I would look into the study and speak good-bye to Laurence; then I would –

I pushed open the door. He was lying on the couch where a short time previously he had sat, white and speechless, listening to Father Paul. I moved towards him softly. God in heaven, he was already asleep. As I bent over him the fullness of his perfect beauty impressed me for the first time; his slender form, his curving mouth that almost laughed even in sleep, his fair, tossed hair, his smooth, strong-pulsing throat. God! how I loved him!

Then there arose the picture of the factor's daughter. I hated her. I hated her baby face, her yellow hair, her whitish skin. "She shall not marry him," my soul said. "I will kill him first – kill his beautiful body, his lying, false heart." Something in my heart seemed to speak; it said over and over again, "Kill him, kill him; she will never have him then. Kill him. It will break Father Paul's heart and blight his life. He has killed the best of you, of your womanhood; kill *his* best, his pride, his hope – his sister's son, his nephew Laurence." But how? how?

What had that terrible old man said I was like? A *strange snake.* A snake? The idea wound itself about me like the very coils of a serpent. What was this in the beaded bag of my buckskin dress? this little thing rolled in tan that my mother had given me at parting with the words, "Don't touch much, but some time maybe you want it!" Oh! I knew well enough what it was – a small flint arrow-head dipped in the venom of some *strange snake.*

I knelt beside him and laid my hot lips on his hand. I worshipped him, oh, how, how I worshipped him! Then again the vision of *her* baby face, *her* yellow hair – I scratched his wrist twice with the arrow-tip. A single drop of red blood oozed up; he stirred. I turned the lamp down and slipped out of the room – out of the house.

* * *

I dream nightly of the horrors of the white man's hell. Why did they teach me of it, only to fling me into it?

Last night as I crouched beside my mother on the buffalo-hide, Dan Henderson, the trapper, came in to smoke with my father. He said old Father Paul was bowed with grief, that with my disappearance I was suspected, but that there was no proof. Was it not merely a snake bite?

They account for it by the fact that I am a Redskin.

They seem to have forgotten I am a woman.

## From *The Shagganappi* (1913)[3]

### LITTLE WOLF-WILLOW

Old Beaver-Tail hated many things, but most of all he hated the North-West Mounted Police. Not that they had ever molested or worried him in his far corner of the Crooked Lakes Indian Reserve, but they stood for the enforcing of the white man's laws, and old Beaver-Tail hated the white man. He would sit for hours together in his big tepee counting his piles of furs, smoking, grumbling and storming at the inroads of the palefaces on to his lands and hunting grounds. Consequently it was an amazing surprise to everybody when he consented to let his eldest son, Little Wolf-Willow, go away to attend the Indian School in far-off Manitoba. But old Beaver-Tail explained with rare appreciation his reasons for this consent. He said he wished the boy to learn English, so that he would grow up to be a keen, sharp trader, like the men of the Hudson's Bay Company, the white men who were so apt to outwit the redskins in a fur-trading bargain. Thus we see that poor old Beaver-Tail had suffered and been cheated at the hands of the cunning paleface. Little Wolf-Willow was not little, by any means; he was tall, thin, wiry, and quick, a boy of marked intelligence and much ability. He was called Little Wolf-Willow to distinguish him from his grandsire, Big Wolf-Willow by name, whose career as a warrior made him famed throughout half of the great Canadian North-West. Little Wolf-Willow's one idea of life was to grow up and be like his grandfather, the hero of fifty battles against both hostile Indian tribes and invading white settlers; to have nine scalps at his belt, and scars on his face; to wear a crimson-tipped eagle feather in his hair, and to give a war-whoop that would echo from lake to lake and plant fear in the hearts of his enemies. But instead of all this splendid life the boy was sent away to the school taught by paleface men and women; to a terrible, far-away, strange school, where he would have to learn a new language and perhaps wear clothes like the white men wore. The superintendent of the school, who had persuaded old Beaver-Tail to let the boy come, brought him out from the Crooked Lakes with several other boys. Most

3 Dedicated to The Boy Scouts.

of them could speak a few words of English, but not so Little Wolf-Willow, who arrived from his prairie tepee dressed in buckskin and moccasins, a pretty string of white elks' teeth about his throat, and his long, straight, black hair braided in two plaits, interwoven with bits of rabbit skin. A dull green blanket served as an overcoat, and he wore no hat at all. His face was small, and beautifully tinted a rich, reddish copper color, and his eyes were black, alert, and very shining.

The teachers greeted him very kindly, and he shook hands with them gravely, like a very old man. And from that day onward Little Wolf-Willow shut his heart within himself, and suffered.

In the first place, the white people all looked sick to him – unhealthy, bleached. Then, try as he would, he could not accustom his feet to the stiff leather shoes he was induced to wear. One morning his buckskin coat was missing, and in its place was a nice blue cloth one with gleaming golden buttons. He hated it, but he had to wear it. Then his green blanket disappeared; a warm, heavy overcoat in its place. Then his fringed buckskin "chaps" went; in their place a pair of dreadful grey cloth trousers. Little Wolf-Willow made no comment, but he kept his eyes and ears open, and mastered a few important words of English, which, however, he kept to himself – as yet. And then, one day, when he had worn these hated clothes for a whole month, the superintendent who had brought him away from his father's tepee sent for him to come to his little office. The boy went. The superintendent was so kind and so gentle, and his smile was so true, that the boy had grown somewhat attached to him, so, without fear of anything in the world, the little Cree scholar slipped noiselessly into the room.

"Ah, Little Wolf-Willow," said the superintendent, kindly, "I notice that you are beginning to understand a little English already." The boy smiled, and nodded slightly. "You are very quick and smart, my boy – quick as a lynx, smart as a fox. Now tell me, are you happy here? Do you like the school?" continued Mr. Enderby.

There was a brief silence, then a direct, straight look from the small Cree eyes, and the words, "I like you – me."

Mr. Enderby smiled. "That's good; I like you, too, Little Wolf-Willow. Now tell me, do you like your new clothes?"

"No good," said the boy.

Mr. Enderby looked grave. "But, my boy, that is what you must wear if you are to be educated. Do you know what the word 'education' means? Have you ever heard the teachers or boys here use it?"

"White man, English," came the quick reply.

"That's it; you have described it exactly. To become educated you must try and wear and do what the white people do – like the English, as you say," Mr. Enderby went on. "Now what about your hair? White men don't wear long hair, and you see all the Cree boys in the school have let me cut their hair. Wouldn't you like to be like them?"

"No; hair good," said the boy.

"Well, how about a 'white' name?" asked Mr. Enderby. "The other boys have taken them. Wouldn't you like me to call you John? I'd like to."

"Me Wolf-Willow, same grandfather," came in tones of pronounced decision.

"Very well, Little Wolf-Willow, you must do as you like, you know; but you said when you came in that you liked me, and I like you very much. Perhaps some day you will do these things to please me." Then Mr. Enderby added softly to himself, "It will all come in time. It is pretty hard to ask any boy to give up his language, his clothes, his customs, his old-time way of living, his name, even the church of his fathers. I must have patience, patience."

"You speak?" asked the boy.

"Just to myself," said Mr. Enderby.

"I speak," said the little Indian, standing up and looking fearlessly into the superintendent's face. "I speak. I keep hair, good. I keep name Wolf-willow, good. I keep skin Indian color. I not white man's skin. English skin no good. My skin best, good."

Mr. Enderby laughed. "No, no, Little Wolf-Willow, we won't try to change the color of your skin," he said.

"No good try. I keep skin, better skin than white man. I keep skin, me." And the next instant he was gone.

Miss Watson, the matron, appeared at the door.

"What have you done to Little Wolf-Willow?" she asked in surprise. "Why, he is careering down the hall at breakneck speed."

"I believe the child thought I was going to skin him, to make a white boy out of him," laughed Mr. Enderby.

"Poor little chap! I expect you wanted to cut off his hair," said Miss Watson, "and perhaps call him Tom, Dick, Harry, or some such name."

"I did," answered the superintendent. "The other boys have all come to it."

"Yes, I know they have," agreed Miss Watson, "but there is something about that boy that makes me think that you'll never get his hair or his name away from him."

And she was right. They never did.

It was six years before Little Wolf-Willow again entered the door of his father's tepee. He returned to the Crooked Lakes speaking English fluently, and with the excellent appointment of interpreter for the Government Indian Agency. The instant his father saw him, the alert Cree eye noted the uncut hair. Nothing could have so pleased old Beaver-Tail. He had held for years a fear in his heart that the school would utterly rob him of his boy. Little Wolf-Willow's mother arose from preparing an antelope stew for supper. She looked up into her son's face. When he left he had not been as high as her ear tips. With the wonderful intuition of mothers the world over, she knew at the first glance that they had not made him into a white man. Years seemed to roll from her face. She had been so fearful lest he should not come back to their old prairie life.

"Rest here," she said, in the gentle Cree tongue. "Rest here, Little Wolf-Willow; it is your home."

The boy himself had been almost afraid to come. He had grown accustomed to sleeping in a house, in a bed, to wearing shoes, to eating the white man's food; but the blood of the prairies leaped in his veins at the sight of the great tepee, with its dry sod floor spread with wolf-skins and ancient buffalo hides. He flung himself on to the furs and the grass, his fingers threading themselves through the buckskin fringes that adorned old Beaver-tail's leggings.

"Father," he cried out, in the quaint Cree tongue, "father, sire of my own, I have learned the best the white man had to give, but they have not changed me, or my heart, any more than they could change the copper tint of my skin."

Old Beaver-Tail fairly chuckled, then replied, between pipe puffs, "Some of our Cree boys go to school. They learn the white man's ways, and they are of no more use to their people. They cannot trap for furs, nor scout, nor hunt, nor find a prairie trail. You are wiser than that, Little Wolf-Willow. You are smarter than when you left us, but you return to us, the old people of your tribe, just the same – just the same as your father and grandfather."

"Not quite the same," replied the boy, cautiously, "for, father, I do not now hate the North-West Mounted Police."

For answer, old Beaver-Tail snarled like a husky dog. "You'll hate them again when you live here long enough!" he muttered. "And if you have any friends among them, keep those friends distant, beyond the rim of the horizon. I will not have their scarlet coats showing here."

Wisely, the boy did not reply, and that night, rolled in coyote skins, he slept like a little child once more on the floor of his father's tepee.

For many months after that he travelled about the great prairies, visiting with the Government Indian Agent many distant camps and Cree lodges. He always rode astride a sturdy little buckskin-colored cayuse. Like most Indian boys, he was a splendid horseman, steady in his seat, swift of eye, and sure of every prairie trail in all Saskatchewan. He always wore a strange mixture of civilized and savage clothes – fringed buckskin "chaps," beaded moccasins, a blue flannel shirt, a scarlet silk handkerchief knotted around his throat, a wide-brimmed cowboy hat with a rattlesnake skin as a hatband, and two magnificent bracelets of ivory elks' teeth. His braided hair, his young, clean, thin, dark face, his fearless riding, began to be known far and wide. The men of the Hudson's Bay Company trusted him. The North-West Mounted Police loved him. But, most of all, he stood fast in the affection of his own Indian people. They never forgot the fact that, had he wished, he could have stayed with the white people altogether, that he was equal to them in English education, but he did not choose to do so – he was one of their own for all time.

But one dreadful night Corporal Manan of the North-West Mounted Police rode into barracks at Regina with a serious, worried face. He reported immediately to his captain. "A bad business, captain," he said, coming to attention, "a very bad business, sir. I have reports from old 'Scotty' McIntyre's ranch up north that young Wolf-Willow, that we all know so well, has been caught rustling cattle – cut out two calves, sir, and – well, he's stolen them, sir, and old Scotty is after him with a shotgun."

"Too bad, too bad!" said the captain, with genuine concern. "Young Wolf-Willow gone wrong! I can hardly believe it. How old is he, Corporal?"

"About sixteen or seventeen, I should say, sir."

"Too bad!" again said the captain. "Well educated; fine boy, too. What good has it done him? It seems these Indians *will* cut up. Education seems to only make them worse, Corporal. He'll feel arrest less from you than most of us. You'll have to go. Start early, at daylight, and bring him in to prison when you return."

"*I?*" fairly shouted Corporal Manan. "*I* arrest young Wolf-Willow? No, sir! You'll have to get another policeman."

"You'll do as you receive orders," blurted the captain, then added more graciously, "Why, Manan, don't you see how much better it is to arrest him? Scotty is after him with a shotgun, and he'll kill the boy on sight. Wolf-Willow is safest here. You leave at daylight, and bring him in, if you have to handcuff him to do it."

Corporal Manan spent a miserable night. Never had a task been so odious to him. He loved the bright, handsome Cree boy, and his heart was sore that he had gone wrong, after giving such promise of a fine, useful manhood. But the white settlers' cattle must be protected and orders were orders – a soldier must obey his superior officer. So, at daybreak, the fastest horse in the service was saddled, and Corporal Manan was hard on the trail of the young Cree thief.

But Little Wolf-Willow knew nothing of all this. Far away up the northern plains a terrible bit of news had come to him. At the Hudson's Bay post he had been told that his old grandfather had been caught stealing cattle, that the North-West Mounted Police were after him, that they would surely capture him and put him in Regina jail. The boy was horrified. His own old grandfather a thief! He knew that old warrior well enough – knew that he was innocent of intentional crime; knew that, should the scarlet-covered police give chase, the old Indian would never understand, but would probably fire and kill the man who attempted to arrest him. The boy knew that, with his own perfect knowledge of English, he could explain everything away if only he could be at his grandfather's in time, or else intercept the police before they should arrest him. His grandfather would shoot; the boy knew it. Then there would be bloodshed added to theft. But Big Wolf-Willow's lodge was ninety miles distant, and it was the middle of a long, severe winter. What was to be done? One thing only – he, Little Wolf-Willow, must ride, ride, ride! He must not waste an hour, or the prison at Regina would have his grandfather, and perhaps a gallant soldier of the king would meet his death doing his duty.

Thrusting a pouch of pemmican into his shirt front, and fastening his buckskin coat tightly across his chest, he flung himself on to his wiry little cayuse, faced about to the north-east, and struck the trail for the lodges of his own people. Then began the longest, most terrible ride of his life. Afterwards, when he became a man, he often felt that he lived through years and years during that ninety-mile journey. On all sides of him stretched the blinding white, snow-covered prairie. Not a tree, not an object to mark the trail. The wind blew straight and level directly down from the Arctic zone, icy, cutting, numbing. It whistled past his ears, pricking and stinging his face like a whiplash. The cold, yellow sunlight on the snow blinded him, like a light flashed from a mirror. Not a human habitation, not a living thing, lay in his path. Night came, with countless stars and a joyous crescent of Northern Lights hanging low in the sky, and the intense, still cold that haunts the prairie country. He grudged the hours of rest he must give his horse, pitying the poor beast for lack of food and water, but compelled to urge it on and on. After what seemed a lifetime of hardship, both boy and beast began to weaken. The irresistible sleepiness that forebodes freezing began to overcome Little Wolf-Willow. Utter exhaustion was sapping the strength of the cayuse. But they blundered on, mile after mile, both with the pluck of the prairies in their red blood; colder, slower, wearier, they became. Little Wolf-Willow's head was whirling, his brain thickening, his fingers clutching aimlessly. The bridle reins slipped from his hands. Hunger, thirst, cold, exhaustion, overpowered both horse and rider. The animal stumbled once, twice, then fell like a dead weight.

* * *

At daybreak, Corporal Manan, hot on the pursuit of the supposed young cattle thief, rode up the freezing trail, headed for the north-east. A mile ahead of him he saw what he thought was a dead steer which the coyotes had probably killed and were eating. As he galloped nearer he saw it was a horse. An exclamation escaped his lips. Then, slipping from his own mount, stiff and half frozen himself, he bent pityingly above the dead animal that lay with the slender body of an Indian hugging up to it for warmth.

"Poor little chap!" choked the Corporal. "Poor Little Wolf-Willow! Death's got him now, I'm afraid, and that's worse than the Mounted Police."

Then the soldier knelt down, and for two long hours rubbed with snow and his own fur cap the thin, frozen face and hands of the almost lifeless body. He rolled the lithe young body about, pounding it and beating it, until consciousness returned, and the boy opened his eyes dully.

"That's better," said the Corporal. "Now, my lad, it's for home!" Then he stripped himself of his own great-coat, wrapped it snugly about the young Indian, and, placing the boy on his own horse, he trudged ahead on foot – five, ten, fifteen miles of it, the boy but half conscious and freezing, the man tramping ahead, footsore, chilled through, and troubled, the horse with hanging head and lagging step – a strange trio to enter the Indian camp.

From far off old Beaver-Tail had seen the approaching bit of hated scarlet – the tunic worn by the North-West Mounted Police – but he made no comment as Corporal Manan lifted in his strong arms the still figure from the saddle, and, carrying it into the tepee, laid it beside the fire on the warm wolf skins and buffalo hides. It took much heat and nourishment before Little Wolf-Willow was able to interpret the story from the Cree tongue into English, then back again into Cree, and so be the go-between for the Corporal and old Beaver-Tail. "Yes, my grandfather, Big Wolf-Willow, is here," said the boy, his dark eyes looking fearlessly into the Corporal's blue ones. "He's here, as you see, and I suppose you will have to arrest him. He acknowledges he took the cattle. He was poor, hungry, starving. You see, Corporal, he cannot speak English, and he does not understand the white man or their laws. He says for me to tell you that the white men came and stole all our buffaloes, the millions of beautiful animals that supplied us with hides to make our tepees, furs to dress in, meat to eat, fat to keep us warm; so he thought it no harm to take two small calves when he was hungry. He asks if anyone arrested and punished the white man who took all his buffaloes, and, if not, why should he be arrested and punished for doing far less wrong than the wrong done by the white man?"

"But – but – " stammered Corporal Manan, "I'm not after *him*. It is *you* I was told to arrest."

"Oh, why didn't I know? Why didn't I know it was I you were after?" cried the boy. "I would have let you take me, handcuff me, anything, for I understand, but he does not."

Corporal Manan stood up, shaking his shoulders as a big dog shakes after a plunge. Then he spoke: "Little Wolf-Willow, can you ever forgive us all for thinking you were a cattle-thief? When I think of your grandfather's story of the millions of buffaloes he has lost, and those two paltry calves he took for food, I make no arrests here. My captain must do what he thinks best."

"And you saved me from freezing to death, and brought me home on your own horse, when you were sent out to take me to prison!" muttered the boy, turning to his soldier friend with admiration.

But old Beaver-Tail interrupted. He arose, held out his hand towards the once hated scarlet-coated figure, and spoke the first words he had ever voiced in English. They were, "North-West Mounted Police, good man, he. Beaver-Tail's friend."

## Sons of Savages

### Life Training of the Redskin Boy-Child

The Redskin boy-child who looks out from his little cradle-board on a world of forest through whose trails his baby feet are already being fitted to follow is not many hours old before careful hands wrap him about with gay-beaded bands that are strapped to the carven and colored back-board that will cause him to stand erect and upright when he is a grown warrior. His small feet are bound against a foot support so that they are exactly straight; that is to start his walk in life aright.

He is but an atom in the most renowned of the savage races known to history, a people that, according to the white man's standard, is uncivilized, uneducated, illiterate, and barbarous. Yet the upbringing of every Red Indian male child begins at his birth, and ends only when he has acquired the learning considered essential for the successful man to possess, and which has been predetermined through many ages by many wise ancestors.

His education is twofold, and always is imparted in "pairs" of subjects – that is, while he is being instructed in the requisites of fighting, hunting, food getting, and his national sports, he takes with each "subject" a very rigid training in etiquette, for it would be as great a disgrace for him to fail in manners of good breeding as to fail to take the war-path when he reaches the age of seventeen.

#### First, Courage

The education of an Iroquois boy is begun before he can even speak. The first thing he is taught is courage – the primitive courage that must absolutely despise fear – and at the same time he is thoroughly grounded in the first immutable law of Indian etiquette, which is that under no conditions must one ever stare, as the Redskin races hold that staring marks the lowest level of ill-breeding.

#### Second, Religious Training

His second subject is religious training. While he is yet a baby in arms he is carried "pick-a-back" in his mother's blanket to the ancient dances and festivals, where he sees for the first time, and in his infant way participates in, the rites and rituals of the pagan faith, learning to revere the "Great Spirit," and to anticipate the happy hunting grounds that await him after death.

At the end of a long line of picturesque braves and warriors who circle gracefully in the worshipping dance, his mother carries him, her smooth, soft-footed, twisting step lulling him to sleep, for his tiny, copper-colored person, swinging to every curve of the dance, soon becomes an unconscious bit of babyhood. But the instant he learns to walk, he learns, too, the religious dance-steps. Then he rises to the dignity of being allowed to slip his hand in that of his father and take his first important steps in the company of the men.

Accompanying his religious training is the all-important etiquette of accepting food without comment. No Indian talks of food, or discusses it while taking it. He must neither commend nor condemn it, and a child who remarks upon the meals set before him, however simple the remark may be, instantly feels his disgrace in the sharpest reproof from his parents. It is one of the unforgiveable crimes.

#### Tricks of Food-Getting

His third subject is to master the tricks of food-getting. His father, or more often his grandfather, takes him in hand at an early age, and minutely trains him in all the art and artifice of the great life-fight for food both for himself and for those who may in later years be dependent on him. He is drilled assiduously in hunting, fishing, trapping, in game calls, in wood and water lore; he learns to paddle with stealth, to step in silence, to conceal himself from the scent and sight of bird and beast, to be swift as a deer, keen as an eagle, alert as a fox.

He is admonished under no conditions, save in that of extreme hunger or in self-defence, to kill mating game, or, in fact, to kill at all save for food or to obtain furs for couch purposes. Wanton slaying of wild things is unknown among the uncivilized Red Indian. When they want occupation in sport or renown, they take the warpath against their fellow-kind, where killing will flaunt another eagle-feather in their crest, not simply another pair of antlers to decorate their tepee.

With this indispensable lesson in the essentials of living always comes the scarcely less momentous one of the utter unimportance of youth. He is untiringly disciplined in the veneration of age, whether it be in man or woman. He must listen with rapt attention to the opinions and advice of the older men. He must keep an absolute silence while they speak, must ever watch for opportunities to pay them deference.

### Age Before Lineage

If he happen, fortunately, to be the son of a chief of ancient lineage, the fact that he is of blood royal will not excuse him entering a door before some aged "commoner." Age has more honor than all his patrician line of descent can give him. Those lowly born but richly endowed with years must walk before him; he is not permitted to remain seated if some old employee is standing even at work; his privilege of birth is as nothing compared with the honor of age, even in his father's hireling.

The fourth thing he must master is the thorough knowledge of medicinal roots and herbs – antidotes for snake-bite and poison – also the various charms and the elementary "science" of the medicine man, though the occupation of the latter must be inherited, and made in itself a life study. With this branch of drilling also is inculcated the precept of etiquette never to speak of or act slightingly of another's opinion, and never to say the word "No," which he is taught to regard as a rude refusal. He may convey it by manner or action, but speak it – never.

And during the years he is absorbing this education he is unceasingly instructed in every branch of warfare, of canoe-making, of fashioning arrows, paddles and snow-shoes. He studies the sign language, the history and legends of his nation; he familiarizes himself with the "archives" of wampum belts, learning to read them and to value the great treaties they sealed. He excels in the national sports of "lacrosse," "bowl and beans," and "snow snake," and when, finally, he goes forth to face his forest world he is equipped to obtain his own living with wisdom and skill, and starts life a brave, capable, well-educated gentleman, though some yet call him an uncivilized savage.

## From *Legends of Vancouver* (1922)

### The Lost Salmon-Run

Great had been the "run," and the sockeye season was almost over. For that reason I wondered many times why my old friend, the klootchman,[4] had failed to make one of the fishing fleet. She was an indefatigable work-woman, rivalling her husband as an expert catcher, and all the year through she talked of little else but the coming run. But this especial season she had not appeared amongst her fellow-kind. The fleet and the canneries knew nothing of her, and when I enquired of her tribes-people they would reply without explanation, " She not here this year."

But one russet September afternoon I found her. I had idled down the trail from the swans' basin in Stanley Park to the rim that skirts the Narrows, and I saw her graceful, high-bowed canoe heading for the beach that is the favourite landing-place of the "tillicums"[5] from the Mission. Her canoe looked like a dream-craft, for the water was very still, and everywhere a blue film hung like a fragrant veil, for the peat on Lulu Island had been smouldering for days and its pungent odours and blue-grey haze made a dream-world of sea and shore and sky.

---

[4] "Woman" or "female" in the trading language of the North-west Indians.

[5] Friends.

I hurried up-shore, hailing her in the Chinook, and as she caught my voice she lifted her paddle directly above her head in the Indian signal of greeting.

As she beached, I greeted her with extended eager hands to assist her ashore, for the klootchman is getting to be an old woman; albeit she paddles against tide-water like a boy in his teens.

"No," she said, as I begged her to come ashore. " I will wait – me. I just come to fetch Maarda; she been city; she soon come – now." But she left her "working" attitude and curled like a school-girl in the bow of the canoe, her elbows resting on her paddle which she had flung across the gunwales.

"I have missed you, klootchman; you have not been to see me for three moons, and you have not fished or been at the canneries," I remarked.

"No," she said. " I stay home this year." Then, leaning towards me with grave import in her manner, her eyes, her voice, she added, "I have a grandchild, born first week July, so – I stay."

So this explained her absence. I, of course, offered congratulations and enquired all about the great event, for this was her first grandchild, and the little person was of importance.

"And are you going to make a fisherman of him?" I asked.

" No, no, not boy-child, it is girl-child," she answered with some indescribable trick of expression that led me to know she preferred it so.

"You are pleased it is a girl?" I questioned in surprise.

"Very pleased," she replied emphatically. "Very good luck to have girl for first grandchild. Our tribe not like yours; we want girl-children first, we not always wish boy-child born just for fight. Your people, they care only for war-path; our tribe more peaceful. Very good sign first grandchild to be girl. I tell you why girl-child may be some time mother herself; very grand thing to be mother."

I felt I had caught the secret of her meaning. She was rejoicing that this little one should some time become one of the mothers of her race. We chatted over it a little longer and she gave me several playful "digs" about my own tribe thinking so much less of motherhood than hers, and so much more of battle and bloodshed. Then we drifted into talk of the sockeye and of the hyiu chickimin the Indians would get.

"Yes, hyiu chickimin," she repeated with a sigh of satisfaction. "Always; and hyiu muck-a-muck when big salmon run. No more ever come that bad year when not any fish."

"When was that?" I asked.

"Before you born, or I, or" pointing across the park to the distant city of Vancouver that breathed its wealth and beauty across the September afternoon – "before that place born, before white man came here – oh! long before."

Dear old klootchman! I knew by the dusk in her eyes that she was back in her Land of Legends, and that soon I would be the richer in my hoard of Indian lore. She sat, still leaning on her paddle; her eyes, half closed, rested on the distant outline of the blurred heights across the Inlet. I shall not further attempt her broken English, for this is but the shadow of her story, and without her unique personality the legend is as a flower that lacks both colour and fragrance. She called it "The Lost Salmon-run."

"The wife of the Great Tyee[6] was but a wisp of a girl, but all the world was young in those days; even the Fraser River was young and small, not the mighty water it is to-day; but the pink salmon crowded its throat just as they do now, and the tillicums caught and salted and smoked the fish just as they have done this year, just as they will always do. But it was yet winter, and the rains were slanting and the fogs drifting, when the wife of the Great Tyee stood before him and said:

" 'Before the salmon-run I shall give to you a great gift. Will you honour me most if it is the gift of a boy-child or a girl-child?' The Great Tyee loved the woman. He was stern with his people, hard with his tribe; he ruled his council-fires with a will of stone. His medicine-men said he had no human heart in his body; his warriors said he had no human blood in his veins. But he clasped this woman's hands, and his eyes, his lips, his voice, were gentle as her own, as he replied:

" 'Give to me a girl-child – a little girl-child – that she may grow to be like you, and, in her turn, give to her husband children.'

---

6 Chief.

"But when the tribes-people heard of his choice they arose in great anger. They surrounded him in a deep, indignant circle. 'You are a slave to the woman,' they declared, 'and now you desire to make yourself a slave to a woman-baby. We want an heir – a man-child to be our Great Tyee in years to come. When you are old and weary of tribal affairs, when you sit wrapped in your blanket in the hot summer sunshine, because your blood is old and thin, what can a girl-child do, to help either you or us? Who, then, will be our Great Tyee?'

"He stood in the centre of the menacing circle, his arms folded, his chin raised, his eyes hard as flint. His voice, cold as stone, replied:

" 'Perhaps she will give you such a man-child, and, if so, the child is yours; he will belong to you, not to me; he will become the possession of the people. But if the child is a girl she will belong to me – she will be mine. You cannot take her from me as you took me from my mother's side and forced me to forget my aged father in my service to the tribe; she will belong to me, will be the mother of my grandchildren, and her husband will be my son.'

" 'You do not care for the good of your tribe. You care only for your own wishes and desires,' they rebelled. 'Suppose the salmon-run is small, we will have no food; suppose there is no man-child, we will have no Great Tyee to show us how to get food from other tribes, and we shall starve.'

" 'Your hearts are black and bloodless,' thundered the Great Tyee, turning upon them fiercely, 'and your eyes are blinded. Do you wish the tribe to forget how great is the importance of a child that will some day be a mother herself, and give to your children and grandchildren a Great Tyee? Are the people to live, to thrive, to increase, to become more powerful with no mother – women to bear future sons and daughters? Your minds are dead, your brains are chilled. Still, even in your ignorance, you are my people: you and your wishes must be considered. I call together the great medicine-men, the men of witchcraft, the men of magic. They shall decide the laws which will follow the bearing of either boy or girl-child. What say you, oh! mighty men?'

"Messengers were then sent up and down the coast, sent far up the Fraser River, and to the valley lands inland for many leagues, gathering as they journeyed, all the men of magic that could be found. Never were so many medicine-men in council before. They built fires and danced and chanted for many days. They spoke with the gods of the mountains, with the gods of the sea; then 'the power' of decision came to them. They were inspired with a choice to lay before the tribes-people, and the most ancient medicine-man in all the coast region arose and spoke their resolution:

" 'The people of the tribe cannot be allowed to have all things. They want a boy-child and they want a great salmon-run also. They cannot have both. The Sagalie Tyee has revealed to us, the great men of magic, that both these things will make the people arrogant and selfish. They must choose between the two.'

" 'Choose, oh! you ignorant tribes-people,' commanded the Great Tyee. 'The wise men of our coast have said that the girl-child who will some day bear children of her own will also bring abundance of salmon at her birth; but the boy-child brings to you but himself.'

" 'Let the salmon go,' shouted the people, 'but give us a future Great Tyee. Give us the boy-child.'

"And when the child was born it was a boy.

" 'Evil will fall upon you,' wailed the Great Tyee. 'You have despised a mother-woman. You will suffer evil and starvation and hunger and poverty, oh! foolish tribes-people. Did you not know how great a girl-child is?'

"That spring, people from a score of tribes came up to the Fraser for the salmon-run. They came great distances – from the mountains, the lakes, the far-off dry lands, but not one fish entered the vast rivers of the Pacific Coast. The people had made their choice. They had forgotten the honour that a mother-child would have brought them. They were bereft of their food. They were stricken with poverty. Through the long winter that followed they endured hunger and starvation. Since then our tribe has always welcomed girl-children – we want no more lost runs."

The klootchman lifted her arms from her paddle as she concluded; her eyes left the irregular outline of the violet mountains. She had come back to this year of grace – her Legend Land had vanished.

"So," she added, "you see now, maybe, why I am glad my grandchild is girl; it means big salmon-run next year."

"It is a beautiful story, klootchman," I said, "and I feel a cruel delight that your men of magic punished the people for their ill choice."

"That because you girl-child yourself," she laughed.

There was the slightest whisper of a step behind me. I turned to find Maarda almost at my elbow. The rising tide was unbeaching the canoe, and as Maarda stepped in and the klootchman slipped astern, it drifted afloat.

"Kla-how-ya," nodded the klootchman as she dipped her paddle-blade in exquisite silence.

"Kla-how-ya," smiled Maarda.

"Kla-how-ya, tillicums," I replied, and watched for many moments as they slipped away into the blurred distance, until the canoe merged into the violet and grey of the farther shore.

## THE SEA-SERPENT

There is one vice that is absolutely unknown to the red man; he was born without it, and amongst all the deplorable things he has learned from the white races, this, at least, he has never acquired. That is the vice of avarice. That the Indian looks upon greed of gain, miserliness, avariciousness, and wealth accumulated above the head of his poorer neighbour as one of the lowest degradations he can fall to is perhaps more aptly illustrated than anything I could quote to demonstrate his horror of what he calls "the white man's unkindness." In a very wide and varied experience with many tribes, I have yet to find even one instance of avarice, and I have encountered but one single case of a "stingy Indian," and this man was so marked amongst his fellows that at mention of his name his tribespeople jeered and would remark contemptuously that he was like a white man – hated to share his money and his possessions. All red races are born Socialists, and most tribes carry out their communistic ideas to the letter. Amongst the Iroquois it is considered disgraceful to have food if your neighbour has none. To be a creditable member of the nation you must divide your possessions with your less fortunate fellows. I find it much the same amongst the Coast Indians, though they are less bitter in their hatred of the extremes of wealth and poverty than are the Eastern tribes. Still, the very fact that they have preserved this legend, in which they liken avarice to a slimy sea-serpent, shows the trend of their ideas; shows, too, that an Indian is an Indian, no matter what his tribe; shows that he cannot, or will not, hoard money; shows that his native morals demand that the spirit of greed must be strangled at all cost.

The chief and I had sat long over our luncheon. He had been talking of his trip to England and of the many curious things he had seen. At last, in an outburst of enthusiasm, he said: "I saw everything in the world – everything but a sea-serpent!"

"But there is no such thing as a sea-serpent," I laughed, "so you must have really seen everything in the world."

His face clouded; for a moment he sat in silence; then, looking directly at me, said, "Maybe none now, but long ago there was one here – in the Inlet."

"How long ago?" I asked.

"When first the white gold-hunters came," he replied. "Came with greedy, clutching fingers, greedy eyes, greedy hearts. The white men fought, murdered, starved, went mad with love of that gold far up the Fraser River. Tillicums were tillicums no more, brothers were foes, fathers and sons were enemies. Their love of the gold was a curse."

"Was it then the sea-serpent was seen?" I asked, perplexed with the problem of trying to connect the goldseekers with such a monster.

"Yes, it was then, but – " he hesitated, then plunged into the assertion, "but you will not believe the story if you think there is no such thing as a sea-serpent."

"I shall believe whatever you tell me, Chief," I answered. "I am only too ready to believe. You know I come of a superstitious race, and all my association with the Pale-faces has never yet robbed me of my birthright to believe strange traditions."

"You always understand," he said after a pause.

"It's my heart that understands," I remarked quietly.

He glanced up quickly, and with one of his all too few radiant smiles, he laughed.

"Yes, skookum tum-tum." Then without further hesitation he told the tradition, which, although not of ancient happening, is held in great reverence by his tribe. During its recital he sat with folded arms, leaning on the table, his head and shoulders bending eagerly towards me as I sat at the opposite side. It was the only time he ever talked to me when he did not use emphasizing gesticulations, but his hands never once lifted: his wonderful eyes alone gave expression to what he called "The Legend of the 'Salt-chuck Oluk' " (sea-serpent).

"Yes, it was during the first gold craze, and many of our young men went as guides to the whites far up the Fraser. When they returned they brought these tales of greed and murder back with them, and our old people and our women shook their heads and said evil would come of it. But all our young men, except one, returned as they went – kind to the poor, kind to those who were foodless, sharing whatever they had with their tillicums. But one, by name Shakshak (The Hawk), came back with hoards of gold nuggets, chickimin,[7] everything; he was rich like the white men, and, like them, he kept it. He would count his chickimin, count his nuggets, gloat over them, toss them in his palms. He rested his head on them as he slept, he packed them about with him through the day. He loved them better than food, better than his tillicums, better than his life. The entire tribe arose. They said Shak-shak had the disease of greed; that to cure it he must give a great potlatch, divide his riches with the poorer ones, share them with the old, the sick, the foodless. But he jeered and laughed and told them No, and went on loving and gloating over his gold.

"Then the Sagalie Tyee spoke out of the sky and said, 'Shak-shak, you have made of yourself a loathsome thing; you will not listen to the cry of the hungry, to the call of the old and sick; you will not share your possessions; you have made of yourself an outcast from your tribe and disobeyed the ancient laws of your people. Now I will make of you a thing loathed and hated by all men, both white and red. You will have two heads, for your greed has two mouths to bite. One bites the poor, and one bites your own evil heart; and the fangs in these mouths are poison – poison that kills the hungry, and poison that kills your own manhood. Your evil heart will beat in the very centre of your foul body, and he that pierces it will kill the disease of greed for ever from amongst his people.' And when the sun arose above the North Arm the next morning the tribes-people saw a gigantic sea-serpent stretched across the surface of the waters. One hideous head rested on the bluffs at Brockton Point, the other rested on a group of rocks just below the Mission, at the western edge of North Vancouver. If you care to go there some day I will show you the hollow in one great stone where that head lay. The tribes-people were stunned with horror. They loathed the creature, they hated it, they feared it. Day after day it lay there, its monstrous heads lifted out of the waters, its mile-long body blocking all entrance from the Narrows, all outlet from the North Arm. The chiefs made council, the medicine-men danced and chanted, but the salt-chuck oluk never moved. It could not move, for it was the hated totem of what now rules the white man's world – greed and love of chickimin. No one can ever move the love of chickimin from the white man's heart, no one can ever make him divide all with the poor. But after the chiefs and medicine-men had done all in their power and still the salt-chuck oluk lay across the waters, a handsome boy of sixteen approached them and reminded them of the words of the Sagalie Tyee, 'that he that pierced the monster's heart would kill the disease of greed for ever amongst his people.'

" 'Let me try to find this evil heart, oh! great men of my tribe,' he cried. 'Let me war upon this creature; let me try to rid my people of this pestilence.'

"The boy was brave and very beautiful. His tribes-people called him the Tenas Tyee (Little Chief) and they loved him. Of all his wealth of fish and furs, of game and hykwa (large shell-money) he gave to the boys who had none; he hunted food for the old people; he tanned skins and furs for those whose feet were feeble, whose eyes were fading, whose blood ran thin with age.

" 'Let him go!' cried the tribes-people. 'This unclean monster can only be overcome by cleanliness, this creature of greed can only be overthrown by generosity. Let him go!' The chiefs and the medicine-men listened, then consented. 'Go,' they commanded, 'and fight this thing with your strongest weapons – cleanliness and generosity.'

---

[7] Money [Johnson's note].

"The Tenas Tyee turned to his mother. 'I shall be gone four days,' he told her, 'and I shall swim all that time. I have tried all my life to be generous, but the people say I must be clean also to fight this unclean thing. While I am gone put fresh furs on my bed every day, even if I am not here to lie on them; if I know my bed, my body, and my heart are all clean I can overcome this serpent.'

" 'Your bed shall have fresh furs every morning,' his mother said simply.

"The Tenas Tyee then stripped himself, and, with no clothing save a buckskin belt into which he thrust his hunting-knife, he flung his lithe young body into the sea. But at the end of four days he did not return. Sometimes his people could see him swimming far out in midchannel, endeavouring to find the exact centre of the serpent, where lay its evil, selfish heart; but on the fifth morning they saw him rise out of the sea, climb to the summit of Brockton Point, and greet the rising sun with outstretched arms. Weeks and months went by, still the Tenas Tyee would swim daily searching for that heart of greed; and each morning the sunrise glinted on his slender young copper-coloured body as he stood with outstretched arms at the tip of Brockton Point, greeting the coming day and then plunging from the summit into the sea.

"And at his home on the north shore his mother dressed his bed with fresh furs each morning. The seasons drifted by; winter followed summer, summer followed winter. But it was four years before the Tenas Tyee found the centre of the great salt-chuck oluk and plunged his hunting-knife into its evil heart. In its death-agony it writhed through the Narrows, leaving a trail of blackness on the waters. Its huge body began to shrink, to shrivel; it became dwarfed and withered, until nothing but the bones of its back remained, and they, sea-bleached and lifeless, soon sank to the bed of the ocean leagues off from the run of land. But as the Tenas Tyee swam homeward and his clean young body crossed through the black stain left by the serpent, the waters became clear and blue and sparkling. He had overcome even the trail of the salt-chuck oluk.

"When at last he stood in the doorway of his home he said, 'My mother, I could not have killed the monster of greed amongst my people had you not helped me by keeping one place for me at home fresh and clean for my return.'

"She looked at him as only mothers look. 'Each day, these four years, fresh furs have I laid for your bed. Sleep now, and rest, oh! my Tenas Tyee,' she said."

* * *

The chief unfolded his arms, and his voice took another tone as he said, "What do you call that story – a legend?"

"The white people would call it an allegory," I answered. He shook his head.

"No savvy," he smiled.

I explained as simply as possible, and with his customary alertness he immediately understood. "That's right," he said. "That's what we say it means, we Squamish, that greed is evil and not clean, like the salt-chuck oluk. That it must be stamped out amongst our people, killed by cleanliness and generosity. The boy that overcame the serpent was both these things."

What became of this splendid boy?" I asked.

"The Tenas Tyee? Oh! some of our old, old people say they sometimes see him now, standing on Brockton Point, his bare young arms outstretched to the rising sun," he replied.

"Have you ever seen him, Chief?" I questioned.

"No," he answered simply. But I have never heard such poignant regret as his wonderful voice crowded into that single word.

# Mabel Washbourne Anderson (Cherokee, 1863–1949)

*Anderson was born in Arkansas to a family of prominent Cherokee forebears, including John Ridge, her maternal grandfather, who was a member of the Treaty Party that agreed to move from traditional Cherokee lands in Georgia to Indian Territory. Her paternal grandfather, Cephus Washburn (Anderson's father changed the spelling), was a well-known early missionary and the founder of Dwight Mission in Arkansas, as she describes briefly in a piece about her uncle, Edward Pason Washbourne, "The Southern Artist." The daughter of Josiah Woodward and Catherine Ridge Washbourne, Anderson grew up in the Cherokee Nation in what is now Oklahoma. Like Lucy Lowrey Hoyt Keys, she attended the Cherokee Female Seminary, graduating in 1883 and later beginning a teaching career in the Cherokee Schools in Vinita, where she taught for several years. After her marriage in 1891 to John Carlton Anderson, she continued to teach and began to write in a variety of forms. Her affirmation of Cherokee history emerges in much of her writing, including her brief but informative volume,* The Life of General Stand Watie, the Only Indian General of the Confederate Army and the Last General to Surrender *(1915). Stand Watie was her grandfather's cousin; in 1913, she organized a chapter of the United Daughters of the Confederacy in his name.*

*Like Ora Eddleman Reed and Narcissa Owen, Anderson appeared to value her Southern heritage. Her interest in history is also evident from essays like "Old Fort Gibson on the Grand," and her desire to preserve Cherokee traditions emerges in "Nowita, the Sweet Singer," a publication that was widely reprinted. As a member of the local Sequoyah Literary Society, Anderson wrote and read on a variety of Cherokee topics, also contributing her work to a range of local and regional periodicals such as* Indian Chieftain, Talequah Arrow, Twin Territories, Sturm's Oklahoma Magazine, *and* Vinita Weekly Chieftain. *Her ability as a children's author emerges in "Joe Jamison's Sacrifice." The Andersons moved to Pryor Creek, Oklahoma in 1904, and she continued to publish, mostly on American Indian subjects, including an appreciation of the poet John Rollin Ridge, her uncle, and to teach in the local high school. After 1930, when she and her husband moved to Tulsa, she dropped from sight as a writer; when she died in 1949, the local newspaper elided her Cherokee heritage, describing her only as a "colorful pioneer."*

## Bibliography

### Primary


"The Cherokee Poet and 'Mt. Shasta.'" *Sturm's Oklahoma Magazine* 6 (March 1908): 23–5.

"Joe Jamison's Sacrifice." *Sturm's Oklahoma Magazine* 6 (July 1908): 44–8.

*The Life of General Stand Watie, the Only Indian General of the Confederate Army and the Last General to Surrender*. Mayles County Republican, 1915; rev. ed., 1931.

"Nowíta, the Sweet Singer." *Twin Territories* 5 (January 1903): 1–2.
"Old Fort Gibson on the Grand." *Twin Territories* 4 (September 1902): 249–55.
"The Southern Artist." *Sturm's Oklahoma Magazine* 4 (June–July 1907): 5–7.

Secondary

Boren, Lyle H. and Dale Boren. *Who is Who in Oklahoma*. Cooperative Publishing, 1935.
Littlefield, Daniel F., Jr. "Mabel Washbourne Anderson." In *Native American Women: A Biographical Dictionary*. Ed. Gretchen Bataille. Garland, 1993.
Littlefield, Daniel F., Jr., and James W. Parins. *A Biobibliography of Native American Writers, 1772–1924*. Scarecrow, 1986.
"Sketch of Mrs. Mabel W. Anderson." *Twin Territories* 3 (June 1901): 99.

## Nowita, the Sweet Singer – A Romantic Tradition of Spavinaw, Indian Territory (*Twin Territories*, January, 1903)

Spavinaw is the most beautiful stream in the Cherokee Nation. Nourished by the sparkling waters of the many springs in that locality, it winds like a shining thread of crystal through the narrow valleys between the hills which bear its name; curving its way by circuitous route, as if reluctant to leave its native hills, the murmur of whose pines chant a tuneful accompaniment to the music of its waters. Nestled among the hills, and within these valleys are the homes of many of the full blood Cherokees, who seek the seclusion and the quiet of the forests in preference to the open prairies, dotted with farms and towns and traversed by railroads. These little Indian cabins are scarcely less difficult to locate than are the haunts of the deer. Secluded in the summer by the luxuriant foliage of the forest trees, the unfamiliar traveler might well imagine, by the whispering of the pines, that "This is the forest primeval." In one of the most picturesque spots of this section of the country stands a lonely Indian cabin which possesses more than ordinary interest to the stranger, for "all the world loves a romance as well as a lover." Tall pines and moss grown rocks shelter the building from the gaze of the intruder. Fate seems to have chosen this site as a fit setting for the gem of romance that has made this cabin an object of interest and curiosity. It was once the home of a young Indian girl, the heroine of a romance that had its origin in the National High Schools of the Cherokee Nation, which are located at Talequah, the national capitol. 'Tis the pathetic story of Nowita, a sweet singing Cherokee maiden, a pupil in the Female Seminary, and a young professor from the east, who taught in the Male Seminary. The Male and Female Seminaries were originally situated three miles from the town of Talequah, and separated from each other by the same distance of lonely prairie, lonely in the winter when the unbroken landscape lay bleak and colorless, but beautiful in the summer when you might gaze as far as eye could reach over the green billows of waving grass, brightened with the variegated hues of many wild flowers, away in the distance to the purple line of the Boston and Ozark mountains. It was an old custom years ago at the Female Seminary, to give a reception to the teachers and pupils of the Male Seminary once every quarter, and every year, on the 7th day of May, the anniversary of the founding of the two schools, was celebrated by a picnic upon the beautiful banks of the winding Illinois, three miles away. Thus it came about that Nowita, the sweet singer, sang ballads in her own native tongue to the pale faced stranger on "Reception Days," and on May day picnics they wandered side by side down the lovely stream, allured from the society of the others by the music of its waters, gathering the spring violets as they went, which they afterwards made into a wreath for Nowita's dusky braids, all unconsciously weaving a bleeding heart among the purple blossoms, for the little Indian maid had learned the language of love more rapidly than she had acquired English, though unusually bright and advanced for her age, and environments, her broken sentences and quaint expressions amused and charmed her admirer as much as the musical cadences of her voice. So time went by and the young man realized that he welcomed with an indefinable eagerness every opportunity that threw him in the society of the young Indian girl, and noted too that her dark eyes, usually so serene and melancholy, shone with a happy lustre in his presence, and he found a vague and pathetic pleasure in the thought that the school days were almost over, and that their final parting was near. But fate, that with cruel and relentless hand had brought together these two young people so dissimilar by environments and nationality, decreed that one of them, at least, should fulfill the destiny allotted her. So when the summer vacation came, and Nowita returned to the primitive home of her parents among the hills, contrary to the advice of his friend and the accusing memory of a pair of blue eyes, among the green mountains of New Hampshire, the young professor joined a camping party for a fortnight's recreation on the banks of the Spavinaw, ostensibly to gather "Indian lore and legends." It is needless to say that he soon sought and found the home of Nowita, and the object of his thoughts. The old story begun at the school was renewed and continued among more romantic surroundings, and with fewer obstructions, save for the grave rebuke and distrust written upon the austere faces of the girl's parents and acquaintances which found no expression in words, for whatever may be said of the refining influence of civilization upon the Indian, the dignity and native pride of a full-blood Cherokee are conceded by all who are at all familiar with their character. Cruel and revengeful they may be, when under oppression, and perhaps treacherous, but coarse or vulgar never. This Indian romance of local celebrity, is given below in parodical form:

Should you ask me whence this story,
Whence this romance and tradition
Of the sad eyed Indian maiden
Of Nowita, the sweet singer,
I should answer, I should tell you
Of a pale and handsome stranger
Teaching in an Indian college
In the village of Tahlequah
At the time that you shall hear of;
I should speak up; I should tell you;
How this fair and fickle stranger
Trifled with this child of nature,
Singing with her gay and thoughtless,
Every moment when together,
Never weary grew the maiden,
Singing with the handsome stranger,
And their voices sweetly blending,
Could be heard throughout the building,
Singing old love songs together
Ballads old and ever lovely.
He pronouncing words in English
She expressing them in Indian,
And he praised her voice and beauty
Whispering words which mean to flatter,
And Nowita sweet and childlike,
Listened to his honeyed speeches
Knew no word which meant deceiving,
And her heart to love unlettered
Filled with new and dreamy music,
And she called him Ska-kle-los-ky
Ska-kle-los-ky, the sweet speaker.

Listening in the halls below them

Stood the friend of Ska-kle-los-ky,
With a cynic's face he listened
To their voices softly singing,
Through his shadow dark and chilling
Like an evil spirit near them,
As a thorn upon a rose stem,
So his presence stung the maiden,
For she felt his disapproval
Of the friendship they were forming,
And she called him Oo-naw-whee-hee
Oo-naw-whee-hee, cold and cruel.
When the sultry days of summer
Came with all their brilliant splendor,
And upon the green prairie
Danced the vexing "Lazy Lawrence"
When her school mates all departed
To their homes and to their parents
None were half so heavy-hearted
As this gentle Indian maiden –
As Nowita, the sweet singer;
All the wild birds of the forest
All the singing brooks and rivers
And the breath of bursting blossoms
From the sweet wild honey suckle[1]
And the calling of the pine trees
From her home among the mountains
Failed to interest their comrade
Or her homeward steps to hasten.
Sad at heart this forest maiden
Left the village of Tahlequah,
Went back to her home and people,
To her home among the pine trees.
And she fancied she was dreaming,
Dreaming of the vanished hours,
When one evening in the twilight
Came her pale and handsome hero –
"Tis his spirit that appeareth,
And my love is dead," she murmured.

Then he told her all the story,
How his friend and other comrades
Had encamped within the valley
Seeking rest and recreation,
How with eagerness he joined them
That again he might be near her,
Saying, "Won't you give me welcome
To the shelter of your pine trees?

[1] "Wild Honeysuckle," a lovely species of the honeysuckle found in the Cherokee's Nation among the rocks of Spavinaw [Anderson's note].

I have come to know your people,
Learn your language, customs, habits,
Learn your legends and traditions,
Will you be my skillful teacher?
I will help you with your English
With your books of prose and verses,
And we'll while away the hours
Helping, teaching, one another."
And he quickly read his answer
In the lovelight on her features.
He abandoned all the future
To the pleasures of the present.
Thus the days they spent together,
Like the ancient days of Eden,
Passed in guileless blissful pleasure
With no shadow to disturb them,
Save the stolid disapproval
Of her own suspicious people,
For her parents and grand parents
Looked with stern disapprobation,
Looked with distrust at the stranger –
With a jealous eye they watched them.
Then she told him all their story,
Why against the "Pale-faced" nation
All this prejudice had arisen,
Of their former home in Georgia,
On the banks of the Osternarly,
Further westward they'd been driven
Like the hunted deer and bison
And their home was now uncertain
Soon it would be taken from them.

She must pour him "connoh-ha-neh,"[2]
She must make him sweet "Con-nutch-chee"[3]
He must smoke the pipe taloneh[4]
And a magic chain of wampum[5]
From her ancient beads she gave him;
He must dive with "Ooch-a-latah"[6]
He must friendly be among them,
So they might begin to trust him,
And her people be his people.
So she made him buckskin slippers –
"Moccasins all brightly beaded,"

[2] The national drink of the Cherokees, made from the pounded grits of new Indian corn. An old adage says, Drink Connoh-ha-neh with a Cherokee, and you will ever be among them [Anderson's note].

[3] A Cherokee dish prepared from the beaten meat of the hickory nut, including both the kernel and the shell [Anderson's note].

[4] A mixture of tobacco and dried leaves of the red sumach. Another old adage, current among the Cherokees says, Smoke Ta-lo-neh from the same pipe with a Cherokee and you will be friends forever [Anderson's note].

[5] Made by the Cherokees many years ago from the bones of the squirrel and colored different shades. They were supposed to possess the magic power of preserving the wearer from the evil one and keeping him in health [Anderson's note].

[6] The last full blood chief of the Cherokee Nation [Anderson's note].

And a hunting shirt of home spun[7]
From her mother's loom she made him;
"Taught him to flint and feather arrows"
"How to shoot them when completed."

Down the river in the moonlight
In her own canoe they glided
While she sang him songs so dreamy
That the great rocks caught the echo
And in phonographic measure
Still repeats them to the forest.

Thus the days of summer glided
Onward towards the coming autumn,
And the day of his departure
Dawned with its foreboding shadows.

But he vowed unto his sweetheart:
"I'll be true to thee, my song bird,
Never love another maiden,
Never sing with any other,
Soon will come the happy spring time
When I will return to wed thee,
And we'll live and sing together.
And will never more be parted."
So with many vows he left her,
Standing lonely in the twilight
"Looking back as he departed" –
With her solemn faith unshaken.
Each day waited fond Nowita;
Happy was the little singer,
Looking forward to the spring time.
Thus the long and dreary winter
Passed away with leaden footsteps,
And again the hills and valleys
Wakened from their chilly slumbers,
And the laughter of the waters
Called to her with happy voices.
And she answered with her singing
Till the song birds in the forest
Caught and mocked the happy echo,
But the voice she loved and longed for,
And the step for which she listened,
And the man for whom she waited,
Never would come again to greet her.
And the maiden sadly singing
In the star light in the morning,

[7] "Hunting Shirt," an ornamental article of apparel used in olden times by the Cherokees, which took the place of a coat. Now in disuse [Anderson's note].

Seemed to draw him near in spirit
From his distant home and people.
But the grand dame of the maiden
Looked with sorrow on her grand child
Looked with sadness at her fading
Looked with anguish at her pining.
She who had been so light-hearted
Till she met the pale faced stranger,
Till she met the handsome Yankee –
Till she met with "Ska-kle-los-ky."
"My dear daughter," said the grand dame,
"Choose a young of your own tribe,
Do not waste your youth in pining,
Wait not for the fickle stranger,
Weep not for your fair faced lover –
Awful queer folks are the white-folks."

Many springs and many winters
Passed away in swift rotation.
And the gentle Indian maiden
Grew into a sad faced woman.
No more twilight found her singing,
Silent was her voice forever.

Said the men among her people,
"Let him come once more among us
To deceive us with his friendship;
When he comes again he'll tarry –
Tarry in these hills forever."

All the powers of the magician
All the pleadings of her people
Failed to change the silent singer,
Or arouse her admiration,
For the tall and handsome suitors –
Chiefs from far and distant nations –
Who had learned her hapless story
And had travelled far to woo her,
But she heeded not nor heard them,
For her thoughts were with the stranger,
And the echo of his whispers
Silenced all the other voices.

Thus in melancholy sadness,
With her mind to memory wedded,
And in patient resignation
So her days alike were numbered;
Thus she passed away in silence
To the land of the hereafter.

Still her sad, unhappy story
Is repeated to the traveler,

And her home among the mountains
To this day is sought by strangers.
If you go alone at twilight
To the cave beside the river[8]
Where the lovers in the evening
Rowed together in the gloaming,
You may hear the repetition
Of the songs as they were uttered,
By this charming Indian maiden,
By Nowita, the sweet singer.

## Joe Jamison's Sacrifice (*Sturm's*, January, 1906)

Muggins was an intelligent little dog with a curly brown coat and soft brown eyes. He belonged to Joe Jamison, one of the brightest and poorest boys in the town, and was the pride and delight of Joe's life, who had taught him many cunning and useful tricks.

Muggins could carry a letter to the postoffice, or a small package to a neighbor, as nicely as anyone; he could play "hide and seek" with the children as well as any boy; he could sit on his hind legs and make a bow with a wisdom and dignity wonderful to see. All these and many other "accomplishments" Joe had taught him during his idle hours, for the little dog was the only play fellow he had ever known. Muggins wore no collar, but he carried his head as high as if he did, and always managed to escape the watchful eye of the tax collector.

He was known from one end of the town to the other, and it would have seemed almost an inhuman act to have put Muggins in the "pound." Certain it is that his young master would have pawned the small hoard of his earthly possessions to have redeemed him.

Muggins was the envy of every small boy in the town, and many a bat and ball and target gun had been offered his little master in exchange for him, but Joe scorned all these offers, and as long as the benefit to be derived concerned only himself, he continued to reject them. But temptation came to him in a way he had least expected. At the hotel in the town a gentleman and his little son had been boarding for several weeks. One evening as Joe was returning from his work of selling papers, he was met by this gentleman, who said, "I believe you are the owner of the little dog, Muggins, that all the little boys in town seem acquainted with? I was out for a walk with my little son yesterday. You remember we stopped at your gate to watch you and the dog play together; Charley was perfectly fascinated with your little pet, and has coaxed me ever since to buy him a dog just like him. Muggins is a very wonderful little fellow, is he not, and what else can he do besides the tricks you so kindly had him perform for us yesterday?"

Joe was charmed and delighted that a grown-up gentleman, and one so richly dressed and distinguished looking, should have noticed and remembered his little dog, and he fell at once into an excited recital of Muggins' accomplishments, little dreaming that he was sowing seeds for the bitterest harvest of tears his eyes had ever known.

"Well," said the gentleman, when Joe had finished, "I have just been out your way to see you and to ask you what you would take for your dog. I want to buy him for my son. I have never denied him anything that he ever asked for, and rather than disappoint him I will give you ten dollars for your little dog."

Had the man for a moment dreamed of the tempest of conflicting emotions he had aroused in the manly little breast, he would never have broached the subject so abruptly, or, perhaps he might not have done so at all; but he knew Joe only as a poor little boy, whose mother lived in a tiny house on the out-

[8] A cave on the shores of Spavinaw, where a low sound as of singing may be heard borne on the waters of the interior of the cave, called by the natives De-cu-na-gus-ky-skilly, or, Singing Spirit [Anderson's note].

skirts of the town and did plain sewing for a living; he thought he would be doing a kindness to buy the dog, not only to his little son, but to Joe as well.

It would be difficult to describe the boy's emotions during this time; he thought of his sister Nellie, older than himself, of her worn old shoes, and thin, faded dress; he remembered how his hard working mother had saved, and planned to keep them both in comfortable clothes in order that they might attend the Sabbath School, and how she had hoped, with the aid of his small earnings, to buy books so that Nellie might attend the public school. With a few books, the remnant of better days, his mother had taught them to read and to write. This she had done in the evenings while she plied her needle. But Nellie would soon be thirteen, and her heart's desire was to be able to buy books and fresh aprons and go to school.

Ten dollars! That was more money than little Joe had ever seen at one time in all his life before, and it opened up an avenue of possibilities to his childish mind: books and aprons for Nellie; warm mittens and shoes and stockings, too – and what would it not buy for mother beside? Only last night he had heard her say if she only had the money to buy her some new glasses she could do neater and swifter work.

In fact, several ten dollar bills would scarcely have covered all the comforts that followed each other in rapid succession through Joe's imagination into the little home where care and want had sat side by side, twin guests since the death of his father six years before. And then Joe thought of Muggins – dear, cunning little Muggins, who had been his constant companion, play-fellow and friend since he was a tiny puppy three years before. And what a comfort he had been to him in his lonely life, no one but the child himself knew. How often had he come home from work, sick at heart from the jesting taunts of some larger and more fortunate boy, with brand new sled and brand new boots, and found comfort and consolation in teaching new tricks to Muggins, and pouring out his troubles in the ears of his little pet; and Muggins had returned his affection and attention with dog-like devotion. He had shared all his griefs and sorrows with his little dog, as well as many a meager meal.

Seeing the boy's hesitation, the gentleman said, "Well, what do you say, my little man? Is not ten dollars sufficient for your dog?"

"Yes sir, O yes, sir, but – but – I will come and see you tomorrow. I must hurry home now, or mother will be uneasy about me. Good evening, sir."

Poor Joe slept but little that night though Muggins lay on a bit of a quilt at his feet. He would wake from his fitful, feverish sleep, haunted by dreams of the loss of his pet. The next day passed, and the next, and still Joe had not found courage to take Muggins to the hotel. Young as he was he must pass through his struggle alone. He knew that if he consulted his mother and Nellie, they would never suffer him to make the sacrifice. No, it would never do to tell them.

Over and over again did he weigh the question in his childish mind. If he sold Muggins, Nellie could go to school that winter; mother could get her glasses, and what a comfort and help that would be to them both. Did he not love his mother and sister better than anything else in life? But to part with Muggins was so hard, and how lonely he should be without him.

On the evening of the third day, after his meeting with the gentleman, Joe summoned all his courage, and with a heroism worthy an older heart, took Muggins in his arms, stepped unnoticed from the house, and walked rapidly away in the direction of the hotel, as if afraid his good resolution might fail him. It was costing his manly little soul no small struggle to part with his beloved pet.

"Muggins, little dog, my dear little dog, you know I don't want to sell you. I would never sell you for myself. I would rather go on forever, wearing a ragged coat and worn old shoes, than to part with you; but we are so poor, and mother works so hard, and, Muggins, ten dollars is a heap of money. I must think of what it will do for mother and Nellie. I know it is right for me to take the money for their sake, and yet, it would not have hurt me so much if you had died, Muggins," and tears fell fast upon the curly brown head upon his arm; "you will never love another little boy as you love me, will you? And I will never, never own another little dog, and, oh Muggins, how I shall miss you when I come home at night, and find you gone."

They had reached their destination by this time, and, drying his eyes, Joe walked up to the clerk and timidly asked for the gentleman, Mr. Williams. The clerk stared at the small figure in silence for a moment, and then said: "Oh, yes; the gentleman and his little son left this morning, and he bade me tell you, if you called, that he was sorry you had changed your mind about the price of your dog; his little son – " Joe waited to hear no more, but turned and hurriedly left the room, with Muggins held close to his beating heart. For the moment he thought of nothing but the fact that he was not returning with empty arms, but his little dog held close and warm within them. But his heart was heavy with self-reproach when he thought of his mother and Nellie. He ought to have gone sooner to see the gentleman. He had not been as brave as he meant to be.

Oh, why had the man ever proposed to buy his dog?

Joe sold papers in the evenings, and through the day he worked in the office of old Mr. Forest, the town magistrate. He had been so proud to hand in his small earnings to his mother, and had thought of all sorts of ways and means by which he might help her, but the thought of selling his dog had never occurred to him.

They were crossing the railroad now, in front of the evening train that had just pulled in. As the light from the engine shone full upon the boy's tear-stained face, a kind voice said, "Hello, my little chap, what is the trouble, and what are you going to do with that dog?" In another moment the engineer was at his side, and laid his hand kindly upon Joe's shoulder. Before he knew what he was doing, he had told him all the story of his mission to the hotel and finding the gentleman gone. "There, there, never mind," said the stranger, "I will buy your dog and give you ten dollars for him, too. My sister is an invalid and will be delighted with just such a pet." And before Joe realized the situation, the engineer was back at his post with Muggins in his arms; the train whistled and was off, leaving Joe standing, gazing, with wide, astonished eyes, at the fast retreating train, and the crisp ten dollar bill in his hand.

It had all happened so suddenly and unexpectedly that Joe stood as if paralyzed, watching the head-light of the train now rapidly disappearing in the darkness and gloom. His arms were empty, and, alas, for the present, his heart felt equally so. "I have done right," he kept repeating to himself, as he vainly sought for comfort.

On reaching home he complained of headache, and went at once to bed. He dared not look at the little pallet at the foot, where, for three years, Muggins had been wont to lie; but, hastily undressing, he covered his head and cried himself to sleep.

The next morning he came to breakfast later than usual; when he had finished, his sister came in to the room and said, "Here are some bones, Joe, I saved for Muggins, but where is he this morning?" For the first time Joe failed to answer her, and, swallowing a big "lump" in his throat, he went out where his mother was at work, and, handing her the ten dollars, said in a husky voice, "Mother a gentleman gave me this money last night for Muggins. He wanted to take him to his sick sister in the city; now you can buy your glasses, and Nell can get her books and aprons and start to school." And, kissing her on the cheek, he hurried upon his way to Mr. Forest's office.

Mrs. Jamison was too much astonished for words; she knew how fondly her little boy had loved his dog, and the mother's heart comprehended in one moment the struggle that had been taking place in the child's heart for days, when she had thought him sick.

No, his sacrifice should not be in vain; she would buy with the money earned at such a cost, the very things he wished her to purchase; her eyes filled with tears of sympathy, her heart thrilled with honest pride. Was he not a noble little fellow of whom any mother might be justly proud? She would show him in a thousand ways, that only a mother can, how she appreciated the sacrifice which cost him such genuine sorrow.

The winter passed and spring found the Jamisons more comfortable than they had been for some time. Nellie had gone to school all winter; Joe still held his position with Mr. Forest, who had found him so indispensable that he increased his wages.

One evening towards the end of May, Joe and Nellie were sent to the hotel to take some sewing that their mother had finished for a sick lady who was stopping there. It was the first time Joe had been to that hotel since the memorable evening when he had carried Muggins there in his arms; and his eyes filled with sudden tears at the recollection.

In response to their knock upon the door, a faint voice called "come in." A lady with a pale and gentle face sat in an easy chair, and half-hidden by a shawl at her feet lay a little brown dog. There was no deceiving Joe's eyes – there was only one dog in the world that looked like that. "Mother sent us to bring home the sewing, please," said Joe, with eyes fixed not upon the lady's face, but upon the little brown ball at her feet.

Scarcely had Joe finished speaking, and before the lady could reply, the little dog opened his eyes, pricked up his ears, and with one bound was in Joe's arms – an old trick he had often practiced before.

Such barking and jumping, such frantic efforts to show his delight at the sight of his beloved little master! How he had listened all these long months for the sound of that familiar voice, for it was none other than Muggins himself, and Joe was so astonished and delighted that he could not control his voice to speak, when the lady asked, "This is little Joe Jamison, is it not, and this is your sister Nell? I sent the sewing to your mother with the express desire of bringing about this happy surprise." Then she had them sit down, and she told them, between intervals of coughing, all the story as her brother had had it from Joe's own lips, and Nellie realized for the first time what a little hero her brother was.

This was the beginning of many happy half hours Joe spent with Muggins, and when, later in the summer, the sick lady went to Colorado for her health, she left Muggins in Joe's care. She had become much attached to the two children, and thought she saw in Joe the elements of a noble and useful man.

Late in September Joe received the first letter he had ever gotten in his life. It was from Mr. White, the engineer, and was as follows:

"Dear Little Joe – You remember when my sister started upon her journey last summer, she committed her little dog to your care; she has gone upon a longer journey, Joe, from which she will never more return. I was with her when she died, and she bade me tell you that she willed Muggins to you, and that you must never part with him again.

A part of her property, which is amply sufficient for your education, she willed to you, with the earnest hope that you may grow up to be a good and useful man. Although I only saw you once, and then only for a few minutes, I trust you will not be sorry to learn that I have been appointed your curator.

I shall endeavor to carry out the wishes of my beloved sister concerning you.

Sincerely yours,
Cecil D. White."

# Sophia Alice Callahan
# (Muscogee/Creek, 1868–1894)

*Our knowledge of Callahan's life is slender at present. The daughter of a one-eighth Creek father, Samuel Benton Callahan, and a white mother, Sarah Elizabeth Thornberg or McAllester (depending on the source), Callahan enjoyed a privileged upbringing in an affluent and well-educated family. Her father was a captain in the first Creek Confederate regiment and a delegate to the Confederate Congress at Richmond, Virginia, where he represented both the Creek and Seminole nations. During the Civil War, his wife and children remained in Texas, where he joined them after his service, and where Callahan was born in January 1868.*

*Moving from Texas to the Creek Nation in 1885, the family lived on a farm near Okmulgee in Indian Territory (now Oklahoma), and Samuel Callahan assumed various positions of responsibility, including the superintendent of Wealaka Boarding School, a Methodist mission school for Creeks. Like many of their wealthy Cherokee counterparts, the group of affluent Creeks to which the Callahans belonged pointed to their Indian heritage with pride and attempted to ameliorate conditions for the less fortunate. We see some familiar patterns emerging in Callahan: like Narcissa Owen, she became a teacher in Indian Territory, working in Okmulgee in 1886 and later in Muskogee in 1891. Also like Susette LaFlesche, she traveled east for educational opportunities, attending the Wesleyan Female Institute in Staunton, Virginia, in 1887. Her early death from pleurisy, at the age of twenty-six, interrupted her plans for further education prior to opening her own school.*

Wynema*, the first known novel to be published by a Native American woman, reflects a variety of literary traditions and speaks from a complex multiple position. On the one hand a romantic novel centering on two love affairs – one between a white hero and heroine, and another between the Creek heroine, Wynema, and the other heroine's brother –* Wynema *also positions itself as a political text in its depictions of debates swirling around women and American Indians. In the chapter "A Conservative," Genevieve Weir, the white heroine, confronts the racism and sexism of her eastern fiancé, whom she ultimately rejects for her kind and open-minded counterpart, Gerald Keithly, who has helped open the Indian school at which she teaches. "Shall We Allot?" depicts the debate swirling around the Dawes Act, or General Allotment Act, of 1887, in which Indians were given land in severalty, but which also served as an opportunity for whites to grab more of the Indians' land in the west.*

Wynema *also reflects Callahan's position as both an insider and outsider to Creek culture. The chapter entitled "Some Indian Dishes" reveals considerable ambivalence about Creek food, while "An Indian Burial" reflects the conjunction of Creek and Christian burial practices. Unlike Mary Jemison and Zitkala-Ša, Callahan seems more approving of Christianity; at the same time, however, she appears critical of whites' hypocrisy. Perhaps because of its overtly political nature, or perhaps because readers could not easily categorize it,* Wynema *appears to have garnered no reviews, and the novel disappeared until recently. An important milestone in American literature,* Wynema *offers a rich mixture of voices and genres, challenging the reader as it seeks to rewrite American history from a perspective sympathetic to Native Americans.*

Bibliography

## Primary

Callahan, S. Alice. *Wynema: A Child of the Forest.* H. J. Smith, 1897. Rpt. ed. A. LaVonne Brown Ruoff. Nebraska, 1997.

## Secondary

Ruoff, A. LaVonne Brown. "Early Native American Women Authors: Jane Johnston Schoolcraft, Sarah Winnemucca, S. Alice Callahan, E. Pauline Johnson, and Zitkala-Ša." In *Nineteenth-Century American Women Writers: A Critical Reader*. Ed. Karen L. Kilcup. Blackwell, 1998. 81–111.

——. "Editor's Introduction." *Wynema: A Child of the Forest.* Ed. A. LaVonne Brown Ruoff. Nebraska, 1997.

——. "Justice for Indians and Women: The Protest Fiction of Alice Callahan and Pauline Johnson." *World Literature Today* 66:2 (1992): 249–55.

——. "S. Alice Callahan." In *Dictionary of Literary Biography*. Vol. 175. Ed. Kenneth M. Roemer. Gale, 1997. 35–7.

——. "Two Ideas above an Oyster: Gender Roles in S. Alice Callahan's *Wynema*." In *Native American Women in Literature and Culture*. Ed. Susan Castillo and Victor M. P. Da Rosa. Fernando Pessoa, 1997.

Van Dyke, Annette. "An Introduction to *Wynema, a Child of the Forest*, by Sophia Alice Callahan." *Studies in American Indian Literatures* (*SAIL*) 4:2–3 (1992): 123–8.

# From *Wynema, A Child of the Forest* (1891)

*"For right is right, since God is God,*
*And right the day* must *win."*[1]

### [Dedication]

To the Indian tribes of North America who have felt the wrongs and oppression of their pale-faced brothers, I lovingly dedicate this work, praying that it may serve to open the eyes and heart of the world to our afflictions, and thus speedily issue into existence an era of good feeling and just dealing toward us and our more oppressed brothers.

*The Author*

### Publisher's Preface

In offering "Wynema" for your perusal, reader, the publishers have no apologies to offer for what literary critics may term the crudeness or incompleteness of the work. The fact that an Indian, one of the oppressed, desires to plead her cause at a tribunal where judge and jury are chosen from among the oppressors is our warrant for publishing this little volume.

---

1 From the hymn "The Right Must Win," by Frederick William Faber (1814–63).

Honest opinions which come from careful thought and deep study are worthy of respectful consideration even though they be the opinions of an Indian, and whoever reads these pages will be convinced that this protest against the present Indian policy of our government is sincere, earnest, and timely.

The Red Men have not been without champions and defenders in the relentless war which the white men's greed has waged unceasingly against them since the landing of Columbus, yet never before, so far as we can learn, have our Red brothers had their story told by the pen of one of their own people. We shall claim then, for this little volume this: It is the Indians' side of the Indian question told by an Indian born and bred, and told none the less potently because the author has borrowed the garb of fiction to present the cause of truth. Her picture of the home-life of this simple people, of their customs and ceremonies, of their aspirations for a higher life, of their inherent weaknesses, of their patient endurance of injustice, oppression and suffering, of their despair and hopelessness, of their last defiance of governmental authority, and of the magnificent results accomplished by those who have gone among them to teach and preach is worthy of the reader's most careful attention.

*Chicago, April 1, 1891*

## Chapter I

### Introductory

In an obscure place, miles from the nearest trading point, in a tepee, dwelt the parents of our heroine when she first saw the light. All around and about them stood the tepees of their people, and surrounding the village of tents was the great, dark, cool forest in which the men, the "bucks," spent many hours of the day in hunting, or fishing the river that flowed peacefully along in the midst of the wood. On many a quiet tramp beside her father, did this little savage go, for she was the only child, and the idol of her parents' hearts. When she was quite small, and barely able to hold a rifle, she was taught its use and spent many happy hours hunting with her father, who occasionally allowed her to fire a shot, to please her.

Ah, happy, peaceable Indians! Here you may dream of the happy hunting-grounds beyond, little thinking of the rough, white hand that will soon shatter your dream and scatter the dreams.

Here is a home like unto the one your forefathers owned before the form of the white man came upon the scene and changed your quiet habitations into places of business and strife.

Here are no churches and school-houses, for the "heathen is a law unto himself," and "ignorance is bliss," to the savage; but the "medicine man" tells them of the Indian's heaven beside the great mountain, and points them to the circuitous trail over its side which he tells them has been made by the great warriors of their tribe as they went to the "happy hunting ground."

Sixteen miles above this village of tepees stood another and a larger town in which was a mission-school, superintended by Gerald Keithly, a missionary sent by the Methodist assembly to promote civilization and christianity among these lowly people. Tall, young and fair, of quiet, gentle manners, and possessing a kindly sympathy in face and voice, he easily won the hearts of his dark companions. The "Mission" was a small log-house, built in the most primitive style, but it accommodated the small number of students who attended school; for the Indians long left to follow after pleasure are loth to quit her shrine for the noble one of Education. It was hard to impress upon them, young or old, the necessity of becoming educated. If their youths handled the bow and rifle well and were able to endure the greatest hardships, unmurmuringly, their education was complete; hence every device within the ken of an ingenious mind, calculated to amuse and attract the attention of the little savages, and to cause them to desire to remain near the school-room, was summoned to the aid of this teacher, "born not made." He mingled with the Indians in their sports whenever practicable, and endeavored in every way to show them he had come to help and not to hinder them. Nor did he confine himself to the village in which his work lay, for he felt the command "Go ye into *all* the world and preach the gospel to *every* creature,"[2]

---

[2] Mark 16:15.

impelling him onward. The village of tepees, Wynema's home, knew him and welcomed him; in the abode of her father he was an honored guest, where, with a crowd gathered about him, he holds of the love and mercy of a Savior of the home that awaits the faithful, and urged his dusky brethren to educate their children in the better ways of their pale-faced friends. At first he talked through an interpreter, but feeling the greater influence he would gain by speaking to the Indians in their own tongue, he mastered their language and dispensed with the interpreter. But to Wynema he always spoke the mother tongue – English; for, he reasoned, she is young and can readily acquire a new language, and it will profit her to know the English. His was the touch that brought into life the slumbering ambition for knowledge and for a higher life, in the breast of the little Indian girl. Her father and mother carried her to the "Mission" to hear Gerald Keithly preach, and missing her when they started off the following day, they found her in the school-room, standing near her friend, listening eagerly and attentively to all he said and wonder-struck at the recitations of the pupils, simple though they were.

"Father," she said, "let me stay here and listen always; I want to know all this the pupils are talking about." "No, my child," answered her father, "your mother and I could not get along without you; we can build a school at home, and you may stay there and listen."

"When, father, when?" Wynema asked eagerly. "Ask Gerald Keithly when he comes," he answered, to divert her attention from himself. Then the days became weeks to Wynema, impatiently awaiting the coming of her friend.

Every day she thought with delight of the school her father would build, and every day planned it all for the benefit of her little friends and playmates, who had become anxious also, from hearing Wynema's description of school life, to enter "learning's hall." When Gerald Keithly finally came, he found a small school organized under Wynema, waiting for a house and teacher.

"Do you really wish to go to school so much, little girl?" he asked Wynema, only to see her cheeks flush and her eyes flash with desire.

"Oh, so much!" clasping her hands; "may I?" she asked.

"If your father wishes," Gerald answered gladly.

"Father says ask you, and now you say, if father wishes," she began disappointedly.

"Well, then, you may, for I shall send off for you a teacher, right away. Now, then, go tell your playmates;" and he patted her cheek.

"Oh, I am so glad!" and she looked at him, her eyes full of grateful tears; then ran gleefully away.

Gerald Keithly then went to the father, stalwart Choe Harjo, and asked:

"Do you want a school here? and will you build a house? If so, I will send and get you a teacher."

"Yes," he answered, "the child wishes it; so be it."

"Would you like a man or a woman for teacher?" Gerald questions.

"Let it be a woman, and she may live with us; I want the child to be with her always, for she is so anxious to learn. We will do all we can for the teacher, if she will live among us."

"I am sure of that," answered Gerald, warmly pressing the Indian's hand.

So the cry rang out in the great Methodist assembly; "A woman to teach among the Indians in the territory. Who will go?" and it was answered by one from the sunny Southland – a young lady, intelligent and pretty, endowed with the graces of heart and head, and surrounded by the luxuries of a Southern home. Tenderly reared by a loving mother, for her father had long ago gone to rest, and greatly loved by her brother and sisters of whom she was the eldest, she was physically unfit to bear a life of hardships of a life among the Indians; but God had endowed her with great moral courage and endurance, and she felt the call to go too strenuously, to allow any obstacles to obstruct her path.

She understood the responsibility of the step she was about to take, but, as she said to her mother who was endeavoring to persuade her to change her resolve, and pleading tearfully to keep her daughter with her:

"God has called me and I dare not refuse to do his bidding. He will take care of me among the Indians as he cares for me here; and he will take care of you while I am gone and bring me back to you again. Never fear, mother, dear, our Father takes care of his obedient, believing children, and will not allow any harm to befall them."

Thus came civilization among the Tepee Indians.

## Chapter II

### The School

Genevieve Weir stood at her desk in the Indian school-house, reflecting: How shall I make them understand that it is God's word that I am reading and God to whom I am talking? She deliberated earnestly. What do they know about the Supreme Being?

Poor little girl! She made the common mistake of believing she was the only witness for God in that place. Wynema often spoke of Gerald Keithly in her broken way; but Genevieve believed him to be miles away.

"I shall begin the exercises with the reading of the Word, and prayer, at any rate, and perhaps they will understand by my expression and attitude," she determined at length, calling the school to order.

She read a portion of the fourteenth chapter of St. John – that sweet, comforting gospel – then clasping her hands and raising her eyes, she uttered a simple prayer to the "all-Father," asking that he open the hearts of the children, that they might be enabled to understand His word; and that He give her such great love for her dusky pupils, that her only desire be in dividing this Word among them. The pupils understood no word of it, but the tone went straight to each one's heart and found lodgment there. At recess Wynema came and stood by her teacher's side with deep wonder in her great, black eyes.

"Mihia," (teacher) she asked, "you talk to God?" and she clasped her hands and raised her eyes, imitating Genevieve's attitude.

"Yes, dear," Genevieve answered, delightedly surprised at the acute understanding of the child. "God is our good Father who lives in heaven, up there," pointing upward, "and is all around us now and all the time. Do you know anything about God, dear?"

"Gerald Keithly talk to God when he come here," the child answered her.

"Does he come here often?" questioned the teacher next.

"Yes, sometime. But, Mihia," returning to the subject matter nearest her heart, "you 'fraid God?"

"Why, no, Wynema," she replied putting her hand on the child's shoulder; "why should I be afraid of the all-Father who loves me so? Are you afraid of your father and mother?"

"O, no; but when I am bad girl, I feel sorry and go off to left them," she said soberly.

"Why do you wish to leave them then? Do you go off when you are a good girl?" Genevieve asked.

"Not when I am good girl, when I am bad. Then my ma and pa ought whip me, but they don't," the child replied.

"Well, dear, God loves you more than your father and your mother can possibly love you; yes, He loves you when you are bad, and when you are good. Sometimes, when you are bad, he will punish you, but He will love you always. Don't be afraid of God, little one, but try to love Him and be a good girl," – with that she stooped and kissed the child, who ran and told her playmates all the words of her teacher.

After this the children seemed to listen to the morning services more seriously and attentively, and before many weeks elapsed were able to join with their teacher in repeating a prayer she taught them.

To many persons the difficulty of teaching our language to any foreigner seems almost insurmountable, and teaching the Indians seems especially difficult. Thus Genevieve Weir's faraway friends thought, and many were the inquiries she received concerning her work.

"How did she make them understand her, and how could she understand them? How could she teach them when they could not understand a word she said? Wasn't she afraid to live among those dark savages?" etc., etc. To all of which she gave characteristic replies.

"God made the Indians as he made Caucasian – from the same mold. He loves the work of His hands and for His sake I love these 'dark savages,' and am, therefore, not in the least afraid of them. They know that I have come to live among them for their good, and they try to show their gratitude by being as kind to me as they know how. I talk to the older ones mostly by signs, but the children have gotten so they can understand me when I speak to them. Sometimes it is rather difficult to make the people at home, at Choe Harjo's, understand me, when Wynema is not by to interpret for me. For instance: yesterday I wanted an egg. I spoke the word egg, slowly several times, but the Indians shook their heads and said something in their language which as greatly puzzled me. Then taking some straw I made a nest and put some feathers in it; you have no idea how quickly they grasped my meaning, and laughing at my device, brought what I had asked for. Then taking the egg, I held it up before them, pronouncing the word egg, slowly, which they all repeated after me. You may be sure they always understand what I want when I call for an egg now. It is remarkable what bright minds these 'untaught savages' have. I know you would be surprised at the rapid progress my pupils make, notwithstanding their great drawback of being ignorant of our own language.

"My little Wynema, of whom I have spoken before, had only to hear a word and she has it. She learns English very rapidly and can understand almost anything I say; and she is a great help to me, as she often interprets for me at home and at school.

"It would be rather amusing and interesting to my friends to come into my school-room when I am hearing the language lesson. It taxes my ingenuity to the uttermost, sometimes, to accurately convey my meaning and make myself understood. I have no advanced classes, yet, but I intend to teach the ancient and modern languages and higher mathematics before I quit this people – you see I do not intend leaving *soon*, and I will never leave them for fear or dislike."

## Chapter III

### Some Indian Dishes

"What have you there, Wynema?" asked Genevieve Weir of her pupil one evening as she stepped into the "cook-room" and found Wynema eagerly devouring a round, dark-looking mass, which she was taking from a corn-shuck. All around the wide fire-place sat Indian women engaged in the same occupation, all eating with evident relish.

"Oh, Mihia! It is blue dumpling. I luf it. Do you luf it?" she asked offering the shuck to Genevieve.

"I do not know what it is. I never saw any before. How is it made?" she made answer.

"It is meal beat from corn, beat fine, and it is beans with the meal. Shell the beans an' burn the shells of it, an' put it in the meal, an' put the beans in an' wet it an' put it in a shuck, an' tie the shuck so tight it won't spill out an' put it in the water an' boil it," the child replied, out of breath with her long and not very lucid explanation.

"What makes the dumpling so dark?" asked the teacher, eying the mass which she held in her hand, rather curiously.

"That is the burn shells; we burn it an' put the meal an' it makes it blue. Goot! eat some, Mihia. It is so goot."

Miss Weir took a small morsel of the dumpling in her mouth, for she was not prepossessed with its looks, and ate it with difficulty for it was tough and tasteless.

"No I don't want any; thank you, dear, I think I don't like it very well because I never ate any; I should have to practice a long time before I could eat blue dumpling very well;" and she smiled away the frown on the child's brow.

Soon after this, supper was announced and the family gathered around a table, filled with Indian dainties.

There in the center of the table, stood the large wooden bowl of sofke,[3] out of which each one helped himself or herself, eating with a wooden spoon, and lifting the sofke from the bowl directly to the mouth. This dish, which is made of the hardest flint corn, beaten or chopped into bits, and boiled until quite done in water containing a certain amount of lye, is rather palatable when fresh, but as is remarkable, the Indians, as a general thing, prefer it after it has soured and smells more like a swill-barrel than anything else. Besides the sofke, were soaked corn bread, which is both sour and heavy; dried venison; a soup with an unspellable name, made of corn and dried beef, which is really the most palatable of all the

[3] A fermented mixture of corn and water; the most important Muscogee food.

Indian dishes; and opuske, a drink composed of meal made from green corn roasted until perfectly dry and brown, and beaten in a stone mortar until quite fine; mixed with water.

Not a very inviting feast for Genevieve Weir, or indeed, for any person unaccustomed to such fare; but that the Indians, surrounding the board considered it such, was evident by the dispatch with which they ate.

And it is strange that, though always accustomed to such fare, the Indians are not a dyspeptic people. We of this age are constantly talking and thinking of ways and means by which to improve our cookery to suit poor digestive organs. How we would hold up our hands in horror at the idea of placing blue dumplings on the table! And yet, we are a much more dyspeptic people than the "blue dumpling" eaters, struggle though we do to ward off the troublesome disease.

"Mihia, the sun is far up. We must go to school. You no get up?" Wynema coming into her teacher's bedroom late one morning. She had waited for Miss Weir to make her appearance at the breakfast-table, and, as she did not do so, went in search of her. There she lay tossing and moaning, with a raging fever, but still conscious. The child, who was unaccustomed to illness in any form, stood looking at her in surprise.

"Come here, dear," said Genevieve, calling her to the bed. "Tell your mamma I am sick, and cannot teach to-day. Your father will please go to the school-house and tell the children. I hope I shall be all right by to-morrow, but I cannot stand on my feet to-day."

Wynema ran to tell her mother, who soon came into the sick-room.

"Seek?" questioned the mother. "What eat?"

"Yes; I do not care for anything to eat," Miss Weir replied; thinking, "Oh, I shall starve to death here if I am sick long!"

"Send for the medicine man, he cure you quick," the woman urged.

Wynema then spoke up; "Medicine man make you well, Mihia, get him come. He make Luce well when she sick."

"Well, send for him, please; for I do want to get well right away," she smiled feebly.

The "medicine man" came in directly and looking at the patient closely, took his position in the corner, where with a bowl of water, a few herbs and a small cane, he concocted his "cure alls." Genevieve watched him curiously and with good reason, for a more queerly dressed person or a more curious performance, it would have been hard to find. With his leggins, his loose, fringed, many-colored hunting-shirt, his beaded moccasins, his long, colored blanket sweeping the ground, and his head-dress with the fringe touching his eyebrows, he was both picturesque and weird. His performance consisted of blowing through a cane into the water in which he had mixed the herbs, and going through an incantation in a low, indistinct tone. What the words were could not be told by any of the Indians – except the medicine man – but all of them had great faith in this personage and held him rather in awe.

After the blowing had been going on for some time and the incantation repeated and re-repeated the medicine was offered to the patient, who made a pretense of taking it.

"Tell him I am better now, Wynema, and he may go," she said to the child who was taking the performance in.

After that dignitary, the "medicine man," had retired, Genevieve used the few simple remedies at hand, known to herself, and to her joy and surprise, was able to resume her school duties on the following day.

The "medicine man" was never called in to wait upon Miss Weir again.

## Chapter VI

## An Indian Burial

Years passed on with the same round of school duties for Genevieve Weir – duties crowned with joy and pride, as she watched the gradual unfolding of mind and soul to the touch of her magic wand – the influence of love opening doors that giant force could not set the least ajar. Wynema continued to be her greatest joy and pride and was more than ever her *vade mecum*,[4] of whom she wrote often to her home friends.

"She learns faster and retains more of what she learns, than any child of whatever hue it has been my fortune to know. She is a constant reader and greets a new book with the warmth of a friend. I have directed her course of reading, and I venture to say, there is not a child in Mobile or anywhere else who has read less spurious matter than she. It is amusing to see her curl up over Dickens or Scott, and grow animated over Shakespeare, whose plays she lives out; and it is interesting to watch the different emotions, in sympathy with the various characters, chase each other over her face. Of the good ones she will say, 'This is you, Mihia, but you are better.' Dear child; would that I were as perfect as she believes me to be!"

One evening as Miss Weir and her pupil were returning from school, they heard strange sounds – such a groaning, wailing, lamenting and sobbing – proceeding from a cabin not far from the roadside; and Miss Weir turned to Wynema for explanation.

"Some one must be dead, and they are singing the death-chant," said Wynema. "Mamma said Sam Emarthla was very sick – so I suppose – so I suppose it is that he is dead." She always spoke brokenly when she was touched. "Shall it be that we may go and look upon the dead?"

"Yes, dear," responded her teacher; "and it may be that we can speak a comforting word to the bereft ones. But tell me before we go in, what is the meaning of the death-chant."

"The death-chant? How can I tell you, Mihia? It begins by telling the good deeds of the dead person; of his virtues; what a good hunter he was; how brave he always was; and ends by carrying him over the mountain side to the happy hunting-ground, there to live forever, among dogs and horses, with bows and arrows and game of all kinds in abundance."

By the time she finished speaking they had reached the cabin door, and on looking in, they beheld the room full of sympathizing friends, who pushed aside and made an entrance for the new-comers.

Going up to the bed where the corpse lay dressed and decorated for burial, Genevieve found the stricken wife lying face downward on the breast of her dead husband. Not a sound escaped her lips, for she seemed stunned by her grief. Here was no fashionable grief with its dress of sable hue, its hangings of crepe, and stationary with its inch-wide band of black, such as Madison-Square widows use. Ah! no, here was real, simple, heart-felt grief such as the ignorant and uneducated feel; grief such as Eve felt over the death of her well-beloved son.

Ranged around the bed were the mourners, noisy at first, but now awed into silence by the presence of a real grief. In a corner of the room Genevieve noticed the medicine man, going through his incantations as usual, in a very subdued voice. Genevieve motioned to Wynema who stood apart looking reverently on, and the girl came and stood by her teacher's side.

"Tell Chineka for me," Miss Weir said, "that God, the good Father above, knows her grief and will help her bear it if she will ask Him; that He has only taken Emarthla for a while, when she can go and join him and live forever above." All this and more Miss Weir spoke and Wynema interpreted to the sorrowing wife, who only glanced up gratefully at the teacher's face.

After asking a few questions relative to the burial, and finding that all things had been prepared for interment the following day, Genevieve and Wynema departed from the bereaved home.

Early in the forenoon of the following day Choe Harjo, his family and Genevieve, repaired to the burial-ground where they found quite a number of the friends and relatives of the deceased man. In a few moments, strong pall-bearers carrying the corpse which was placed in a rude wooden box, appeared, followed by the widow and the nearest of kin. Arriving at the grave, the box would have been immediately lowered, had not a friendly hand stopped the pall-bearers, and a voice said something which caused them to put the coffin down and stand with uncovered heads. Looking up in surprise, Genevieve beheld Gerald Keithly with bible in hand, proceeding in reverent way to conduct the burial services. The Indians listened to him with fixed attention, and when, as he finished reading, he spoke a few words in their own language concerning the dead, words of praise for his good deeds, and words of sympathy for

[4] Traveling companion.

the sorrowing wife and loved ones, the tears ran softly down the cheeks of many, and a moisture gathered in the eyes of Chineka who, for the first time since her bereavement, showed some signs of being conscious of her surroundings.

When the service was over, after the prayer had been offered and the hymn sung, friends of the dead man placed inside the grave beside the coffin, his gun and ammunition, bows and arrows, and a sufficient amount of provision to carry him on his journey to the happy hunting-ground.

Then the coffin was well sprinkled with rice, and the company disbanded and went home.

It would be well to say here what should have been said before; in preparing a man for burial, the Indians dress him in full hunting-suit, boots, and hat. Near him in the coffin, lies his pipe and tobacco, so that when he is ready to start to his final home, he has all things at hand to cheer and comfort him.

## Chapter VII

## A Strange Ceremony

"Why do the Indians go by the creek on their way home?" asked Miss Weir of Gerald Keithly as he rode by her side on the way home from the burial.

"Wait and you will see," he answered briefly.

When the Indians reached the creek they all dismounted and walked into the water, some of them bathing themselves and some only throwing the water on their heads and faces; after which procedure they walked out of the water backward and turned homewards.

"Mihia, you don't drive away disease or illness – throw the water over yourself," and Wynema sprinkled herself generously. Genevieve looked toward Gerald, as if to ask advice, when she saw him gravely going through the same ceremony. She did not speak until they were again riding side by side, when she said in a strained surprised tone:

"Surely, Mr. Keithly, you do not believe in any such ceremony as the one I have just witnessed."

He laughed heartily at her tone. "Surely, Miss Genevieve," he replied, "when I am in Rome I strive to do as Rome does when the doing so does not harm me nor any one else. The Indians believe that the water will keep off the disease, and they have an inkling of the truth. I don't mean to say that I believe the sprinkling of water, as I did just now, will have any effect, either good or bad, on the human system; but it is declared in Holy Writ that 'Cleanliness is next to godliness,' and truly a clean body is almost proof against disease."

"But don't you think that by participating in their strange ceremonies, you only encourage the Indians to keep up their barbaric customs?" Genevieve asked.

"What was wrong with this ceremony?" he asked by way of reply. "Surely you would not wish to deprive these people of all their customs and ceremonies. The ceremony to-day was simple and innocent; there was no harm done to any one – and if it pleases them to keep such a custom, I say, let them do so. Now, if it were the scalp-dance or war-dance or any of their ceremonies calculated to harm themselves or others, I should use all my influence in blotting it out; but these Indians have long ago laid aside their savage, cruel customs and have no more desire to practice them than we have to see them do so."

"Right, as ever," said Genevieve, frankly extending her hand. "I did not think of it as you present the matter; but I see I should have strengthened my influence over my Indian friends, by pleasing them in performing their water-ceremony. It seems I can never see things as they are, in the true light."

"Now don't blame yourself so. I'll act 'father confessor,' and give absolution if you wish; you took the same view of the case that many others of our race have taken, and you have not done any harm. I may be wrong in the view I take of the matter," he added, "but I have thought often and long over it, and my course seems best to me."

"And to me," she hastened to say. "I think if we always do what seems best to us, after investigating to the best of our ability, and praying it all out to the great 'Father confessor,' we shall not go far wrong." There was a mist in her eyes as she said this in a low tone.

"Amen," he exclaimed soberly and reverently.

This gave the conversation a more serious turn and the speakers a kindlier regard for each other.

## CHAPTER IX

### SOME CHANGES

"Wynema, I am going home this vacation, and want you to go with me; would you like to go?" asked Miss Weir one morning, as she and Wynema were on their way to the school-house.

By the way, this school-house deserves some notice, for a great change has taken place in it. In place of the little log-cabin, chinked with mud, stood a large frame building, constructed from the most approved modern plan and furnished with every convenience. The attendance had grown so large that another teacher had to be employed, and Wynema, who was at that time well qualified to fill the position, was chosen in preference to a stranger. And the change did not stop with the school-house, for everywhere, all around their building, were neat residences in place of the tepees; and to the right of the school-building stood a fine new church, adorned with steeple and bell, whose sound called together the people every sabbath to worship beneath the arched roof of the holy edifice. Miss Weir had organized a sabbath-school which met in the school-house, soon after she came among these people; but the school increased so much in numbers that she hardly recognized in it her small beginning. White people had settled among these Indians, and being peaceful and law-abiding, the Indians welcomed them and gave them a helping hand. A young missionary, Carl Peterson by name, a teacher in Mr. Keithly's school, came over every Sabbath and expounded Scripture to an attentive congregation. This same missionary deserves mention, as he had toiled five years among the Sioux Indians, and was giving his whole life to spreading the Gospel among the Indians.

This little village of Tepees had grown so much that its inhabitants wished to dignify it by a name whose orthography English-speaking people could master, and by a post-office. So they applied to Miss Weir to know if she would object to having the town called for her.

"No," said she; "Weir does not sound well as the name of a town; but if you do not care, I will suggest another and a better. Call it Wynema. That is pretty enough for any town," and so it was called.

But we have wandered afar off and must return to the present.

Wynema looked wistfully at the one whom she still called Mihia, and clasping her hands said:

"Oh, wouldn't I? Oh, Mihia. To go with you among your people, to see your dear mother, your brother, and sisters of whom you often tell me – that would be joy; but my poor father and mother! what would become of them if I should never return?"

"But we shall come back, Wynema. I am coming back if God spares me. Your mother and father will be glad to have you see something of the world beyond this little village, and I know they would rather trust you with me than with any one. Only consent to go and all can be arranged for us to have a pleasant trip and visit. My little girl has grown so dear to me that I dislike to part with her for even a short while," – and Genevieve placed her hand on her friend's arm.

That stroke won the battle and Genevieve had her way. The friends talked animatedly of their projected visit until they reached home that afternoon, after the school duties were performed. The plan was submitted to Wynema's parents' inspection, and after some natural reluctance they gave it their hearty approval. Then as the holidays were near, preparations were made for the friends' departure.

## CHAPTER XI

### IN THE OLD HOME

"Oh, how nice it is to be home again!" cried Genevieve, looking into every remembered nook and cranny about the place "Nothing changed, but everything seems to nod a familiar 'How d'ye do.' I declare, I don't feel a day older than when I ran up the attic stairs and crawled out of the window into the old elm tree, where Robin and I had our 'Robinson Crusoe's house,' and I was the 'man Friday.' Do you remember the day you fell out, Robin, when the bear got after you and you climbed out on the bough, when it broke? It would seem as yesterday if Robin were not such a tall, broad-shouldered fellow, really towering over us all; and I, a cross-grained, wrinkled spinster; and Toots putting on young lady's airs – I suppose we shall have to call her Bessie, now; and even Winnie, our dear little baby, is laying aside her dolls and – I do really believe it Miss – is smiling at Charley or Willie or Ted. Ah, no wonder the little Mith feels so ancient when she views such a group of grown folks and realizes they are her children. But let's hear a report of yourselves, and I'll satisfy the baby's curiosity to see my Indian relics," – and a laughing, happy group, they recount experiences, compare notes and enjoy themselves generally.

Back at the old home, Genevieve is the light-hearted girl of long ago, to be teased and petted, and to tease and pet in return. And in all this merriment and happiness is our little Indian friend forgotten or pushed aside because of her dark skin and savage manners? Ah, no; she is the friend of their dear one, and for that reason, at first, she was warmly welcomed and graciously entertained, and afterward she was loved for her own good qualities. Many were the rambles and rides, the drives and picnics these young people enjoyed. Generally Robin, Bessie and Wynema formed these excursion parties, for Genevieve preferred remaining at home or had a "previous engagement."

After "the visitor," – as Winnie still called Wynema much to her discomfiture and amusement – had been with them for some weeks, she and Robin, with Winnie for propriety, for Bessie was detained at home, were out rowing on the bay, when Robin glancing up at his companion, asked: "Doesn't the rippling of the waves make your head swim? make you 'drunk' as Winnie says?"

"No, I am accustomed to being on the water; I often row alone. I don't ever remember of feeling 'drunk.' What kind of a feeling is it?" she smiled inquiringly.

"Oh, I can't tell exactly – only you feel as if the ground were slipping from under you, and the world and everything therein, spinning like a top for your amusement. It isn't a pleasant feeling, I assure you," and he put his hand to his head as if he were then experiencing the feeling.

"No, I presume not, from your description. But where and how did you gain so much information about it? Personal experience?" mischievously.

"No," Winnie spoke up in defense of her favorite, "Robin never was drunk. But Mr. Snifer, oh, he gets just awful drunk, and he just falls down, and fights his wife, and I'm awful afraid of him," clasping her hands earnestly.

"Thank you, Pet, for defending my character," said her brother lovingly. "You see, Miss Wynema, our little girl has been studying grammar and makes much progress."

"I am sure of one thing," said Wynema, taking the child's hand; "that is, though this little maid may not be perfectly correct in the use of words, she will never be deficient in the depth of her affection. Dear, am sorry your neighbor is such a beastly man; but that reminds me of some of my people when they become intoxicated – 'get drunk,' as you term it – only my people act much worse. They ride through the streets, firing pistols and whooping loudly, and often kill many people. 'Firewater' is an awful thing among your people who are more civilized than we are, and you can imagine what a terrible influence it exerts among my people." The child shuddered and shut her eyes.

"But, Miss Wynema – "

"Don't call me that; I am not accustomed to it," she interrupted.

"Well, but Wynema, I thought it was against the law of the United States to carry whisky or any intoxicant into your country," Robin said surprisedly.

"So it is against the treaty made by the U. S. government with the Indians; but, notwithstanding all this, the whisky is brought into our country and sold to our people."

"Are not the smugglers ever apprehended and punished?" he asked.

"Oh, yes, often; but that does not materially affect the unholy and unlawful practice. Only last Christmas, as your sister can tell you better than I, drunken Indians and white men were to be seen on the streets of all our towns. Oh, it is terrible," shuddering. "The only way I can see, of exterminating the evil is to pull it up by the roots; stop the manufacture and of necessity the sale of it will be stopped."

"I believe you would make a staunch Woman's Christian Temperance Unionist, for that is their argument," he replied admiringly.

"Indeed, I am a member of that union. We have a small union in our town and do all we can against the great evil – intemperance; but what can a little band of women, prohibited from voting against the ruin of their husbands, sons and firesides, do, when even the great government of Uncle Sam is set at defiance?" Wynema waxed eloquent in defense of her "hobby."

"I am afraid you are a regular suffragist!" Robin said, shrugging his shoulders.

"So I am," emphatically; "but it does me very little good, only for the principle's sake. Still, I believe that, one day, the 'inferior of man,' the 'weaker vessel' shall stand grandly by the side of that 'noble lord of creation,' his equal in *every* respect."

"Hear! Hear! How much the 'cause' loses by not having you to publicly advocate it! Say, didn't sister teach you all this along with the rest? I think you must have imbibed those strong suffrage principles and ideas from her," said Robin, teasingly.

She went on earnestly, ignoring his jesting manner: "Your sister and I hold many opinions in common, and doubtless, I have imbibed some of hers, as I have the greatest respect for her opinions; but the idea of freedom and liberty was born in me. It is true the women of my country have no voice in the councils; we do not speak in any public gathering, not even in our churches; but we are waiting for our more civilized white sisters to gain their liberty, and thus set us an example which we shall not be slow to follow." She finished, her cheeks flushed and her eyes sparkling with earnestness and animation. Robin looked at her with admiration shining in his dark blue eyes.

"I am sure of that, if you are a fair representative of your people," he said. "But I will not jest about the matter any longer for I am as truly interested in it as you are. I think it will only be a matter of time, and a short time, too, when the question as to whether our women may participate in our liberties, help choose our officers, even our presidents, will be settled in their favor – at least, I hope so. There is no man who is enterprising and keeps well up with the times but confesses that the women of to-day are in every respect, except political liberty, equal to the men. It could not be successfully denied, for college statistics prove it by showing the number of women who have borne off the honors, even when public sentiment was against them and in favor of their brother-competitors. And not alone in an intellectual sense are you women our equals, but you have the energy and ambition, and far more morality than we can claim. Then you know so well how to put your learning in practice. See the college graduates who make successful farmers, vintners, etc. Indeed, you women can do anything you wish," he said, in a burst of admiration.

"Except to vote," she replied quietly.

"And you would do that if I had my way," Robin said warmly.

"It seems to me somebody else would make a splendid lecturer on Woman's Rights. You had better enlist," tauntingly.

"By taking one of the women? I should like to," and he looked into her eyes his deep meaning.

## Chapter XII

### A Conservative

Soon after Genevieve's return, Maurice Mauran came over to bid her welcome, and to renew the tie that once bound them, but which Genevieve severed when she departed to dwell among the Indians. Genevieve was rejoiced to be with him again, and noted all changes in him for the better, with pride and delight; but she noticed his indifferent and slighting manner of speaking about religion and secular matters, temperance and her much-loved Indians; and it troubled her. All the questions of the day were warmly discussed during his visits, which were of frequent occurrence, when finally, a short while before Genevieve's departure, the subject of woman's suffrage came up, and Genevieve warmly defended it.

"Why, Genevieve," said Maurice, "I fear you are a 'real live,' suffragist! I wonder that you have not cut off your hair and started out on a lecturing tour; I'm sure you would do well. Really, little girl," he said more seriously, "you are too pronounced in your opinions on all subjects. Don't you know ladies are not expected to have any ideas except about house-keeping, fancy-work, dress and society, until after they are married, when they only echo the opinions of their husbands? As for woman's rights, I don't want my little wife to bother her head about that, for it is immodest and unwomanly. You look surprised, but what would a woman out of her sphere be, but unwomanly?"

"I look and am surprised, Maurice, at your statement," Genevieve replied quietly. "I am surprised that a man of your culture could entertain such 'old-fogy' opinions as you have expressed. It is just such and like sentiments that have held women back into obscurity for so long; but, thank God!" she added fervently, "sensible men are beginning to open their eyes and see things in a different light from what their ancestors saw them. The idea of a woman being unwomanly and immodest because she happens to be thoughtful and to have 'two ideas above an oyster,' to know a little beyond and above house and dress is perfectly absurd and untrue. Is Mrs. Hayes,[5] wife of ex-president Hayes, and president of the Woman's Mission Board immodest because she does not devote her time to cleaning house or planning dresses, but prefers doing missionary work? And is the great leader of temperance work, Frances E. Willard,[6] World's and National president of the Women's Christian Temperance Union, of whom one of your great men said 'I think she is one of the most remarkable women the century has produced,' and another called her 'that peerless woman of the earth, that uncrowned queen,' – I say, is she unwomanly because she prefers to devote her life to temperance work instead of keeping house for some man for her 'victuals and clothes?' As for that matter, who of our leaders, our truly great women, can be truthfully called immodest or unwomanly? Their very womanliness is their passport to the hearts of their fellow-men – their insurance of success. Ah, my friend, you will have to change your opinion on this question for a newer and better one, for yours is decidedly old-fashioned and out of taste," she concluded warmly.

"Well, we won't quarrel about it, for I know you are not so interested in these questions as to be disagreeable about them. I don't and cannot believe in a woman coming out in public in any capacity; but so long as I have my little wife at home, I will keep my sentiments to myself."

And the subject passed without more notice; but the seeds of discord were planted in the hearts of two who were "Two children in a hamlet bred and born," and should have been "Two hearts that beat as one."[7]

It seemed very strange to Genevieve that she should be constantly comparing Maurice Mauran to Gerald Keithly, and not always in Maurice's favor. She thought how differently these two men believed, and one was buried among the Indians where it would be thought he had no opportunity for keeping up with the times; and still – and then she sighed and did not finish.

## CHAPTER XIII

## SHALL WE ALLOT?

"What is it you are reading, Mihia, that you look so troubled?" queried Wynema coming in one afternoon from a stroll she had taken with Robert[8] and Bessie, and looking very pretty with her bright, merry eyes and rosy cheeks. She came and looked over her friend's shoulder in her loving way. "Oh, what a long article!" drawing down her face. "Shall we allot? allot what? Oh, that is a home paper! Surely it cannot mean allot our country?"

"That is just what it means, dear," replied her friend. "Some United States Senators are very much in favor of allotting in severalty the whole of the Indian Territory, and, of course, that would take in your country also. I don't like the idea, though it has been talked of for a long time. It seems to me a plan by which the 'boomers' who were left out of Oklahoma are to be landed. For years the U. S. Senators and citizens have been trying to devise ways and means by which to divide the Indians' country, but, as yet, nothing has been done. Now the matter assumes a serious aspect, for even the part-blood Indians are in favor of allotment; and if the Indians do not stand firmly against it, I fear they will yet be homeless," and Miss Weir sighed and gazed abstractedly at her listener.

---

[5] Lucy Ware Webb Hayes (1831–79), wife of President Rutherford B. Hayes.

[6] Frances E. Willard (1839–98) was often called "the Uncrowned Queen of America," presumably for her great influence on American culture.

[7] From *Der Sohn der Wildnis*, by Friedrich Halm, Baron von Münch-Bellinghausen (1806–71); translated by Maria Lovell in 1854 as *Ingomar the Barbarian*.

[8] Probably the formal version of "Robin."

"But I don't see how dividing our lands can materially damage us," said Wynema looking thoughtfully back again. "We should have our own homes, and contrary to ruining our fortunes I think it would mend them. See! This is the way I see the matter. If I am wrong, correct me. There are so many idle, shiftless Indians who do nothing but hunt and fish; then there are others who are industrious and enterprising; so long as our land remains as a whole, in common, these lazy Indians will never make a move toward cultivating it; and the industrious Indians and 'squaw men' will inclose as much as they can for their own use. Thus the land will be unequally divided, the lazy Indians getting nothing because they will not exert themselves to do so; while, if the land were allotted, do you not think that these idle Indians, knowing the land to be their own, would have pride enough to cultivate their land and build up their homes? It seems so to me;" and she looked earnestly at Genevieve, awaiting her reply.

"I had not thought of the matter in the way you present it, though that is the view many congressmen and editors take of it. Then again in support of your theory that allotment will be best, this paper says the Indians *must* allot, to protect themselves against the U. S. Government, and suggests that the more civilized apply for statehood; for it says 'if the protection provided for in the treaties be insufficient, more certain protection should be secured.' Another paper says, 'Gen. Noble,[9] Secretary of the Interior, in his recent report, strikes a blow at "Wild West" shows by recommending an act of congress, forbidding any person or corporation to take into employment or under control any American Indian. He advocates a continuance of the policy of exclusion in connection with the Indian Territory cattle question; suggests that the period now allowed a tribe to determine whether it will receive allotment be placed under the control of the President, so that it may be shortened if *tribes give no attention to the subject or cause unreasonable delays;* and discountenances the employment of attorneys by the Indians to aid in negotiations with, or to prosecute claims against, the government.' This sounds like the lands will be allotted whether the Indians like or no. I cannot see the matter as it has been presented by you, and as these papers advocate it, my idea is, that it will be the ruin of the poor, ignorant savage. It will do very well for the civilized tribes, but they should never consent to it until their weaker brothers are willing and able. Laws are made for people and not people for laws. The South Sea Islander could not be governed by the laws of England, nor can the North American Indian become a fit subject of the United States. Do you not see, my friend, that if your land were divided, your territory would then become a fit subject of the United States Government. Do you think the western tribes sufficiently tutored in the school of civilization to become citizens of the United States, subject to its laws and punishments?"

"Oh, no indeed! Far from it! What a superficial thinker I am not to have understood this!" answered the girl vehemently.

"Then there is another objection to this measure," continued Miss Weir, "that seems very weighty to me. Were the land divided, these poor, ignorant, improvident, short-sighted Indians would be persuaded and threatened into selling their homes, piece by piece, perhaps, until finally they would be homeless outcasts, and then what would become of 'Poor Lo!'[10] None of his white brothers, who so sweetly persuaded away his home, would give him a night's shelter or a morsel of food." Genevieve was so intensely earnest that she had risen and was pacing the room, her hands clasped together, her brows knit. Wynema, who seldom saw her in such moods, was frightened, and reproached herself with having been the cause of it.

"Oh, I am so sorry, dear Mihia – so sorry I was so foolish! Pray, forgive me! It is always the way with me, and I dare say I should be one of the first to sell myself out of house and home;" and the girl hung her head, looking the picture of humiliation.

"No, dear, I am the one to ask forgiveness for needlessly disturbing you so. Now go along and enjoy yourself, for I dare say nothing will come of all this;" and Genevieve kissed her friend, hoping that she might never have cause to be less light-hearted than at present.

---

9 John Willock Noble (1831–1912), Secretary of the Interior from 1889 to 1893, spoke out against Wild West shows in an annual report of 1890.

10 In "An Essay on Man," Alexander Pope (1688–1744) laments, "Lo, the poor Indian!"

## Chapter XIV

### More Concerning Allotments

When Maurice Mauran came over to make his accustomed visit, Genevieve brought up the subject of allotment, incidentally, and showed him the paper she had been reading. She spoke calmly and indifferently, striving to hide her own sentiments that she might obtain his free opinion.

"You are an able lawyer, one of the lights of your profession, and more able to form a correct opinion as to whether it would be legal for the United States Government to allot the Indians' land against the expressed desire of this people."

When he had finished reading, he threw the paper down, saying, "Pshaw! I hope you do not waste your time reading such stuff as this. Why, don't you see that this allotment would be the best thing that ever happened to the Indian, for it would bring him out and educate him? As it is, he will remain just as he is and has been since the 'year one,' – nothing but an uncouth savage. Why, don't you know, Genevieve, the Indian in an uncivilized state is nothing more than a brute? He hasn't as much sense as Prince, there," pointing to his dog which came and laid his head on his master's knee. "You see he understands that I am talking about him; don't you, old fellow. And if," said he, resuming his argument, "if by constant contact and intercourse with white people the Indians do not become civilized, why, let them go to the dogs, I say, for they are not worth spending time and money on; and what is the use of their cumbering lands that white people might be cultivating? Why, what's the matter with you, Genevieve? you look as if you had been struck," he said suddenly turning to her.

"Nothing is the matter," she replied in an ominously quiet tone. "I am waiting for you to go on. I want to hear your full opinion."

"Well, then don't look at me so;" she withdrew her eyes. "I am afraid, Genevieve," he went on, "that your sojourn among the Indians was not at all beneficial to you. You will excuse me, I hope, for saying it, but I don't want my affianced wife to hold such opinions regarding so important a matter as this Indian question, as you evidently hold. You lived among them; you know them to be idle, trifling, a people whom no amount of cultivation could civilize, and yet you wish to go back and add to the disgrace of your former stay among them. Forgive me, my dear girl, if I offend you by my plain language, but it is best we should understand each other. I cannot but feel it a disgrace for you to have lived and labored among such a people – a people very little superior to the negro in my opinion. I am fond of you, you know, and proud of your gifted mind, but I do not want my wife to stock her mind with sentiments that, if held by all, would be injurious to the commonwealth." He spoke in the patronizing way men usually adopt when reasoning with women. "I have looked forward to your home-coming and comforted myself during our separation with the thought that soon that separation would be over forever; that, one in mind and heart we would wander peacefully down the hill of time together, and side by side rest at its foot when our journey is done; but despite my great affection for you, my dear, I cannot overlook – "

"Stop!" cried Genevieve, her eyes flashing and her cheeks flaming with indignation. "I have had enough of that. I asked you your opinion on the Indian question and instead you are giving me the model by which you expect to mold your future wife. You had better get one of clay or putty as that will turn into any shape you wish to mold it. You say I have disgraced myself by laboring among the ignorant, idle, treacherous Indians; but never in all the years I have dwelt among these savages have I been subjected to the insult your words imply. I asked you for an opinion; you have given me vituperation; and not being content with slandering the poor, ignorant, defenseless Indians, you begin on me. Oh, if I pretended to be a man, I'd be a *man,* and not a sniveling coward. If you were a man, I would reason with you, but you do not understand the first principles of logic. Your wife, indeed! I have never promised to be such, and please heaven! I never will. My husband must be a man, full-grown – a man capable of giving an opinion, just and honest, without using insult to do so. Good evening! I have no time to spend in arguing about a people who have not the intellect of a dog," and with a curl of her lip, and a toss of the head, she swept from the room, righteously angry.

The young man, left to himself, was hardly able to conduct himself to the door, for so sudden had been Genevieve's attack that it left him stunned with surprise – not so stunned, however, but that he was able to understand that his long-cherished hope of "owning" this girl was crushed forever.

There was no mistaking the tone of her voice and her emphatic words.

Very different from his opinion was that of Gerald Keithly as expressed in a letter which she received a few days after her quarrel with Maurice. He said:

"You will see by this that I am still with my charge. I did not get off as I desired, for the country is so disturbed over the threatened measure – allotment in severalty – that I thought it best to stay and see the matter settled, though I do not believe the land will be divided soon. I think it is a mere question of time, when it will be; and God knows what will become of these poor savages when it is! For, as you know, they have so little providence or shrewdness or any kind of business sense, that their sharper white brothers would soon show them 'the way the land lies.' I cannot but admit that this measure would be best for the half-bloods and those educated in the ways of the world, able to fight their own battles; but it would be the ruin of the poor, ignorant full-bloods. 'The strong should protect the weak' says chivalry; but there seems to be very little if any chivalric spirit shown in the case of these Indians. Little Fox came over yesterday to ask my opinion concerning the probability of the passage of this measure. I told him just what I thought about it, and he said, straightening back proudly: 'But the United States Government cannot take our lands and divide them, for they are ours. They made a treaty with us to the effect that this land should be ours and our children's so long as grass grows and water runs; if it be ours, what right has congress to take it and divide it? They cannot force us to divide, against our will, legally, either, and we will never consent to this measure. We know what it means. It means statehood first, and it means homeless Indians, last. Have not the white people pushed us farther and farther away, until now we are in this little corner of the world? And do they now wish to deprive us of it? Why do they not go to Texas when homes are offered for the making, and a welcome extended to the homeless? Do you think the whites would furnish us homes if we gave them ours? Not much. No, we will never agree to this measure; I will fight it with my last breath,' he added fiercely.

"'Well,' I said, 'if you all stand firmly against this measure it cannot be passed legally, for that would stake the honor of the United States Government. But the Indians can be threatened and bribed into agreeing to divide their lands; and the tide is so strong against them I fear they cannot weather it. I will do all I can for them, in the way of advising and helping, and fighting if need be. Byron fought for the emancipation of Greece and gave his life to the cause.[11] Even so, will I, a much more humble person, give mine for the liberty of the poor Indian.'

"Pray for us, Genevieve, dear, that God may open the eyes of our oppressors to see the great wrong they are doing, and spare this people. I don't want to be selfish, nor see you in danger; but I – that is we – do want you back badly, very badly – more than you can imagine."

Ah, thought Genevieve after reading this letter over many times, here is a man after my own heart! Noble, generous, self-sacrificing and withal, *tender* and *true.* Oh, Maurice if it were only you! and it is to be feared she thought more of the writer than of the contents of the letter, for she was only human, after all, and it was so nice to be loved.

Ah, Gerald Keithly, if you could have only known! – how much heaviness of heart it would have spared you!

[11] Dying of a fever in Greece, George Gordon Byron, Lord Byron (1788–1824), supported the movement for Greek independence from Turkey.

# Fox Indian Woman (Mesquakie/Fox; fl. 1918)/Truman Michelson

*In 1918, anthropologist Truman Michelson collected the short life story of an anonymous Mesquakie (Fox) Indian woman in Tama, Iowa. Michelson recorded numerous such narratives from members of midwestern tribes. Still relatively young compared to many of the women whose life stories were recorded by ethnographers and anthropologists around the turn of the century, the woman who speaks here was born in the late 1800s, and we learn in the course of the narrative that she had three husbands and several children. Often published by the Bureau of American Ethnology, Michelson's work required him to seek out tribal members for assistance in obtaining informants and translating their stories; the names of informants were frequently kept secret, in part because they may sometimes have revealed information that was not supposed to leave the tribe. The degree of his editorial intervention is unclear; however, one feature of this narrative, its explicit description of sexual norms and practices, elicited the following terse remark from Michelson: "It may be noted that at times the original autobiography was too naive and frank for European taste, and so a few sentences have been deleted." This comment suggests the relatively light hand of the editor elsewhere, and we can have a reasonable amount of confidence that the narrative accurately reflects the voice of the speaker. Michelson notes, "No attempt was made to influence the informant in any way; so that the contents are the things which seem of importance to herself."*

*Important matters included education, especially in matters pertaining to female roles and responsibilities, while the story avoids the complex political situation of the tribe at the end of the century. Conflict between traditionalists and progressives caused continuing strife, especially over such matters as the selection of a chief and the public education of their children. In 1898 the federal government opened a boarding school, but because the Mesquakie ("The Red Earth People") refused to send their children, the school was closed by 1911. None of this political material appears in the autobiography, which focuses on more personal concerns such as the education of children and the mutual support of family. However gentle Michelson's editorial hand may have been, the method of collection of the story virtually guaranteed some introduced errors. Related in the Mesquakie language to Harry Lincoln (half Mesquakie and half Winnebago), corrected by his wife, Dalottiwa (Mesquakie), and translated by Horace Poweshiek (Mesquakie) before coming to Michelson and being published in a process that took over two years, the story epitomizes a form of bicultural composite composition. Poweshiek was a progressive, and we cannot be certain how this perspective may have influenced his translation. Even more significantly, the presence of men in elements of the composition process may have informed the narrator's choice of materials, as well as the selection of materials they considered important in the final product.*

*We should note that the narrative contains some gaps and some misinterpretations by Michelson. For example, the passage in which the narrator is cautioned not to sleep in different places reflects the Mesquakie belief that such behavior may result in a young woman's unchaste behavior when she grows older. In relation to the passages about menstruation,*

*Michelson imposed the disparagement more characteristic of white patriarchal society than reflective of the tribe's beliefs. For the Mesquakie as for many other Indian tribes, menstruation was a time of power, potentially both beneficial and harmful – as we saw, for example, with the traditional Cherokee narrative above – reflected in the isolation the narrator endures because of the necessity to keep the power contained. Another important element of the narrative is its emphasis on the importance of women in the narrator's life, her mother being the most significant. As we see in the menstruation section, however, other women also figure significantly; the "grandmother" in this section – "grandmother" being a title signifying respect and highlighting wisdom rather than specifying a blood relationship – aids and comforts the fearful girl and educates her about her future responsibilities and proper behavior. Finally, although the narrative appears to emphasize roles and events characteristic of the Mesquakie more generally, moments of individuality appear, perhaps most notably in the narrator's description of leaving her first, abusive husband, and her desire for children. Despite the complexity of the story's composition and the difficulty of locating the narrator's intentions, the narrative offers a moving account of a woman's life that contributes importantly to a tradition of American Indian women's autobiography.*

## Bibliography


### Primary

Michelson, Truman. "The Autobiography of a Fox Indian Woman." *Bureau of American Ethnology Fortieth Annual Report, 1918–1919* (1925): 291–349.

### Secondary

Bataille, Gretchen M. and Kathleen Mullen Sands. *American Indian Women: Telling Their Lives*. Nebraska, 1984.

Brown, Richard Frank. "A Social History of the Mesquakie Indians, 1800–1963." MA thesis, Iowa State University, 1964.

Brumble, H. David, III. *American Indian Autobiography*. California, 1988.

Hagen, William T. *The Sac and Fox Indians*. Oklahoma, 1958.

Jones, William. *Ethnography of the Fox Indians*. Smithsonian Institution, Bureau of American Ethnology Bulletin 125, 1939.

Krupat, Arnold, ed. Introduction to *Native American Autobiography*. Wisconsin, 1994.

Wong, Hertha Dawn. *Sending My Heart Back Across the Years: Tradition and Innovation in Native American Autobiography*. Oxford, 1992.


# The Autobiography of a Fox Indian Woman (1918; with Dalottiwa, Horace Poweshiek, and Truman Michelson)

Well, I shall now tell what happened to me. From the time when I was six years old is perhaps when I begin to recollect it. Of course (I do) not (recollect it) fully; I forget once in a great while (some days) each year back.

Well, I played with dolls[1] when I made them. (And) when I played with them I would make one large doll. Now they would be supposed to be many children. And that large doll, I would pretend, would do the cooking. Of course I would do the cooking in my play. And many of us would eat together when we ate, I pretended. And then I made little wickiups[2] for the dolls to live in.

---

[1] Dolls were formerly made of corn husks in the fall; their clothing was made of muskrat and squirrel skins [Michelson's note].

[2] To-day a good many families live in shacks and there are a few good frame houses; but still nearly half the Foxes live in wickiups of rush mats in winter and "bark houses" in summer. [Planks now take the place of bark. The above remarks held true at the time this paper was prepared for press, but now (fall of 1924) the bulk of the Foxes live in shacks (Michelson's note)].

When I was perhaps seven years old I began to practice sewing for my dolls. But I sewed poorly. I used to cry because I did not know how to sew. Nor could I persuade my mother to (do it) when I said to her, "Make it for me." "You will know how to sew later on; that is why I shall not make them for you. That is how one learns to sew, by practicing sewing for one's dolls. That is why one has dolls, namely, to make everything for them – their clothing and moccasins." And so I would always practice sewing for my dolls.

When I was perhaps eight years old I began to like to swim. If we were living near where a river flowed by, we girls always would swim. There were many of us. Although we were scolded, yet when we could do so secretly we would go swimming. Some would be whipped because they did not mind. As for me, I was never whipped[3] as I was the only girl (my parents) had. I would only be severely scolded when I did not mind when I was forbidden (anything). And I was made to fast when I did not pay attention. And I was forbidden to go with the other little girls, that is, the very naughty ones. "They might get you (into their habits), as they will not know how to make anything when they grow up in the future if they do not try to make anything. That is the way you will be if you do not try to make anything, if you merely loaf around,"[4] I would be told when I was made to fast. I was fed at noon. But soon, within several days, I had forgotten what I was forbidden. Again I was told, "Do not sleep anywhere (in the wickiups) of the little girls with whom you play. Come back to where we live while it is still daylight. Do not be out some place in the night. Play with them now and then."

Well, when I was nine years old I was able to help my mother. It was in spring when planting was begun that I was told, "Plant something to be your own." Sure enough I did some planting. When they began to hoe weeds where it was planted, I was told "Say! You weed in your field." My hoe was a little hoe. And soon the hoeing would cease. I was glad.

When (we) ceased bothering where it was planted, I was unwilling to do anything. But when I would be told, "When you finish this, then you may go and play with the little girls," I was willing. I then surely played violently with the children. We played tag[5] as we enjoyed it.

And at the time when what we planted was mature, I was told, "Say! You must try to cook what you have raised." Surely then I tried to cook. After I cooked it, my parents tasted it. "What she has raised tastes very well," they said to me. "And she has cooked it very carefully," I would be told. I was proud when they said that to me. As a matter of fact I was just told so that I might be encouraged to cook. And I thought, "It's probably true."

And when I was ten years old I ceased caring for dolls. But I still liked to swim. But when I said to my mother, "May I go swimming?" she said to me, "Yes. You may wash your grandmother's waist for her, and you may wash mine also," I was told. I was made to wash (anything) little. Surely I would not feel like asking, "May I go swimming," as I was afraid of the washing. Now as a matter of fact the reason why I was treated so was to encourage me to learn how to wash.

"That is why I treat you like that, so that you will learn how to wash," my mother told me. "No one continues to be taken care of forever. The time soon comes when we lose sight of the one who takes care

---

3 Even at the present day Fox children are rarely whipped; they are made to fast instead. Formerly their cheeks were painted with charcoal; in this way the entire village would know they were fasting, and accordingly no lodge would offer them meals [Michelson's note]. We see this preference for reasoning over corporal punishment expressed repeatedly in this collection.

4 Lazy girls are disliked [Michelson's note].

5 "Tag" is played in the following way: If there are ten, they get nine short sticks all of which are the same length, and one long one. They are held between the thumb and index finger; the tops are seen. The one who makes the sticks does so secretly. When the one with the sticks comes to where the other children are he tells them to pull out one each. Whoever gets the long one is to be the chaser. They will make marks on a tree or post. All assemble there except the one who has the long stick. If any child wants to run, the one who has the sticks will chase him (or her); or all can run out at the same time; in the latter case the chaser will chase any one he (or she) thinks he (or she) can catch. The rule is that the one chased must be touched squarely on the head. The one thus touched becomes the chaser's partner, and helps in chasing. After all are caught, new sticks will be made; or if there chances to be a swift runner left they say he must be the chaser [Michelson's note].

of us. I never got to know how my mother looked. My father's sister brought me up. To-day I treat you just as she treated me. She did not permit me to be just fooling around. Why, even when I was eight years old I knew how to cook very well. When my father's sister was busy with something, I did the cooking," she said to me. I did not believe her when she said that, for I was then ten years old and was just beginning to cook well, and I knew how to sew but I was poor at it. At that time when my mother woke up, she said to me, "Wake up, you may fetch some water. And go get some little dry sticks so we may start the fire," she said to me. When I was unwilling I was nevertheless compelled. That is the way I was always treated.

Soon, moreover, I was told, "This is your little ax," when a little ax was brought. I was glad. "This is your wood-strap," I was told. My mother and I would go out to cut wood; and I carried the little wood that I had cut on my back. She would strap them for me. She instructed me how to tie them up. Soon I began to go a little ways off by myself to cut wood.

And when I was eleven years old I likewise continually watched her as she would make bags. "Well, you try to make one," she said to me. She braided up one little bag for me. She instructed me how to make it. Sure enough, I nearly learned how to make it, but I made it very badly. I was again told, "You make another." It was somewhat larger. And soon I knew how to make it very well. Then surely I was unwilling to make them. At first I was willing to make them as I did not know how to make them very well. But I was constrained to keep on making them. During the winters I kept on making them. Moreover, at that time a little rush mat was woven for me. "Make this," I was told. I tried to make it. Later on I finished it. I made it extremely poorly. Soon I began to help my mother after I knew how to make rush mats.

She would be very proud after I had learned to make anything. "There, you will make things for yourself after you take care of yourself. That is why I constrain you to make anything, not to treat you meanly. I let you do things so that you may make something. If you happen to know how to make everything when you no longer see me, you will not have a hard time in any way. You will make your own possessions. My father's sister, the one who took care of me, treated me so. That is why I know how to make any little thing. 'She is in the habit of treating me meanly,' I thought, when she ordered me to make something all the time. Now as a matter of fact she treated me well. When I knew about it, I would think, 'why she must have treated me very well.' And that is why I treat you so to-day. So very likely when you think of me, you think, 'she treats me meanly.' It is because I am fond of you and wish you to know how to make things. If I were not fond of you, I would not order you around (to do things). (If I were not fond of you) I would think, 'I don't care what she does.' If you are intelligent when you are grown and recollect how I treated you, you will think, 'I declare! My mother treated me well.' Or if you are bad you will not remember me when I am gone. And this. Though you know how to make things you will not make anything. That is what you will do if you are bad. I do not wish you to be that way. I desire that you take care of yourself quietly," my mother told me.

And again, when I was twelve years old, I was told, "Come, try to make these." (They were) my own moccasins. "You may start to make them for yourself after you know how to make them. For you already know how to make them for your dolls. That is the way you are to make them," I was told. She only cut them out for me. And when I made a mistake she ripped it out for me. "This is the way you are to make it," I was told. Finally I really knew how to make them.

And then a small belt of yarn was put on the sticks for me. A little was started for me. "Try to make this one," I was told. I began to try to make it. Later on I surely knew how to make it. Then I kept on making belts of yarn. My mother was pleased when I learned how to make anything.

At that time I knew how to cook well. When my mother went any place, she said to me, "You may cook the meal." Moreover, when she made mats I cooked the meals. "You may get accustomed to cooking, for it is almost time for you to live outside. You will cook for yourself when you live outside," I would be told.

Soon I was told, "Well, begin to try to weave; you may wish to make these mats." Then I began to try to weave. Later I knew how to weave very well. Then I began to help my mother all the time. She was proud when I continued to learn how to make anything.

And then I was thirteen years old. "Now is the time when you must watch yourself; at last you are nearly a young woman. Do not forget this which I tell you. You might ruin your brothers if you are not careful. The state of being a young woman is evil. The manitous hate it. If any one is blessed by a manitou, if he eats with a young woman he is then hated by the one who blessed him and the (manitou) ceases to think of him.[6] That is why it is told us, 'be careful' and why we are told about it beforehand. At the time when you are a young woman, whenever you become a young woman, you are to hide yourself. Do not come into your wickiup. That is what you are to do." She frightened me when she told me.

Lo, sure enough when I was thirteen and a half years old, I was told, "Go get some wood and carry it on your back." It was nearly noon when I started out. When I was walking along somewhere, I noticed something strange about myself. I was terribly frightened at being in that condition. I did not know how I became that way. "This must be the thing about which I was cautioned when I was told," I thought.

I went and laid down in the middle of the thick forest there. I was crying, as I was frightened. It was almost the middle of summer after we had done our hoeing. After a while my mother got tired of waiting for me. She came to seek me. Soon she found me. I was then crying hard.

"Come, stop crying. It's just the way with us women. We have been made to be that way. Nothing will happen to you. You will have gotten over this now in the warm weather. Had it happened to you in winter you would have had a hard time. You would be cold when you bathed as you would have to jump into the water four times. That is the way it is when we first have it. Now, to-day, as it is warm weather, you may swim as slowly as you like when you swim," I was told. "Lie covered up. Do not try to look around. I shall go and make (a wickiup) for you," I was told.

I was suffering very much there in the midst of the brush. And it was very hot.

It was in the evening when I was told, "At last I have come for you. I have built (a place) for you to live in. Cover your face. Do not think of looking any place." I was brought there to the small wickiup. And I was shut off by twigs all around. There was brush piled up so that I could not see through it. There was only a little space where I lived to cook outside. My grandmother must have made it a size so that there was only room for us to lie down in.

"I shall fetch your grandmother to be here with you," my mother told me. It was another old woman.[7] As a matter of fact the reason she was brought there was for to give me instructions. I did not eat all day long. The next day I was told, "We shall fetch things for you to use in cooking." I was not hungry as I was frightened. The next day my grandmother went to eat. It was only as long as she (took) when she went to eat that I was alone, but I was afraid. In the evening I was brought little buckets to cook with, any little thing to eat, water and wood. Then for the first time I cooked.

And my grandmother would keep on giving me instructions there, telling me how to lead a good life. She really was a very old woman. Surely she must have spoken the truth in what she had been saying to me. "My grandchild," she would say to me, "soon I shall tell you how to live an upright life. To-day you see how old I am. I did exactly what I was told. I tried and thought how to live an upright life. Surely I have reached an old age," she told me. "That is the way you should do, if you listen to me as I instruct you. Now as for your mother, I began giving her instructions before she was grown up, every time I saw her. Because she was my relative is why I gave her instructions, although she was well treated by her father's sister by whom she was reared. That is why she knows how to make things which belong to the work of us women. If you observe the way your mother makes anything, you would do well, my grandchild. And this. As many of us as entered young womanhood, fasted. It was very many days: some fasted

---

[6] It is not lawful for a woman who is menstruating to eat with others; she secludes herself in a little lodge, and it is not considered proper for a man to linger about there, and a man is not to enter such a lodge . . . [Michelson's note; the note goes on to discuss the power of menstruating women]. A manitou is a supernatural being or deity, especially one who controls nature.

[7] The girl's maternal grandmother was dead; the term grandmother in the present instance is only a courtesy-term [Michelson's note].

ten days, some four, five, every kind of way. To-day, to be sure, things are changing. When I was a young woman I fasted eight days. We always fasted until we were grown up," my grandmother told me.

My mother only came to fetch me water and little sticks of wood so that I might kindle a fire when I cooked. And we made strings. That is what we did.

"Do not touch your hair: it might all come off. And do not eat sweet things. And if what tastes sour is eaten, one's teeth will come out. It is owing to that saying that we are afraid to eat sweet things," my grandmother told me. She always gave me good advice from time to time. "Well, there is another thing. Now the men will think you are mature as you have become a young woman, and they will be desirous of courting you. If you do not go around bashfully, for a long time they will not have the audacity to court you. When there is a dance, when there are many boys saying all sorts of funny things, if you do not notice it, they will be afraid of you for a very long time. If you laugh over their words, they will consider you as naught. They will begin bothering you right away. If you are immoral your brothers will be ashamed, and your mother's brothers.[8] If you live quietly they will be proud. They will love you. If you are only always making something in the same place where you live, they will always give you something whenever they get it. And your brothers will believe you when you say anything to them. When one lives quietly the men folks love one. And there is another thing. Some of the girls of our generation are immoral. If one goes around all the time with those who are immoral, they would get one in the habit of being so, as long as one has not much intelligence. Do not go around with the immoral ones, my grandchild," my grandmother told me. "And this. You are to treat any aged person well. He (she) is thought of by the manitou; because he (she) has conducted his (her) life carefully is why he (she) reached an old age. Do not talk about anyone. Do not lie. Do not steal. If you practice stealing, you will be wretched. Do not (be stingy) with a possession of which you are fond. (If you are stingy) you will not get anything. If you are generous you will (always) get something. Moreover, do not go around and speak crossly toward anyone. You must be equally kind to (every) old person. That, my grandchild, is a good way to do," my grandmother said to me. She was indeed always instructing me what to do.

Soon I had lived there ten days. "Well, at last you may go and take a bath," my mother said to me. We started to the river. "Take off your waist," I was told. After I had taken it off I leaped into the water. Then, "I am going to peck you with something sharp," I was told. I was pecked all over. "And now on your lower part," I was told. "Only use your skirt as a breechcloth," is what I was told. I was also pecked on my thighs. "It will be that you will not menstruate much if the blood flows plentifully," I was told. I was made to suffer very much. I put on other garments.

I threw away those which I had formerly been wearing around. And then for the first time I looked around to see. And again I had to cook alone for myself outside for ten days. After ten days I again went to bathe. And then for the first time I began to eat indoors with (the others).

I told my mother, "My grandmother has always been instructing me what I should do," I said to her. She laughed. "That is why I went after her, so she would instruct you thoroughly in what is right. 'She might listen to her,' is what I thought of you."

And I began to be told to make something more than ever. Moreover, when she made a basket, she said to me, "You (make one)." I would make a tiny basket. Later on the ones which I made were large ones. And then I was fifteen years old.

"You may now try to sew bead and appliqué ribbon work. If you know how to sew you are to make things to wear when you dance. If it is known that you can already sew, (people) will hire you. Not merely that. You will be paid. You will be benefited by knowing how to sew," my mother told me. Then indeed I began to practice sewing. It took me a long time to sew well. It (must have) taken me two years to sew well. From then I was always making something.

I was sixteen years old when we were making mats in the summer. In the winter we were making

[8] In an extended note, Michelson highlights the particularly close relationship between a girl and her maternal uncles in Fox culture.

sacks and yarn belts, (and) we were sewing appliqué ribbon work and bead work. Behold, it was true that I was constantly asked (to make) something, (and) I would be paid. "That is why," I would be told, "I continuously told you to learn to know how to make things. After these mats are completed, and any one is given them, soon he (she) (will) give something in return. And also in regard to these sacks, when (anyone) is given them, he (she) gives something in return, no doubt. That is why one is willing to make things, because they are benefited by what is made," I was told. Lo, surely when I began to realize it, what I had been told was true.

Now when I was more than seventeen, while living outside somewhere, after two days, late at night while I was still sleeping, (some one) said to me, "Wake up." (The person) was holding a match, and lit it. Lo, it was a man when I looked at him.[9] I was as frightened as possible. I trembled as I was frightened. When I ordered him away, (my voice) did not (sound) natural when I spoke. I was barely able to speak to him. And from then on, now and then men tried to come to me. I always had been instructed what was proper. When it was known (what kind of a person) I (was), they began to try to court me.

Then I was instructed, "Well, when you are twenty,[10] then you may desire to take a husband. Whoever is the one whom you are going to take as your husband, he alone is the one with whom you are to talk when you begin to talk with (a man). Do not talk to many. It is not right for women to have many friends. Their husband(s) will not treat them well as they are jealous when they know what (their wives) have been doing. That indeed is why (women) are forbidden to have many friends." That is what I was told.

Then soon when I was eighteen, in the spring at the time when (people) begin to pick strawberries, I accompanied a young woman when we were strawberrying.[11] "We will see one," she would say to me. Then she would say to me, "I am just joshing you." As a matter of fact she and one young man had made arrangements to see each other over there.

Soon he came over there. They were well acquainted with each other and treated each other kindly. She was helped by him when she was picking strawberries. She kept coming to me to get me to go with her some place. Soon he came with another young man. Then this young woman got me to talk to his fellow young man. "He will not do anything; you may talk together quietly," that woman told me. As often as we went anywhere those men came. Finally I surely began to talk to that young man. And then we four went around (together) a great deal. It surely was enjoyable (to hear them) say funny things. Then it was that I always wished to see him right away when I went anywhere, that is after I had seen him.

Of course many men tried to get me to talk with them. Soon it was known (what kind of person I was). My, but they scolded me severely. Another young man had been selected for me to take as husband. (The other one) and I were already well acquainted.

"You had better take a husband right away," I was told, "'When you are twenty, you shall take a husband,' I told you formerly when I was instructing you. And I forbade you to go around with immoral (girls). Surely you are already not doing right. I desired to see you well-married while I was still living. But now I do not expect you to be well-married to one (man). The father of the one with whom you talk is evil. He (your lover) might beat you. That is the way his father is. He is always beating his wife.[12] And when anything is taking place, he will not allow his wife to go there. Moreover, that man is extremely lazy.[13] That is why I think the son will be like that. He is always merely walking around. I have never known him to do any work. If you took him as your husband, you would probably be taking care of him. He would cheat you,

9 It is considered improper for a boy and girl, unless very young, to be seen talking together. A young man cannot meet his inamorata openly; it must be in the brush or at night when the old people are asleep [Michelson's note].

10 Most Fox girls even to-day marry much earlier than this, and this has been the case from at least 1820 onward [Michelson's note].

11 A girl is not supposed to go off by herself unless she has some good reason. If a girl gads about and does no housework she soon acquires an unenviable reputation [Michelson's note].

12 Wife beating is not common among the Foxes, but it occurs sporadically . . . [Michelson's note].

13 In the early days girls wished to marry young men that were successful in killing game, who trapped and sold furs, thereby gaining an easy livelihood; but to-day girls are told to try to marry young men who have homes, horses, and everything they want. The young man who can support a wife is the one to marry. It is bad form for a young girl to marry a divorced man, and vice versa [Michelson's note].

for you already know how to do all the work that belongs to us women. You really must not take him for your husband. You must take the other one as your husband, the one with whom I think it proper for you to live. You must stop talking with the one you are trying to love. If, however, I learn that you talk again with him, you will cease to have control over any of our things. I shall not believe anything you say to me. Now I know in the past that you listened to what I told you. That is why I believed you when you said anything to me. And this. As many things as you have learned to make, I am very proud of (them). That is why I would forbid you to go around with immoral (girls). Surely as soon as you began to go around with them we found it out. You are no longer afraid of men. You formerly were afraid to go anywhere because of them. But now you always desire to go somewhere. You will be thought of as naught if you are immoral. The ones who are moral are those whom men want to live with (i. e., marry). And they will only make sport of the immoral ones. That is why they bother them, to have a good time with them, not to marry them. You might as well quickly take as your husband the one whom I permit you," I was told.

I was nineteen years old. Then I made up my mind to begin talking with the one I was permitted. I did not like him very well. I thought more of the other one. Always I would think, "Would that I might talk (with him)." I really couldn't stop talking with him. I worried about him. And I again went around with the one I was permitted, when I went anywhere. Later on I became acquainted with him. But I always thought more of the other one, the one they hated on my account.

Soon the one I was permitted began to try to have me accompany him to his home. He always asked me to go with him when ever I saw him. Then I said to him, "I am very much afraid of your parents." "Well, I will go with you to your home," he said to me, "we do not speak a different language, so it is not right for us to be afraid of each other. As for me, I am not afraid of your parents. For I have done nothing evil to you. As long as we have been talking together, I have been quiet with you. You know it too. I intend that we shall live quietly with each other. I always think, 'Oh that she were willing.' You are the only one with whom I wish to live. I shall treat you very nicely. Whatever you tell me, I shall do. And I shall always work. And I shall not hate your parents. I am not fooling you. What I say to you this day, I shall surely do," he said to me. Soon I consented. At night we departed. When it was daylight, I was (rather) ashamed to go where we lived with him. The next day when he was seen, he surely was treated very nicely, for I had for a husband the one they had wished me to.

Then he gave me his horse, and the clothing which he used at dances, his finery. And I gave that horse to my brothers. Soon my mother-in-law came to summon me. "Go over there," my mother said to me. I departed. When I arrived there, "Right here," I was told. "Sit down," I was told. I sat down comfortably. Well, they began to clothe me in finery. I was clad all over in finery. Then; "You may also take this kettle (home)," I was told. There were also some dry goods in it, and a bridle was in the kettle. I had a very large bundle on my back when I departed. I arrived where we lived clad in finery. My mother looked at (the bundle). When she saw the bridle (she said), "Now you have two horses. If you had taken the other (man) as your husband, you wouldn't have been given anything." Soon I likewise was told, "I say, you take this (to them)." Food was placed in a sack, mattings (were to go), and several belts of yarn were tied around them. Then we were through (with the wedding ceremonies). And then only the relatives of my husband gave me each something, usually dry goods. And I would take a sack or basket full of food, beans, pumpkins (to his people), and mattings and corn.

Surely my husband for a long time treated me nicely. And my mother strongly forbade me to keep on talking with the other one. She watched me closely. But I couldn't stop thinking of him, for he was the one I loved. I did not love my husband. That is why I always thought of the other one. When anything was going on, I went around with my mother as she was watching me so that I should not talk with the other one again. And she forbade me to go any place by myself. "Go with your husband when you go any place. They might say something about you. Some one might say of you, 'she goes around with another man.' Those who desire to make trouble for married couples are smart," I would be told.

And when I had been living with him for half a year, soon I ceased having catamenial flows. Thereupon I was given instructions again, "Well, this is what has happened: probably you are to have a child.

When anything is cooked and it is burned, it must not be eaten so that children's afterbirths will not adhere. And nuts are not to be eaten, so that the babies will be able to break through the caul. And in winter, one is not to warm their feet, so that the babies will not adhere (to the caul). And (women) are not to join their feet to those of their husbands, so that (the babies) will not be born feet-first. And the feet of no (animals) are to be eaten. And one must be careful not to touch crawfish. Also, if these are touched when one is enceinte, the babies will be born feet-first. It is said that (women) have a hard time when they are born that way. That is why one believes and fears (what one has been told), so that one will not suffer a long time at childbirth. It is better to do what we are told. And no corpse is to be touched. If it is touched the babies would die after they are born, by inheriting it. And if the dead are looked at, they are to be looked at with straight eyes. Also it is said that if they are looked at slantingly, the babies will be cross-eyed. And if cranes are touched, the babies will always look upward. The children will not be able to look upon the ground. And when anyone drowns, if he is touched, the babies would die. These are the number of things one is forbidden to do. And it is told that one should carry wood always on one's back so that the babies will be loosened (i. e., born easily) . Again, after (a woman) knows that she is pregnant, she is to cease to have anything to do with her husband. (Otherwise) the babies will be filthy when they are born. When their parents do not observe this, (the babies) begin to move around. That is the rule when that happens. For we women have a hard time at childbirth. We suffer. Some are killed by the babies. But we are not afraid of it, as we have been made to be that way. That is probably the reason why we are not afraid of it. Oh, if we were all afraid of it, when we all became old, that is as far as we could go. We should not be able to branch out (to a new generation). So at childbirth we should do only what we are told. The ones who do not do as they are told are the ones who are injured by their children."

I have now told you all how it is, though I did not know about this, namely, how hard childbirth is. Even at this time I was not able to know about it. Only after I had given birth (to a child) would I know how hard it is. Soon surely my abdomen grew large. I was ashamed. When there was a dance I did not go there as I was ashamed.

Soon after eight months were by, my mother-in-law came. She came to talk with my mother. "Now is the time when she is on the point of giving birth (to a child). We should build (a little wickiup) beforehand for her so that she may be delivered there. That is why I took my time coming, (thinking) she might be sick at night," she said to my mother. They built it. After they built it, she said to my mother, "Well, you may summon me whenever she is sick."

Soon I became sick in the evening when lying alone. I did not tell of it. Soon I was told, "You might be sick?" "Yes," I answered, "I am sick and have a little pain in the small of my back," I said to my mother. "Oh ho," she said, "very likely now is the time when you are to have a child. I shall summon her. For she said, ' you will summon me.'" In a little after she came, she said to me, "Come, go to the little wickiup." (Blankets) were spread for me. When I sat down comfortably a strap was fastened from above. "You are to hold on to this when you begin to feel intense pain," I was told. I then felt more intense pain. After a while I was told, "Lie down. When you begin to suffer acute pain you are to try to sit up. You are to sit on your knees and you are to sit erect." I did so. I would hold on to the strap. (The child) could not be born.

After midnight I was nearly unable to get up. The women who were attending me became frightened. Then they said among themselves, " We shall pray (for help)." My mother-in-law took Indian tobacco and went to a woman skilled in obstetrics for help. And when that woman came, she at once boiled some medicine. After she had boiled it, she said: "Let her in any case sit up for a while. You must hold her so that she will not fall over." After I was made to sit up, she spat upon my head; and she gave me (the medicine) to drink. After she had given me (the medicine) to drink, she began singing. She started to go out singing and went around the little wickiup singing. When she danced by where I was, she knocked on the side. "Come out if you are a boy," she would say. And she would again begin singing. When she danced by she again knocked the side. "Come out if you are a girl," she would say again. After she sang four times in a circle, she entered (the wickiup). And she gave me (medicine) to drink. "Now it will be born. She may lie down. Only lay her down carefully. You must hold her knees straight up," she said. Lo, sure enough, a little boy was born.

Then I knew how painful childbirth was. After I had borne (the child) I was not in pain in any spot. I was well. They cut off the baby's navel with one inch of the cord on it. A brand-new pair of scissors was used. They tied up the place where he was cut. His belly was washed. The next day he was placed in a cradle. And they tied a little piece of meat on his navel with a cloth going around (his body), tying it on his abdomen. "You must moisten him once in a while so that his umbilical cord will drop off soon," I was told. I did so to him. I did not wash him myself. My mother attended to him for me. In three days his umbilical cord dropped off. He could not draw the milk out for two days when I nursed him.

Then, "You must always keep him in a cradle: (otherwise) he might have a long head, (or) he might be humpbacked, (or) he might be bow-legged. That is why they are placed carefully, so they will (not) be that way. When they are tied that way they will be straight. They are kept in cradles for nearly one year. Again, they are not to be held all the time. They are placed in a swing after they suckle so that they will not be a nuisance. They become trained to be left alone when one goes some place, if they are not cry-babies. And when they are constantly held some cry when they are laid down. (People) are bothered by them when they get them used to being constantly held," I was told.

I lived outside for thirty-three days.[14]

Then soon my husband began to act differently. He did not treat me at all the way he had done when he was acting nicely. The fact of the matter is that the young woman with whom I used to go around before I was married had been telling him something. "You are treating her so well, but your wife formerly was the same as married to another man. (That is) what I know about her. 'We shall never stop talking to each other even if we marry other (persons),' they said to each other," she kept on telling him. Finally he apparently really believed her. From that time on he began to treat me badly. That young woman was made jealous because he treated me well. That was why she kept on telling him stories. As for her, the men would not marry her as she was immoral. Finally (my husband) began to beat me.

" That is why I formerly forbade you to talk to any men. That is why I said to you, 'You must talk only to the one whom you are to marry,'" my mother said to me. "Finally you will make your son angry if you are always having trouble with each other. Babies die when they become angry," I was told.

Soon, when our little boy nearly knew how to talk, he became ill. I felt very sorrowful. Later on, indeed, he died. It is surely very hard to have death (in the family). One can not help feeling badly. "That is why I told you about it when you were both unfortunately frightening him," I was told. "That is why children are not struck. One would feel worse if one had beaten (the child)," I was told. I felt worse after he was buried. The fourth day we fed those who buried him in the evening. We began to make every kind of new finery. After we had made it, I began to think over the one whom we should adopt. I thought of all the babies. I found one as if this way: "This one perhaps is loved as much as I loved my baby," I thought. Then we adopted him, so that we in a way had a son.

And then later on (my husband) became meaner. He was lazy. But my mother forbade me to be divorced. And soon my mother died. I was twenty-five years old. I felt terribly. I remembered everything she told me from time to time.

And from that time I really began taking care of myself. It was very hard. Work never ended. (A person) could not just stay around (and do nothing). "Surely my mother treated me well in teaching me how to make things. What would have happened to me if I had not known work suitable for women? I should have been even poorer, if my mother had not instructed me," I thought all the while. Whenever I made anything I surely was given clothing to wear in exchange. And when I made something, I gave it away. In the spring when I planted anything I attended to it carefully. Surely I cooked it when it grew. In winter I did not lack things to cook.

[14] It is at this point that Michelson notes, "the Indian text is too naïve [that is, too explicit] for European taste"; he has deleted a portion. He implies that the narrative relates to sexual customs following childbirth.

And my husband did nothing but act meanly. When there was a dance he would not allow me to go and see it. Soon I thought, "Well, now that my mother has gone, this fellow treats me meanly. It was because my mother forbade me to become a divorcee that (I allowed) this fellow to ill-treat me. Besides I do not love him. Now no one would scold me. And I love the other one. I hate this one." I began to see dances in spite (of what he had said). He was fearfully angry . "It's because you may see that man is why you are perverse in going there," he said to me. "I want to see him," I would say to him. I began to chase him away.

"You may marry other (women) who are quiet (i. e., moral). We shall never be able to live nicely together. While I was living quietly (i. e., morally) with you, you began to act badly. And it was not my idea to live with you. It was because I was told. I suppose I was permitted so that you would treat me well and not abuse me. So now we will be divorced. You must go. You could have behaved nicely if you had wished us to live together always. You might have been working quietly so that we should not be poor. You know how I have been doing. I have been working quietly. And you without reason began to be jealous. I have not talked to anyone as long as we have been living together. But now we must surely be divorced," I said to him.

"Truly from now on I shall stop acting that way. I shall begin to treat you nicely. And I shall work diligently. I shall not be able to refuse what you ask me. From now on you shall have control of what we shall continue to do," he said to me. "No, I shall not believe you though you may do your best to speak nicely. You have ill-treated me too long," I said to him. I was not able to chase him away. As I was leaving he came and seized me. "Believe me," he said to me. "No, indeed," I said to him. He held me there. "You are not going off any place," he said to me. I cried bitterly and he let me go.

I went where my uncle (mother's brother) lived and slept there. The next day my uncle said to me, "It is strange that you came and slept with us. Something has happened to you." "My husband treats me very badly. That is why I was unwilling (to keep on living with him)," I said to him. "It is known broadcast that he abuses you. No one will reproach you if you think of being divorced. I myself will not scold you. It is a rule that a married couple should alike treat each other well. As for me, I treat the one with whom I live (i. e., wife) well and she treats me well. She always cooks for me when I am working. And if I were suddenly to treat her badly while she was still treating me well and while she was still living morally, were I to become jealous over something without reason, her relatives would not like it. For I surely would be doing wrong. If she cast me off none of her relatives would scold her. Every one, all over, would be glad of what happened to me. Certainly I should not find one (woman) who behaved as well. Surely I should always want back the one who behaved well. (But) I might have angered her. I alone should be thinking of her. Surely she would not think of me. She would hate me as much as possible," my uncle said to me. "Well, my niece (sister's daughter), now you are of sufficient age to listen attentively," he said to me. "You probably still think of what your mother told you. You may foolishly begin to be immoral. You should look at men quietly (i. e., without an immoral purpose). Whomever you think will treat you well is the one whom you should take for your husband. If he happens to treat you well, you should live quietly with him. Do not again desire another (husband). For it also is not right for you women to have many husbands. A woman who does that is gossiped about a good deal. It is the same as if she goes from man to man. That, my niece, is what I want you to do. Because your mother is gone is why I tell you as I understand it. And if you are now divorced you should stay (single) for at least one or two years. You should just be working diligently. Then you might marry that one," my uncle said to me.

And so I became divorced. Of course (my former husband) was always trying to get me, but I could not be kind again to him. I hated him tremendously.

And the wife of the (man) with whom I talked when I was still a virgin died. After I had been divorced for one year and he had become a widower free from death-customs, he again began to (court) me. Of course others courted me but I did not talk to them. And soon I began talking with him, for we were already acquainted with each other while we were young. And soon he asked me why I became divorced. I told him exactly how it was that I became divorced.

"Well! He was entirely wrong in what he thought of us. I ceased seeing you when you were married. Even if I had seen you I should not have been able to screw up my courage to say anything to you. You surely would have reported me. You acted that way when you were married. If I had persuaded you (to marry me) at the time, I should not have beaten you. Now you must be willing for us to do that," he said to me. "I suppose you too will beat me, that is why you are courting me," I said to him. "Why, how often have you heard of me striking the one with whom I was living? I never struck her even once. Nor did I scold her. She danced vigorously at dances also before she became ill. That is how I should treat you too. You might dance vigorously if you felt like dancing vigorously. To dance vigorously is natural. I do not know of anyone being married (at the dances). How, pray, could anyone act in a courting way as there would be many people? No one would fail to be seen if he courted there. I should think that way myself. If you are willing we shall do that. I want you to consent very much. I have always thought, 'I wish I might live with her,' " he said to me. "Well, I might consent in a year, but not now," I said to him. For a long time we were merely talking with each other.

The one with whom I formerly lived never gave up. He always tried to court me. But I could not think kindly of him again. For he had angered me as he already had treated me badly. I hated him thoroughly.

Soon the time came which I had set for us to live together. When we saw each other, he said to me, "Well, at last it is the time you set for your consent. To-night at night do not latch your door firmly. I shall come to you." That is what I did. He came. And sometimes he would sleep far off in a wickiup where his relatives lived. And at any time I went and visited my relatives. He never spoke crossly to me. So I loved him dearly. The other one, the one with whom I first lived, was sensual. That is why I hated him.

And after I married the other one I was so well. When there was a dance, he said to me, "Go and dance. I should be made ashamed by their talk if you were not seen when something is going on. 'He is probably jealous,' is what they would say of me. I am ashamed to have that said of me," he would say to me. "Clothe yourself in fine apparel," he would also say to me.

And soon when we were talking together, he said to me, "I wish I had been able to persuade you long ago, for we first talked with each other." "Well," I said to him, "I was not master of my own person while my mother was yet living. They soon found out that I was talking with you. I was scolded and I was told, 'you must marry the other fellow.' It was that good-for-nothing. The fact is that had I been master of myself, I couldn't have married him. Perhaps you might have persuaded me, for I had already become acquainted with you. For I was always thinking of you, especially at first. When I first stopped talking to you I was lonely," I said to him. "Well, let it be, for we have each other nicely at last," he said to me. My, but he talked so nicely. I had been living with him for two years. I continued to love him more and more as he treated me well.

Soon we had another child, a little girl, but it died after it was four months old. Then they had me drink medicine so that I would not have a child again as they died when I had them.

I never heard my husband speak crossly. Even when there were Shawnee dances[15] at night, he said to me, "Have a fine time dancing." "Well, I have surely found a man," I thought. "If this (man) were to cast me off to-day, I should tag after him anyhow," I thought. When he went to any place for a long time, I yearned for him. And I thought, "He has made me happy by treating me well." Then I began to make things for him, his finery, his moccasins, his leggings, his shirt, his garters, his cross-belt. After I had made finery of every kind for him, (I said), "These are what I have made for you as you have made me happy as long as I have lived with you, (and) because you have never made me angry in any way. 'You

[15] The Shawnee dance is the same as the Snake dance . . . which the Foxes acquired while in Kansas. Formerly it was pretty likely to be rough; and girls and their lovers would meet on such occasions. The husband's confidence in his wife could not be shown to greater advantage than by permitting, or rather urging, his wife to be present [Michelson's note].

must dance vigorously,' I thought. That is why I made them for you." "You please me very much. That is how I was told when given instructions. 'If you live with a woman, if she likes the way you act and you treat her well, she will also care for you if she is intelligent. If she is immoral, you will not please her; she will only think of treating you meanly,' I was told. Now I see what I was told," he said to me.

I had more and more charge over everything. It seems as if he was a good hunter, for he brought in much game when he went hunting. So we never were in want of meat, as he knew how to hunt. I was rightly married to him. I was married to him a good many years. Soon a drum was brought. And suddenly he said to me, "If we join in (the ceremony of that) drum we might be worshipping." We were just about doing it. I did not even think of divorce as I liked his ways so much.

Soon he fell ill. I felt very sorry for him. I felt terribly. Soon he became sicker and sicker. I cried in vain, as I felt so badly about him. And he died. Soon it was terrible for me. I undid my hair and loosened it. For several nights I could not sleep as I was sorrowful. On the fourth day I called the men. "You are to divide all these possessions of ours among you," I said to my male relatives. And then the female relatives of my dead husband came to comb my hair. And they brought other garments for me to wear. I wore black clothing. And soon those male relatives of mine to whom I had given our possessions brought food of every kind. The women brought all things which women raise. I went over to those (women) who had combed my hair and told them to take that food. I felt as wretched as possible. I was fasting. Soon I would walk far off to cry, it was far off so that it would not be known, (and) so that it should not be said about me, "Heavens! she must be very sorry, even as if she were related to him." And I became lazy. I only wanted to lie down. I kept on sleeping as I was lonely.

That uncle (mother's brother) mentioned before probably heard about it. "She is very poorly since her husband died. She acts differently (from what she did formerly). To-day she is as if sick," is what he heard. He came to me. "I have come to see, my niece (sister's daughter), whether you are sick. You are losing much weight," he said to me. "No," I said to him. "I have come to instruct you as to what you should do. I know that you listened to what I told you when you were divorced. As you believed me you did exactly as I told you. You have made me very happy. Now this is what you are to do, my niece. Do not think so very much of him all the time, for it is dangerous to do that. That will happen to you if you dream that you are sleeping with him. You will cease to live very soon. That is why it is forbidden to do that. If you are sorry for your husband while still bound by death ceremonies, you would not go where something is going on," he said to me. "And do not talk much, and do not laugh as long as you are bound by death ceremonies. You must be merely always quietly making something. Nor must you look around too much. Perhaps it was because you were not careful that no one straightway instructed you what you should do when your husband first died. I myself was busy at the time; that is why I did not come and instruct you what you should do. This is what is (supposed to be) done when one's husbands (wives) die. When they are taken to be buried (those surviving) accompany them when the (dead) are brought there. After they are placed on top of the hole, they begin to speak to those ghosts. After they have spoken to them, first the relatives (of the dead) begin to throw tobacco to them, then others afterwards. After all have offered tobacco to them, then last of all the husbands (wives) offer tobacco to them. They walk around in a circle where the (dead) is. Then they walk toward the East. They continue to go any place in the brush. They go through very thick brush. They are never to look backward. If they were to look backward they would die soon. It is far off where they are to go, and turn to go back. That is what they (are supposed to) do. Perhaps you did not do that, so I have heard," my uncle said to me.

"I did not know that that was the way. For I did not hear my mother, when she was alive, speak of how those unreleased from death-ceremonies should act. That is why I did not know what should be done. I did not go there when (my husband) was buried. I stayed here in the wickiup," I told my uncle.

"This is why they do that, so they may run and hide from that soul, and why they wander around in thick brush," he said to me. "So that is why you feel so badly. If you had done as I now tell you, you would not be that way. And when you eat always put some on the fire for him. Do not forget (to do this) as long as an adoption-feast has not been held and as long as you are not freed from death-ceremonies.

That is what you must do," my uncle said to me. "Well, that is all. I shall soon come again to give you instructions," he said to me. And he departed.

And then always when I ate I put (food) on the fire for my husband. And I tried to cease to think of him all the time as I was afraid to die early.

Later on when I heard that an adoption-feast was about to take place, sure enough they soon came to summon me. When I came there, there were many Indians. When I went in there, the ones who were adopted were eating there. When they fed me it was as if we were eating with my husband for the last time, in order that he might be released. After I had eaten, I was told, "Take off your clothing." Then they began to clothe me in fresh clothes, and my hair was combed and my face was washed. And then I was told, "Well, do not take off your (clothing). For (now) you are to be clad like this. You may begin to wear finery. You may go and do whatever you please. If you are desirous of marrying anyone, you may marry him. Some one will take care of you if you marry him. Do not be afraid of us. You have pleased us by treating our relative well while he was alive. So why should we be against you? So you must believe what we say to you this day." And then I departed.

For the first time I began to wear fresh clothing. And I began to be careful again. And that uncle of mine came again. "At last I have come to give you instructions again, my niece. This day you have ceased to be restricted by death-ceremonies. You know how hard it was to find a good man who treated you well. So you must feel very badly. Do not stop thinking of him (in a little while). A good man is hard to find. You know how your first husband treated you in the past. He abused you badly. So you should not forget your last husband for a long time. The men will begin to court you. Do not think of beginning to respond to them right away. For four years try not to forget your husband of whom you have sight. For you are still young. It will be nothing if you do not marry any one for a long time. Your next husband will not be as good. That is why I have come to tell you how sorry I am for your husband. So you must try to do that. And I am very proud that you believed me when I told you to do what was right. Some (women) become immoral when their mothers die, as they cease to be guided by anyone. And they do not listen to others when they are instructed. That is also why I think my niece will watch out for herself. Well, my niece, I have finished instructing you. If you do that, you will lead a straight life."

I did as he told me. None of the men who were courting me was able to get my consent. I sharply scolded anyone who courted me. For four years I remained (single), (showing) how sorry I was for my husband. If I had had a child I should have never married again. As it was, I was too much alone all the time. "That is why," I thought, "I am always lonely." When more than four years were up, I again began to be kind to one man. Soon he asked that we should marry. "Now I began to be kind to you so that we should be married. Your husband was my friend. We used to talk together a great deal. He said to me, 'if I die first, you must court the one with whom I live, so as to marry her. She behaves very well. She is your sister-in-law as we are friends.[16] It is because I do not want other men to marry her as she is too good. That really is why I say it to you. It might happen that I should die first, for we do not know when we are to die,' he said to me, 'and you must treat her nicely as I love her dearly as she is good,' he said to me. So I am trying to get you ( to agree) for us to do so. As I was told, 'you must treat her well,' I could not begin to treat you meanly. I should try (to treat you) as my friend treated you," he said to me. Then I consented.

Oh, he never became angry, but he was rather lazy. He was slow in making anything. And he was a gambler. I did not love him as much as I did the one who was dead.

And I began to wish to have a child again. "If I had a child I should have it do things for me. Surely they will not all die," I thought. Soon I asked an old woman who knew about medicine. "Is there perhaps a medicine whereby one might be able to have a child if one drank it?" I said to her. "Surely I know one," she said to me, "you might have a child if you drink it, for you already have had children," she said to me. "It was because I drank a medicine that I ceased having children," I said to her. "That is nothing. You might easily have a child," she said to me. "You might have relatives if you had children," she said to me. She gave me (medicine) to drink. Sure enough, I began to have children.

After we had many children then my husband died. "Well, I shall never marry again," I thought, "for now these children of mine will help me (get a living)," I thought.

---

[16] That is, the two men were like brothers.

# Owl Woman (Juana Manwell; Papago, fl. 1880)/Frances Densmore (1867–1957)

*In 1920 ethnomusicologist Frances Densmore recorded the work of elderly Papago healer Owl Woman, who lived on the San Xavier reserve in Arizona. About 1880, after the death of her husband, Owl Woman had been taken by spirits to the spirit land for consolation. Showing her where her husband lived, these guides also, via the spirit of a man who had died near Tucson, gave her three songs with which to heal illnesses caused by Papago spirits. Owl Woman's communication with the spirit world continued, and she received numerous songs from people who had died under various circumstances – both patients she knew and had failed to cure as well as many unfamiliar to her. Because of these gifts of song, she regarded herself not as their author but as their transmitter. Her treatment followed a prescribed pattern: first she sang four songs, then she stroked the patient with a bunch of owl feathers sprinkled with ashes. Moving through four segments – that is, following the pattern of sacred numbers corresponding to the four compass points – she alternated songs and treatment throughout the night. If the patient failed to improve, Owl Woman felt that she could not effect a cure.*

*Spending nearly forty years in recording Native American traditional music, Frances Densmore was one of the most distinguished turn-of-the century women ethnologists (including Harriet Maxwell Converse {1836–1903} and Alice Fletcher {1838–1923}) who sought to preserve the oral traditions of Native American tribes across North America. Born in Minnesota and educated at the Oberlin Conservatory from 1886 to1889, Densmore's translations of Owl Woman's songs reflected the influence of modernist (and especially imagist) movements in European American literary traditions; like Mary Hunter Austin, whose versions of Indian songs were especially influential during this period, she both reported and shaped the form. Densmore used portable cylinder equipment to record a vast amount of material coming from tribes ranging from the Seminoles in Florida to the Sioux, the Mandan and Hidatsa, and the pueblo peoples of the southwestern United States. Although we might question the degree to which her own voice informed her translations, we must acknowledge her influence in helping to preserve the traditional music of many tribes and in ensuring that Native American music would not be read merely as a historical curiosity, but heard as a dynamic art form with powerful links to spiritual life.*

## Bibliography

### Primary

Densmore, Frances. *The American Indians and Their Music*. Woman's Press, 1926.
——. *Chippewa Music.* Bulletin 45. Smithsonian Institution Bureau of American Ethnology, 1910–13.
——. *Papago Music*. Bulletin 90. Smithsonian Institution Bureau of American Ethnology, 1929.

——. *Pawnee Music.* Bulletin 93. Smithsonian Institution Bureau of American Ethnology, 1929.
——. *Teton Sioux Music.* Bulletin 61. Smithsonian Institution Bureau of American Ethnology, 1918.

Secondary

Austin, Mary. Introduction to *American Indian Poetry: An Anthology of Songs and Chants.* Ed. George W. Cronyn. Fawcett, 1991.
——. *The American Rhythm.* Harcourt, 1923.
Densmore, Frances. Preface to *Music of the Maidu Indians of California.* Southwest Museum, 1958.
Fletcher, Alice. "Indian Songs and Music." *Journal of American Folk-Lore* 11 (April–June 1898): 85–104.
Hofman, Charles. *Frances Densmore and American Indian Music: A Memorial Volume.* Museum of the American Indian, 1968.
Krupat, Arnold. *The Voice in the Margin: Native American Literature and the Canon.* California, 1989.
Parezo, Nancy J., ed. *Hidden Scholars: Women Anthropologists and the Native American Southwest.* New Mexico, 1993.
Winters, Yvor. "The Indian in English." *Uncollected Essays and Reviews.* Ed. Francis Murphy. Chicago, 1975.

# From *Papago Music* (1929)

## Songs for Treating Sickness, Sung during the Four Parts of the Night

### Parts One and Two: Beginning Songs and Songs Sung before Midnight

#### No. 72 "Brown Owls"

Brown owls come here in the blue evening,
They are hooting about,
They are shaking their wings and hooting.

#### No. 73 "In the Blue Night"

How shall I begin my song
In the blue night that is settling?
I will sit here and begin my song.

#### No. 74 "The Owl Feather"

The owl feather is rolling in this direction and beginning to sing.
The people listen and come to hear the owl feather
Rolling in this direction and beginning to sing.

#### No. 75 "They Come Hooting"

Early in the evening they come hooting about,
Some have small voices and some have large voices,
Some have voices of medium strength, hooting about.

## No. 76 "In the Dark I Enter"

I can not make out what I see.
In the dark I enter.
I can not make out what I see.

## No. 77 "His Heart is Almost Covered with Night"

Poor old sister, you have cared for this man and you want to see him again, but now his heart is almost covered with night. There is just a little left.

## No. 78 "I See Spirit-Tufts of White Feathers"

Ahead of me some owl feathers are lying,
I hear something running toward me,
They pass by me, and farther ahead
I see spirit-tufts of downy white feathers.

## No. 79 "Yonder Lies the Spirit Land"

Yonder lies the spirit land.
Yonder the spirit land I see.
Farther ahead, in front of me,
I see a spirit stand.

## NN/NT[1]

Sadly I was treated, sadly I was treated,
Through the night I was carried around,
Sadly I was treated.

## No. 80 "Song of a Spirit"

A railroad running west,
He travels westward.
When he gets a certain distance
He flaps his wings four times and turns back.

## No. 81 "We Will Join Them"

Yonder are spirits laughing and talking as though drunk.
They do the same things that we do.
Now we will join them.

1 "NN/NT": there is no number or title.

### No. 82 "My Feathers"

I pity you, my feathers,
I pity you, my feathers, that they make fun of,
They must mean what they say,
Or perhaps they are crazy in their hearts.

### No. 83 "The Women are Singing"

On the west side people are singing as though drunk. The women are singing as though they were drunk.

### NN/NT

In the great night my heart will go out,
Toward me the darkness comes rattling,
In the great night my heart will go out.

### NN/NT

On the west side they are singing, the women hear it.

### No. 84 "I Am Going to See the Land"

I am going far to see the land,
I am running far to see the land,
While back in my house the songs are intermingling.

### No. 85 "I Run Toward Ashes Hill"

Ashes Hill Mountain, toward it I am running,
I see the Ashes Hill come out clearer.

### No. 86 "The Waters of the Spirits"

They brought me to the waters of the spirits.
In these waters the songs seem to be stringing out.

## Parts Three and Four: Songs Sung between Midnight and Early Morning

### No. 87 "There Will I See the Dawn"

A low range of mountains, toward them I am running.
From the top of these mountains I will see the dawn.

## No. 88 "I Run Toward the East"

I am not sure whether I am running west or east but I run on and on.
I find that I am running east.

## No. 89 "I Die Here"

I am dead here, I die and lie here,
I am dead here, I die and lie here,
Over the top of *Vihuliput* I had my dawn.

## No. 90 "I Could See the Daylight Coming"

Black Butte is far. Below it I had my dawn.
I could see the daylight coming back of me.

## No. 91 "The Dawn Approaches"

I am afraid it will be daylight before I reach the place to see.
I feel that the rays of the sun are striking me.

## No. 92 "The Owl Feather is Looking for the Dawn"

The owl feather is likely to find the daylight.
He is looking for it.
He is looking to see the dawn shine red in the east.

## No. 93 "The Morning Star"

The morning star is up.
I cross the mountains into the light of the sea.

## No. 94 Song of a Medicine Woman on Seeing that a Sick Person Will Die

I think I have found out.
I think I have found out.
With the owl songs I have found out and will return home.

# Zitkala-Ša (Red Bird, Gertrude Simmons Bonnin; Sioux, 1876–1938)

*Zitkala-Ša was born Gertrude Simmons on the Yankton Reservation in South Dakota, the third child of Ellen Simmons (Tate I Yohin Win, or Reaches for the Wind), a full-blood Yankton Dakota, and a white man who deserted the family before his daughter was born. Raised traditionally until the age of eight, she successfully pleaded with her mother to be allowed to attend a white school and entered White's Manual Labor Institute in Indiana, a Quaker missionary school. Published in 1900 in the prominent periodical, the* Atlantic Monthly, *"The School Days of an Indian Girl" describes the traumatic experiences that opened a wedge between her and the culture in which she had been raised – described in vivid and nostalgic terms in "Impressions of an Indian Girlhood" – and especially between herself and her mother. Zitkala-Ša also recounts both her mother's resistance to her daughter's return east to Indiana's Earlham College to pursue further education from 1895 to 1897, and the virulent racism that she endured in spite of academic success. Becoming a teacher at Carlisle Indian Industrial School from 1898 to 1899, she continued to be critical of the system of Indian education, seen here in "An Indian Teacher Among Indians," a criticism that may ultimately have cost her her position. Also a talented musician, after leaving Carlisle she studied violin during 1900 and 1901 at the New England Conservatory of Music, where she flourished in Boston's artistic environment.*

*After breaking her engagement to the Yavapai physician Carlos Montezuma, whom she had met at Carlisle and who wished her to move to Chicago as the assimilated wife of a doctor, she returned to the reservation to care for her mother and gather materials for a book of traditional narratives,* Old Indian Legends. *Working as an issue clerk, she met and married another Yankton Sioux employee of the Indian Service, Raymond T. Bonnin, in 1902. Zitkala-Ša found little time to write during the first decade of her marriage, when the Bonnins worked on the Uintah and Ouray Reservation in Utah, and after the birth of her son, Raymond O. Bonnin, in early 1903. She managed in 1913 to collaborate with William Hanson on an Indian opera,* The Sun Dance, *which would be performed by the New York Light Opera Guild as American opera of the year in 1937. In 1914 she joined the Society of American Indians (SAI), an organization dedicated to Indian self-determination that nevertheless, as her political writing reveals, was fundamentally assimilationalist. After her election as Secretary-Treasurer of the SAI in 1916, and her acceptance of the editorship of its journal,* American Indian Magazine, *from 1918 to 1919, she began to write again, this time focusing on political activism, which was assisted by the couple's move to Washington, DC. A tireless worker for Indian rights, Bonnin served as a lobbyist for Indian legislation, a community organizer, and a spokesperson for reform, participating in efforts for peyote suppression, Indian citizenship, education reform, and land ownership rights. During this time, as a member of the General Federation of Women's Clubs, within which she had created an Indian Welfare Committee, she went to Oklahoma with co-investigators Charles Fabens and Matthew Sniffens to report on the corruption of whites who served as putative guardians for Oklahoma Indians; their volume,* Oklahoma's Poor Rich Indians, *helped prompt the government to appoint a federal investigation. Although the*

*SAI dissolved in 1920, her political work continued through the rest of her life. In 1926 she founded the National Council of American Indians, of which she served as president until her death. She was buried in Arlington National Cemetery.*

*Zitkala-Ša's writing offers today's readers an intense and complex combination of styles, genres, and voices. Her first published narratives, "Impressions of an Indian Girlhood," "The School Days of an Indian Girl," and "An Indian Teacher Among Indians," reveal a richly textured and evocative autobiography that, rather than representing Indians merely as victims, challenges the treatment of Indians in American culture and underscores the resistance of Indians to assimilation. At the same time, like "The Soft-Hearted Sioux" and many stories by Johnson and Reed, they poignantly depict the dilemma of individuals caught between cultures. Other stories, such as "A Warrior's Daughter," also parallel the work by those writers that emphasizes the strength of Indian people, especially women, in the face of great adversity. Like these stories, her poems sometimes draw upon a sentimental tradition to indict white mistreatment of Indians, while "The Red Man's America" rewrites a familiar nationalist song with powerful irony. The pieces collected in* Old Indian Legends *about Iktomi, the Dakota trickster, indicate her desire to reach an audience across cultures, as she transforms them from traditional stories told in the evening to written narratives that teach both the children for whom they were intended, and their adult counterparts, about important Indian values. Varying with its audience, her political writing ranges from persuasive and community-oriented in tone to sharply critical, speaking on subjects ranging from community service to Indian citizenship to Indian patriotism in World War I. In spite of her nearly lifelong discomfort with her intercultural situation, Zitkala-Ša composed a memorable and diverse body of work, often informed by oratorical power, that anticipated and helped enable the renaissance of American Indian writing in recent years.*

## Bibliography

### Primary


"Address by Mrs. Gertrude Bonnin." *American Indian Magazine* (Fall, 1919): 153–7.

"America, Home of the Red Man." *American Indian Magazine* (Winter, 1919): 165–7.

*American Indian Stories*. Hayworth, 1921. Rpt. Nebraska, 1985.

"Chipeta, Widow of Chief Ouray: With a Word About a Deal in Blankets." *American Indian Magazine* (July–September, 1917): 168–70.

"Editorial Comment." *American Indian Magazine* (July–September, 1918): 113–14.

"Editorial Comment." *American Indian Magazine* (Winter, 1919): 161–2.

The Gertrude Simmons and Raymond T. Bonnin Papers. University Archives, Brigham Young University, Provo, Utah.

"Impressions of an Indian Childhood." *Atlantic Monthly* (January, 1900): 37–47.

"Indian Gifts to Civilized Man." *American Indian Magazine* (July–September, 1918): 115–16.

"An Indian Teacher Among Indians." *Atlantic Monthly* (March, 1900): 381–6.

"The Indian's Awakening." *American Indian Magazine* (January–March, 1916): 57–9.

"Letter to the Chiefs and Head-men of the Tribes." *American Indian Magazine* (Winter, 1919): 196–7.

*Oklahoma's Poor Rich Indians: An Orgy of Graft and Exploitation of the Five Civilized Tribes – Legalized Robbery* [with Charles N. Fabens and Matthew K. Sniffen]. Indian Rights Association, 1924.

*Old Indian Legends*. Ginn, 1901. Rpt. Nebraska, 1985.

"The Red Man's America." *American Indian Magazine* (January–March, 1917): 64.

"The School Days of an Indian Girl." *Atlantic Monthly* (February, 1900): 185–94.

"A Sioux Woman's Love for Her Grandchild." *American Indian Magazine* (October–December, 1917): 230–1.

"The Soft-Hearted Sioux." *Harper's* (March, 1901): 505–8.

"The Trial Path." *Harper's* (October, 1901): 741–4.

"A Warrior's Daughter." *Everybody's Magazine* (April, 1902): 346–52.

"Why I Am a Pagan." *Atlantic Monthly* (December, 1902): 801–3.

"A Year's Experience in Community Service Work Among the Ute Tribe of Indians." *American Indian Magazine* (October–December, 1916): 307–10.

## Secondary

Bataille, Gretchen, and Kathleen Mullen Sands. *American Indian Women: Telling Their Lives*. Nebraska, 1984.

Bernadin, Susan. "The Lessons of a Sentimental Education: Zitkala-Ša's Autobiographical Narratives." *Western American Literature* 32:3 (1997): 212–38.

Cutter, Martha J. "Zitkala-Ša's Autobiographical Writings: The Problems of a Canonical Search for Language and Identity." *MELUS: The Journal for the Study of the Multi-Ethnic Literatures of the United States* 19:1 (1994): 31–44.

Fisher, Dexter. "The Transformation of Tradition: A Study of Zitkala-Ša and Mourning Dove, Two Transitional American Indian Writers." In *Critical Essays on Native American Literature*. Ed. Andrew Wiget. Hall, 1985. 202–11.

Hoefel, Roseanne. "Writing, Performance, Activism: Zitkala-Ša and Pauline Johnson." In *Native American Women in Literature and Culture*. Ed. Susan Castillo and Victor M. P. Da Rosa. Fernando Pessoa, 1997. 107–18.

Lukens, Margaret A. "The American Story of Zitkala-Ša." In *In Her Own Voice: Nineteenth-Century American Women Essayists*. Ed. Sherry Lee Linkon. Garland, 1997. 141-55.

Lukens, Margo. "Zitkala-Ša (Gertrude Simmons Bonnin)." In *Dictionary of Literary Biography*. Vol. 175. Ed. Kenneth M. Roemer. Gale, 1997. 331–6.

Meisenheimer, D. K., Jr. "Regionalist Bodies/Embodied Regions: Sarah Orne Jewett and Zitkala-Ša." In *Breaking Boundaries: New Perspectives on Women's Regional Writing*. Ed. Sherrie Inness and Diana Royer. Iowa, 1997. 109–23.

Okker, Patricia. "Native American Literatures and the Canon: The Case of Zitkala-Ša." In *American Realism and the Canon*. Ed. Tom Quirk and Gary Scharnhorst. Delaware, 1994. 87–101.

Ruoff, A. LaVonne Brown. "Early Native American Women Authors: Jane Johnston Schoolcraft, Sarah Winnemucca, S. Alice Callahan, E. Pauline Johnson, and Zitkala-Ša." In *Nineteenth-Century American Women Writers: A Critical Reader*. Ed. Karen L. Kilcup. Blackwell, 1998. 81–111.

Spack, Ruth. "Re-Visioning Sioux Women: Zitkala-Ša's Revolutionary American Indian Stories." *Legacy: A Journal of American Women Writers* 14:1 (1997): 25–42.

Stout, Mary A. "Zitkala-Ša." In *Dictionary of Native American Literature*. Ed. Andrew Wiget. Garland, 1994. 303–7.

Susag, Dorothea M. "Zitkala-Ša (Gertrude Simmons Bonnin); A Power(full) Literary Voice." *Studies in American Indian Literatures* 5:4 (1993): 3–24.

Udall, Catherine. "Zitkala-Ša." In *Native American Women: A Biographical Dictionary*. Ed. Gretchen Bataille. Garland, 1993. 31–2.

# Poetry

## From *American Indian Magazine*

### The Indian's Awakening (January–March, 1916)

I snatch at my eagle plumes and long hair.
A hand cut my hair; my robes did deplete.
Left heart all unchanged; the work incomplete.
These favors unsought, I've paid since with care.
Dear teacher, you wished so much good to me,
That though I was blind, I strove hard to see.
Had you then, no courage frankly to tell
Old race-problems, Christ e'en failed to expel?

My light has grown dim, and black the abyss
That yawns at my feet. No bordering shore;
No bottom e'er found by hopes sunk before.
Despair I of good from deeds gone amiss.
My people, may God have pity on you!
The learning I hoped in you to imbue
Turns bitterly vain to meet both our needs.
No Sun for the flowers, – vain planting seeds.

I've lost my long hair; my eagle plumes too.
From you my own people, I've gone astray.
A wanderer now, with no where to stay.
The Will-o-the-wisp learning, it brought me to rue.
It brings no admittance. Where I have knocked
Some evil imps, hearts, have bolted and locked.
Alone with the night and fearful Abyss
I stand isolated, life gone amiss.

Intensified hush chills all my proud soul.
Oh what am I? Whither bound thus and why?
Is there not a God on whom to rely?
A part of His Plan, the atoms enroll?
In answer, there comes a sweet Voice and clear,
My loneliness soothes with sounding so near.
A drink to my thirst, each vibrating note.
My vexing old burdens fall far remote.

"Then close your sad eyes. Your spirit regain.
Behold what fantastic symbols abound,
What wondrous host of cosmos around.
From silvery sand, the tiniest grain
To man and the planet, God's at the heart.
In shifting mosaic, souls doth impart.
His spirits who pass through multiformed earth
Some lesson of life must learn in each birth."

Divinely the Voice sang. I felt refreshed.
And vanished the night, abyss and despair.
Harmonious kinship made all things fair.
I yearned with my soul to venture unleashed.
Sweet Freedom. There stood in waiting, a steed
All prancing, well bridled, saddled for speed.
A foot in the stirrup! Off with a bound!
As light as a feather, making no sound.

Through ether, long leagues we galloped away.
An angry red river, we shyed in dismay,
For here were men sacrificed, (cruel deed),
To reptiles and monsters, war, graft, and greed.
A jungle of discord drops in the rear.
By silence is quelled suspicious old fear,
And spite-gnats' low buzz is muffled at last.
Exploring the spirit, I must ride fast.

Away from these worldly ones, let us go,
Along a worn trail, much travelled and, – Lo!
Familiar the scenes that come rushing by.
Now billowy sea and now azure sky.
Amid that enchanted space, as they spun
Sun, moon and the stars, their own orbits run!
Great Spirit, in realms so infinite reigns;
And wonderful wide are all His domains.

Hark! Here in the Spirit-world, He doth hold
A village of Indians, camped as of old.
Earth-legends by their fires, some did review,
While flowers and trees more radiant grew.
"Oh, You were all dead! In Lethe you were tossed!"
I cried, "Every where 'twas I told you were lost!
Forsooth, they did scan your footprints on sand.
Bereaved, I did mourn your fearful sad end."

Then spoke One of the Spirit Space, so sedate.
"My child, We are souls, forever and aye.
The signs in our orbits point us the way.
Like planets, we do not tarry nor wait.
Those memories dim, from Dust to the Man,
Called Instincts, are trophies won while we ran.
Now various stars where loved ones remain
Are linked to our hearts with Memory-chain."

"In journeying here, the Aeons we've spent
Are countless and strange. How well I recall
Old Earth trails: the River Red; above all
The Desert sands burning us with intent.
All these we have passed to learn some new thing.
Oh hear me! Your dead doth lustily sing!
'Rejoice! Gift of Life pray waste not in wails!
The Maker of Souls forever prevails!' "

Direct from the Spirit-world came my steed.
The phantom has place in what was all planned.
He carried me back to God and the land
Where all harmony, peace and love are the creed.
In triumph, I cite my Joyous return.
The smallest wee creature I dare not spurn.
I sing "Gift of Life, pray waste not in wails!
The Maker of Souls forever prevails!"

## The Red Man's America (January–March, 1917)[1]

My country! 'tis to thee,
Sweet land of Liberty,

[1] An ironic version of the familiar hymn, "America," composed by Baptist minister Samuel F. Smith (1808–1905) in 1832. The hymn became widely popular after the Civil War.

My pleas I bring.
  Land where OUR fathers died,
  Whose offspring are denied
  The Franchise given wide,
  Hark, while I sing.

My native country, thee,
Thy Red man is not free,
Knows not thy love.
  Political bred ills,
  Peyote in temple hills,
  His heart with sorrow fills,
  Knows not thy love.

Let Lane's Bill swell the breeze,
And ring from all the trees,
Sweet freedom's song.
  Let Gandy's Bill[2] awake
  All people, till they quake,
  Let Congress, silence break,
  The sound prolong.

Great Mystery, to thee,
Life of humanity,
To thee, we cling.
  Grant our home-land be bright,
  Grant us just human right,
  Protect us by Thy might,
  Great God, our kind.

## A Sioux Woman's Love for Her Grandchild (October–December, 1917)

Loosely clad in deerskin, dress of flying fringes,
Played a little blackhaired maiden of the prairies;
Plunged amid the rolling green of grasses waving,
Brimming o'er with laughter, round face all aglowing.
Thru the oval teepee doorway, grandma watched her,
Narrowed aged eyes reflecting love most tender.

Seven summers since a new-born babe was left her.
Death had taken from her teepee, her own daughter.
Tireless love bestowed she on the little Bright eyes, –
Eagerly attended her with great devotion.
Seven summers grew affection intertwining.
Bent old age adorned once more with hopes all budding.

---

2 "Lane's Bill" and "Gandy's Bill" were probably Congressional bills related to Indian rights. "Lane" likely refers to Henry Smith Lane, a Representative and Senator from Indiana. He served from 1861 to 1867 in the 37th through 39th Congresses; he was also special Indian commissioner from 1869 to 1871. Harry Luther Gandy was a Representative from South Dakota from 1915 to 1921, serving in the 64th through 68th Congresses. Because individual bills were often known only colloquially by their sponsors' names, I have been unable to locate the specific bills to which Zitkala-Ša refers here.

Bright Eyes spied some "gaudy-wings" and chased them wildly.
Sipping dew and honey from the flowers, gaily
Flit the pretty butterflies, here now, then yonder.
"These, the green, wee babes," old grandma mused in wonder.
"One time snug in winter slumber, now in season
Leave their silken cradles; fly with gauzy pinion."

Shouting gleefully, the child roamed on fearlessly
Glossy, her long hair, hung in two braids o'er each ear,
Zephyrs whispered to the flowers, at her passing,
Fragrant blossoms gave assent with gracious nodding.
Conscious lay the crystal dew, on bud and leaflet,
Iridescent joys emitting 'till the sun set.

Monster clouds crept in the sky; fell shadows in the prairie.
Grandma, on her cane, leaned breathless, sad and weary.
Listened vainly for the laughter of her darling.
"Where, Oh where, in sudden desert's endless rolling,
Could the wee girl still be playing?" cried she hoarsely,
Shaking as with ague in that silence somber.

Sobbing bitterly, she saw not men approaching.
Over wrought by sorrow, scarcely heard them talking.
Gusts of wind rushed by; cooled her fever;
Loosed her wisps of hair befitting to a mourner.
"In God's infinitude, where, Oh where is grandchild?"
Winds caught up her moaning, shrieked and shook the teepee.

"Dry your tears, old grandma, cease excessive wailing."
(Empty words addressed they to an image standing.)
"Chieftain's word of sympathy and warning, hear you!
Moving dust-cloud of an army is on coming;
Though you've lost your grandchild, tempt no useless danger.
In the twilight, we must flee hence." This the order.

Duty done, they paused with heads bowed sadly.
These strong men were, used to meeting battles bravely,
Yet the anguish of the woman smote them helpless.
Setting of the sun made further searching fruitless,
Darkness, rife with evil omens surging tempest
Came, obliterating hope's last ray for rescue.

Fleeing from the soldiers startled Red Man hurried
Riding travois, ponies face the lightnings, lurid
'Gainst the sudden flashing, angry fires, a figure
Stood, propped by a can. A soul in torture
Sacrificing life than leave behind her lost one
Greater love hath no man; love surpassing reason.[3]

[3] This incident occurred upon the coming of Custer's army, preliminary to the battle known erroneously in history as "Custer's Massacre" [Zitkala-Ša's note].

# Fiction and Prose Nonfiction

## From *Old Indian Legends* (1904)

### Iktomi and the Ducks

Iktomi is a spider fairy. He wears brown deerskin leggins with long soft fringes on either side, and tiny beaded moccasins on his feet. His long black hair is parted in the middle and wrapped with red, red bands. Each round braid hangs over a small brown ear and falls forward over his shoulders.

He even paints his funny face with red and yellow, and draws big black rings around his eyes. He wears a deerskin jacket, with bright colored beads sewed tightly on it. Iktomi dresses like a real Dakota brave. In truth, his paint and deerskins are the best part of him – if ever dress is part of man or fairy.

Iktomi is a wily fellow. His hands are always kept in mischief. He prefers to spread a snare rather than to earn the smallest thing with honest hunting. Why! he laughs outright with wide open mouth when some simple folk are caught in a trap, sure and fast.

He never dreams another lives so bright as he. Often his own conceit leads him hard against the common sense of simpler people.

Poor Iktomi cannot help being a little imp. And so long as he is a naughty fairy, he cannot find a single friend. No one helps him when he is in trouble. No one really loves him. Those who come to admire his handsome beaded jacket and long fringed leggins soon go away sick and tired of his vain, vain words and heartless laughter.

Thus Iktomi lives alone in a cone-shaped wigwam upon the plain. One day he sat hungry within his teepee. Suddenly he rushed out, dragging after him his blanket. Quickly spreading it on the ground, he tore up dry tall grass with both his hands and tossed it fast into the blanket.

Tying all the four corners together in a knot, he threw the light bundle of grass over his shoulder.

Snatching up a slender willow stick with his free left hand, he started off with a hop and a leap. From side to side bounced the bundle on his back, as he ran light-footed over the uneven ground. Soon he came to the edge of the great level land. On the hilltop he paused for breath. With wicked smacks of his dry parched lips, as if tasting some tender meat, he looked straight into space toward the marshy river bottom. With a thin palm shading his eyes from the western sun, he peered far away into the lowlands, munching his own cheeks all the while. "Ah-ha!" grunted he, satisfied with what he saw.

A group of wild ducks were dancing and feasting in the marshes. With wings outspread, tip to tip, they moved up and down in a large circle. Within the ring, around a small drum, sat the chosen singers, nodding their heads and blinking their eyes.

They sang in unison a merry dance-song, and beat a lively tattoo on the drum.

Following a winding footpath near by, came a bent figure of a Dakota brave. He bore on his back a very large bundle. With a willow cane he propped himself up as he staggered along beneath his burden.

"Ho! who is there?" called out a curious old duck, still bobbing up and down in the circular dance.

Hereupon the drummers stretched their necks till they strangled their song for a look at the stranger passing by.

"Ho, Iktomi! Old fellow, pray tell us what you carry in your blanket. Do not hurry off! Stop! halt!" urged one of the singers.

"Stop! stay! Show us what is in your blanket!" cried out other voices.

"My friends, I must not spoil your dance. Oh, you would not care to see if you only knew what is in my blanket. Sing on! dance on! I must not show you what I carry on my back," answered Iktomi, nudging his own sides with his elbows. This reply broke up the ring entirely. Now all the ducks crowded about Iktomi.

"We must see what you carry! We must know what is in your blanket!" they shouted in both his ears.

Some even brushed their wings against the mysterious bundle. Nudging himself again, wily Iktomi said, "My friends, 't is only a pack of songs I carry in my blanket."

"Oh, then let us hear your songs!" cried the curious ducks.

At length Iktomi consented to sing his songs. With delight all the ducks flapped their wings and cried together, "Hoye! hoye!"

Iktomi, with great care, laid down his bundle on the ground.

"I will build first a round straw house, for I never sing my songs in the open air," said he.

Quickly he bent green willow sticks, planting both ends of each pole into the earth. These he covered thick with reeds and grasses. Soon the straw hut was ready. One by one the fat ducks waddled in through a small opening, which was the only entrance way. Beside the door Iktomi stood smiling, as the ducks, eyeing his bundle of songs, strutted into the hut.

In a strange low voice Iktomi began his queer old tunes. All the ducks sat round-eyed in a circle about the mysterious singer. It was dim in that straw hut, for Iktomi had not forgot to cover up the small entrance way. All of a sudden his song burst into full voice. As the startled ducks sat uneasily on the ground, Iktomi changed his tune into a minor strain. These were the words he sang:

"Ĭštokmus wacipo, tuwayatunwanpi kinhan ĭšta nišašapi kta," which is, "With eyes closed you must dance. He who dares to open his eyes, forever red eyes shall have."

Up rose the circle of seated ducks and holding their wings close against their sides began to dance to the rhythm of Iktomi's song and drum.

With eyes closed they did dance! Iktomi ceased to beat his drum. He began to sing louder and faster. He seemed to be moving about in the center of the ring. No duck dared blink a wink. Each one shut his eyes very tight and danced even harder. Up and down! Shifting to the right of them they hopped round and round in that blind dance. It was a difficult dance for the curious folk.

At length one of the dancers could close his eyes no longer! It was a Skiska who peeped the least tiny blink at Iktomi within the center of the circle. "Oh! oh!" squawked he in awful terror! "Run! fly! Iktomi is twisting your heads and breaking your necks! Run out and fly! fly!" he cried. Hereupon the ducks opened their eyes. There beside Iktomi's bundle of songs lay half of their crowd – flat on their backs.

Out they flew through the opening Skiska had made as he rushed forth with his alarm.

But as they soared high into the blue sky they cried to one another: "Oh! your eyes are red-red!" "And yours are red-red !" For the warning words of the magic minor strain had proven true. "Ah-ha!" laughed Iktomi, untying the four corners of his blanket, "I shall sit no more hungry within my dwelling." Homeward he trudged along with nice fat ducks in his blanket. He left the little straw hut for the rains and winds to pull down.

Having reached his own teepee on the high level lands, Iktomi kindled a large fire out of doors. He planted sharp-pointed sticks around the leaping flames. On each stake he fastened a duck to roast. A few he buried under the ashes to bake. Disappearing within his teepee, he came out again with some huge seashells. These were his dishes. Placing one under each roasting duck, he muttered, "The sweet fat oozing out will taste well with the hard-cooked breasts."

Heaping more willows upon the fire, Iktomi sat down on the ground with crossed shins. A long chin between his knees pointed toward the red flames, while his eyes were on the browning ducks.

Just above his ankles he clasped and unclasped his long bony fingers. Now and then he sniffed impatiently the savory odor.

The brisk wind which stirred the fire also played with a squeaky old tree beside Iktomi's wigwam.

From side to side the tree was swaying and crying in an old man's voice, "Help! I'll break! I'll fall!" Iktomi shrugged his great shoulders, but did not once take his eyes from the ducks. The dripping of amber oil into pearly dishes, drop by drop, pleased his hungry eyes. Still the old tree man called for help. "Hĕ! What sound is it that makes my ear ache!" exclaimed Iktomi, holding a hand on his ear.

He rose and looked around. The squeaking came from the tree. Then he began climbing the tree to find the disagreeable sound. He placed his foot right on a cracked limb without seeing it. Just then a whiff of wind came rushing by and pressed together the broken edges. There in a strong wooden hand Iktomi's foot was caught.

"Oh! my foot is crushed!" he howled like a coward. In vain he pulled and puffed to free himself.

While sitting a prisoner on the tree he spied, through his tears, a pack of gray wolves roaming over the level lands. Waving his hands toward them, he called in his loudest voice, "Hĕ! Gray wolves! Don't you come here! I'm caught fast in the tree so that my duck feast is getting cold. Don't you come to eat up my meal."

The leader of the pack upon hearing Iktomi's words turned to his comrades and said:

"Ah! hear the foolish fellow! He says he has a duck feast to be eaten! Let us hurry there for our share!" Away bounded the wolves toward Iktomi's lodge.

From the tree Iktomi watched the hungry wolves eat up his nicely browned fat ducks. His foot pained him more and more. He heard them crack the small round bones with their strong long teeth and eat out the oily marrow. Now severe pains shot up from his foot through his whole body. "Hin-hin-hin!" sobbed Iktomi. Real tears washed brown streaks across his red-painted cheeks. Smacking their lips, the wolves began to leave the place, when Iktomi cried out like a pouting child, "At least you have left my baking under the ashes!"

"Ho! po!" shouted the mischievous wolves; "he says more ducks are to be found under the ashes! Come! Let us have our fill this once!"

Running back to the dead fire, they pawed out the ducks with such rude haste that a cloud of ashes rose like gray smoke over them.

"Hin-hin-hin!" moaned Iktomi, when the wolves had scampered off. All too late, the sturdy breeze returned, and, passing by, pulled apart the broken edges of the tree. Iktomi was released. But alas! he had no duck feast.

## Iktomi and the Muskrat

Beside a white lake, beneath a large grown willow tree, sat Iktomi on the bare ground. The heap of smouldering ashes told of a recent open fire. With ankles crossed together around a pot of soup, Iktomi bent over some delicious boiled fish.

Fast he dipped his black horn spoon into the soup, for he was ravenous. Iktomi had no regular meal times. Often when he was hungry he went without food.

Well hid between the lake and the wild rice, he looked nowhere save into the pot of fish. Not knowing when the next meal might be, he meant to eat enough now to last some time.

"How, how, my friend!" said a voice out of the wild rice. Iktomi started. He almost choked with his soup. He peered through the long reeds from where he sat with his long horn spoon in mid-air.

"How, my friend!" said the voice again, this time close at his side. Iktomi turned and there stood a dripping muskrat who had just come out of the lake.

"Oh, it is my friend who startled me. I wondered if among the wild rice some spirit voice was talking. How, how, my friend!" said Iktomi. The muskrat stood smiling. On his lips hung a ready "Yes, my friend," when Iktomi would ask, "My friend, will you sit down beside me and share my food?"

That was the custom of the plains people. Yet Iktomi sat silent. He hummed an old dance-song and beat gently on the edge of the pot with his buffalo-horn spoon. The muskrat began to feel awkward before such lack of hospitality and wished himself under water.

After many heart throbs Iktomi stopped drumming with his horn ladle, and looking upward into the muskrat's face, he said:

"My friend, let us run a race to see who shall win this pot of fish. If I win, I shall not need to share it with you. If you win, you shall have half of it." Springing to his feet, Iktomi began at once to tighten the belt about his waist.

"My friend Ikto, I cannot run a race with you! I am not a swift runner, and you are nimble as a deer. We shall not run any race together," answered the hungry muskrat.

For a moment Iktomi stood with a hand on his long protruding chin. His eyes were fixed upon something in the air. The muskrat looked out of the corners of his eyes without moving his head. He watched the wily Iktomi concocting a plot.

"Yes, yes," said Iktomi, suddenly turning his gaze upon the unwelcome visitor; "I shall carry a large stone on my back. That will slacken my usual speed; and the race will be a fair one."

Saying this he laid a firm hand upon the muskrat's shoulder and started off along the edge of the lake. When they reached the opposite side Iktomi pried about in search of a heavy stone.

He found one half-buried in the shallow water. Pulling it out upon dry land, he wrapped it in his blanket.

"Now, my friend, you shall run on the left side of the lake, I on the other. The race is for the boiled fish in yonder kettle!" said Iktomi.

The muskrat helped to lift the heavy stone upon Iktomi's back. Then they parted. Each took a narrow path through the tall reeds fringing the shore. Iktomi found his load a heavy one. Perspiration hung like beads on his brow. His chest heaved hard and fast.

He looked across the lake to see how far the muskrat had gone, but nowhere did he see any sign of him. "Well, he is running low under the wild rice!" said he. Yet as he scanned the tall grasses on the lake shore, he saw not one stir as if to make way for the runner. "Ah, has he gone so fast ahead that the disturbed grasses in his trail have quieted again?" exclaimed Iktomi. With that thought he quickly dropped the heavy stone. "No more of this!" said he, patting his chest with both hands.

Off with a springing bound, he ran swiftly toward the goal. Tufts of reeds and grass fell flat under his feet. Hardly had they raised their heads when Iktomi was many paces gone.

Soon he reached the heap of cold ashes. Iktomi halted stiff as if he had struck an invisible cliff. His black eyes showed a ring of white about them as he stared at the empty ground. There was no pot of boiled fish! There was no water-man in sight! "Oh, if only I had shared my food like a real Dakota, I would not have lost it all! Why did I not know the muskrat would run through the water? He swims faster than I could ever run! That is what he has done. He has laughed at me for carrying a weight on my back while he shot hither like an arrow!"

Crying thus to himself, Iktomi stepped to the water's brink. He stooped forward with a hand on each bent knee and peeped far into the deep water.

"There!" he exclaimed, "I see you, my friend, sitting with your ankles wound around my little pot of fish! My friend, I am hungry. Give me a bone!"

"Ha! ha! ha!" laughed the water-man, the muskrat. The sound did not rise up out of the lake, for it came down from overhead. With his hands still on his knees, Iktomi turned his face upward into the great willow tree. Opening wide his mouth he begged, "My friend, my friend, give me a bone to gnaw!"

"Ha! ha!" laughed the muskrat, and leaning over the limb he sat upon, he let fall a small sharp bone which dropped right into Iktomi's throat. Iktomi almost choked to death before he could get it out. In the tree the muskrat sat laughing loud. "Next time, say to a visiting friend, 'Be seated beside me, my friend. Let me share with you my food.'"

## From *American Indian Stories* (1921)

### Impressions of an Indian Childhood

#### I. My Mother

A wigwam of weather-stained canvas stood at the base of some irregularly ascending hills. A footpath wound its way gently down the sloping land till it reached the broad river bottom; creeping through the long swamp grasses that bent over it on either side, it came out on the edge of the Missouri.

Here, morning, noon, and evening, my mother came to draw water from the muddy stream for our household use. Always, when my mother started for the river, I stopped my play to run along with her. She was only of medium height. Often she was sad and silent, at which times her full arched lips were compressed into hard and bitter lines, and shadows fell under her black eyes. Then I clung to her hand and begged to know what made the tears fall.

"Hush; my little daughter must never talk about my tears"; and smiling through them, she patted my head and said, "Now let me see how fast you can run today." Whereupon I tore away at my highest possible speed, with my long black hair blowing in the breeze.

I was a wild little girl of seven. Loosely clad in a slip of brown buckskin, and light-footed with a pair of soft moccasins on my feet, I was as free as the wind that blew my hair, and no less spirited than a bounding deer. These were my mother's pride, – my wild freedom and overflowing spirits. She taught me no fear save that of intruding myself upon others.

Having gone many paces ahead I stopped, panting for breath, and laughing with glee as my mother watched my every movement. I was not wholly conscious of myself, but was more keenly alive to the fire within. It was as if I were the activity, and my hands and feet were only experiments for my spirit to work upon.

Returning from the river, I tugged beside my mother, with my hand upon the bucket I believed I was carrying. One time, on such a return, I remember a bit of conversation we had. My grown-up cousin, Warca-Ziwin (Sunflower), who was then seventeen, always went to the river alone for water for her mother. Their wigwam was not far from ours; and I saw her daily going to and from the river. I admired my cousin greatly. So I said: "Mother, when I am tall as my cousin Warca-Ziwin, you shall not have to come for water. I will do it for you."

With a strange tremor in her voice which I could not understand, she answered, "If the paleface does not take away from us the river we drink."

"Mother, who is this bad paleface?" I asked.

"My little daughter, he is a sham, – a sickly sham. The bronzed Dakota is the only real man."

I looked up into my mother's face while she spoke; and seeing her bite her lips, I knew she was unhappy. This aroused revenge in my small soul. Stamping my foot on the earth, I cried aloud, "I hate the paleface that makes my mother cry!"

Setting the pail of water on the ground, my mother stooped, and stretching her left hand out on the level with my eyes, she placed her other arm about me; she pointed to the hill where my uncle and my only sister lay buried.

"There is what the paleface has done! Since then your father too has been buried in a hill nearer the rising sun. We were once very happy. But the paleface has stolen our lands and driven us hither. Having defrauded us of our land, the paleface forced us away.

"Well, it happened on the day we moved camp that your sister and uncle were both very sick. Many others were ailing, but there seemed to be no help. We traveled many days and nights; not in the grand, happy way that we moved camp when I was a little girl, but we were driven, my child, driven like a herd of buffalo. With every step, your sister, who was not as large as you are now, shrieked with the painful jar until she was hoarse with crying. She grew more and more feverish. Her little hands and cheeks were burning hot. Her little lips were parched and dry, but she would not drink the water I gave her. Then I discovered that her throat was swollen and red. My poor child, how I cried with her because the Great Spirit had forgotten us!

"At last, when we reached this western country, on the first weary night your sister died. And soon your uncle died also, leaving a widow and an orphan daughter, your cousin Warca-Ziwin. Both your sister and uncle might have been happy with us today, had it not been for the heartless paleface."

My mother was silent the rest of the way to our wigwam. Though I saw no tears in her eyes, I knew that was because I was with her. She seldom wept before me.

## II. The Legends

During the summer days my mother built her fire in the shadow of our wigwam.

In the early morning our simple breakfast was spread upon the grass west of our tepee. At the farthest point of the shade my mother sat beside her fire, toasting a savory piece of dried meat. Near her, I sat upon my feet, eating my dried meat with unleavened bread, and drinking strong black coffee.

The morning meal was our quiet hour, when we two were entirely alone. At noon, several who chanced to be passing by stopped to rest, and to share our luncheon with us, for they were sure of our hospitality.

My uncle, whose death my mother ever lamented, was one of our nation's bravest warriors. His name was on the lips of old men when talking of the proud feats of valor; and it was mentioned by younger men, too, in connection with deeds of gallantry. Old women praised him for his kindness toward them; young women held him up as an ideal to their sweethearts. Every one loved him, and my mother worshiped his memory. Thus it happened that even strangers were sure of welcome in our lodge, if they but asked a favor in my uncle's name.

Though I heard many strange experiences related by these wayfarers, I loved best the evening meal, for that was the time old legends were told. I was always glad when the sun hung low in the west, for then my mother sent me to invite the neighboring old men and women to eat supper with us. Running all the way to the wigwams, I halted shyly at the entrances. Sometimes I stood long moments without saying a word. It was not any fear that made me so dumb when out upon such a happy errand; nor was it that I wished to withhold the invitation, for it was all I could do to observe this very proper silence. But it was a sensing of the atmosphere, to assure myself that I should not hinder other plans. My mother used to say to me, as I was almost bounding away for the old people: "Wait a moment before you invite any one. If other plans are being discussed, do not interfere, but go elsewhere."

The old folks knew the meaning of my pauses; and often they coaxed my confidence by asking, "What do you seek, little granddaughter?"

"My mother says you are to come to our tepee this evening," I instantly exploded, and breathed the freer afterwards.

"Yes, yes, gladly, gladly I shall come!" each replied. Rising at once and carrying their blankets across one shoulder, they flocked leisurely from their various wigwams toward our dwelling.

My mission done, I ran back, skipping and jumping with delight. All out of breath, I told my mother almost the exact words of the answers to my invitation. Frequently she asked, "What were they doing when you entered their tepee?" This taught me to remember all I saw at a single glance. Often I told my mother my impressions without being questioned.

While in the neighboring wigwams sometimes an old Indian woman asked me, "What is your mother doing?" Unless my mother had cautioned me not to tell, I generally answered her questions without reserve.

At the arrival of our guests I sat close to my mother, and did not leave her side without first asking her consent. I ate my supper in quiet, listening patiently to the talk of the old people, wishing all the time that they would begin the stories I loved best. At last, when I could not wait any longer, I whispered in my mother's ear, "Ask them to tell an Iktomi story, mother."

Soothing my impatience, my mother said aloud, "My little daughter is anxious to hear your legends." By this time all were through eating, and the evening was fast deepening into twilight.

As each in turn began to tell a legend, I pillowed my head in my mother's lap; and lying flat upon my back, I watched the stars as they peeped down upon me, one by one. The increasing interest of the tale aroused me, and I sat up eagerly listening to every word. The old women made funny remarks, and laughed so heartily that I could not help joining them.

The distant howling of a pack of wolves or the hooting of an owl in the river bottom frightened me, and I nestled into my mother's lap. She added some dry sticks to the open fire, and the bright flames leaped up into the faces of the old folks as they sat around in a great circle.

On such an evening, I remember the glare of the fire shone on a tattooed star upon the brow of the old warrior who was telling a story. I watched him curiously as he made his unconscious gestures. The blue star upon his bronzed forehead was a puzzle to me. Looking about, I saw two parallel lines on the chin of one of the old women. The rest had none. I examined my mother's face, but found no sign there.

After the warrior's story was finished, I asked the old woman the meaning of the blue lines on her chin, looking all the while out of the corners of my eyes at the warrior with the star on his forehead. I was a little afraid that he would rebuke me for my boldness.

Here the old woman began: "Why, my grandchild, they are signs, – secret signs I dare not tell you. I shall, however, tell you a wonderful story about a woman who had a cross tattooed upon each of her cheeks."

It was a long story of a woman whose magic power lay hidden behind the marks upon her face. I fell asleep before the story was completed.

Ever after that night I felt suspicious of tattooed people. Wherever I saw one I glanced furtively at the mark and round about it, wondering what terrible magic power was covered there.

It was rarely that such a fearful story as this one was told by the camp fire. Its impression was so acute that the picture still remains vividly clear and pronounced.

## III. The Beadwork

Soon after breakfast mother sometimes began her beadwork. On a bright, clear day, she pulled out the wooden pegs that pinned the skirt of our wigwam to the ground, and rolled the canvas part way up on its frame of slender poles. Then the cool morning breezes swept freely through our dwelling, now and then wafting the perfume of sweet grasses from newly burnt prairie.

Untying the long tasseled strings that bound a small brown buckskin bag, my mother spread upon a mat beside her bunches of colored beads, just as an artist arranges the paints upon his palette. On a lapboard she smoothed out a double sheet of soft white buckskin; and drawing from a beaded case that hung on the left of her wide belt a long, narrow blade, she trimmed the buckskin into shape. Often she worked upon small moccasins for her small daughter. Then I became intensely interested in her designing. With a proud, beaming face, I watched her work. In imagination, I saw myself walking in a new pair of snugly fitting moccasins. I felt the envious eyes of my playmates upon the pretty red beads decorating my feet.

Close beside my mother I sat on a rug, with a scrap of buckskin in one hand and an awl in the other. This was the beginning of my practical observation lessons in the art of beadwork. From a skein of finely twisted threads of silvery sinews my mother pulled out a single one. With an awl she pierced the buckskin, and skillfully threaded it with the white sinew. Picking up the tiny beads one by one, she strung them with the point of her thread, always twisting it carefully after every stitch.

It took many trials before I learned how to knot my sinew thread on the point of my finger, as I saw her do. Then the next difficulty was in keeping my thread stiffly twisted, so that I could easily string my beads upon it. My mother required of me original designs for my lessons in beading. At first I frequently ensnared many a sunny hour into working a long design. Soon I learned from self-inflicted punishment to refrain from drawing complex patterns, for I had to finish whatever I began.

After some experience I usually drew easy and simple crosses and squares. These were some of the set forms. My original designs were not always symmetrical nor sufficiently characteristic, two faults with which my mother had little patience. The quietness of her oversight made me feel strongly responsible and dependent upon my own judgment. She treated me as a dignified little individual as long as I was on my good behavior; and how humiliated I was when some boldness of mine drew forth a rebuke from her!

In the choice of colors she left me to my own taste. I was pleased with an outline of yellow upon a background of dark blue, or a combination of red and myrtle-green. There was another of red with a bluish-gray that was more conventionally used. When I became a little familiar with designing and the various pleasing combinations of color, a harder lesson was given me. It was the sewing on, instead of beads, some tinted porcupine quills, moistened and flattened between the nails of the thumb and forefinger. My mother cut off the prickly ends and burned them at once in the centre fire. These sharp points were poisonous, and worked into the flesh wherever they lodged. For this reason, my mother said, I should not do much alone in quills until I was as tall as my cousin Warca-Ziwin.

Always after these confining lessons I was wild with surplus spirits, and found joyous relief in running loose in the open again. Many a summer afternoon a party of four or five of my playmates roamed over the hills with me. We each carried a light sharpened rod about four feet long, with which we pried up certain sweet roots. When we had eaten all the choice roots we chanced upon, we shouldered our rods and strayed off into patches of a stalky plant under whose yellow blossoms we found little crystal drops of gum. Drop by drop we gathered this nature's rock-candy, until each of us could boast of a lump the size of a small bird's egg. Soon satiated with its woody flavor, we tossed away our gum, to return again to the sweet roots.

I remember well how we used to exchange our necklaces, beaded belts, and sometimes even our moccasins. We pretended to offer them as gifts to one another. We delighted in impersonating our own mothers. We talked of things we had heard them say in their conversations. We imitated their various manners, even to the inflection of their voices. In the lap of the prairie we seated ourselves upon our feet, and leaning our painted cheeks in the palms of our hands, we rested our elbows on our knees, and bent forward as old women were most accustomed to do.

While one was telling of some heroic deed recently done by a near relative, the rest of us listened attentively, and exclaimed in undertones, "Han! han!" (yes! yes!) whenever the speaker paused for breath, or sometimes for our sympathy. As the discourse became more thrilling, according to our ideas, we raised our voices in these interjections. In these impersonations our parents were led to say only those things that were in common favor.

No matter how exciting a tale we might be rehearsing, the mere shifting of a cloud shadow in the landscape near by was sufficient to change our impulses; and soon we were all chasing the great shadows that played among the hills. We shouted and whooped in the chase; laughing and calling to one another, we were like little sportive nymphs on that Dakota sea of rolling green.

On one occasion I forgot the cloud shadow in a strange notion to catch up with my own shadow. Standing straight and still, I began to glide after it, putting out one foot cautiously. When, with the greatest care, I set my foot in advance of myself, my shadow crept onward too. Then again I tried it; this time with the other foot. Still again my shadow escaped me. I began to run; and away flew my shadow, always just a step beyond me. Faster and faster I ran, setting my teeth and clenching my fists, determined to overtake my own fleet shadow. But ever swifter it glided before me, while I was growing breathless and hot. Slackening my speed, I was greatly vexed that my shadow should check its pace also. Daring it to the utmost, as I thought, I sat down upon a rock imbedded in the hillside.

So! my shadow had the impudence to sit down beside me!

Now my comrades caught up with me, and began to ask why I was running away so fast.

"Oh, I was chasing my shadow! Didn't you ever do that?" I inquired, surprised that they should not understand.

They planted their moccasined feet firmly upon my shadow to stay it, and I arose. Again my shadow slipped away, and moved as often as I did. Then we gave up trying to catch my shadow.

Before this peculiar experience I have no distinct memory of having recognized any vital bond between myself and my own shadow. I never gave it an afterthought.

Returning our borrowed belts and trinkets, we rambled homeward. That evening, as on other evenings, I went to sleep over my legends.

## IV. The Coffee-Making

One summer afternoon my mother left me alone in our wigwam while she went across the way to my aunt's dwelling.

I did not much like to stay alone in our tepee for I feared a tall, broad-shouldered crazy man, some forty years old, who walked loose among the hills. Wiyaka-Napbina (Wearer of a Feather Necklace) was harmless, and whenever he came into a wigwam he was driven there by extreme hunger. He went nude except for the half of a red blanket he girdled around his waist. In one tawny arm he used to carry a heavy bunch of wild sunflowers that he gathered in his aimless ramblings. His black hair was matted by the winds, and scorched into a dry red by the constant summer sun. As he took great strides, placing one brown bare foot directly in front of the other, he swung his long lean arm to and fro.

Frequently he paused in his walk and gazed far backward, shading his eyes with his hand. He was under the belief that an evil spirit was haunting his steps. This was what my mother told me once, when I sneered at such a silly big man. I was brave when my mother was near by, and Wiyaka-Napbina walking farther and farther away.

"Pity the man, my child. I knew him when he was a brave and handsome youth. He was overtaken by a malicious spirit among the hills, one day, when he went hither and thither after his ponies. Since then he can not stay away from the hills," she said.

I felt so sorry for the man in his misfortune that I prayed to the Great Spirit to restore him. But though I pitied him at a distance, I was still afraid of him when he appeared near our wigwam.

Thus, when my mother left me by myself that afternoon I sat in a fearful mood within our tepee. I recalled all I had ever heard about Wiyaka-Napbina; and I tried to assure myself that though he might pass near by, he would not come to our wigwam because there was no little girl around our grounds.

Just then, from without a hand lifted the canvas covering of the entrance; the shadow of a man fell within the wigwam, and a large roughly moccasined foot was planted inside.

For a moment I did not dare to breathe or stir, for I thought that could be no other than Wiyaka-Napbina. The next instant I sighed aloud in relief. It was an old grandfather who had often told me Iktomi legends.

"Where is your mother, my little grandchild ?" were his first words.

"My mother is soon coming back from my aunt's tepee," I replied.

"Then I shall wait awhile for her return," he said, crossing his feet and seating himself upon a mat.

At once I began to play the part of a generous hostess. I turned to my mother's coffeepot.

Lifting the lid, I found nothing but coffee grounds in the bottom. I set the pot on a heap of cold ashes in the centre, and filled it half full of warm Missouri River water. During this performance I felt conscious of being watched. Then breaking off a small piece of our unleavened bread, I placed it in a bowl. Turning soon to the coffeepot, which would never have boiled on a dead fire had I waited forever, I poured out a cup of worse than muddy warm water. Carrying the bowl in one hand and cup in the other, I handed the light luncheon to the old warrior. I offered them to him with the air of bestowing generous hospitality.

"How! how!" he said, and placed the dishes on the ground in front of his crossed feet. He nibbled at the bread and sipped from the cup. I sat back against a pole watching him. I was proud to have succeeded so well in serving refreshments to a guest all by myself. Before the old warrior had finished eating, my mother entered. Immediately she wondered where I had found coffee, for she knew I had never made any, and that she had left the coffeepot empty. Answering the question in my mother's eyes, the warrior remarked, "My granddaughter made coffee on a heap of dead ashes, and served me the moment I came."

They both laughed, and mother said, "Wait a little longer, and I shall build a fire." She meant to make some real coffee. But neither she nor the warrior, whom the law of our custom had compelled to partake of my insipid hospitality, said anything to embarrass me. They treated my best judgment, poor as it was, with the utmost respect. It was not till long years afterward that I learned how ridiculous a thing I had done.

## V. The Dead Man's Plum Bush

One autumn afternoon many people came streaming toward the dwelling of our near neighbor. With painted faces, and wearing broad white bosoms of elk's teeth, they hurried down the narrow footpath to Haraka Wambdi's wigwam. Young mothers held their children by the hand, and half pulled them along in their haste. They overtook and passed by the bent old grandmothers who were trudging along with crooked canes toward the centre of excitement. Most of the young braves galloped hither on their ponies. Toothless warriors, like the old women, came more slowly, though mounted on lively ponies. They sat proudly erect on their horses. They wore their eagle plumes, and waved their various trophies of former wars.

In front of the wigwam a great fire was built, and several large black kettles of venison were suspended over it. The crowd were seated about it on the grass in a great circle. Behind them some of the braves stood leaning against the necks of their ponies, their tall figures draped in loose robes which were well drawn over their eyes.

Young girls, with their faces glowing like bright red autumn leaves, their glossy braids falling over each ear, sat coquettishly beside their chaperons. It was a custom for young Indian women to invite some older relative to escort them to the public feasts. Though it was not an iron law, it was generally observed.

Haraka Wambdi was a strong young brave, who had just returned from his first battle, a warrior. His near relatives, to celebrate his new rank, were spreading a feast to which the whole of the Indian village was invited.

Holding my pretty striped blanket in readiness to throw over my shoulders, I grew more and more restless as I watched the gay throng assembling. My mother was busily broiling a wild duck that my aunt had that morning brought over.

"Mother, mother, why do you stop to cook a small meal when we are invited to a feast?" I asked, with a snarl in my voice.

"My child, learn to wait. On our way to the celebration we are going to stop at Chanyu's wigwam. His aged mother-in-law is lying very ill, and I think she would like a taste of this small game."

Having once seen the suffering on the thin, pinched features of this dying woman, I felt a momentary shame that I had not remembered her before.

On our way I ran ahead of my mother and was reaching out my hand to pick some purple plums that grew on a small bush, when I was checked by a low "Sh!" from my mother.

"Why, mother, I want to taste the plums!" I exclaimed, as I dropped my hand to my side in disappointment.

"Never pluck a single plum from this bush, my child, for its roots are wrapped around an Indian's skeleton. A brave is buried here. While he lived he was so fond of playing the game of striped plum seeds that, at his death, his set of plum seeds were buried in his hands. From them sprang up this little bush."

Eyeing the forbidden fruit, I trod lightly on the sacred ground, and dared to speak only in whispers until we had gone many paces from it. After that time I halted in my ramblings whenever I came in sight of the plum bush. I grew sober with awe, and was alert to hear a long-drawn-out whistle rise from the roots of it. Though I had never heard with my own ears this strange whistle of departed spirits, yet I had listened so frequently to hear the old folks describe it that I knew I should recognize it at once.

The lasting impression of that day, as I recall it now, is what my mother told me about the dead man's plum bush.

## VI. The Ground Squirrel

In the busy autumn days my cousin Warca-Ziwin's mother came to our wigwam to help my mother preserve foods for our winter use. I was very fond of my aunt, because she was not so quiet as my mother. Though she was older, she was more jovial and less reserved. She was slender and remarkably erect. While my mother's hair was heavy and black, my aunt had unusually thin locks.

Ever since I knew her she wore a string of large blue beads around her neck, – beads that were precious because my uncle had given them to her when she was a younger woman. She had a peculiar swing in her gait, caused by a long stride rarely natural to so slight a figure. It was during my aunt's visit with us that my mother forgot her accustomed quietness, often laughing heartily at some of my aunt's witty remarks.

I loved my aunt threefold: for her hearty laughter, for the cheerfulness she caused my mother, and most of all for the times she dried my tears and held me in her lap, when my mother had reproved me.

Early in the cool mornings, just as the yellow rim of the sun rose above the hills, we were up and eating our breakfast. We awoke so early that we saw the sacred hour when a misty smoke hung over a pit surrounded by an impassable sinking mire. This strange smoke appeared every morning, both winter and summer; but most visibly in midwinter it rose immediately above the marshy spot. By the time the full face of the sun appeared above the eastern horizon, the smoke vanished. Even very old men, who had known this country the longest, said that the smoke from this pit had never failed a single day to rise heavenward.

As I frolicked about our dwelling I used to stop suddenly, and with a fearful awe watch the smoking of the unknown fires. While the vapor was visible I was afraid to go very far from our wigwam unless I went with my mother.

From a field in the fertile river bottom my mother and aunt gathered an abundant supply of corn. Near our tepee they spread a large canvas upon the grass, and dried their sweet corn in it. I was left to watch the corn, that nothing should disturb it. I played around it with dolls made of ears of corn. I braided their soft fine silk for hair, and gave them blankets as various as the scraps I found in my mother's workbag.

There was a little stranger with a black-and-yellow-striped coat that used to come to the drying corn. It was a little ground squirrel, who was so fearless of me that he came to one corner of the canvas and carried away as much of the sweet corn as he could hold. I wanted very much to catch him and rub his pretty fur back, but my mother said he would be so frightened if I caught him that he would bite my fingers. So I was as content as he to keep the corn between us. Every morning he came for more corn. Some evenings I have seen him creeping about our grounds; and when I gave a sudden whoop of recognition he ran quickly out of sight.

When mother had dried all the corn she wished, then she sliced great pumpkins into thin rings; and these she doubled and linked together into long chains. She hung them on a pole that stretched between two forked posts. The wind and sun soon thoroughly dried the chains of pumpkin. Then she packed them away in a case of thick and stiff buckskin.

In the sun and wind she also dried many wild fruits, – cherries, berries, and plums. But chiefest among my early recollections of autumn is that one of the corn drying and the ground squirrel.

I have few memories of winter days at this period of my life, though many of the summer. There is one only which I can recall.

Some missionaries gave me a little bag of marbles. They were all sizes and colors. Among them were some of colored glass. Walking with my mother to the river, on a late winter day, we found great chunks of ice piled all along the bank. The ice on the river was floating in huge pieces. As I stood beside one large block, I noticed for the first time the colors of the rainbow in the crystal ice. Immediately I thought of my glass marbles at home. With my bare fingers I tried to pick out some of the colors, for they seemed so near the surface. But my fingers began to sting with the intense cold, and I had to bite them hard to keep from crying.

From that day on, for many a moon, I believed that glass marbles had river ice inside of them.

## VII. The Big Red Apples

The first turning away from the easy, natural flow of my life occurred in an early spring. It was in my eighth year; in the month of March, I afterward learned. At this age I knew but one language, and that was my mother's native tongue.

From some of my playmates I heard that two paleface missionaries were in our village. They were from that class of white men who wore big hats and carried large hearts, they said. Running direct to my mother, I began to question her why these two strangers were among us. She told me, after I had teased much, that they had come to take away Indian boys and girls to the East. My mother did not seem to want me to talk about them. But in a day or two, I gleaned many wonderful stories from my playfellows concerning the strangers.

"Mother, my friend Judéwin is going home with the missionaries. She is going to a more beautiful country than ours; the palefaces told her so!" I said wistfully, wishing in my heart that I too might go.

Mother sat in a chair, and I was hanging on her knee. Within the last two seasons my big brother Dawée had returned from a three years' education in the East, and his coming back influenced my mother to take a farther step from her native way of living. First it was a change from the buffalo skin to the white man's canvas that covered our wigwam. Now she had given up her wigwam of slender poles, to live, a foreigner, in a home of clumsy logs.

"Yes, my child, several others besides Judéwin are going away with the palefaces. Your brother said the missionaries had inquired about his little sister," she said, watching my face very closely.

My heart thumped so hard against my breast, I wondered if she could hear it.

"Did he tell them to take me, mother?" I asked, fearing lest Dawée had forbidden the palefaces to see me, and that my hope of going to the Wonderland would be entirely blighted.

With a sad, slow smile, she answered: "There! I knew you were wishing to go, because Judéwin has filled your ears with the white man's lies. Don't believe a word they say! Their words are sweet, but, my child, their deeds are bitter. You will cry for me, but they will not even soothe you. Stay with me, my little one! Your brother Dawée says that going East, away from your mother, is too hard an experience for his baby sister."

Thus my mother discouraged my curiosity about the lands beyond our eastern horizon; for it was not yet an ambition for Letters that was stirring me. But on the following day the missionaries did come to our very house. I spied them coming up the footpath leading to our cottage. A third man was with them, but he was not my brother Dawée. It was another, a young interpreter, a paleface who had a smattering of the Indian language. I was ready to run out to meet them, but I did not dare to displease my mother. With great glee, I jumped up and down on our ground floor. I begged my mother to open the door, that they would be sure to come to us. Alas! They came, they saw, and they conquered!

Judéwin had told me of the great tree where grew red, red apples; and how we could reach out our hands and pick all the red apples we could eat. I had never seen apple trees. I had never tasted more than a dozen red apples in my life; and when I heard of the orchards of the East, I was eager to roam among them. The missionaries smiled into my eyes and patted my head. I wondered how mother could say such hard words against him.

"Mother, ask them if little girls may have all the red apples they want, when they go East," I whispered aloud, in my excitement.

The interpreter heard me, and answered: "Yes, little girl, the nice red apples are for those who pick them; and you will have a ride on the iron horse if you go with these good people."

I had never seen a train, and he knew it. "Mother, I am going East! I like big red apples, and I want to ride on the iron horse! Mother, say yes!" I pleaded.

My mother said nothing. The missionaries waited in silence; and my eyes began to blur with tears, though I struggled to choke them back. The corners of my mouth twitched, and my mother saw me.

"I am not ready to give you any word," she said to them. "Tomorrow I shall send you my answer by my son."

With this they left us. Alone with my mother, I yielded to my tears, and cried aloud, shaking my head so as not to hear what she was saying to me. This was the first time I had ever been so unwilling to give up my own desire that I refused to hearken to my mother's voice.

There was a solemn silence in our home that night. Before I went to bed I begged the Great Spirit to make my mother willing I should go with the missionaries.

The next morning came, and my mother called me to her side. "My daughter, do you still persist in wishing to leave your mother?" she asked.

"Oh, mother, it is not that I wish to leave you, but I want to see the wonderful Eastern land," I answered.

My dear old aunt came to our house that morning, and I heard her say, "Let her try it."

I hoped that, as usual, my aunt was pleading on my side. My brother Dawée came for mother's decision. I dropped my play, and crept close to my aunt.

"Yes, Dawée, my daughter, though she does not understand what it all means, is anxious to go. She will need an education when she is grown, for then there will be fewer real Dakotas, and many more palefaces. This tearing her away, so young, from her mother is necessary, if I would have her an educated woman. The palefaces, who owe us a large debt for stolen lands, have begun to pay a tardy justice in offering some education to our children. But I know my daughter must suffer keenly in this experiment. For her sake, I dread to tell you my reply to the missionaries. Go, tell them that they may take my little daughter, and that the Great Spirit shall not fail to reward them according to their hearts."

Wrapped in my heavy blanket, I walked with my mother to the carriage that was soon to take us to the iron horse. I was happy. I met my playmates, who were also wearing their best thick blankets. We showed one another our new beaded moccasins, and the width of the belts that girdled our new dresses. Soon we were being drawn rapidly away by the white man's horses. When I saw the lonely figure of my mother vanish in the distance, a sense of regret settled heavily upon me. I felt suddenly weak, as if I might fall limp to the ground. I was in the hands of strangers whom my mother did not fully trust. I no longer felt free to be myself, or to voice my own feelings. The tears trickled down my cheeks, and I buried my face in the folds of my blanket. Now the first step, parting me from my mother, was taken, and all my belated tears availed nothing.

Having driven thirty miles to the ferryboat, we crossed the Missouri in the evening. Then riding again a few miles eastward, we stopped before a massive brick building. I looked at it in amazement, and with a vague misgiving, for in our village I had never seen so large a house. Trembling with fear and distrust of the palefaces, my teeth chattering from the chilly ride, I crept noiselessly in my soft moccasins along the narrow hall, keeping very close to the bare wall. I was as frightened and bewildered as the captured young of a wild creature.

## The School Days of An Indian Girl

### I. The Land of Red Apples

There were eight in our party of bronzed children who were going East with the missionaries. Among us were three young braves, two tall girls, and we three little ones, Judéwin, Thowin, and I.

We had been very impatient to start on our journey to the Red Apple Country, which, we were told, lay a little beyond the great circular horizon of the Western prairie. Under a sky of rosy apples we dreamt of roaming as freely and happily as we had chased the cloud shadows on the Dakota plains. We had anticipated much pleasure from a ride on the iron horse, but the throngs of staring palefaces disturbed and troubled us.

On the train, fair women, with tottering babies on each arm, stopped their haste and scrutinized the children of absent mothers. Large men, with heavy bundles in their hands, halted near by, and riveted their glassy blue eyes upon us.

I sank deep into the corner of my seat, for I resented being watched. Directly in front of me, children who were no larger than I hung themselves upon the backs of their seats, with their bold white faces toward me. Sometimes they took their forefingers out of their mouths and pointed at my moccasined feet. Their mothers, instead of reproving such rude curiosity, looked closely at me, and attracted their children's further notice to my blanket. This embarrassed me, and kept me constantly on the verge of tears.

I sat perfectly still, with my eyes downcast, daring only now and then to shoot long glances around me. Chancing to turn to the window at my side, I was quite breathless upon seeing one familiar object. It was the telegraph pole which strode by at short paces. Very near my mother's dwelling, along the edge of a road thickly boarded with wild sunflowers, some poles like these had been planted by white men. Often I had stopped, on my way down the road, to hold my ear against the pole, and, hearing its low moaning, I used to wonder what the paleface had done to hurt it. Now I sat watching for each pole that glided by to be the last one.

In this way I had forgotten my uncomfortable surroundings, when I heard one of my comrades call out my name. I saw the missionary standing very near, tossing candies and gums into our midst. This amused us all, and we tried to see who could catch the most of the sweetmeats.

Though we rode several days inside of the iron horse, I do not recall a single thing about our luncheons.

It was night when we reached the school grounds. The lights from the windows of the large buildings fell upon some of the icicled trees that stood beneath them. We were led toward an open door, where the brightness of the lights within flooded out over the heads of the excited palefaces who blocked our way. My body trembled more from fear than from the snow I trod upon.

Entering the house, I stood close against the wall. The strong glaring light in the large whitewashed room dazzled my eyes. The noisy hurrying of hard shoes upon a bare wooden floor increased the whirring in my ears. My only safety seemed to be in keeping next to the wall. As I was wondering in which direction to escape from all this confusion, two warm hands grasped me firmly, and in the same moment I was tossed high in midair. A rosy-cheeked paleface woman caught me in her arms. I was both frightened and insulted by such trifling. I stared into her eyes, wishing her to let me stand on my own feet, but she jumped me up and down with increasing enthusiasm. My mother had never made a plaything of her wee daughter. Remembering this I began to cry aloud.

They misunderstood the cause of my tears, and placed me at a white table loaded with food. There our party were united again. As I did not hush my crying, one of the older ones whispered to me, "Wait until you are alone in the night."

It was very little I could swallow besides my sobs, that evening.

"Oh, I want my mother and my brother Dawée! I want to go to my aunt!" I pleaded; but the ears of the palefaces could not hear me.

From the table we were taken along an upward incline of wooden boxes, which I learned afterward to call a stairway. At the top was a quiet hall, dimly lighted. Many narrow beds were in one straight line down the entire length of the wall. In them lay sleeping brown faces, which peeped just out of the coverings. I was tucked into bed with one of the tall girls, because she talked to me in my mother tongue and seemed to soothe me.

I had arrived in the wonderful land of rosy skies, but I was not happy, as I had thought I should be. My long travel and the bewildering sights had exhausted me. I fell asleep, heaving deep, tired sobs. My tears were left to dry themselves in streaks, because neither my aunt nor my mother was near to wipe them away.

## II. The Cutting of My Long Hair

The first day in the land of apples was a bitter-cold one; for the snow still covered the ground, and the trees were bare. A large bell rang for breakfast, its loud metallic voice crashing through the belfry overhead and into our sensitive ears. The annoying clatter of shoes on bare floors gave us no peace. The constant clash of harsh noises, with an undercurrent of many voices murmuring an unknown tongue, made a bedlam within which I was securely tied. And though my spirit tore itself in struggling for its lost freedom, all was useless.

A paleface woman, with white hair, came up after us. We were placed in a line of girls who were marching into the dining room. These were Indian girls, in stiff shoes and closely clinging dresses. The small girls wore sleeved aprons and shingled hair. As I walked noiselessly in my soft moccasins, I felt like sinking to the floor, for my blanket had been stripped from my shoulders. I looked hard at the Indian girls, who seemed not to care that they were even more immodestly dressed than I, in their tightly fitting clothes. While we marched in, the boys entered at an opposite door. I watched for the three young braves who came in our party. I spied them in the rear ranks, looking as uncomfortable as I felt.

A small bell was tapped, and each of the pupils drew a chair from under the table. Supposing this act meant they were to be seated, I pulled out mine and at once slipped into it from one side. But when I turned my head, I saw that I was the only one seated, and all the rest at our table remained standing. Just as I began to rise, looking shyly around to see how chairs were to be used, a second bell was sounded. All were seated at last, and I had to crawl back into my chair again. I heard a man's voice at one end of the hall, and I looked around to see him. But all the others hung their heads over their plates. As I glanced at the long chain of tables, I caught the eyes of a paleface woman upon me. Immediately I dropped my eyes, wondering why I was so keenly watched by the strange woman. The man ceased his mutterings, and then a third bell was tapped. Every one picked up his knife and fork and began eating. I began crying instead, for by this time I was afraid to venture anything more.

But this eating by formula was not the hardest trial in that first day. Late in the morning, my friend Judéwin gave me a terrible warning. Judéwin knew a few words of English; and she had overheard the paleface woman talk about cutting our long, heavy hair. Our mothers had taught us that only unskilled warriors who were captured had their hair shingled by the enemy. Among our people, short hair was worn by mourners, and shingled hair by cowards!

We discussed our fate some moments, and when Judéwin said, "We have to submit, because they are strong," I rebelled.

"No, I will not submit!" I will struggle first!" I answered.

I watched my chance, and when no one noticed I disappeared. I crept up the stairs as quietly as I could in my squeaking shoes, – my moccasins had been exchanged for shoes. Along the hall I passed, without knowing whither I was going. Turning aside to an open door, I found a large room with three white beds in it. The windows were covered with dark green curtains, which made the room very dim. Thankful that no one was there, I directed my steps toward the corner farthest from the door. On my hands and knees I crawled under the bed, and cuddled myself in the dark corner.

From my hiding place I peered out, shuddering with fear whenever I heard footsteps near by. Though in the hall loud voices were calling my name, and I knew that even Judéwin was searching for me, I did not open my mouth to answer. Then the steps were quickened and the voices became excited. The sounds came nearer and nearer. Women and girls entered the room. I held my breath and watched them open closet doors and peep behind large trunks. Some one threw up the curtains, and the room was filled with sudden light. What caused them to stoop and look under the bed I do not know. I remember being dragged out, though I resisted by kicking and scratching wildly. In spite of myself, I was carried downstairs and tied fast in a chair.

I cried aloud, shaking my head all the while until I felt the cold blades of the scissors against my neck, and heard them gnaw off one of my thick braids. Then I lost my spirit. Since the day I was taken from my mother I had suffered extreme indignities. People had stared at me. I had been tossed about in the air like a wooden puppet. And now my long hair was shingled like a coward's! In my anguish I moaned for my mother, but no one came to comfort me. Not a soul reasoned quietly with me, as my own mother used to do; for now I was only one of many little animals driven by a herder.

## III. The Snow Episode

A short time after our arrival we three Dakotas were playing in the snowdrift. We were all still deaf to the English language, excepting Judéwin, who always heard such puzzling things. One morning we learned through her ears that we were forbidden to fall lengthwise in the snow, as we had been doing, to see our own impressions. However, before many hours we had forgotten the order, and were having great sport in the snow, when a shrill voice called us. Looking up, we saw an imperative hand beckoning us into the house. We shook the snow off ourselves, and started toward the woman as slowly as we dared.

Judéwin said: "Now the paleface is angry with us. She is going to punish us for falling into the snow. If she looks straight into your eyes and talks loudly, you must wait until she stops. Then, after a tiny pause, say, 'No.' " The rest of the way we practiced upon the little word "no."

As it happened, Thowin was summoned to judgment first. The door shut behind her with a click.

Judéwin and I stood silently listening at the keyhole. The paleface woman talked in very severe tones. Her words fell from her lips like crackling embers, and her inflection ran up like the small end of a switch. I understood her voice better than the things she was saying. I was certain we had made her very impatient with us. Judéwin heard enough of the words to realize all too late that she had taught us the wrong reply.

"Oh, poor Thowin!" she gasped, as she put both hands over her ears.

Just then I heard Thowin's tremulous answer, "No."

With an angry exclamation, the woman gave her a hard spanking. Then she stopped to say something. Judéwin said it was this: "Are you going to obey my word the next time?"

Thowin answered again with the only word at her command, "No."

This time the woman meant her blows to smart, for the poor frightened girl shrieked at the top of her voice. In the midst of the whipping the blows ceased abruptly, and the woman asked another question: "Are you going to fall in the snow again?"

Thowin gave her bad password another trial. We heard her say feebly, "No! No!"

With this the woman hid away her half-worn slipper, and led the child out, stroking her black shorn head. Perhaps it occurred to her that brute force is not the solution for such a problem. She did nothing to Judéwin nor to me. She only returned to us our unhappy comrade, and left us alone in the room.

During the first two or three seasons misunderstandings as ridiculous as this one of the snow episode frequently took place, bringing unjustifiable frights and punishments into our little lives.

Within a year I was able to express myself somewhat in broken English. As soon as I comprehended a part of what was said and done, a mischievous spirit of revenge possessed me. One day I was called in from my play for some misconduct. I had disregarded a rule which seemed to me very needlessly binding. I was sent into the kitchen to mash the turnips for dinner. It was noon, and steaming dishes were hastily carried into the dining-room. I hated turnips, and their odor which came from the brown jar was offensive to me. With fire in my heart, I took the wooden tool that the paleface woman held out to me. I stood upon a step, and, grasping the handle with both hands, I bent in hot rage over the turnips. I worked my vengeance upon them. All were so busily occupied that no one noticed me. I saw that the turnips were in a pulp, and that further beating could not improve them; but the order was, "Mash these turnips," and mash them I would! I renewed my energy; and as I sent the masher into the bottom of the jar, I felt a satisfying sensation that the weight of my body had gone into it.

Just here a paleface woman came up to my table. As she looked into the jar, she shoved my hands roughly aside. I stood fearless and angry. She placed her red hands upon the rim of the jar. Then she gave one lift and strode away from the table. But lo! the pulpy contents fell through the crumbled bottom to the floor! She spared me no scolding phrases that I had earned. I did not heed them. I felt triumphant in my revenge, though deep within me I was a wee bit sorry to have broken the jar.

As I sat eating my dinner, and saw that no turnips were served, I whooped in my heart for having once asserted the rebellion within me.

## IV. The Devil

Among the legends the old warriors used to tell me were many stories of evil spirits. But I was taught to fear them no more than those who stalked about in material guise. I never knew there was an insolent chieftain among the bad spirits, who dared to array his forces against the Great Spirit, until I heard this white man's legend from a paleface woman.

Out of a large book she showed me a picture of the white man's devil. I looked in horror upon the strong claws that grew out of his fur-covered fingers. His feet were like his hands. Trailing at his heels was a scaly tail tipped with a serpent's open jaws. His face was a patchwork: he had bearded cheeks, like some I had seen pale faces wear; his nose was an eagle's bill, and his sharp-pointed ears were pricked up like those of a sly fox. Above them a pair of cow's horns curved upward. I trembled with awe, and my heart throbbed in my throat, as I looked at the king of evil spirits. Then I heard the paleface woman say that this terrible creature roamed loose in the world, and that little girls who disobeyed school regulations were to be tortured by him.

That night I dreamt about this evil divinity. Once again I seemed to be in my mother's cottage. An Indian woman had come to visit my mother. On opposite sides of the kitchen stove, which stood in the center of the small house, my mother and her guest were seated in straight-backed chairs. I played with a train of empty spools hitched together on a string. It was night, and the wick burned feebly. Suddenly I heard some one turn our door-knob from without.

My mother and the woman hushed their talk, and both looked toward the door. It opened gradually. I waited behind the stove. The hinges squeaked as the door was slowly, very slowly pushed inward.

Then in rushed the devil! He was tall! He looked exactly like the picture I had seen of him in the white man's papers. He did not speak to my mother, because he did not know the Indian language, but his glittering yellow eyes were fastened upon me. He took long strides around the stove, passing behind the woman's chair. I threw down my spools, and ran to my mother. He did not fear her, but followed closely after me. Then I ran round and round the stove, crying aloud for help. But my mother and the woman seemed not to know my danger. They sat still, looking quietly upon the devil's chase after me. At last I grew dizzy. My head revolved as on a hidden pivot. My knees became numb, and doubled under my weight like a pair of knife blades without a spring. Beside my mother's chair I fell in a heap. Just as the devil stooped over me with outstretched claws my mother awoke from her quiet indifference, and lifted me on her lap. Whereupon the devil vanished, and I was awake.

On the following morning I took my revenge upon the devil. Stealing into the room where a wall of shelves was filled with books, I drew forth The Stories of the Bible. With a broken slate pencil I carried in my apron pocket, I began by scratching out his wicked eyes. A few moments later, when I was ready to leave the room, there was a ragged hole in the page where the picture of the devil had once been.

## V. Iron Routine

A loud-clamoring bell awakened us at half-past six in the cold winter mornings. From happy dreams of Western rolling lands and unlassoed freedom we tumbled out upon chilly bare floors back again into a paleface day. We had short time to jump into our shoes and clothes, and wet our eyes with icy water, before a small hand bell was vigorously rung for roll call.

There were too many drowsy children and too numerous orders for the day to waste a moment in any apology to nature for giving her children such a shock in the early morning. We rushed downstairs, bounding over two high steps at a time, to land in the assembly room.

A paleface woman, with a yellow-covered roll book open on her arm and a gnawed pencil in her hand, appeared at the door. Her small, tired face was coldly lighted with a pair of large gray eyes.

She stood still in a halo of authority, while over the rim of her spectacles her eyes pried nervously about the room. Having glanced at her long list of names and called out the first one, she tossed up her chin and peered through the crystals of her spectacles to make sure of the answer "Here."

Relentlessly her pencil black-marked our daily records if we were not present to respond to our names, and no chum of ours had done it successfully for us. No matter if a dull headache or the painful cough of slow consumption had delayed the absentee, there was only time enough to mark the tardiness. It was next to impossible to leave the iron routine after the civilizing machine had once begun its day's buzzing; and as it was inbred in me to suffer in silence rather than to appeal to the ears of one whose open eyes could not see my pain, I have many times trudged in the day's harness heavy-footed, like a dumb sick brute.

Once I lost a dear classmate. I remember well how she used to mope along at my side, until one morning she could not raise her head from her pillow. At her deathbed I stood weeping, as the paleface woman sat near her moistening the dry lips. Among the folds of the bedclothes I saw the open pages of the white man's Bible. The dying Indian girl talked disconnectedly of Jesus the Christ and the paleface who was cooling her swollen hands and feet.

I grew bitter, and censured the woman for cruel neglect of our physical ills. I despised the pencils that moved automatically, and the one teaspoon which dealt out, from a large bottle, healing to a row of variously ailing Indian children. I blamed the hard-working, well-meaning, ignorant woman who was inculcating in our hearts her superstitious ideas. Though I was sullen in all my little troubles, as soon as I felt better I was ready again to smile upon the cruel woman. Within a week I was again actively testing the chains which tightly bound my individuality like a mummy for burial.

The melancholy of those black days has left so long a shadow that it darkens the path of years that have since gone by. These sad memories rise above those of smoothly grinding school days. Perhaps my Indian nature is the moaning wind which stirs them now for their present record. But, however tempestuous this is within me, it comes out as the low voice of a curiously colored seashell, which is only for those ears that are bent with compassion to hear it.

## VI. Four Strange Summers

After my first three years of school, I roamed again in the Western country through four strange summers.

During this time I seemed to hang in the heart of chaos, beyond the touch or voice of human aid. My brother, being almost ten years my senior, did not quite understand my feelings. My mother had never gone inside of a schoolhouse, and so she was not capable of comforting her daughter who could read and write. Even nature seemed to have no place for me. I was neither a wee girl nor a tall one; neither a wild Indian nor a tame one. This deplorable situation was the effect of my brief course in the East, and the unsatisfactory "teenth" in a girl's years.

It was under these trying conditions that, one bright afternoon, as I sat restless and unhappy in my mother's cabin, I caught the sound of the spirited step of my brother's pony on the road which passed by our dwelling. Soon I heard the wheels of a light buckboard, and Dawée's familiar "Ho!" to his pony. He alighted upon the bare ground in front of our house. Tying his pony to one of the projecting corner logs of the low-roofed cottage, he stepped upon the wooden doorstep.

I met him there with a hurried greeting, and, as I passed by, he looked a quiet "What?" into my eyes.

When he began talking with my mother, I slipped the rope from the pony's bridle. Seizing the reins and bracing my feet against the dashboard, I wheeled around in an instant. The pony was ever ready to try his speed. Looking backward, I saw Dawée waving his hand to me. I turned with the curve in the road and disappeared. I followed the winding road which crawled upward between the bases of little hillocks. Deep water-worn ditches ran parallel on either side. A strong wind blew against my cheeks and fluttered my sleeves. The pony reached the top of the highest hill, and began an even race on the level lands. There was nothing moving within that great circular horizon of the Dakota prairies save the tall grasses, over which the wind blew and rolled off in long, shadowy waves.

Within this vast wigwam of blue and green I rode reckless and insignificant. It satisfied my small consciousness to see the white foam fly from the pony's mouth.

Suddenly, out of the earth a coyote came forth at a swinging trot that was taking the cunning thief toward the hills and the village beyond. Upon the moment's impulse, I gave him a long chase and a wholesome fright. As I turned away to go back to the village, the wolf sank down upon his haunches for rest, for it was a hot summer day; and as I drove slowly homeward, I saw his sharp nose still pointed at me, until I vanished below the margin of the hilltops.

In a little while I came in sight of my mother's house. Dawée stood in the yard, laughing at an old warrior who was pointing his forefinger, and again waving his whole hand, toward the hills. With his blanket drawn over one shoulder, he talked and motioned excitedly. Dawée turned the old man by the shoulder and pointed me out to him.

"Oh, han!" (Oh, yes) the warrior muttered, and went his way. He had climbed the top of his favorite barren hill to survey the surrounding prairies, when he spied my chase after the coyote. His keen eyes recognized the pony and driver. At once uneasy for my safety, he had come running to my mother's cabin to give her warning. I did not appreciate his kindly interest, for there was an unrest gnawing at my heart.

As soon as he went away, I asked Dawée about something else.

"No, my baby sister, I cannot take you with me to the party tonight," he replied. Though I was not far from fifteen, and I felt that before long I should enjoy all the privileges of my tall cousin, Dawée persisted in calling me his baby sister.

That moonlight night, I cried in my mother's presence when I heard the jolly young people pass by our cottage. They were no more young braves in blankets and eagle plumes, nor Indian maids with prettily painted cheeks. They had gone three years to school in the East, and had become civilized. The young men wore the white man's coat and trousers, with bright neckties. The girls wore tight muslin dresses, with ribbons at neck and waist. At these gatherings they talked English. I could speak English almost as well as my brother, but I was not properly dressed to be taken along. I had no hat, no ribbons, and no close-fitting gown. Since my return from school I had thrown away my shoes, and wore again the soft moccasins.

While Dawée was busily preparing to go I controlled my tears. But when I heard him bounding away on his pony, I buried my face in my arms and cried hot tears.

My mother was troubled by my unhappiness. Coming to my side, she offered me the only printed matter we had in our home. It was an Indian Bible, given her some years ago by a missionary. She tried to console me. "Here, my child, are the white man's papers. Read a little from them," she said most piously.

I took it from her hand, for her sake; but my enraged spirit felt more like burning the book, which afforded me no help, and was a perfect delusion to my mother. I did not read it, but laid it unopened on the floor, where I sat on my feet. The dim yellow light of the braided muslin burning in a small vessel of oil flickered and sizzled in the awful silent storm which followed my rejection of the Bible.

Now my wrath against the fates consumed my tears before they reached my eyes. I sat stony, with a bowed head. My mother threw a shawl over her head and shoulders, and stepped out into the night.

After an uncertain solitude, I was suddenly aroused by a loud cry piercing the night. It was my mother's voice wailing among the barren hills which held the bones of buried warriors. She called aloud for her brothers' spirits to support her in her helpless misery. My fingers grey icy cold, as I realized that my unrestrained tears had betrayed my suffering to her, and she was grieving for me.

Before she returned, though I knew she was on her way, for she had ceased her weeping, I extinguished the light, and leaned my head on the window sill.

Many schemes of running away from my surroundings hovered about in my mind. A few more moons of such a turmoil drove me away to the eastern school. I rode on the white man's iron steed, thinking it would bring me back to my mother in a few winters, when I should be grown tall, and there would be congenial friends awaiting me.

## VII. Incurring My Mother's Displeasure

In the second journey to the East I had not come without some precautions. I had a secret interview with one of our best medicine men, and when I left his wigwam I carried securely in my sleeve a tiny bunch of magic roots. This possession assured me of friends wherever I should go. So absolutely did I believe in its charms that I wore it through all the school routine for more than a year. Then, before I lost my faith in the dead roots, I lost the little buckskin bag containing all my good luck.

At the close of this second term of three years I was the proud owner of my first diploma. The following autumn I ventured upon a college career against my mother's will.

I had written for her approval, but in her reply I found no encouragement. She called my notice to her neighbors' children, who had completed their education in three years. They had returned to their homes, and were then talking English with the frontier settlers. Her few words hinted that I had better give up my slow attempt to learn the white man's ways, and be content to roam over the prairies and find my living upon wild roots. I silenced her by deliberate disobedience.

Thus, homeless and heavy-hearted, I began anew my life among strangers.

As I hid myself in my little room in the college dormitory, away from the scornful and yet curious eyes of the students, I pined for sympathy. Often I wept in secret, wishing I had gone West, to be nourished by my mother's love, instead of remaining among a cold race whose hearts were frozen hard with prejudice.

During the fall and winter seasons I scarcely had a real friend, though by that time several of my classmates were courteous to me at a safe distance.

My mother had not yet forgiven my rudeness to her, and I had no moment for letter-writing. By daylight and lamplight, I spun with reeds and thistles, until my hands were tired from their weaving, the magic design which promised me the white man's respect.

At length, in the spring term, I entered an oratorical contest among the various classes. As the day of competition approached, it did not seem possible that the event was so near at hand, but it came. In the chapel the classes assembled together, with their invited guests. The high platform was carpeted, and gayly festooned with college colors. A bright white light illumined the room, and outlined clearly the great polished beams that arched the domed ceiling. The assembled crowds filled the air with pulsating murmurs. When the hour for speaking arrived all were hushed. But on the wall the old clock which pointed out the trying moment ticked calmly on.

One after another I saw and heard the orators. Still, I could not realize that they longed for the favorable decision of the judges as much as I did. Each contestant received a loud burst of applause, and some were cheered heartily. Too soon my turn came, and I paused a moment behind the curtains for a deep breath. After my concluding words, I heard the same applause that the others had called out.

Upon my retreating steps, I was astounded to receive from my fellow-students a large bouquet of roses tied with flowing ribbons. With the lovely flowers I fled from the stage. This friendly token was a rebuke to me for the hard feelings I had borne them.

Later, the decision of the judges awarded me the first place. Then there was a mad uproar in the hall, where my classmates sang and shouted my name at the top of their lungs; and the disappointed students howled and brayed in fearfully dissonant tin trumpets. In this excitement, happy students rushed forward to offer their congratulations. And I could not conceal a smile when they wished to escort me in a procession to the students' parlor, where all were going to calm themselves. Thanking them for the kind spirit which prompted them to make such a proposition, I walked alone with the night to my own little room.

A few weeks afterward, I appeared as the college representative in another contest. This time the competition was among orators from different colleges in our State. It was held at the State capital, in one of the largest opera houses.

Here again was a strong prejudice against my people. In the evening, as the great audience filled the house, the student bodies began warring among themselves. Fortunately, I was spared witnessing any of the noisy wrangling before the contest began. The slurs against the Indian that stained the lips of our opponents were already burning like a dry fever within my breast.

But after the orations were delivered a deeper burn awaited me. There, before that vast ocean of eyes, some college rowdies threw out a large white flag, with a drawing of a most forlorn Indian girl on it. Under this they had printed in bold black letters words that ridiculed the college which was represented by a "squaw." Such worse than barbarian rudeness embittered me. While we waited for the verdict of the judges, I gleamed fiercely upon the throngs of palefaces. My teeth were hard set, as I saw the white flag still floating insolently in the air.

Then anxiously we watched the man carry toward the stage the envelope containing the final decision.

There were two prizes given, that night, and one of them was mine!

The evil spirit laughed within me when the white flag dropped out of sight, and the hands which hurled it hung limp in defeat.

Leaving the crowd as quickly as possible, I was soon in my room. The rest of the night I sat in an armchair and gazed into the crackling fire. I laughed no more in triumph when thus alone. The little taste of victory did not satisfy a hunger in my heart. In my mind I saw my mother far away on the Western plains, and she was holding a charge against me.

## An Indian Teacher Among Indians

### I. My First Day

Though an illness left me unable to continue my college course, my pride kept me from returning to my mother. Had she known of my worn condition, she would have said the white man's papers were not worth the freedom and health I had lost by them. Such a rebuke from my mother would have been unbearable, and as I felt then it would be far too true to be comfortable.

Since the winter when I had my first dreams about red apples I had been traveling slowly toward the morning horizon. There had been no doubt about the direction in which I wished to go to spend my energies in a work for the Indian race. Thus I had written my mother briefly, saying my plan for the year was to teach in an Eastern Indian school. Sending this message to her in the West, I started at once eastward.

Thus I found myself, tired and hot, in a black veiling of car smoke, as I stood wearily on a street corner of an old-fashioned town, waiting for a car. In a few moments more I should be on the school grounds, where a new work was ready for my inexperienced hands.

Upon entering the school campus, I was surprised at the thickly clustered buildings which made it a quaint little village, much more interesting than the town itself. The large trees among the houses gave the place a cool, refreshing shade, and the grass a deeper green. Within this large court of grass and trees stood a low green pump. The queer boxlike case had a revolving handle on its side, which clanked and creaked constantly.

I made myself known, and was shown to my room, – a small, carpeted room, with ghastly walls and ceiling. The two windows, both on the same side, were curtained with heavy muslin yellowed with age. A clean white bed was in one corner of the room, and opposite it was a square pine table covered with a black woolen blanket.

Without removing my hat from my head, I seated myself in one of the two stiff-backed chairs that were placed beside the table. For several heart throbs I sat still looking from ceiling to floor, from wall to wall, trying hard to imagine years of contentment there. Even while I was wondering if my exhausted strength would sustain me through this undertaking, I heard a heavy tread stop at my door. Opening it, I met the imposing figure of a stately gray-haired man. With a light straw hat in one hand, and the right hand extended for greeting, he smiled kindly upon me. For some reason I was awed by his wondrous height and his strong square shoulders, which I felt were a finger's length above my head.

I was always slight, and my serious illness in the early spring had made me look rather frail and languid. His quick eye measured my height and breadth. Then he looked into my face. I imagined that a visible shadow flitted across his countenance as he let my hand fall. I knew he was no other than my employer.

"Ah ha! so you are the little Indian girl who created the excitement among the college orators!" he said, more to himself than to me. I thought I heard a subtle note of disappointment in his voice. Looking in from where he stood, with one sweeping glance, he asked if I lacked anything for my room.

After he turned to go, I listened to his step until it grew faint and was lost in the distance. I was aware that my car-smoked appearance had not concealed the lines of pain on my face.

For a short moment my spirit laughed at my ill fortune, and I entertained the idea of exerting myself to make an improvement. But as I tossed my hat off a leaden weakness came over me, and I felt as if years of weariness lay like water-soaked logs upon me. I threw myself upon the bed, and, closing my eyes, forgot my good intention.

## II. A Trip Westward

One sultry month I sat at a desk heaped up with work. Now, as I recall it, I wonder how I could have dared to disregard nature's warning with such recklessness. Fortunately, my inheritance of a marvelous endurance enabled me to bend without breaking.

Though I had gone to and fro, from my room to the office, in an unhappy silence, I was watched by those around me. On an early morning I was summoned to the superintendent's office. For a half-hour I listened to his words, and when I returned to my room I remembered one sentence above the rest. It was this: "I am going to turn you loose to pasture!" He was sending me West to gather Indian pupils for the school, and this was his way of expressing it.

I needed nourishment, but the midsummer's travel across the continent to search the hot prairies for overconfident parents who would intrust their children to strangers was a lean pasturage. However, I dwelt on the hope of seeing my mother. I tried to reason that a change was a rest. Within a couple of days I started toward my mother's home.

The intense heat and the sticky car smoke that followed my homeward trail did not noticeably restore my vitality. Hour after hour I gazed upon the country which was receding rapidly from me. I noticed the gradual expansion of the horizon as we emerged out of the forests into the plains. The great high buildings, whose towers overlooked the dense woodlands, and whose gigantic clusters formed large cities, diminished, together with the groves, until only little log cabins lay snugly in the bosom of the vast prairie. The cloud shadows which drifted about on the waving yellow of long-dried grasses thrilled me like the meeting of old friends.

At a small station, consisting of a single frame house with a rickety board walk around it, I alighted from the iron home, just thirty miles from my mother and my brother Dawée. A strong hot wind seemed determined to blow my hat off, and return me to olden days when I roamed bareheaded over the hills. After the puffing engine of my train was gone, I stood on the platform in deep solitude. In the distance I saw the gently rolling land leap up into bare hills. At their bases a broad gray road was winding itself round about them until it came by the station. Among these hills I rode in a light conveyance, with a trusty driver, whose unkempt flaxen hair hung shaggy about his ears and his leather neck of reddish tan. From accident or decay he had lost one of his long front teeth.

Though I call him a paleface, his cheeks were of a brick red. His moist blue eyes, blurred and bloodshot, twitched involuntarily. For a long time he had driven through grass and snow from this solitary station to the Indian village. His weather-stained clothes fitted badly his warped shoulders. He was stooped, and his protruding chin, with its tuft of dry flax, nodded as monotonously as did the head of his faithful beast.

All the morning I looked about me, recognizing old familiar sky lines of rugged bluffs and round-topped hills. By the roadside I caught glimpses of various plants whose sweet roots were delicacies among my people. When I saw the first cone-shaped wigwam, I could not help uttering an exclamation which caused my driver a sudden jump out of his drowsy nodding.

At noon, as we drove through the eastern edge of the reservation, I grew very impatient and restless. Constantly I wondered what my mother would say upon seeing her little daughter grown tall. I had not written her the day of my arrival, thinking I would surprise her. Crossing a ravine thicketed with low shrubs and plum bushes, we approached a large yellow acre of wild sunflowers. Just beyond this nature's garden we drew near to my mother's cottage. Close by the log cabin stood a little canvas-covered wigwam. The driver stopped in front of the open door, and in a long moment my mother appeared at the threshold.

I had expected her to run out to greet me, but she stood still, all the while staring at the weather-beaten man at my side. At length, when her loftiness became unbearable, I called to her, "Mother, why do you stop?"

This seemed to break the evil moment, and she hastened out to hold my head against her cheek.

"My daughter, what madness possessed you to bring home such a fellow?" she asked, pointing at the driver, who was fumbling in his pockets for change while he held the bill I gave him between his jagged teeth.

"Bring him! Why, no, mother, he has brought me! He is a driver!" I exclaimed.

Upon this revelation, my mother threw her arms about me and apologized for her mistaken inference. We laughed away the momentary hurt. Then she built a brisk fire on the ground in the tepee, and hung a blackened coffeepot on one of the prongs of a forked pole which leaned over the flames. Placing a pan on a heap of red embers, she baked some unleavened bread. This light luncheon she brought into the cabin, and arranged on a table covered with a checkered oilcloth.

My mother had never gone to school, and though she meant always to give up her own customs for such of the white man's ways as pleased her, she made only compromises. Her two windows, directly opposite each other, she curtained with a pink-flowered print. The naked logs were unstained, and rudely carved with the axe so as to fit into one another. The sod roof was trying to boast of tiny sunflowers, the seeds of which had probably been planted by the constant wind. As I leaned my head against the logs, I discovered the peculiar odor that I could not forget. The rains had soaked the earth and roof so that the smell of damp clay was but the natural breath of such a dwelling.

"Mother, why is not your house cemented? Do you have no interest in a more comfortable shelter?" I asked, when the apparent inconveniences of her home seemed to suggest indifference on her part.

"You forget, my child, that I am now old, and I do not work with beads any more. Your brother Dawée, too, has lost his position, and we are left without means to buy even a morsel of food," she replied.

Dawée was a government clerk in our reservation when I last heard from him. I was surprised upon hearing what my mother said concerning his lack of employment. Seeing the puzzled expression on my face, she continued: "Dawée! Oh, has he not told you that the Great Father at Washington sent a white son to take your brother's pen from him? Since then Dawée has not been able to make use of the education the Eastern school has given him."

I found no words with which to answer satisfactorily. I found no reason with which to cool my inflamed feelings.

Dawée was a whole day's journey off on the prairie, and my mother did not expect him until the next day. We were silent.

When, at length, I raised my head to hear more clearly the moaning of the wind in the corner logs, I noticed the daylight streaming into the dingy room through several places where the logs fitted unevenly. Turning to my mother, I urged her to tell me more about Dawée's trouble, but she only said: "Well, my daughter, this village has been these many winters a refuge for white robbers. The Indian cannot complain to the Great Father in Washington without suffering outrage for it here. Dawée tried to secure justice for our tribe in a small matter, and today you see the folly of it."

Again, though she stopped to hear what I might say, I was silent.

"My child, there is only one source of justice, and I have been praying steadfastly to the Great Spirit to avenge our wrongs," she said, seeing I did not move my lips.

My shattered energy was unable to hold longer any faith, and I cried out desperately: "Mother, don't pray again! The Great Spirit does not care if we live or die! Let us not look for good or justice: then we shall not be disappointed!"

"Sh! my child, do not talk so madly. There is Taku Iyotan Wasaka,[4] to which I pray," she answered, as she stroked my head again as she used to do when I was a smaller child.

## III. My Mother's Curse upon White Settlers

One black night mother and I sat alone in the dim starlight, in front of our wigwam. We were facing the river, as we talked about the shrinking limits of the village. She told me about the poverty-stricken white settlers, who lived in caves dug in the long ravines of the high hills across the river.

A whole tribe of broad-footed white beggars had rushed hither to make claims on those wild lands. Even as she was telling this I spied a small glimmering light in the bluffs.

"That is a white man's lodge where you see the burning fire," she said. Then, a short distance from it, only a little lower than the first, was another light. As I became accustomed to the night, I saw more and more twinkling lights, here and there, scattered all along the wide black margin of the river.

Still looking toward the distant firelight, my mother continued: "My daughter, beware of the paleface. It was the cruel paleface who caused the death of your sister and your uncle, my brave brother. It is this same paleface who offers in one palm the holy papers, and with the other gives a holy baptism of firewater. He is the hypocrite who reads with one eye, 'Thou shalt not kill,' and with the other gloats upon the sufferings of the Indian race." Then suddenly discovering a new fire in the bluffs, she exclaimed, "Well, well, my daughter, there is the light of another white rascal!"

She sprang to her feet, and, standing firm beside her wigwam, she sent a curse upon those who sat around the hated white man's light. Raising her right arm forcibly into line with her eye, she threw her whole might into her doubled fist as she shot it vehemently at the strangers. Long she held her outstretched fingers toward the settler's lodge, as if an invisible power passed from them to the evil at which she aimed.

## IV. Retrospection

Leaving my mother, I returned to the school in the East. As months passed over me, I slowly comprehended that the large army of white teachers in Indian schools had a larger missionary creed than I had suspected.

It was one which included self-preservation quite as much as Indian education. When I saw an opium-eater holding a position as teacher of Indians, I did not understand what good was expected, until a Christian in power replied that this pumpkin-colored creature had a feeble mother to support. An inebriate paleface sat stupid in a doctor's chair, while Indian patients carried their ailments to untimely graves, because his fair wife was dependent upon him for her daily food.

I find it hard to count that white man a teacher who tortured an ambitious Indian youth by frequently reminding the brave changeling that he was nothing but a "government pauper."

Though I burned with indignation upon discovering on every side instances no less shameful than those I have mentioned, there was no present help. Even the few rare ones who have worked nobly for my race were powerless to choose workmen like themselves. To be sure, a man was sent from the Great Father to inspect Indian schools, but what he saw was usually the students' sample work *made* for exhibition. I was nettled by this sly cunning of the workmen who hoodwinked the Indian's pale Father at Washington.

My illness, which prevented the conclusion of my college course, together with my mother's stories of the encroaching frontier settlers, left me in no mood to strain my eyes in searching for latent good in my white co-workers.

At this stage of my own evolution, I was ready to curse men of small capacity for being the dwarfs their God had made them. In the process of my education I had lost all consciousness of the nature world about me. Thus, when a hidden rage took me to the small white-walled prison which I then called my room, I unknowingly turned away from my one salvation.

Alone in my room, I sat like the petrified Indian woman of whom my mother used to tell me. I

[4] An absolute Power [Zitkala-Ša's note].

wished my heart's burdens would turn me to unfeeling stone. But alive, in my tomb, I was destitute!

For the white man's papers I had given up my faith in the Great Spirit. For these same papers I had forgotten the healing in trees and brooks. On account of my mother's simple view of life, and my lack of any, I gave her up, also. I made no friends among the race of people I loathed. Like a slender tree, I had been uprooted from my mother, nature, and God. I was shorn of my branches, which had waved in sympathy and love for home and friends. The natural coat of bark which had protected my oversensitive nature was scraped off to the very quick.

Now a cold bare pole I seemed to be, planted in a strange earth. Still, I seemed to hope a day would come when my mute aching head, reared upward to the sky, would flash a zigzag lightning across the heavens. With this dream of vent for a long-pent consciousness, I walked again amid the crowds.

At last, one weary day in the schoolroom, a new idea presented itself to me. It was a new way of solving the problem of my inner self. I liked it. Thus I resigned my position as teacher; and now I am in an Eastern city, following the long course of study I have set for myself. Now, as I look back upon the recent past, I see it from a distance, as a whole. I remember how, from morning till evening, many specimens of civilized peoples visited the Indian school. The city folks with canes and eyeglasses, the countrymen with sunburnt cheeks and clumsy feet, forgot their relative social ranks in an ignorant curiosity. Both sorts of these Christian palefaces were alike astounded at seeing the children of savage warriors so docile and industrious.

As answers to their shallow inquiries they received the students' sample work to look upon. Examining the neatly figured pages, and gazing upon the Indian girls and boys bending over their books, the white visitors walked out of the schoolhouse well satisfied: they were educating the children of the red man! They were paying a liberal fee to the government employees in whose able hands lay the small forest of Indian timber.

In this fashion many have passed idly through the Indian schools during the last decade, afterward to boast of their charity to the North American Indian. But few there are who have paused to question whether real life or long-lasting death lies beneath this semblance of civilization.

## The Soft-Hearted Sioux

### I

Beside the open fire I sat within our tepee. With my red blanket wrapped tightly about my crossed legs, I was thinking of the coming season, my sixteenth winter. On either side of the wigwam were my parents. My father was whistling a tune between his teeth while polishing with his bare hand a red stone pipe he had recently carved. Almost in front of me, beyond the center fire, my old grandmother sat near the entranceway.

She turned her face toward her right and addressed most of her words to my mother. Now and then she spoke to me, but never did she allow her eyes to rest upon her daughter's husband, my father. It was only upon rare occasions that my grandmother said anything to him. Thus his ears were open and ready to catch the smallest wish she might express. Sometimes when my grandmother had been saying things which pleased him, my father used to comment upon them. At other times, when he could not approve of what was spoken, he used to work or smoke silently.

On this night my old grandmother began her talk about me. Filling the bowl of her red stone pipe with dry willow bark, she looked across at me.

"My grandchild, you are tall and are no longer a little boy." Narrowing her old eyes, she asked, "My grandchild, when are you going to bring here a handsome young woman?" I stared into the fire rather than meet her gaze. Waiting for my answer, she stooped forward and through the long stem drew a flame into the red stone pipe.

I smiled while my eyes were still fixed upon the bright fire, but I said nothing in reply. Turning to my mother, she offered her the pipe. I glanced at my grandmother. The loose buckskin sleeve fell off at her elbow and showed a wrist covered with silver bracelets. Holding up the fingers of her left hand, she named off the desirable young women of our village.

"Which one, my grandchild, which one?" she questioned.

"Hoh!" I said, pulling at my blanket in confusion. "Not yet!" Here my mother passed the pipe over the fire to my father. Then she, too, began speaking of what I should do.

"My son, be always active. Do not dislike a long hunt. Learn to provide much buffalo meat and many buckskins before you bring home a wife." Presently my father gave the pipe to my grandmother, and he took his turn in the exhortations.

"Ho, my son, I have been counting in my heart the bravest warriors of our people. There is not one of them who won his title in his sixteenth winter. My son, it is a great thing for some brave of sixteen winters to do."

Not a word had I to give in answer. I knew well the fame of my warrior father. He had earned the right of speaking such words, though even he himself was a brave only at my age. Refusing to smoke my grandmother's pipe because my heart was too much stirred by their words, and sorely troubled with a fear lest I should disappoint them, I arose to go. Drawing my blanket over my shoulders, I said, as I stepped toward the entranceway: "I go to hobble my pony. It is now late in the night."

## II

Nine winters' snows had buried deep that night when my old grandmother, together with my father and mother, designed my future with the glow of a camp fire upon it.

Yet I did not grow up the warrior, huntsman, and husband I was to have been. At the mission school I learned it was wrong to kill. Nine winters I hunted for the soft heart of Christ, and prayed for the huntsmen who chased the buffalo on the plains.

In the autumn of the tenth year I was sent back to my tribe to preach Christianity to them. With the white man's Bible in my hand, and the white man's tender heart in my breast, I returned to my own people.

Wearing a foreigner's dress, I walked, a stranger, into my father's village.

Asking my way, for I had not forgotten my native tongue, an old man led me toward the tepee where my father lay. From my old companion I learned that my father had been sick many moons. As we drew near the tepee, I heard the chanting of a medicine-man within it. At once I wished to enter in and drive from my home the sorcerer of the plains, but the old warrior checked me. "Ho, wait outside until the medicine-man leaves your father," he said. While talking he scanned me from head to feet. Then he retraced his steps toward the heart of the camping-ground.

My father's dwelling was on the outer limits of the round-faced village. With every heartthrob I grew more impatient to enter the wigwam.

While I turned the leaves of my Bible with nervous fingers, the medicine-man came forth from the dwelling and walked hurriedly away. His head and face were closely covered with the loose robe which draped his entire figure.

He was tall and large. His long strides I have never forgot. They seemed to me then the uncanny gait of eternal death. Quickly pocketing my Bible, I went into the tepee.

Upon a mat lay my father, with furrowed face and gray hair. His eyes and cheeks were sunken far into his head. His sallow skin lay thin upon his pinched nose and high cheekbones. Stooping over him, I took his fevered hand. "How, Ate?" I greeted him. A light flashed from his listless eyes and his dried lips parted. "My son!" he murmured, in a feeble voice. Then again the wave of joy and recognition receded. He closed his eyes, and his hand dropped from my open palm to the ground.

Looking about, I saw an old woman sitting with bowed head. Shaking hands with her, I recognized my mother. I sat down between my father and mother as I used to do, but I did not feel at home. The place where my old grandmother used to sit was now unoccupied. With my mother I bowed my head. Alike our throats were choked and tears were streaming from our eyes; but far apart in spirit our ideas and faiths separated us. My grief was for the soul unsaved; and I thought my mother wept to see a brave man's body broken by sickness.

Useless was my attempt to change the faith in the medicine-man to that abstract power named God. Then one day I became righteously mad with anger that the medicine-man should thus ensnare my father's soul. And when he came to chant his sacred songs I pointed toward the door and bade him go! The man's eyes glared upon me for an instant. Slowly gathering his robe about him, he turned his back upon the sick man and stepped out of our wigwam. "Ha, ha, ha! my son, I can not live without the medicine-man!" I heard my father cry when the sacred man was gone.

## III

On a bright day, when the winged seeds of the prairie-grass were flying hither and thither, I walked solemnly toward the centre of the camping-ground. My heart beat hard and irregularly at my side. Tighter I grasped the sacred book I carried under my arm. Now was the beginning of life's work.

Though I knew it would be hard, I did not once feel that failure was to be my reward. As I stepped unevenly on the rolling ground, I thought of the warriors soon to wash off their war-paints and follow me.

At length I reached the place where the people had assembled to hear me preach. In a large circle men and women sat upon the dry red grass. Within the ring I stood, with the white man's Bible in my hand. I tried to tell them of the soft heart of Christ.

In silence the vast circle of bareheaded warriors sat under an afternoon sun. At last, wiping the wet from my brow, I took my place in the ring. The hush of the assembly filled me with great hope.

I was turning my thoughts upward to the sky in gratitude, when a stir called me to earth again.

A tall, strong man arose. His loose robe hung in folds over his right shoulder. A pair of snapping black eyes fastened themselves like the poisonous fangs of a serpent upon me. He was the medicine-man. A tremor played about my heart and a chill cooled the fire in my veins.

Scornfully he pointed a long forefinger in my direction and asked:

"What loyal son is he who, returning to his father's people, wears a foreigner's dress?" He paused a moment, and then continued: "The dress of that foreigner of whom a story says he bound a native of our land, and heaping dry sticks around him, kindled a fire at his feet!" Waving his hand toward me, he exclaimed, "Here is the traitor to his people!"

I was helpless. Before the eyes of the crowd the cunning magician turned my honest heart into a vile nest of treachery. Alas! the people frowned as they looked upon me.

"Listen!" he went on. "Which one of you who have eyed the young man can see through his bosom and warn the people of the nest of young snakes hatching there? Whose ear was so acute that he caught the hissing of snakes whenever the young man opened his mouth? This one has not only proven false to you, but even to the Great Spirit who made him. He is a fool! Why do you sit here giving ear to a foolish man who could not defend his people because he fears to kill, who could not bring venison to renew the life of his sick father? With his prayers, let him drive away the enemy! With his soft heart, let him keep off starvation! We shall go elsewhere to dwell upon an untainted ground."

With this he disbanded the people. When the sun lowered in the west and the winds were quiet, the village of cone-shaped tepees was gone. The medicine-man had won the hearts of the people.

Only my father's dwelling was left to mark the fighting-ground.

## IV

From a long night at my father's bedside I came out to look upon the morning. The yellow sun hung equally between the snow-covered land and the cloudless blue sky. The light of the new day was cold. The strong breath of winter crusted the snow and fitted crystal shells over the rivers and lakes. As I stood in front of the tepee, thinking of the vast prairies which separated us from our tribe, and wondering if the high sky likewise separated the soft-hearted Son of God from us, the icy blast from the North blew through my hair and skull. My neglected hair had grown long and fell upon my neck.

My father had not risen from his bed since the day the medicine-man led the people away. Though I read from the Bible and prayed beside him upon my knees, my father would not listen. Yet I believed my prayers were not unheeded in heaven.

"Ha, ha, ha! my son," my father groaned upon the first snowfall. "My son, our food is gone. There is no one to bring me meat! My son, your soft heart has unfitted you for everything!" Then covering his face with the buffalo-robe, he said no more. Now while I stood out in that cold winter morning, I was starving. For two days I had not seen any food. But my own cold and hunger did not harass my soul as did the whining cry of the sick old man.

Stepping again into the tepee, I untied my snow-shoes, which were fastened to the tentpoles.

My poor mother, watching by the sick one, and faithfully heaping wood upon the centre fire, spoke to me:

"My son, do not fail again to bring your father meat, or he will starve to death."

"How, Ina," I answered, sorrowfully. From the tepee I started forth again to hunt food for my aged parents. All day I tracked the white level lands in vain. Nowhere, nowhere were there any other footprints but my own! In the evening of this third fast-day I came back without meat. Only a bundle of sticks for the fire I brought on my back. Dropping the wood outside, I lifted the door-flap and set one foot within the tepee.

There I grew dizzy and numb. My eyes swam in tears. Before me lay my old gray-haired father sobbing like a child. In his horny hands he clutched the buffalo-robe, and with his teeth he was gnawing off the edges. Chewing the dry stiff hair and buffalo-skin, my father's eyes sought my hands. Upon seeing them empty, he cried out:

"My son, your soft heart will let me starve before you bring me meat! Two hills eastward stand a herd of cattle. Yet you will see me die before you bring me food!"

Leaving my mother lying with covered head upon her mat, I rushed out into the night.

With a strange warmth in my heart and swiftness in my feet, I climbed over the first hill, and soon the second one. The moonlight upon the white country showed me a clear path to the white man's cattle. With my hand upon the knife in my belt, I leaned heavily against the fence while counting the herd.

Twenty in all I numbered. From among them I chose the best-fattened creature. Leaping over the fence, I plunged my knife into it.

My long knife was sharp, and my hands, no more fearful and slow, slashed off choice chunks of warm flesh. Bending under the meat I had taken for my starving father, I hurried across the prairie.

Toward home I fairly ran with the life-giving food I carried upon my back. Hardly had I climbed the second hill when I heard sounds coming after me. Faster and faster I ran with my load for my father, but the sounds were gaining upon me. I heard the clicking of snowshoes and the squeaking of the leather straps at my heels; yet I did not turn to see what pursued me, for I was intent upon reaching my father. Suddenly like thunder an angry voice shouted curses and threats into my ear! A rough hand wrenched my shoulder and took the meat from me! I stopped struggling to run. A deafening whir filled my head. The moon and stars began to move. Now the white prairie was sky, and the stars lay under my feet. Now again they were turning. At last the starry blue rose up into place. The noise in my ears was still. A great quiet filled the air. In my hand I found my long knife dripping with blood. At my feet a man's figure lay prone in blood-red snow. The horrible scene about me seemed a trick of my senses, for I could not understand it was real. Looking long upon the blood-stained snow, the load of meat for my starving father reached my recognition at last. Quickly I tossed it over my shoulder and started again homeward.

Tired and haunted I reached the door of the wigwam. Carrying the food before me, I entered with it into the tepee.

"Father, here is food!" I cried, as I dropped the meat near my mother. No answer came. Turning about, I beheld my gray-haired father dead! I saw by the unsteady firelight an old gray-haired skeleton lying rigid and stiff.

Out into the open I started, but the snow at my feet became bloody.

## V

On the day after my father's death, having led my mother to the camp of the medicine-man, I gave myself up to those who were searching for the murderer of the paleface.

They bound me hand and foot. Here in this cell I was placed four days ago.

The shrieking winter winds have followed me hither. Rattling the bars, they howl unceasingly: "Your soft heart! your soft heart will see me die before you bring me food!" Hark! something is clanking the chain on the door. It is being opened. From the dark night without a black figure crosses the threshold. . . . It is the guard. He comes to warn me of my fate. He tells me that tomorrow I must die. In his stern face I laugh aloud. I do not fear death.

Yet I wonder who shall come to welcome me in the realm of strange sight. Will the loving Jesus grant me pardon and give my soul a soothing sleep? or will my warrior father greet me and receive me as his son? Will my spirit fly upward to a happy heaven? or shall I sink into the bottomless pit, an outcast from a God of infinite love?

Soon, soon I shall know, for now I see the east is growing red. My heart is strong. My face is calm. My eyes are dry and eager for new scenes. My hands hang quietly at my side. Serene and brave, my soul awaits the men to perch me on the gallows for another flight. I go.

## A Warrior's Daughter

In the afternoon shadow of a large tepee, with red-painted smoke lapels, sat a warrior father with crossed shins. His head was so poised that his eye swept easily the vast level land to the eastern horizon line.

He was the chieftain's bravest warrior. He had won by heroic deeds the privilege of staking his wigwam within the great circle of tepees.

He was also one of the most generous gift givers to the toothless old people. For this he was entitled to the red-painted smoke lapels on his cone-shaped dwelling. He was proud of his honors. He never wearied of rehearsing nightly his own brave deeds. Though by wigwam fires he prated much of his high rank and widespread fame, his great joy was a wee black-eyed daughter of eight sturdy winters. Thus as he sat upon the soft grass, with his wife at his side, bent over her bead work, he was singing a dance song, and beat lightly the rhythm with his slender hands.

His shrewd eyes softened with pleasure as he watched the easy movements of the small body dancing on the green before him.

Tusee is taking her first dancing lesson. Her tightly-braided hair curves over both brown ears like a pair of crooked little horns which glisten in the summer sun.

With her snugly moccasined feet close together, and a wee hand at her belt to stay the long string of beads which hang from her bare neck, she bends her knees gently to the rhythm of her father's voice.

Now she ventures upon the earnest movement, slightly upward and sidewise, in a circle. At length the song drops into a closing cadence, and the little woman, clad in beaded deerskin, sits down beside the elder one. Like her mother, she sits upon her feet. In a brief moment the warrior repeats the last refrain. Again Tusee springs to her feet and dances to the swing of the few final measures.

Just as the dance was finished, an elderly man, with short, thick hair loose about his square shoulders, rode into their presence from the rear, and leaped lightly from his pony's back. Dropping the rawhide rein to the ground, he tossed himself lazily on the grass. "Hunhe, you have returned soon," said the warrior, while extending a hand to his little daughter.

Quickly the child ran to her father's side and cuddled close to him, while he tenderly placed a strong arm about her. Both father and child, eyeing the figure on the grass, waited to hear the man's report.

"It is true," began the man, with a stranger's accent. "This is the night of the dance."

"Hunha!" muttered the warrior with some surprise.

Propping himself upon his elbows, the man raised his face. His features were of the Southern type. From an enemy's camp he was taken captive long years ago by Tusee's father. But the unusual qualities of the slave had won the Sioux warrior's heart, and for the last three winters the man had had his freedom. He was made real man again. His hair was allowed to grow. However, he himself had chosen to stay in the warrior's family.

"Hunha!" again ejaculated the warrior father. Then turning to his little daughter, he asked, "Tusee, do you hear that?"

"Yes, father, and I am going to dance tonight!"

With these words she bounded out of his arm and frolicked about in glee. Hereupon the proud mother's voice rang out in a chiding laugh.

"My child, in honor of your first dance your father must give a generous gift. His ponies are wild, and roam beyond the great hill. Pray, what has he fit to offer?" she questioned, the pair of puzzled eyes fixed upon her.

"A pony from the herd, mother, a fleet-footed pony from the herd!" Tusee shouted with sudden inspiration.

Pointing a small forefinger toward the man lying on the grass, she cried, "Uncle, you will go after the pony tomorrow!" And pleased with her solution of the problem, she skipped wildly about. Her childish faith in her elders was not conditioned by a knowledge of human limitations, but thought all things possible to grown-ups.

"Hähob!" exclaimed the mother, with a rising inflection, implying by the expletive that her child's buoyant spirit be not weighted with a denial.

Quickly to the hard request the man replied, "How! I go if Tusee tells me so!"

This delighted the little one, whose black eyes brimmed over with light. Standing in front of the strong man, she clapped her small, brown hands with joy.

"That makes me glad! My heart is good! Go, uncle, and bring a handsome pony!" she cried. In an instant she would have frisked away, but an impulse held her tilting where she stood. In the man's own tongue, for he had taught her many words and phrases, she exploded, "Thank you, good uncle, thank you!" then tore away from sheer excess of glee.

The proud warrior father, smiling and narrowing his eyes, muttered approval, "Howo! Hechetu!"

Like her mother, Tusee has finely pencilled eyebrows and slightly extended nostrils; but in her sturdiness of form she resembles her father.

A loyal daughter, she sits within her tepee making beaded deerskins for her father, while he longs to stave off her every suitor as all unworthy of his old heart's pride. But Tusee is not alone in her dwelling. Near the entrance-way a young brave is half reclining on a mat. In silence he watches the petals of a wild rose growing on the soft buckskin. Quickly the young woman slips the beads on the silvery sinew thread, and works them into the pretty flower design. Finally, in a low, deep voice, the young man begins:

"The sun is far past the zenith. It is now only a man's height above the western edge of land. I hurried hither to tell you tomorrow I join the war party."

He pauses for reply, but the maid's head drops lower over her deerskin, and her lips are more firmly drawn together. He continues:

"Last night in the moonlight I met your warrior father. He seemed to know I had just stepped forth from your tepee. I fear he did not like it, for though I greeted him, he was silent. I halted in his pathway. With what boldness I dared, while my heart was beating hard and fast, I asked him for his only daughter.

"Drawing himself erect to his tallest height, and gathering his loose robe more closely about his proud figure, he flashed a pair of piercing eyes upon me.

"'Young man,' said he, with a cold, slow voice that chilled me to the marrow of my bones, 'hear me. Naught but an enemy's scalp-lock, plucked fresh with your own hand, will buy Tusee for your wife.' Then he turned on his heel and stalked away."

Tusee thrusts her work aside. With earnest eyes she scans her lover's face.

"My father's heart is really kind. He would know if you are brave and true," murmured the daughter, who wished no ill-will between her two loved ones.

Then rising to go, the youth holds out a right hand. "Grasp my hand once firmly before I go, Hoye. Pray tell me, will you wait and watch for my return?"

Tusee only nods assent, for mere words are vain.

At early dawn the round camp-ground awakes into song. Men and women sing of bravery and of triumph. They inspire the swelling breasts of the painted warriors mounted on prancing ponies bedecked with the green branches of trees.

Riding slowly around the great ring of cone-shaped tepees, here and there, a loud-singing warrior swears to avenge a former wrong, and thrusts a bare brown arm against the purple east, calling the Great Spirit to hear his vow. All having made the circuit, the singing war party gallops away southward.

Astride their ponies laden with food and deerskins, brave elderly women follow after their warriors. Among the foremost rides a young woman in elaborately beaded buckskin dress. Proudly mounted, she curbs with the single rawhide loop a wild-eyed pony.

It is Tusee on her father's warhorse. Thus the war party of Indian men and their faithful women vanish beyond the southern skyline.

A day's journey brings them very near the enemy's borderland. Nightfall finds a pair of twin tepees nestled in a deep ravine. Within one lounge the painted warriors, smoking their pipes and telling weird stories by the firelight, while in the other watchful women crouch uneasily about their center fire.

By the first gray light in the east the tepees are banished. They are gone. The warriors are in the enemy's camp, breaking dreams with their tomahawks. The women are hid away in secret places in the long thicketed ravine.

The day is far spent, the red sun is low over the west.

At length straggling warriors return, one by one, to the deep hollow. In the twilight they number their men. Three are missing. Of these absent ones two are dead; but the third one, a young man, is a captive to the foe.

"He-he!" lament the warriors, taking food in haste.

In silence each woman, with long strides, hurries to and fro, tying large bundles on her pony's back. Under cover of night the war party must hasten homeward. Motionless, with bowed head, sits a woman in her hiding-place. She grieves for her lover.

In bitterness of spirit she hears the warriors murmuring words. With set teeth she plans to cheat the hated enemy of their captive. In the meanwhile low signals are given, and the war party, unaware of Tusee's absence, steal quietly away. The soft thud of pony-hoofs grows fainter and fainter. The gradual hush of the empty ravine whirrs noisily in the ear of the young woman. Alert for any sound of footfalls nigh, she holds her breath to listen. Her right hand rests on a long knife in her belt. Ah, yes, she knows where her pony is hid, but not yet has she need of him. Satisfied that no danger is nigh, she prowls forth from her place of hiding. With a panther's tread and pace she climbs the high ridge beyond the low ravine. From thence she spies the enemy's camp-fires.

Rooted to the barren bluff the slender woman's figure stands on the pinnacle of night, outlined against a starry sky. The cool night breeze wafts to her burning ear snatches of song and drum. With desperate hate she bites her teeth.

Tusee beckons the stars to witness. With impassioned voice and uplifted face she pleads:

"Great Spirit, speed me to my lover's rescue! Give me swift cunning for a weapon this night! All-powerful Spirit, grant me my warrior-father's heart, strong to slay a foe and mighty to save a friend!"

In the midst of the enemy's camp-ground, underneath a temporary dance-house, are men and women in gala-day dress. It is late in the night, but the merry warriors bend and bow their nude, painted bodies before a bright center fire. To the lusty men's voices and the rhythmic throbbing drum, they leap and rebound with feathered headgears waving.

Women with red-painted cheeks and long, braided hair sit in a large half-circle against the willow railing. They, too, join in the singing, and rise to dance with their victorious warriors.

Amid this circular dance arena stands a prisoner bound to a post, haggard with shame and sorrow. He hangs his disheveled head.

He stares with unseeing eyes upon the bare earth at his feet. With jeers and smirking faces the dancers mock the Dakota captive. Rowdy braves and small boys hoot and yell in derision.

Silent among the noisy mob, a tall woman, leaning both elbows on the round willow railing, peers into the lighted arena. The dancing center fire shines bright into her handsome face, intensifying the night in her dark eyes. It breaks into myriad points upon her beaded dress. Unmindful of the surging throng jostling her at either side, she glares in upon the hateful, scoffing men. Suddenly she turns her head. Tittering maids whisper near her ear:

"There! There! See him now, sneering in the captive's face. 'Tis he who sprang upon the young man and dragged him by his long hair to yonder post. See! He is handsome! How gracefully he dances!"

The silent young woman looks toward the bound captive. She sees a warrior, scarce older than the captive, flourishing a tomahawk in the Dakota's face. A burning rage darts forth from her eyes and brands him for a victim of revenge. Her heart mutters within her breast, "Come, I wish to meet you, vile foe, who captured my lover and tortures him now with a living death."

Here the singers hush their voices, and the dancers scatter to their various resting-places along the willow ring. The victor gives a reluctant last twirl of his tomahawk, then, like the others, he leaves the center ground. With head and shoulders swaying from side to side, he carries a high-pointing chin toward the willow railing. Sitting down upon the ground with crossed legs, he fans himself with an outspread turkey wing.

Now and then he stops his haughty blinking to peep out of the corners of his eyes. He hears some one clearing her throat gently. It is unmistakably for his ear. The wing-fan swings irregularly to and fro. At length he turns a proud face over a bare shoulder and beholds a handsome woman smiling.

"Ah, she would speak to a hero!" thumps his heart wildly.

The singers raise their voices in unison. The music is irresistible. Again lunges the victor into the open arena. Again he leers into the captive's face. At every interval between the songs he returns to his resting-place. Here the young woman awaits him. As he approaches she smiles boldly into his eyes. He is pleased with her face and her smile.

Waving his wing-fan spasmodically in front of his face, he sits with his ears pricked up. He catches a low whisper. A hand taps him lightly on the shoulder. The handsome woman speaks to him in his own tongue. "Come out into the night. I wish to tell you who I am."

He must know what sweet words of praise the handsome woman has for him. With both hands he spreads the meshes of the loosely woven willows, and crawls out unnoticed into the dark.

Before him stands the young woman. Beckoning him with a slender hand, she steps backward, away from the light and the restless throng of onlookers. He follows with impatient strides. She quickens her pace. He lengthens his strides. Then suddenly the woman turns from him and darts away with amazing speed. Clinching his fists and biting his lower lip, the young man runs after the fleeing woman. In his maddened pursuit he forgets the dance arena.

Beside a cluster of low bushes the woman halts. The young man, panting for breath and plunging headlong forward, whispers loud, "Pray tell me, are you a woman or an evil spirit to lure me away?"

Turning on heels firmly planted in the earth, the woman gives a wild spring forward, like a panther for its prey. In a husky voice she hissed between her teeth, "I am a Dakota woman!"

From her unerring long knife the enemy falls heavily at her feet. The Great Spirit heard Tusee's prayer on the hilltop. He gave her a warrior's strong heart to lessen the foe by one.

A bent old woman's figure, with a bundle like a grandchild slung on her back, walks round and round the dance-house. The wearied onlookers are leaving in twos and threes. The tired dancers creep out of the willow railing, and some go out at the entrance way, till the singers, too, rise from the drum and are trudging drowsily homeward. Within the arena the center fire lies broken in red embers. The night no longer lingers about the willow railing, but, hovering into the dancehouse, covers here and there a snoring man whom sleep has overpowered where he sat.

The captive in his tight-binding rawhide ropes hangs in hopeless despair. Close about him the gloom of night is slowly crouching. Yet the last red, crackling embers cast a faint light upon his long black hair, and, shining through the thick mats, caress his wan face with undying hope.

Still about the dance-house the old woman prowls. Now the embers are gray with ashes.

The old bent woman appears at the entrance way. With a cautious, groping foot she enters. Whispering between her teeth a lullaby for her sleeping child in her blanket, she searches for something forgotten.

Noisily snored the dreaming men in the darkest parts. As the lisping old woman draws nigh, the captive again opens his eyes.

A forefinger she presses to her lip. The young man arouses himself from his stupor. His senses belie him. Before his wide-open eyes the old bent figure straightens into its youthful stature. Tusee herself is beside him. With a stroke upward and downward she severs the cruel cords with her sharp blade. Dropping her blanket from her shoulders, so that it hangs from her girdled waist like a skirt, she shakes the large bundle into a light shawl for her lover. Quickly she spreads it over his bare back.

"Come!" she whispers, and turns to go; but the young man, numb and helpless, staggers nigh to falling.

The sight of his weakness makes her strong. A mighty power thrills her body. Stooping beneath his outstretched arms grasping at the air for support, Tusee lifts him upon her broad shoulders. With half-running, triumphant steps she carries him away into the open night.

## The Great Spirit (1921)

When the spirit swells my breast I love to roam leisurely among the green hills; or sometimes, sitting on the brink of the murmuring Missouri, I marvel at the great blue overhead. With half-closed eyes I watch the huge cloud shadows in their noiseless play upon the high bluffs opposite me, while into my ear ripple the sweet, soft cadences of the river's song. Folded hands lie in my lap, for the time forgot. My heart and I lie small upon the earth like a grain of throbbing sand. Drifting clouds and tinkling waters, together with the warmth of a genial summer day, bespeak with eloquence the loving Mystery round about us. During the idle while I sat upon the sunny river brink, I grew somewhat, though my response be not so clearly manifest as in the green grass fringing the edge of the high bluff back of me.

At length retracing the uncertain footpath scaling the precipitous embankment, I seek the level lands where grow the wild prairie flowers. And they, the lovely little folk, soothe my soul with their perfumed breath.

Their quaint round faces of varied hue convince the heart which leaps with glad surprise that they, too, are living symbols of omnipotent thought. With a child's eager eye I drink in the myriad star shapes wrought in luxuriant color upon the green. Beautiful is the spiritual essence they embody.

I leave them nodding in the breeze, but take along with me their impress upon my heart. I pause to rest me upon a rock embedded on the side of a foothill facing the low river bottom. Here the Stone-Boy, of whom the American aborigine tells, frolics about, shooting his baby arrows and shouting aloud with glee at the tiny shafts of lightning that flash from the flying arrow-beaks. What an ideal warrior he became, baffling the siege of the pests of all the land till he triumphed over their united attack. And here he lay, – Inyan our great-great-grandfather, older than the hill he rested on, older than the race of men who love to tell of his wonderful career.

Interwoven with the thread of this Indian legend of the rock, I fain would trace a subtle knowledge of the native folk which enabled them to recognize a kinship to any and all parts of this vast universe. By the leading of an ancient trail I move toward the Indian village.

With the strong, happy sense that both great and small are so surely enfolded in His magnitude that, without a miss, each has his allotted individual ground of opportunities, I am buoyant with good nature.

Yellow Breast, swaying upon the slender stem of a wild sunflower, warbles a sweet assurance of this as I pass near by. Breaking off the clear crystal song, he turns his wee head from side to side eyeing me wisely as slowly I plod with moccasined feet. Then again he yields himself to his song of joy. Flit, flit hither and yon, he fills the summer sky with his swift, sweet melody. And truly does it seem his vigorous freedom lies more in his little spirit than in his wing.

With these thoughts I reach the log cabin whither I am strongly drawn by the tie of a child to an aged mother. Out bounds my fourfooted friend to meet me, frisking about my path with unmistakable delight. Chän is a black shaggy dog, "a thoroughbred little mongrel" of whom I am very fond. Chän seems to understand many words in Sioux, and will go to her mat even when I whisper the word, though generally I think she is guided by the tone of the voice. Often she tries to imitate the sliding inflection and long-drawn-out voice to the amusement of our guests, but her articulation is quite beyond my ear. In both my hands I hold her shaggy head and gaze into her large brown eyes. At once the dilated pupils contract into tiny black dots, as if the roguish spirit within would evade my questioning.

Finally resuming the chair at my desk I feel in keen sympathy with my fellow-creatures, for I seem to see clearly again that all are akin. The racial lines, which once were bitterly real, now serve nothing more than marking out a living mosaic of human beings. And even here men of the same color are like the ivory keys of one instrument where each resembles all the rest, yet varies from them in pitch and quality of voice. And those creatures who are for a time mere echoes of another's note are not unlike the fable of the thin sick man whose distorted shadow, dressed like a real creature, came to the old master to make him follow as a shadow. Thus with a compassion for all echoes in human guise, I greet the solemn-faced "native preacher" whom I find awaiting me. I listen with respect for God's creature, though he mouth most strangely the jangling phrases of a bigoted creed.

As our tribe is one large family, where every person is related to all the others, he addressed me: –

"Cousin, I came from the morning church service to talk with you."

"Yes?" I said interrogatively, as he paused for some word from me.

Shifting uneasily about in the straight-backed chair he sat upon, he began: "Every holy day (Sunday) I look about our little God's house, and not seeing you there, I am disappointed. This is why I come today. Cousin, as I watch you from afar, I see no unbecoming behavior and hear only good reports of you, which all the more burns me with the wish that you were a church member. Cousin, I was taught long years ago by kind missionaries to read the holy book. These godly men taught me also the folly of our old beliefs.

"There is one God who gives reward or punishment to the race of dead men. In the upper region the Christian dead are gathered in unceasing song and prayer. In the deep pit below, the sinful ones dance in torturing flames.

"Think upon these things, my cousin, and choose now to avoid the after-doom of hell fire!" Then followed a long silence in which he clasped tighter and unclasped again his interlocked fingers.

Like instantaneous lightning flashes came pictures of my own mother's making, for she, too, is now a follower of the new superstition.

"Knocking out the chinking of our log cabin, some evil hand thrust in a burning taper of braided dry grass, but failed of his intent, for the fire died out and the half-burned brand fell inward to the floor. Directly above it, on a shelf, lay the holy book. This is what we found after our return from a several days' visit. Surely some great power is hid in the sacred book!"

Brushing away from my eyes many like pictures, I offered midday meal to the converted Indian sitting wordless and with downcast face. No sooner had he risen from the table with "Cousin, I have relished it," than the church bell rang.

Thither he hurried forth with his afternoon sermon. I watched him as he hastened along, his eyes bent fast upon the dusty road till he disappeared at the end of a quarter of a mile.

The little incident recalled to mind the copy of a missionary paper brought to my notice a few days ago, in which a "Christian" pugilist commented upon a recent article of mine, grossly perverting the spirit of my pen. Still I would not forget that the pale-faced missionary and the hoodooed aborigine are both God's creatures, though small indeed their own conceptions of Infinite Love. A wee child toddling in a wonder world, I prefer to their dogma my excursions into the natural gardens where the voice of the Great Spirit is heard in the twittering of birds, the rippling of mighty waters, and the sweet breathing of flowers.

Here, in a fleeting quiet, I am awakened by the fluttering robe of the Great Spirit. To my innermost consciousness the phenomenal universe is a royal mantle, vibrating with His divine breath. Caught in its flowing fringes are the spangles and oscillating brilliants of sun, moon, and stars.

## From Various Periodicals

### A YEAR'S EXPERIENCE IN COMMUNITY SERVICE WORK AMONG THE UTE TRIBE OF INDIANS (*AMERICAN INDIAN MAGAZINE*, OCTOBER–DECEMBER, 1916)

We began our Community Center work in the fall of 1915, by starting sewing classes among the women. There was no time to consult the fashion books. We met one day each week, devoting it to charity work for the aged members of the tribe. Plain, warm garments cut in the loose style they are accustomed to wear, were made for those who could neither see to sew nor buy their clothing ready made, with money they did not have. Sometimes members of the sewing classes helped one another with their necessary sewing. Later they learned very rapidly to crochet little caps, jackets and bootees for their babies. Old comforters were repaired; new quilts were pieced and quilted quite creditably by the women.

Many funny little stories were told at these sewing classes. With laughter they stitched away upon the article in hand. As the autumn advanced into winter and snow, we found new work to do in addition to our weekly sewing.

Every Monday, Indians from far and near came to the Government office. Some came to receive their monthly subsistence checks, others to sign papers or to give testimony in an heirship hearing. There was no rest-room to accommodate these "Monday Indians." All day the mothers with their babies, stood outdoors in the snow. There is nothing so tiresome as waiting. At noon the "Monday Indians" flocked by the tens and twenties to the homes of the Indian employees. Now the salaries of the Indian police, Indian interpreter, janitor and stableman are the smallest in the Government service – scarcely enough to support the families of these employees. This enforced hospitality of the Indian employees was very unfair. The longer an Indian employee stayed in the government service, the deeper into debt he got. Yet since there is no employment by which ready money may be earned, they are tempted to try the Government jobs, thinking to get a few dollars thereby.

The wives of these Indian employees agreed with me that by locking up their homes and donating their services to prepare and serve a simple, wholesome lunch to these "Monday Indians," a mutual benefit would be gained to all concerned. The Monday lunch and rest-room were started. The soup, pies and coffee were prepared by the Indian women under my supervision. This was really a practical demonstration in domestic science. The women learned improved methods of preparing food in their own homes. The Indian men hauled the wood and cut it up for us. They were good enough to carry buckets of water for us, too.

At the close of the day enough provision had been saved in the homes of the Indian employees to last them a whole week. Moreover, the visiting Indians had been provided a legitimate accommodation. They had a comfortable place to rest without imposing upon any one.

We are grateful to Superintendent Kneale for his kindness in allowing us the use of a Government building, and encouraging us by sometimes coming to our lunches. Mrs. Kneale was always there to help us serve the lunches. There was a great rush at the noon hour and each of us wished we had more than a single pair of hands.

With the coming of springtime, when the Indians were busy with their farming, their trips to the Agency being less regular, we changed our plan. Then we ceased our sewing classes and lunch and rest-room work. We organized a local branch of the Society of American Indians which met once a month.

Our programs were both instructive and social. We spent part of the evening in a study of local conditions. We read papers upon selected subjects. We argued in favor of sending all Indian children to school. We talked also of the innumerable benefits to a tribe that held its annual fairs. We mentioned here the good work started by the Commissioner of Indian Affairs in emphasizing the vital importance to the future race, by the saving of the babies. We encouraged co-operation in this, for it was so unmistakably in the right direction. The evening's discussions were interspersed with music and readings in a lighter vein.

Throughout the entire year I made regular visits to the Indians at their camps. The territory is great and much time and energy is lost on the road.

During the year, three donations were made to the Community Center work by members of the Society of American Indians, which totaled $23.00. I wish to submit this itemized account:

| | |
|---|---|
| $ 5.00 | Sewing materials, needles, thimbles, thread scissors, easy patterns for children's dresses and aprons. |
| $ 8.00 | Subscription to newspapers used in lunch and rest-room. |
| $10.00 | Applied on purchase of dishes for lunch-room. |
| $23.00 | |

Dishes purchased for the Community Center work were:

4 doz. tablespoons
4 doz. Teaspoons
4 doz. Cups and saucers . . . . . . . . . . $9.20

50 soup bowls . . . . . . . . . . . . . . . . . . 7.00
25 yds. Oilcloth . . . . . . . . . . . . . . . . . 5.50
Carpenter hire . . . . . . . . . . . . . . . . . . 2.00

——

$23.70
10.00 pd. by donation

——

$13.70 pd. by lunches

There remains on hand a credit balance of $1.30

During the summer the Community Center property was carefully packed away. With our acquired wealth of dishes and experience the first year, we are better prepared for the second year's work.

The lunch and rest-room should operate in such a way as to furnish wholesome lunch to the Indians at a minimum cost, allowing only a small margin of gain, that the work may sustain itself.

Under the direct supervision of the Society of American Indians, I made my effort in Community Center work. There were no funds to carry on this experimental work; nor was there any salary attached to my assignment of duty.

I mention these merely as interesting items though they are only incidentals after all. "Where there is a will there is a way."

The field chosen for my work was not a new one. There were others who had already devoted years to the uplift of the race. They were not lacking in time-tested experience nor means either.

The Government had its salaried employees here. The Church had also provided for its self-sacrificing missionaries, too.

The question naturally arose as to the advisability of the National organization of Indians diverting their energy upon a line of work already taken care of by able bodies. And perhaps there would be some to whom such an endeavor might appear as an interference with workers in the field, more especially, since there were phases of our problem that urgently demanded our undivided attention.

The thought of interference with any good work is wholly foreign to our high motive; nor do we presume any superiority to those already in the field.

We have awakened, in the midst of a bewildering transition, to a divine obligation calling us to love, to honor our parents. No matter how ably, how well others of God's creatures perform their duties, they never can do our duty for us; nor can we hope for forgiveness, were we to stand idly by, satisfied to see others laboring for the uplift of our kinsmen. Our aged grandparents hunger for tenderness, kindness and sympathy from their own offspring. It is our first duty, it is our great privilege to be permitted to administer with our own hands, this gentle affection to our people. There is no more urgent call upon us; for all too soon these old ones will have passed on. It is possible, indeed, to combine with practical systematic effort, a bit of kindness and true sympathy.

Our Community Center work is non-sectarian and non-partisan. For this reason we are in a position to lend unobtrusively, very beneficial aid toward uniting and welding together the earnest endeavors of various groups of educators and missionaries.

Our chief thought is co-operation with all constructive uplift work for humanity. Therefore, in our attempt to do our very own duty to our race, we do so with a full appreciation of all kindnesses and gratitude for all that good people have done and are still doing in behalf of our race.

## CHIPETA, WIDOW OF CHIEF OURAY, WITH A WORD ABOUT A DEAL IN BLANKETS (*AMERICAN INDIAN MAGAZINE*, JULY–SEPTEMBER, 1917)

A year ago this fall it was my special privilege to be the guest of Chipeta. I had gone to her for a heart to heart talk about the use of peyote, a powerful narcotic, used by the Ute people. Within her nephew's tepee where she gave me audience were gathered friends, relatives and neighbors, – for word had gone out that I was coming to talk about matters of large importance with Chipeta. And Chipeta is an honored woman for she is the widow of Chief Ouray, a red patriot who had many times saved the lives of white settlers and who had in many an emergency saved his tribe from disaster.

Our conversation drifted pleasantly to the days of Chipeta's girlhood. It is an old time custom among Indians to enter upon a subject slowly and not rush to discussion at once, nor try to say all one desired to voice in one breath.

Chipeta was not boastful. More often she sat silently smiling and nodding her assent to the stories one related of her wild rides through the hills, risking her own personal safety to give warning to her white friends of impending raids. With these stories told, came the plunge into the talk about present day conditions. I told of the rumors that she and her brother McCook had been deceived into the use of a dangerous drug and that they were being fleeced by the mercenary traffickers in peyote buttons.

Earnestly she scanned my face as I told them of the inevitable degeneration that follows the habitual and indiscriminate use of narcotics. Frankly she told me that peyote eased her brother's rheumatism and hers. Admitting the truth of my statements she said, "I have noticed that the pains return when I stop the use of the drug."

McCook then spoke. Terse and deeply significant was his reply: "When the Great White Father in Washington sent a letter to me telling me that whiskey was bad, I stopped our people from its use. When the Great White Father sent a letter to me telling me that gambling was bad, I forbade our people to play cards." There was a momentary pause. I wondered what he would say next. I hoped he would say he now decided to give up the drug, peyote and stop its use among his people. He concluded briefly:

"Now the Great White Father has sent me no letter telling me peyote is bad. Therefore, as long as he permits its use, we will continue to use it."

It was with a sad heart that I returned to the Agency. All along the journey questions presented themselves to my mind. Did you ever try giving a serious talk or lecture to an audience that was more or less under the influence of a drug? In such a case what results may you expect? Did you ever hear of an evangelist addressing a class of drug users who in their abnormal condition were helplessly unable to receive his message? What do civilized communities do with their drug victims? Do not they legislate for the protection of society and for the protection of the drug user? A great longing filled me for some message from the Great White Father telling his red children that peyote was bad for them and asking them to refuse to use or sell it. Federal action is needed. Chief Ouray, friend of the white man, would that your old friends might befriend your aged widow and the people whom you loved. Would that federal action might be taken before it is too late. These were the burden of my thoughts as I rode back from my visit with Chipeta.

Some time later, while conversing with a friend who had been interested in my visit I heard an amazing story. It was about my friend Chipeta. It was like a tale in a night-mare and I could scarcely believe it. For Chipeta, for Chief Ouray and his people my indignation arose but I could not speak. This is what I heard told:

"In some way the idea was started that the Government ought to give a gift to Chipeta in grateful memory to Chief Ouray, faithful friend of the border settlers and loyal advocate of obedience to Federal orders. It was to be a token of regard also to Chipeta for the valuable service, she, too had rendered. The plan was presented to the Great White Father in Washington and was approved.

"The question then came up as to the kind of gift that would be useful to Chipeta and at the same time suitable as a memento."

I heard the story of the discussion and light streamed into my heart. My fancy moved ahead of the story and I thought of the kind of gifts that were within range of possibility. What if the gift should be a genuine guarantee of water rights to the Ute Indians, or the title to their 250,000 acres of grazing lands to be held intact for the future unallotted children, or a message from the Great White Father giving news of Federal action against the peyote drug? All these things and more were needed and any one would have been a royal gift to the royal Chipeta. Then dimly in my ears the story went on.

With a sudden shock I heard that the gift chosen was a pair of trading store shawls. Scarcely could I believe my ears, for was this a suitable gift with which to honor loyal service through a period of many years?

"The shawls were purchased at a little trading station and sent to Washington where they were tagged as a gift from the Great White Father, in honor of the past friendship of Chief Ouray and of Chipeta to the white people. Then the shawls were reshipped to their starting point in Utah.

"With what innocent joy Chipeta received them. At once she returned the compliment by sending the donor a large and expensive Navajo blanket. It was a free will offering, paid for by personal money and given out of the gratitude of her heart for the little token that someone in Washington had given her.

"Little did Chipeta realize that she had never really received a gift, but that without her consent she had been made to pay for the 'gift shawls.'

"The bill for the shawls was sent to the Government office at Uintah and Ouray Agency and the money in settlement was paid out of Ute money known as 'Interest on the Ute 5% Funds.'"

If the spirit eyes of Chief Ouray can see his heart must be made sad. His widow has given away a beautiful blanket rug to reciprocate what she thinks a gift of tender sentiment.

Poor unsuspecting Chipeta, loyal friend of the white in the days when Indian friendship counted! Your shawls derived even so cover your head like a royal mantle and it is not for you to bow your head in shame. Your reward for faithful service is the recollection of your husband's integrity and the consciousness of having within your light always done well. No shawl is big enough to obscure or to cover the gifts you have given freely and for which no material thing will ever repay you.

## Indian Gifts to Civilized Man
### (*The Indian Sentinel*, July, 1918; also in *Tomahawk*, July, 1919)

Changing Woman, according to American Indian mythology, has once more rejuvenated herself. Out of old age she springs up in her former youthful beauty. In a royal robe of green, she adorns herself with gorgeous flowers. Changing Woman is the personification of the seasons.

This Indian Mother-Nature has ever been much adored by the red men. In turn she has loved her black eyed children well. Many secrets she has told them in her secret bowers. Centuries of communion with her, in Indian gardens under primeval forests, have brought forth from insignificant plants, the acclimated and perfected corn and potato. Today they are important food for the people of the earth. They are a contribution from the Red Man of America. He does not crave any praise for the benefits we derive from his labors. It is for our own soul's good that we would give him due credit, at this acceptable time.

Food conservation of the hour is our immediate duty. Mr. Hoover clearly points out how we may very materially aid our allies in saving wheat for them by our own usage of more corn and potatoes. For a brief moment thought reverts to the red man who gave us his corn and potato. Our real appreciation may not find expression in words. We are so absorbed and busily engaged in urgent war activities. We have scarcely a minute to spare for anything else. Notwithstanding these circumstances, our gratitude to the Indian for these gifts is demonstrated by our vast fields, so eloquent in their abundant annual crops. Truly, these speak louder than words.

The patriotic farmer, planting his garden and his field, may wonder as he toils in the blistering sun what service, if any, the American Indian is giving to America in her defense of world democracy. The red man, citizen or non-citizen of our United States, is a loyal son of America. Five thousand Indian men are in our army. Some have already spilled their life blood in the trenches. Others have won military medals "Over There." Indian women are courageously knitting sweaters, helmets and socks for our brave soldiers. The Indian has subscribed about ten million dollars in liberty bonds.

The Commissioner of Indian Affairs, Hon. Cato Sells, visiting four army camps in Texas, found 1,500 Indian soldiers there. Eighty-five per cent of this number are volunteers. Of the remaining fifteen per cent, some there are who did not claim their exemption, so eager were they to serve their country. Notwithstanding the difficulties that arise from the complicated system of classifying the government's wards, the Indian is in the front ranks of American patriotism. For absolute loyalty to the Stars and Stripes, the Indian has no peer.

It is especially gratifying that our great government did not segregate our Indian soldiers into Indian units, but permitted them to serve as Americans, shoulder to shoulder with their white brothers in khaki. Such a close companionship promises mutual benefits. The Indian is an adept at finding natural protection and hiding places. He inherits from his forefathers a wonderfully fine sense of direction which enables him to return to his starting point. Being thus so much at home in the out-of-doors, he may be an invaluable guide to our boys born and bred indoors. On the other hand, the Indian may learn much practical white man's knowledge from first hand experience; and, in their united struggle, will be gained a bond of sympathy that never was found in any book of learning.

The Indian race, once numbering about a million and a half has dwindled to about three hundred thousand. Yet in proportion to his numbers, he is unexcelled in his response to the country's call for fighting men. Were a patriotism like his to sweep through our entire population of millions, we would have in a day, an invincible army of twelve and a half million men. When we realize that the only future hope of the red man is in his educated, physically strong men, we marvel at his heroic response. This undaunted self-sacrifice of America's aboriginal son challenges your patriotism and mine. The sterling quality of his devotion to America is his most inspiring gift to the world. Well may we strive to cultivate in our hearts a better acquaintance with the Indian in our midst. He is just as worth while as the potato patch we are weeding and the cornfield we are plowing.

## Editorial Comment (*American Indian Magazine*, July–September, 1918)

The Pierre, (S.D) Conference is an accomplished fact. In these trying war times it was a privileged sacrifice to journey there.

Three of the S.A.I. officers absent are in military service. Arthur C. Parker, President, is on military duty "Somewhere in America"; John M. Oskison, First Vice-President, is serving "Somewhere in France"; Margaret Frazier, Vice-President on Membership, is a trained nurse in the Red Cross work at Camp Bowie, Texas.

The Honorary President, Rev. Sherman Coolidge, presided over the meetings.

The delegation of members though numerically small, was strikingly representative. There were gathered together in behalf of Indian welfare work – Arapahoe, Apache, Oklahoman, Ojibway, Ute, Pottowatomie, Sioux from different tribes and others.

It was gratifying and significant that in the face of the Conference dates having been designated for country fairs on all Indian reservations under Indian Bureau management, a successful conference was possible. Faithful Associate members crossed the continent to attend the American Indian Conference. Many new members were added to the rolls during the meeting.

The hospitality of the citizens of Pierre will ever be cherished in memory.

The spirit of a great united American brotherhood fighting in a common cause, – the defense of world democracy, pervaded the whole affair. American Indians are watching democracy, baptized in fire and blood overseas. They are watching the christening with mingled feelings of deepest concern, – the thing lies so close to their hearts it is difficult to give it expression. Indian soldiers lie dead on European battlefields, having intermingled their blood with that of every other race in the supreme sacrifice for an ideal.

Surely, the flaming shafts of light typifying political and legal equality and justice, – government by the people, now penetrating the dark cloud of Europe are a continuous revelation. The light grows more effulgent, emanating as it does from the greatest of democracies, – America. The sunburst of democratic ideals cannot bring new hope and courage to the small peoples of the earth without reaching the remotest corners within America's own bounds.

Frank discussions are apt to call forth suppressed emotions of the American Indian but need not thereby create ruffled feelings. The Society of American Indians is compelled by stress of the times to consider and discuss higher education for the Red Man and the rights of small peoples at its Annual Conference.

It is needful to thrash out the truth about Indian matters. Truth and justice are inseparable component parts of American ideals. As America has declared democracy abroad, so must we consistently practise it at home.

The American government is one where the voice of the people is heard. It is therefore not a radical step nor a presumption for the native Red Man today to raise his voice about the welfare of his race. The Red Man has been mute too long. He must speak for himself as no other can, nor should he be afraid to speak the truth and to insist upon a hearing for the utterance of truth can harm no one but must bless all mankind.

The future success of the Indian as a full-fledged American citizen depends largely upon what he does for himself today. If he is good enough to fight for American ideals he is good enough for American citizenship now.

Our Conference was honored by the presence of an Indian Bureau official, Mrs. Wilma R. Rhodes, Field Supervisor. This representative of our government repeatedly took the floor of the Conference to differ from the expressed opinions of the Indian members. These debates were marked with intense feeling. The difference seemed to be the natural result of a difference of viewpoint and interest.

The Indian Bureau system was naturally defended by its representative. The members of the Conference expressed a decided preference for Public Schools and American institutions. The Bureau representative advocated the alleged sweet oil of Government Schools under the Bureau System, while the Conference members protested against what they believed to be the fat fly of paternalism in this particular brand of ointment.

The Society of American Indians appreciates every true friend but were the organization to begin naming them it would be an undertaking. The great object and purpose of the Conference is to study the interest of the race as a whole and to devise means and methods for its practical advancement and the attainment of its rightful position among the peoples of the world.

## America, Home of the Red Man (*American Indian Magazine*, Winter, 1919)

To keep the home fires burning, the Society of American Indians held its annual conference this fall at Pierre, South Dakota. While en route to the West, the Secretary[5] was accosted by a traveler whose eyes fairly gleamed under the little service pin she wore. At length curiosity spoke. The only preliminary introduction was a clearing of the throat. "You have a relative in the war?" asked the voice. "Yes, indeed," was the quick reply. "I have many cousins and nephews somewhere in France. This star I am wearing is for my husband, who is a volunteer in Uncle Sam's Army." A light spread over the countenance of the pale-faced stranger. "Oh! Yes! You are an Indian! Well, I knew when I first saw you that you must be a foreigner."

The amazing speech dropped like a sudden curtain behind which the speaker faded instantly from my vision. In figures of fire, I saw, with the mind's eye, ten thousand Indian soldiers swaying to and fro on European battlefields – finally mingling their precious blood with the blood of all other peoples of the earth, that democracy might live. Three-fourths of these Indian soldiers were volunteers and there was those also who did not claim exemption, so eager were they to defend their country and its democratic ideals. The Red Man of America loves democracy and hates mutilated treaties.

Twelve million dollars had been subscribed by the American Indians to the Liberty Loans. Generous donations they made to war funds of the Red Cross, Y.M.C.A. and other organizations.

I beheld rapidly shifting pictures of individual sacrifices of Indians, both young and old.

An old grandmother, whom someone dubbed a "Utah squaw" now appeared wonderously glorified. Her furrowed face was aglow with radiance. Her bent form, clad in pitiful rags, changed in a twinkling of an eye to strength and grace. Her spirit shining through earthly misfortunes, revealed an angel in disguise. She donated five hundred dollars to the Red Cross and had left only thirteen dollars. "Thirteen dollars left? That is enough for me," the toothless old grandmother lisped in her own native tongue. It was her mite in this cause of world democracy.

Beside her stood an Indian brave in the Army uniform. Early he went over seas for active service at the front. A treasured file of his letters filled the air like white-winged pigeons, telling a story stranger than fiction.

---

5 That is, Zitkala-Ša. A footnote indicates that this piece was "Written for *The Home Mission Monthly*." This periodical was published in New York from 1886 to 1924 by the Woman's Board of Home Missions of the Presbyterian Church in the United States.

He was a machine gunner. It was his duty to stand by his gun till he should drop. One day he fell, but the wound was not fatal. After his recovery he served as an infantryman. A Hun shrapnel found him again. His time, apparently, had not yet come to die. He recovered. Undaunted, he was glad when he was re-assigned to the Remount Station. "I have nothing to do now," his letters read, "only to break army horses for riding." True, he was an expert horseman, but with a crippled knee, no telling what moment he might ignominiously break his own neck. This thought never occurred to him. Later a message came again from France. "I am no longer in the Remount. I have been assigned to garden work. I am digging spuds to help win the war."

And now I saw little French orphans, babes with soft buckskin moccasins on their tiny feet. Moccasins, that Indian women of America had made for them, with so much loving sympathy for an anguished humanity.

Time and distance were eliminated by the fast succession of pictures crowding before me. The dome of our nation's Capitol appeared. A great senator of Indian blood[6] introduced upon the floor of the United States Senate a resolution that all Indian funds in the United States Treasury be available to our government, if need be, for the prosecution of the war. From coast to coast throughout our broad land not a single voice of the Red Man was raised to protest against it.

America! Home of the Red Man! How dearly the Indian loves you! America! Home of Democracy, when shall the Red Man be emancipated? When shall the Red Man be deemed worthy of full citizenship if not now?

A slight motion of the strange pale-face standing before me attracted my notice. I scanned him closely, to see what part of the dream he was. I wondered if a part of any dream could be cognizant of the rest of the actors, dream fellows, beheld by the dreamer or seer of visions. A pity he could not have seen the pictures that held me spell-bound a moment ago. Alas, I did not have the courage to try to put them into words. When at last I spoke, the luster of his eye grew less bright. He was fast losing interest. From the questions with which I plied him, he probably guessed I was a traveling book agent.

Did you ever read a geography? The Red Man is one of four primary races into which the human family has been divided by scientists. America is the home of the Red Man. Have you read the June *Designer*, 1918, about Indian children in Red Cross work? Have you read the April *National Geographic Magazine*, 1918, in which the Secretary of the Interior, Hon. Franklin K. Lane, has contributed an article entitled, "What is it to be an American?" In the third paragraph of this article we are told "There has been nothing of paternalism in our government." I would like to ask, "How does this apply to the Red Men in our midst?"

Slowly shaking his head, the stranger withdrew cautiously, lest he be snared into subscribing for one or all of these publications.

## Letter to the Chiefs and Head-men of the Tribes
## (*American Indian Magazine*, Winter, 1919)

From Gertrude Bonnin, Secretary of the Society of American Indians.

My friends and kinsmen:

This little letter is written to you that each may receive a direct message today. There are two things I wish to bring to your special attention. These are English-speaking and retaining ownership of a portion of our Indian lands.

Since the close of the great war, in which our Indians fought so bravely, there is much talk among our White brothers about the importance of all Americans learning to speak English. There are many languages among the White people just as there are among our different Indian tribes. Plans are being

[6] Possibly Robert L. Owen (1856–1947), son of Narcissa Owen and one of the first senators from Oklahoma. Elected in 1907, Owen was reelected in 1912 and 1918.

made and our government is supporting this new movement to educate all foreigners who now are American citizens, by the study of the English language.

In all their papers, many of which I read, they are urging the returned soldiers and girl war-workers to go back to the schools. Night schools are opened for the working men and women. No one is ever too old to learn.

Friends, if the White people have found it worth while to do this, isn't it even more worth our while to renew our efforts to speak English? No doubt there have been occasions when you wished you could have expressed your thought in English. Remembering this experience, will you now encourage other Indians to make the effort to learn this language?

Very often I have wished that you could write to me in a language we both would understand perfectly. I could then profit by your advice in many things, and you would know you were not forgot.

And now, I have a word to say about Indians holding permanently a small portion of their inherited lands. Sometimes I fear they are selling their lands too fast and without consideration for the future children of our race. Indians are an out-of-doors people, and though we may become educated in the White man's way and even acquire money, we cannot really be happy unless we have a small piece of this Out-of-Doors to enjoy as we please. For the sake of our children's children we must hold onto a few acres that they may enjoy it as we have. –

Many times as I walk on the paved streets of the city, I long for the open Indian country in which I played as a child. I wonder how our White brothers can be content, being born and bred In-Doors. I understand that it is their fast increasing population that necessitates building houses, larger and higher, to accommodate them. The White man is a wonderful builder of stone houses, which to me are better to look upon from the outside than to live in, as they shut out the sky and sunshine.

I shall be glad to hear from you, should you feel interested in these two things about which I have taken the liberty to write you.

Yours for the Indian Cause.

Gertrude Bonnin

## From *Oklahoma's Poor Rich Indians: An Orgy of Graft and Exploitation of the Five Civilized Tribes – Legalized Robbery* (1924; with Charles H. Fabens and Matthew K. Sniffen)

### Summary

As the result of a careful, first-hand investigation of Indian conditions in the Eastern Oklahoma by the undersigned, it is found –

That because Congress, by the Act of May 27, 1908, took from the Interior Department all jurisdiction over Indian probate matters in Eastern Oklahoma and transferred it to the local county courts, the estates of the members of the Five Civilized Tribes are being, and have been, shamelessly and openly robbed in a scientific and ruthless manner.

That all efforts by the Department of the Interior to have the County Courts follow rules of procedure that would afford a measure of protection to the Indians have failed. The rules promulgated by the State Supreme Court in 1914 were soon weakened, and then were annulled on July 10, 1923, by action of the Oklahoma State Supreme Court, leaving each County Court a law unto itself.

That in many of the Counties the Indians are virtually at the mercy of groups that include the county judges, guardians, attorneys, bankers, merchants – not even overlooking the undertaker – all regarding the Indian estates as legitimate game.

That an examination of 14,229 probate cases in six counties where the Indian population is the largest shows the average cost of administration to be Twenty per cent, and in some instances it has been as high as Seventy per cent. That there is no provision limiting the cost of administering an Indian estate in Oklahoma: the amount is optional with the county courts. Incidentally, the cost for probating Indian estates in other sections of the country cannot exceed a total of $75. In most cases the cost is not over $20 – which is less than two per cent.

That excessive and unnecessary administrative costs, unconscionable fees and commissions, are allowed by many of the County Courts to professional guardians, attorneys, et al.

That even in cases where there is no actual dishonesty or collusion between these judges and guardians, the results show a flagrant disregard of the Indians' welfare highly lucrative to those empowered to protect Indian interests.

That Indian children have been allowed to die for lack of nourishment because of the heartlessness and indifference of their professional guardians, who had ample funds in their possession for the care of the wards.

That young Indian girls (mere children in size and mentality) have been robbed of their virtue and their property through kidnapping and a liberal use of liquor.

That to the grafters "the quick and the dead" are all the same. On one occasion they waited literally at the beside of a dying woman, and hardly the breath left her body when her thumb was pressed upon an ink pad and an impression from it made on an alleged will, which was later offered for probate.

That a woman, after being dead for four years, was resurrected as a man and able to sign a lease – all attested by witnesses and a notary public.

That the undertakers were solicitous to see that a deceased Indian had a first-class funeral, and they thoughtfully provided a "solid bronze casket" for $2600 or $2700, with a $75 silk flag (worth not more than $25) to float over the grave – and other accessories in proportion. The best is none too good for an Indian When Dead, if he leaves any property. Dead or alive, however, the grafters manage to "get" the Indian.

That in one respect, at least, the actions of these informal organizations are consistent; sex or age makes no difference, the young child, the adult, the incompetent (mentally or physically) are all treated alike.

That many of the county courts are influenced by political considerations, and that Indian guardianships are the plums to be distributed to the faithful friends of the judges as a reward for their support at the polls. The principal business of these county courts is handling Indian estates. The judges are elected for a two-year term.

That "extraordinary services" in connection with the Indian estates are well paid for; one attorney, by order of the court, received $35,000 from a ward's estate, and never appeared in court.

That in the case of smaller estates, in many instances when the ward becomes of age he is in debt to his guardian; his property has been squandered and nothing is left for him.

That frequently in disposing of tracts of inherited Indian land, the purchase price has been four-tenths of its actual value, as proved by mortgages placed on the property a few days after the sale was approved by the Court, – according to the records of twenty cases, taken at random from various counties.

That when oil is "struck" on an Indian's property, it is usually considered prima facie evidence that he is incompetent, and in the appointment of a guardian for him his wishes in the matter are rarely considered.

That every effort made by the Federal authorities to safeguard the interests of these Indians has been thwarted.

That the Interior Department is powerless, under existing law, to protect these helpless Indians from this wholesale plundering, because Congress vested exclusive jurisdiction over probate matters in the county courts of Oklahoma.

That while the Interior Department maintains a staff of probate attorneys, they are without any specific authority. The Court will hear them out in a perfunctory manner and then usually ignores their protests.

That there are "divorce promoters" going around among the Indians drumming up cases for their attorney friends, for the fees to be secured.

That some attorneys co-operate with "flappers" to ensnare wealthy young Indian men into matrimony, making free use of bootleg whiskey as an aid. Soon thereafter a divorce usually follows and the court allows liberal alimony to the flapper wife, which she shares with her co-partner, the attorney.

## THE PROFESSIONAL GUARDIAN

The professional guardian is a class that seems to be indigenous to the soil of but one State – Oklahoma. At one time there was no limit to the number of estates that could be intrusted to his "tender" hands, but it was such a profitable business that the Oklahoma legislature interfered by passing an act providing that "no person shall be appointed guardian for any minor or minors, or other person or persons, who is, at the time of the hearing of the application for appointment, the guardian of as many as five persons other than his or her own family and relatives."

This "reform" may have been brought about by the jealousy of those "hungry for good things," but it was not with a view to protecting the Indians. Still, with five good estates, the professional guardian is able to assume the rôle of "leading citizen," own a fine house, and a high-priced automobile, and live in luxury. They are usually quite alert, and do not wait to be called by an Indian. Let oil be discovered on an Indian allotment, and one of the profession will promptly file a petition in Court to have the individual declared incompetent (if it is the case of an adult) and ask to be appointed guardian. Of course, as the court wants to "protect" the Indian, the petition is usually granted. There are probably 4000 of these professional guardians, and the estates trusted to them vary from a few thousand dollars up into the millions.

These grafters often keep a "birthday book" so they will know when the minors with estates become of age (which means the restrictions on the lands of mixed-blood are automatically removed). They have been known to go to the Government Indian schools to call on these minors, and promise them presents of gold watches, or invite them to share their homes after they leave school, or become of age. Sometimes this "come into my parlor" invitation is accepted, but where competition among the grafters is keen, it helps to open the eyes of the prospective victims.

However, it is believed that the professional guardianship game is a very profitable one; and we learned of one instance where a man said to be a "King of the Bootleggers" gave up that supposedly lucrative business to join the ranks of the Guardians. It may be that he considered the latter trade to be more lucrative and safer!

Each guardian usually has an attorney steadily retained – probably to advise him how far he can go and be within the law. It is believed that if the guardian was honest and competent there would be no need for the regular services of an attorney. But there are many, many attorneys in Eastern Oklahoma, and they have to live somehow!

One case came to our attention where grafters were ready to pay a man well for his services if he would steal or kidnap an infant half-blood Indian or Mexican child, for the purpose of giving it to a white adventuress married to a rich Indian, so that the woman could claim to have a "blood heir" to the estate in question.

The professional guardian is catered to by banks, who desire his account; by the merchants who want to secure the ward's trade; his friends want liberal loans on questionable security – and in this way the whole community is interested – not forgetting the judge, who is anxious to be re-elected.

Many of the County judges appear to be quite lenient in their attitude toward these guardians; there is no real auditing of the accounts presented for the judges' approval, and usually "everything goes."

An attorney living in Okmulgee, who has been a resident of Oklahoma since 1898, declared that guardians for Indians do not need attorneys. He stated that the cost of administering Indian estates was at least twice what it ought to be; that the fees allowed were excessive, referring to an instance where an attorney received a commission of $1800, when $180 would have been a proper charge. He also said that many attorneys in Okmulgee made their money from collecting fees of ten per cent from bonuses on oil leases, and that all they had to do to earn it was to put an advertisement in the local papers. He further declared that many of the buildings in Okmulgee were erected from Indian money; that as a matter of fact the town was built on Indian money, and that the same can be said about Tulsa, Muskogee, and other cities of Oklahoma.

It is impossible to state the total number of Indians who have been plundered, or the value of their property, but of the 64,339 whose restrictions were removed in 1908, probably not more than five or ten per cent have anything left. Now most of them are living back in the hills, or being cared for by friends and relatives.

There are about 18,000 restricted Indians, who have property – their children, born since the rolls closed, do not appear on the records. As these adults die, however, their property becomes unrestricted, and the grafters, like vultures, are soaring around awaiting the visit of the Grim Reaper, ready to swoop down on the incompetent full-blood heirs the instant the breath leaves the relative's body. These grafters usually aim to have the heirs sign a contract to pay them fifty per cent of the amount to be automatically transferred to them, and yet they render no service in the transaction.

## The System at Work

The whole system of guardianship turns upon the county judges. These judges are elected for a two-year term by popular vote and the guardianships are regarded as political plums. The judge depends for his election on the persons whom he has promised to appoint guardians, and once he has appointed them he will depend on them for his re-election, and so will not remove them even if they are incompetent. The guardian makes whatever purchases needed for his ward at certain stores, or tells his ward that he must purchase at these stores, and thus the storekeeper is anxious to have the guardianship continued and to have the county judge re-elected. Thus an informal organization is built up so that every member of the community of any influence has interest in protecting the system.

There are two evils that result from this system: One is the charging of excessive guardian fees, attorneys' fees and administrative costs; the other is the actual abuse of the trust by dishonesty, petty graft and negligence. There are plenty of cases of this sort to be found in every county.

The first step in any guardianship case is to make application to the county court for appointment. In the case of a minor it is only necessary to show that there is some money to be handled. In case the Indian is of age and has property, it is necessary to show that he is incompetent to handle his own property. Although incompetents are not specifically referred to in the Act of 1908, the practice of the Oklahoma Courts has been to regard them as included in the term "minors" in Section 6 of that Act. The County Courts, in general, have little hesitation in declaring any Indian incompetent to handle more than a very limited sum of money, and no Indian for whom a guardianship is sought has any likelihood of avoiding it. As an example of this, take the case of Susanna Butler and the case of Munnie Bear:

Susanna Butler nee Dacon, is a full-blood Creek girl, about twenty years old, with an income from the Department of $500 a month, and also some land leased on a crop-share agreement.

An action was brought to declare her incompetent. Testimony showed that she usually spent all the $500 in the first part of the month and had a few unpaid bills and that a large part of the expenses came in taking motor trips around the country with other Indian girls, her own age, in which she paid all the expenses.

A garage keeper testified that she bought things from him at excessive prices, but on cross-examination denied he overcharged and said that she merely bought the best in the market instead of something just as good at a lower price.

Susanna admitted that she did not know some details of oil leases which were handled by the Department for her. There was no other evidence of incompetency of weight. It was held by the County Court that she was incompetent and a guardian appointed. An appeal is pending in this case.

Munnie Bear, a young, shrewd full-blood Creek woman, with the help of her half-brother, ran a farm which she inherited from her aunt, her own allotment being leased.

When oil was discovered on her allotment, an action was started to appoint a guardian for her. The testimony shows that although she did not speak English, or read or write, she had managed to save enough in three or four years to buy some $2000 worth of livestock and a Ford truck for use on the farm, and had at least $2500 more in the bank. Her half-brother, Lonie, testified that she kept all the money in the bank in her own name; that she never let him keep any of it; that he took care of the stock and that she kept account of it and that he did not sell any of it without seeing her first, and that if she agreed to the sale he handed her the money and she put it in the bank. On this evidence, it was held that she was incompetent to handle her own property and a guardian was appointed. The case was reversed on appeal.

The principle of Munnie Bear's case seems to be that if she never spent any money, she did not know the value of it, and the principle of Susanna Dacon's case would seem to be that if she always spent all the money, she did not know the value of it.

Both cases were decided by the same judge, William L. Seawell, of Okfuskee County, in February and March, 1923.

## A SEVEN-YEAR-OLD VICTIM

The smothered cries of the Indians for rescue from legalized plunder comes in a chorus from all parts of eastern Oklahoma. The case cited above is from Tulsa County. And now follows another outrage perpetrated under cover of a County Court in the southern part of eastern Oklahoma.

Little *Ledcie Stechi*, a Choctaw minor, seven years old, owned rich oil property in McCurtain County. She lived with her old grandmother in a small shack back in the hills about two and a half miles from Smithville. They lived in dire poverty, without proper food or clothing and surrounded by filth and dirt. Ledcie Stechi inherited lands from her mother, including twenty acres which became valuable oil property. Other lands she inherited were sold by her uncle, Noel Samuel, for a consideration of $2000 which was deposited in the bank subject to control by the County Judge, who allowed $10 a month for the support of Ledcie Stechi.

After the discovery of oil on the twenty acres above mentioned, her uncle, Noel Samuel, who was her guardian, was induced to resign through a combination of various tactics, force, persuasion and offer of reward which he never got. Mr. Jordon Whiteman, owner of the First National Bank of Idabel, whose attorney was instrumental in Noel Samuel's resignation, was appointed guardian. At the time of Mr. Whiteman's appointment, July, 1921, Ledcie lived with her old grandmother in the hills, and until 1923 they were in a semi-starving condition. Once a week the old grandmother walked to Smithville to buy food on the monthly credit of $15 allowed them by Mr. Whiteman, at Blake's store. They had no conveyance. Sometimes she was too tired to walk back. Then she hired some one to take her home, which cost fifty or sixty cents. During this period from 1921 to 1923, the guardian did nothing to make them more comfortable or to educate the little Indian heiress.

In the fall of 1922 the guardian attempted to sell ten acres of Ledcie's oil land which was producing at the time, and appraised at $90,000, for a consideration of $2000. This attempt was defeated, and with the result that Ledcie Stechi's monthly allowance was increased to $200, from which the guardian allowed the child and grandmother a credit of $15 monthly at a local store. Still, throughout the following year, Ledcie and her grandmother fared no better than prior to the $200 allowance to the guardian. In April, 1923, they were brought to Idabel, the County seat. The rich little Choctaw girl, with her feeble grandmother, came to town carrying their clothes, a bundle of faded rags, in a flour sack. Ledcie was dirty, filthy, and covered with vermin. She was emaciated and weighed about 47 pounds.

A medical examination showed she was undernourished and poisoned by malaria. After five weeks of medical treatment and nourishment Ledcie gained 11 pounds. Her health improved, she was placed by an employee of the Indian Service in the Wheelock Academy, an Indian school. Mr. Whiteman, evidently fearing to lose his grasp on his ward, demanded the child, and Ledcie Stechi, child of much abuse, was returned to the custody of her legal guardian 24 hours after she was taken to the school where she would have had good care. The last time the aged grandmother had seen Ledcie, and only for a few minutes, was on the 12th of July.

A month later, on the 14th of August, word was brought to the hills that Ledcie was dead. There had been no word of the girl's illness and the sudden news of her death was a terrible blow to the poor old grandmother.

The following day, at dawn, before the corpse had arrived, parties of grafters arrived at the heretofore unknown hovel in the hills and harassed the bereaved old grandmother about the future disposal of Ledcie's valuable properties.

Rival speculators went over the body of Ledcie Stechi. Some of them sent flowers to be placed on the grave of her, who though but a child, had known only of poisonous thorns. The floral offerings were too late for the child of sorrows, but they were made by hypocrites who hoped thereby to play upon the heart of the aged grandmother, who was now the sole heir to Ledcie Stechie's vast estate.

Greed for the girl's lands and rich oil property actuated the grafters and made them like beasts surrounding their prey, insensible to the grief and anguish of the white-haired grandmother. Feebly, hopelessly, she wailed over the little dead body – its baby mouth turned black, little fingernails turned black, and even the little breast all turned black! In vain she asked for an examination of the body, believing Ledcie had been poisoned. "No use. Bury the body," commanded the legal guardian.

The Court has already appointed a guardian for the grandmother, – against her vehement protest. She, too, will go the way of her grandchild, as sheep for slaughter by ravenous wolves in men's forms, unless the good people of America intervene immediately by remedial Congressional action. Such action is the duty of all loyal Americans for the protection of America's wards.

Incidentally, another heir has been put forward in a contest suit; but whichever way the case is decided the attorneys expect to come in for fat fees.

## In Osage County

Having heard a great deal about the questionable tactics of County Judges, and having read many records in the County Court files, I naturally wanted to attend a hearing that I might get facts first hand. By inquiry I learned that numerous cases were on the Court calendars of the different counties of Eastern Oklahoma. I selected one in which I did not know any of the parties concerned or the nature of the case.

On November 19, 1923, I attended the court hearing of the case of Martha Axe Roberts (nee Washington), in Osage County held in Pawhuska, Oklahoma. Martha, – a Shawnee, and widow of an Osage from whom she inherited one and one-half shares in the Osage Nation, – did not appear in person. She was represented by her attorney, Mr. T.A. Chandler, a former Congressman from Oklahoma. This case involved an effort to remove the present guardian and transfer jurisdiction over Martha's estate from the Osage County to the Craig County Court. It was surprising at the outset when her attorney, identifying Martha, offered a government record of her enrollment that the Court would not allow it. The continued protest of Judge Sturgill, attorney for L.T. Hill, guardian of Martha, made it next to impossible to give any evidence for the Indian woman. The court would not hear the story of her deprivations and poverty.

Though Martha had inherited wealth (an annual income of at least $15,000), it was so manipulated by her white guardian, L.T. Hill, of Hominy, Oklahoma, that instead of her weekly allowance of $75, she was told she had no money. Mr. Hill let her have $1.50 and sometimes as much as $2.50, claiming it was a personal loan to her.

Dissatisfied and lonely, Martha left Hominy and went to live with her father and mother in Craig County. She moved her household goods to White Oaks, among the Shawnee Indians. Her guardian went to Vinita, a nearby town, and there finding Martha in her Packard car, put her out on the street and took her car away under a writ of replevin.[7] Martha got a conveyance, through the kindness of a friend, and went home only to find an empty house. Her household goods had been taken by her guardian, even to the kitchen stove. For her and her two small children there was not a bed nor a chair nor food in the house. Her "professional" guardian further placed a notice in the newspaper warning the public against giving Martha any credit. He wrote her a letter; told her she would get no money from him until she returned to Osage County.

During these troubled times her fourteen months' old baby got sick. In her extremity, Martha again telephoned to her guardian for money, as she could get no one to attend her child except a negro doctor who, upon hearing of the notice in the newspaper, left the case. Mr. Hill refused to pay Martha any of her money.

This Indian woman of ample means in her own right, with an annual income of at least $15,000, was

---

7 An action for the recovery of goods or chattels wrongfully taken or detained; here the guardian uses US law to engage in corrupt activities.

thrown upon public charity, while the court allowed $1900 to her guardian for replevining her property. Without proper food or medical care, the baby died. When Mr. Hill heard of the child's death he telephoned to his ward to hold the dead body a day and wait until he came when he would make all the funeral arrangements. So obstinate in not letting his ward have her money when the baby was yet alive and there was hope of saving its life – now, so ready to spend her money after the baby was forever lost to its broken-hearted mother. The Osage County court would not hear the tragic story of the Shawnee woman whose identification it had refused to recognize. Like countless other Indians, she was but a fly upon the chariot wheel of her legal guardian.

Mr. Hill was represented by Judge Sturgill, a former judge of Osage County, under whom he had been appointed guardian for Martha Axe Roberts, nee Washington. The objections of Judge Sturgill to most of the evidence offered in Martha's case were sustained by the court and therefore stricken from the record. The Court stenographer forgot to take down statements of Mr. Chandler, Martha's attorney, until he requested her to do so. Plainly, the court was dominated by Judge Sturgill. It is common talk that the present judge owes his appointment to the influence of this same Judge Sturgill, following his resignation. Whenever Judge Sturgill spoke, the Court's hearing improved and much went into its records about John Washington, Martha's father, being a worthless drunkard and also that Martha had no sense of the value of money, nor of right and wrong; that she was crazy. Within a short half-hour, the Court dismissed the case. Mr. Chandler gave notice that the case would be appealed to the State District Court.

I felt an overwhelming indignation at the legal helplessness of a poor, rich Indian woman.

Yet, there was a question in my mind lest Martha be mentally unbalanced under the strain and humiliation of her situation; that there might be some foundation for this official statement against her that she was crazy. To satisfy myself on this point I went to Vinita. There I met a gentle, bright-eyed Indian woman. After hours of conversation with her, in the course of our visit together, I found her very intelligent, though unlettered.

I spent the evening with her, her little child and her father and mother. Many things were told to me of her guardian, Mr. Hill. She said he had a store in Hominy to which he limited all her purchases. He sold her faded shopworn blankets that had holes in them at full price and refused to exchange them when she protested. When she wanted to buy a Singer sewing machine, Mr. Hill told her she had no money. He bought her, out of her own funds, however, an expensive Packard car, and submitted to the Court a gas bill for eight months amounting to $2750. Judge Sturgill, then on the bench, approved it. Mr. Hill's father-in-law sells gasoline. This item was later protested.

Martha further said her guardian bought high-grade hogs, paying as much as $90 for a six months' old pig, when she was not interested in stock raising and only wanted a few hogs on the farm to use for meat. Now Mr. Hill is paying a man $50 a month, out of her funds, to care for the stock she did not want.

Martha says her estate is being mismanaged by her guardian, and, while he is not guardian of her person, Mr. Hill is trying to force her to return to Osage County. Her own desire is to remain in Craig County with her father and mother, and to live among her people, whose language she speaks. Martha has more than enough means for herself and child. She is to be admired in her wish to live with her father and mother, who are no longer young, to make them more comfortable in their advancing age.

Her father, John Washington, is a bricklayer and stone cutter by trade. He is a man well-informed in practical business methods and has a keen memory. He did not deny the charge against him that he uses intoxicating liquors, but he told me of many occasions, which he has not forgotten, when Mr. Hill, Martha's guardian, supplied him with his whiskey in the name of friendship. It appears that Mr. Hill would make use of the habit he encouraged now to discredit John Washington.

I called the Farmers State Bank in Vinita and asked the cashier, Mr. Martin, if he knew John Washington. He said "yes." Mr. Martin had been born and raised there and knew everybody. I asked him if the charge against John Washington was true, that he was a worthless drunkard? He said, "I have never seen him drunk. On the contrary, I consider Martha and her father intelligent and above the average Indian."

My conclusion is that Martha is not crazy but perfectly sane, and her love for her parents, which draws her to them, is wholly admirable. She is a victim of exploitation.

Under the present bias of the County Court, where Judge, ex-judge and "professional" guardian combine their forces, the Indian is legally bound and gagged. There is no hope of justice so long as these conditions are permitted to remain. Legalized robbery of the rich Indian is an ugly practice and abhorred by all self-respecting Americans.

The human cry of this Shawnee woman is a call to America for defence and protection.

## In Briefer Form

To cite all the cases investigated would be monotonous repetition; suffice it to say, their number is legion, and while there may be variation as to harrowing details, the general result is the same, so far as it concerns the plundering of the Indians, under the "system" as developed in eastern Oklahoma.

A brief summary, which follows, of a number of glaring cases will show that in the activities of the informal organization of grafters, sex or age make no difference; the young child, the adult, the incompetent (mentally or physically) are all robbed in the same thorough, nonchalant scientific manner. The "system" has but one object – GET THE MONEY AND GET IT QUICK!

In the case of HILLY BEAR the grafters waited almost at the bedside of the woman, and when the breath left her body they took her thumb, pressed it on an ink pad and then made the finger-print signature on a document alleged to be her last will. When an investigation was made the ink was found on Hilly Bear's dead finger. Fortunately, this atrocious effort was defeated; but it illustrates some of the methods that have been used by the grafters.

AKEY ULTEESKEE, full-blood Creek, No. 4231, had land adjoining Bartlesville. When she was four years old she was taken by a man named Lannom and raised as his own child. Her land had oil on it. When she became of age her guardian owed her $22,000. The guardian was also the father of Akey's illegitimate child – he robbed her of her money and her virtue. The child was given away. When last heard of it was at Fort Smith, Ark. Akey is now of age; has no guardian for obvious reasons, and is living at Willowbrook, Calif. She has a small income of about four or five dollars a month, which is handled by the Muskogee office.

SINA BATTIEST died November 8l, 1918. She left a child (about one year old at the time of her death), Malvina Battiest, now Billy.

FOUR YEARS LATER Sina Battiest, according to the certificate of a Notary Public, appeared in person, AS A MAN, and executed a lease to one Charles S. Lynch, and "his" signature is duly attested to by two witnesses. This document is in Book 110, page 39, Records of Stephens County, Oklahoma.

Thus, it will be seen that the grafters can bring the dead to life, and even change the sex!

FANNIE TIGER, full-blood Creek, widow of Palmer Tiger, inherited one-half interest in her husband's estate. The Court approved a purported Oil and Gas lease for $4000 paid over County Judge's desk; the money was put in an envelope; taken to bank by her and when counted only $1500 was found. This purported oil and gas lease was later found to be a deed to the property.

The case was contested in Court; the district Court decided against Fannie Tiger. Motion for a new trial is now pending.

ROBERT THOMPSON, an incompetent restricted Quapaw Indian, about fifty years old. He was sent to an Insane Asylum. When the present guardian took charge of this estate, a little over two years ago, $24,000 was receipted for. The Liberty Bonds and all securities have been disposed of, and the balance now on hand (November, 1913) amounted to $54.40.

CHRISTINE BENNETT (mixed-blood Choctaw) became of age in May, 1923. Oil was developed on her property a few years prior to that date, and from the available records it would appear that the amount received from the estate was $151,000, out of which Christine received less that $15,000. The remaining 90 percent went to attorneys, or was loaned by the guardian to worthless securities.

SABER JACKSON (Creek full-blood) received $50,000 for his courtesy right in the property inherited by his daughter. A guardian, of course, was appointed to handle the money. By order of the Court, the guardian paid himself approximately $8000. Five thousand dollars was paid to certain attorneys, in addition to their expense accounts. Then the guardian is alleged to have loaned out practically all of the balance of the security that was wholly inadequate.

The indifference of a County Court to the interest of a full-blood Indian is illustrated in the case of ISRAEL LEWIS, a Choctaw Roll N. 11,925. Under existing law, a deed from a full-blood heir must be approved by the County Court having jurisdiction. A petition was presented to the Pontotoc County Court in the name of Israel Lewis, to sell a tract of inherited land for $2800. The land was appraised at $4502, and another bid for $3500 had been submitted. The Court ignored the probate attorney's protest, and the land was sold for $2800.

## In Conclusion

These cases, we think, are sufficient to show the hopelessness of the present situation. In the same section of the Act giving jurisdiction to the county courts was a provision for the appointment of probate attorneys to watch the interests of the Indian wards. The Oklahoma Courts have held that they are not bound to pay any attention to the recommendations of these probate attorneys, and the latter informed us it is only by keeping on friendly terms with the judges that they are able to accomplish anything whatever for the benefit of the Indians. In one case an attorney told us that the court had held that a brief which he filed as probate attorney for the United States, and as Amicus Curiae was entitled to no consideration as filed by the Probate Attorney of the United States, but would be considered as he had added the words "Amicus Curiae"; or, in substance, that they would hear him as a friend of the Court but would not hear the United States by its Attorney.

## The Remedy

There is no hope of any reformation of the present system, and if action is delayed for a few years there will be no Indians with property to be protected. Legislation should be enacted at once giving the Department of the Interior as complete control of all Indian property and Indian minors and incompetents as constitutional limitations will permit, and this should apply to all Indians in Oklahoma.

Respectfully Submitted,

Gertrude Bonnin,
Research Agent, Indian Welfare Committee, General Foundation of Women's Clubs

Charles H. Fabens,
For American Indian Defense Ass'n.

Matthew K. Sniffen,
For Indian Rights Association.

# Ora V. Eddleman Reed
# (pseud. Mignon Schreiber; Cherokee, 1880–1968)

*One of the most prolific writers in this collection, Ora Eddleman Reed was born near Denton, Texas. Like many of her female Cherokee counterparts, she was well educated, attending Henry Kendall College, which would later become the University of Tulsa. Reed's father, David Jones Eddleman, was a prominent figure in the pioneer community of Denton, being elected mayor twice, leading in the organization of the First Christian Church, and acting as a Masonic Grand Lecturer of Texas from 1871 to 1880. During the Civil War, he and his two brothers served in the Confederate army, as did several of Reed's maternal relatives. Reed's strong-willed Cherokee–Irish mother, Mary Daugherty, came to Denton from Missouri. We know little about this early part of Reed's life other than that she attended school with her younger sister, to whom she was close all her life.*

*After the passage of the General Allotment Act, the family debated the move to Indian Territory, in part because Mary and her brothers wished to fulfill a family dream of rejoining the Cherokees. Although David had other ideas, Mary prevailed, and when Ora was about fourteen, the family returned to Muskogee. The move played a crucial role in the events of the writer's later life, for in 1897, David, his two children Myrta and George, and Mary's cousin, Charles L. Daugherty, bought the* Muskogee Daily Times, *in part to repay the debt owed them by the struggling newspaper's first owners. None of these partners was a strong business manager, however, and the paper continued to flounder until Mary Eddleman became the manager. With David's excellent editorship and Mary's management abilities, the paper began to prosper.*

*While still in her teens, Reed took on jobs as telegraph editor, proofreader, society editor, city editor, and production person. Ironically, the ownership of the paper ultimately stood in the way of fulfillment of the family dream of enrollment as Cherokees, for it reprinted an article that criticized the judge who heard their case when it came to court. Nevertheless, the Eddlemans remained proud of their Cherokee heritage, which Reed would highlight in much of her later writing. While Ora worked on the* Muskogee Daily Times, *her sister Myrta and her husband Walter Sams founded the newspaper,* Twin Territories, *of which Reed would eventually assume editorial responsibility. Involved from the beginning, she was listed as editor beginning in 1900, at the same time becoming active in the Territory Press Association. Much of the writing published in the early issues may have been composed by her, although she rarely signed her work and often assumed the pseudonym of Mignon Schreiber (meaning "little writer"), an accurate pen name for someone who was five feet tall and weighed 100 pounds. Under Ora's editorship, which appears to have occurred between 1898 to 1904, with some brief gaps, the magazine flourished; she not only contributed pieces herself, but drew together some of the most talented writers in the territories, including Chinnubbie Harjo and Alexander Posey.*

*Because* Twin Territories *sought and gained an audience both in the territories and from the East – the latter often investors – the contents reveal a broad amalgamation of materials. Reed's own writing included romantic short fiction, novellas, humor, essays, and tribal stories. Some of her fiction focuses on independent heroines who nevertheless find love. Themes of mistaken identity, or the relationship of mixed blood women to white men, appear frequently, as in "Only an Indian Girl" and "Her Thanksgiving Visit." Narratives such as "Indian Wit and Wisdom" and "Aunt Mary's Christmas Dinner" delight in telling stories of Indians' one-upmanship over whites – a version of the coup tale – while "Billy Bearclaws, Aid to Cupid," represents both a romantic narrative and a reinvention of the trickster tale. Anticipating some of Zitkala-Ša's political writing, "Father of 90,000 Indians" and "Daughters of Confederacy" provide readers with tribal and territorial history, while "What the Curious Want to Know," a regular feature of the newspaper, addressed questions sent to the young editor, often by people outside the territories. Here Reed's wry and sometimes caustic voice emerges in full force. Although in aesthetic terms much of the fiction may appear relatively conventional, we need to remember that most of the work collected here was written when Reed was fairly young; nevertheless, it often has some kind of twist, or displays a complex use of voice and perspective, emerging, perhaps, from Reed's identity as an educated and progressive mixed-blood Cherokee. Like Callahan and Owen, Reed appears to have less of the ambivalence about her bicultural status than does Zitkala-Ša; like many of the writers here, however, Reed frequently invokes the image of the proper Victorian lady combined with the independent woman. We should also be attentive to the fact that novellas like "A Pair of Moccasins" and "Lucy and I As Missionaries" were published serially, and thus require of us a different kind of attentiveness to plot development, character, and genre than narratives published originally in complete form.*

*Sometime in the latter years of her editorship, the writer met her future husband, Charles LeRoy Reed, a reporter for the* Kansas City Star *and later an assistant manager for the Associated Press. Although Ora's father initially opposed the marriage, he finally consented, and the couple were married in Muskogee on April 6, 1904. Ora moved briefly to Kansas City, where she was unhappy, before she and Charles returned to Muskogee, where Charles worked for the US Indian Agency until about 1916. In the early years of the marriage, Ora continued to work in journalism, editing the "Indian Department" of* Sturm's *from September 1905 to November 1906. Ill health and then motherhood – two sons – eventually prompted her to give up this work. When Charles finally obtained a good job with the Gulf Oil Company, the family moved to Ponca City, and later, to Casper, Wyoming. As her sons grew up, Ora had time to contribute to various local newspapers, and she initiated and hosted what may have been the first "talk radio" show in the United States.*

*After Charles Reed retired in 1942, the family returned to Muskogee, where he died in 1949. Ora moved to Tulsa and contributed a few essays and articles to local newpapers and magazines. Sometime during her long life, she completed a novel manuscript and an unpublished volume of poetry still held by the family. Reed's important contributions to the traditions of Cherokee writing, Native American writing, and American literature richly deserve the attention they are only beginning to receive.*

## Bibliography

### Primary

Aunt Mary's Christmas Dinner (*Twin Territories*, December, 1899).
Billy Bearclaws, Aid to Cupid (*Sturm's Oklahoma Magazine*, September, 1909).
The Choctaw People (*Twin Territories*, June, 1899).
A Christmas Legend (*Twin Territories*, December, 1902).
[Daugherty Canyon] (*Twin Territories*, May, 1899).
Daughters of Confederacy (*Sturm's Oklahoma Magazine*, June, 1910).
Do Not Want Them (*Twin Territories*, June, 1899).
A Face at the Window (*Twin Territories*, July, 1899).
Father of 90,000 Indians (*Sturm's Oklahoma Magazine*, July, 1906).
Her Mother's Daughter (*Twin Territories*, July, 1900–January, 1901; with Harriet Bradley).
Her Thanksgiving Visit (*Twin Territories*, November, 1899).
The Honor of Wynoma (*Twin Territories*, November, 1902).
The Indian Orphan (*Sturm's Oklahoma Magazine*, January, 1908).
Indian Proverbs (*Sturm's Statehood Magazine*, March, 1906).
Indian Tales Between Pipes (*Sturm's Oklahoma Magazine*, November, 1906).
Indian Wit and Wisdom (*Sturm's Statehood Magazine*, March, 1906).

Lizonka (*Twin Territories*, May–October, 1899).
Lucy and I as Missionaries (*Twin Territories*, March–August, 1900).
Only an Indian Girl (*Twin Territories*, February–July, 1900; with Barton Langford).
A Pair of Moccasins (*Twin Territories*, August–December, 1899).
[Talequah] (*Twin Territories*, June, 1899).
What the Curious Want to Know (*Twin Territories*, 1900–2).
When the Cowboy Reigned (*Sturm's Statehood Magazine*, April, 1906).

Secondary

Kosmider, Alexia. "Strike a Euroamerican Pose: Ora Eddleman Reed's 'Types of Indian Girl.'" *American Transcendental Quarterly* 12:2 (1998): 109–31.
——. "'What the Curious Want to Know': Cherokee Writer, Ora Eddleman Reed Writes Back to the Empire." *Literature and Psychology* 41:4 (1995): 51–72.
Littlefield, Daniel F., Jr., and James W. Parins. "Ora V. Eddleman Reed." In *Native American Writing in the Southeast: An Anthology, 1875–1935*. Mississippi, 1995.
Mihesuah, Devon A. *Cultivating the Rosebuds: The Education of Women at the Cherokee Female Seminary*. Illinois, 1993.
Morrison, Daryl. "*Twin Territories: The Indian Magazine*, and Its Editor, Ora Eddleman Reed." *Chronicles of Oklahoma* 60 (1982): 136–66.
Perdue, Theda. *Cherokee Women: Gender and Culture Change, 1700–1835*. Nebraska, 1998.
——. *Nations Remembered: An Oral History of the Five Civilized Tribes, 1865–1907*. Greenwood, 1980.
——. *Slavery and the Evolution of Cherokee Society, 1540–1866*. Tennessee, 1979.

# Fiction

## From *Twin Territories*

### A Face at the Window (July, 1899)

"Why, come right in, Mr. Franklin. It is cooler out here on the porch than in the house, though. Will you be seated?"

"Yes, thank you Mrs. Ansley. You have a very pleasant place. I haven't been here for quite a while have I? All well?"

"Quite well, thank you. You should come oftener to see us. True there are no young folks here – that is, young ladies, so that even Tom, who has just returned from college, finds it dull and is seldom at home. But – "

"No young ladies, you say? Why, there is one, for as I came up the road now I saw in the upper window of this house the most beautiful face I ever beheld. Is she a guest of yours?"

"Guest! Why, indeed you must be mistaken. There is not a woman on this place but myself; and as for a young lady, there has not been one at this old farm house for over a week."

Mr. Franklin jumped up excitedly. "My dear Mrs. Ansley, I am not mistaken. As sure as I am here looking at you, just so sure did I see a face at the window upstairs. Come out here in the yard, perhaps it is still visible."

He clutched her arm and together they gazed at the upstairs window, but nothing was to be seen there.

Mrs. Ansley looked nervously at her caller. He was a tall handsome brunette, well dressed and a well known man in the little village and surrounding country. Everybody who knew him admired and respected him. Mrs. Ansley knew he was perfectly sane, so how could she account for this sudden nonsensical whim, as she termed it?

She was greatly relieved when she saw Tom coming up the road. Mr. Franklin scarcely greeted him, so intently was he looking at the window.

"He declares he saw the face of a woman at the window up there, Tom," Mrs. Ansley whispered to her son. "Do you see any one?"

"Why, no indeed. What kind of a looking creature was she, Franklin?"

Mr. Franklin turned round quickly and in an excited voice said:

"I was coming up the road there when I happened to glance up and at that window just above us I saw gazing down at me the loveliest face I have ever seen. She appeared to be rather young and had something white over her head. She was a perfect blond – that was all I could tell, for she was there only a half a minute or so. As soon as I started on she vanished.

"You are aware that I am an admirer of beautiful faces, but I had never hoped to see any thing half so lovely as this vision. Pardon me, but will you allow me to search that room?" Mrs. Ansley hesitated.

"Oh course you may both come with me," he added.

"Very well. Come;" and Mrs. Ansley led the way to a pretty little bedroom on the second floor of the house. This room was searched, and, in fact, the whole house, but it was of no use. No young lady was to be seen. Somewhat crestfallen, but still firmly protesting that he had seen a young lady at that window, young Franklin took his departure, accompanied by Tom.

Mrs. Ansley stood at the front gate watching them.

Franklin seemed to be telling Tom just how and where he was when he saw the face.

When he came to a certain turn in the road he stopped, wheeled round facing the window, and for a few seconds stood there pointing silently toward the window.

Mrs. Ansley saw it all and flew down to the bend in the road. She grasped Franklin's arm, but he shook her off, saying wildly: "Look and be convinced! There she stands in exactly the same position as before."

Tom looked and Mrs. Ansley looked. Then the latter gave one faint little scream and her hands fell heavily to her sides. For there in the window was the face Franklin had described.

Finally they recovered and started towards the house, determining to search it once more. But strange to say she vanished as quickly as they left the bend in the road.

The news quickly spread over the village and country, and crowds flocked to see "the face at the window."

Mrs. Ansley and Tom moved to another town, and for many years their old home was known as the "famous haunted house."

As for Franklin, he had fallen desperately in love with the face. He would sit for hours and hours at the bend in the road watching the window and talking tenderly about his love for the fair blue-eyed maiden.

A curious feature of the affair was that the face was not visible on cloudy days or from any other point than the bend in the road.

The papers said: "Absolutely nothing can be seen from the inside of the house, and though venturesome people sit on the outside sill and carefully examine the glass from the outside, there is nothing to account for the appearance of the face."

The excitement grew intense and exciting tales were scattered afar over the adjoining country about the old house. All kinds of experiments were made, but no one could account for the appearance of the lovely face. Everybody for miles around knew of Walter Franklin's love for the fair one. While he remained perfectly sane on every other point, he was insane whenever the "face at the window" was mentioned. He never allowed it to interfere with his business affairs, however, and he lost not a particle of respect and admiration he had always commanded. But his health was fast sinking, and the doctor ordered a change of climate and scene.

It was with great difficulty that Mr. Franklin was persuaded to leave "his lady." At first he refused outright, but when he was told that Mrs. Ansley wanted him to come to her home in a town far distant, he gave in and soon found himself comfortably established in her new home.

Whenever the "face at the window" was mentioned, Mrs. Ansley would get nervous and plead for it to be hushed. So it happened that Franklin, ever gallant and thoughtful, never mentioned his "love." He secretly confided to Tom that he'd marry no one until that mystery was cleared up and he found a face as beautiful as his vision.

One evening he strolled out alone. The surrounding country was beautiful and the cool evening air felt refreshing. Mrs. Ansley lived in a pretty country place with very few neighbors, so Walter walked nearly a mile before he came upon a house. When he found himself so far from home, and it nearly supper time, he decided to enter the house, get a drink and perhaps stay there for supper, for well he knew the country people's hospitality.

When he entered and made himself known, they were just on the point of sitting down to their evening meal, and, as he expected, he was urged to eat. In the course of the meal the farmer, and head of the house asked, "Where is Bessie, wife?"

"Oh, lawsy, I forgot. She was so tired when she got here that she asked me to let her sleep till supper, and here I have done and gone and forgot her. I'll go get her." And, rising from the table, the old lady left the room and soon returned with a young woman.

"Mr. Franklin," the old farmer said, "this is my niece, Bessie Jonwell, who is visitin' us for a spell. Now, let's all eat supper."

Mr. Franklin raised his eyes to her face for the first time, and then grasping the back of the chair for support, stood leaning there, heavy and unconscious. No one could account for this sudden action. When he had revived sufficiently to speak, he found himself on a bed, and the startled farmer and his wife near his bedside. They begged him not to speak, but he feebly inquired, "Where's my Bessie?"

Bessie came in scared and white and stood trembling before him. "Where's the window, Bessie?" he asked, stroking her hand. "When I wanted you so, why did you stand so quietly at the window? Why didn't you let me find you?"

All night he tossed and murmured and called for Bessie, if she were absent from the room.

Next morning Mrs. Ansley and Tom were sent for. When they entered Walter Franklin's room no one was there but the old farmer and Walter. As soon as the latter saw them he sat up in bed and said, "Oh, Mrs. Ansley, I've found her. She hasn't been at the window all the time; she's here. Why don't you bring her in, sir?" turning to the farmer. "Go bring Bessie to me!"

The old man left the room and returned with Bessie. Mrs. Ansley covered her face with her hands when she gazed on her, but Tom recovered himself in time to shake hands with her and lead her to a chair.

"Don't you see?" cried Walter feverishly: "This is Bessie! I found her! See her hair – so fine and golden, and her sweet blue eyes!" Then he would sink back on his pillow and rest quietly for a while if she remained by him.

"Can you, Mrs. Ansley, Mr. Ansley, explain all this to us? He hasn't been right since he saw her, and she firmly protests that she never saw or heard of him before. What can it all mean, ma'am?"

"Sir," began Tom, for his mother was too weak to talk. "I might just as well tell you all. Mr. Franklin is asleep, and if mother would rather she may leave the room."

"No, I will stay," whispered Mrs. Ansley. So Tom commenced:

"Some years ago my mother and I were living in the little village of M—, and this Mr. Franklin was a good friend of ours and came to see us quite often. One day he came, and in course of the conversation inquired who our guest was. We had no guest, but he declared he had seen a young lady at the upstairs window as he came up the road in front of our house. We allowed him to search the house, and the result was he found no one. If we had not afterwards seen the face ourselves, we would have declared him insane. But the whole village saw it from a bend in the road, from which point only it was visible. Of course, the house was declared haunted, and we moved here, but have not been able to sell the house to this day – ."

"And the mystery remains a mystery still?" interrupted the farmer.

"It does. And I fear it will never be cleared up. Many have tried different experiments, but I have never bothered with it. I – "

"What sort of face had she?" inquired the now thoroughly excited farmer.

"Oh, yes; that's the most exciting part," put in Mrs. Ansley; "the face in the window was exactly the same as your niece's here. How can it be, I wonder?"

"I used to live in the village you mentioned," said the farmer – Mr. Randell – who was by no means ignorant, "when I was a boy. I have not been to the old place for many years, but if you wish I will go with you and help clear this up, for I believe it can be done. I believe that all phenomena can be accounted for on scientific principles."

"You have heard of this before, then?" questioned Tom.

"No, never. Not even when I was living there did anything like this occur. But I would like to see this face, and if you will go with me we will start in a few days. This young man will be better soon."

"Don't you think it is strange that the face is like mine, uncle?" inquired Bessie.

"It is, very. But there may be some mistake in regard to that, if they never got nearer it than the road, because the window woman was blonde and you are a blonde may make it seem as you and she resembled."

Turning to Tom he inquired: "But why did it affect Mr. Franklin so when he met Bessie last evening?"

"Why," exclaimed Tom, "he fell in love with the window woman, and upon seeing a face so like his 'love's' he fainted."

"Humph!" ejaculated the farmer.

In about a week Mr. Randall and Mr. Ansley started for M—.

Mrs. Ansley had Walter moved to her house and Bessie went, too, to stay by him. It was plain the nursing was not distasteful to her.

When Tom came to his old home he scarcely knew it, it was so overgrown with weeds and so deserted looking. But as soon as they came to the bend in the road, there in the window was the same face that had been there for many years.

The farmer was greatly excited and anxious to examine the window glass.

Then they hurried up to the place, and Tom noticed the farmer wore a puzzled expression.

"Have you any clue to this mystery, sir?" he asked respectfully.

"No, " shortly answered the farmer. "But," he continued, "I have seen this place before. In fact, I was born in this very room."

"What! Is this your old home? Why did you not tell me before?"

"Because I did not know. You never told me in what part of the village your 'haunted house' was."

"True. But now maybe you know the cause of the appearance of this face?"

"Can't say that I do. But I'm going to know before I leave. This property is too valuable for you to lose in this way."

"Oh! as for the property, it isn't so valuable as you think; still, I don't like losing it. You would perhaps prize it more than I would. To think of your having been born here and spent your boyhood days!"

"Were you not born here, too?"

"No. And I haven't been here very much either – always been away to college. Mother moved here after father died, you know. The old place might be made pretty. Don't know but that I shall build here some day."

During this conversation the farmer had been carefully examining the glass. In the days that followed he made many discoveries after trying many experiments. Among other things he discovered that the face was always in one window pane – there were four in the lower sash, each being about 14x18. He immediately removed the glass and put it to various tests without being enlightened.

But one day, while turning it carefully, he was electrified to see the face appear. He immediately saw the resemblance between it and Bessie's face. It was faint and shadowy, but as he gazed at it he suddenly recognized – his sister, Bessie's mother. He called to Tom: "It is explained – the mystery is cleared!"

"You can't mean it," cried Tom, rushing up the stairs.

"Yes, I can. Come here."

Tom came and, gazing at the faintly outlined face on the glass, he listened while his friend explained the mystery of years.

"As I told you," began the farmer, "I used to live here. My father was a photographer. I am surprised that I did not think of this before, but it is all clear to me now. When my sister, Bessie's mother, was about twenty-two she had father make a large picture of her. When this pane of glass was broken I remember now that he replaced it with a negative on which was the life-size face of my sister.

"How we all laughed at him! The plate was an overexposure, you know, and the negative was too 'thin' to print. Such negatives are not unlike the old-fashioned 'daguerreotype,' and if you were a professional or amateur photographer, you would easily understand how, under certain conditions, the face would appear and disappear. That explains it all, doesn't it?"

"Yes, I understand now. It is the likeness of Miss Jonwell's mother, and that is why the face resembles her. Well, well."

The news soon spread through the village that the "old Ansley house mystery" was satisfactorily cleared up, and that young Ansley was having the house torn away, and a beautiful new residence was being erected. The grounds were once more made pretty, new walks were laid, new shrubbery put out, and the place was not the same. Mrs. Ansley was overjoyed when she heard of it all. When the farmer and Tom returned to their home they found Mr. Franklin quite well and quite in love with blue-eyed Bessie.

It need scarcely be added that in a few months the engagement between Walter Franklin and Bessie was made known. Mrs. Ansley and Tom, together with Mr. and Mrs. Franklin are now living happily in the new house at M—, and Walter Franklin often says that "loving a pretty face is all well enough, but loving a sweet, pretty girl is far better."

## A Pair of Moccasins (August–December, 1899)

### Chapter I

It was considerably past sundown, and a cool, refreshing wind was rising; clouds that betokened rain were gathering in the east. The stillness of evening was settling over the earth; in the deep, dark wood were to be heard the weird sounds that so fascinate the lover of nature. In its recesses, near a little spring, a frog school was in session. The master, a great fellow, sat on a log, and hundreds of pupils, some near, some far, answered his hoarsely-asked questions. Up in the tree-tops the birds sang softly; an owl hooted; the air was full of insects' humming.

Later on, when the birds had almost ceased their chirpings, when even the frogs had become quieter and only the mournful "whoo?" and perhaps a sad "whip-poor-will" broke the stillness, two children entered the wood. The sky was clearing now and the moon shone flickeringly through the forest. The two figures paused, breathless, under the largest of the oaks which seemed almost to bend down to them and ask them what their mission was at that hour, and to whisper, caressingly, that if sorrow or trouble brought them hither, protection would be given them by the huge giants of the forest.

The children were a boy and a girl, the latter taller and perhaps several years older than the former.

The girl gazed about her in rapture.

"Oh, Timber! Isn't this glorious? Isn't it beautiful? were the words she uttered, although in an Indian tongue, and the boy answered:

"Yes, my sister. And to think it is ours, ours."

"Yours, Timber, not mine, for I cannot stay to own it," answered the girl, sadly. "I love the forest – I love every tree in it. I wish I knew that I could always live out here, a child of nature. Oh, Timber! To think I have to go away and may never see you again."

"Yes, yes, you will see me again some day. We shall not be separated for long. Let us not think of the future now, but build a fire and enjoy our last moments with our friends, the trees."

So saying, the little fellow, for he was not more than ten years of age, began to gather dry leaves and sticks and piling them high, set fire to them, and soon the cheerful blaze lighted up fully one-half the forest. The children, wrapped in their blankets, sat before it several hours. After awhile the girl arose and bade the boy stamp down the fire, which had burned low, and together the two left the woods.

When morning came the sun shone through an Indian tepee, and his bright beams played lightly upon the dark faces of the boy and girl as they lay sleeping side by side. The girl woke first.

"Timber, Timber," she called, as she shook the boy. "Wake up, it is morning and the sun is high. Besides, don't you remember what day this is? Wake Timber!"

The boy sat up, rubbing his eyes.

"Oh, Chinka, this is the day you are going away!" he cried, suddenly remembering.

An hour afterward, when a slight breakfast had been prepared by Chinka and partaken of by herself, Timber and their aged grandmother, who had slept in another part of the tepee, a man rode up, dismounted, and leaving his horse to graze near by, entered the tepee. He was a young man, with a kind, good-natured, though not handsome, face. He was tall, but slightly built. The smile he bestowed upon the occupants was such as to inspire confidence. He held out his hand to Chinka, the only one of the three who could understand or speak English, and asked:

"Are you almost ready to go, Chinka? We must be off before noonday."

"Ready go now," she answered shyly. The English was hard for her to speak.

"Tell your grandmother and brother that I have made all the necessary arrangements for taking you away. I have seen the chief and the agent and have secured the papers. Tell them, too, that they must not be uneasy about you. Good care will be taken of you and you can come back to see them some day, or send for them to come to you. Tell them goodbye, and then we must go."

The girl uttered a few sentences in Indian, to which the woman listened unmoved, only grunting. The boy threw his arms about his sister's neck. She put him gently from her and went to her grandmother. The old woman pulled off her moccasins and handed one of them to Chinka, saying, "Take it, my daughter, and never be separated from it. No matter where you go, keep your moccasin. Your brother here will keep its mate, so that when I am dead and gone, and you two are far apart you can each look on your moccasin and think of one another. Then, if you should grow out of each other's knowledge and should meet some day, you could match your moccasins and know that you are brother and sister. Remember, children, let nothing part you from your moccasins."

The white man, who had stood looking on, was somewhat amused, although he could not understand one word the old Indian uttered. He asked no questions, but when Chinka had again embraced both her brother and grandmother, he took her by the hand and led her to where his horse was grazing. One small bundle was all she carried away with her. In that she had placed her moccasin and a blanket, and her companion tied it to the horn of his saddle, and with Chinka behind him he galloped off.

The quaint old tepee, with its bark-covered sides, was soon lost to view. Timber and his grandmother stood long in front of it, gazing after the quickly disappearing horse; then, when only a distant cloud of dust could be seen, Timber turned and fled to the forest.

On and on the travelers rode. Hotter and hotter grew the sun and by the time they came in sight of a settlement, it was the noon hour.

"Are you very tired?" asked the man kindly, as he lifted Chinka off the horse when they had reached the town. She nodded her head.

"We have a long way to go yet, child. We will stop here for dinner and then we take the stage to the nearest railroad. You will see so many new sights and people that you will not be tired, I hope."

He took her into the small, dirty tavern, where a pale, sweet-looking woman met them.

"Did you bring her, Charlie? Yes, there she is," she added, as she caught a glimpse of Chinka. "Bless her little heart! Come here, my dear; are you glad you are going home with us?" She stooped down before Chinka and pinched her round cheeks.

"Poor little girl! You are hot and tired. Come in my room and bathe and rest a little before dinner." She led her away and the man went to look after his horse.

Charles Kimberlain and his wife had been missionaries among the Indians a number of years and had known Chinka since she was a little girl of seven or eight. She had attended their school and there had learned to understand English. With much difficulty they had persuaded her to accompany them to their home, for dearly they loved the child and much wished to educate her. She yielded at last, with the promise that if they decided to keep her, her brother would be sent for also, to share her privileges.

After dinner the three – Charles Kimberlain, his wife and Chinka climbed into the high stage coach and started on their journey to the railway station. Chinka always remembered that drive. It was long and tedious; besides, every tree, every rock, rill and river reminded her of some happy day she and Timber had spent together, while the torturing reminder that she was leaving it all – seemed to be in the very atmosphere; even the birds seemed to be singing, "never come back – you'll never come back – never come back again!" in a sorrowful sort of way.

At last the station was reached. It was quite dark and they were just in time for the night train. The puffing, blowing, whistling and shrieking frightened Chinka, who clung to the missionaries' hands as if she would never let go. Seated in the cars, she was less timid and looked about. There were thousands of things to interest her, and for awhile she forgot Timber, who at that moment was lying in the tall grass in front of the tepee, thinking of her.

## Chapter II

"Little girl, won't you tell me your name?"

The voice was kind, and Chinka looked up, to see a tall stranger bending over her.

He repeated the question, but Chinka shook her head.

"Won't you talk to the gentleman?" asked Mrs. Kimberlain, persuasively.

"Name Chinka," answered the girl, blushing painfully. The gentleman seated himself by her and propounded a number of questions, a few of which she understood and answered. Then he turned to Mr. Kimberlain, with:

"I have often wanted to get a pair of Indian moccasins. I wonder if this little one hasn't a pair she can let me have?"

"I don't know, I am sure, but I hardly believe she has. Where is the moccasin your grandmother gave you, Chinka? Show it to the gentleman."

She hesitated.

"You need not give it to him," he added, and she immediately produced the beautifully beaded slipper. The stranger examined it critically, admiring its odd beauty and curiously stitched sides.

"I would give her anything for it," he said.

"I do not believe she would part with it for any sum. It is the last gift of her aged grandmother," answered Mr. Kimberlain decidedly, and the man returned it to Chinka, who had been eyeing it jealously while he handled it.

That night she slept but little, for she was thinking over the events of the day, so far the most exciting one in all her twelve years.

At last she dozed, and was waked by a sudden crash. She sat up straight and tried to peer through the darkness. Many people were shouting, and some were crying and screaming. Some one reached out his arms to her and said firmly:

"This way, Chinka. There has been a wreck and we must get out. Don't be afraid of me, but give me your hands."

She could not see his face, but the voice she knew belonged to the strange gentleman who had asked her for her moccasin the night before. It was nearly morning now. She reached out her hands and he took her in his arms and carried her into the open air. She did not know what "wreck" meant, but something of its awfulness dawned upon her when she saw the piles of debris, under some of which were writhing, groaning human beings, and still, white corpses, who an hour ago were sleeping peacefully in their berths, little dreaming of their terrible fate. The stranger carried Chinka away from it all, explaining to her as he went, how another train had collided with theirs, and thus the fearful wreck. He left her in a little house by the wayside, bidding her stay there until he returned.

She sat down, tired and frightened, and wondered vaguely how many miles away from Timber she was. She eagerly scanned the faces of those about her, anxious to find Mr. and Mrs. Kimberlain. But nowhere could she find them. She shivered as she thought of the dead people under the piles of broken glass and timbers, and wondered if they were there. Soon the stranger returned.

"Chinka," he said, "you must try to understand me and must be a brave little girl, for I have sad news for you. You must hear what I have to tell you. This is not a time to give down. Your kind friends – I did not learn their names – have suffered much in this wreck. They died a little while ago. The lady was killed almost instantly, but the gentleman lived to see me carry you away. When I went back he called me to him and asked me if you were hurt. When I told him no, that you were quite safe and uninjured, he said, 'Thank God,' and died with a sweet smile of relief on his face. This is hard for you, I know, little one, but you must be thankful that we two have escaped unhurt. You shall be well cared for by me. I shall take you home with me, to be my own little girl."

He spoke so kindly that Chinka could not help being glad she had fallen into such good hands, although the poor child was sorely grieved to know her dearest friends were dead. She clung to her new friend, crying bitterly.

"Come, we must see what we can do for these poor mortals," said Mr. Huntington – for such was his name – as he again lifted Chinka in his arms.

Suddenly she hushed crying and a look of utter despair crossed over her dark face.

"What is it, my child?"

"Oh, oh, moccasin gone!" she cried.

"Perhaps we can find it," he said, "don't worry so."

But he did not know of how much consequence that one moccasin was to Chinka.

## Chapter III – Part II

Chinka's journey with her new friend was long and would have been very tedious for the child, had not the gentleman been kindness and patience personified. No spot of beautiful scenery was too small to escape his notice, and be pointed out to her; no subject, however childish, was too foolish for him to discuss; no wish of hers, even though unspoken, was too slight to be granted, and at last the girl began to look upon him as a sort of being that was not human – a Great Spirit, in her vivid imagination, who did what mortals could not do.

She became freer in his presence than she had ever been, even with her first kind friends and teachers. He seemed to have a faculty for bringing her out of herself and inspiring confidence, and soon he was on the best of terms with her.

Their journey had lasted three days when one morning he came into the car, after having purchased an appetizing breakfast for her, and said in his usual cheery tones:

"Well, my little girl, we are almost home. Are you glad?"

"Glad," she repeated, nodding her head.

"I have another little girl at home," he continued. I imagine she is about your age – twelve years. She will be delighted to see you, I know."

When in the afternoon of that day Mr. Huntington lifted Chinka off the train, they were greeted by a daintily dressed girl, whom Mr. Huntington kissed and called daughter, and a boy, a few years his sister's senior. With surprise the two gazed at Chinka, dusty and travel-stained, and the Indian girl clung to their father's hand.

"Veda and Donald," said Mr. Huntington, leading Chinka forward. "I have brought you a new sister. I will tell you more about her later on. Let it suffice now for me to say that she is friendless and alone in the world, so far as I know, and you must both be kind to her. Come, speak to her."

Veda shrank back, but Donald said, with something like his father's frank smile:

"We are very glad to see her, father. But come, the carriage is waiting, and you must want to get home as quickly as possible."

"That is true, my son. This way, Chinka."

In the carriage, while Mr. Huntington conversed with his children, asking them questions regarding home affairs, telling them of his journey, the wreck, and so on, he watched the shy Indian girl.

He wondered, as he compared her with his own dainty, pretty daughter, if his decision to take her into the family had not been an unwise one. He would reconsider his plan, he told himself.

The mansion, for indeed the Huntington home was a mansion, to which they were driven was grander and more wonderful than anything Chinka could possibly have imagined, and she was painfully ill at ease, when she was led into the broad halls and Mr. Huntington rang for a servant.

"Take this child to the nursery and have her bathed and dressed with as much care as Miss Veda is," he commanded, and Chinka was led away. Her appearance in the household had caused much comment among the servants. Donald, too, and Veda, had wondered, rather uncomfortably, if "that Indian" was going to stay with them all the time, and "what mama would say."

While Chinka was having her garments changed and was being freely discussed in the servants' quarters, Mr. Huntington was telling her story to three listeners in the sitting-room.

The children listened sympathetically, but Mrs. Huntington was almost unwilling to hear him through.

"Ralph," she at last broke out, impatiently interrupting him, "you have, as usual, let your sympathy get the better of you. Why in the world need you have concerned yourself? Weren't there other people near the scene who could take care of the unfortunates? Would you have our daughter associate with that girl? Would you bring her into the family as one of us – would you? Well, if you would, I won't, so there! You can spend money on her if you want to, but she shan't be educated in the same room with my daughter, and the sooner your trot her off to some school for unfortunate waifs, the better for all!"

She would undoubtedly have said more, for she was a high-tempered woman, but she could not find words expressive enough just then and was compelled to think a moment. Mr. Huntington's quiet voice broke the awful stillness that followed her angry words.

"That is enough, Blanche. This subject need receive no further discussion, especially before our children. I want my son and daughter to be refined, noble and generous to sympathize with the poor and unfortunate, and to be willing, if necessary, to share their mite of this world's goods with them. This Indian child needs somebody's attention and she shall receive it. There are more ways than one of settling a matter."

His voice had a ring of determination to it, and no one spoke. The dinner bell rang at that moment; once seated around the table, other subjects were introduced by Mr. Huntington and a very peaceable meal was partaken of. As soon as it was over Mr. Huntington had a servant prepare a dinner for Chinka, and he himself carried it up to the nursery to the lonely girl. She was pleased to see him again and greeted him joyfully. The servants had plied her with questions, and then laughed at her queer pronunciation, or perhaps, her inability to answer them at all, and she had spent a very uncomfortable hour. She ate little of the food, and kept clinging to her one true friend, saying in a trembling voice,

"Want go away! Want go way!"

"Poor little girl," he said soothingly, "you shall go away, for life at this place would be more than misery for you just now."

The next day found Mr. Huntington and Chinka on the cars again, and before the week was over she was placed in school. Other Indian children by the hundreds were there and she was at last persuaded to part with Mr. Huntington. The teachers were kind and patient; her own language was spoken by a number of the pupils.

Thus she left forever her old life in the forest, her tepee home in the wilds, and drifted into a new, strange and changeful life.

## Chapter IV. A Lapse of Five Years

In a luxurious room in a fashionable young ladies' school a girl sat reading. Her book rested on a table and, with her elbows on either side of her, her fingers playing on the dark hair resting so gracefully on her forehead, she seemed to be entirely unconscious of her surroundings. A knock at the door only partly aroused her, and without taking her eyes off her book she called, "Come in."

"Oh, at it again!" exclaimed a dashing, pretty girl tripping into the room and pausing behind her friend's chair. "My dear girl, you study entirely too hard. Put your book away, for I've great, grand and glorious news to tell you!" Gently she closed her friend's book and drew her into an easy chair.

"But, Agnes," remonstrated the girl, "I ought to finish that les – "

"Never mind the lesson, my dear. If you study so much your eyes won't be so bright and I've a particular reason for wishing them so to-night. Now listen. Some new pupils have arrived, and Miss Oppenheim is going to give us a recep–"

Her friend raised her hands in affected horror.

"You ought to study grammar, Agnes," she interrupted, smiling. "But pardon me; go on. When is this reception? It seems to me we have had enough of them already,"

"Oh, Eloise, how can you say so! I could go to 'em every night in the week! And this one is something special. Several of the college boys will be here to meet the new girls, and incidentally, to greet the old ones" – slyly pointing to herself and Eloise – "And we expect to have a good time."

"Well, said Eloise, "I hope you will not be disappointed."

"Oh, but you're coming down – I know you will. You must not let what the girls say annoy you. They don't mean half of it. They're just silly, envious school girls, and you're superior to any girl in this school – I don't care if you are part Indian!"

A deep flush crept over Eloise's face, but she straightened herself proudly.

"Everyone doesn't take the same view that you do, Agnes. You have always been kind to me – always the same, everywhere, when others acted queerly and left me to myself. If I were not learning so much I would leave this place to-day – at once. But I must complete my education, in spite of everything, and it would be no better anywhere else."

She spoke sadly, yet earnestly, and her friend, unused to anything serious, was awed into silence. Presently she spoke.

"Eloise, I wish you would tell me something about yourself. You never did, you know, except that you could remember no father or mother, and that some friend helped you, and to him you owed a great debt of gratitude, and must needs study your eyes out to repay it." Eloise smiled.

"That is about all there is to tell, Enhesse, (my friend)" she said sadly. "At least, you would not be interested in any of the incidents pertaining to my life since I – was civilized."

She spoke the last words slowly, and a queer smile lurked in the corners of her mouth. Her friend laughed slightly.

"I cannot imagine you being uncivilized, my dear," she said, "surely you are joking."

"No, indeed I am not," replied the dark-haired girl, "when I was very, very young I was, in a way, uncivilized, for I was born in an uncivilized part of the world. I was, of course, taken charge of by kind missionaries at an early age, and under their influence and teachings I was raised to a higher mode of living. Then, when I was twelve, or thereabouts, a good friend brought me away from my home and placed me in a mission school for Indians – then to complete my – my civilization, I came here."

"But, your family," persisted the fair-haired Agnes, "had you no brothers or sisters?"

It was several moments before Eloise spoke, and when she did there were tears in her eyes and voice.

"I had one little brother, whom I have not seen since I left him that morning, when I came away. He clung to me and cried and begged me to send for him, too. I have done that, repeatedly, but having long ago lost the one clue I had to him, I am unable to find him, and am afraid I shall never see him again."

"Poor girl! What was this clue, Eloise, by which you would know your brother?"

"A moccasin. When we parted our old grandmother gave each of us one of her own moccasins, which were exactly alike, but entirely different from any ever made, I know. If ever we met again, we could compare our moccasins and thus prove our identity, she said. But unfortunately for me, I lost my moccasin in a wreck and have never found it yet."

"But, if you should ever meet your brother and he should display his moccasin, the loss of yours would not matter so much; his would be sufficient proof."

"That is true, and I had thought of it before; but I am afraid I shall never see him."

"Maybe you will," answered Agnes, with a comforting gesture. "At any rate, put away sad thoughts for to-day and dress for to-night's gayities. 'Drive dull care away' in a merry dance with some college 'Fresh.' That is my advice. Your brother will come around all right some day. I wouldn't worry a minute about him. Boys always turn up where you least expect them, anyway."

Eloise, whose name had been changed from Chinka, in the Indian school, and who was no other than our Indian heroine, turned now to her friend and smiled.

"You always make me feel better, Agnes. I will go down with you to-night, if only for a little while."

"That's a dear!" exclaimed Agnes. "Dress your prettiest and be ready when I come for you. I must leave you now, for there's the dinner-bell. Bye-bye." And she tripped out as she had come in, laughing and leaving good cheer behind her.

Eloise did not turn immediately to her lessons, but sat with her hands clasped above her head, half a smile, half a frown on her face. Her life since leaving her far-away Indian home had been spent mostly in schools – first, three years in the Indian Mission in which Mr. Huntington placed her, another in a private school for girls, and another in the place where we now find her, and where she is entering upon her sixth year. Being thus continually thrown in the society of refined, educated people, the girl, had she been even less inclined to learn, could not have remained unimproved. As it was, she showed wonderful aptness for learning; combine that with what is the secret of all success: a willingness to work, and work hard, and it is not surprising that awkward little Chinka, the unlearned, became Eloise, the tall, graceful, accomplished girl, with a purpose in life. She was not beautiful, nor pretty, but in her face was intelligence and refinement, and in her movements a womanly grace and charm that attracted strangers and bound her friends to her. Mr. Huntington was proud of his young charge and had invested her money, coming from her Indian claims, wisely and well, so that she had repaid him for his early kindnesses to her, and was now quite independent of anyone. But of her Mr. Huntington never spoke to his family – never since that day when his wife denounced her had her name passed his lips when in the presence of his family. He told them she was in good hands – and there the matter rested.

Eloise did not go down to dinner, but when, an hour afterward, Agnes called for her, she found her ready for the party, dressed with unusual pains and looking the embodiment of health and girlish grace.

"You have excellent taste, Eloise," said Agnes, holding her at arm's length to admire her. "I am glad you look so well to-night. There is some one I want you to meet." And together they descended the stairs.

## Chapter V

Miss Oppenheim's receptions were always very informal, for these the pupils enjoyed most. The girls and boys were made to associate together as companions and as long as mere comradeship existed, parties were given them frequently, so that this particular reception was only one of many. But Eloise could seldom be persuaded to be present on these occasions. She dreaded to meet strangers.

As she was standing alone by a window she saw Agnes approaching, accompanied by a good looking young man, whom she at once recognized, by many descriptions from Agnes, as the "handsomest fellow going – Chester Grant!" She turned, but already Agnes lay a detaining hand on her arm and was presenting her companion.

"Don't run away from us, Miss Landon," said Chester, as Eloise was about to slip away after the introduction. "Miss Agnes has told me about you so much – won't you talk to me awhile?"

"Why, yes, I suppose so. I am not much used to talking to any one excepting those I am well acquainted with, but I shall be glad to hear you talk." Her simplicity charmed him and her quiet, unassuming manner, as she looked up to him and listened gravely to his conversation, pleased him.

He was rather curious concerning her, for Agnes had told him that she was an Indian by birth, and as he talked he made a mental note of every particular regarding her – her dress, her hair and eyes and movements, and the fastidious Chester was satisfied. All evening he was near her and others, who had once shunned her, were now glad to make her acquaintance, since Chester had seen fit to show a preference for her.

How like the world is a school room! The comparison has been drawn more than once, by more than one observer.

During the long term that followed, Eloise was the supreme favorite among teachers and pupils. Standing high in her classes, applying herself with redoubled energy to her studies, it is no wonder that she merited her changed and exalted position. Yet, as is always the case, there were those who sought to down her.

Among the new pupils who entered for the winter term, was a tall, dignified girl whose name was entered on the books as "Veda Huntington." Stylishly clothed, haughty in bearing and cool of manner, Miss Huntington impressed her classmates with a certain degree of awe, differing little from dislike. But as wealth is invariably attractive, and as every evidence of wealth clung to Miss Huntington, from the top of her proud head to the tips of her daintily slippered feet, she was soon surrounded by would-be friends.

It was a few days after her arrival that Agnes was discussing her, as she sat with Eloise after study hour.

"I can't like her," Agnes was saying. "I've tried to, but it's no use. There's something repelling about her."

"You should not form opinions so quickly, unless they be good ones," answered Eloise.

"Yes I should, too. I liked you from the very first and I was right in doing so. And, when I form a bad opinion, I am usually right. You see," laughingly, "I am a good judge of human nature."

"Well, I hope not in this case," quietly remarked Eloise.

Agnes stared. "Why? What is this Huntington girl to you?"

"She is the daughter of one of the best friends I ever had. Agnes, will you keep a secret?"

"Why, yes, dozens of 'em," exclaimed Agnes, all curiosity.

"Well, you have often asked me who it was that brought me away from my wild home and educated me, and I will tell you. It was Mr. Huntington, the father of Veda."

"And does she know it?"

"No, indeed, and that is the secret you must keep. I am sure Mr. Huntington has never told his family who or where I am, and I do not care to tell them myself, as they were greatly opposed to his doing anything for me." Eloise then described her first meeting with Mr. Huntington's family, and Agnes exclaimed vehemently!

"I knew I was right. I can't bear her!"

"But that is wrong. You must not be prejudiced. The girl is not to blame, for she was too young to have an opinion in the matter. And then, again, you must remember your promise. Don't tell anyone what I have told you."

"I won't," answered her friend, as they separated for the night.

For many days Eloise and Veda were thrown apart, as the latter was below the former in her classes. But there came a time when the entire school was making preparations for a concert which was to be by far the grandest that had ever been given at Miss Oppenheim's School for Girls. "It shall exceed any former effort," said busy Miss Oppenheim, as she assisted the members of the faculty in arranging the program.

A pretty play was decided upon, in which it happened that two girls were the leading characters. "The part of the brunette shall be given Eloise," said one of the teachers, "for it suits her perfectly; but where shall we find the blonde. There are a number of blondes here, but none who can play this part well."

"Why not Miss Huntington?" asked some one.

"The very one. I had not thought of her. Won't she make a charming maid for our dark queen?"

So Miss Huntington was sent for. A half dozen girls had assembled in the room, among whom were Eloise and Agnes, when Veda came to see what was required of her.

"Here she is," exclaimed several as she entered.

"My dear, we have decided upon a little play – here is a copy of it that you may look over, You are to take the part of 'Christine.' "

Veda took the book and glanced over the 'dramatis personae,' while the others began to talk happily over the coming concert. Presently her firm voice was heard by all in the room, as she returned the book to Miss Oppenheim.

"I shall not play the part, for I won't be maid to any one, not even in a play. Especially not to Miss Landon," she added, with some hauteur.

"Why, I am astonished!" exclaimed Miss Oppenheim, while the others almost held their breath.

"You will have to explain yourself," continued her teacher.

"I have no explanation to make, except that I cannot play the part of maid to Eloise Landon," and the offended young lady left the room.

There was silence for a few seconds and then Miss Oppenheim said, "Miss Huntington shall explain what she meant or she shall leave this school. I'll have no such silly nonsense here. Emma, go to her room and tell her I said return here immediately. The rest of you may retire, as I wish to speak to the young lady alone."

The girls filed reluctantly out of the room and gathered in little knots in the hall, discussing the exciting event.

"What in the world did she mean?" asked several, and Agnes, with flashing eyes, exclaimed, "I know what she meant – the little simpleton! How I'd like to shake her."

"Tell us, tell us! Is it because she dislikes Eloise? Or, is it," the girl lowered her tone and glanced around to be sure Eloise was not within hearing, "or is it because Eloise is an Indian girl?"

They remembered their own aversion when the dark Indian girl had first come to this school and wondered if Miss Huntington entertained the same foolish idea.

"It just is," answered Agnes. "And she'll learn like some of the rest of you little idiots that Eloise is superior to, or on an equality with any of us."

Fortunately the girls were used to plain spoken Agnes and had discovered long ago that retorts only made her more pointed in her speech; therefore, those whom the shoe fitted, wore it with as much grace as possible, quietly ignoring her thrust.

Only Eloise had remained with Miss Oppenheim when the girls were dismissed, and while the discussion went on in the hall, she was pleading Veda's cause with flushed face and bright eyes.

"Miss Oppenheim, we all know what she meant – don't ask her to repeat it. It hurt me, but I shall not hold it against her. Please do not send her away, with the disgrace of expulsion upon her. It would break her father's heart. Only her ignorance led her to talk so."

Miss Oppenheim was surprised, for well she knew the sensitive, yet proud nature of the girl before her. "What do you know of her father?"

Eloise faltered, then said quickly, "Miss Oppenheim, five or six years ago, Mr. Huntington was in the far West on business. On the cars returning to his home he found a poor little Indian girl whose only friends had been killed in a wreck. He brought the child home with him, placed her in school and protected her like a daughter, with no hope of reward."

## Chapter VI

Eloise paused in her earnestness. "Miss Oppenheim, no person, no matter how great or good, could have been kinder to the timid, shrinking little Indian girl than was Mr. Huntington. He looked faithfully after her interests and when he found that she owned lands and money he placed it all to her credit, using not a cent of it himself. All this and more he did, out of pure sympathy, even when his family protested to the extent that he had to keep his knowledge of the girl's whereabouts a secret from them. Miss Oppenheim, I am that Indian girl. Do you wonder that I would save my dearest friend's daughter from disgrace, even to the humbling of my own pride?"

"My dear," said Miss Oppenheim, her eyes wet, "I am glad you told me this. Go now."

"But you will not be too harsh with her?" Eloise lingered to ask the question.

"I know better now how to deal with her," answered her teacher, smiling. As Eloise passed out, Veda, with head erect, entered and stood before Miss Oppenheim. "Veda," began that lady, looking squarely into the blue eyes before her. "Tell me why you spoke as you did. Give me a straightforward answer." "I think my words were plain enough. I said I would not play the part of maid to Miss Landon. Surely you cannot compel me." "No, I would not do that, but I can at least tell you that politeness to each and every pupil in this school is my strictest rule. Unkindness is neither lady like nor dignified. False pride is worse than none at all. Your foolish speech this morning was both unkind and undignified and, I am sorry to say, showed the lack of womanliness which every girl wishes to cultivate. I would not be a true teacher did I not tell you that the only polite thing for you to do is to make an apology to Eloise for your hasty speech." Veda stood unmoved. "And if I refuse to do this?"

Miss Oppenheim tapped her foot impatiently. "You cannot remain here and refuse to obey rules," she answered quickly. Veda's face grew pale with anger. "You shall not expel me on this girl's account! She is only an Indian girl – and I won't stand it!"

"It is on your own account, Veda. Eloise is in no way to blame. You may go to your room now and if you have not apologized to Eloise by this hour tomorrow, I shall enforce my rules. You are dismissed."

Veda quitted the room immediately, and when she passed Eloise in the hall, she turned her head haughtily in the opposite direction.

"Now, what do you think of that Huntington girl?" It was Agnes' rather triumphant exclamation as she burst into Eloise's room during study hour the following evening, and found Eloise, as usual, buried in her lessons. Eloise's dark eyes saddened. "Oh, Agnes," she began, but was interrupted. "Now Eloise, there's a dear, don't begin to excuse the hateful little spider! She hasn't got good manners, not even common politeness, in spite of all her airs, and you needn't say a word in her favor to me."

"It's true that she is unkind and impolite, but are we not becoming so, too, when we say unkind things about her?"

Agnes laid her arms about her friend's neck. "I'd be a perfect terror without you, Eloise. You always set one right. Of course it is mean to say things about her, but she's so silly, I can hardly help it. Guess what I heard today?"

"I don't know, I'm sure," said Eloise, wondering.

"Why, Veda's brother has entered college. I saw Chester today and he told me; said he wanted us to meet him. I hope he ain't like his sister."

"Oh, he isn't – or rather he wasn't when they were children. I remember he was very kind to me when I was there."

"I'll like him, then," exclaimed Agnes impulsively.

"And Oh, Eloise," continued Agnes, drawing closer to her friend, "Chester told me something else. You know I told him about your brother – about poor little Timber – and he was very much interested and said he was going to do what he could to help you find him."

"Yes, yes – go on, Agnes," Eloise cried, as Agnes paused.

"Well, Chester told me that this brother of Veda's had in his possession a peculiar moccasin – only one – which he prizes very greatly. Chester happened to see it while Mr. Huntington was unpacking his trunk – they are to be room mates. He said he hated to ask questions about it, but he was anxious to see your moccasin so that he could compare them." "Oh, Agnes, I must see it! What if it belongs to Timber? I wonder if there's any possible chance of speaking to Mr. Huntington or Mr. Chester?" Eloise had risen in her excitement and diving down into her trunk had pulled out her precious moccasin and was holding it up to the light.

"Not to-night, dear," smiled Agnes. "But of course he will be coming over to see Veda soon and you might get Miss Oppenheim to let you speak to him. You'd have to tell her all the circumstances, though."

"Oh, I shouldn't mind that. Let's go to her room. Come on, hurry!" and almost before Agnes could rise and follow her, Eloise was half way down the long hall.

They found Miss Oppenheim alone in her room and quite willing to listen to whatever they had to tell.

"What is it girls?" she asked kindly, drawing them to her side, adding, "Why, you are trembling Eloise; what has happened?"

Eloise poured forth her story, beginning at the first when she and Timber were separated, leading on up with Chester's discovery. Miss Oppenheim listened with interest.

"My poor little girl! Of course you may speak to Mr. Huntington," she said, when Eloise had finished. "Stay," as the girls rose to go. "I'll find out from Veda whether he is coming tomorrow. You will rest more peacefully if you know," and touching a bell, she bade a servant send Miss Huntington to her.

It was several minutes ere Veda appeared and when she did finally come she merely asked, "Did you wish to see me?" utterly ignoring Eloise and Agnes.

"Have you not met the young ladies, Veda?" asked Miss Oppenheim, in well-feigned surprise. "If not, allow me to present them – ."

"I have had the – I have met them," replied Veda, slightly inclining her head.

"Oh, very well, then. I sent for you to enquire whether or not your brother intends to call here tomorrow. I am informed that he has entered college in this city."

"He will call on me in the morning at ten," Veda answered in a friendlier voice than the girls had ever heard her use, and they began to think that, after all, she might not be such a terrible girl as she appeared.

"That is good. After you have had your little visit with him, I wish you would detain him, as I wish to speak to him on an important matter."

"Very well. Is that all?"

Miss Oppenheim was a shrewd woman and had made a study of human nature – especially the dispositions of young girls, so now she was quick to see that Veda had, in a degree, repented of her hasty action heretofore related, and wished as much as possible for a girl of her nature, to bring about a reconciliation, but knew not how to proceed. Miss Oppenheim was unable to determine whether this change had come from fear of her brother learning about her actions, or a natural desire to be at peace with her school mates. At any rate, she was glad to note the change and hastened to help matters along with her own tact.

"No Veda, that is not all. Don't hurry away, for we girls are anxious to know more about this brother of yours, whose arrival seems to have set the whole college afire with excitement. I hear praises of him on all sides. Stay here and let's all get better acquainted."

Veda paused, irresolutely, and then throwing herself into a chair, burst into tears.

"There, there, don't cry, dear child. What is the matter? Have you been lonely?"

"Yes," sobbed Veda, "Nobody seemed to want to really love me and when – I saw – all the girls – so nice and – and – chummy – it made me – hate them – for they – didn't seem – to want me around – "

"And that is why you drew off so proudly to yourself? You did wrong – but there! we'll forget it all, won't we girls? We were homesick ourselves when we first came here, and we know how it feels!"

Eloise had risen quickly and was sitting on the arm of Veda's chair. "Please don't cry, Miss Veda, for you shan't be lonely any more," she was saying softly, while Agnes sat immovable across the room, glaring sarcastically.

Suddenly Veda stood up and exclaimed, "Don't do that Miss Landon, until I have apologized to you." She twisted her handkerchief nervously. Agnes' expression changed and she leaned forward.

"Don't!" began Eloise, but Miss Oppenheim said gently, "Go on Veda. That is right."

"I'm sorry I said what I did, for brother told me this afternoon in the park who you are – I didn't tell him I treated you badly, but I was just telling him about you – and he told me now nobly and generously you had helped papa by making him use your money when he would have failed if he hadn't accepted it and brother said I ought to be very nice to you, for I wouldn't be in school now if it hadn't been for you helping papa. I just nearly died when he told me, to think how mean and – and uppish I'd been, but I couldn't tell brother, for oh, you don't know how manly he is and how good! He never would have forgiven me for slurring you!" Veda was weeping again, but this time she was not alone, for Miss Oppenheim's eyes were wet, while Agnes was fairly snubbing.[1]

"You dear girl!" cried Agnes, flinging her arms about Eloise, "you never told me this! I knew you were good, but I never dreamed you were quite so angelic as this!"

Eloise looked puzzled. "Why isn't it what anyone with a speck of gratefulness, would have done?" she asked.

"Oh yes, but others wouldn't have kept so mum about it. I'd have flown at Veda Huntington the first thing and told her of it."

"Come girls, I think we'll all be better friends in the future, don't you? I am very much relieved and I hope there won't be any more differences."

"There won't" said Veda; "at least I won't be the cause of them."

"And you may chum with Eloise and me, now that you have apologized like a good fellow!" exclaimed Agnes, in a fit of goodness, slipping her arm about Veda's waist.

"Oh, may I? Do you know, I never thought you'd like me!"

"So I shouldn't if you hadn't done the right thing," answered plain spoken Agnes, as, after kissing Miss Oppenheim good night the three tripped down the hall together.

But as Eloise lay awake after retiring that night, it was not of Veda, nor of Agnes, nor of the wonderful reconciliation she was thinking. She thought of a slender, dark faced little lad, standing as she last saw him, amid the tall grasses beside a rude tepee, his arms outstretched and crying pitifully, "Chianka, Chianka!"[2] Where was he now?

## [Chapter VII]

It was fifteen minutes past 10 o'clock the following morning when Agnes knocked at Eloise's door.

"Miss Oppenheim has sent for us, lovey," cried Agnes, clapping her hands. "Mr. Huntington has been

---

1 Perhaps Reed means "sobbing."

2 Possibly a nickname for "Chinka."

here a quarter of an hour, for I saw him when he came. Susie, who brought me the message from Miss Oppenheim, says that they're waiting for us in the parlor. Oh, 'Loise, you've been crying, I know you have!"

"Well, Agnes, I have, I must confess, but they were tears of joy; for, do you know, I feel just like Mr. Huntington is going to tell me some news of my brother this morning, and you can't imagine how light hearted I feel."

"Yes, I can too. Oh, I hope he knows where he is! Didn't Veda behave like a little lady last night? I tell you, Eloise, her brother must be a good fellow to make her relent like that."

"He is. I remember distinctly how nice he was to me when I first saw him. But come, dear, I am quite ready. We must not keep them waiting."

"You've been looking awfully stunning this morning, 'Loise," remarked Agnes, as the two started for the parlor.

"I should not want to look otherwise on such an a occasion," playfully answered Eloise, as they reached the parlor door.

Eloise's breath came quick as Donald Huntington rose to be presented to her. He had the easy grace of a well bred gentleman and his cordial manner put her quite at ease.

"I think I have had the honor of knowing Miss Landon, when we were both several years younger," he remarked, "Indeed," he continued, "I think I am not presuming when I say I consider us old friends."

"I have been telling Mr. Huntington about your moccasin, Eloise," said Miss Oppenheim, "and I think he has good news for you."

"Oh, have you? Can you tell me anything about my poor little Timber?"

Eloise's eyes fairly sparkled, as she came nearer Donald and trembling with excitement, asked the questions. Donald looked away a moment, then, turning suddenly, he said, "Miss Landon, about a year ago I was sent by my father to attend to some business out west. It was my first trip to that country and I lingered longer than was completely necessary, hunting and traveling about. One day I came upon a boy – I suppose about fourteen or fifteen. He was sitting alone by the road side and looked tired and dejected. I knew at first glance that he was an Indian boy – there were many around there. I stopped and spoke to him, but at first he wouldn't answer me. At last, however, I got him to talking, and 'twas a pitiful tale he told me – of how he had struggled up alone, after his sister had been taken away by missionaries and how his aged grandmother had died. He said the white people had always treated him well and he had gone to school some, but he was tired out and so disappointed in never hearing of his sister that he didn't care to live. In some way the boy's face was familiar, but I did not connect him with you – for, to tell the truth, I barely remembered my meeting with you when we were children. I persuaded the boy not to give up all hope, that perhaps I could help him find his sister. I got him interested in a farm which I had purchased, as an investment merely, and when I came away, a few weeks afterward, I left him manager of that, and a more contented fellow than when I first met him. In parting he gave me a curiously stitched and beaded moccasin, saying his sister, wherever she was, possessed one exactly like it. I promised to do all I could to find her and came away. Since then I have spent much time away from home and not until a day or so ago, when I came here to enter college, have I heard anything about the mate to Timber's moccasin."

He paused and unwrapped a small package he carried in his pocket, while Eloise, with flushed face and tearful eyes, pressed nearer and compared her moccasin with the one Donald held up.

"Are they not exactly alike?" he asked.

"They could not be more so," declared Miss Oppenheim and Veda.

Eloise pressed them to her bosom, while Donald continued.

"When I was unpacking the other night, Chester – you all know him, of course – pounced down on this moccasin, exclaiming, 'Why, old boy, where did you get this?' I told him a friend of mine gave it to me and he remarked, 'I could tell you where its mate is.' 'Where?' I asked. And then he told me as much as he knew about Miss Landon and her brother and wound up with: 'I was fortunate enough to be the one to restore to Miss Landon her moccasin, only a few weeks ago, after she had given up ever seeing it again; 'twould be queer if you are the one to bring its mate, wouldn't it?' Some one called him away just then, and I have not yet had a chance to continue our conversation. How did he assist you in finding your moccasin, and how did you become separated from it in the first place, Miss Landon?"

Eloise told him the story about the wreck and how she lost her one clue to her brother.

"Until three weeks ago I hadn't the slightest idea of ever seeing my moccasin again. I had told Agnes about it, and Mr. Chester, too, knew of it. He was deeply interested and often encouraged me, by saying that some day I'd have my moccasin again. And one day he brought it up to me. I was in the park. He came up behind me and dropped it in my lap.

" 'Does that look anything like your lost moccasin?' he asked, and I could have screamed for joy, for at first glance I recognised my treasure. Mr. Chester had been poking about in an old shop on a side street and came across that one moccasin, and he purchased it, not thinking for a minute that it could be the one I once owned. The clerk said it had been sold to them by an old crippled man, and we, Mr. Chester and I, have come to the conclusion that the man must have been in the wreck and found my moccasin among his belongings. At any rate, here it is, and here is its mate," and she looked lovingly at the old moccasins she held.

"Mr. Huntington, tell me more about Timber. When can I see him?" she continued, eagerly. Donald looked at her a few seconds and then replied by asking: "Do you want to go to him, or shall we send for him to come here? I am at your service in the matter and you may depend upon me to do anything in my power for you."

Eloise flushed.

"Thank you," she murmured.

"Oh Eloise, send for him," cried Agnes. "It will be loads nicer than going out there."

But Eloise's expression showed that she had already made her decision. Turning to Miss Oppenheim, she said:

"Miss Oppenheim, it lacks but a few weeks of the Christmas holidays. May I leave earlier – may I go at once to Timber?"

"Oh, my dear," began her teacher, "how – but yes, we can spare you. You know already how glad I am for you – how pleased we all are that you have at last realized the one wish of your heart. To detain you would be selfish, indeed. Go, my dear, whenever you think best."

"Thank you, dear, kind Miss Oppenheim," answered Eloise, smiling lovingly on her teacher.

"And now, Mr. Huntington, I shall ask you to arrange the trip for me, for I know comparatively nothing about it."

"I would suggest that you wire my father to meet you here and go with us. When do you wish to start?"

"Wish? Why, I'd start today – now – this minute, if it were possible. But I can wait till tomorrow I suppose, or until your father comes."

Eloise's voice was joyful and her whole being throbbed with pleasure. Donald could not resist smiling at her in her pretty eagerness.

"I had better go immediately and attend to your telegram for you."

"Oh, if you will! And, Mr. Huntington, it is so good of you to be willing. I shall never forget the services you have done me. I shall always remember your kindness to my brother. How can I thank you enough?"

Donald's countenance grew serious, and extending his hand to her in parting he said gravely, "Miss Eloise, it is I – Veda and I – who should thank you. We, too, shall never forget the kindness you have done us."

After adieus to the others, he was off and Agnes exclaimed, as she helped Eloise pack a grip shortly afterward: "Well, Eloise, he is one gentleman, if there is one."

As soon as Mr. Huntington arrived and the situation was explained to him, he willingly accompanied his son and Eloise on their trip west.

How can we describe the meeting between the long-separated brother and sister? Separation had only increased their love for each other. Again Eloise spoke her mother tongue, Timber laughingly correcting her numerous mistakes. Again they visited their old haunts and the forest so familiar to both.

But Eloise felt that she could not tarry long. She was quick to realize that Timber needed the advantages which school life would give him, and she accordingly made arrangements for him to return with her.

Carlisle was decided upon as the best place for him to go, and ere many weeks had rolled around, he was a happy inmate of that school.

When Eloise found herself again among her school mates, it was with a light, happy heart and the prospects of a bright future.

* * *

"You might continue and tell us how they turned out!" exclaimed a friend of the writer, after reading over the manuscript. But why can the reader not guess the rest?

"Of course, Eloise and Donald married," my friend continued. But no. The bright-haired Agnes, so laughing and gay, won the heart of that serious young man, and Mr. Chester, who played so great a part in reuniting Eloise and Timber, had, long ere school closed, won a sweet promise from Eloise, which was fulfilled in due time and the two lived a happy, peaceful life.

And Veda? A foreigner carried her away, and she became a leader in high social circles.

A life of single blessedness awaited Timber, who, after a course at college, returned to the home of his fathers and there, dwelling among his own people, he, by an exemplary life, did much to educate and in various ways to elevate them.

But always there existed between himself and his sister a bond unbreakable. And Eloise's children cherish an old, torn pair of moccasins – and often clamor for this story.

## AUNT MARY'S CHRISTMAS DINNER (DECEMBER, 1899)

"I wonder who can have written me this?" mused Aunt Mary, as she picked up the letter her nephew had placed at her plate.

"Suppose you open it and find out?" suggested the older of her two big nephews, smiling across the table at her puckered, bewildered face.

"But it's such a queer post mark," continued Aunt Mary, slowly breaking the seal. "T-a-l-e-q-u-a-h – how do you pronounce it? Must be somewhere in the Indian Territory – capital, ain't it Joe? I don't remember my maps very well."

"Let me see it, Aunt. Shall I read it for you?" asked Joe, the younger: and his aunt willingly gave it to him. He glanced hurriedly down the sheet and then exclaimed! "Listen, aunt:

> "Miss Mary Jenkins, Dear Madam – I have to inform you of the death of James Jenkins, in this city on the 15th inst. His burial took place today. Mr. Jenkins, just before his death, told me, his attending physician, that you are his only living relative, and desired me to make all arrangements for you to have the care of his only child, a girl, and requested that you rear her as your own. Her mother, a Cherokee woman, died in the child's infancy. You may expect the Miss five days from date. I shall arrange her property matters, as per Mr. Jenkins' request.
>
> "I have the honor to be,
>
> "Your obedient servant,
>
> "J. G. Lambert, M.D.
>
> "Talequah, Ind. Ter., Dec. 16, 18— "

"Oh, ho, another child to raise! I should think you'd had your share of that, after rearing two naughty nephews from infancy. Too bad, I say!" exclaimed Frank, as Joe finished reading the letter.

"It is kind of hard on aunt, but I think it'll be mighty nice to have a little girl about the house again," mused Joe, who had tender recollections of a bright-haired little sister who never grew to young ladyhood. "Who was this James Jenkins, aunt?"

"He was my father's cousin. He left his home when a very young man and none of us ever heard from him again until he wrote home from the Indian Territory and said he had married a Cherokee Indian woman. His people thought that was dreadful and refused to have any more to do with him. That's the last I heard of him until this letter tells me of his death. Poor old Jim! He had a hard time."

"But of course you'll take the child?" questioned Joe.

"Of course," readily assented Aunt Mary, whose heart seemed big enough to hold all the orphan children in existence, if her home would not.

When her only sister had died, leaving two little boys, Aunt Mary had willingly shared her home with them and was now being amply rewarded, as both had grown into excellent young men and were supporting themselves and her by means of business of their own.

"Let's see, the little Cherokee girl will reach us shortly before Christmas, won't she? I wonder if she knows anything about Santa, or dolls – "

"In other words, you wonder if she's civilized," laughingly interrupted Joe.

"I wonder how old she is. It would seem queer to have a very little girl about," remarked Aunt Mary.

"Well. I suppose we had better order up a cradle, a doll, a box of toys and a few other things for the young lady's inspection," said Frank, rising.

"No; not yet. But you must answer this letter for me today and bid Dr. Lambert send the child as early as he will and assure him of her welcome."

Later in the day a delivery wagon stopped at Aunt Mary's front door and unloaded a doll, a cradle and various other articles delightful to children's eyes. Aunt Mary smiled at her nephew's eagerness to do the proper thing for their distant relative's reception. In the days that followed little else was spoken of but the coming of the little Cherokee girl. Frank took less interest, but Joe's greatest delight was to prepare for her coming and he purchased toys and dolls galore.

The holidays were rapidly approaching and the day on which "Cherokee," as the boys had named her, the doctor having failed to mention the child's name, was to arrive, had dawned bright and clear. As Aunt Mary and her nephews sat at breakfast that morning, they talked of little else save her.

"I have arranged for her to go to the Kindergarten after Christmas," said Joe, proudly.

"And, in case she is old enough, I have made arrangements with Miss Lange for her music lessons," put in Frank, and Aunt Mary followed up with:

"I have made her the coziest little play room imaginable in one corner of the attic. You ought to take a peep at it. I shall show it to her the first thing Christmas morning. The Christmas tree is all ready for the candles to be lighted – and her dolls and toys are placed where she can't help being delighted at first glance."

"Why, I believe her coming is going to make our Christmas brighter than ever," declared Joe, and the others nodded their heads.

"I do hope she won't be too backward," continued Joe. "I bet she'll come wearing a little red shawl and buckskin moccasins and will raise the mischief when we try to convert her into an up-to-date little girl, and teach her to speak English correctly," ventured Frank, who was not quite sure how he was going to enjoy having "a little Indian" about him.

"I wish I had studied more about the Indians and was better posted regarding them. I should judge –" Aunt Mary's speech was cut short by a sharp ring at the side door.

"Gracious!" exclaimed the old lady: "how that frightened me! I suppose it's the new cook I'm expecting. Open the door, will you, Joe?" In the doorway stood a young girl, neatly dressed, carrying a small grip in one hand.

"Good morning ma'am," said Joe, politely, who had been taught the highest respect for a woman, whether a princess or housemaid.

"Good morning, sir. Does Miss Jenkins live here?" The girl's voice was a trifle timid.

"Yes, come in. Just step into the kitchen. Aunt will see you in a few moments." He placed her a chair by the stove, and, not noticing her puzzled expression, passed on into the dining room.

"I say, Aunt, that's a rather stunning looking cook you've got this time. Looks more like one of your young lady acquaintances than a house-maid. Ready to go, Frank?"

"Yes, let me get my hat. Good bye, aunt."

"Good bye, boys. Don't forget – " But the front door closed.

"I'm so glad you came early, for I've lots of work to do. I hope you're good at pastry work?"

"Yes ma'am, I can do anything in the way of cooking."

"What shall I call you?"

The girl paused, "Oh, my name? Call me Nannie," she stammered.

The old lady looked at her sharply over her glasses and said: "You had better put on some kitchen clothes, if you have them. Go up the back stairway to your room – and hurry down, mind!"

"Goodness me! I didn't think of hiring out when I left home," thought the girl, as she hastily slipped into a neat calico dress and brushed her shining black hair. "Funny, but I can't resist a joke and I'm going to enjoy this one thoroughly."

Having finished her simple preparations for the kitchen, she started from her attic-bedroom – which was plainly that occupied by Aunt Mary's "help," when a queer sight met her eyes, and she stopped. She was staring at the corner fitted up by Aunt Mary with dolls, toys and other play things. She wondered a moment, and then a light broke in upon her, and she burst into a low, merry laugh. "Too bad to spoil such plans! I should have enjoyed those things about twelve years ago."

"Well, Nannie," began Aunt Mary, as the girl entered the kitchen "we'll spend most of the day baking. We'll have only a light lunch at noon," and she proceeded to give further directions, Nannie listening intently and respectfully. All morning she labored with cakes; delicacies of every description, and by noon the pantry was fragrant with the odor of good things, and a dainty, appetizing lunch awaited the nephews. The good cook fairly flew about her work, and won golden opinions from Aunt Mary, who admired, not only her excellent understanding of kitchen work, but also her bright, pretty face and obliging manners.

But the nephews came in without the expected "Cherokee," and Aunt Mary's face assumed a look of disappointment.

"Are you sure, Joe, that she wasn't there? It would have been so easy to miss her."

"I am sure, aunt. The doctor said she would be there and would know me, but no child, girl, or woman approached me, nor did I see anyone who resembled an Indian in the least."

"Maybe she'll come in the morning," suggested Frank. "The last letter from Dr. Lambert stated that it might be possible that connections could not be made and that she would be delayed: so let's not worry. I'll bet the 'Cherokee' is all right. Come, let's taste this inviting lunch. That new cook must be a jewel, aunt."

"So she is, and I thank my stars I was lucky enough to get her. Why, I tell you, she's out of the ordinary, and I wish I could keep her in the family all the time." The old lady then proceeded to give her nephews a detailed account of the new cook's morning's work, the young men listening in respectful silence, although the subject of cooks did not especially interest them. But before starting down town, Joe had occasion to go to the kitchen for some misplaced article, which, of course, he was unable to find. The new cook was standing demurely by the window, her girlish form outlined against the white curtains. Joe glanced at her. He remembered his aunt had called her Nannie.

"Er-er – Nannie," he began, "I say, have you seen anything of – of my shaving mug? I can't tell for the life of me how it got misplaced."

"Why – let me see. I saw it – where did I see it? Oh, yes, here it is," and darting into a closet she brought forth the desired article.

"Thank you," replied Joe, taking it from her hands. The event was trifling – so outside parties would say – yet who can tell? In that brief second their eyes met – and, well, Joe found occasion to go to the kitchen oftener than was his custom – and it wasn't always a-hunting shaving mugs that he went.

* * *

"I declare, I am worried to death. Boys, you must send a telegram today to Dr. Lambert and tell him that 'Cherokee' has not come. Did you mail your letter, Joe?" said Aunt Mary, as she went down to the third of Nannie's delicious breakfasts.

"To be sure, and I should get an answer today. I am worried myself."

"Tomorrow is Christmas day, too, and we had counted on her being here. But cheer up. Maybe she'll come yet," said Frank, with an attempt at cheerfulness.

Down in the kitchen the new cook was sitting disconsolate by the stove, wondering how best she could undo the harm her foolish joke had already done. She had, on several occasions overheard the conversations between Aunt Mary and her nephews, and their uneasiness scared her. Her first intention had been to tell them the true state of affairs the first day, but several words that had dropped carelessly from Frank's lips while she was waiting at table, had made her resentful, and she had impulsively decided never to tell. "I'll bet that little 'Injun' will be a fright, with her uncivilized ways," had been a part of the sentence he uttered, and she, passing behind his chair, could hardly refrain from dashing the cup of hot coffee she was carrying into his face. But for Aunt Mary's sake she felt she must do something. But that day a thing happened that saved her from revealing her secret.

Dinner that day, it seemed to her was dull and gloomy – an unusual feeling to pervade that household – something terrible and awful. As she was passing the open door she heard Frank say: "Yes, aunt, I'm a ruined man today. I didn't tell you and Joe how near the clash was, for I thought I could raise the money – but I can't!" His head sank on the table and all was silent, save for his sobs. Nannie paused outside and listened. Presently Joe said: "Old man, I wish you had told me sooner. I might have helped you – but now, I can't do much. You're welcome to all I have – "

Nannie listened for no more. She realized what the awful matter was. Rushing to her little room she snatched up her grip and flew down stairs. Her eyes were bright and as she ran, she kept repeating to herself: "He's Joe's brother. I can do it for him – he's Joe's brother!"

She burst into the dining room like a young cyclone, waving her grip as she came.

"Aunt Mary!" she exclaimed, ignoring their surprise. "Frank! Joe! I've got it! Here's the money – at least, I can give you a check for it – right now! See here!" and opening the grip she produced several letters – one from Dr. Lambert, introducing her, and another written by her father just before his death.

Aunt Mary, Frank and Joe stared.

"You can't be – Cherokee?" gasped Frank.

"I am Nannie Jenkins, a Cherokee Indian girl, sir," she returned proudly. Then followed her explanations of how she had come alone and finding no one to meet her on the early train, had inquired the way to their home.

"You seemed to take me for a cook, so just for a joke, I played the role of a kitchen maid – "

"Successfully," finished Aunt Mary, rapturously kissing her.

"And, Frank, you must tell me about your trouble, for I can help you. I have money enough to keep me always – my Cherokee claim, you know."

Frank took her hand. "I oughtn't to allow this," he said, "but I'll have to – and oh, I am so thankful to you!"

"Don't mention it," she said. "Just let me get another plate and we'll finish dinner together."

She skipped away to the kitchen. Joe on some pretense, followed, and neither returned for some time. But in they came at last, both blushing and laughing. Neither of them carried a plate.

There was an awkward pause, and finally Joe, taking Nannie's hand, led her to his aunt.

"I think, Aunt Mary," he said, "we'll keep her in the family!"

"Oh, ho!" cried his aunt, and she shook them both.

"Now who says we won't have a happy Christmas dinner!" exclaimed Nannie, as they sat down to finish their interrupted meal.

## THE HONOR OF WYNOMA
## A THANKSGIVING STORY BY A CHEROKEE GIRL (NOVEMBER, 1902) [3]

### Chapter I

"An Indian wife – could anything be more preposterous! It was all well enough for Horton to go west, for he could get a better start there, but who ever dreamed of his falling in love with an Indian girl? He shan't marry her with my consent – that's certain."

---

[3] Although Reed did not sign this story, textual evidence suggests that it is likely she wrote it – as well as the anonymous nonfiction pieces "Daugherty Canyon," "Do Not Want Them," and "Talequah" below – as she did much of the anonymous copy for *Twin Territories*.

Mrs. Boynton threw down her son's letter with contempt and looked across the table at her husband, who was contentedly munching his toast. He smiled under her angry gaze and finished his toast.

"I'll have another cup of coffee, please," he remarked placidly.

His wife filled his cup and passed it back. There was silence.

"Well, can't you say anything?" Mrs. Boynton demanded.

"Yes, I could say a number of things, but I've learned that in a case like this, it doesn't turn out well when a man's mother and father step in and tell him he shan't marry the woman he loves – or thinks he loves – it amounts to the same thing. You'll have to learn to take it easy, Mary."

Mrs. Boynton stared in astonishment. "Then, are we to sit quietly by and see our only son – our eldest, of whom we are so proud, obey a foolish whim and bring home as his bride an Indian girl – a rough, uncouth Indian?"

Mr. Boynton stirred uneasily and avoided his wife's eyes. She went on. "Must we call an Indian daughter, and put her on a level with our own refined daughter? Must our first grandchildren have the blood of savages in their veins? Good heavens! Don't you see that it is all wrong? Horton must have lost his mind."

Mr. Boynton was saved the trouble of answering his wife's very pointed questions by the entrance of a maid. "Please ma'am," she said, handing her mistress a letter. "Here is a letter as I forgot to bring in. It was caught in the bottom of the bag."

There was another brief silence, and as Mrs. Boynton's eyes scanned the letter her countenance changed. "It is from Madge," she explained to her husband. "She says her class is to have fortnight's holiday at Thanksgiving and she wants to know if she may bring a friend home with her. Oh, dear, these children! If it isn't one it's the other – and sometimes both, as in this case. I don't approve of this gayety in the midst of the term. There'll be a perfect round of parties and dances – the more so since there will be a guest in the house."

"Well, tell her she can't bring the girl," suggested Mr. Boynton, rising.

"Oh, I can't do that. I wouldn't refuse her so small a pleasure. There's no reason why she shouldn't have her, except that it puts extra work on me. Now, Henry, do write to Horton today and tell him he musn't do this dreadful thing. Tell him how disappointed we should all be. Why, we could never receive her in our home, and think of how Madge – dainty Madge who wouldn't touch an Indian – would be estranged from her only brother. Oh, I'm sure Horton would never do it if he could come home awhile and get his eyes opened."

"Well, I'll write," promised Mr. Boynton as he closed the side door behind him.

A few mornings afterward Horton Boynton sat at his desk in a certain western town, opening his mail. One letter was from Madge, and he read it with interest.

"Dear old Bud," (it began)

"I'm with you, heart and soul. Who wouldn't be, after your doleful letter, poor boy? If she's all you say – and of course she is – she's a peach, and can't fail to win My Lady mother's heart. I'm going home the Monday before Thanksgiving. Tell Miss Indian to be ready. If you love her, I will too. Don't be a goose and give up.

"Hurriedly,

"Madge."

"Bless my little sister's heart!" he exclaimed as he refolded the letter. "Now, for 'Miss Indian's' home to tell her my plan."

"Miss Indian," otherwise Miss Wynoma Littleheart, the beautiful daughter of John Littleheart, a prominent half-breed Indian, met her lover at the gate. Her home, instead of the tepee which Mrs. Boynton had pictured, was a spacious white house surrounded by grounds as lovely as Mrs. Boynton's own. The interior furnishings, too, were equal in taste, beauty and value to those found in other homes – for John Littleheart belonged to a progressive tribe, and his daughter had had lavished upon her every advantage that money could buy.

"Something pleases you this morning, Horton?" she called as she tripped down the walk toward him.

"Yes, and no," he answered, drawing her to a seat in the shelter of an evergreen. The morning was warm and pleasant for the time of year, and the sun smiled down upon the lovers.

"You have heard from your people?" she divined quickly.

"Yes."

"And – and they are unwilling?"

"Remember, they have never seen you, dear – ," he began.

"Ah, yes – but I know." She looked away sadly, trying to keep back the tears. It is hard for a woman to feel that she is not welcome in her husband's family – it takes away part of the girlish romance, she delights in. "It was that way at school; at first, the girls looked askance, because I was Indian. They couldn't see what I had done with my paint and feathers. It wore away, though, Horton, and they liked me in the end!" She turned a suddenly radiant face toward him.

"Yes, and they'll like you at home," he reassured her. "It's their confounded ignorance, Wynoma, nothing else in the world. We'll teach them a few things."

Then their heads went closer together, and after that their voices were lower. They talked and nodded, and at last Horton arose.

"You will, then, Wynoma?"

And she smiled and answered, "I'll be ready, dear, when your sister comes."

"That's my brave little girl," he exclaimed. Then a bird trilled wildly in the evergreen, as if threatening to tell what happened.

* * *

"Let's see; I'll call you 'Noma, and you call me Madge. It's lucky Horton didn't mention your name in his letter to mom and dad. We'd have had to get you another one for this trip. Heigho! Here we are, and there's dad to meet us."

There were two well dressed young ladies among those who alighted when the train stopped. Mr. Boynton smilingly advanced to meet them – for they were Madge and her friend come for a holiday at the Boynton home.

"Papa, this is my friend, Miss 'Noma Littleheart; and let's hurry home, for I'm hungry as a bear!"

A few days later when Madge and Wynoma were out Mr. and Mrs. Boynton sat by the fire together. Suddenly Mrs. Boynton sighed.

"If only Horton were here," she said. "I know I could make him see his error – the absurd boy!"

"How do you like Miss Littleheart – Madge's friend?" asked Mr. Boynton, by way of diverting her mind, if possible, from the unpleasant subject.

"I was just thinking of her," answered Mrs. Boynton. "Now, if Horton had chosen a girl like Miss 'Noma – she asked me to call her 'Noma, but I won't just yet – if he had chosen a girl like her, I say – bright, intelligent, vivacious and entertaining – I shouldn't have objected one bit. She's our kind. Why, I am real proud that she and Madge are good friends, for she is, I am sure, a strong, noble character. Her manners are perfect – so well bred and gentle. And such eyes – did you ever see such clearness – so much expression? I must confess I'm charmed. Madge tells me she is a Western girl, although she has received her education in the East – a very liberal one, as you can easily tell. Her people must have wealth – it is evident that she is accustomed to ease, one might say luxury. Again, I say that I wish Horton were here, for he wouldn't be human if he could withstand her charms. Perhaps he would then forget this girl whose forefathers were savages and who can never move in our circle. Oh, it runs me wild to think of it! I could never bear for him to marry a girl with a drop of Indian blood."

"Oh, well," soothed Mr. Boynton, " 'there's many a slip,' you know. Maybe the Indian girl isn't so bad, after all. Why, Mary, I knew an Indian once – " Mr. Boynton laid down his pipe and would have started one of his oft told "stories," but Mrs. Boynton interrupted.

"Yes, I've no doubt you knew a perfectly wonderful Indian, in his way, Henry, but I'm not in the mood to hear about him. There's no good among them – the savage lot!"

"What's that about savages?" It was Miss Littleheart's gay voice, as she entered, followed by Madge.

They had just returned from a drive, and turned fresh, rosy faces to their elders. But a close observer would have noted a frightened look in the dark eyes of Wynoma. She feared her secret had been guessed. The answer dispelled her fear.

"My wife feels like a savage today, her favorite expression when she is not quite well," explained Mr. Boynton, placidly.

"Oh!" exclaimed Wynoma. Then, "Can't I relieve you – do anything for you dear Mrs. Boynton?"

"Perhaps, – after awhile, dear. For the present, a cup of tea is all I ask of you."

Madge and Mr. Boynton exchanged sudden glances. After awhile Mr. Boynton was called to his study, and Madge went to change her dress. Mrs. Boynton and Wynoma – she of the dark, dreamy eyes – sat alone in the gathering twilight. The lamps were not yet lighted, and the firelight flashed fitfully. Outside a November storm was gathering; inside was warmth, cheer, comfort – and the semi-darkness that invites confidence. Suddenly Mrs. Boynton put out a hand to touch the dark hair of the girl seated at her feet.

"My dear," she began, and halted.

"Yes?" breathed Wynoma.

"I am going to tell you my troubles, if you will listen. Then I have a request to make."

"I – I am sure, Mrs. Boynton, I appreciate the confidence." She could say no more. His mother? Ah, she had dreamed that some day she would lay her hands lovingly on her head, but under different circumstances!

"Yes, I am troubled about my son, Horton. Oh, Wynoma, I wish you knew him. He is so good, so handsome – everything a mother could wish." (Wynoma's breath caught. Could the woman be trying her?)

"But," the mother continued, "he has just written to us (he is in the West in business), of his engagement to an Indian girl! Think of it, I, to receive a low born Indian girl as my daughter? The very thought makes me shudder. You can perhaps realize how I feel. I won't attempt to tell you. But, if I can prevent it, he shall never marry her – and here comes my request of you. First, my dear – pardon me, I beg of you – but are you engaged?"

Wynoma laughed merrily. "In talking to you – yes. But go on," she answered, evasively.

"Well, I shall telegraph my son to come home for Thanksgiving Day. Then," she added meaningly, "when he meets you and mingles again among civilized people, I hope he will forget this wild Indian girl."

Wynoma was silent for a few moments. She was thinking of the cold-hearted, calculating woman by her side. At last she found her voice.

"Aren't you playing with dangerous tools? What is to become of the poor Indian girl, should your plan succeed, and what of me, should I love your son and he remain faithful to the other one?"

"Those questions Fate must answer," Mrs. Boynton said, and the lights which the maid brought in at that moment revealed her cold, determined expression.

* * *

Horton Boynton acknowledged very formally the introduction to his sister's friend, Miss Littleheart. Mrs. Boynton had arranged every plan whereby the two should be thrown together – long drives and walks, while she watched secretly, so she thought, the progress of her little play. She noted, in the days that followed, their growing interest in each other; noted that her son spoke less and less of his Indian sweetheart and sought continuously Miss Littleheart's side. Could she only have seen the two when they knew there were no prying eyes! But she was content with what she saw. So their Thanksgiving passed merrily, with no cloud. Even Mrs. Boynton was lighthearted and smiled on every one.

## Chapter II

Several days before the return of Horton to his business in the West and Madge and Miss Littleheart to their school and home respectively, Horton and Miss Littleheart went for a drive. For the first time, there was silence between them.

"Well, Wynoma, haven't we waited long enough?" Horton spoke first. Wynoma turned her face away.

"I've been thinking, Horton," her voice sounded cold and odd. "I've decided that we can't be married."

"Oh, the mischief you have!" exclaimed Horton. "Why what's the matter? Just when everything is settled – when Mother is willing – ."

"That's just it – we've deceived your mother into willingness! She knows you are going to marry, and she had rather it would be I than, to quote her, 'a low-born Indian girl!' I can't bear it. Only this morning she told me that she was so glad to see the change in you – so glad she was 'rid of that Indian girl.' I tell you, Horton, I'm sick of it! I am an Indian girl, but I am not the kind that deceives! It was weakness this plan of ours. I should have owned my Indian blood, and accepted the consequences. As it is, my honor has asserted itself in time. I shall go no further. If you could not take me in the face of your mother's prejudice and opposition, you are not deserving of me, and it is best that we part."

"But, sweetheart – when she finds out you are one and the same – don't you see it will be all right?"

"No, I don't see. It will never be all right to me. I never liked your mother's plan from the start, and was weak to acquiesce in it. Somehow, I can't help feeling like there is a forlorn, mistreated little Indian girl out there in my Western home who has been deceived by herself and her lover. I must go back and tell her that she at least has her old self back again, if she did have to give up her – lover." She was near to sobbing, but her head was erect, and her eyes shining. Horton never loved her more than at that moment.

A boy on a bicycle called to them, waving a yellow envelope.

"I've a telegram for Miss Littleheart," he said as he alighted beside the buggy. "They told me at the house that I'd find you on this road perhaps."

Wynoma tore open the telegram. "Drive on fast, Horton," she said calmly. "I must catch that noon train. My father – is – dying!"

There was not time for many explanations that morning, but Wynoma went calmly to Mrs. Boynton and told her all. "Of course," she concluded, "it is needless for me to add that I will trouble you no more. Your son is free, so far as I am concerned. Have no more uneasiness on account of 'the low-born Indian girl' your son loves. You will find that, although some white blood is mingled with that of my Indian ancestors, I can still be unrelenting, brave and true to my promise, though the heavens fall." She would not allow Horton to return to her home with her. That night there was a storm in the Boynton household, and Horton left on the midnight train.

* * *

Another Thanksgiving Day was approaching. In her Western home Wynoma Littleheart a year older, a year stronger in determination, a year lovelier, sat by her fire, alone. Much had happened in that year – and yet so little, she thought listlessly. Horton, unable to change her, had moved his business to a distant town. Her father had recovered from his illness, and with him she lived, and led an apparently happy life. Like a proud, stern warrior, she had waited for the flag of truce from Mrs. Boynton; but the days dragged by and no word came.

A step roused her from her revery. Then a closely veiled woman entered the room. In the twilight Wynoma did not recognize her, and in gentle tones bade her to be seated. But the woman at once removed her veil.

"Wynoma, don't you know me?"

Wynoma stood erect. "It is Mrs. Boynton," she said, stiffly.

"Yes, and I want your forgiveness. I was wrong, but I was ignorant and prejudiced, too. I have come all this distance, alone, to make another request of you before another Thanksgiving Day comes around. This year has been a horrible nightmare. I have been afraid that I would die ere pride would let me make reparation. I am unhappy, Horton is miserable – and you – you love him still? Ah, yes, I know you do. Then, come back with me, and let's give thanks that the past is gone – that a miserable, selfish mistake is blotted out, and that – see, I acknowledge it, Wynoma – the Indian girl is my daughter's equal, yes, in some respects, my daughter's mother's superior!"

The appeal was pathetic. Wynoma's eyes were swimming in tears. She stretched out both her hands.

"Oh," she cried, "You are not alone to blame, I have been too stern. Forgive? I am so glad, glad there is such a word in your language as 'forgive.'"

The next day found them journeying Northward.

# From *Sturm's*

## Billy Bearclaws, Aid to Cupid (September, 1909)

Little Eagle Tom sat by the roadside and dug his brown toes into the sand. Before him stretched the billowy Oklahoma prairie; behind him, more prairie, and to the eastward loomed the grim, gray buildings of the government Indian school. As Little Eagle glanced toward them, he twisted his small brown features into an expression of contempt.

Little Eagle was a truant – just a disgusted little Indian truant. He had tired of the white man's civilization which for several months had been administered to him in regular doses by the big, mustached school superintendent. Little Eagle had tired of it all – the daily routine in the boarding school, the lessons and other duties imposed upon these wards of the government in Uncle Sam's well-meant effort to lead them out of the paths of savagery. Little Eagle didn't want to be civilized, so he decided to run away to where he could live out his life in idle enjoyment.

It hadn't been a difficult matter to come thus far – but then he had come only a few miles from the big school buildings. He was resting until he could continue his journey under cover of the darkness. He had it all very nicely planned. They wouldn't miss him for an hour or so yet – not till all the boys and girls filed into the big dining room for supper at 6:30. Then they wouldn't investigate before morning; it was too frequent an occurrence to cause alarm. The superintendent would think he had merely gone home to his parents, as all the boys did when they ran away. He would send, or go himself, in the morning, to bring him back. And his parents would compel him to come back, too. Aye, that was where Little Eagle planned to foil them. He was not going home!

Among the teachers at the government school was the young and rarely beautiful daughter of the superintendent. Little Eagle was in her classes, and to him she was – he expressed it in a very musical Indian word – "The One To Be Adored." Ever since that day when he came to school for the first time and she had led him, a shy little brown boy, to the classes, she had held the supreme place in his childish heart. Indeed, but for her, he would long ago have forsaken the paths of learning. Now, as Little Eagle was only twelve years old, and pretty Betty Merwin was twenty, his love was without alloy; it even extended to and included those she loved, instead of harboring jealousy, as might have been the case with an older lover. For instance, Little Eagle concealed – the word is used advisedly, as all emotions were faithfully concealed by this little stoic – the deepest respect and profoundest admiration for a certain well-to-do young ranchman, Martin Strong, who stood high in the affections of Miss Merwin.

Perhaps no one but Little Eagle knew just how well the ranchman stood in Miss Betty's estimation, since her father had forbidden him to come to the school to see his daughter. But Little Eagle knew. Miss Betty took frequent walks alone, and Little Eagle, feeling she needed protection, skulked along behind in the dusk, like a faithful dog, until Martin Strong stepped forth to meet her. Once Mr. Strong had observed him, and tossed him a dollar with the hand that was not holding Miss Betty's. "Vamoose," he had said, adding, "and keep mum."

"He will, never fear," Miss Betty had said, smiling at him brightly. And forty government superintendents couldn't have dragged her secret between Little Eagle's close-set lips.

Little Eagle's plan was to go to Mr. Strong's ranch for a few months, until the superintendent gave up the search for him. He believed the ranchman would keep his secret as he had kept his; also, he thought that in keeping close to the ranchman, he would not always be very far from Miss Betty. He felt, too, that he could trust Mr. Strong – he could do no more than "keep mum" if Little Eagle asked it.

As darkness gathered, Little Eagle thought he heard a horse galloping far off. The sounds came nearer, and soon the horse and rider came into view. Behind some scrubby bushes Little Eagle darted, until the rider's face was discernible, then he crawled out and uttered a sound something between a friendly salutation and a grunt. The man pulled his horse to a standstill and peered down into the boy's face.

"What the – why, Little Bearclaws, or whatever's-your-name, what are you doing here – running away?"

Little Eagle assented gravely. Then he quietly and evenly explained, in as dignified English as he could command. The young ranchman laughed and took off his hat to him.

"You young schemer!" he exclaimed. "And yet they say the Indian is dull. You've led me into a pretty trap. If I refuse to take you, you'll have to go back to school eventually, and might very effectually put my dream o' love to an end by telling the old man of our meetings. If I take you, I may get arrested for harboring an outlaw. But you wait here till I come back in about an hour, and I reckon you can jump on behind and go with me. Poor little devil," he added as he turned into the road again, "I was savage enough myself once to hate 'rithmetic and g'ography."

Little Eagle retreated to the clump of bushes to wait. When he had waited about an hour and a half, he sleepily concluded that this must have been Miss Betty's evening to go for a walk.

"Well, Billikins, hop on," said a voice, and Little Eagle rubbed his eyes. In a jiffy he was sitting behind Mr. Strong on the wiry little pony. Not another word was spoken on the ten-mile ride, until, as they turned in at the big gate, the ranchman said, seriously, "Sonny, you're Billy Bearclaws now, for diplomatic reasons, and you never saw a government school. The boys here may jibe you at first, but, as I've said before, keep mum."

Billy Bearclaws grunted and slid off to shut the gate.

For many days the Boss had been worried. The boys had noticed it, for where heretofore he had "jollied" and made merry with them, he now sat apart and smoked and looked glum.

"Sick, Boss?" asked "Long Jim," sympathetically. But Martin shook his head.

"Not very, I guess," he replied; and the cowboy walked away. To the others he said, "Cain't imagine what it is. Things wuz never in better shape – cleaned up a cool thousand last shipment. Cain't be money matters as troubles him. He must be sick." The other boys shook their heads, as if the problem was too deep for them.

Billy Bearclaws watched the Boss narrowly with those beady little jet eyes of his. Being somewhat on the inside of Mr. Strong's personal affairs, he thought he held the solution to his trouble. Something was wrong concerning Miss Betty – of that much he was certain. But what? He waited. He observed that the Boss did not leave the ranch often and then not long at a time. Consequently, he did not go to meet Miss Betty any more. And why? Was Miss Betty sick, dead – these thoughts harassed him as he idled around the ranch. His staying there had been accepted with little comment. "The Boss had picked the Injun up somewhere," was what the boys said, and as strangers came seldom, no one recognized in him the former school boy, Little Eagle, for he had cast away his government clothes and donned Indian togs before he was five miles from the school buildings. The ranch hands had ceased to wonder about him, and he amused himself happily all through the long days. The first cloud in his new existence was now enveloping him.

The Boss was not one to be questioned, nor Billy Bearclaws one to question. So matters drifted gloomily along, until at last Billy could stand it no longer. He arose one morning with the fire of determination in his eyes. No one else was up on the ranch, for it was quite early. Stealthily, the little Indian crept to the big barn and began to bridle one of the cow ponies. He was wrestling with an obstinate buckle, when he heard the Boss's voice.

"What are you doing, Bearclaws?" he asked sternly. The boy turned quickly.

"Goin' back to gov'ment school," he answered promptly.

The Boss chuckled. "Are you? And going on one of my best ponies? And slipping away without saying goodbye? I guess that is what we might call 'Indian leave' eh? Take the bridle off, Billy, and wait till after breakfast," he added kindly.

Billy stood silent, while the Boss came close and laid his hand on the child's shoulder.

"Poor little kiddie; are you tired of us here? Tell me, honest Injun – where were you going?"

Billy Bearclaws threw his head back dramatically, and the fire of oratory, which is the heritage of every Indian, burned in his whole expression. "I go," he began, "for you an' Miss Betty. The Sweet-Angel-of-Light, The-One-To-Be-Adored, The-Bright-One-Of-Your-Heart. I see you, yesterday, today, tomorrow, silent and unhappy. I know something wrong. I go to see. To prepare place for you. I return back again." He finished with a flourish of his hands, having glibly mixed his Bible knowledge with his small stock of ready English. The Boss sat down on a box, and when he raised his head presently, his cheeks were wet – that they were tears of mirth, Bearclaws never knew.

"Well, well, Billy you're all right," he said. "I'm no end obliged to you, old chap. Sit down here, and let's have a talk. I believe a fellow could trust you, all right. Now, tell me, what possible good could your going back to the school do for me? If you are properly penitent for running away, and want to go back, why, that's well and good, and I'll send you over any time. But I don't see how that could help me and Miss Betty."

Bearclaws had no answer. Evidently his one object had been to satisfy himself that Miss Betty was well and safe, and to return when he could, with the news for the ranchman.

"You see, Billy," continued the boss, almost as if reasoning with himself, "the superintendent has forbidden her seeing me any more, and has even made it impossible for us to meet as we've been doing. No letter I send her is delivered, and she believes me untrue to my word to see her and write to her. It is a sad predicament, and I wouldn't stand for it one minute – I'd tear up the earth or go to her – except," his voice grew wistful, "I've thought maybe – maybe the old man's about right. I'm not much for a pretty girl like Betty. She loves me, but maybe she'd forget me if she didn't see me any more. Her father has notified me that as soon as this term of school is closed she is to return to an aunt in Washington and be married to one of those high-up, rich ducks, and she'll be about the same as Queen somebody, and can do the society stunt every day in the year. Who am I to stand in her way to better herself? What could I offer her to equal all that? She'd be almost the same as buried here on the ranch, just plain Mrs. Strong, and only a lot of cow punchers to kowtow to her. So I've just made up my mind not to see her again. I won't stand in her way. It's about to kill me to do this, but maybe when I know she's gone away and I'll never see her again – "

The words were like an electric shock to Billy. "No, no," he cried, springing up; "You go get her. She loves you and me."

"Oh, come," said the Boss half angry that he had said so much to a mere Indian boy. "Clear out now and go to breakfast. And keep mum – do you hear?"

But Billy clung to him. "Why you not steal her from the super'ntendent?" he insisted.

"It seems the idea of stealing always appeals to an Indian," muttered the Boss, turning away.

At breakfast everybody was silent. The Boss rode away soon after the meal was over, the men went to their duties, and Billy Bearclaws was left to himself. Nothing amused him this morning – he was doing some deep thinking. Suddenly a plan of action evolved in his active brain, and he darted to the barn. One little pony stood in a stall munching hay. Billy led him out, jumped on his back and was off like someone suddenly gone mad.

By noon he drew rein in front of Big Elk Joe's grass house. The huge Indian greeted him pompously.

"Greeting to you, Little-Boy-From-Spirit-Land," he said. "You have been mourned as dead. First the big superintendent send to your father's house to find truant Indian boy. He no find you there. Then send here, there, everywhere. He offer reward. Nobody get that reward. Little Eagle Tom dead, then. Indians make big cry. Now here you come from happy hunting ground. Tell me, what must Big Elk do for spirit boy?"

Since the belief that he was dead evidently had been generally accepted, Little Eagle Tom, alias Bearclaws, lost no time in dispute of explanation. He slid off the tired pony and began a serious conference with the big Indian. An hour they talked together, Billy apparently explaining, the man nodding and grunting comprehendingly. After a while Big Elk called two others to his side. They were brave braves indeed, in their gorgeous trappings, and when introduced to Billy as the "Returned-Spirit-Boy," gave no evidence of fear or surprise. Big Elk spoke a few words to them, and they nodded, going away presently. Billy, after eating with Big Elk, went out to the little mustang, removed his halter, and with a waving motion of his arms, frightened the animal off the premises. With a dreamy expression in his pathetic dark eyes, he watched the pony loping, riderless, toward the ranch.

The afternoon was drawing to a close, and at the government school the Indian boys were busy with their various chores. The superintendent, stern looking, yet kind withal, was among them, giving suggestions and help when necessary. Glancing down the big road leading to the school, he noticed three Indians riding single file. They rode into the yard and the superintendent went to greet them.

"Come in, Big Elk," he called, and nodded to the others. But Big Elk shook his head gravely, and motioned to the boys all about them.

"Do you want to see me alone?" asked the superintendent. The Indian nodded.

"Then tie your horse and come into the office." The three Indians followed him into the house.

"Now then," said the superintendent, seating himself and speaking pleasantly, not knowing exactly what to expect, since these Indians often came to him with troubles of one kind or another. "What is it, Big Elk?"

"Little Eagle Tom, he want to come back to school," calmly announced Big Elk.

"Little Eagle Tom! Why, sir, the boy is dead, isn't he? At least you Indians all reported such to me. The agent and I have kept a pretty faithful watch for him, and I am quite positive that his own father and mother think he is dead. His name has even been entered on the roll of deceased Indians – he is bound to be dead!"

But Big Elk stolidly shook his head. "Little Eagle Tom not dead. He come back today from spirit land. He say to me he will come back to super'ntendent's school."

"Oh, all right then; of course, I am very glad to know he is alive and certainly the thing is to get him back into school. But it's really too bad he's got onto that deceased roll. I suppose you've come to know if that reward is still good. Well, bring the boy to me tomorrow, and the reward is yours." He closed the roll top desk and rose, as if to end the conference. But Big Elk's head was again shaking solemnly.

"We come not for reward. Little Eagle very sorry he run away. He love you and your school and your daughter, his teacher. He now very ill in my grass house. Tomorrow he may go again to spirit land." Big Elk paused, as Miss Betty, passing in the hall, heard his words and came in and stood beside her father. Then he continued, very impressively,

"Little Eagle does not forget the teaching of The-One-To-Be-Adored. In his sickness he talks of her, he calls for her. If she will come to him, he will return to school as soon as he is able. 'Will she come quick?' he ask, through me."

The big Indian folded his arms. He had delivered his message. He awaited its effect. Miss Betty's blue eyes opened wide, and she turned from the solemn-visaged Indian to her father.

"Is it true, father? Is the poor little fellow sick, and asking for me? Oh, it must be, or Big Elk would not say so," she added, casting a quick glance at the Indian, who nodded.

"Yes, I suppose it is true, Betty," responded her father; "the little rascal has probably been in hiding till he's sorry of his action and will be glad enough to come back to us. Of course, our duty is to get him back into school, where he can be properly cared for."

"He ask only for Miss Betty," put in Big Elk. "For her he call to see before he died again."

"Oh, I must go to him, father – may I not?"

"I hardly think it advisable," began the superintendent, frowning.

"Oh, but surely it is our duty to look after him – mine as much as yours; he was my pupil and so loyal to me," she faltered, almost tearfully. "Father, surely you can trust me with Big Elk – he has been such a faithful friend to you. He would take me safely there."

"Yes," assented the Indian.

"I cannot allow you to go alone, Betty," said her father firmly, and Big Elk saw that he had failed in his errand. "Tomorrow we will drive to Big Elk's house – as early in the morning as we can start. Go back, Big Elk and tell Little Eagle we rejoice to know he is alive, but regret his illness. Tell him I will bring Miss Betty to see him tomorrow morning and if possible he shall return with us here. See that he is well taken care of through tonight."

The Indians bowed and went out. And with her father's decision Betty had to be content, yet there were ill forebodings in her tender heart, for she feared the boy might die before she reached him. Also, why had he left the ranch – for she had known all along where he was concealed. Was Martin Strong really so heartless as to turn the child out, even as he had apparently so ruthlessly banished her from his heart? Oh, if the boy only lived for her to see him and ask him one little word concerning Martin – these were her harassing thoughts as she lay awake that night.

The following day being Sunday there were no classes, and Betty was ready early to accompany her father to Big Elk's house. Just as they were starting, however, the mail was delivered, and some of it proved to be so urgent that at the last moment the superintendent decided he would remain at home to attend to it, and send one of the boys with her.

"These letters are extremely important – I can't afford to delay them so much as a day. John Makes Brave can take you over. It isn't far – you can drive it in an hour and a half. Don't stay too long. Take some food with you. See if Little Eagle is able to be moved. Find out all about the case. Big Elk assured me it was nothing contagious. I'll send the agency physician over, if you think it's necessary."

With these hurried instructions he went back to his desk and Betty drove off with the solemn John Makes Brave.

On a rug in one corner of Big Elk's grass house lay Little Eagle Tom. When Miss Betty bent over him, he smiled shyly. The medicine man had been there, and some concoction of his had almost made Little Eagle sick, but his black eyes were bright enough. While Miss Betty was talking to him in low, gentle tones, and noting inwardly that for a sick boy he was looking unusually well, some one entered the grass house – someone tall and erect and handsome. When he spoke, Miss Betty's heart almost stopped beating, and Little Eagle turned eagerly. It was Martin Strong, and he came quickly to Miss Betty's side.

"Betty, dear!" was all he could say, and with the words the tired look that had recently come to his eyes disappeared. Betty crept close to him and laid her hand on his arm. Big Elk walked outside. Little Eagle lay quite still. In the dim light of the grass house it seemed to him he could discern but one figure, so close-clasped were the lovers. Presently he coughed cautiously. Betty turned quickly.

"Oh, Martin, how shameful of us! The poor little fellow is quite, quite ill, and we selfish people almost forgot him. What shall we do for him? Father said I must bring him back with me to the school, if he was able to be moved. I wonder – "

Little Eagle blinked at the ranchman appealingly.

"Wait, Betty mine, let me talk to this boy. You may be able to teach this little rascal to read and write, but when it comes to really understanding him, I believe I have you bested. Billy Bearclaws, look at me!" he commanded, turning to Little Eagle. The boy gazed back at him through half-shut lids.

"Are you sick, kiddie?" The boy shook his head.

"You ran off from my ranch, on one of my ponies. You came here and pretended sickness to Big Elk. You sent after Miss Betty. You then sent word to me to come here this morning. Isn't it all so?"

Again the boy nodded, and the small brown face was almost permitted to show signs of smiling.

"You see, Betty, dear," continued Martin Strong, "the best friend you and I have in all the world is Billy Bearclaws, once Little Eagle. He is sort of partner of Cupid – looks after Cupid's affairs out west here; he is an – "

"He is an angel!" exclaimed Miss Betty rapturously, as she realized Little Eagle's maneuverings to bring her to her lover. But instantly her face clouded.

"What good will it do, Martin, after all?" she asked, the big tears very near the surface in her wide blue eyes. "I must return to the school, and Little Eagle must go, too. And after that you know how hard it is for me to see you."

"Betty," said Martin Strong firmly, taking both her hands into his own. "I have you now, and I don't intend you shall ever leave me. I have given your father every opportunity to treat me well, and at least the chance to investigate my character before he utterly condemned me. He will do neither. Now I shall simply take matters into my own hands. For a while I had almost decided to try to give you up, for I thought he might be right – you might not be happy out here with me – and I wanted to do the thing that would give you the greatest happiness. I will not always be a ranchman, but I want to make good out here, and it seems a selfish thing to ask a girl to stay with a man like me, not specially good nor interesting, when she might choose a richer man and live a life of pleasure and ease. So I hesitated to ask you to take the step, when I found your father had made such dazzling plans for you. But now, Betty, I ask you to make the decision – do you love me well enough to live with me in obscurity and share, it may be, a life of hardship?"

And Miss Betty answered bravely and unhesitatingly, "Yes, Martin." He drew her closely to him. When they turned presently, guiltily, to Little Eagle's couch, he was no longer there. They found him sitting with Big Elk outside.

"Well, little sick boy," called Martin Strong, "jump into the buggy there. Miss Betty and I will take you back to school." Little Eagle looked dazed and hurt. Betty turned inquiring eyes on her lover.

"Surely, Martin, I thought –"

"I am going with you, certainly, Betty. Didn't I say you were not to leave me any more? Your driver may ride my horse. I will take his place in the buggy with you."

"But father – "

"That is why I am going with you, dear child. I would carry you off with me instead, this very minute, but – I will steal no man's property – it would be a bad example to set for Billy here," he added whimsically. "Besides, I must see your father regarding our immediate marriage."

Betty said no more, except to coax Little Eagle to go with them. He finally got into the buggy, but he wasn't very buoyant about it.

When the stern and dignified superintendent saw the returning buggy, he went out to meet it pleasantly enough; but his expression changed to anger when he recognized Martin Strong. He gruffly ordered Betty to go into the house, but Martin Strong put his hand on her arm.

"I ask your pardon, Mr. Merwin, but I cannot allow Betty to leave me. I found her, through no arrangement of hers, at the bedside of this little sick chap here. I have loved your daughter ever since I first saw her, and she loves me. Two people who love as we do can never be happy apart, no matter how much they would like to consider other people's wishes. So Betty and I will be married this evening at six o'clock, at Rev. Bryson's, over at the agency. I suppose you realize that we could have gone on over there without telling you anything about it, but we want to treat you fair and square. I do not forget that she is your daughter; it honestly makes me rather like you, when I think of it. And please don't forget that she is my affianced wife."

He was quite calm, while the superintendent was growing white with rage.

"You – you – " he stammered wrathfully.

"Martin Strong is my name," supplied that young man promptly. "And it might interest you to know that my father is James M. Strong, the copper miner of Montana; that my family connection is the equal of yours, and that your daughter is not exactly marrying a pauper. I never told you these things before, for I don't thrust my credentials in every man's face; and I like to stand on my own worth. But you seemed to take me for a rascal from the first. The facts may make a difference in your opinion of me, but that doesn't count with me now. I like to remember that Betty accepted me for myself alone."

With a movement of the reins he started the horse. Betty looked back at her father, standing there alone, and her heart ached for him. After all, he was getting old, and he had tried to father and mother both, for all his harsh, stern way. Tears came into her eyes, and she leaned close to the one man she loved better than her father. "Dear," she said, and her voice trembled, "when we are married, won't you bring me back to him – tonight – for his forgiveness and blessing? He will like you now – and remember, he's my father."

Martin Strong bent over her and kissed her tenderly. "You dear little girl," he murmured. "Yes, we will drive back tonight if you wish, child. Your happiness is my law."

And Billy Bearclaws, little brown-faced aid to Cupid, slipped down onto his knees in front of the dashboard, picked up the fallen reins, and guided the tired horses along the prairie road.

# Nonfiction

## From *Twin Territories*

### [Indian Land Selection] (May, 1899)

The *Indian Citizen*[4] asks: "How are the Choctaws and Chickasaws going to select their lands? They know nothing about township lines, range lines, section lines or subdivision of sections. They have no familiarity with maps or plans. They have had no opportunity to become familiar with them. They know

[4] Presumably the *Indian Citizen* newspaper in Atoka, Indian Territory, published under various names from 1889 to 1909.

nothing about field notes or surveys. They have been raised with a prejudice against these things, as their national pride has led them to think that the absence of such things was their surest and safest guarantee of the continuance of their existence as tribes and nations, and they fought against this dismemberment as long as they could." The *Citizen* certainly underestimates the intelligence of its people of the native class. If its editor will take a run up to Muskogee, and hang about this neighborhood a few days, he will see that the Creeks are fully equal to the emergency of finding THEIR land. A Creek employed as pressman in the Times office managed to find 920 acres, allotted to himself and family, which virtually makes this man independent during the remainder of his life.

## DAUGHERTY CANYON (MAY, 1899)[5]

If it be possible to obtain a photo in time, the June number of TWIN TERRITORIES will contain one picture, at least, of Daugherty Canyon – the loveliest spot in all the Chickasaw Nation. We have had so much trouble in getting photos and engravings on time since the magazine was started, the publishers feel almost afraid to make promises of this character. Daugherty Canyon, however, is worthy of considerable effort to secure photographic reproduction and we shall make the effort.

This famous canyon is located twenty miles north of Ardmore, on the Washita river. The canyon is over a mile in length, and the Santa Fe railway traverses the gorge from end to end, following the windings of the river in its tortuous course through the limestone gap, or gorge, that severs as with a knife the Arbuckle Mountains at this point.

Here is a scene worthy of the brush of the most gifted painter. For a full half-mile, the Santa Fe roadbed is literally carved out of the solid face of the cliff, which rises to a distance of 300 feet above the track, while on the other, not a dozen feet from the steel rails, the noisy river brawls and foams above the rocky bed. At intervals the channel narrows and the turbulent stream deepens into quiet pools, whose mirror-like depths reflect the giant white sycamores that clothe the northern margin of the river. These deeper pools are alive with fine fish of a dozen varieties. Almost every Sunday afternoon crowds of young people take the train at Ardmore and run out here for a half-day's recreation after a week's worry with business cares and home duties. A clamber to the top of the cliffs is rather tiresome, but young hearts and youthful limbs do not mind it, and when once at the top the magnificent view well repays the trouble. There is no regular railway station at the canyon, but any Santa Fe conductor, with the usual courtesy of the officials of that road, finds it a pleasure instead of an annoyance to stop his train and allow pleasure-seekers to get off at a switch which has been put in at the north extremity of the gorge.

Never will the writer forget his last visit to the canyon. The day had been a sultry one, and the shade of the sycamore's foliage was indeed delightful. We were a party of three, who lounged upon the grassy banks of the stream, and alternately smoked and dozed over the lazy task of watching three bobbing corks. Up to three o'clock in the afternoon, not a cloud marred the blue of a perfect June day. On the granite peaks across the river the summer heat glimmered and danced in little waves. A long roll of distant thunder broke the quiet, warning us that a storm was approaching, and in the southwest great masses of inky clouds were piling, one upon the other, mountain high. Soon the blue of the June sky was hid by a canopy of wildly charging, purple-crested storm clouds, all whirling and tossing like the giant waves of the sea. A ragged tongue of flame shot from the bosom of the black mass that hung above the pinnacles of the lofty gray cliff, and with the deafening crash of thunder which accompanied the descending bolt, a towering oak that stood upon the very edge of the precipice toppled and fell with a mighty crash down the full three hundred feet and lay at the foot of the cliff, a mass of "kindling wood." Then rain began to descend in torrents, and the face of the "everlasting rocks" was literally ablaze with lightning. The tall crags seemed, through the rain-sheets, to be a thousand feet high, and lit up by the electric display, reminded us of one of Doré's[6] illustrations in Dante's Inferno. A half-hour the storm

---

[5] See note 3 above. Reed's brother-in-law may have written this piece, although he often signed his work; some nineteenth-century women writers used the first-person masculine pronoun.

[6] Gustave Doré (1832–83) was a celebrated nineteenth-century French illustrator, whose works included engravings for an 1861 edition of Dante's *Inferno*.

continued thus, and then the blue sky showed in patches between the dark masses as they sullenly retired toward the east. An hour later the sun came out hotter than ever; but it was welcome, for once, as we were all wet to the skin. It is safe to say that neither of us will ever forget that visit to Daugherty canyon, the most beautiful spot in the land of the Chickasaws.

## DO NOT WANT THEM (JUNE, 1899)

Durant[7] is stirred up over the question of allowing or not allowing negroes in that city. The *Durant Times* bitterly opposes the introduction of colored people into the community, and invites a discussion of the matter by citizens and subscribers throughout its columns. One citizen writes as follows on the subject:

> "Having no negroes has been one of the causes of the prosperity of our city and to now bring them in by force would be working an injustice on us who have settled here because this was a white man's town. If negroes are brought here I fear there will be trouble and may be loss of life; this I sincerely hope will be avoided. Let everyone think seriously over this matter. Some one has suggested that a vote be taken and if a majority of the people want negroes then let them come, but if a majority of the people do not want them, then we should make it as it has been in the past, and enforce the rule – keep them out."

The question is, how are you going to keep them out, and at the same time avoid resorting to lawlessness? Negroes may be ever so much a curse to a town or a country, but in this land of the free, especially in Indian country, it is utterly impossible to enforce discrimination against them in the matter of residence without violating the law. Should the whites attempt to bar the negroes from coming into or residing in this country, it would simply result in a race war that would in a short time place the Indian Territory under martial law, and, indeed, bring about untold complications and dangers. No matter how much we might deplore and protest against their presence, there is no way to avoid it except by an organized "make-it-too-hot-for-them" policy, which leads directly and instantly into white-capism with its consequent terrors and annoyances.

And right here, while we are talking on this subject, TWIN TERRITORIES will make a prediction , and you will live to see the prophecy fulfilled: Before another two years roll around we shall witness serious trouble between the three races in the Indian country.

The white man has sought and obtained the right to lay out townsites and build for himself homes in this country, and when these towns begin to fill up with a large per cent of whites, they will naturally want to control things to the exclusion of any opinion from the negro. Now, this won't suit the colored gentleman, for the reason that hitherto he has, in common with the Indian, called this his home and country. We have been the guests of the red man, so to speak, and the negro has had full and equal rights with ourselves, and in many instances more, as there are thousands who may have become citizens. Now, when the white man steps in, builds towns and proposes to exclude the negro from the council lodge, Mr. Negro will in all probability make a vigorous protest.

## TALEQUAH (JUNE, 1899)

Talequah, home of the Cherokees, is not a city – it is hardly more than a village, but it is one of the prettiest towns in the beautiful Indian Territory. In point of scenery, no other place in the Cherokee, or in any other of the Indian Nations, can excel Talequah. It is unlike most of Indian Territory towns. Its streets are quiet and all are shaded by immense trees, while gurgling brooks flow musically down the main streets, or cool, refreshing springs are hidden in among rocks that have lain for ages in the same

---

7 At the time in Indian Territory, Durant is in southern Oklahoma near the Texas border, roughly midway between Oklahoma City and Dallas. The *Durant Times* was published from 1896 to sometime in the first decade of the 1900s.

place and have formed stepping stones for the inhabitants ever since Talequah has existed. It is a romantic old place, such as tourists delight in visiting, and indeed many an interesting story there is clinging to the rocks, the rills, the rivulets and ancient buildings.

The residents are mostly Cherokees and some of the wealthiest of this race of Indians dwell there.

The capitol building is in Talequah. The Cherokee Male and Female seminaries, two of the largest schools in the Indian Territory, are situated at this place, besides the Presbyterian Mission and other schools.

Talequah has another attraction – its beautiful women. Verily, the Cherokee women are the prettiest under the sun. Intelligent, tall, graceful, bright-eyed brunettes most of them are, while sometimes one meets a blonde Cherokee and feels that this is surely talking with an angel on earth. Such are the Cherokee people and such is Talequah.

## THE CHOCTAW PEOPLE (JUNE, 1899)

Little is known of the early history of the Choctaws. Like the Chickasaws, their neighbors, they occupied a small portion of the State of Mississippi before their removal to Indian Territory, and their customs, habits and modes of government at that time are almost without record.

Like the other aboriginal races the Choctaws had faith in a Great Spirit, which they worshiped in a manner not unlike that of the Chickasaws and other tribes. Their medicine man, too, was popular up till 1837, when a law was passed which forbade him to receive fees, such as horses, hogs or cattle, if the patients were not cured when placed under his care. Should he succeed in restoring them to health, however, nothing was too good for him to receive and often whole herds of cattle and vast amounts of other property were given him by grateful patients. But the medicine man, like nearly all the other ancient rites, customs and superstitions of this race, has become a thing of the past and the bright, intelligent little Choctaws of today think, and indeed know, as little about them as do white people who come here.

The Choctaws are a much enduring people and they have undergone many hardships. When their lands in Mississippi were allotted and the United States laws were adopted, the Choctaws awoke to a realization of their position. Being always an active people, they did not wait long to determine what to do, so they petitioned the United States to remove them to a new country. The treaty of Dancing Rabbit Creek was the result of this petition. Their land in Mississippi was sold and that which they now occupy in the Indian Territory was purchased.

The toilsome journey from their old home to the new we will not undertake to describe. Old and young alike shared in the trials, the hardships and the privations connected with this trip, always patient, and urged forward by the hope that the new land would be a happier and better one than the old. But the long march proved too much for many of the old and infirm who perished on the way and were laid to rest before the new land was reached.

About 1845 all the Choctaws had arrived and settled in their new domain.

A proud but conquered race it was that set about at once to making its own laws and selecting its rulers. Wonderful was the change in that people during the years that followed.

The Choctaws have developed into one of the most powerful and intelligent races of all the Indians. The grand privileges of self-government, the influence of missionaries and the example of many good white families who settled in their midst, did much to bring about the marvelous change – and all in a little more than fifty years.

Many of the Choctaws of today are equal in point of intelligence and independence to any citizen of the United States. The majority of them are very wealthy and own homes that are up-to-date in every particular.

Rich tracts of land are to be found in their nation while the country throughout is abundantly watered and well adapted to stock raising and farming.

The chief wealth of the nation is, however, its inexhaustible coal beds. The income from this source is truly immense. Besides this a large quantity of timber is cut down and shipped out of the nation annually. Walnut, pine and oak abound mostly.

In point of natural scenery, also, the Choctaw Nation is unsurpassed by anything this side of the Sierra Madre mountains. The diversity of landscape is remarkably wonderful.

Some of the busiest towns of Indian Territory are in the Choctaw nation. Schools and churches have long ago been established and this race of people is in every respect up to date, and civilized.

The men of this nation are courteous, well-bred and highly educated. The women, while not as beautiful as their Cherokee sisters, are highly accomplished, being often thorough musicians, excellent artists and brilliant conversationalists. They are almost foolishly modest, it seems, not wishing to "air" their accomplishments.

Twin Territories has tried repeatedly to secure photographs of some of these dark and queenly women, but each attempt has been a failure so far, although we have not yet given up this idea by any means. We hope soon to present likenesses of a number of the Choctaw people – Governor McCurtain, his brilliant sons and daughter; also other prominent families of this noble race. Then, and not until then, can our readers fully realize the truth of our words in regard to this people.

## FROM "WHAT THE CURIOUS WANT TO KNOW . . . A DEPARTMENT DEVOTED TO ENQUIRERS." (1990–1902)

Edited by Yours Candidly, from *Twin Territories*

### from December, 1900

So much is being written and reported to the great daily and weekly newspapers published in the northern and eastern states concerning Indian Territory which is absolutely false and misleading that *Twin Territories* deems it an imperative duty resting upon the editors of papers and periodicals published in Indian Territory to contradict and denounce all such fabrications. To any such person acquainted with the facts as they exist, it seems hardly necessary to devote any time or attention to these fabrications, but seeing that they are read and believed by many unsophisticated youths in the north and east, a demand arises for the truth.

. . . Of course, periodicals and papers which attempt to increase their circulation by the publication of fabrications and fictitious stories, pandering to the whims and whimsical, sensational temperaments of their readers, are to some extent excusable as no one with any brains would expect to find truth in their columns, but the great dailies and weeklies which propose to give the truth in their columns, truth for the edification of their readers, ought to be more careful than to allow their columns filled with their ridiculous and sensational fabrications, . . . articles sent to them no doubt by unreliable reporters, who resort to the fertility of their brain and inventive genius to compose articles from which they hope to gain a paltry nine pence.

Even now *Twin Territories* would not dwell on this subject were it not for the fact that the chiefs of the several tribes of Indians and Indian agents are continually in receipt of letters written by verdant youths and cast-off old bachelors living in the northern and eastern states who haven't brains enough to discern the truth nor comprehension enough to judge human nature, who are the misguided victims of the stories referred to in this article. What ordinary common sense youth reared in the western country would ever be guilty of entertaining the foolish idea that anywhere among any people could be found a wealthy maiden foolish enough to purchase a husband? . . .

#### ARCHIE, HADDAM, CONN.

(a) I don't know of any Indian girl with great wealth who is looking for a handsome husband. The story you read was no doubt untrue. The Indian girls out here have better sense than to advertise themselves in that manner. As you suggest, you might "come out and look around for yourself," but unless you have some sense with your good looks, I won't be responsible for the result. (b) No, please don't send your photograph. Your description sufficed.

J.A.K., Westfield, Mass.

(a) It is no more dangerous to live in Indian Territory than any part of the United States (b) Yes, you are safe in bringing your wife with you – so far as I know. I am not acquainted with her, but if she doesn't whip you, no one here will, so long as you are a law-abiding citizen.

## from January, 1901

Enquirer, Decater, Indiana.

I have been in the home of the gentleman [whom you mention], a number of times, and I didn't have to crawl around in a dirty wigwam, either, as you suggest. A prominent leader among his people, the Creeks; and the son and grandson of like leaders – he is a gentleman of rare attainments. His home is filled with choice books and his parlor contains a number of elegant paintings . . . The stories you have read of him are truly stories – or the word might be stronger, if I weren't a woman.

## from January, 1902

Milliner, Oakhill, N.Y.

You ask what kind of a stock of millinery you should select to settle in a town in Indian Territory; "also" you add, "if lots of beads and such things are required as trimmings, and if it is true that the Indians like only the brightest colors of Ribbon?" Really, I ought not to pay attention to your questions. What do you take us for? Where have you been the last half century? Seriously, I wouldn't advise you to come here with a stock of millinery. You're needed in that place, I am sure, where you won't be misunderstood – and unappreciated. The poor Indians'll manage to get head-gear in some way or other, without you – and if they don't, they can go bare-headed. It would be a pity to have you sacrifice yourself to come way out here in order to educate them in wearing up-to-date hats. It wouldn't pay you my dear madam – but you might learn a whole lot!

## from July, 1902

Many letters are received every day from our subscribers in the states in which are asked questions concerning Indian and Oklahoma Territories, and the various Indian tribes, and it will be a pleasure to answer same under this head. The editor of this department will give the questions the best possible attention, since it is the purpose of Twin Territories to increase interest in these two territories and the people living here. All questions relative to this country and the Indians whose home it is, will be cheerfully answered. Address Twin Territories, Query Department, Muskogee, Indian Territory.

Violet, Columbia, Minn.

Don't believe the "chief" you mention wants "a white wife." He has one already and a most charming family.

Anita, Mooredale, Conn.

Musicians among the Indians are very numerous. Perhaps the most accomplished ones are among the Cherokees, and the other civilized tribes, and those who have been to the Mission and Government schools. The girls learn rapidly both piano and stringed instruments. Their natural talent for music, however, is not remarkable, and they master the art simply by application, as a rule. The Indians are more literary than musical. There are many excellent writers of prose and poetry among the various tribes.

## from September, 1902

### Miss Anxiety, N.Y.

The young man's failure to write to you is, I am sure, not due to his having been "devoured by the savages out here." He can't possibly have been in some danger – except the danger of some Indian maid's bright eyes! You will pardon me if I do not give you the advice you asked for. My answers must be confined to questions relative to Indian or Oklahoma Territories. However, should I ever meet the young man, will let you know.

### Old Bachelor, St. Louis, Mo.

I do not know of any Indian girl who would like to correspond with you. Don't trouble to send your picture.

## from November, 1902

### Indian Territory's Admiring Friend, Geneva, N.Y.

I don't know whether to advise you to come here or not. I'd rather not advise at all, for if you should come, and the Indians here "ate you up," then you'd blame me, and I don't want to be responsible. However, I'll say this much – if the shocks of sudden surprises are shattering to your nerves, don't come to Indian Territory with your present idea of wildness. Read up a little.

## from December, 1902

### G. A. Brenninger, Chamberlain, S. D.

In my opinion, Indian students who have a desire to receive a higher education than that afforded them in the Indian Government schools should be given it. There is no reason why the Indian should not advance rapidly, and it has been proven beyond a doubt that the Indian girl or boy, when given an equal chance with their white cousins, can accomplish just as much as can the white boy or girl. There have been exceptions, of course, where the Indian has proven lazy, careless and indifferent to the opportunities afforded him; but cannot the same be said of the white girl and boy in hundreds of thousands of cases? So I answer you, yes, I believe the Indian student who shows an aptness for the arts or the professions should be given the best advantages the land affords. Yes, I believe it would be a wise move for the Government, to either establish a Conservatory of Music for Indians or to furnish scholarships in some good Conservatory already established, so that those Indian boys and girls who are desirous of education along that line could receive such an advantage. The better the education, the more thorough and complete, the sooner the Indian will be able to prove to the world – as indeed, he has already begun to do – his capabilities and his usefulness in the new life he has entered upon.

## From *Sturm's* [*Sturm's Statehood*[8] *Magazine* to June, 1906, and *Sturm's Oklahoma Magazine* to May, 1911]

### Indian Wit and Wisdom (March, 1906)

Because the Indian talks little and is sometimes slow to answer is no sign of dullness. It is only that he considers it improper to show haste. Once a missionary preached a long sermon to some full-bloods. He

[8] Oklahoma did not become a state until November 16, 1907.

told of the fall of Adam, the coming of Christ to atone for man's sins, His miracles, etc. At last he finished and an Indian rose to thank him. This is what he said: "What you have told us is good. It is a bad idea to eat apples. They should be made into cider. Then cider should be allowed to stand a while. It is better so. We thank you for coming so far to tell us these things that you have heard from your mother."

Once when Quanah Parker, the white-Comanche chief, had, on a very hot day just taken a drink of ice water, a bystander, a white man, remarked, "White man pretty smart, ain't he?" "Yes," Quanah replied, "white man smarter than God."

"Oh, no, not smarter than God. Why do you think so?" returned the white man.

"Why," said Quanah, "God, He made ice in winter time; white man he makum summer time all same." The white man made no reply.

## Indian Proverbs (March, 1906)

The coward shoots with shut eyes.
No Indian ever sold his daughter for a name.
Before the pale-face came, there was no poison in the Indian's corn.
There is no cure for the firewater's burn.
Small things talk loud to the Indian's eye.
When a fox walks lame, old rabbit jumps.
The pale-face's arm is not longer than his word.
A squaw's tongue runs faster than the wind's legs.
There is nothing so eloquent as a rattlesnake's tail.
If the Indian would lie like the pale-face he would rule the earth.
The Indian scalps his enemy; the pale-face skins his friends.
The Indian takes his dog to heaven; the pale-face sends his brother to hell.
There will be hungry pale-faces so long as there is any Indian land to swallow.
When a man prays one day and steals six, the Great Spirit thunders and the evil one laughs.
A starving man will eat with the wolf.
There are three things it takes a strong man to hold; a young warrior, a wild horse and a handsome squaw.

## When The Cowboy Reigned (April, 1906)

Within Indian Territory's broad domains millions of cattle have been pastured. Here, upon nature's luxuriant herbage, these kings and queens of the plains have browsed and grown fat, tossing their horns in the freedom of almost unlimited pasturage. In the old days of leasing grass lands to the white cattlemen, multiplied thousands of poor cattle from Texas and other points were shipped to Indian Territory, and here they soon became sleek, and away their prosperous owners sent them to the great marts of the North. Indian Territory grazing land was considered by cattlemen as among the finest in the world; and so great ranches were established, and over Indian Territory's broad prairies reigned the lordly cowboy of the old type, now nearly extinct.

Many tales could be told of those old days, when such types of outlaws as Belle Starr, the famous female bandit, "Bill" Cook, Cherokee Bill, the Younger boys, Tom Story, Ned Christie and others noted for their desperate and daring deeds of murder and theft, ran riot in the Territory. Stealing cattle was among the smaller crimes of those bands of outlaws, and with them the hardy cowboy had to deal, and many is the lively skirmish that is recalled by the few survivors of the ranch house in the Indian Territory.

With the allotment of lands to the Indians, the ranch house, with its crew of jolly good-natured cowboys, gradually disappeared. The change that is to end in Statehood for Indian Territory, the dissolution of tribal customs and laws, and United States citizenship for the Indians, was first noted by these ranchmen, whom it first affected. The cowboy, who braved the territory in days of danger and lawlessness, who once galloped over its far-reaching prairies, lord of his ranch kingdom, has had to move on.

He saw, as he sat on his faithful cow pony, his kingdom usurped by the progress of civilization. His domain has been converted into neat farms. Instead of the isolated ranch house where, after the roundup, the boys gathered to "spin yarns," sing rollicking songs, to play a friendly game of cards, and to dream sometimes of homes far away in the States – this has been displaced for comfortable farm houses. Industrious farmers from the States are moving in as rapidly as Indian lands are available and around the doors of the new homes little children are playing and busy housewives sing within. The pasture lands are being converted into corn fields, wheat fields, cotton fields. The Indians, learning of their white neighbors, are waking up and their homes, too, put on a more prosperous appearance.

Not only do numerous farms dot the fair prairie land, but a huge motor, propelled by steam, comes bounding across the once vast prairie, scattering the few remaining herds. The cowboy pulls up his pony and together they watch the train, the little pony "shying" and dilating his nostrils at the unusual sight. In the track of the "monster" little towns spring up in a night. A depot is "run up," a rude church is constructed, a pine grocery store, with one corner for ribbons and dress goods for the women, is soon ready for business, and thus it is the cowboy finds himself in the midst of onrushing civilization.

Tiny houses dot the country adjacent to the "depot" – little, hastily built "shacks" that will serve as shelter till more commodious homes can be afforded. Often tents gleam in the sunshine for these newcomers – "home-seekers" – are not overly particular. Soon the village is a thriving town, and before the cowboy has had time to realize the great change in his country, he rides into a busy city one day, and his sturdy bronco rears and plunges at the sight of the electric cars, and he himself gazes in wonder at the imposing homes along the paved avenues.

So it has been in this fair new country in the last quarter of a century or less. The old-time "cowpunch" is gone. The ranch house, with memories of the stirring early-day episodes, is a thing of the past. The allotment of lands, the progress of the Indians, the onrush of civilization, the incoming of thousands of investors, capitalists – and grafters – all this has changed the old order of things, and the cow-man is dethroned. But, when you find the survivor of those days he will tell you all the tales of the early days when he galloped over the plains as free as he was light-hearted, listened to the bellowing of his herds and felt the wind as it tanned his cheek. He will tell you of the "hold-ups" and of the cattle stealing, when he faced desperadoes in protection of his interests, and all the old stories of the "wild" Indian Territory, but which conditions, happily for all, exist no more.

## Father of 90,000 Indians (July, 1906)

One of the most unique, it might be said stupendous, positions authorized by the United States Government is that occupied by the man who supervises the 90,000 Indian inhabitants of Indian Territory. These Indians are the members of the Five Civilized Tribes, viz., Cherokee, Creeks, Choctaws, Chickasaws and Seminoles, who, by treaty stipulations with the United States early in the nineteenth century, relinquished their rights to soil in Alabama, Georgia, Tennessee, North and South Carolina and Mississippi and accepted some twenty million acres of land in what now comprises Indian Territory.

Mr. J. George Wright, United States Indian Inspector for the Indian Territory, is the man who holds the peculiar position of father for 90,000 Indians, and his authority is found in section 27 of the act of June 28, 1898 (30 stat., 495), which reads:

> That the Secretary of the Interior is authorized to locate one Indian inspector in Indian Territory, who may, under his authority and direction, perform any duties required by the Secretary of the Interior by law, relating to affairs therein.

The inspector reviews and transmits to the Secretary of the Interior all reports of the agent in charge of Union Agency, the superintendent and supervisors of schools, revenue inspectors, mining trustees of the Choctaw and Chickasaw nations and supervising engineer of townsites – in fact he recommends just what is best for Poor Lo and administers to his wants accordingly.

The individual Indian, however, hardly knows that there is such a man as the inspector. Almost the first English words the full-blood learned in Indian Territory were "the agent," and they come to him for their every want as does a small boy to his father. The agent is greater than the president of the United States in the eyes of the red man.

In truth, the agent is the right hand man of the inspector and upon him falls the brunt of the work of administering to nearly one hundred thousand Indian citizens, ranging from fullblood to 1/128 Indian by blood. Mr. Dana H. Kelsey, agent in charge of Union Agency, therefore in reality is the foster father, or rather federal guardian, of the members of the Five Civilized Tribes of Indians in Indian Territory, the largest Indian agency in the United States.

To enumerate the different branches of the work of the Indian agent would require much more space than this article can devote. Briefly, he manages all affairs pertaining to the Indian, handles his money, builds his houses, pays his debts, sells his land and sees that he gets the highest market price for it, or if some greedy white man has taken "squatter's" rights, the agent must escort him out of the territory – in fact he is the red man's guardian.

The agent receives and disburses more than three million dollars each year. A large per cent of this money is derived from royalties on coal, asphalt and other minerals, oil and gas, tribal taxes and through the sale of lots in government townsites. In addition to this money the agent is required to make from time to time special payments to the Indians, ranging from a few thousand to nearly a million dollars. One of these was recently finished in which he paid $600,000 to the so-called "loyal Creeks," these being, as one would imply from the term, the Creek Indians and their descendants who were loyal to the United States during the civil war. Another payment to the Choctaw allottees of $900,000 is just being completed, while still another of about the same sum is being prepared.

The Indian agent has under his direct employ one hundred persons (not including field men or Indian police). Eight of these are Indians by blood, three of whom are high grade stenographers. More than 150,000 letters are received by the agent each year and there is mailed from his office 250,000.

When one considers the peculiar conditions of this Indian country and the individuality of the territory – there never was another like it in the world – it is easier to comprehend or realize in a way the difficulties which one man must encounter in administering to the inhabitants. In the first place Indian Territory has never been nor is it now an organized territory; no local government exists except in incorporated towns, and no taxes other than for municipal purposes and the different tribal laws are imposed which latter are enforced by the Secretary of the Interior. It has neither counties nor political status, and with the exception of certain tribal laws, all laws are made by congress, and the territory has no representative in that body. The administration of certain other federal statutes applicable to the territory, are enforced through the United States courts, divided into four judicial districts.

As the situation and laws pertaining to each tribe are different, Indian Territory is in fact five distinct Indian reservations, and the man who occupies the position of agent must fully understand the peculiar and particular needs of each tribe.

And the most peculiar phase of the unique situation is that every Indian in Indian Territory is a citizen of the United States (Act of March 3, 1901, 31 stat., L., 1447).

It is interesting to spend a few hours in the office of the Indian agent. At all times during the day can be found a line of Indians waiting their turn to see "the agent." The first may be a fullblood Cherokee, who, through an interpreter, asks how much royalty he is to receive for the month. He is informed $1,400 (this amount being the average monthly royalty received by some four or five Cherokees, while many others receive as much as $1,000 each month). The agent tells him that the money is on deposit in one of the United States depositories for this purpose, whereupon the lucky Indian endeavors by every story possible to get possession of it. He can build him a home to cost every cent of the money to his credit and the agent, after ascertaining that he has received "a square deal," will pay the cost; or he may purchase stock and farming implements and have his land improved or make any other judicious investment with the approval of the agent, but he cannot handle his money. He is incompetent as a child in money matters.

The next in line is a Creek woman with a dozen scared youngsters clinging to her skirts. She has a grievance. A white man has taken possession of her land and will pay her nothing for the use of it. The "intruder" is called in and after vainly endeavoring to prove that possession is nine points of the law, is turned over to a squad of swarthy Indian policemen, who march him and his cattle across the Kansas line.

A handsome young Choctaw, in a neat business suit, then demands the attention of the agent and asks that the restrictions upon the alienation of his surplus allotment be removed. He is questioned under oath relative to his education, intelligence, business capacity, etc., to the satisfaction of the agent, who duly makes a favorable report to the Secretary of the Interior through the inspector and the commissioner of Indian affairs. If the secretary approves the agent's findings the applicant is free to use his land (other than that portion designated as his homestead) in any manner he may choose.

The Creek Indians can list their surplus land for sale with the agent without having the restrictions removed. He secretly appraises the tract which the Indian wishes to sell, and for sixty days advertises the land in the daily papers. The bids are then opened and the highest bidder (if his price be above the appraised value) gets the plum.

There are every day dozens of each of the above specified matters, as well as hundreds of others of different nature, reviewed and reported upon by the agent.

In less than another year tribal government and affairs will be dissolved in the Indian Territory. The present is the period of transition. Titles are passing to the occupants of town lots; the allotments are practically completed (a fair per cent of which are alienable under certain conditions). Congress is working overtime in the endeavor to legislate for the territory and the red man, and the Indian agent and Poor Lo will mutually be happy when the strenuous life is over.

## Indian Tales Between Pipes (November, 1906)

Many are the amusing stories told by the field parties of the Dawes Commission[9] relative to their experiences with the full blood Indian. A party of these boys recently met at a corn dance down in the Hickory Grove district, and "swapped" experiences as they sat around the fire and smoked their pipes. In some of these stories it was evident that the ignorant (?) full blood got the best of the white man, and demonstrates that his native wit and shrewdness to a large extent compensates his lack of learning acquired from school books.

Mr. H. Van Smith, for several years disbursing clerk for the Commission, came in for a goodly share of the narratives, and said that more than once he was "bested" in an argument with a red man.

Mr. Smith was sent down in Mississippi a year ago to bring to the Territory the few remaining Choctaws who had successfully evaded former officials. After beating the brush for several weeks he succeeded in getting together sixty-four of the natives, and by promising to give them almost anything from a cap pistol to an upright piano, got their promise to be at the railroad station on a certain date. Everything appeared to be moving lovely and according to schedule until the day before the trip to the Territory was to take place. On this day a hungry looking wearer of the blanket approached Smith and after inspecting him for a few minutes said: "Maybe so, Injun take him dog." Smith was preoccupied and merely answered, "all right, take your dog if you want to." However, the Indian was not fully satisfied, and again said, this time with more emphasis: "Maybe so, Injun take him dog." Smith replied with like emphasis that as far as he was concerned he could take all the dogs he wanted to, and then promptly dismissed the matter from his mind.

The next day Smith was detained in the town until nearly train time. When he arrived at the depot, however, he understood why his full blood friend had been so persistent on the day previous, for lo and behold – sixty-four Indians and sixty-five dogs. A dog for each Indian, and they had thoughtfully brought an extra one for Smith.

On another occasion a stalwart full blood, laboring under a fair load of Peruna, or some other similar beverage that gives a man nerve to face a visit from his mother-in-law, entered one of the departments and without further ceremony announced that he wanted to file for his twenty-four children. As the

[9] Led by Massachusetts Senator Henry Dawes, who sponsored the Dawes Act (or General Allotment Act) of 1887, the Dawes Commission was initiated in 1893. Its initial function was to determine citizenship claims and prepare a roll for the Five Civilized Tribes. Later it was also to survey and divide the land among those on the roll. The aim of the Dawes act was to allot tribal lands in severalty as a means of making the Indians more "civilized."

applicant appeared scarcely more than thirty-years of age himself, the clerk in charge told him there must be some mistake; that he surely did not have twenty-four children. The Indian insisted, and the clerk told him to go home and think it over a few days, then to come back when he felt better, and they would talk it over.

The Indian evidently recognized that he was properly equipped with that which cheers, for he promptly replied; "No, talk it over today. Maybe so come back when I feel better and I no talk any."

Realizing it was best to hear him out the clerk told him to go ahead and explain it to him. The Indian did so in this manner: "Maybe so I have four children, and squaw she die. I take another squaw with eight children. Then her children mine, maybe so?" The clerk agreed that when he married a widow with eight children the children were then his. This pleased the Indian and he continued:

"Well so, my children hers, maybe so?"

The clerk also agreed that his new wife would be the mother of his own children. The Indian then promptly closed the argument with, "well so, she have twelve children, mine and hers. Maybe so you give land for twenty-four children."

A delegation had come in from the Eucha district to protest to the agent against a white man who would not keep his hogs fenced up, and consequently they were creating havoc with the crops being planted by the Indians. Some of the Creek Indians are great on oratory and in this delegation was one of this kind – an old white headed King of the town. The younger members explained their mission and endeavored to demonstrate how very necessary it was that immediate steps be taken to compel this white man to pen up his hogs. The old King kept shaking his head in a dissatisfied manner, and finally demanded that he be heard. The younger members respectfully withdrew and the old fellow advanced to the center of the floor, pulled a bandanna handkerchief of about the dimensions of an ordinary tablecloth from his pocket, deliberately wiped his mouth and hands, and striking a pose, commenced: "You young fellows don't know what you is talking about. You explanations you'se'f about as clear as mud. Talk about hogs! Why you don't know the first principle of a hog. Mr. Agent, let a man talk who has been raised among hogs."

It is needless to say the remainder of his speech was lost, owing to the office force being convulsed with laughter.

I. N. Ury, a Kansas politician, an Indian Territory investor, a resident of Muskogee, and an all around good fellow, has also had some dealings with the full blood. Mr. Ury is gentleness itself wherever the weaker sex is concerned, but he is apt to lose patience when dealing with men, and especially if his feeding has not been up to the standard required by an active politician.

On one occasion Mr. Ury was driving overland in the Creek Nation with a party of friends. When they reached the north fork of the Canadian river they found the water too high to ford with safety, so drove several miles up the river before crossing. Consequently they lost their way and drove about aimlessly until sundown, when they pitched camp, relit their pipes for supper, and discussed their predicament. In the morning they tried another smoke for breakfast, and started out in the hope that they would soon meet some one who would direct them to their intended destination. They passed a number of houses, but being in the full blood settlement, the Indian women, according to custom in the absence of their husbands, grabbed their children and made for the brush.

Along about high noon the party was overjoyed by seeing a wagon, drawn by two fine mules, approaching them. Mr. Ury hailed the driver, who stopped his mules and politely waited. Ury asked him several questions, but was answered each time with "ugh" and the dull Indian shake of the head.

Finally Ury lost what little patience remained and began swearing, (and being a politician he has a fair "cussing" vocabulary, by the way.) He cussed every Indian within the bounds of Indian Territory, then jumped from the Atlantic to the Pacific coast, from Canada to the Gulf of Mexico and back. It is difficult to state just where he would have ended had he not exhausted his breath and stopped for a moment.

During this time the Indian had been sitting in his wagon, watching Ury with all interest possible. When the swearing ceased he asked in excellent English and with the most bland manner, "what is the name of the town you gentlemen are desirous of reaching?"

He then directed them on their journey, which happily was of short duration, as they were within two miles of their desired destination. Ury, however, he who had fought many political campaigns to a finish, had bought and sold land of Freedmen, had met the Indian Territory lawyer on equal ground and been victorious, – Ury was the most subdued one of the party. Since then he has become wary of the "dull" full blood.

## The Indian Orphan (January, 1908)

Amid so much confusion of ideas now entertained by the world at large concerning the Indians of the new state of Oklahoma there is no more erroneous belief than that the Indians are all fabulously wealthy, from the smallest stolid faced little full blood up to the intelligent, fully civilized one-sixty-fourth blood Indian. In the estimation of most people, in other words, to be an Indian, of whatever tribe simply means to be the possessor of rich oil lands, fine farm lands and a big bank account with Uncle Sam. To ask for charity for any purpose where Indians are concerned is, therefore almost considered a form of graft. No one seems to be able to comprehend an Indian in destitute circumstances or without the actual necessities.

Columbus found Lo, the poor Indian, the undisputed possessor of an entire continent, and the romantic idea from that time to the present has been that no matter what his other conditions, Lo was independently rich in this world's goods.

It is easy to see how such an idea has become general. Almost every day one may read in the papers of some wealthy "Indian Princess" or may find articles in which the wealth of individual Indians is estimated in large figures.

As a matter of fact there are a few remnant tribes, small in numbers, as for example, the Osages, whose individual wealth is quite extensive. But there is real poverty among the great portion of the full bloods of the new state, and actual suffering for the necessities of life in many instances. To have an allotment is one thing – for it is true, of course that the Indians all have their pro rata share of land – but when you are a full blood, maybe you may know where your land is and maybe you don't; and when you don't know how to make a living off that land even if you do know where it is located; and when maybe the land is productive and maybe it is rocky and sterile; and when you can't sell any of it to get money to work it – granted you have the inclination – you see, taking all these things into consideration, I say you wouldn't feel like such a very rich Indian.

We do not wish to be understood as implying or intimating that the Five Civilized Tribes of Oklahoma Territory – that is the Cherokees, Creeks, Choctaws, Chickasaws and Seminoles are a degenerate people. Far from it. In truth they are in advance in civilization of the other tribes. They possess average intelligence and ambition. Civilization was embraced by them more than a hundred years ago, and among the mixed bloods of these tribes are some very bright men and women.

But with all their possessions their condition is not that of dazzling wealth. The turning point has come in the lives of the Indians. They are American citizens now. Those who are prepared to meet the great change – who have Yankee shrewdness combined with Indian keenness – will no doubt be able to look after their affairs and will accumulate wealth. But what of the unlettered, the untutored? They do not understand the value of their lands and are encumbering them for mere pittances – enough, perhaps, for immediate needs. In a country where almost every other man is a grafter, the ignorant class is easy prey. What is the future of the Red American citizen?

Beyond doubt the worst phase of this Indian question is the condition of the Indian orphans. They will be the chief sufferers from the present cheating and robbing by "grafters." There are thousands of poor full blood Indian orphan children. Many of them are utterly homeless, helpless, hopeless and friendless. Their relations, if they have any, don't want them or can't take care of them. Their allotments are probably tied up by some grafter in a long time lease; or their guardians fail in their duty. No one can believe the great number of little Indian children thus thrown on the mercy of the world.

It is a very serious matter – that of the Indian orphan – more serious indeed than people realize. While the Territory trips merrily into statehood, some of her red skinned citizens are in dire distress out there in the hills, and the cry of the orphan can be heard. If the true condition of the full blood Indian orphan was known to one-half the missionary societies and charitable organizations of this country, it is certain that less money would go out for foreign missions. Not that it isn't needed in foreign fields, but because charity begins at home. It is a crime to let those at our very doors suffer, when we are expecting to mold them into good, staunch American citizens.

Rev. J. S. Murrow, of Atoka, Indian Territory, is one of the oldest living missionaries to the Indians. He has devoted more than fifty years of his life to the Southern tribes and is thoroughly acquainted with their conditions and needs. Of recent years he has been devoting his efforts toward establishing a home for Indian orphans, and in fact has succeeded in so far as he has a few temporary buildings erected on a tract of land located about nine miles from Coalgate, Oklahoma. This is the only Indian orphan home in the United States. This industrial home is the only hope for the full blood orphan Indian children of the new state. It is open to all orphan children of full blood parentage or those not more than one-half white. It has been a long, hard struggle to get the institution established and even now its founder and his co-workers, who have this matter so close at heart, are heartsick because they have means to care for just a limited number of children and indigent old people when there are hundreds seeking admittance.

Rev. Murrow is an old man now, but his zeal is unabated. He has lived very close to these full blood Indians – has studied their conditions and knows their needs. This orphan's home is the only thing he is now devoting his time and attention to, and the one thing he hopes to accomplish for them before he lays down his life's work. The old missionary is cheery and optimistic, but when he tells of the mistreatment of these orphans and of the terrible condition in which he has found many of them, his eyes are dim, and one is quite convinced that even if these children might be considered "rich" in land, they are indeed poor if they have no guiding influences, no home training, no protector to save for them their little heritages.

Three thousand acres of land have been donated to the Home; part of this given by the Chickasaw and Choctaw Nations and the remainder given in small quantities out of allotments of Indians who appreciated the needs of the Home. By the favor of the Secretary of the Interior these donations have been filed together. The title is in the home and the land, and the buildings to be erected thereon cannot be sold or mortgaged as long as there are any full blood Indian orphan children to need the protection and care of this institution. It will be one spot that thieves cannot steal from the Indians – one little spot the Indians cannot be driven from; a place of refuge and a Christian industrial home for the orphan children of the passing race.

But how to erect sufficient buildings and to put the home on a self supporting basis is the brain puzzling question. It takes money to do this. The question of a location settled and the land secured, it must be fenced and cleared and put into shape for cultivation. The land is what is termed "second grade." It is very rocky; partly covered with small timber and a small percent is prairie. The rocks will be used for building purposes.

If the institution is once established on a reasonable basis it will be self supporting, but the farm in its unsettled condition, with its raw undeveloped land, cannot be very remunerative. The cost to fence it alone will be a big item, not mentioning the other expenses necessary to put it upon a solid footing. Meanwhile the faithful few are gathered together in a few small buildings that have been hastily erected in that secluded spot already known as The Murrow Indian Orphans' Home, with the orphans who are glad to be thus cared for.

Small need to suggest what willing hands and hearts might do for this worthy undertaking. One has only to investigate ever so slightly to be convinced that a home for Indian orphans is the crying need of this country. Go out among the full bloods and look into their affairs for yourself and you will wonder that the home has not long ago been a reality. Then investigate the brave efforts of "Father Murrow" and you will no longer hesitate where your charity funds shall be sent.

## DAUGHTERS OF CONFEDERACY (JUNE, 1910)

In the young state of Oklahoma, the population of which is composed of people from every state in the Union, there are at least one thousand women who are banded together as a part of the great organization of the Southland, the United Daughters of the Confederacy. In every town and village, even those that have miraculously sprung up in a night, as it were, a chapter of the Daughters of the Confederacy has been organized along with other women's clubs.

The women who are active in the work have come to Oklahoma from the old southern states, where loyalty to the cause for which the South suffered, bled and died, has never faltered; where heroic women stepped forth directly after the war and picked up the thread of broken fortunes, made new homes in places left desolate by cruel war; buoyed the helpless, and by womanly strength and courage have done a noble part in the upbuilding of the South. How inconceivably hard that task was, only the women themselves, perhaps, know, for they walked unfalteringly over all obstacles. Not only were there homes to be remade, but soldier's widows and children to be cared for, and places of refuge for wounded, sick and needy must be prepared. Want and destitution were on every hand. The southern states were not in position to provide pensions for the southern soldiers or their widows, so it was the Confederate veterans who, as the years went by and the need of the Confederate veterans became more pitiful as age came upon them, inaugurated the move of establishing a chain of homes for Confederate veterans throughout the South. Today these stand, monuments grander than any marble, to the untiring efforts of the Daughters of the Confederacy. Old soldiers, too ill to work, or left alone and needy in their old age, are lovingly cared for in these homes.

Schools and dormitories were also established by the Daughters and many bright young men and women today owe their education to this organization. Among the poor mountain whites of the South, the good accomplished in the schools that the Daughters have established has been marvelous, and the good work is going steadily on.

Although philanthropy came first and was the real reason for the organization of the Daughters of the Confederacy, they are patriotic, too, and their loyalty to Dixieland and her brave soldiers has found expression in monuments and tablets of marble and bronze. Nearly every spot in the southern states which the Civil war made famous has been so marked. The Daughters gave $5,000 of the $75,000 that went to erect a monument to Jefferson Davis at Richmond. A splendid monument to Robert E. Lee will soon be erected at Arlington by the Daughters of the South. An earnest effort has been made, too, that not only the textbooks in the schools, but public opinion also should become fair and just toward the South, and southern women have written upon the subject of their work until most people have come to realize what it means to be a Daughter of the Confederacy. They were not organized in a spirit of antagonism toward the North, but simply to answer the distressing call for help among the aged and infirm soldiers who had given their health, wealth and all to their country.

Organized with nothing but good as its motive, it has reached out and out until, wherever there is a little band of southern women, a chapter of the Daughters of the Confederacy is organized, always with these thoughts in mind: to make comfortable the last days of the Confederate veteran, to care for his widow, and to educate the youth of the South; to present the cause of Dixie to the world in its true light, devoid of prejudice, that history may hand down to the ages a fair and just record of the southern soldiers – than whom all the world must acknowledge there have been no braver men.

The women of the South, thus organized have been able to accomplish great and good deeds that will live forever. Their influence has been felt all over the nation in cementing the terrible break in the national friendship caused by the Civil war. Whenever northern women have come South, they have found hospitality and good will; whenever a southern woman has gone North, it was with such loyalty and praise in her heart for her beloved Southland that soon any prejudice that might have found lodgment in her new northern neighbors was dispelled. Woman's attitude means almost as much in national affairs as in any other sphere, and the women of the South have played an important part in the rebuilding of that once ruined section.

Peculiar conditions existed at the time of the admission of Oklahoma to statehood. While not strictly a southern state, the oldest families of the Indian Territory were, mostly, people from the real South; and the Five Civilized Tribes, whose territory the state originally was, were the southern tribes of Indians, coming from Georgia, Alabama, Florida, the Carolinas and Tennessee. These tribes furnished the South with some of her best soldiers, notable among them being Stan Waitie, a full-blooded Cherokee, the only Indian who ever attained the rank of brigadier general. He was a grand soldier and he and his men gave the South excellent service.

Others who came more recently to the new state are from every part of the world; but here, as in the older states, the daughters of the South have found work to do as they did "down home," and are seriously going about it. The old Indian Territory had been the scene of several battles during the war, and a number of skirmishes, and investigation proved that many Confederate soldiers' graves were unmarked, and, what was worse, numbers of Confederate veterans were living in want, exposed in their old age to the chill winters without the necessities of life. Naturally, the first organized effort of the Oklahoma division of the Daughters has been to allay the suffering of the veterans and build a refuge for them. Before statehood, several of the abler veterans assisted the Daughters in maintaining a cottage home near McAlester, which furnished an abiding place for a number of these old soldiers whose last days would otherwise have been spent most miserably. Out of that grew the idea of a State Confederate Veteran's Home, and now the plan is almost a reality.

In the special session of the second state legislature, what is known as house bill No. 41 was passed, which provides that the state shall maintain, at a cost of $25,000 per year, for the period of twenty-five years, a Home for Confederate Veterans, and their wives and widows. The Home is to cost not less than $20,000. It will be built at Ardmore, this place having made the best inducements of any for its location. The town donated twenty-five acres of ground, $5,000 cash, and free water piped to the building.

While the state does not provide the funds to erect this building, the fact that its maintenance is assured is an incentive that has stirred the hearts of every Oklahoma southerner, and of many who are not of the South but whose sojourn here has convinced them that the institution is a worthy one. The originators of the bill are W. F. Gilmer, a son of the Confederacy, who is a representative of Carter county in the state legislature; J. H. Maxey, of Pottawatomie county, Frank Casteel, of Cimarron county, of the house, and H. J. Allen, of the senate. Mr. Gilmer, who was appointed financial agent, has worked tirelessly in the interest of the Home, soliciting and collecting funds. He has found noble helpers everywhere – in the veterans themselves, whose hearts are stirred for their unfortunate comrades to whom this home will prove a God's blessing in their old age; in the Sons of Veterans, buoyant young men of a young commonwealth, who desire this Home as a monument to their hero-fathers; but in the Daughters of the Confederacy more than all others, who are willing to do everything to raise money for the Home, from serving pink teas to peddling cook books – as one plucky woman did.

In all the efforts toward arousing interest and enthusiasm in the work, no one has been more faithful than the state president of the Daughters, Mrs. Culbertson. She has traveled from one end of the state to the other, organizing chapters, enthusing them to renewed effort, until one might almost say the credit of furnishing the greater portion of the funds for the building may be given the Oklahoma chapters. When a chapter in one town that has only sixteen members, can raise $300; another, of twelve members, gives $200; others as much as $500 to $800, all secured in a year's time, and in woman's way – teas, socials, recitals, old fashioned southern dances – surely, the southern woman's energy matches that of their northern sisters.

By these means, the Oklahoma Confederate Veteran's Home will be built soon. The governor signed the maintenance bill on February 14th – and the pen with which he signed it is a precious possession of the Oklahoma Daughters. The contract for the building was let March 18th, and ground was broken on April 12 – just forty-nine years to the day since the Civil war was broken out! On June 24th – St. John's day – the corner stone will be laid, with appropriate ceremonies, under the auspices of the Masonic fraternity. The Home will be completed by October 15th, so that the veterans needing a home may have one before another winter. It is to be a home in the truest sense, where the old soldier may not even have to be separated from his faithful wife, if it be the two are cast upon the world, for it is a home for the wives and widows as well as for the veteran.

So much the Daughters of the Confederacy stand for that it would seem their work will never be ended. The Oklahoma Daughters feel that there is much educational work for them to do, and they expect to follow the precedent of other southern states and establish scholarships in the state schools. Pictures of southern heroes are being placed in all the schools of the state, to hang side by side with the great leaders of the northern army – as in the New York University one finds Robert E. Lee's name on a bronze tablet in the university's hall of fame, while beside it another tablet contains the name of his opponent, U. S. Grant. Southern soldiers' graves are being sought out and marked by the Daughters, and are strewn with flowers each Confederate decoration day, April 26.

At the meetings of the Daughters of the Confederacy there is no thought but for the betterment and uplifting of the South. True womanhood composes the organization, with hearts of love and courage. The stars and stripes are as dear to the southern woman as to any other citizen of the United States – united now in the truest sense – and that flag always waves side by side with the relic flag of the South, the beautiful stars and bars, at all national and state meetings. If anyone doubts the loyalty of southern mothers, let him count the southern sons who went unfalteringly to the front in the late war. But as long as southern women find work to do among their people they will stand banded together as United Daughters of the Confederacy, and will proudly trace their ancestry back to the veteran of the Confederate army.

The Oklahoma state officers of the Daughters of the Confederacy are: Mrs. W. T. Culbertson, Kiowa, president; Mrs. A. S. Riddle, Chickasha, first vice president; Mrs. W. O. Deason, Shawnee, second vice president; Mrs. W. A. Johnson, Wagoner, third vice president; Mrs. Lewis Paulin, Durant, fourth vice president; Mrs. W. R. Clement, Oklahoma City, recording secretary; Mrs. Zol. J. Woods, Purcell, treasurer; Mrs. T. D. Davis, McAlester, corresponding secretary; Mrs. Fanny Catlett, Pawnee, registrar; Mrs. K. J. Bass, Lawton, historian; Mrs. Charles Reed, Muskogee, recorder of the cross of honor; Mrs. M. Moore, Tulsa, Custodian of flags; Mrs. T. C. Harrill, Wagoner, children's auxiliary director.

# Various Authors

*In the time period encompassed by this anthology, Native Americans published, edited, and wrote for numerous periodicals, as the previous selections by individual authors indicate. We can locate the beginning of the Native press either with the publication of the* Cherokee Phoenix, *begun in 1828 by Elias Boudinot, or* The Literary Voyager or Muzzeniegun, *initiated in 1826 by ethnologist Henry Rowe Schoolcraft. Periodicals edited or published by Indians ranged from tribal newspapers such as the* Phoenix *and the* Cherokee Advocate *to literary journals like* A Wreath of Cherokee Rose Buds. *During this period, many other publications not edited or published by Native Americans emerged that were devoted to Indians and Indian culture, such as Schoolcraft's weekly; reform periodicals such as* The Indian's Friend, *published by the National Indian Association; government-supported newspapers, such as* The Carlisle Arrow *and* Red Man; *and independent newspapers, often from the western part of the United States. Including such publications as the* American Indian Magazine *(the journal of the Society of American Indians which Zitkala-Ša edited and in which she published much of her reform writing) some of the Indian or Indian-related periodicals were quite influential – whether for good or for bad – in national Indian affairs, supporting such causes as education, allotment, and citizenship.*

*Along with* Twin Territories, *edited and published by Ora Eddleman Reed, and* Sturm's, *the monthly to which Reed contributed regularly, the major periodicals represented here include the literary papers of the Cherokee Female Seminary; the weekly paper of the US Indian Industrial School at Carlisle, Pennsylvania; and the periodical of the Haskell Institute in Lawrence, Kansas. The first of these,* Cherokee Rose Buds, *emerged during the 1853–4 school year, being advertised as an annual by 1855, when it became* A Wreath of Cherokee Rose Buds. *Edited and written by the students of the Seminary, it included poems, essays, and stories on a wide range of subjects, from intemperance to nature. The Seminary closed at the end of the 1856–7 school year and did not reopen until after the Civil War. In spite of the protest offered by Na-Li in "An Address to the Females of the Cherokee Nation," the students often belonged to the families of the Cherokee elite, who were progressive in outlook; their contributions to the paper reflect this relatively privileged status. Their writing includes the deliciously ironic essay "The Gardening Season – A Great Time Among All Matrons" and the intriguing poem, "Literary Day Among the Birds."*

*The Haskell Institute, begun in 1884 as the vocationally oriented Indian Training School, sponsored* The Indian Leader, *a publication that emerged in 1897 with many of the same goals as today's college alumni magazines: to keep in touch with graduates, to highlight the achievements of students and graduates, and to promote the institution to those on the outside by demonstrating the progressive nature of Haskell and its alumni. While many numbers of the* Leader *contained such everyday materials as notes on campus activities and descriptions of sports events, others included more literary selections. The editors during the time-span encompassed here were white school officials, and the degree of control that contributors had in determining the substance or tone of their work is unclear; narratives such as "An Indian Girl's History, Written by Herself," with its odd third-person perspective, suggest a high degree of teacher intervention, while others, such as "Left Overs From Good English Week," underscore the periodical's (and the school's) interest in Indian acculturation. "A Fish Story," on the other hand, intimates a critical perspective on norms of white middle-class femininity.*

*Publications of the Carlisle Indian Industrial school, which in various incarnations included the* Carlisle Arrow *(known first as* The Arrow*), the* Red Man, *the* Red Man and Helper, *and* The Carlisle Arrow and Red Man, *had a range of goals, including that of showcasing the positive results of US Indian education policy and underscoring the achievements of the "progressive" Indian. Some of the journals contained campus information such as class and sports listings, school calendars, and descriptions of school celebrations. Including versions of traditional tales, they also promoted Indian education, urged Indian self-help and good moral deportment, described various Indian activities outside of the institution, and published traditional stories by students. The Carlisle journals received broad public attention, with many Eastern newspapers reprinting selections similar to "The Story of the Deerskin" and "A Seneca Tradition." Overall, the diverse selections from these periodicals, ranging from autobiography to advice writing, utopia, and traditional narratives, and including texts by child as well as adult authors, enrich our understanding of the larger tradition of Native American women's writing.*

## BIBLIOGRAPHY

### Primary

*The Arrow* (Carlisle, PA, 1904–8).
*The Carlisle Arrow* (Carlisle, PA, 1908–17).
*The Carlisle Arrow and Red Man* (Carlisle, PA, 1917–18).
*Cherokee Rose Buds* (Park Hill, OK, 1848–54).
*The Indian Helper* (Carlisle, PA, 1885–1900).
*The Indian Leader* (Lawrence, KS, 1897–1982).
*Red Man* (Carlisle, PA, 1910–17).
*The Red Man and Helper* (Carlisle, PA, 1900–4).
*Twin Territories* (Muskogee, IT [Indian Territory], 1899–1904).
*A Wreath of Cherokee Rose Buds* (Park Hill, OK, 1855–7).

### Secondary

*Carlisle Indian Industrial School Periodicals and Publications*. R. Christopher Goodwin, 1998.
Foreman, Carolyn Thomas. *Oklahoma Imprints, 1835–1907*. Oklahoma, 1936.
Littlefield, Daniel F., Jr., and James W. Parins. *American Indian and Alaska Native Newspapers and Periodicals, 1826–1924*. Greenwood, 1984–6.
Mihesuah, Devon A. *Cultivating the Rosebuds: The Education of Women at the Cherokee Female Seminary, 1851–1909*. Illinois, 1993.
Murphy, James E. and Sharon M. Murphy. *Let My People Know: American Indian Journalism, 1828–1978*. Oklahoma, 1981.
Ray, Grace Ernestine. *Early Oklahoma Newspapers*. Oklahoma, 1928.

## From *Cherokee Rose Buds* (1854)

### Our Wreath of Rose Buds

Corinne

I

We offer you a wreath of flowers
Culled in recreation hours,
Which will not wither, droop, or die,
Even when days and months pass by.

II

Ask you where these flowers are found?
Not on sunny slope, or mound;
Not on prairies bright and fair
Growing without thought or care.

III

No, our simple wreath is twined
From the garden of the mind;
Where bright thoughts like rivers flow
And ideas like roses grow.

IV

The tiny buds which here you see
Ask your kindly empathy;
View them with a lenient eye,
Pass each fault, each blemish by.

V

Warmed by the sunshine of your eyes,
Perhaps you'll find to your surprise,
Their petals fair will soon unclose,
And every bud become – a Rose.

VI

Then take our wreath, and let it stand
An emblem of our happy band;
The *Seminary*, our *garden* fair,
And *we*, the *flowers* planted there.

VII

Like roses bright we hope to grow,
And o'er our home such beauty throw
In future years – that all may see
Loveliest of lands, – the Cherokee.

## [Editorial]

We hope we shall not be thought presumptuous in having our Paper printed, as it is not because we consider it so valuable, but as an incentive to our own exertions and for the pleasure we might hereafter derive from comparing the past with the present; the improvement of those who shall take our places with our first attempts and to recall pleasant associations which may be connected with it. Yet we shall be much gratified with the patronage of all those friends who feel willing to encourage our laudable efforts: The more so as we wish to add our . . . few drops in the great stream which is going abroad to make the desert places of other lands bud and blossom as the Rose.

## An Osage Wedding

Ka-Ya-Kun-Stah

Every nation and race of the world has its peculiar customs, and none are more striking than some of the marriage ceremonies of the red race. Take for instance, an Osage wedding. The brave who has won the young squaw's heart calls at her mother's lodge and throws from his back a freshly killed deer, the fruits of his morning hunt. The mother at once believes him to be a great man. The daughter timidly glances a welcome and a smile. How pleased seems the mother as she is consenting to give up her child for the price of ten mules.

He rises, takes a hasty leave, but in a short time is seen returning, mounted on his war horse and driving before him the prize which is to gain for him his heart's Hope. As he arrives, the mother receives and examines her gain. The father stands silently looking on, yielding in all his wife consents to do. The next day the marriage must come off and she must before that time erect a new lodge in which to receive the bridal couple. Early the next morning the people of the town are up and in motion. After uttering their devotions to the Great Spirit, they begin preparing a feast, for all are invited. A wild and unbridled horse is led out and the bride comes forth to mount him; she is dressed in scarlet cloth; her skirt short and her pantalets of the same; her foot displays an ornamental moccasin, while her wrist and fingers are decked with jewels and her neck with wampum. All are collected to witness the scene. The horse, with a halter around his nose is held for her while she mounts him. Four bridesmaids stand near the horse holding the four corners of a scarlet blanket. Nearby stand the groomsmen. At a given signal four guns are fired by the groomsmen; the horse, being frightened, starts off; the bride if not inclined to show her expert riding throws herself into the blanket and is borne by the bridesmaids to the lodge which is her new home, the spectators following. The Brave, enters first, and then other near friends, showing their great joy. The nuptials are over; songs and feasting commence. Every variety of wild game is procured; all partake freely without ceremony to the satisfaction of their appetites. The happy couple are now ready to enter upon the various duties of their wild life.

## An Address to the Females of the Cherokee Nation

### Na-Li

It is sometimes said that our Seminaries were made only for the rich and those who were not full Cherokees, but it is a mistake. I thought I would address a few lines to the other class in the Nation. My beloved parents were full Cherokees. They belonged to the common class: and, yet, they loved their children as well [as] the rich; but they had never attended school, and therefore did not know the value of learning; and probably would never have made provision for me to attend school. But these beloved parents have been called from this world and left me a lonely orphan. I was very young and have but a faint remembrance of my mother's long and wearisome sickness of the consumption. At the time of my mother's death, a kindly missionary teacher came and took me under her care. Under the influence and teaching of the missionaries, I was prepared to enter this institution.

I should not have said so much about myself; but I feel a great many of the full Cherokees can have the benefit of the Seminary as well as I. Our Chief and directors would like very much that they should come and enjoy the same privileges as those that are here present, and the teachers would take as much pains in instructing you. I feel it is no disgrace to be a full Cherokee. My dark complexion does not prevent me from acquiring knowledge and of being useful hereafter.

I write this, hoping that it will persuade you to attend school and thus prepare to enter this Institution. We can give you a hearty welcome. You can be instructed in Mathematics, History and studies of various characters for the improvement of our minds; and though we may not see their use for the present, we will in years to come. I am much interested in the studies thus set before me. But a year and a half will soon pass away and then I am to go out into the Nation and endeavor to be useful; and, although I sometimes think I cannot be; yet I am required to try.

Once more I urge you to attend some *Public School*; be studious and persevering, and then after awhile you will probably be well prepared to enter our Institution. If you should not succeed the first time, "try; try again."

## View from our Seminary

### Edith

Our Seminary commands a most delightful and varied prospect of the surrounding country. On the north, stretching away as far as the eye can reach is a wood; and though within the few years past many demands have been made upon its wealth of noble trees, yet for years to come will an inexhaustible number continue to lift their lofty tops proudly to the blue sky in defiance of the devastating stroke of the woodman's axe.

This wood is one of our favorite resorts in the Spring and Summer days, where, when school duties are finished, we often wander, a merry troop, over hill and dale in search of the woodland flowers and delicious berries. Then, laden with our treasures we set out homeward as the loud tones of the Seminary bell warn us to hasten on that we may be in time for *Supper*, which is relished with a much keener appetite after the exercise in the fresh open air.

But the most picturesque part of the scenery is the *prairie* encompassed on the south by a range of green hills rising one above another, the most noted of which is Park Hill, elevated into a peak several hundred feet above the level of the ground. From its summit a much wider view is presented: the prairie extends in front and on either side; its surface by gently rising hills and sloping valleys and covered over with flowers of every hue. Scattered in all directions are green fields, meadows and groves; and peeping from among the trees of the latter, instead of the rudely constructed *wigwams* of our forefathers which stood there not more than half a century ago, elegant white dwellings are seen. Every thing around denotes taste, refinement and the progress of civilization among our people: well may they vie with the long enlightened inhabitants of the *east*.

One of the most handsome and beautiful situated of these dwellings is the residence of our Chief and his white bride, who left her native land and friends a few years since to come and dwell with him in his wild prairie home among his own tribe, the Cherokees.

## Childhood

### Wah-Lie

Nothing is more delightful to think about than the joyous hours of childhood, when nought prevailed within our little bosoms save pleasant thoughts of sport and play. Fond memory brings to mind the many, many pleasant hours that I have spent together with my little brothers (for I have no sisters,) the many times that we have played beneath some large oaks, just at the end of a broad lane, upon the green grass, beside a large spring of clear cool water. I remember how much pleasure it gave me to take a walk, or a ride, with my parents or brothers, to a majestic river about a half a mile from the house, and see *boats* passing, and at other times men fishing along the bank. It also filled our hearts with glee to hear them planning a walk in search of flowers, berries &c, in the *prairie*, or upon a beautiful hill just in front of the house from which you could see several houses and the Grand Prairie. How often one longs to be a child again, and it is not strange when all those dear scenes are brought to mind. When childhood's years are past, many are the trials and troubles of this life, and, perhaps of the next. When I see little children running and skipping about so full of life and joy, the scenes of my own childhood years come before me, and I cannot help saying with others, "Oh! would I were a child again."

## The Gardening Season – A Great Time Among All Matrons

### Letilla

Dear me, what busy airs and looks they do carry about them. Early betimes they are out in their gardens if it is only to see what must be accomplished during the coming day. After the beds are made and walks levelled, the seed box that was so carefully stored away is again brought forth to light. Every little bag and paper is opened to see what this and that is. Although they prize their seeds so much, they are very liberal to their neighbors, and like to see *them* have an abundance also. If some less fortunate dame steps in to *beg* a little *bean* or *pea* seed, as she terms it, the bean basket is set forth for her use at pleasure. "Now," says the owner of the basket, "I'm going to give you some of my *choice* kinds, for I am certain that you will like them, and agree with me that they are a great bean." "This is" holding forth one in two fingers, "this is my favorite slick bean, they do make the best snaps, and stay tender longer than any other kind I know, and do not get stringy till they are most ripe." (Wonderful bean!) "This," holding another forth, "is the best bean ever was; do take some and try them. Miss — got the seed from Mrs. Somebody, and she gave me just a *few* last year; now I have an abundance – they bear so well." "I *must* have some certain," says the neighbor. After they have talked over the basket for half an hour or longer, about what time of the moon is best for planting, and praised so many kinds of beans, that one would think *all* beans were the best *ever was*, and Mrs. — has got all she wants, she takes her leave looking as if she had been very fortunate *that* day *indeed*.

## A Dialogue Between Susan and Ellen

(Susan.) Good morning, cousin E. Do you intend going to the Seminary to improve your mind and prepare for usefulness?

(Ellen.) I don't know about all that. I intend going, but I shall want to engage in the fun I understand they have there sometimes; for I like to pass much of my time away in high glee, and not be poring over these "old books" all the time.

(Susan.) But, Ellen, I understand the great object of the School funds and those who manage it is to improve the mind, manners and morals, and not to instruct at a great expense for funny purposes and the mere gratification of youthful feelings, yet you will have plenty of innocent amusements and exercises to break the monotony of study.

(Ellen.) But I expect to do things sometimes to my own notions, without having the eyes or ears of the teachers know them all. I cannot confine myself to many rules or too much restraint.

(Susan.) Now let me tell you dear, cousin, these teachers sometimes "mark a scholar all up" who does not like "rules and restraints," and is sly and artful in going beyond them. And then your case might be brought up before the directors and you be disgraced by [being] expelled from the Seminary. Then, oh! how badly you and your friends would feel.

I have been here some time, and I think I know what is about the truth, that the directors would have you do nothing but for your own good; and what you do not wholly approve now, you will a few years hence. Come to the Seminary, then, and be faithful in your studies, upright in your deportment, obedient to rule, and you will find no difficulty. And at the close of the four years, you will leave with honors to yourself and friends, prepared to exert a good influence, and to be useful to those around you.

## Dissipation

### Cherokee

It is something very common to see dissipated persons in our little villages by half dozens or more every week, especially on the Sabbath, that day appointed for sacred rest. Dissipation or intemperance is one of the greatest evils in our Nation. Just look around and see how many families have been deprived of their happiness and peace by this one habit. Ought we not all try to lend our aid in putting down this great evil? If we are young, we have an influence (our teachers say,) so let us one and all give our utmost influence for this noble cause. How I love the very word "Temperance." How often it restores comfort to our nearly ruined families. How many hearts would beat with pleasure to hear of our little Nation becoming one in heart and hand in the cause of Temperance. If those dissipated persons only knew of one half the pleasure it would give to their parents and sisters, they would shrink from the deadly poison and become a true hearted people in this noble cause. Just look at a regular rum drinker. His step is feeble and unsteady, his eyes swollen, his face red, and, perhaps, bruised from some recent fight, and his whole frame tells that rum has done its work and he, a ruined man. Who of you would look thus? Will you not then all sign the Temperance Pledge or join the Sons of Temperance, leave off intoxicating drinks and let it be told abroad that this Nation for one is a Temperance one; that there is not one within its bounds who *condescends* to dissipation.

## Kate M—'s Composition

### Lusette

A bright, laughter loving body was Kate M—. You could see fun in abundance peeping from her blue eye and playing around her mouth. But Kate did not love study, and composition day was almost a terror. A strange thing was it if she was not delinquent.

Tired of constant reproof, one day the bright idea, (for so she thought it at the time) came into her mind, that it would be very nice to copy a real good composition from several different books. It was soon finished and taken to her teacher who was surprised to see Kate so punctual. But after reading it over she was much disappointed. Here, she found a quotation from "Fanny Fern," and there, another from Grace Greenwood,[1] and a host of others scattered all along. When Kate was sent for, she came with the expectation of being greeted with something like this:–

---

1 Fanny Fern (Sara Payson Willis Parton, 1811–72) and Grace Greenwood (Sara Jane Clarke Lippincott, 1823–1904), were popular Eastern white writers; the author indicates here her familiarity with current literary trends.

"I am very glad you are so punctual." Or "I have had to make so few corrections." But she found her teacher looking very grave indeed. How quickly those fringed lids dropped over the laughing eyes; and the crimson blush stole upon the cheeks when she saw she had been detected. As a punishment the teacher required her to bring the several books from which she had copied and read each piece separately after she herself read from the composition. But poor Kate had not gone too far before the hot tears began to roll down her cheeks, her voice was choked with sobs and she entreated her teacher to forgive her this time and it should be the last attempt at deception. Her teacher felt that she was in earnest and with a few kind words of caution dismissed her to her room.

## A Peep into the Future

### Inez

Here are gathered together, a happy youthful group. Sorrow has scarcely touched us: hope, bright sunny hope shines along our path and casts its rays far into the future. But let us pass from 1854 to '58 and see what change the Wizard Time has wrought in these *four* short years. Our happy Section has been disbanded and we are widely scattered. Stop for a moment, and hear a little of our altered situations.

The first, — a fair, gay blue eyed girl is to be the bride of him who was once the school teacher at Our —.

Black eyed "Dora" and her school companion took such a fancy to see the "golden caves and diamond cells [?]" of California that they could not be satisfied till they had taken a peep into them.

The regular thoughtful Louisa is teaching a public school.

I have just heard from "rosy cheeked Lide," she is soon to be a bride and that *neat lady* that lived on the hill has already taken upon herself the responsibilities of a married life.

"Alina" is teaching school successfully somewhere in the Nation.

The witty "Nan" is also engaged in the same occupation, but expects to return home shortly, to be bridesmaid for her sister.

The destiny of one, fairy like creature with auburn hair, is hard to tell, I heard it reported that she was traveling in "Sunny Italy."

I had long ago given up all hopes of hearing from the little, smiling "Grace" when I was pleasantly surprised by a letter from her. It was frequently spoken of that she had a correspondent *somewhere* in the neighborhood, and I think it must have been true, for she tells me that they are living very happily together.

"Liddy," "the very picture of our ancestors," lives in a beautiful cottage at the foot of a hill where she enjoys the sweet songs of the birds and other pleasant companions.

"Maggie" is at home teaching her little brothers and sisters.

As for *me*, my dear companions, I had always taken great delight in reading and thinking of the beautiful land of Mexico, and I resolved *one* day to go there. So I sit 'neath the delicious orange trees that blossom all the year round, thinking of you, and hoping that the coming years may bring changes as slightly tinged with sadness as those that are already here.

## A Dream

### Flora Green

The glorious sun had shed his last rays o'er our happy world. Birds had ceased to warble their notes of love. The summer breeze gently rocked the tall forest trees; "Sending forth a low sweet murmur like the soft breathings of a Seraph's harp." The moon had risen in the clear sky, shedding her silver beams on all below. After gazing on those myriads of bright stars and the beauties of surrounding nature, I was soon wrapped in a quiet slumber, and seemed transported by an unearthly being to a celestial region. It was not the *real heaven*, but a kind of fairy land. It had some resemblance to some scenes of earth, but was more bright, more beautiful, more fair. The grass was as the softest velvet; streams of pure water ran like threads of silver amidst its verdure, all proceeding from a clear spring that gushed from out of a mountainside. Its margin was crowned with fragrant flowers; soft sweet music was to be heard; nymphs of the wood and little merry fairies laughed and danced in the bright moonlight to the sound of the musical chimes. Suddenly a cloud passed over this beautiful dell and I was awaked from my slumbers, to find the sunbeams stealing gently into my pleasant room. Songs of birds were heard among the leafy bowers; and as I looked out upon this beautiful world in her earthly summer robe, I could scarcely tell which was the brightest, the *real* world or the Fairy land of my dreams.

### QUEER MATTY

Dora

Matty was queer; and the many funny things she did and said were enough to bring a smile to the demure face of Miss Puss, had she possessed a wee bit more of intelligence, even though she, herself was often the subject of Matty's cunning pranks.

One day, her mother going out for a few moments, left her alone with Grandma who was quietly dozing in her arm chair, and Puss who was also indulging in a nap upon the rug. Matty sat for a while as if thinking of something.

Then, suddenly starting up she went on tiptoe behind Grandma and with a roguish smile slipped her spectacles off her nose and her knitting from her lap; then going to Puss, she gave her a rap with her dimpled hand. Puss rose looking very much bewildered at being so unceremoniously roused; but Matty told her to come and play "Grandma." Puss was then placed in a chair, the spectacles on her nose, and the knitting between her paws. Puss did not like her predicament and struggled with all her might to free herself but in vain; her paws were all tangled in the yarn and she could not get them high enough to pull her spectacles off.

And there stood Matty, clapping her hands and sending out peal after peal of merry laughter, so that spectacles and knitting had well nigh perished had not Matty's Mother stepped in at that moment. Grandma, whose cozy nap had of course been disturbed, looked very grave when she saw the mischief and heard Matty reproved by her mother for being so naughty. Matty said she would never do so again and she kept her word about an hour.

On going out into the yard she came across a hen with a fine brood of little chicks and, seeing no one looking on, she seized a pretty little one and running off to a basin of water plunges it in. When she took it out and found its bright feathers all dripping and lying close together, she thought it did not look half so *pretty* as before and she began to pick them off. Poor little chick was almost bare when her father came along and seeing Matty exclaimed, "Why, Matty, what *are* you doing?" "Oh! nothing," she says, "only I have given chick a washing but its feathers looked so ugly that I's picking them off so that *pretty* ones may come." Oh, little Matty was so queer, always doing something which she promised never to do again and then going away and forgetting it. But Matty had a good loving little heart after all if she was mischievous.

## From *A Wreath of Cherokee Rose Buds* (August, 1855)

### [EDITORIAL]

Another Spring term has drawn to a close, and we present you again with a collection of Rose Buds, gathered from our Seminary Garden. If on examining them, you chance to find a withered or dwarfish bud, please pass it by; attributing the deficiency to the *drought* which prevailed in the early part of the Spring.

We hope our friends out of the Nation will bear in mind how few have been the literary advantages we possessed, until lately. Only four or five years ago, some of our number knew very little of the

English language, and although they have now obtained a good idea of it, and are making progress in some branches of English literature, yet we hope for lenient judgment, when our efforts are compared with those of our white sisters.

## Two Scenes in Cherokee Land

### Scene I. by Na-Li

On a hill-side, by a merry little brook, stood a rude hut, inhabited by a Cherokee family. There was no fencing to be seen about it; no neat grass-plot bordered with flowers; no shrubbery or rose-bushes to add the beauty of cultivation to the wild scenery of nature. No vine had been taught to twine its delicate tendrils over the doorway. A few large trees were standing about. Here might be seen a broken mortar, and there a pestle, while the ground was strewn with rocks, skins, rags, and a few spears of yellow-looking grass, struggling for life. Every thing about the habitation made it look more wild and desolate.

Now, if you have no objection, we will take a peep within. In rudeness and uncivilization, we find the inmates bearing a striking resemblance to their little hut. In one corner is a roll of buffalo skins, which doubtless serve for beds. The floor is the earth upon which the hut stands.

A woman is seated by the fire-side, smoking a pipe. Stretching along over her head, are a few strings of dried venison, and on the sides of the hut are fastened some beads, feathers, &c. No little stand of books, no vase of flowers, filling the room with fragrance, no neat papers are to be seen; nothing but the mere necessities of life.

Several large, swarthy-looking boys in one corner, are repairing their bows and arrows for a hunt. In another corner stand two girls with mortar and pestle, preparing to beat "*Conihany*." They are dressed in calico skirts with red jackets fastened with silver brooches, their feet are covered with *moccasins*. Their hair is plaited and hanging down their backs.

A whoop starts the boys. They gather up their bows and arrows, get some dried venison, and parched cornmeal, and other necessary articles, and go out where a large company of hunters are waiting for them. Soon the woods seem to be alive with their whoops, yells, and the barking of dogs.

In the mean time the girls have finished beating the Conihany. A large kettle, filled with the Conihany, is placed on the fire; the little ones of the family sit watching it with great eagerness. When it is done it is taken up in a large earthen bowl of home manufacture. Each member of the family then partakes of it with a wooden spoon until their hunger is satisfied.

After two or three weeks of absence, the company of hunters return loaded with the game of the forest, which they throw down for the females to cut up and dry for food.

Thus pass the days of their wild life, without any intellectual pleasure or enjoyments, only varied from the same, monotonous round by some great gathering or public festival. The most noted of these were the "*green corn dances*," as they were called. They were a kind of religious festival, held at the time when the corn began to "silk." At them were gathered young and old, male and female. After making merry several days, they returned to the same passive, un-interesting life.

### Scene II. by Fanny

The birds are singing merrily as they hop from tree to tree in the green woods. The wide prairies are robed in their Spring dress, gemmed with flowers. By the fenced fields of wheat and corn, we see that civilization and nature are here united in our Cherokee land. White cottages peep forth from the same spot, perhaps, where some warrior's rude wigwam once stood. What a contrast to the scenes of olden times! The Missionaries came and brought with them the Bible. They taught our ancestors the precepts of religion and the arts of civilization; to cultivate farms and to erect neat little cottages. They taught them also the knowledge of books, and the value of education. Thus, under the influence of the religion of the Missionaries, the wild Indian was changed and became a new man.

Let us enter one of these white cottages. As you approach it, look around you and take a survey of the yard, enclosed with neat white palings. Here is found, bordering the smooth walks, flowering shrubbery of various kinds, sending forth spicy odors upon the air. Before you is the cottage, with a portico in front. The windows are shaded by vines twining themselves here and there, wherever their tendrils can find a place to cling to.

It is Spring. The tall, noble oaks have clothed their skeleton forms in robes of beautiful green; the claws of Bears and Panthers no more leave their prints upon the bark; the Buffalo and the Deer repose no longer beneath their shade.

Within the cottage we find ourselves in a room most tastefully arranged. Books are here for leisure hours; while flowers from Nature's own garden, the prairie, as well as those most rare, and a musical instrument are their companions. What other evidences of civilization and refinement are needed? Books, flowers, music, and what is far better, the *Holy Word* of God is here to study, showing that religion has shed its pure light over all.

But where are the occupants of the dwelling? Have they gone to celebrate the festival of some *Unknown Power*? Have they gone to a *ball-play*, or to have a gossip at a *green-corn-dance*, as in days gone by? No; for the general observance of these customs has ceased. Other festivals or "gatherings," have taken their places, where the *mind* is exercised instead of the *body*. The Indian lad, in place of his bow and arrow, is now taught to use the pen and wield the powers of eloquence. The girl, instead of engaging in the dance, keeping time with the rattling noise of the *terrapin-shells*, bound to her ancles, keeps time with the *chalk*, as her fingers fly nimbly over the *black-board*, solving some problem in Algebra or Geometry. It is at such a gathering that you will find those for whom we inquire. It is *Examination Day* at the Female Seminary, and here are assembled, father, mother, brother, and friends, listening to the prompt recitations of a daughter and sister. The next day another examination is to be held at a similar institution, where many of the Cherokee youths are now pursuing a course of studies that they may be useful to their nation. And who does not remember another merry gathering in the grove on the *Seventh of May*, to celebrate the Fourth Anniversary of the opening of our Seminaries. The bright, happy faces that were witnessed on that day cannot be very soon forgotten. Other evidences of civilization may be seen among us, and although there are seen dark clouds, I hope we may advance, never faltering, until all the clouds of ignorance and superstition and wickedness flee from before the rays of the Suns of *Knowledge* and *Righteousness*.

## Beauty

### Alice

In creating the world, God made every thing that could contribute to the happiness of his creatures. Over all he threw the mantle of beauty to please the eye.

On every side, are lofty hills and mountains; fertile valleys and spreading prairies covered with their thousand flowers. Here and there, thick forests meet the gaze; the little rippling brooks go singing by, and noble rivers roll on to the mighty ocean. These are *beauties of nature*.

But man, himself, in physical beauty, excels in the works of God. What more admirable than the noble form, "erect in God-like majesty," or the more perfect gracefulness of woman? The blushing smiles that play upon the rosy cheek, the silken hair falling luxuriantly over the shoulders, the sparkling eye; – these are all lovely and call forth many a word of praise.

But there is a beauty which exists within, worth more than all these outward ornaments, and it often appears where they are waiting. It is the *beauty of the intellect*; the reflection of a mind which has gathered knowledge by its piercing glance from all the glorious creations that surround us. It has soared to the shining worlds which fill the universe and brought down wisdom; it has communed with the great intellects of the earth until all that is lovely in mind and matter is stamped upon it.

But there is a *higher* beauty still, – before which physical, and even intellectual beauty grows dim. It is found where right feelings and principles are cherished in the heart. Like flowers, the more they are cultivated the more beautiful they become, and if watered by dews from the *Fountain of Life*, they will spread the radiance of *Moral Beauty* over the soul. Physical beauty may pass away, and intellectual beauty decay; but *moral* beauty will never fade; it will only appear brighter when transplanted from Earth to the gardens of Heaven.

## A Walk

Kate

It was a beautiful evening in April, when one of my school-mates and I concluded to take a walk. As soon as supper was over off we started, determined to have a longer walk than the evening before. In a few minutes we were some distance from the Seminary, out on the prairie, gathering flowers. But we thought that was not far enough. So we walked on. Turning our course into the woods, and following a little path, not knowing where it led to, we soon found ourselves a long way from the Seminary. We thought it best to return; for if we did not we surely would be tardy. But we saw a large tree before us, and wanted to go to it very much; so we made ourselves believe we were very tired and would not be tardy if we should go and rest a while. We went on until we came to the tree. It was a noble looking tree, and its green robe, the soft velvet carpet which was spread underneath it, and the birds singing so sweetly, made it a pleasant resting-place.

We sat down, and were soon so absorbed in the arrangement of our flowers, that when we looked for "old Sol," nothing was to be seen of him except his last rays, which soon disappeared. We quickly set out to return; and as it took us some time to find the place where we turned out into the woods, it was quite dark when we reached the gate. We stopped a few minutes to gather breath enough to speak. The rooms were lighted up, and "study-hour" was over. We knew the first question that would be asked us after entering our rooms. Oh! how we dreaded to go in; but in we *must* go, and so in we went. The "retiring bell" rang just as we reached our rooms. I was glad of that, for I was very tired; but it was some hours before I fell asleep. My room-mates looked pleasant and spoke kindly to me. I did not feel much like talking, but I managed to answer their questions until they told me that my teacher had been inquiring for me, and was very anxious about me; then I could say no more, but I could not keep from *thinking*. My room-mates continued to talk; they did not know how bad I felt. Now and then I could hear a little laugh from the other rooms, but suddenly the "last-bell" struck and every thing was still, nothing was heard but the chirping of the crickets. I was haunted by the thought of what my teacher would say to me next morning, when I went to my classes to recite, and knew nothing about my Geometry lesson; and what little J—'s teacher would say to her, when she went to her Algebra class. The morning came. I went to my class; – my teacher looked at me but said nothing. She did not send me to the "board" first; – there were several girls who went up and "demonstrated" their Propositions. I listened to them very attentively, and tried to remember as much as I could. As last I was called upon to "demonstrate." I knew how to draw the "figure" from having seen it drawn by another, but could remember nothing but, "Let A, B, C, and E, D, F, be two triangles, and the angle A=B – " then I stopped in confusion, and could proceed no farther. My teacher excused me, but said I must remain after the class was dismissed. She asked me where I was at "study-hour." I told her, but could make no excuse, for we had been told not to walk out far after supper, as that was a time for study. She reproved me kindly and dismissed me. I found that little J. knew no more about her lesson than myself. It was the last time we took a walk at a forbidden hour, for we decided that the pleasure was not equal to the pain.

## Female Influence

Qua-Tsy

How often have we heard it reiterated that the destiny of the world depends on woman – that woman is the appointed agent of morality – the inspirer of those feelings and dispositions which form the moral nature of man. These remarks, although so common, are none the less true. The elevation of our race does depend upon the manner in which woman executes this commission. Nor does the destiny of man as an individual, alone depend on *female influence*, but that of nations, kingdoms, and empires.

Many are the instances recorded in history, which may be mentioned in proof of this. I will speak of some of the most notable ones. First, of Aspasia of Athens.[2] Nothing is said of her personal beauty; but in eloquence she far surpassed all her contemporaries. She was an instructress of the philosopher, Socrates. She also assisted Pericles, one eminent among the Greeks, so much, that he could not but acknowledge his indebtedness to her for his mental improvement. Who does not remember the world-renowned Helen, the cause of the long and disastrous Trojan war. In Roman history too, woman often bears a conspicuous part, both for good and evil. It was a notable Roman matron who once saved Rome. Coriolanus having been banished, was on his return to Rome, fully resolved to demolish the city, in spite of entreaties to spare it; for, beside his feeling of revenge, he knew that if he yielded the penalty was death. But when Veturia, his mother, came and fell down before him, and begged him to desist, her pleadings prevailed. He exclaimed, "Oh! my mother! thou hast saved Rome, but lost thy son." Cleopatra was another eminent character. She was very fascinating; perhaps more so than any of her sex. Her influence over some of the leading men of Rome was almost boundless. But did this influence tend to elevate the nation? No, it was such that it brought only remorse and sorrow, especially to Mark Antony, who, in consequence of her influence, became totally dead to honor and morality.

Even in later periods, the effects of female influence may be seen. The proudest monarch of France would tremble before a single female sooner than he would at the approach of armed foes. That female was Madam de Stael. This same monarch when asked, what he thought ought to be done to elevate their country, replied, "Elevate the mothers." And indeed it is the mothers who influence and elevate their children. Who does not admire the character of George Washington's mother, to whom he is not a little indebted for the praise and honor ascribed to his name. This instance might be added to instance almost without number, but let these suffice.

If this influence has been so universal in past ages, is it not equally powerful in our day. If so, how careful should the females of our little nation be in regard to the manner in which each one exerts her influence. The elevation of the Cherokee people also depends upon the females; and, perhaps, particularly upon those who are just springing into active life, and who enjoy the privileges of this Institution. How necessary is it that each one of us should strive to rightly improve and discipline our minds while at school, and to be governed by principle and not by impulse, so that when we are called to other stations and our field of efforts widens, *our influence* may have an elevating and ennobling effect upon all with whom we come into contact.

## Critics and Criticism

### Lelia

How many things there are in the world to find fault with. According to some people, every thing is wrong. But nothing is more vexatious than *criticism*. In the literary world, no writer can put his thoughts before the public, but what his work is pounced upon by some merciless *critic*, who takes delight in bringing out, not the beauties of a piece, but its defects. The best of poets and writers have had their feelings lacerated by these severe attacks; and it has even caused the death of some. It is doubtful if the critics possess half the genius of those whose literary efforts they attack.

Even our poor little *Rose Bud* cannot escape, but has to receive its full share of criticism. "Well, that's copied, I know," when they don't know any thing about it; or, "She must have been to the upper regions;" or, "She has tried very hard to have a little touch of sublimity," Or, perhaps they please themselves with some slight grammatical blunder.

2 Born sometime between 460 and 455 BC, Aspasia was the beloved mistress of Pericles, leader of Athens during the classical age. She was an educated woman who participated in public life. Coriolanus (fl. late fifth century BC) was a famous Roman military hero, while Madame de Stael (1766–1817) was an admired French writer.

We have faults, to be sure,
We very well know it;
  We don't expect to vie
With proser and poet.

[That *poetry* was not stolen from any one.] But if these terrible fault-finders could only be here on "composition" day, and note the deep lines of care on the countenances of those who are trying to grasp some thought, or the despairing looks of others as they find, after all their efforts, bright thoughts have taken to themselves wings, I think they would be more sparing of their cutting remarks, and inclined to speak a word of encouragement, instead of withering the Rose Bud with their icy breath.

## LITERARY DAY AMONG THE BIRDS

Lily Lee

Dark night at last had taken its flight,
Morn had come with her earliest light;
Her herald, gray dawn, had extinguished each star,
And gay banners in the east were waving afar.

That lovely goddess, Beautiful Spring,
Had fanned all the earth with her radiant wing;
"Had calmed the wild winds with fragrant breath,"
And gladden'd nature with an emerald wreath.

Within the precincts of the Bird Nation,
All was bustle and animation;
For that day was to witness a literary feast,
Where only Birds were invited guests.

The place of meeting was a leafy nook,
Close by the side of a sparkling brook.
Soon were assembled a merry band,
Birds from every tree in the land.

Mrs. DOVE came first, in soft colors drest;
Then Mr. CANARY, looking his best.
The family of MARTINS, dressed in brown,
And Mr. WOODPECKER, with his ruby crown.

The exercises opening with a scientific song,
By the united voices of the feathered throng.
Then was delivered a brilliant oration,
By 'Squire RAVEN, the wisest bird of the nation.
Master WHIP-POOR-WILL next mounted the stage,
Trying to look very much like a sage.

Eight pretty green PARROTS then spoke with art;
Though small, with credit they carried their part.
Again an oration by Mr. QUAIL,
Spoken as fast as the gallop of snail.
And lastly, Sir BLACKBIRD whistl'd off an address,
Of twenty odd minutes, more or less.

Then came the applause, so loud and long,
That the air echoed the joyous song.
But the sun was low, so soon they sped
To their quiet nests and their grassy beds;
And rocked by the breeze, they quietly slept,
Ere the firstling star in the blue sky crept.

## INTEMPERANCE

### Grace

In taking this subject I fear it may be remarked as it was of a temperance meeting, some weeks ago, "that it is old and worn out." But that is not so. The subject cannot be worn out so long as the material is furnished for it.

It is well known how ruinous Intemperance is, and that many feel its power.

What is a more distressing sight than that of an old man whose white locks indicate his near approach to eternity, tottering from one side of the road to the other, as he returns to the grog shop, his constant resort.

Go to his dwelling, and there you will see one half of the chimney lying on the ground, the chinking fallen from the cracks it was designed to stop, and the windows stuffed with rags.

Look at his field; a rail lying here, another there; and the weeds growing as rank as if they had been sown and cultivated instead of grain.

All this would not have been, if the little, smoky hut in some secret nook, had never been visited, or the private jug or bottle never kept.

This bent and feeble man was once as strong and happy as many of our friends and brothers now are; but he yielded, step by step, to the influence of Intemperance until he has become too weak to retrace his path or turn aside from his destroyer.

Not many months ago, on a cold night, the sleet falling thick and fast; a company of young men tried the experiment of yielding themselves to the influence of Intemperance, for the sake of the merry feeling it produces. In their wanderings they found themselves in a swamp. One of the party being weary from his efforts to extricate himself, decided to "make himself at home," and so dismounted and retired to a mud-hole. It would be well if the party would be satisfied with the experience of that night.

How many there are among us, of the young and intelligent, who thus degrade themselves, and cause pain and misery to others.

Think of the sighs and tears, the aching heart of a mother, or a sister, as they behold that father or brother, who ought to be their comfort and pride, reeling on the brink of a *Drunkard's Grave*.

## THE MOUSE'S WILL

### Leonora

In a dark corner of an old cellar, there lived the large family of Mrs. Mouse. Very cunning they were and worthy to possess such a title. But Miss Puss equalled them in this. She would sit dozing away, her eyes half shut, pretending that she did not see them peeping at her with their cunning little black eyes; but just as soon as one came near enough she would be sure to have it within her claws, growling away at a great rate, as she had her paw upon it. The old lady mouse from the experience of a long life, had grown quite too cunning for this great enemy of her race. Quite fortunate was she; but old age had shrunk up her frame, and the poor creature could scarcely move about.

One day, as usual, the family departed on a ransacking expedition. They were gone a long time, and when they returned they found their old mother dead. No tears streamed down their furry faces; but as soon as they saw she was gone the way of all mice, a squeaking conversation took place as to what was to be done with the property; for Madam Mouse was a great miser. Soon the consultation closed, and off they went into the old hiding-place; and there, among a lot of yellow looking documents, they found her *will*, written on a bit of parchment, which they remembered she purloined from a lawyer's office, making the instrument quite legal. A piece of old mouldy cheese, two inches long and about the same in thickness, she bequeathed to the eldest daughter. Next, came half a dozen sweet potatoes, carried off one night from a neighboring cellar, to another. A piece of pound-cake, from Miss Kate's wedding-supper, was the portion of another; then came corn by the bushel. O! what a thievish set they were. And, lastly, a long list of rare and curious things, gathered from various places, were to be divided among them as they wished.

When the reading of the will was finished, without waiting for further form or ceremony, they all scampered off in search of their share of this immense property. It was found, and, as is usually the case, it was soon scattered.

## From *The Indian Helper* (June 20, 1890)

### A TRIP TO THE MOON
### A COMPOSITION BY ONE OF OUR IMAGINATIVE SIOUX GIRLS

Nellie Robertson

Of the many strange lands and queer places I have visited in my life, the strangest and the one [in which] I have experienced [most] pleasure was my trip to the moon in 1900.

I got on board an air ship which was bound for the moon, one fine morning in June. Quite a number of people were starting for the same place.

For many days we sailed through the air. The scenery all the way was delightful both day and night, but the motion of the ship in air having the same effect as the motion of the ship on water, we did not enjoy the sights very much on the way.

After many days of travelling, we landed in a large city called Ujipa, which means in our language, Greentown.

The lunarians resemble the people of the earth in every way but the color of their eyes and hair. The color of their eyes is a bright green and their hair a very bright yellow.

Both men and women dress alike, in a loose gown, but you can distinguish them by their way of wearing their hair. The men have long hair and wear it in two or three plaits in the back. The women have short hair and wear little caps to match their eyes. They are a very kind and polite people.

Up in the moon they have no school-houses nor books of any kind from which to read or study. They are a blissful people. They know nothing outside of what is going on in their own world. Money is of no use to them there. Food of every kind grows all the year round.

A sort of fruit something like our cheese grows on trees very abundantly, and they call it bread. Corn, potatoes, cabbage and numerous vegetables grow wild. Water-melons, pumpkins and squashes grow on trees, apples, oranges, peaches and grapes may be found in abundance.

The people do not work very hard for their food.

Their clothes are made from the leaves of a very large plant. These leaves measure about 20 square feet. They make very strong and durable clothes.

The houses are built only of wood and beautiful. The people are ruled over by their king, Nonboose Kiang, which we know as "The Man in the Moon." He is a good, kind man and is liked by all his people.

The amusements and habits of the lunarians are very much like ours. They were so kind to us that when the time came for us to leave we were very sorry. I hope sometime in the future to take another trip and see more things of interest.

# From *The Indian Leader* (June, 1897)

## Autobiography of an Indian Girl

[Bright Eyes – such is the name which the author of this story gives to herself – is now about nineteen years old. She has been at Haskell Institute for about ten years; is now a member of the ninth grade, that is the highest degree of the grammar school, and will finish the course this summer. Having been asked to write an oration to be delivered before her fellow students in the assembly hall, she said she did not know what theme to write upon, unless it was her own life experience. The idea having been approved, she wrote the story which is here reproduced from her manuscript as she wrote it herself. The plain school-girl style in which it is written greatly enhances the interest awakened by the pleasing recital. The story is valuable as a proof taken from the actual life experience of a full-blood Indian, demonstrating the effective manner in which the rising generation of the American Indian can be, and actually is, being introduced into civilized life by the training they receive at the US government schools for Indians.]

In one of the tribes of Indians was a family who were not civilized, and you can imagine how they lived. Their home was a small tepee with no furniture to make it comfortable and with no bed to sleep on. In this family a little girl was born, whom the father and mother thought much of. They had other children, too, but this little baby girl was the pet of the father. As she grew older she was loved and petted more than ever. Her father used to get her everything she wanted and he tried to please her in every way he could. Oh, I must not forget to tell you her name Her father thought that "Bright-Eyes" was the best, so he gave her that name. Bright-Eyes has black hair and a dark complexion. When she was about six years old she was left motherless for her dear mother died. She then stayed at home with her father and the rest of the family.

About three years after the death of her mother her father thought it was best to send little Bright-Eyes to school. He had a very hard time to make her go. At first she would not go at all, but at last her father persuaded her and she went. When he took her to the train, she cried and was afraid of the engine, for she had never seen one before. They had a hard time getting her in the car. The next thing was that little Bright-Eyes could not speak a word of English for she had not been to school yet. She could only say a few words and the first English word she had learned was "pincushion."

After Bright-Eyes was in school awhile she became more used to it and learned to love her new home. The school was quite a large one and at first she felt lost to find herself among so many. She soon learned the English Language and began her school work of A, B, C. She would go to school all day long and sit and try to read her letters and to write her name. She grew and became more interested in her studies.

Bright-Eyes stayed in school about three years and at the end of that time she had grown to be quite a large girl and was given permission to go home. She was so glad when she was told that she could go home and see her parents. That night she could not sleep. Early next morning she was up and could hardly await the time for her to start. She started in the morning and on her way she was so lonesome that she wished she was back at her old school home. On the following day she arrived at the agency. Her parents were not there to meet her so she was taken to a school near by. About two days after, her parents knowing that she was there, came up to see her. Bright-Eyes was reading in the reception room when a big, stout, looking man with Indian clothes on and a woman looking just like the man came in at the door with a white woman. The white lady said: "Bright-Eyes, here are your father and mother."

Poor little Bright-Eyes' eyes at once filled with tears. She could not realize that this man was her father. She had not thought of seeing him in that condition. Slowly she arose from her seat and went and shook hands with the man, who sat near with big tears rolling down his face. It was such a pitiful sight. Bright-Eyes had forgotten her Indian language and she could not speak to them. Her father said something in Indian and pointed to his wife. Poor little Bright-Eyes could not understand but she supposed that he wanted her to shake hands with her and she shook her head "No," and sat there looking at the woman. A sad thought came to her. Could that be her mother? No, she could never call her mother; her own dear mother was dead and gone, and a woman looking like the one before her could not be her mother.

The father and mother of Bright Eyes went home. They wanted to take their daughter, but she could not go. After they went Bright-Eyes threw herself in the white lady's arms and burst out into a most pitiful cry and said: "Could that be my father, and has he married again? Could I stay here with them? I could not!" And she told the lady to send her back to her dear old school home, where she could be happy. The lady talked to her and told her to go and stay with them awhile.

The next day her father came up again and so poor little Bright-Eyes went with them. They lived about four miles from town, and Bright-Eyes sat on the front seat of the wagon with her father, and his wife sat in the back. The two jabbered away in Indian while Bright-Eyes was so quiet. Every once in a while Bright-Eyes would understand a few words and she knew that they were talked about her. Soon they came in sight of a small, white, frame house and Bright-Eyes's father said something in Indian and pointed to the house. She supposed that he said, that was their home, and she shook her head "yes," and thought: "Can it be possible, that is my home? When I went away we were living in a tepee!" They soon arrived at the house and before she could get out of the wagon, two Indian women came running out and took her down and sat right down on the ground and commenced to cry. They cried so loud that for a moment Bright-Eyes could not realize what was the matter; at least she thought they were crying for joy, so she joined in with them.

Bright-Eyes was so lonesome that she didn't know what to do with herself. It was so warm in the house, that they had a tepee outside, and they all slept in it. The old woman made Bright-Eyes a bed by the side of hers, and little Bright-Eyes went to bed early for she was quite tired, but she could not sleep for the bed was too hard. She lay there thinking of her old school home and her dear school friends. The bed was hard and the noise across the creek kept her awake. After a while she fell asleep. Early the next morning she awoke, and she thought she was at her school home but found herself lying on the hard ground. She said: "How I wish I was back to my dear old school home and could lie between two clean white sheets instead of on the ground."

The mother got up and prepared breakfast and when it was ready she called Bright-Eyes to eat it, but she would not go. She cried and cried and her father came in and talked to her in Indian, but Bright-Eyes could not understand a word and she would not eat any breakfast and her father would not eat either.

Soon after the breakfast was over her father hitched up the wagon and took little Bright-Eyes to visit her other relations. They were glad to see her. Little Bright-Eyes stayed at home about four months with her parents. All the time she was with them she was afraid they might make her dress in Indian but they did not. Her father did all he could for her. He took her to see the Indian dances and she got all the pleasures she wanted.

Early in the fall she went back to school at the Agency, and stayed there about two months and then she coaxed her father to let her go back to her old school home. At last she got word from him that he would let her go. With a sad parting from her parents, whom she had learned to love for their kindness to her, she returned and about two days after she found herself back in her dear home and was with her old friends once more. And it is said that Bright-Eyes is still in school and has learned all she can and that she has nearly completed the Grammar school course.

## From *The Indian Leader* (October 27, 1899)

### The Story of Columbus

Myrtle Dixon

The following uncorrected story was written by a little girl in the Second Grade:[3]

Nearly five hundred years ago the little boy Columbus lived in Italy.

---

3 This sentence is obviously the editor's or teacher's interpolation.

He lived in a pretty town by the sea shore.

His mother and father were poor and had to work very hard to get money to send him to school, they wanted him to have education.

He liked to go the sea shore and watch the ships come and go, he used to have dreams of what he was going to do.

Christopher Columbus learned these studies[:] drawing, Arithmetic and geography.

He used to say I wonder what's over there.

When I get big I will go and see.

People used to get the sailors perfumes and silk, spices, jewels, they used to get all these things from India, they carried all these things on camels back.

Columbus friends told him storys about the sea and told him that he had to study hard before he could become a sailor and told him that had to learn about the stars and other things. When he first took his journey he was only fourteen years old. Columbus became a sailor. He did not go to India because he did not have a ship of his own.

The Queen of Spain and the King helped Columbus.

He had three ships and had two hundred and twenty sailors. They had to cross the Atlantic ocean.

It took them nearly two months to cross the Atlantic ocean.

October 12, 1492 was when they first saw land. When they came to the shore they set up the flag of Spain to show that island belonged to Spain. The Indians said welcome white men in Indian, they were proud of him they called him Spain. They were good to Columbus at first and they treated him mean afterward.

## From *The Indian Leader* (October, 1899)

### AN INDIAN GIRL'S HISTORY, WRITTEN BY HERSELF

The girl was born Dec. 28, 1878, in an Indian teepee. Her mother died when she was eight months old and she was left with her father alone. Her father took her to her aunt's. She lived happily with her aunt. When she was old enough to talk she called her aunt "Mother," for she did not know that her mother was dead. She was raised on rice from childhood until she could feed herself. Her father went up north to stay and she hasn't seen him since. Her mother had plenty of ponies just like the rest of the Indians. They were all given to her. When she was six years old her aunt died and her sister took her and has kept her ever since. She used to go to ghost dances and thought she had good times. She did not intend to go to school for she thought it was terrible to go. While at home she would sometimes go out horseback riding or be out in the woods picking berries. Whenever the white folks came to their house she would go out in the woods to hide, for fear they would take her to school. Her sister wanted her to go to school but she refused to go. Her sister had four sons; she was the only girl in the family, but she wasn't one of their own children. They raised her. But these boys treated her like a sister. They did not go to school and of course they did not know a word of English. They lived in a house made out of bark. The time came when the youngest boy and the girl were to go to school. They did not like to go so they ran off from home. They thought by doing this they would not need to go. But they were brought back home, and were allowed to wait until they went of their own accord. One day when they were at home alone they thought of stealing some sugar to make taffy. These boys cooked the taffy for the girl was too small to do it.

Their mother had gone to see her brother who lived next to their house. So the children stayed at home alone. They cooked so much taffy and were trying to eat it up before their mother came, for they knew she would not like it if she saw them. When they thought it was about time for her to be back they hid some and the rest they gave to the dogs. The dogs did not know what it was, so they ate it, but could not very well chew it, for it would soon stick their jaws together. They soon gave out chewing and just sat there and did not know what to do next. The children thought it was fun but the dogs did not. The children took pity on them and gave them some warm water to melt the taffy.

These boys were very naughty and loved to play tricks on anyone. After that time this girl's sister and the boys all went down to the field and she was to stay home and look after the house. A white man happened to come when she was alone and she was afraid of him, but she took courage to go and see what he wanted. He said something to her in English about her brother-in-law, but she only pointed towards the field and said a few words in her language. She was sorry she didn't go to school when she was asked to go and now how she wished to go. At the age of ten years they took her to school. She was very proud to think she went. She did not dress like an Indian girl now. She could not speak a word of English but she tried to talk and she soon learned how. She began her schooling in 1890 and from this time on she has been going to school. In 1893 she started for Haskell and she is now here with us. She is very glad to think she has the privilege of going to school.

## From *The Indian Leader* (May 3, 1901)

### A Fish Story

Edith Tourtillotte

It was on a bright July morning during my vacation at home that I went on my first trout fishing trip. Having hooks, lines and bait in readiness and for company my two brothers and an old Haskell friend, I was ready for my trip. Of course we had to have a lunch so we took enough of it. I had never gone fishing so did not know that I would have to array myself in a rainy day skirt, sunbonnet and a great big handkerchief. I managed some way after receiving good advice from my brother to be in full uniform, with the exception of the boots. As we were just about to leave I spied some white kid slippers, or rather gray, with French heels. I thought to myself that they would take the place of the boots as they were much lighter, and I told the boys, as they were all boys, that I could walk much faster, although I was not used to walking three miles for trout. We walked in sand, and up and down hills for about three miles before we came to our stopping place for awhile. I was very tired and worn out when I reached the creek, and those French heels were the cause of my being so tired. I told Allie that he would have to dispose of them some way, so he out with his jack knife and cut them off, and then I was in solid comfort. After getting me a fish pole in the woods Allie told me to go very quietly down to the creek near by and throw my hook into the water very lightly. Girls are girls, so I rushed to the edge of the creek, threw my hook in, and not only the hook went, but the girl did too. Well I wasn't hurt, so I tried it again, but went with more caution this time and I got a bite but didn't get the fish. In a short time Allie came to me and asked me if I had had a bite. I told him the sad story and of course he said, "Just like a girl." I was pretty quiet after that and Allie and I went down the creek while Chamie and my younger brother went up the creek. We went through bushes and tall grass and by the time we had traveled a mile I had begun to wonder if I couldn't stop and catch fish in the mud. After going a little farther I dropped my hook into the water and I was surprised to get another bite. I waited until I thought Mr. Trout had a good hold, and then I pulled out my hook and line and to my surprise I saw a nice big trout. I called to Allie and told him of my good luck, and you can imagine how pleased I was when I took the fish off my hook, as that was the first fish I had ever caught. We fished for some time and by the time we had traveled three miles I had been quite successful and caught five fish. We soon grew hungry as it was past noon, so after finishing our toilet, we sat down near the creek and ate our share of the lunch and left enough of it for the two boys. We had left them up the creek but knew that they would come down as far as we went, and in order to have them get their lunch we stuck a piece of wood into the mud and pinned to it a note with this written on it, "Look under bridge at the northeast corner for your lunch." After putting their lunch away Allie and I walked a ways down the road leading toward home, and sat down to rest. We counted our fish and we found that Allie had caught twenty-one and I caught eight. We saw in a short time, Chamie and my brother coming in the distance. They had eaten their lunch we had hid for them and knew we were on our way home. They counted their fish and Wallie caught eleven and Chamie eight. We had quite a little chat over our trip and I told the boys of the many misfortunes I had, and I had a lot of them. I fell into the creek twice, lost my rubbers in the mud, caught my fish hook onto a branch of a tree, besides many other misfortunes. We then started for home as I was tired of fishing trout. We reached home about 2:30 o'clock and we looked like tramps coming into town covered with mud. I was very tired when I did get home, and I told Allie I would never go trout fishing with him again, and if any of the girls present have never gone fishing I would advise you not to go if you have to wear slippers with French heels, or if you have to walk as far as I did and only catch eight fish and fall in the creek besides.

## From *The Indian Leader* (January 31, 1902)

### AN AUTOBIOGRAPHY

Elena Byanuaba

I was born at Galisteo, New Mexico. My father and mother were born at the same place.

My father is an Indian man and my mother is a Mexican woman.

My childhood days were spent at home. While three of my brothers were at school I had to be at home and help both father and mother with the home work. There I learned how to plant corn, beans, wheat, etc.

Many times while helping throw in the seeds I had to jump for there were so many snakes and I used to be afraid for fear I should step on them. But all the same I thought it more fun to help my father with his work than mother with her cooking.

Then I used to think that school would not do me any good and that I was just as happy at home without going to school.

After my brothers were three years at school, the same man that took them to school began to ask father and mother to let me go; at first they refused to let me go; especially mother thought it impossible to let me go.

Well, any way, they agreed to let me go to school in the year 1896. It was then the first time I ever stepped into a school. At first, when I entered the Sante Fe Indian school I was very lonesome; every little thing would bring my tears out, but my brothers used to talk to me and try to console me and they did try so hard to make me happy. At last I got used to it; and after I got interested in my studies and began to understand a little bit of English I began to like it.

In less than a year I spoke pretty good English and by the end of that year I was in the Second Grade.

The second year I had sore eyes for about three months and I was out of school, but when they got well and strong, I studied hard through vacation. I didn't go home that summer but used to go to my teacher's room for help. Her name was Miss Silcott and she helped me so much; and since, I feel so thankful to her, and I am so glad that I have learned and am learning something.

I think that Uncle Sam is very good to the Indians.

I came to Haskell this year on September 3, and I think that Haskell is all right; all the studies are fine, and I think any body that has common sense will surely learn something here. Of course I miss the mountains of the dear home so much.

I hope that I will succeed at Haskell and I wish that my brothers could come here some time. I have four brothers and a little sister at Sante Fe Indian school.

I like algebra best of all my studies in school, although I don't understand it very well yet, and I like the sewing work very much.

I have read these books: "Self Help," "To Have and to Hold," "Ramona," "Ben Hur," "When Knighthood Was in Flower," "Uncle Tom's Cabin" and a few others.

I will give you a few descriptions of myself: I am dark complexioned and have black hair. I am about five feet and three inches high; I have solid teeth but they are uneven, and I weigh about 115 pounds.

I admire these virtues: The best of character, a good Christian girl, honesty, cleanliness, promptness and politeness, and I do the best I can.

## From *Twin Territories* (December, 1902)

### LEGEND OF THE CRICKET

Alice Phillips (A Klamash River Cal. Indian girl)

All the trees are bare now, and ready for winter, the autumn winds having stripped them of their pretty colored leaves. The wild flowers all have gone into their dark homes, beneath the sod, to sleep till the cold, frosty weather is past, and gentle spring returns with her showers of rain and sunshine, to awaken them into bloom, and delight the hearts of nature lovers once more. And all the sweet-singing birds have, likewise, taken their departure for sunny climates, leaving none to cheer our gloomy hours, but the little cricket, whose shrill, musical chirp makes the twilight hours so pleasant and cheerful. It would be lonely indeed, were it not for this small creature. Almost every one is familiar with him; on every homely hearth, in every garden and field, in the grass, his shrill piping is heard and recognized. But, perhaps not every one is familiar with the history of his color, which we all know is black.

The Klamath River Indians have a fable, which, they, doubtless, have handed down from generations unknown, and which is still repeated to their young children. It is amusing for one to consider what strange ideas these Indians had formed about the origin of such things, and yet they, like other people, had their fairy stories, legends and stories of war, with which to entertain the younger members on cold, wintry evenings, – it was contrary to their rules to tell stories at any other season. This is the story told of the cricket, "chit-eep, chit-eep."

Once, a long, long time ago, when the animals first came upon the earth, there was a cricket and her only son, who lived very happily in the grass, singing all day long, till one day the young cricket fell ill and died. Now, the poor mother was grieved very much over the death of her only child, and tried to discover a way of bringing him to life again. She went to Penephitche, the wolf, who was then chief and ruler over all the small animals and insects, and begged him to come and cure her son of death, for they had great faith in their "medicine men," and "yus-atotta." But the selfish cayote only shook his head and said:

"Awth! Why would you wish the dead back again? There are too many of us now; there will not be any room on earth for us; we will be crowding each other into fire and water pretty soon!"

The little thing went away very sad, and, since he could return to life no more, she buried her child, and, after the Indian mode of mourning, cropped her hair closely and painted herself black, and wears to this day, that same hue.

## From *Twin Territories* (April, 1903)

### FOR THE LITTLE CHIEFS AND THEIR SISTERS

The following poem was written by a little Cherokee girl just eight years of age – Hellen Rebecca Anderson, daughter of Mrs. Mabel Washbourne Anderson, a contributor to Twin Territories. The poem is entirely original with little Hellen, and we give it just as she submitted the manuscript to Twin Territories.—Editor.[4]

[4] Ora Eddleman Reed.

### THE UNRULY PIGS.

Billy Wiggs once caught some pigs.
    And he put them in a pen,
But the pen was not strong,
    And so all went wrong,
And the pigs were gone again.

He followed them fast,
    And found them at last
And put them in another;
    They ate and they fussed,
As if they would bust,
    And he sold them to his mother.

## From *Sturm's* (September, 1905)

### A SUMMER DAY

Adella Washee

The cherries are ripe in the orchard,
    The wild birds are calling to me,
And out in the meadow the grasses
    Are rippling like waves on the sea;
The daisies are shaking so gayly
    Their white-ruffled caps in the sun,
And over the tall weeds beside me
    A long silken line has been spun.

I watch it sway upward and downward,
    And fancy a message so sweet
Has come to the bee, seeking honey
    In blossoms not far from my feet.
I sit in wonderful silence,
    And softly o'er wires none can see
The many-toned voices of summer
    Are telling their story to me.

## From *The Indian Leader* (December, 1908)

### A CHRISTMAS FESTIVAL AMONG THE INDIANS

Julia Seelatsee

I will try to tell of the way the Indians spend their Christmas on the Yakima Reservation. Of course this only refers to the Indians who have not yet been civilized, those who still cling to their old Indian ways and customs.

Their religious belief is entirely different from the white people's. They believe there is no such thing as God, but they think that there is a heaven, and everyone who goes there is equal, that there is no one to look up to. But anyhow on Christmas they have a good time. The men during the hunting season kill deer, bear, and other animals and some move to the Columbia River, to dry and salt salmon.

The women in the spring go out digging roots. There are ever so many kinds; some are good, too. They gather all kinds of berries, and dry them and put them up. Then on Christmas day they all bring them to a "long church;" they call it the "Bom-bom" church. Here they do their cooking. They boil almost everything they cook. They have their Indian bread made of roots, which in their own tongue they call "a-moe-mell." The bread is in a round form about the size of a small marble. The roots when dug and washed they pound, and mold into different shapes. Then it is dried in the sun. After it is dry it is just as crisp and looks so white. Sometimes they put sugar in it to make it taste sweet. Well, when everything is prepared, they set the table on the ground and they all squat around.

Before they begin eating, usually the chief makes a little speech. After he has finished they begin eating in this manner: They first eat the salmon, till that is all gone; then the meat of the deer, bear, or whatever it may be; then the roots, then the berries and last comes water. On great occasions they don't use coffee, but take water instead.

After the dinner is over they dance all kinds of dances. Some of them are very pretty to witness, especially when they are dressed in their native costumes. They also sing some pretty religious Indian songs.

This dancing and singing goes on for almost two weeks after Christmas. Every year Christmas is celebrated in this manner.

## From *Red Man* (September, 1910)

### A Seneca Tradition

Evelyn Pierce

Many years ago the Senecas believed in witchcraft. Old men and women were usually the ones on whom suspicion rested. A particular case was that of an old woman who lived apart from the others. She had two daughters who looked very much like her. A peculiarity of the woman was her eyes. They were very round and set close together, so they looked somewhat like an owl's eyes. This woman was supposed to take the form of a black dog when making her raids, and she usually went out on the darkest nights.

One dark autumn night a woman, from no apparent cause, was taken ill. During the day she seemed better, but later, as night came on, she began to rave about a large black dog that she insisted was coming to take her away. This very naturally led the people, who were caring for her to think the witchwoman had paid her a visit. Accordingly, three men were asked if they would not be willing to steal over to the woman's house on the first dark night and capture her – or if out, await her return.

Finally the dark night longed for came, and the three men went forth into the darkness to visit the woman's house. On arriving, they peered in at the windows to see if the witchwoman was at home. A thorough search revealed only the two daughters sitting before the kitchen fire. The house, having three entrances, a man was posted at each, so that the woman would be caught by one of the three whenever she returned.

About midnight they heard faint footsteps near them. Each man waited until he heard the click of the latch, then dashed for the door the click had come from. The woman did not have time to change her form back to her natural self, so she was caught in an assumed form – an enormous black dog.

The woman was so enraged at being caught, and also to avoid punishment, she changed herself and her daughters into owls, so that she could still prowl about at night. This she did before the men had time to bind her.

The old Indians tell this story when asked why they consider the hoot of an owl near a home the sign that someone in that home is to die soon.

This may be because the woman taken ill died about the time the witchwoman and her two daughters flew about as hooting owls.

## From *Red Man* (October, 1910)

### The Story of the Deerskin

Emma LaVatta, Shoshoni

Once upon a time a family of deer lived near a large river. The family was of the buck, doe, and three fawns. Whenever the doe went in search of food she always left the fawns at home and told them not to let any one in, no matter who came, because not very far from them, across the river, lived an old bear who might devour the young fawns. As the mother had said, the bear came and tried to get in, but they kept so still he went away thinking no one was at home.

Finally, one day he watched the doe go away and noticed the fawns were not with her, so as soon as she was out of sight the bear went over and pawed until he broke in and killed the three fawns. He then left.

When the doe returned and found her children dead she knew it was the bear's mischief and started to go to the bear's cave where she might kill him, but when she came to the river she saw she could not cross. As she stood there meditating what to do, two eagles, knowing her trouble, told her they would carry her across, but when they reached the middle of the river they dropped her and she was drowned. While all this was happening the buck was on the other side of the mountain and when he reached home he found the fawns dead and the doe gone, so he buried the fawns and went to find the doe. On reaching the river the same eagle offered to assist him who had attempted to carry the doe across. This time they succeeded. When they reached the other side he found a large gathering of animals and the bear told him to stay inside of the cave and not to look out because they were going to have a war and he might be killed if he did not obey. When the war began, however, it was too much of a temptation, so he went out and was killed. The bear took the skin and stretched it over his door, so no one could look out when inside.

Usually you will find a deerskin stretched over the door of an Indian's wigwam.

## From *The Indian Leader* (January 20, 1911)

### A Pima Legend

Luciana Cheerless

Once there lived a very beautiful young lady who did not wish to get married. Near her home lived a young man, who wished to have this beautiful girl for a wife, but she did not like him because he always gambled.

Near her home was a lake, and every time she went to get water he would follow her and ask her to be his wife. She got so tired of this that she told her brother about it and he told her to grind some corn very fine and make *pinole.* Then he took some eagle feathers and scraped them into it. He told his sister to go to the lake, and if this young man came again and asked her to marry him, to tell him she would if he would drink some of her *pinole.* She did as her brother had told her, and found this young man gambling as usual. He said to the men "I must have a drink." When he reached the lake he asked her to marry him. She said "If you will drink some of my pinole I will marry you," and he was willing to drink it. When he took the first swallow he shivered; at the second swallow his flesh was covered with little pimples; the third time little eagle feathers began to grow and the fourth he was a full-fledged eagle. Then he flew to the top of a low hill. The girl went and told the people and then the men got their bows and arrows to kill the eagle, but every time they shot he caught the arrows in his claws. Then he flew away and tried to rest on the trees but the branches broke off. That is why the eagle on every dollar has arrows and a branch of a tree in his talons. He was the largest eagle that ever lived, his wings being several feet in length. He was so heavy that he could find no tree nor hill safe enough for him to rest on, so he flew away to the top of a very high cliff which no one could climb and made his home there. The cliff shook and rocked with his weight, but soon settled down and then he knew he was safe.

When he made himself at home he started eating little animals that were on the cliff. At first he ate rabbits and small animals and then he began flying down on the people and carrying them home to kill them. He caught the beautiful maiden and carried her home alive and kept her for his wife. They had one little baby eagle. As the people were getting scared, they said, "We must kill the eagle or all the people will be killed." They went to Sur-ur-huh, "The Little Old Man," and asked him to help them. The first time they asked him, he did not answer them; the second time he shook his rattle; the third time he coughed; the fourth time he promised to help them. He told them, "If I kill him, you will see clouds." He took some iron-wood, made some large nails and drove them into the high rock so that he had a ladder to climb to the top. He found the woman and the little eagle alone and asked the former what she usually did for the eagle when he came home. She told him that she combed his head and he always went to sleep.

Then Sur-ur-huh turned himself into a butterfly and hid among the bushes but the woman told him she could see him. Then he turned into a fly and hid under the lung of one of the people.

The eagle came home and his wife did as usual. The little eagle tried to tell his father that some one had been there. The old eagle asked what the little eagle meant. The woman told him that when babies first learn to talk they always talk that way, but they didn't know what they are saying. He soon went to sleep, but when she whistled, he woke up and asked her why she whistled.

She said, "Nothing, only I am proud because you have brought so many people today." The fourth time she whistled he did not waken. She pinched him and found he was fast asleep. Then she called for Sur-ur-huh, who came and cut his head off and killed the little eagle. The cliff began to rock again. When it stopped, he took water and boiled it and bathed the bodies. The last ones the eagle brought came to life quickly, and he sent them home. Those that had been there a long time had forgotten where they came from and who their people were. Their eyes had decayed and changed color. These were the white people and that is why they have blue eyes.

Sur-ur-huh took a feather from the eagle and some bark from a tree and wrote on it, and told the white people they could talk to each other in English. Then they came down and went to their homes. The people had been watching, and when they saw the smoke they all rejoiced and went out to welcome Sur-ur-huh to his home.

## From *The Indian Leader* (March 3, 1911)

### Saquavicha, the Fox-Girl

Clara Talavenska Keshoitewa, Hopi

Once upon a time there lived at Oraibi two young girls who were in love with a handsome boy that lived near them. The girl Saquavicha, who lived to the east of his home, married him, and when Palavicha heard of it she was jealous.

While Saquavicha was at the boy's home doing the cooking for the family, Palavicha, who was jealous of the married one, asked Saquavicha to go with her for water, so both of them went to the spring which the Hopi call the spider spring because an old spider-woman lived near by. Usually she was seen in the form of a spider, but she could change her self to a woman whenever she wished. The jealous girl, Palavicha, then told her companion that she was going to roll the sacred emblem which she had brought with her, which was a wreath of thorns. She rolled it and told Saquavicha, who sat at the bottom of the hill, to catch it when it reached her. But it bounced over Saquavicha's head and changed her to a fox.

Now Palavicha, who was a hard-hearted girl, laughed at Saquavicha and told her that she had no right to marry the boy. Palavicha came home along and the people in the village asked her what had become of Saquavicha. She answered that she was coming along and she did not know why she lingered. It was now getting dark and the relatives of the boy went to search for Saquavicha, but could not find her anywhere.

The poor fox-girl, crying, went southward towards the cornfield as far as the little house, where she slept that night. The next morning nothing could be seen but snow and she did not know where to go, for when it snows the men always go hunting. She knew that if they found her they would be sure to kill her. Just then she heard the footsteps of the hunters along the road and all she could think of was how she might get away and not be killed. Just then came two men with guns to kill her. When they looked the other way, she jumped out, but not in time to get out of their sight. Just as she went behind the house, the men shot at her, but she cried out in her human voice and the men did not kill her. They knew that it must be a person, for if it were a fox it would not cry out like a human being, and they caught her and took her home to the old spider-woman, who was their grandmother. As soon as they got into the house the grandmother knew at once who it was. She put some water on to boil for a long time and then after it had cooled a little she put Saquavicha into it. Then the fox's skin came off and left a beautiful girl. After this the spider-mother bathed Saquavicha and dressed her in pretty clothes.

The girl stayed with them for many years and the two hunters were ever watching for her people. Every time they asked her if she were lonesome for her people, she would tell them she was, but that she did not want to see Palavicha again. But it made her feel sorry to know that her people were grieving for her.

The old spider-woman had made some things ready for Saquavicha to take when she should leave them. One evening the two grandsons came again and wanted to take her home, for her people, whom they had at last found, were in great sorrow for the loss of their child. And in the night when everybody was asleep, they took her to her home.

As they came near the house the door was shut and no light could be seen through the windows. Saquavicha was very anxious to see her people and so when she got near the door, she called to them, but no answer came. She called again and again, still nobody came until she knocked at the door. Then her father came and found his dear daughter, and the two men vanished.

The next day all the people came to see her. She was very different and could hardly talk. Towards evening she told her father to kill some sheep, as the spider-woman had told her to do. The following day they had a big feast and Palavicha, who had turned Saquavicha into a fox, came also. Saquavicha put some medicine into Palavicha's cup and poured water into it for her to drink. As Palavicha drank the water she was changed into an owl. She looked around and it seemed to her that she was in a cave alone, and then she flew away and never returned.

To this day the Indians fear the owl, believing that if one comes near the village some one in the family will die or that some other misfortune will come to them.

## From *The Indian Leader* (January, 1912)

### IN A SNOW DRIFT

Minnie Pike, Eut

Once upon a time there was a family of Indians lost in a snow drift. The family consisted of the father and mother, two little children, a boy and a girl, and their grandmother.

They were on their way to another village when the snow began to fall. It fell faster and faster until the father thought they had better stop and put up their tent. They thought they would camp there all night and the next morning go on if it stopped snowing. But when morning came the snow was falling faster and the tent was almost covered, and by the next morning the tent was entirely covered with snow.

They thought of no way to get out of the tent. They stayed there for many days until their food gave out, then the father fell sick and died. After his death the mother died. They couldn't take the bodies out so they left them in the tent side by side. The poor grandmother didn't know what to do. At last a thought came to her, that she would not give up trying to dig a hole from the tent door to the top. So she set to work with her hatchet cutting blocks of snow out. There was no food left so she boiled the hatchet and made the children drink the water and let them chew on some hides. She said that the iron would make them strong, that is why she boiled the hatchet. At last, after many days of hard work, the grandmother had dug a hole large enough for them to get out. She took the children and hatchet with her. They went on and came to the village where they had started to go. Her sad story was told to all. The children were once more happy. It was said that these two children were the strongest Indians that ever lived, because they drank the water that the iron hatchet was boiled in and the iron made them strong.

## From *The Carlisle Arrow* (December 27, 1912)

### Babetta's Christmas

Isabel LaVatta

My story opens on a beautiful winter day with the sun shining so brightly upon the snow-covered ground that everything as far as the eye could see seemed to wear a crown of glittering jewels. The streets of the town were filled with busy people, hurrying to and fro, bearing countless boxes which told of Christmas gifts and Christmas joys. The bells were jingling and tinkling through the frosty air, telling everyone that this was merry Christmastide, the happiest time of all the year.

Away from the noisy bustling town, out in a lonely little shack far in the woods, there was one to whom Christmas meant nothing. Misfortune had fallen upon little Babetta, and she had been left a lonely, helpless orphan. What was Christmas to her? She knew that this was the holiday season, but to her it was bringing only sorrow and grief. Lonely she sat there, wondering if there was any place on earth for a child so poor and solitary as she, and while she was thinking this she fell asleep and dreamed of all the beautiful things of which she was bereft. She saw in her dream a magnificent palace where luxury abounded. In one of the rooms was a glorious Christmas tree, sparkling with lights and laden with gifts, and in another was a table sumptuously spread with the food which Babetta so sorely needed. She reached out her hand to touch the table, the dream vanished, and the little girl awoke to the realization of her poverty and grief.

The memory of the dream lingered in Babetta's mind so long that at last she decided to go into town to see if she could not banish it from her thoughts. Putting on her poor ragged coat, she went out and made her way slowly into the noisy town. The snow was falling. Little Babetta was not warmly clad, so she made slow progress on her journey. Suddenly, she heard a moan, and looked about her to see whence it came. She heard it again and immediately went toward the spot from which it seemed to come. She had gone only a few steps when she came on an old man moaning with pain and crying for help. Babetta bent over him and asked what a little girl like her could do to help him. The man, whose clothing proclaimed him a man of wealth, bade her go in a certain direction and find his carriage, which he had left a few moments before. It was really quite a distance away, but pity lent wings to Babetta's feet and the time seemed short as she sped on her errand. When she reached the carriage, the coachman bade her get in and guide him to the spot where his master lay. And now Babetta's Christmas joys began, for the old gentleman, with his wound comfortably bandaged, listened to her pitiful story, took her to his home, and brought her up as his cherished daughter.

## From *The Red Man* (December, 1912)

### THE MERMAN'S PROPHECY

Emma M. Newashe

The spring had not arrived in all its splendor, but its coming was clearly seen, for the buds on the trees were beginning to show that everything would be full of life.

One cool morning before sunrise, two devoted brothers decided to go hunting and at the same time keep fast.

They traveled for six days, and at the end of the sixth day, the younger became tired and hungry. That night they had their usual night's rest but ate nothing.

The seventh morning, while the brothers sat beside each other, the younger cast his wistful eyes up to a large tree. Just where three of the limbs branched from the trunk, he saw an unusual sight. A fish! Owning to his curiosity, he asked his brother to climb the tree and see if he could not get the fish. The elder was tired and so nearly exhausted from hunger and travel that he failed after five times to climb the tree. The younger was anxious to obtain the fish and resolved to climb. He was not long in accomplishing the feat. He threw the fish down to his brother who was very much frightened at discovering that it was really a fish. He knew at once that there was some mystery connected with it.

It happened that they were near a village. The younger brother suggested that they boil the fish; but the older was very much opposed to the proposition on account of breaking fast, but because his brother insisted, he suggested that he might go and borrow a copper kettle to use in carrying water from a lake near-by. They agreed on this, and while the elder was gone, he cleaned the fish.

After they had their meal, the younger became very thirsty. He asked his brother to get some water for him and without delay the elder went to the lake. His brother drank and drank water and his brother kept on carrying water for him until he was overcome with fatigue. At last the elder said that he must go to the lake and drink as much water as he desired. This, he did, but he could not quench his thirst. His brother who did not accompany him became very uneasy about his stay. He went to the lake and here saw his brother lying with his head down to the water's edge.

When the younger saw his brother, he gave one leap into the lake. He tried to catch him but it was of no avail. He waited a few minutes and in the middle of the lake he saw his brother changed to a merman. His countenance was stronger and wiser.

Then, in a commanding yet merciful voice, the Merman asked his brother to call all his people to assemble around the lake. The next day all the Sacs gathered around him ready to hear what he had to say.

He began by saying that he had always been happy with them, but his saddest days concerning his people were rapidly approaching. He told them so long as they were north of where the white-barked (sycamore) trees grow, he could constantly watch over them. He told them so long as they stayed north of the Missouri River, they would continue to adopt the customs of their ancestors; but, as soon as the tribe crossed, they would no longer have his beneficent influence. Their worship, language and customs would change. The prophecy extends to where he said that the tribe would settle near a large body of water (supposed to be the Gulf of Mexico), and that this would be a final resting place of the Sacs.

So many parts of this prophecy have come true that it is considered very wonderful by the tribe.

## From *The Indian Leader* (December 26, 1919)

### Left Overs From Good English Week.
### Slogans and Rhymes by Vocational IV, Girls

1. Hang,
Slang!
2. While slang is in the atmosphere,
We must treat it with a sneer.
3. Here's to the class of 1920!
Good English we must have aplenty.
4. Be a good walker
And a good talker.
5. Do not slave for master "Slanguage."
Be your own master, uphold good language.
6. S—stands for spelling important for all,
P—perseverance, for patience, and pull.
E—stands for effort put forth on our words.
L—stands for leaders of which you have heard.
L—stands for loyal, applied to this class,
If we can spell, perhaps we shall pass.
7. Be clean in your speech
Our slogan this week.
8. Hail to the class of '20!
We're studious far than some.
And when we speak, we'll use no slang,
And chew no chewing gum.

## From *The Indian Leader* (December 26, 1919)

### A Story of Modern Knights

By Evelyn Leary, Vocational IV

Once there were two great bands of knights. One band was composed of good knights, who tried in every way possible to help the people. The other band was composed of bad knights who dragged the people down and taught them bad things.

The leader of the first band of knights went by the name of "Good Speech." He had many followers. Some of the most popular ones went by the names; "I can," "All right," "Haven't," "Is it not," "Wouldn't you," "Have to," "Look there," "Where," "Going," "Far," "If and Just."

These knights spent one week each year in trying to overcome the bad knights, who had been so well fed and protected that they were very strong and hard to overthrow. Their leader's name was "Bad Speech"; he also went by the name of "Slang." He, too, had many followers, but they were very different from the followers of the first leader, because they were working for a different purpose. They tried to undo the work of the good knights and often times succeeded. Some of the supporters of "Bad Speech" were, "I kin," "Awright," "Ain't got," "Ain't it," "Wouldn't," "Gott," "Luk ther," "Whar," "Goin," "Fer," If and Jest."

Year after year these knights battled and every year some of the followers of "Bad Speech" were killed.

Some were only wounded and by the next year's battle were strong enough to fight again. Oftentimes a few of "Good Speech" knights were wounded, but not many killed, because right almost always overcomes wrong. Sometimes when some of the followers of "Bad Speech" were cornered and saw that they would either have to surrender or be lost, they would yield. When a knight was overcome, he had to take the names of the knight who had overcome him, so many of the followers of "Bad Speech" had to change their names. At first it was very awkward for them but as time went on they began to like their new names and would not have them changed if they could. They joined the good knights and went out to help Good Speech in his cause.

Good Speech and his knights are still fighting. In time they hope to bring all the followers of Bad Speech to their side. Join the forces of Good Speech and help him win.

# Index